Everyman, I will go with thee,
and be thy guide

FEMALE PLAYWRIGHTS
OF THE NINETEENTH CENTURY

Edited by
ADRIENNE SCULLION
University of Glasgow

EVERYMAN
J. M. DENT • LONDON
CHARLES E. TUTTLE
VERMONT

Selection and apparatus © J. M. Dent, 1996

J. M. Dent
Orion Publishing Group
Orion House, 5 Upper St Martin's Lane,
London WC2H 9EA
and
Charles E. Tuttle Co., Inc.
28 South Main Street,
Rutland, Vermont 05701 USA

Typeset by Deltatype Ltd, Ellesmere Port, Cheshire
Printed in Great Britain by
The Guernsey Press Co. Ltd, Guernsey, C. I.

British Library Cataloguing-Publication Data
is available upon request.

ISBN 0 460 87729 1

CONTENTS

NOTE ON THE PLAYWRIGHTS AND EDITOR

Details of the lives of Joanna Baillie, Marie-Thérèse De Camp, Fanny Kemble, Anna Cora Mowatt, Mrs Henry Wood (with T. A. Palmer), Florence Bell, Elizabeth Robins and Pearl Craigie (John Oliver Hobbes) appear in the Introduction.

ADRIENNE SCULLION is British Academy Postdoctoral Fellow in the Department of Theatre, Film and Television Studies at the University of Glasgow.

CHRONOLOGY OF THE PLAYWRIGHTS' LIVES

Year	Life
1762	11 September – birth of Joanna Baillie at Bothwell, Lanarkshire, Scotland
1769	The Baillie family move to Hamilton
1772	Around this time Joanna Baillie is sent to boarding school in Glasgow
1773	
1775	17 January – birth of Marie-Thérèse De Camp in Vienna. As a child she moves with her family to London
1776	Joanna Baillie's father appointed Professor of Divinity, University of Glasgow
1777	
1778	Death of Joanna Baillie's father
1779	Matthew Baillie begins studies at Balliol College, Oxford; William Hunter assumes guardianship of the family; Dorothea, Agnes and Joanna Baillie move to Long Calderwood, the Hunter's estate outside Glasgow
1783	Matthew Baillie inherits William Hunter's School of Anatomy, Windmill Street, London; Dorothea, Joanna and Agnes move to London
	Marie-Thérèse De Camp begins stage career as a child-dancer
1786	Marie-Thérèse De Camp, achieving success as Zélie in de Genlis's *La Colombe* at Le Texier, is engaged at the Royal Circus; she makes her debuts at the Haymarket (14 June) and at Drury Lane (24 October), where she plays Julie in Burgoyne's *Richard, Coeur de Lion*

CHRONOLOGY OF THEIR TIMES

Year	Artistic Events	Historical Events
1772	Mercy Otis Warren, *The Adulateur*	
1773	Hannah More, *The Search After Happiness*; Mercy Otis Warren, *The Defeat*	Tea Act incites Boston Tea Party
1775	Debut of Sarah Siddons Premiere: Beaumarchais, *Le Barbier de Séville* Birth of Charles Kemble, Jane Austen	Skirmishes at Lexington and Concord preface the American Revolution; the Battle of Bunker Hill
1776	David Garrick retires and Richard Brinsley Sheridan assumes control of Drury Lane	American Declaration of Independence and Revolutionary War (definitive peace in 1783 with Treaty of Paris)
1777	Premiere: Hannah More, *Percy*	
1779	Death of David Garrick	
1783	John Philip Kemble's debut as Hamlet	

Year	Life
1787	October – death of Marie-Thérèse De Camp's father
1790	Joanna Baillie publishes, anonymously, her first book, *Fugitive Poems*
1791	Joanna Baillie, with her sister and mother, moves to Hampstead; they reside there for the rest of their lives
1792	15 August – Marie-Thérèse De Camp's adult success is assured when she appears as Captain MacHeath in a travesty version of *The Beggar's Opera* at the Haymarket
1798	Joanna Baillie publishes, anonymously, the first volume of her *Plays on the Passions* – it includes *Count Basil*, *The Trial* and *De Montford*
1799	3 May – Marie-Thérèse De Camp's comedy, *First Faults*, premieres at Drury Lane
1800	29 April – Joanna Baillie's *De Montford* produced at Drury Lane with Sarah Siddons and John Philip Kemble
1802	Joanna Baillie publishes the second volume of *Plays on the Passions*, which includes *The Election*, *Ethwald* and *The Second Marriage*
1804	Joanna Baillie publishes *Miscellaneous Plays*, which includes *Constantine Paleologus* and *Rayner*

Year	Artistic Events	Historical Events
1787	Premieres:Royall Tyler, *The Contrast* Birth of Edmund Kean, Mary Russell Mitford	
1791		Paine, *The Rights of Man*
1792	Death of Goldoni	
1793	Birth of Felicia Dorothea Hemans	
1798	Establishment of Park Theatre, New York Coleridge and Wordsworth, *Lyrical Ballads*	
1799	Premiere: Sheridan, *Pizarro* Birth of Catherine Gore	
1800	Marie Edgeworth, *Castle Rackrent*; Schiller, *Maria Stuart*	
1801		Pitt resigns on king's refusal to sign Catholic Emancipation Bill
1802	John Philip Kemble and Sarah Siddons move to Covent Garden *Edinburgh Review* begins	Peace of Amiens
1803	Birth of Dumas, père, Jerrold	War renewed between Britain and France
1804	Dartmouth appointed Lord Chamberlain – his period of office 1804–12 is noted for its leniency, particularly towards the smaller houses Debut of W. H. B. Betty, a.k.a. 'The Infant Rosicus'	Pitt prime minister Napoleon Emperor End of Holy Roman Empire

Year	Life
1805	29 April – Marie-Thérèse De Camp's interlude *Personation; or, Fairly Taken In* premiered at Drury Lane; it is published by Dick's
1806	2 July – Marie-Thérèse De Camp marries Charles Kemble; 1 October – De Camp makes her Covent Garden debut as Maria in *The Citizen* Autumn – death of Joanna Baillie's mother
1808	18 May – Marie-Thérèse De Camp's interlude *The Day After the Wedding; or, A Wife's First Lesson* produced at Covent Garden Joanna Baillie publishes a number of poems in *The Edinburgh Annual Register*
1809	4 October – Kemble's enlarged Covent Garden Theatre opens; 'Old Price' Riots ensue 27 November – birth of Frances Anne (Fanny) Kemble in London
1810	29 January – Joanna Baillie's *The Family Legend* is produced at the Edinburgh Theatre Royal; it is published in the same year
1812	Joanna Baillie publishes a third volume of *Plays on the Passions*
1814	17 January – birth of Ellen Price (Mrs Henry Wood) in Worcestershire, England; much of her early life is spent with her maternal grandmother, Mrs Evans
1815	12 December – Marie-Thérèse De Camp's *Smiles and Tears; or, The Widow's Stratagem* produced at Covent Garden Joanna Baillie's *The Family Legend* performed at the Theatre Royal, Edinburgh and at Drury Lane

Year	Artistic Events	Historical Events
1805	Scott, *Lay of the Last Minstrel* Death of Schiller	Battles of Trafalgar, Ulm and Austerlitz
1806	Webster, *Dictionary* Birth of Elizabeth Barrett Browning	Battle of Jena Death of Pitt
1808	20 September – Covent Garden destroyed by fire Hunt's *Examiner* founded	
1809	Drury Lane destroyed by fire *Quarterly Review* founded Birth of Gogol, Poe, Tennyson	Birth of Darwin Death of Paine
1810	Premiere: Rhodes, *Bombast Furioso* Scott, *The Lady of the Lake* Birth of Chopin, Schumann, de Musset	
1812	Sarah Siddons retires from the stage Rebuilt Drury Lane opens Birth of Browning, Dickens, Edward Lear	War between Britain and US begins Napoleon invades Russia
1814	Edmund Kean's debut as Shylock at Drury Lane; Elisa O'Neill's debut; Dorothy Jordan retires from the stage Jane Austen, *Mansfield Park*; Scott, *Waverly*; Wordsworth, *The Excursion* Birth of Le Fanu, Lermontov, de Sade Death of Mercy Otis Warren	Treaty of Ghent Congress of Vienna begins
1815	Scott, *Guy Mannering* Birth of Trollope	Battle of Waterloo Treaty of Vienna

Year	Life
1816	Around this time Fanny Kemble is sent first to Boulogne then to Paris for formal schooling Death, in London, of Jeanne De Camp, mother of Marie-Thérèse
1818	17 April – Marie-Thérèse De Camp creates the role of Madge Wildfire in Terry's musical version of *The Heart of Midlothian*
1819	March – Anna Cora Ogden (Mowatt Ritchie) born to Samuel and Eliza Ogden, Americans residing in Bordeaux, France 9 June – Marie-Thérèse De Camp retires from the stage with a production of her own *Personation*
1820	Joanna Baillie visits Scotland
1821	Kean produces Joanna Baillie's *De Montford* at Drury Lane; she publishes *Metrical Legends*

Year	Artistic Events	Historical Events
1816	Macready's debut at Covent Garden Premiere: Planché, *Amoroso, King of Little Britain* Jane Austen, *Emma*; Coleridge, *Christabel, Kubla Khan* Birth of Charlotte Brontë	
1818	Jane Austen, *Northanger Abbey, Persuasion*; Susan Ferrier, *Marriage*; Keats, *Endymion*; Mary Shelley, *Frankenstein* Birth of Turgenev, Emily Brontë, Charlotte Mary Sanford Barnes	Birth of Marx
1819	Elisa O'Neill retires from the stage; opening of Adelphi Theatre Scott, *The Bride of Lammermore, Ivanhoe*; Shelley, *The Masque of Anarchy* Birth of Mary Ann Evans (George Eliot), Ruskin, Whitman	Peterloo massacre
1820	Edmund Kean's American debut Premieres: Planché, *The Vampire*; Scribe, *Un Verre d'Eau* Keats, *The Eve of St Agnes, Isabella, Odes*; Shelley, *Prometheus Unbound*	George IV accedes Cato Street conspiracy
1821	Galt, *Annals of the Parish*; Shelley, *Adonais, Epipsychidion, Hellas* Birth of Baudelaire, Dostoevsky, Flaubert Death of Keats, Mrs Inchbald	Death of Napoleon

Year	Life
1822	March – Charles Kemble assumes management of Covent Garden
1823	Joanna Baillie edits and publishes *Poetic Miscellanies*, an anthology containing poems by Scott, Wordsworth, Southey, Felicia Hemans and several others
1825	Fanny Kemble meets Harriet St Leger, her life-long friend and correspondent, for the first time
1826	Joanna Baillie publishes *The Martyr* 17 September – the Ogden family sail for New York
1827	Fanny Kemble resides in Edinburgh
1829	Fanny Kemble returns to London; 5 October – makes her triumphant debut as Juliet at Covent Garden Marie Thérèse De Camp comes out of retirement for one night to play Lady Capulet
1830	Late May – Fanny and Charles Kemble begin their British tour

Year	Artistic Events	Historical Events
1822	Gas lighting at the Paris Opera Daguerre's Diorama opens in Paris De Quincey, *Confessions of an English Opium Eater* Birth of Matthew Arnold, Boucicault Death of Shelley	
1823	Charles Kemble's authentic revival of *King John* Lamb, *Quentin Durward* Birth of Sidney Frances Bateman Death of John Philip Kemble, Anne Radcliffe	Monroe Doctrine Mill, *Elements of Political Economy*
1825	Edmund Kean's second tour to America Hazlitt, *The Spirit of the Age*	
1826	Fenimore Cooper, *The Last of the Mohicans* Death of Royall Tyler	
1827	Debut of Charles Kean E. W. Brayley, *Historical and Descriptive Account of the Theatres of London* Death of Blake, Beethoven	
1829	Premiere: Jerrold, *Black-Eyed Susan* Birth of T. W. Robertson	Catholic emancipation
1830	Madame Vestris begins her management of the Olympic Theatre Cobbett, *Rural Rides*; Stendahl, *Le Rouge et Le Noir* Birth of Emily Dickinson, Christina Rossetti, Hazlitt	William IV accedes Liverpool and Manchester Railway opens
1831	Death of Sarah Siddons, Hegel	Faraday's electromagnetic current

Year	Life
1832	Fanny Kemble creates the role of Julia in Sheridan Knowles's *The Hunchback*. 15 March – *Francis the First* premiered at Covent Garden. 22 June – Fanny Kemble takes leave of the Covent Garden stage; 1 August – Fanny and Charles Kemble (stepping down as manager of Covent Garden), along with Adelaide De Camp, sail for New York. In September Charles and Fanny make their American debuts at the Park Theatre, New York (Fanny's debut 18 September); October – in Philadelphia, Fanny Kemble meets Pierce Butler for the first time Anna Cora Ogden meets James Mowatt (some fourteen years her elder)
1833	On her first visit to the theatre, late 1833 or early 1834, Anna Cora Ogden sees Fanny Kemble at the Park Theatre in Knowles's *The Hunchback*
1834	April – death of Adelaide De Camp. 7 June – Fanny Kemble marries Pierce Butler in Philadelphia 6 October – at the age of 15 Anna Cora Ogden marries James Mowatt secretly in New York
1835	Spring – the Mowatts move to Flatbush, Long Island May – Fanny Kemble Butler gives birth to her first daughter, Sarah; Fanny's *The Journals of a Residence in America* is published in Paris; *The Journals of Frances Anne Butler* published in London
1836	Winter – death of Eliza Ogden. Samuel Ogden marries Julia Fairlie Ellen Price marries Henry Wood at Whittington, near Worcester. They spend much of their married life abroad, chiefly in Dauphiné, France Under the pseudonym of 'Isabel', Anna Cora Mowatt publishes *Pelayo; or, The Cavern of Covadonga* 1 November – Fanny Kemble Butler sails from New York bound for London

Year	Artistic Events	Historical Events
1832	Premieres: Jerrold, *The Rent Day*; Knowles, *The Hunchback*; Peake, *The Climbing Boy* Genest, *Some Account of the English Stage from the Restoration in 1600 to 1830*; Dunlap, *History of American Theatre* Birth of Lewis Carroll Death of Scott, Goethe	First Reform Bill becomes law
1833	Passage of Dramatic Copyright Act secures playwrights control over work Bunn manages both Drury Lane and Covent Garden Death of Edmund Kean, Hannah More	Abolition of slavery in Britain
1834	Birth of G. du Maurier, H. J. Byron Death of Coleridge, Lamb	Peel becomes prime minister
1835	Debut of Charles Matthews Jr at the Olympic; debut of Charlotte Cushman Birth of Mark Twain Death of Cobbett, Hogg, Felicia Dorothea Hemans	
1836	28 October – Charles Kemble appointed Examiner of Plays; 23 December – he retires from the stage playing Benedict to Helen Faucit's Beatrice at Covent Garden Dickens, *Pickwick Papers* (begins); Büchner, *Woyzeck* written (published 1873) Birth of W. S. Gilbert	

Year	Life
	Joanna Baillie's *The Homicide* is produced at Drury Lane and *The Separation* at Covent Garden. She publishes the final volume of *Plays on the Passions* and some *Miscellaneous Plays*, including *Witchcraft*
1837	As 'Isabel', Anna Cora Mowatt publishes *Reviewers Reviewed; a Satire*. She continues to write closet dramas and begins to contribute to magazines using the *nom de plume* 'Cora' Spring – Anna Cora Mowatt travels to Europe 7 August – Fanny Kemble's *The Star of Seville* is produced at the Walnut Street Theatre, Baltimore
1838	May – Fanny Kemble Butler gives birth to her second daughter, Frances. Her second play, *The Star of Seville*, is performed in America 3 September – Marie-Thérèse De Camp dies at Chertsey, near London 30 December – the Butlers arrive at Butler's Island, part of Pierce Butler's estate in the Georgia Sea Islands
1839	April – the Butlers return to Butler's Place, Philadelphia; relations between Fanny and Pierce in terminal decline. May – Fanny threatens to leave for London and to return to the stage
1840	August – the Mowatts sail for New York. Upon his return to America James Mowatt's health fails and he is forced to retire from work. October – Anna Cora Mowatt's *Gulzara; or, The Persian Slave* is mounted as a private performance in celebration of her father's birthday (17 October): the play is subsequently published in the journal *New World*.

Year	Artistic Events	Historical Events
1837	Macready assumes managerial control of Covent Garden Webster begins management of Haymarket First London appearance of Samuel Phelps Premiere: Charlotte Mary Sanford Barnes, *Octavia Brigaldi* in New York Dickens, *Oliver Twist* (begins) Birth of Mary Elizabeth Braddon Maxwell	Victoria accedes to throne
1838	Madame Vestris relinquishes Olympic management Birth of Augustin Daly Premieres: Boucicault, *A Legend of the Devil's Dyke*; Lytton, *The Lady of Lyons* Dickens, *Nicholas Nickelby* (begins)	Formation of Anti-Corn-Law League
1839	Macready ends his Covent Garden management, control assumed by Madame Vestris and Matthews Premiere Lytton, *Richlieu; or, The Conspiracy* Birth of Marie Wilton (later Mrs Squire Bancroft) Death of Dunlap	Chartist riots
1840	Poe, *Tales of the Grotesque and Arabesque* February – Charles Kemble resigns his office as Examiner of Plays in favour of his son, John Mitchell Kemble. 24 March to 10 April – at the invitation of Queen Victoria,	Queen Victoria marries Prince Albert

Year	Life
	Financial ruin forces the Mowatts to sell their property in Long Island
	1 December – Charles Kemble close to death, the Butlers sail for Liverpool
1841	18 October – Anna Cora Mowatt begins her public readings. The Mowatt's summer at Lenox and meet the Sedgwicks, also friends of Fanny Kemble. Anna Cora Mowatt begins to write profesionally
1842	Anna Cora Mowatt publishes the novel, *The Fortune Hunter*
1843	4 May – the Butlers sail for America where they take up residence in a boarding house in Philadelphia
1844	Fanny Kemble Butler separates from Pierce Butler. She publishes a collection of *Poems* in Philadelphia
1845	24 March – Anna Cora Mowatt's *Fashion* premiered at the Park Theatre, New York. 13 June – Mowatt makes her stage debut at the Park Theatre as Pauline in Edward Bulwer-Lytton's *Lady of Lyons*. She publishes the novel, *Evelyn; or, A Heart Unmasked, A Tale of Domestic Life*. 1845/6 – she tours the United States September – Fanny Kemble Butler leaves Philadelphia, on 16 September, for London. 20 December – she travels to Italy, residing with her sister Adelaide Sartoris in Rome
1846	May – Anna Cora Mowatt returns to the Park Theatre. E. L. Davenport becomes her leading man 8 December – Fanny Kemble Butler leaves Rome for London

Year	Artistic Events	Historical Events
	Charles Kemble makes a triumphant return to the stage, playing some of his most popular roles in a short season at Covent Garden Premiere: Lytton, *Money* Birth of Hardy, Zola	
1841	Macready takes over Drury Lane Premiere: Boucicault's *London Assurance* *Punch* begins	Peel becomes prime minister
1842	Premieres: W. Marston, *The Patrician's Daughter*, Pitt, *Sweeney Todd* Tennyson, *Morte d'Arthur* Birth of Mallarmé Death of Stendahl	
1843	Theatre monopoly ended by Theatre Regulation Act Macready ends his management of Drury Lane Birth of Henry James	
1844	Phelps begins 18-year management of Sadler's Wells Dickens, *A Christmas Carol*; Thackeray, *Barry Lyndon* Birth of Sarah Bernhardt	Factory Act restricts working hours for women and children
1845	Disraeli, *Sybil*	Irish famine
1846	Premieres: Archer, *The Black Doctor*; Taylor, *Vanderdecken; or, The Flying Dutchman*	Repeal of the Corn Laws US at war with Mexico

Year	Life
1847	16 February – Fanny Kemble Butler returns to the stage at the Theatre Royal, Manchester. She tours Britain reviving old parts and beginning public readings. She publishes *A Year of Consolation*, about her travels in Italy. April – Pierce Butler initiates divorce proceedings on grounds of wilful desertion. May – Fanny reappears on the London stage
	27 September – Anna Cora Mowatt's *Armand; or, The Child of the People* is produced at the Park Theatre, New York. Davenport is Armand, the role created for him, and Mowatt is Blanche. 1 November – the Mowatts, accompanied by Davenport, sail for England. 7 December – Mowatt and Davenport make their British debuts in *Lady of Lyons* at the Theatre Royal, Manchester
1848	5 January – Anna Cora Mowatt and Davenport make their London debuts in *The Hunchback* at the Princess's Theatre
	April – after a short visit to America, Fanny Kemble Butler begins a series of Shakespearean readings at the Willis Rooms, London
1849	18 January – Anna Cora Mowatt's *Armand; or, The Peer and the Peasant* is produced with great success at the Marylebone Theatre and subsequently published in London
	February – Fanny Kemble Butler begins an engagement playing opposite Macready. 21 November – Fanny Kemble and Pierce Butler divorce. In America Fanny continues her public readings as 'Mrs Kemble'. She subsequently retires to Lenox, Massachusetts
1850	January – Mowatt's *Fashion* is performed at the Olympic. An edition of the play is published in London Fanny Kemble returns to London

Year	Artistic Events	Historical Events
1847	Madame Vestris and Charles Matthews begin their Lyceum management Covent Garden opened as an Opera House Premieres: J. M. Morton, *Box and Cox*; de Musset, *Un Caprice* at the Comédie Française Charlotte Brontë, *Jane Eyre*; Emily Brontë, *Wuthering Heights*; Thackeray, *Vanity Fair* (begins) Birth of Ellen Terry, Bram Stoker	
1848	Dickens, *Dombey and Son*; Elizabeth Gaskell, *Mary Barton*; Mary Sanford Barnes, *Plays, Prose and Poetry* Death of Emily Brontë	Chartists suppressed Public Health Act passed
1849	Electricity introduced to Paris Opera Ibsen completes first play, *Catiline* Dickens, *David Copperfield* (begins); Macauly, *History of England* (begins); Charlotte Brontë, *Shirley* Birth of Ellen Terry, Strindberg Death of Poe, Maria Edgeworth	Gold rush in California begins
1850	Charles Kean begins management of Princess's Premieres: Taylor, *The Vicar of Wakefield*; Wagner, *Lohengrin*, conducted by Liszt Hawthorne, *The Scarlet Letter*; Wordsworth, *The Prelude*	Society for Promoting the Employment of Women formed US Fugitive Slave Law

Year	Life
1851	9 September – birth of Florence Eveleen Eleanore Olliffe (later Lady Bell) in Paris 23 February – Joanna Baillie dies in Hampstead, London. Her complete works are published February – Anna Cora Mowatt performs in Newcastle, James Mowatt dies in London. She undertakes a final tour of the English provinces. 9 July – sails for America. 19 August – returns to the New York stage, at Niblo's Theatre, before touring through Boston, Providence, Philadelphia, Baltimore, Cincinnati and St Louis. 30 December – private production of *Gulzara* staged by Mowatt and her sisters in Philadelphia
1852	January – Anna Cora Mowatt meets William Foushee Ritchie. 1852/3 – Mowatt continues touring throughout the US, often performing in *Armand* and *Fashion*
1853	Summer – Anna Cora Mowatt withdraws from the stage through illness. Whilst recuperating she writes her autobiography. Later in the year she begins her farewell tour From mid-1853 Fanny Kemble and the Sartorises spend a year in Italy
1854	Anna Cora Mowatt retires from the stage. Her final performance, 3 June, at Niblo's Garden, is as Pauline, the role in which she made her debut. On 6 June she marries William Foushee Ritchie. Her *Autobiography of an Actress; or, Eight Years on the Stage* is published. *Fashion* published in New York by Samual French 12 November – death of Charles Kemble

Year	Artistic Events	Historical Events
	Death of Balzac, Wordsworth (Tennyson succeeds as Poet Laureate)	
1851	Macready and Helen Faucit retire from the stage	The Great Exhibition
	Premieres: Lovell, *Ingomar*; Webster, *The Courier of Lyons*	
	Elizabeth Gaskell, *Cranford* (begins); Melville, *Moby Dick*; Wagner *Oper und Drama*	
	Birth of Robert Louis Stevenson	
1852	Ibsen becomes stage director and dramaturg at Bergen's Norsk Theater	
	Premiere: Boucicault, *The Corsican Brothers*	
	Dickens, *Bleak House* (begins); Harriet Beecher Stowe, *Uncle Tom's Cabin*	
	Birth of Lady Gregory, George Moore, W. Poel	
	Death of Gogol	
1853	Buckstone takes over management of Haymarket	
	Boucicault arrives in US	
	Charlotte Brontë, *Villette*; Elizabeth Gaskell, *Ruth*	
	Birth of J. Forbes-Robertson, Lucy Lane Clifford	
1854	Madame Vestris retires	Crimean War begins
	Dickens, *Hard Times*; Gaskell, *North and South* (begins); *The Dramatic Works of Mary Russell Mitford*	
	Birth of Rimbaud,	

Year	Life
1855	Anna Cora Mowatt Ritchie publishes a volume of *Plays* containing both *Fashion* and *Armand*
1856	Fanny Kemble returns to America for a reunion with her daughters who summer with her in Lenox June – Anna Cora Mowatt publishes *Mimic Life; or, Before and Behind the Curtain*, a series of sentimental narratives Mr and Mrs Henry Wood return to England, residing in Norwood
1857	Anna Cora Mowatt publishes *Twin Roses*, a novel of stage life
1859	May – Frances Butler comes of age – Fanny Kemble takes her daughter to Europe, returning in October, whereupon she undertakes another reading tour. Sarah Butler marries Dr Owen J. Wister – their son, Owen Wister (b. 1860), the eminent American novelist
1860	Mrs Henry Wood wins £100 from the Scottish Temperance League for her novella *Danesbury House*

Year	Artistic Events	Historical Events
	Oscar Wilde, David Belasco, Charles Frohman Death of Susan Ferrier	Crimean War begins
1855	Debut of Marie Wilton (later Mrs Bancroft) Dickens, *Little Dorrit* (begins); Kingsley, *Westward Ho!*; Longfellow, *Hiawatha*; Tennyson, *Maud*; Whitman, *Leaves of Grass* (begins); *Saturday Review* begins Death of Charlotte Brontë, Mary Russell Mitford	
1856	Debut of Henry Irving Premiere: Sidney Frances Bateman, *Self* Birth of Freud, Rider Haggard, Bernard Shaw Death of Madame Vestris	The Matrimonial Causes Act
1857	Premiere: Boucicault's *The Poor of New York* Trollope, *Barchester Towers* Birth of Conrad, F. Benson Death of de Musset, Jerrold	Indian Mutiny
1859	Charles Kean retires Premiere: Boucicault, *The Octoroon* Dickens, *A Tale of Two Cities*; Eliot, *Adam Bede*; J. S. Mill, *On Liberty* Birth of A. E. Housman, J. K. Jerome Death of De Quincy, Hunt, Macaulay	Darwin, *On the Origin of the Species*
1860	Premieres: Boucicault, *The Colleen Bawn* (initiating the 'long run'); *The Octoroon* (New York premiere) Collins, *The Woman in White*; Dickens, *Great Expectations* (begins);	Abraham Lincoln elected President of US

Year   *Life*

1861   January – Mrs Henry Wood's novel *East Lynne* is
              serialised in the *New Monthly Magazine*. It is published
              in novel form in the autumn
              Anna Cora Mowatt Ritchie leaves her husband to live
              with her family in the North. Later in the year she
              leaves America: the rest of her life is spent abroad, first
              in Florence, later in England

1862   25 January – an enthusiastic review of *East Lynne* in
              the *Times* assures Mrs Henry Wood's success. She also
              publishes *The Channings* and *Mrs Halliburton's
              Troubles*. December – stage version of *East Lynne* in
              New York
              6 August – birth of Elizabeth Robbins in Louisville,
              Kentucky, to Charles and Hannah Robins

1863   28 March – premiere of Clifton W. Tayleur's
              adaptation of *East Lynne* in New York, with Lucille
              Western as Lady Isabel
              May – Fanny Kemble publishes *Journal of a Residence
              on a Georgian Plantation, 1838–1839*
              Mrs Henry Wood publishes *The Shadow of Ashlydyat*

1864   16 May – production of Fanny Kemble's *English
              Tragedy* at the New Broadway Theatre, New York.
              October – Kemble's adaptation from Dumas,
              Mademoiselle De Belle Isle, produced at the
              Haymarket.
              The Marriage Bells; or, The Cottage on the Cliff, an
              adaptation of *East Lynne* by W. Archer produced in
              London. Mrs Henry Wood publishes *Lord Oakburn's
              Daughters*

Year	Artistic Events	Historical Events
	Eliot, *The Mill on the Floss*; Birth of J. M. Barrie	Abraham Lincoln elected President of US
1861	Debuts of Squire Bancroft and William Kendal George Eliot, *Silas Marner* Death of Elizabeth Barrett Browning, Scribe, Catherine Gore	US Civil War begins Death of Prince Albert
1862	Phelps ends his management of Sadler's Wells Bernhardt's first appearance at the Comédie Français in Racine's *Iphigénie* Debuts of Ellen Terry and Charles Wyndham Hugo, *Les Misérables* Birth of J. T. Grein, Maeterlinck, Edith Wharton Death of Thoreau	Homestead Act opens the West
1863	Premiere: Taylor, *The Ticket-of-Leave Man* (beginning a run of 407 nights) Birth of Stanislavsky Death of Thackeray, Charlotte Mary Sanford Barnes	
1864	Monopoly abolished in Paris Premiere: Robertson, *David Garrick* Browning, *Dramatis Personae*; Dickens, *Our Mutual Friend* (begins); Elizabeth Gaskell, *Wives and Daughters* (begins); Le Fanu, *Uncle Silas* Birth of Janet Achurch	

Year	Life
1865	Anna Cora Mowatt Ritchie publishes the novel *Fairy Fingers*
1866	Premiere of John Oxenford's adaptation of *East Lynne* at the Surrey Theatre. Death of Henry Wood. Mrs Henry Wood moves to South Hampstead, where she lives for the rest of her life
	Anna Cora Mowatt Ritchie publishes the novel *The Mute Singer*
1867	3 November – Pearl Richards (later Mrs Pearl Craigie; pseudonym John Oliver Hobbes) born at Chelsea, near Boston, Massachusetts
	Death of Pierce Butler
	Mrs Henry Wood becomes proprietor and editor of *Argosy*, where she publishes much of her later work. She publishes, anonymously, *A Life's Secret*
	Anna Cora Mowatt Ritchie publishes the anthology *The Clergyman's Wife, and Other Sketches*
1868	February – the Richards family move to London
	Fanny Kemble recommences her public readings in New York
1869	Fanny Kemble retires from public reading, returning to live near Philadelphia
	Mrs Henry Wood publishes *Roland Yorke*
1870	Anna Cora Mowatt Ritchie publishes *Italian Life and Legends*. She dies of tuberculosis, on 29 July, in Twickenham, London, and is buried in Kensal Green Cemetery with her first husband, James Mowatt

Year	Artistic Events	Historical Events
1865	Beginning of Bancroft management of the Prince of Wales (till 1880) Premieres: Boucicault, *Arrah-na-Pogu*; Robertson, *Society* Arnold, *Essays in Criticism*; Carroll, *Alice in Wonderland*; Newman, *The Dream of Gerontias*; Tolstoy, *War and Peace* (begins) Birth of Kipling, Yeats	US Civil War ends President Lincoln assassinated by John Wilkes Booth
1866	Select Committee of House of Commons investigates Theatrical Licences and Regulations Premiere: Robertson, *Ours* Trollope, *The Last Chronicle of Barset* (begins) Birth of H. G. Wells	
1867	Premiere: Robertson, *Caste* Zola, *Thérèse Raquin* Birth of Arnold Bennett, Galsworthy	Disraeli's Reform Act Marx, *Das Kapital* (begins)
1868	Premiere: Robertson, *Play* Birth of Gorky Death of Charles Kean	
1869	Premieres: H. J. Byron, *Uncle Dick's Darling*; Robertson, *School* Arnold, *Culture and Anarchy*; J. S. Mill, *On the Subjection of Women*	Suez Canal opens
1870	Premieres: Albery, *Two Roses*; Gilbert, *The Princess*; Strinberg's first produced	Elementary Education Act Franco-Prussian War begins Vatican Council

Year   *Life*

1871   June – Frances Butler marries the Honourable and
            Reverend James Wentworth Leigh. Fanny Kemble, her
            two daughters and their families visit Adelaide and
            Edward Sartoris in Rome

1872   The Richards summer on the Isle of Wight, beginning
            Pearl's long association with the island
            August – Elizabeth Robins is sent to live with
            grandmother in Zanesville, Ohio, where she attends the
            Putnam Female Seminary
            Mrs Henry Wood publishes *Within the Maize*
1874   Mrs Henry Wood begins to publish her 'Johnny
            Ludlow' stories, anonymously, in *Argosy*. 19
            November – T. A. Palmer's adaptation of *East Lynne*
            produced in Nottingham, with Madge Robertson as
            Lady Isabel

1875   Fanny Kemble begins to publish her 'Old Woman's
            Gossip' in the *Atlantic Monthly*

Year	Artistic Events	Historical Events
	play, *In Rome*, performed at the Dramaten Birth of Belloc Death of Dickens, Dumas père	Birth of Lenin
1871	Irving triumphs in *The Bells* at the Lyceum Premieres: Gilbert, *Pygmalion and Galatea* Darwin, *The Descent of Man*; George Eliot, *Middlemarch*; Hardy, *Desperate Remedies* Birth of Proust Death of T. W. Robertson	Trade Unions legalised Purchase of Army Commissions abolished Paris Commune
1872	Hardy, *Under the Greenwood Tree*; Nietzsche, *The Birth of Tragedy* Birth of Aubrey Beardsley, Beerbohm	
1874	The Meiningen troupe succeeds in Berlin and begins its European tours Premieres: Taylor, *Lady Clancarty*; Boucicault, *The Shaughraun* Hardy, *Far From the Madding Crowd* Birth of Chesterton, Frost, Gertrude Stein	
1875	Ellen Terry's Portia at Prince of Wales Charlotte Cushman retires from the stage Premiere: H. J. Byron, *Our Boys* Tolstoy, *Anna Karenina* (begins) Birth of Jung, Thomas Mann, Rilke Death of Kingsley	

Year	Life
1876	Mrs Henry Wood publishes her most successful later novel, *Edina* 1876/7 – Pearl Richards attends the Misses Godwin's Boarding School, London; she is subsequently educated by private tutors Florence Olliffe marries Hugh Bell
1877	20 January – Fanny Kemble leaves America. She never returns.
1878	Fanny Kemble publishes *Records of a Girlhood*
1880	June – Elizabeth Robins travels with her father to the gold mines of the Rocky Mountains, Colorado. December – Robins visits New York

Year	Artistic Events	Historical Events
1876	Phelps proposes a National Theatre First performance of *Peer Gynt* in Christiania Wagner's Bayreuth Theatre established Premiere: Tennyson, *Queen Mary* George Eliot, *Daniel Deronda*; Twain, *Tom Sawyer* Birth of Jack London Death of George Sand	Edison phonograph invented
1878	Irving assumes control of Lyceum (till 1899) with Ellen Terry as leading lady Debut of Beerbohm Tree Hardy, *Return of the Native* Birth of Lionel Barrymore Death of Charles Matthews, Phelps	Electric street lighting introduced in London Congress of Berlin
1879	Theatrical Reform Association and Church and Stage Guild founded Shakespeare Memorial Theatre opened at Stratford Premiere: Ibsen, *A Doll's House* at Danish Royal Theatre James, *Daisy Miller*; Stevenson, *Travels with a Donkey* Birth of Forster, Ethel Barrymore	First London telephone exchange Birth of Einstein, Stalin, Trotsky
1880	Bancrofts assume management of Haymarket Premieres: A. W. Pinero, *The Money-Spinner*;	Gladstone prime minister

Year	Life
1881	24 August – Elizabeth Robins travels to New York, set to go on the stage. During her journey, she reads Anna Cora Mowatt's *Autobiography*. 26 December – as a member of James O'Neill's company, Robins makes her professional stage debut in *The Two Orphans*
1882	Fanny Kemble publishes *Records of Later Life*
1883	January/February – James O'Neill company disbands. Elizabeth Robins joins H. M. Pitt's company. For the first time she appears under her own name. 25 August – after the collapse of Pitt's company, Robins joins the Boston Museum Company and makes her debut with the company as Adrienne in *A Celebrated Case* Fanny Kemble publishes *Notes on Some of Shakespeare's Plays*
1884	Fanny Kemble moves to Hereford Square, South Kensington, London
1885	12 January – Elizabeth Robins marries fellow actor George Richmond Parks in Salem, Massachusetts. 1 June – Robins leaves the Boston Museum Company. September – Robins joins a new company managed by O'Neill, touring as Mercedes in *The Count of Monte Cristo*
1886	November – Pearl Richards travels in America
1887	February – Pearl Richards returns to London and marries Reginald Walpole Craigie. She begins to write

Year	Artistic Events	Historical Events
	Ibsen's *Pillars of Society* given morning reading at Gaiety Birth of Lytton Strachey, Sean O'Casey Death of George Eliot, Flaubert, Planché, Taylor	
1881	D'Oyly Carte open Savoy Theatre with Gilbert and Sullivan, *Patience* London appearance of the Saxe-Meiningen Company Premieres: *Master Olof*, Strinberg's first major play published and produced in Stockholm; Ibsen, *Ghosts*	Married Women's Property Act Death of Disraeli, Carlyle
1882	Premieres: H. A. Jones, *The Silver King*; Ibsen, *An Enemy of the People* Birth of John Barrymore	
1883	Irving's first US tour	Fabian Society formed
1884		Gladstone's Reform Act
1885	Bancrofts leave Haymarket Premieres: Gilbert and Sullivan, *The Mikado*; Pinero, *The Magistrate*	
1886	James, *The Bostonians* Birth of T. S. Eliot, Lenox Robinson	Gladstone's first Home Rule Bill defeated
1887	Antoine founds Théâtre Libre, Paris	

Year	Life
	professionally and enters University College, London to follow a course in classics
	10 February – Mrs Henry Wood dies in London
	June – suicide of Elizabeth Robins's husband.
	September – Robins joins a touring company led by Edwin Booth and Lawrence Barrett
	Florence Bell publishes the comedy *A Sixpenny Telegram*. Her play *L'Indécis* is produced by Coquelin at the Royalty
1888	July – Elizabeth Robins arrives in Liverpool, spends a week in London before travelling to Norway during August. September – Robins returns to England and London. 20 October – makes her London debut in Poel's *Chieromancy* at St George Hall, Langham Place. December – she plays Portia to Benson's Shylock in Exeter
1889	Fanny Kemble publishes a novel *Far Away and Long Ago*
	17 January – Elizabeth Robins takes over from Mary Rorke as Mrs Errol in *The Real Little Lord Fauntleroy* for Saturday matinées. 5 July – Robins appears in trial matinée of Moore's *Forgotten* at the Islington Grand. 17 July – Robins appears in her first production of Ibsen as Martha Bernick in *The Pillars of Society*
1890	Spring – Elizabeth Robins plays opposite George Alexander in Hamilton Aide's long-running comedy *Dr Bill*. 10 June – Robins meet William Archer for the first time. August – she travels in Europe, visiting Oberammergau
	15 August – Pearl Craigie gives birth to her son, John Churchill Craigie
	Fanny Kemble publishes *Further Records*
	Florence Bell publishes collection of *Chamber Comedies*
1891	27 January – Elizabeth Robins appears as Mrs Linden in *The Dolls House*. 20 April – Robins appears as *Hedda Gabler*. 4 May – *Hedda Gabler* begins a run of evening performances. 26 September – Robins opens as Claire de Cintré in a production of Henry James's *The American*
	May – Pearl Craigie separates from her husband. Using the pseudonym of 'John Oliver Hobbes' for the first time, she publishes her first book, *Some Emotions and a Moral*

Year	Artistic Events	Historical Events
1888	Debut of Mrs Patrick Campbell Birth of James Bridie, Eugene O'Neill Death of Arnold	Eastman-Kodak's box camera invented
1889	Théâtre Libre visit London First English production of Ibsen's *A Doll's House*	
1890	Alexander begins management of the St James's James, *The Tragic Muse* Death of Boucicault	
1891	J. T. Grein's Independent Theatre Society founded – produces Ibsen's *Ghosts*; Conan Doyle, *The Adventures of Sherlock Holmes*; Hardy, *Tess of the D'Urbervilles*; Wilde, *The Picture of Dorian Gray*	Free elementary education

Year	Life
1892	May – Pearl Craigie publishes her second novel, *The Sinner's Comedy* in London and New York
	10 and 12 May – Elizabeth Robins plays the title role in Florence Bell's adaptation of *Karin*, a Swedish story by Alfhild Agrell. 18 August – Robins visits Bell in Yorkshire
	5 July – Pearl Craigie converts to Roman Catholicism: she takes the additional names of 'Mary Teresa'
1893	15 January – Fanny Kemble dies in London. She is buried near her father's grave in Kensal Green
	20 February – Elizabeth Robins appears as Hilda in *The Master Builder*
	28 April – premiere of *Alan's Wife* by Florence Bell and Elizabeth Robins at a matinée at Terry's by the Independent Theatre. Robins appears as Jean. It is repeated on the evening of 2 May. During May and June, in a season of Ibsen at the Opera Comique, Robins revives the role of Hilda Wangel – along with those of Rebecca West in *Rosmersholm*, Hedda in *Hedda Gabler* and Agnes in *Brand*. Bell is one of the sponsors of the event
	May and June – Pearl Craigie publishes the novels *A Study in Temptations* and *A Bundle of Life*
	10 July – Independent Theatre Society production of Florence Bell's *Jerry-Builder Solness*, a parody of Ibsen's *The Master Builder*. She publishes the one-act comedies *Between the Posts* and *A Joint Household*
1894	5 June – Pearl Craigie's first play, *Journey's End in Lovers Meeting*, written in collaboration with George Moore, produced at Daly's, with Johnston Forbes Robertson as Sir Philip and Ellen Terry as Lady Soupsie, and later, at the Lyceum. The first act of a second, uncompleted, play, *The Fool's Hour* (again in collaboration with Moore) is published in April in the first number of *The Yellow Book*. December – Craigie's novel *The Gods, Some Mortals, and Lord Wickenham*, begins serialisation in the *Pall Mall Budget*

Year	Artistic Events	Historical Events
1892	*Charley's Aunt* begins run of 1492 performances at the Royalty Premieres: Independent Theatre Society produces Shaw's *Widower's Houses*; Wilde, *Lady Windermere's Fan* Death of Tennyson	Gladstone prime minister Keir Hardy elected as first Labour MP
1893	Premieres: Wilde, *A Woman of No Importance*; Pinero, *The Second Mrs Tanqueray* with Mrs Patrick Campbell in the title role	Financial panic in America
1894	William Poel's Elizabethan Stage Society formed Premieres: Shaw, *Arms and the Man*; Jones, *The Case of the Rebellious Susan*	Death of Alexander III; accession of Nicholas II

Year	Life
	Summer – publication of Elizabeth Robins's novel *George Mandeville's Husband*, published under the pseudonym 'C. E. Raimond'. She also appears as the Countess Zicka in a revival of *Diplomacy* at the Garrick
1895	July – Pearl Craigie's divorce is finalised, she wins exclusive custody of her son. 1895/6 – Craigie president of the Society of Women Journalists Publication of Elizabeth Robins' second novel, *The New Moon*
1896	*The School for Saints* by Pearl Craigie premiered at the Lyceum. Publishes *The Herb Moon: a Fantasia* 23 November – Robins appears as Asta in *Little Eyolf*, in a cast that also includes Janet Achurch and Mrs Patrick Campbell
1897	3 May – Ibsen's *John Gabriel Borkman* launches the New Century Theatre *The School for Saints* by Pearl Craigie published in novel form
1898	2 June – *The Ambassador* by Pearl Craigie premiered at the St James's Theatre Elizabeth Robins appears in a matinée production of *Hedda Gabler* at the Fifth Avenue Theatre, New York
1899	February – Pearl Craigie's one act drama, *A Repentance*, produced at the St James's: it is poorly received. *Osbern and Ursyne* is published in Lady Randolph Churchill's *Anglo-Saxon Review*

Year	Artistic Events	Historical Events
1895	Premieres: Wilde, *An Ideal Husband*, *The Importance of Being Earnest*; Pinero, *The Notorious Mrs Ebbsmith* 25 May – Wilde convicted for committing homosexual acts and sentenced to 2 years hard labour. Irving knighted on the same day Crane, *The Red Badge of Courage*	Trial of Oscar Wilde Salisbury prime minister
1896	Premieres: Chekhov, *The Seagull* at the Alexandrinsky Theatre, St Petersburg; Jarry, *Ubu Roi*	Klondike Gold Rush
1897	Irish Literary Theatre formed Premieres: Barrie, *The Little Minister*; Shaw, *The Devil's Disciple* James, *What Maisie Knew*	Queen Victoria's Diamond Jubilee
1898	Stanislavsky and Nemirovich-Danchenko found Moscow Arts Theatre Premiere: Pinero, *Trelawney of the 'Wells'* Wilde, *The Ballad of Reading Gaol*; James, *The Turn of the Screw* Birth of Brecht	Spanish-American War
1899	Stage Society founded – proposes a 'theatre of ideas' Premieres: Yeats, *The Countess Cathleen*; Ibsen, *When We Dead Awaken* Birth of Noël Coward Death of Augustin Daly	Freud, *The Interpretation of Dreams* Boar War begins

Year	Life
1900	22 November – Pearl Craigie's *The Wisdom of the Wise* premiered (to a scornful audience) at the St James's: versions of it and *Osbern and Ursyne* are published Elizabeth Robins travels to Alaska to 'rescue' her brother from taking holy orders. In Seattle she falls ill with typhoid fever. She returns to London on 21 November and convalesces in Devon Florence Bell publishes *The Arbiter*, a novel
1901	Spring – Pearl Craigie travels to Italy. She publishes the novel, *The Serious Wooing*. Her essay on 'George Eliot' for the *Encyclopaedia Britannica* is favourably received
1902	*The Bishop's Move* by Pearl Craigie and Murray Carson produced at the Garrick with Violet Vanburgh and Arthur Bourchier. Mrs Craigie publishes the novels *Love and the Soul Hunters* and *Robert Orange* and a collection of short stories and plays (including *Journeys End in Lovers Meeting* written with George Moore), *Tales About Temperaments*. Her essay on 'George Sand' for a series of translations of French novels edited by Edmund Gosse is favourably received 30 October – Elizabeth Robins opens as *Eleanor* in an adaptation of Mrs Humphrey Ward's novel by the author and Julian Russell Sturgis. It runs for 15 performances after which, at the age of 40, Robins retires from the stage.
1903	January – Pearl Craigie is present at the Delhi Durbar. She reports on her travel experiences in the *Daily Graphic* and *Collier's Weekly*: they are subsequently collated in *Imperial India*. Her 'Letters from a Silent Study' appear in the *Academy* being republished in a single volume in 1904. She spends part of the year in Spain Florence Bell publishes a play, *The Dean of St Patrick's*
1904	Hugh Bell knighted 21 April! – Pearl Craigie's comedy, *The Flute of Pan* premiered at the Queen's Theatre, Manchester and, 12 November, produced with little success at the Shaftesbury. It is later published as a novel. Following successful serialisation in *Pall Mall Magazine* she publishes *The Vineyard* as a novel

Year	Artistic Events	Historical Events
1900	Premieres: H. A. Jones, *Mrs Dane's Defence*; Shaw, *You Never Can Tell* Death of Wilde	
1901	Premieres: H. G. Barker, *The Marrying of Anne Leete*; Chekhov, *The Three Sisters*	Death of Victoria, accession of Edward VII
1902	Premieres: Barrie, *The Admirable Crichton, Quality Street*; Gorky, *The Lower Depths*; Shaw, *Mrs Warren's Profession, Man and Superman*	Boer War ends
1903	Premiere: Synge, *The Shadow of the Glen*	Emmeline Pankhurst founds Women's Social and Political Union
1904	Barker and Vedrenne commence management of the Court Theatre (ends 1907) Royal Academy of Dramatic Art founded	Russo-Japanese War begins

Year	Life
	Elizabeth Robins publishes *The Magnetic North*, her most popular novel, based on her experiences, and those of her brother Raymond, in Alaska. It is dedicated to Florence Bell
1905	Pearl Craigie makes a lecture tour in the US. *The Flute of Pan* is published in novel form Elizabeth Robins publishes *A Dark Lantern*
1906	January – Pearl Craigie returns to London. 13 August – death of Craigie and the posthumous publication of her last novel, *The Dream and the Business*
1907	9 April – premiere of *Votes for Women* by Elizabeth Robins at the Court, directed by Harley Granville Barker. It is adapted and published in novel form as *The Convert*. Robins joins the board of the Women's Social and Political Union; moves to Blythe, Surrey Florence Bell publishes *At the Works: a Study of a Manufacturing Town*

Year	Artistic Events	Historical Events
	Abbey Theatre opened in Dublin	
	Premieres: Barrie, *Peter Pan*; Shaw, *John Bull's Other Island*; Synge, *Riders to the Sea*; Chekhov, *The Cherry Orchard*	
	Death of Chekhov	
1905	Actors' Union established	First Russian Revolution
	Aldwych Theatre opened	
	Meyerhold assumes control of Moscow Arts Theatre	
	Premieres: Barker, *The Voysey Inheritance*; Shaw, *Major Barbara, Man and Superman, The Philanderer* Craig, *The Art of the Theatre*; Forster, *Where Angels Fear to Tread*; Wilde, *De Profundis*	
	Death of Henry Irving	
1906	Premieres: Galsworthy, *The Silver Box*; Lady Gregory, *Hyacinth Halvey*; Shaw, *The Doctor's Dilemma*	Labour Party founded Women's Freedom League formed
	Birth of Samuel Beckett, Lillian Hellman, Clifford Odets	
	Death of Ibsen	
1907	Opening season of the Gaiety Theatre, Manchester, supported by Annie Horniman	Medical Inspection Act

Year	Life
1908	Elizabeth Robins publishes *Come and Find Me*, a novel about the quest for the North Pole
1909	Elizabeth Robins moves to Backsettown, Henfield, Sussex. *Votes for Women* is produced in New York and Rome
1910	Premiere of Florence Bell's *The Way the Money Goes*

Year	Artistic Events	Historical Events
1908	Premiere: Cicely Hamilton, *Diana of Dobson's*	Formation of Women's National Anti-Suffrage League, Fabian Women's Group, Actresses' Franchise League and Women Writers' Suffrage League

INTRODUCTION

There has been a general, and rather ungrounded, perception that the nineteenth century is all but a black hole for plays written by women; that no woman wrote a play of any interest in the decades between Mrs Inchbald's numerous and hugely popular works of the 1780s and 1790s and Elizabeth Robins's politically charged *Votes for Women* in 1906; that the history of women and the nineteenth-century stage is that of celebrated actresses and the occasional manager. Of course, this is tangibly untrue. Although the nineteenth century is not, perhaps, the place to look for plays of great literary worth (at least not until the end of the century when the influence of new European drama had an effect), the theatre was a vital, energetic, popular and determinedly profitable environment demanding of a constant supply of new plays. The voices of women playwrights, although less influential than in the Restoration or the eighteenth century, would indeed be heard, and occasionally celebrated, as an important aspect of the theatre culture.

Theatre historian Michael Booth is one of those who have commented upon the unprecedented 'detachment and isolation' from the theatre of the great writers of the nineteenth century. Certainly one can argue that the subordination of the word in favour of production values, the low fixed-fee system of payments and the lack of copyright drove potential dramatists to the more private forms of poetry and the novel.[1] However, the theatre industry was also one of rich diversity and economic strength, a highly organised medium responding more to social and economic factors than to literary and aesthetic principles but still demanding of new plays and playwrights.

Women were employed in all aspects and at all levels of this cultural industry. Their most visible role was certainly that of performer and, as Tracy C. Davis makes clear in her ground-breaking studies, this category encompasses the lowest-paid dancing girl and the greatest, most popular and most powerful stars.[2] The roles adopted by women theatre professionals extended beyond the footlights to include the astute managers of touring companies, grand theatres and local music halls, and the skilled, if undervalued, crafts-workers necessary for any stage production. In short, women were active, sedulous and creative forces in the nineteenth-century stage.

The women whose works appear in this volume reflect this diversity. One was a retiring spinster whose dalliance with the stage was primarily literary and resolutely proper; one a child prodigy, who performed at Drury Lane at the age of eleven; one the celebrated star of London's first house; one the leading lady of the American stage; one a member of the British social elite whose friendship with one of the late-century's most remarkable actresses, led to demanding, new drama; another was an American-born member of London's literary aristocracy whose career as a writer of plays was criticised as a fashionable whim rather than a commitment to the advancement and development of the contemporary stage. These were different women writing different types of drama for a constantly changing, constantly evolving theatre environment.

During the nineteenth century plays were variously written by the leading stars of the period, by theatre managers, by educational reformers, by socialists, by feminists and by the new and outlandish phenomenon of the professional playwright. Women were included in all these categories. Nevertheless, most of the women whose work appears in this volume were performers before they were playwrights. The writing careers of Marie-Thérèse De Camp and her daughter Fanny Kemble were, more or less, dependent on their star status and the indulgence of Kemble managements. But the American Anna Cora Mowatt is more unusual in that her professional writing career preceded, albeit briefly, her ascendancy as America's most popular mid-century actress. Her fellow-countrywoman, Elizabeth Robins, retired from the stage at the relatively young age of forty-one to pursue an equally successful writing career. For most of these practitioners, the stage was a place wherein an industrious and talented woman might earn her keep and more. Some, like Fanny Kemble, were born to the profession, others turned to the theatre for amusement, to advance political ideas or from sheer financial need. For each the stage offered a potentially exciting and independent lifestyle: an active and intellectually and physically demanding career with an opportunity for national and international travel and the possibility of celebrity status and financial independence.

These were opportunities for women that few other professions could equal. As a consequence, the women whose work is included in this anthology were able, at different points in their lives, to make choices their contemporaries could not because of the independence afforded by their earning potential. As a child-performer Marie-Thérèse De Camp contributed ably to her family's income. Fanny Kemble single-handedly saved the Kemble management of Covent Garden from financial ruin. Anna Cora Mowatt supported her ill and financially ruined husband for almost all of their married life and was able to leave her second husband on the expectations that she could earn her own living. The prose-writer Mrs Henry Wood (represented here as the author of *East Lynne*, which was the source material for the definitive melodrama of the late century) wrote for profit from the 1850s and in her middle age seems to have provided her household with its sole income. Elizabeth Robins, a widow at twenty-three, emigrating from the US and emerging in London as one of an influential new generation of actors determined to reform theatre, earned her own income for all of her long life. Pearl Craigie divorced her husband after a short, unhappy match and ploughed for herself a distinctive and independent furrow that included study, travel and journalism. Such choices were possible because of talent and necessity, certainly, but also because of the general, and at the time unique, meritocracy of the theatre world.

The women who wrote for the theatre were of a different mettle than those who wrote the century's significant novels. As Gwen Davis and Beverly A. Joyce argue:

> The commercial stage in the mid-Victorian age did retain something of the unsavoury reputation of the Restoration theatre. The ambiguous social position of the actress may have discouraged some from going on the stage or writing for it, but it continued to attract women for financial reward and for the outlet of their talents.[3]

These were women publicly active and industrious within their chosen field, bold travellers and adventurers, who took advantage of and pushed forward the freedoms and responsibilties gradually admitted to women in the nineteenth century. The expansion and the profes-sionalisation of the stage in the course of the nineteenth-century supported what was, in some respects and for some practitioners, a protofeminist industry. Women could have equal and even greater earning potential than men, women could and did employ and manage theatre companies and theatre buildings; they could and did travel widely in the pursuit of their careers. The women who took these opportunities earlier in the century were often remarkable and ground-breaking figures who built a strong foundation for the more overtly politicised women writers and performers of the 1890s. Their extraordinary and brilliant careers contributed to the advance of theatre as an art form, as a legitimate and respected profession and as a social, economic and increasingly influential cultural force.

The nineteenth-century stage saw great and radical changes in organisation: the emergence of the professions of playwright and director, the industrialisation of the theatre infrastructure – with the rise of the actor-manager and the theatre syndicates – and the move towards respectability. The plays in this volume offer a unique perspective on these developments. From the verse drama and historical tragedy of the early Romantic period to drawing room comedy and satire, from sentimental melodrama to political commentary, they reflect the broad scope of nineteenth-century drama. The plays are wonderfully diverse, describing the lives of women who are by turns heroic, prosaic, comical and tragic; men and women who are evil, foolish, scheming, wronged or just ordinary, and depicting characters who are, indeed, victims of theatrical convention alongside those who are remarkably and radically disruptive of dramatic stereotypes.

In the course of the nineteenth century women provided the stage with plays of great diversity and the audiences with remarkable entertainments. In selecting texts for this volume I have focused on pieces that reflect the different aspects of the theatre environment of the nineteenth century and illustrate the many and varied roles adopted by women within that environment. Readers may rightly conclude that the plays have not been selected merely for their literary worth but because they represent achievements merely by women who worked for and in the nineteenth-century theatre. These works reflect the various strands of dramatic writing encompassed by the nineteenth-century theatre, including a tradition of plays that were written to be published and read privately, plays highlighting the power of the mid-century celebrity, plays displaying clear, generic structure and focusing on fashionable society, as well as plays of social awareness and political intent.

I hope that readers will find in this volume an unexpected and neglected aspect of nineteenth-century culture and that they will enjoy the plays with an appropriate spirit of exploration and rediscovery.

Joanna Baillie

Joanna Baillie was born a daughter of the manse in Bothwell, Lanarkshire, Scotland, in 1762. Her mother was Dorothea Hunter Baillie, whose brothers, William and John Hunter, were the pre-eminent physicians of the age. Although Joanna's younger brother, Matthew, was set for a career in medicine, such an option was imponderable for Joanna and her sister, and lifelong companion, Agnes. Nonetheless, she was educated in the literatures and philosophies of the day, and the depth and quality of this training is reflected in the tone and the scope of her own prose, poetry and drama.

Joanna Baillie was already at a boarding school in Glasgow when, in 1776, her father was appointed Professor of Divinity at the University of Glasgow. The family moved from Hamilton to the environs and society of Glasgow's High Street, but two years later the professor was dead and the family left the precincts of the university. While Matthew went to Balliol College, Oxford, Joanna, her mother and sister retired to Long Calderwood, the Hunter estate outside Glasgow. There they remained until 1783 when William Hunter's death left Matthew heir to his School of Anatomy on Windmill Street, London, and the family moved to the metropolis. In the early 1790s, shortly after the anonymous publication of Joanna's first volume of poetry, the female Baillies moved to Hampstead where they resided for the rest of their lives.

Her first volume of plays, *A Series of Plays; in which it is attempted to delineate the stronger passions of the mind*, was published in 1798 and contains some of Baillie's best known pieces, principally *De Montford* and *Count Basil*. A second volume followed in 1802; her *Miscellaneous Plays* was published in 1804 and a third volume of the so-called *Plays on the Passions* appeared in 1812. Although she did again publish plays in the 1830s, it is on these early publications that Joanna Baillie's reputation as a dramatist rests.

Baillie's first play to be produced for the theatre was *De Montford*, which premiered at Drury Lane with the age's leading tragedians – Sarah Siddons and John Philip Kemble – on 29 April 1800. It is a somewhat stilted heroic verse-tragedy whose success was rather limited. Nevertheless it remained, on and off, in the Kemble repertoire, and was part of John Philip Kemble's farewell tour in 1817, when it achieved particular success in Edinburgh, a city with close ties to the Kemble dynasty. The Theatre Royal was something of an outpost for the Kemble empire, being managed by Sarah Siddons's son, Henry, and, after his death, by his widow, Harriet, and her brother W. H. Murray.

Edinburgh was also a loyal supporter of Baillie. Although so long resident in London, she was celebrated as a Scottish woman of letters. Her friendship with Sir Walter Scott was the flourishing of this identity, and he promoted and sponsored her work both in the Scottish capital and in London. Baillie first met the age's most popular novelist and storyteller in 1806 and a friendship began that was to last until Scott's death in 1832. When the Baillie sisters toured the north (the Lakes, Glasgow and the Highlands) in 1808, they were guests of Scott in Edinburgh. Perhaps inspired by this Highland excursion, Baillie's next play was *The Family Legend*, which became, along with *De Montford*, one of her most successful pieces for the theatre. It was produced, at the Theatre Royal, Edinburgh, in 1810 (at the insistence of Scott), at Drury Lane in 1815 and again at Drury Lane (by Edmund Kean) in 1821. Its first production was particularly celebrated, as its heroically Ossianic tone coincided with the patriotic mood of Edinburgh.[4] It is an eventful tale of clan rivalry, deceit, revenge and retribution, lost loves, innocence at risk, concealed identity and espionage. Its several climaxes – which include the leading lady being abandoned on a rock to await certain drowning, and a dramatic, and potentially rather bloody, duel – assure a spectacular entertainment but little by way of mature character development or sophisticated denouement. Sir Walter, however, knew the value of playing-to-the-balcony and realised the play's potential for sensational staging: Alasdair Cameron notes that for this first production Scott 'had insisted that authentic tartans (green for the Campbells contrasting with red for the Macleans) be used.'[5] The enthusiasm of the period for what appears on the page to be monotonous versification can be explained by such spectacular and energetic stage presentations that transformed the exaggerated drama of verse tragedy through the élan of production.

While most of Joanna Baillie's drama is written in verse, a lively alternative may be found in *Witchcraft*, 1836, a play of a surprisingly different tone and type, though also set in Scotland. The play is one of Baillie's most unusual, notable for a distinctive and sustained attempt at linguistic realism and a very different use of drama than her usual employment of the poetic tragic mode allowed. Although ponderously plotted it is unexpectedly intriguing, something of a psychological thriller set against a backdrop of religious intolerance and the fear of hellish witchcraft. The play offers a remarkably bleak vision of character and community. There is none of the heroics of *De Montford*, *Count Basil* or *The Family Legend*; characters are generally unsympathetic, with dark and often guilty secrets, and demonstrate little by way of tolerance or humanity – at the play's close the townspeople of Paisley are literally baying for blood.

In 1836 Joanna Baillie's career in writing drama ended with the productions of *The Homicide* at Drury Lane and *The Separation* at Covent Garden and the collation of some later works in a three-volume edition of *Dramas*. Although only a minority of her plays were ever performed, her position as *grande dame des lettres* during the early and middle decades of the nineteenth century was secure. The majority of these plays were written to be read, being closer to the genre of 'closet' plays that the era allowed for and celebrated than to active engagements in the theatre industry. Some of her works did hold the stage, but it rested with her substantial publications to assure her a place in the public's imagination. She died in Hampstead, London, on 23 February 1851.

Joanna Baillie is, quite simply and irrespective of gender, the most important playwright in nineteenth-century Scotland. And so it is all the more unfortunate that when she is remembered at all it is in connection with the patronage of Sir Walter Scott and as his *protégé*. His support for 'the best dramatic writer' in Britain since the Jacobeans[6] did secure her stage production and access to Scottish literary circles, but Joanna Baillie's *oeuvre* is large enough and strong enough that her reputation should be considered on its own merits. During her lifetime she was celebrated as *the* female writer of the age, eclipsing the reputations of Hannah More, Anne Yearsley and Felicia Hemans. Byron described her as 'our only dramatist since Otway and Southerne; I don't except Home', concluding that 'Women (save Joanna Baillie) cannot write tragedy.'[7] However, today her work is neither remembered not celebrated, nor is it likely to be revived. It is a type of drama that, despite its heroic intent and assured poetry, is in essence a form of the early nineteenth century. Nevertheless, for those employed in the historiography of the stage and the history of stage theory, her introduction to the *Plays on the Passions* is a remarkably engaging, insightful and salient commentary on the role of the drama. It evidences serious thought and reflection on a genre that the coming century would often dismiss as either tedious and portentous versification or mere and vulgar sensationalism.

Marie-Thérèse De Camp

In an age of child-prodigies, Marie-Thérèse De Camp (later Mrs Charles Kemble)[8] was a precocious child performer who achieved the near impossible by winning significant success in adulthood. Born in Vienna on 17 January 1775, of a French father (Georges De Camp) and Swiss mother (Jeanne Dufour), she was the first of at least six children, some four of whom worked in theatres on both sides of the Atlantic.

When Marie-Thérèse was an infant, the family moved to London in search of theatrical employment for her father, who became a musician in the orchestra at Covent Garden. Her first professional engagement was at the age of eight, on 1 May 1783, when she appeared as Cupid in the opera-ballet *Les Ruses de l'Amour* at the King's Theatre. She worked almost constantly from that time, drawing the attention of the Prince of Wales, shortly to become Prince Regent, whose patronage made the child a particular favourite of his court. In 1786 she appeared as Zélie in a translation of the Countess de Genlis's *La Colombe* at Le Texier's theatre, making her debuts at the Haymarket as a dancer and at Drury Lane as Julie in *Richard, Coeur de Lion* the same year. Her adult success was assured following her performance as MacHeath in a sex-reversal production of *The Beggar's Opera* at the Haymarket on 15 August 1792.

Marie-Thérèse De Camp is described, by biographers of her more famous daughter Fanny, as dedicated to outdoor pursuits (principally angling and riding), moody and, later in life, eccentric in her behaviour. But she was also unimpeachably chaste, virtuous and respectable, a devout member of London's Swiss congregation. Despite this reputation, the whiff of scandal touched her in 1795 when, as one of the young leading-lights of the Drury Lane company, she caught the inebriated attentions of John Philip Kemble. He burst into her dressing room and pressed his unwanted attentions upon the young lady. Whilst she was known for the probity of her character, such an action was equally unusual for the leading actor. The rumpus attracted swift help and little damage was done to either party. Immediately, John Philip Kemble apologised in a remarkably public manner – the *Times* ran an announcement:

> I, JOHN PHILIP KEMBLE, of the Theatre Royal, Drury-lane, do adopt this method of publicly apologizing to MISS DECAMP, for the very improper and unjustifiable behaviour I was lately guilty of towards her; which I do further declare her conduct and character had in no instance authorised, but; on the contrary, I do know and believe both to be irreproachable.
>
> January 27, 1795.[9]

The affair seemed to be over until 1800 when Charles, John Philip Kemble's younger brother, announced his desire to marry his vivacious co-star. His elder brother at first refused to allow the match, eventually agreeing to it if the couple would wait until Charles's thirtieth birthday. Thus, despite both being successful actors, in command of excellent incomes and potentially independent, the couple waited the alloted span to marry, on 2 July 1806, with the blessing of the Kemble clan, and the determinedly patriarchal John Philip gave the bride away.

Shortly thereafter the Kembles transferred their management to Covent Garden and Marie-Thérèse De Camp made her debut in this, the capital's first house, on 1 October 1806. The apotheosis of the Kemble regime at Covent Garden should have occurred on 4 October 1809, when an enlarged and renovated auditorium opened to the public. Instead the evening was marked by unprecedented disturbances and public outcry, immediately described as the 'OP' or 'Old Price' Riots. Persisting for some sixty-seven consecutive performance nights, audiences protested vocally and disruptively against the modernised theatre's raised admission prices. Marie-Thérèse returned to face the unruly audience two nights after the opening in the farce *Who Wins?*, and afterwards retired from the stage to prepare for the birth of her third child and first daughter, Fanny, on 27 November.

Marie-Thérèse De Camp the actress was celebrated for her beauty, her figure and her delightful stage personality. De Camp the playwright was less celebrated but equally in tune with the whims of theatre audiences. She wrote comedies and farces, and she was particularly adept at the short interludes, or one-act plays, that would be interspersed throughout the programme and were so much a feature of the nineteenth-century stage. Her plays are peopled by the types of character she and her husband excelled at playing – members of sophisticated society, clever, witty and vivacious but perhaps slightly put-upon or gullible. In complete command of this genre, De Camp was confident in choosing the premiere of her first full-length comedy, *First Faults*, for her own benefit night[10] on 3 May 1799. This is a slight, if promising, comedy that featured some of Covent Garden's best and most popular comedians: Charles Kemble, Harriot Mellon and Dorothy Jordan. It received just a single performance and was never printed.[11]

De Camp's interlude, a one-act farce titled *The Day After the Wedding; or, A Wife's First Lesson*, was produced at Covent Garden, for the benefit of Charles Kemble, on 18 May 1808. To its traditional tale – taming a shrewish wife and pricking the pomposity of masculinity – was added greater piquancy with the casting of the theatre's favourite couple as the newly-wed protagonists. Colonel Freelove provided Charles Kemble with an archetypally good-hearted if misled romantic lead and the irascible Lady Freelove proved one of

De Camp's most popular roles. Perhaps De Camp's most successful piece, *The Day After the Wedding* continued to hold the stage for several decades with production continuing regularly on both sides of the Atlantic and several editions being published.[12]

The management of Covent Garden lodged De Camp's play *The Lawsuit* with the Lord Chamberlain's office on 27 November 1815. Retitled *Smiles and Tears: or, The Widow's Stratagem*, the play premiered on 12 December. The writer herself seems to have made a solitary appearance as Lady Emily Gerrard – Charles Kemble was again perfectly suited for the role of Sir Henry Chomley – before again withdrawing from the Covent Garden stage until 1818/9 when she returned to her loyal London audiences for her final season and roles that included Madge Wildfire in the premiere of Terry's musical version of *The Heart of Midlothian* (17 April 1819). Her farewell from the stage was on 9 June 1819 when she played Lady Julia in a production of her own 1805 interlude of disguise, mistaken identity and true love, *Personation; or, Fairly Taken In.*

Smiles and Tears is based on Amelia Opie's sentimental novel, *Father and Daughter.*[13] In translation and after adaptation it becomes a delightful comedy, carefully attuned to the demands of the contemporary stage. The play benefits from De Camp's interest in character and from her wit and ample knowledge of what would work on stage. It is a play of two rather different but intimately related plots. The more obviously appealing, and perhaps the better written, is that concerning the love affairs between Lady Emily Gerald and Colonel O'Donolan, Mrs Belmore and Sir Henry Chomley, and turns on themes of concealed and mistaken identity, jealousy and legal wranglings. The other is a tense melodramatic piece concerning Delaval, later Lord Glenthorn, and his abused lover, Cecil Fitzharding. This is a more difficult and perhaps less convincing plot of idiosyncratic emotional excess and consummate sentimentalism. The characters are, on one level, the stock types of melodrama (the duplicitous rake and the virtuous young girl) and, on another, of complex and unexpected psychological depth. Delaval is a demanding role of contradictory motivations and confused morality and, in the lighter plot, O'Donolan is a deeply touching sketch of a foolishly jealous but devoted lover. The conclusion of the plot concerning Cecil and Delaval is unexpectedly dark and emotionally engaging. In stark and deliberate contrast to the happy affairs of Emily and O'Donolan, Mrs Belmore and Sir Henry, Cecil and Delaval are not united. Although Delaval repents his wrong doings and receives forgiveness from Cecil, redemption does not extend to her, and she commits herself to caring for her distracted father, apparently leaving her infant child in the care of the newly ennobled Delaval. Her contrition is at least as sincere as Delaval's but her penance excludes her from society, her seduction having cast her irretrievably as a fallen woman.

Smiles and Tears, De Camp's most substantial and most assured play, also seems to have been her last piece of theatre writing.[14] Given the confidence she displays in handling the intricacies of plot and the complexities of some of her characters, this seems at least unfortunate. Although she retired from the stage in 1819 De Camp maintained a close and expert involvement with the management of Covent Garden, making a celebrated return to that stage just one more time when, at the age of fifty-five, she broke her retirement to play Lady Capulet to her daughter's debut Juliet.

Marie-Thérèse De Camp died at Adlestone, near Chertsey, on 3 September 1838. Fanny was in America.

Fanny Kemble

The nineteenth century saw the rise and rise of the theatrical dynasty. From the Keans, the Macreadys and the Websters to the Batemans, the Terrys and the Barrymores, the children of theatre professionals often followed the family trade. The Kembles were both typical of this tendency and remarkable in that their reputation remains so dominant. So much so that the story of the theatre culture of the late-eighteenth and nineteenth centuries could be told through reference to the Kembles alone, for their extended family tree eventually annexed not only the De Camps but also the Satchells, the Murrays and the Cowells, and through them the Batemans and the Comptons. The fortunes of the Kembles represent the rise of great and celebrated actors (quintessentially that of siblings Sarah Siddons and John Philip Kemble), the geographical and economic spread of the theatre industry (great metropolitan houses, provincial Theatres Royal and lesser circuits were managed by the Kembles, who were also among the first to tour in and emigrate to North America), the influence of state control over the British stage (Charles Kemble held the office of Examiner of Plays for the Lord Chamberlain's office), as well as the technical development of the stage and the theatre industry (under their management Covent Garden was at the forefront of new initiatives in production and management). However, in a family whose parents, aunts, uncles, brothers and sisters were almost all actors, the union of Marie-Thérèse De Camp and Charles Kemble was remarkable in that only their eldest daughter followed their footsteps directly. (Their youngest daughter, Adelaide, achieved notable success as an opera singer, but early and happy marriage to Edward Sartoris ended her professional career.)

Frances Ann Kemble was born on 27 November 1809 when her family's fortunes at Covent Garden were typically uncertain. Perhaps more than any other force, it was this theatre, its financial needs and artistic demands that shaped Fanny Kemble's life and career. Something of a wild and unruly child, she was sent abroad for her education, first to Boulogne and then, for a longer period, to Paris. This was a formative experience for her linguistically, socially and personally, instilling in her the distinctive independence of spirit that so marked her later years. Upon her return, she spent long periods with various relatives: during an 1825 visit to cousins she first met Harriet St Leger, her life-long friend and correspondent; and from 1827 she resided some two years with Mrs Henry Siddons (née Harriet Murray), widow of her aunt Sarah Siddons's actor-manager son and leading lady of the Edinburgh Theatre Royal. Fanny Kemble later recalled this sojourn to Edinburgh as one of the happiest and most contented of her life.

In 1829 she returned to London. The family business was in crisis. Drastic action was called for and drastic action was taken when Marie-Thérèse and Charles Kemble enlisted their eldest daughter to save the family fortune by going on the stage. On 5 October 1829, and not yet twenty-one years of age, Fanny Kemble made a triumphant debut as Juliet on the stage made famous by her aunt and uncle, Sarah Siddons and John Philip Kemble. To show her support of her young and inexperienced daughter, Marie-Thérèse came out of retirement for one night to play Lady Capulet. Charles Kemble played Mercutio. The phenomenal success of this casting coup temporarily secured the fate of the Kemble management of Covent Garden and led to a remarkable outburst of fanaticism for the new star. In late May 1830 Fanny and her father commenced an extensive money-making tour of Britain, playing at major theatres throughout the country and everywhere meeting fashionable society. Fanny Kemble's diaries and journals record her experiences and encounters with enthusiasm and a degree of style: in Edinburgh she met Sir Walter Scott, 'that admirable genius and excellent, kind man';[15] in Manchester, George Stephenson, 'with whom I am most horribly in love'.[16]

During her peak season of 1832, Fanny created the part of Julia in Sheridan Knowles's *The Hunchback*, one of her most popular roles, and premiered (on 15 March) her own play *Francis the First* with herself as Louisa of Savoy, the scheming Queen Mother. It is a play typical of the contemporary fashion for heroic and historical verse drama. It may read poorly, but with the whole of Covent Garden's resources at her disposal the play afforded a great opportunity for sumptuous settings and spectacular action – indeed, the whole of the final act is little more than an extended and action-packed battle scene.

The publication and production of *Francis the First* is a clear example of the nineteenth-century theatre's cult of the star performer. It was staged as a vehicle for the particular talents and reputation of Fanny Kemble, exploiting her fame and celebrity. It is nonetheless revealing that she chose the more interesting, and more challenging, role of the Queen Mother, rather than the traditionally romantic one of Françoise. Despite her protestations that she disliked the stage, Fanny Kemble knew how to distinguish between a demanding, complex role that might stretch and develop her skills, and one that was merely ordinary.

On 22 June 1832 she bid farewell to the Covent Garden audience and on 1 August sailed for New York, where she and her father made their American debuts at the Park Theatre in September. In October, the tour continued to Philadelphia, where Fanny met her future husband, Pierce Butler, for the first time. The expedition was profitable and enjoyable until the unexpected death in April of her aunt, chaperone and friend, Adelaide De Camp. Fanny was consoled by Butler, a Philadelphian who had been besotted with her from the first. He appeared handsome, rich and dashing, interested in the theatre and music, as well as the outdoor activities, including riding, that she enjoyed so much. To friends, however, her marriage on 7 June 1834 to Butler was ill-starred from the start. Kemble retired from the stage, gave her considerable profits from the American tour to her father (who returned to London), and settled down to a less than idyllic rural existence in Pennsylvania. She gave birth to her first daughter, Sarah, in May 1835; a second daughter, Frances, followed in May 1838.

New work continued to be produced, mainly in prose journals (*The Journal of Frances Anne Butler* was published in Philadelphia in 1835) but some plays were presented before the public, notably a production of *The Star of Seville* at the Walnut Street Theatre, Baltimore in 1838. Most of Fanny's time, however, was taken with establishing a home, caring for her family and experiencing the variety and potential of her life in America. This included her shattering journey to the southern states and her visit to the Butler's estate in the Georgia Sea Islands at the beginning of 1839, when she experienced a slave-worked plantation for the first time. Her journals reflect her shock and disgust at the conditions these people endured. These feelings were just some of the factors contributing towards the increasingly certain disintegration of her marriage. When the Butlers returned to Philadelphia in April of that year relations between Fanny and Pierce were in terminal decline, with Fanny threatening to leave Pierce to return to London and the stage. However, the inevitable split did not come until 1844, the year she also published a volume of *Poems* in Philadelphia – a city she did not quit until September of 1845, sailing for London and finally travelling to Italy to stay for almost a year with her sister, Adelaide Sartoris, in Rome. After this sojourn, which she chronicles in *A Year of Consolation* (1847), she returned to the stage first at the Theatre Royal, Manchester, and then in a tour of England during which she revived old parts and began a series of public readings, notably of Shakespeare. In April 1847 Pierce Butler initiated divorce proceeding on the grounds of wilful desertion. In May, Fanny returned to the London stage for the first time since 1832 and, in February 1849, began an engagement playing, somewhat incongruously, opposite the rising-star William Charles Macready.

On 21 November 1849, after a bitter and very public hearing, Fanny and Pierce Butler divorced. Butler gained custody of their two daughters. In America for the proceedings Fanny continued her public readings as 'Mrs Kemble' before retiring to the relative tranquillity and privacy of Lenox, Massachusetts. During 1850 she returned to London, and from mid-1853 spent another year with the Sartorises in Italy, being in London for the death of her father on 12 November 1854. In 1856 she returned to America for a long-anticipated reunion with her daughters, who summered with her in Lenox.

Fanny Kemble's transatlantic lifestyle continued for many years to come. In May 1859, when her second daughter came of age, Fanny took Frances to Europe, returning in October to undertake another money-making reading tour. She crossed and recrossed the Atlantic on many occasions over the next decade or so, and these transitory years were marked by the publication of several important works – a collection of *Plays* (1863) certainly, but more significantly the remarkable *Journal of a Residence on a Georgian Plantation in 1838–1839* (1863).

Continually under financial pressure, Fanny Kemble briefly recommenced her public readings in New York in 1868, finally retiring from the platform the next year when she returned to live near her daughter Sarah and her family outside Philadelphia. Pierce Butler had died in 1867, leaving his diminished estates to the management of his youngest and most devoted daughter, Frances, who married the Honourable and Reverend James Wentworth Leigh in June 1871. Fanny began her travelling once again, and she and both her daughters and their families spent an extended vacation with Adelaide and Edward Sartoris in Rome. During this period she met the novelist Henry James, who famously described her as 'the terrific Kemble' and who was to become the dearest friend of her old age.[17] Upon the families' return to America, Fanny continued to reside close to Sarah in Philadelphia and in 1875, at the age of sixty-six, she began her regular contributions to the *Atlantic Monthly* under the heading of 'Old Woman's Gossip' – an undertaking that earned her some £300 annually.[18] In January 1877 Fanny Kemble left America for the last time, subsequently publishing autobiographical reminiscences, including *Records of a Girlhood* (1878), *Records of Later Life* (1882), the novel *Far Away and Long Ago* (1889) and *Further Records: 1848–1883* (1890). Fanny Kemble died in London on 15 January 1893 and is buried at Kensal Green, close to the grave of her father.

With the possible exception of *Journal of a Residence on a Georgian Plantation*, often cited by historians as contributing to the abolitionist debate, she is remembered more for her phenomenal acting career than for her preferred career as a writer. This is all the more ironic given her distaste for the practice of acting (she infamously described the career of the actress as 'a business unworthy of a woman') and her abiding determination to be considered as a woman of letters.

Anna Cora Mowatt

Anna Cora Mowatt is the most influential of the many women working for the American stage in the nineteenth century. Her importance lies on a number of fronts: one is certainly her play *Fashion*; another her role in the expansion of the provincial circuits of the United States; there are also her various autobiographical books and semi-autobiographical novels describing and illuminating nineteenth-century stage life; and there is her contribution to the rise of the social acceptability and respectability of theatre, which cannot be exaggerated.

Mowatt was born in March 1819[19] to Samuel and Eliza Ogden, Americans living in Bordeaux, France. Business interests kept the family in the Dordogne until the end of 1826 when they returned to America. Her family was prominent both within New York society and American political history. Samuel Ogden had been very nearly ruined when he financed the so-called Miranda Expedition and was subsequently tried for fitting out an expedition against a power (Spain) in amity with the United States; and her mother, Eliza, was the granddaughter of Francis Lewis, one of the signatories of the Declaration of Independence. Despite the family's fashionable interest in elaborate charades and amateur theatricals, this was, in the mid-nineteenth century, an unlikely beginning for one of the age's most popular stage performers. Indeed, religous fervour meant that she had refused even to enter a professional theatre until she was thirteen, at which point her principles relaxed on seeing Fanny Kemble as Julia in *The Hunchback*.

On 6 October 1834, at the age of fifteen, Anna Cora Ogden all but eloped to marry James Mowatt in New York. Under his tutelage she developed her strong interest in poetic and dramatic literature, and wrote and privately published her first play, *Pelayo; or, The Cavern of Covadonga* in 1836. From 1837, using the *nom de plume* of 'Cora', she began to contribute to magazines and journals. However, because of failing health and a diagnosis of consumption, a sea voyage was recommended and she set off for Europe to recuperate. Like any American tourist she was intent on seeing the sights, first of London, where she saw Madame Vestris at the Olympic, and then Paris, where she saw Rachel at the Théâtre Français. In Europe to join his young wife, James Mowatt's health deteriorated and, when the couple returned to New York in August of 1840, became irretrievable, forcing him to retire from work. His almost immediate financial ruin necessitated the sale of their substantial property in Long Island. In the midst of this financial collapse Anna Cora Mowatt's second play, *Gulzara; or, The Persian Slave*, was mounted in a private performance in celebration of her father's birthday. The play was subsequently published in the journal *New World*. Her writing career was galvanised when (often writing as 'Helen Berkley') she became a regular contributor to *Godey's*, *The Democratic Review*, *The Ladies' Companion*, *The Columbian* and other magazines. In 1842 she published her first novel, *The Fortune Hunter*. Recognising the potential of his wife's skills, James Mowatt established a company to promote her work. It was not a success but did issue her volumes on *A Life of Goethe* and *Memoirs of Madame D'Arblay*, which act as a fine contrast to her contemporary guides to homemaking, domestic horticulture and other 'how to' topics.

Motivated almost entirely by financial necessity, and encouraged by the playwright and essayist Epes Sargent, Mowatt began a parallel career as a public reader with an engagement in Boston on 18 October

1841. She subsequently appeared in Providence, Rhode Island, and the tour culminated in New York. Again influenced by Sargent, she wrote a play, and on 24 March 1845 *Fashion; or, Life in New York* premiered at the Park Theatre, New York. It ran for a remarkable eighteen nights, and during its third week in New York was staged simultaneously at the Chestnut Street Theatre in Philadelphia. It was not until 13 June, again at the Park Theatre that Mrs Mowatt made her stage debut as an actress, appearing as Pauline in *Lady of Lyons*. A few nights later she performed at the Walnut Street Theatre in Philadelphia. After a fortnight's engagement, under much public pressure and as a benefit for the stage manager Mr Blake, she appeared as Gertrude in *Fashion*. It was not her favourite role, despite the public's enjoyment of seeing her in her own play, but from this point her career as a performer was assured. Engagements followed at Niblo's Garden, New York, preceding a tour of the United States during 1845 and 1846. After this first year on the stage she left her existing and somewhat unsatisfactory leading man, William H. Crisp, for the rising star of E. L. Davenport, with whom she began another extensive American tour. In this *annus mirabilis* she published her second novel, *Evelyn*.

During 1847 James Mowatt travelled to England to arrange a British tour for his wife. Summering with her father in New York, Anna Cora Mowatt wrote the historical romance, *Armand; or, The Child of the People*. The play was written specially for her partnership with Davenport: she playing Blanche and her co-star the gallant Armand. It was produced at the Park Theatre and in Boston prior to embarkation for England. On 7 November 1847 the pair made their British debuts at the Theatre Royal, Manchester, with Mowatt's most popular role, *Lady of Lyons*. The tour continued on to London where, on 5 January 1848, at the Princess's, they made their metropolitan debuts in one of Fanny Kemble's favourite plays, *The Hunchback*. They then moved on to extended engagements first at the Olympic and subsequently the Marylebone, where on 18 January 1849 her play *Armand*, with some revisions (including the amendment of the dangerously republican subtitle 'The Child of the People' to the more traditionally romantic 'The Peer and the Peasant'), received its British premiere.

After the summer break Mowatt and Davenport returned to the Marylebone. They held another year's contract with the management who was the lessee of both this theatre and the Olympic, and they transferred to the latter venue from December. During this time James Mowatt fell ill and in October travelled to the West Indies. Despite

Mrs Mowatt's popularity as a performer and Davenport's continued rise, when the Olympic staged *Fashion* in January 1850 it was not a great success. Mowatt herself declined to play Gertrude and the production ran for only two weeks before it was withdrawn. Perhaps the specificity of its New York milieu was too foreign for the London audience, its chauvinist Americanism a little too insular and xenophobic. Nevertheless, in February an edition of this play was published in London.

Never a robust figure, Mrs Mowatt's own health failed and she withdrew from the London stage. In terminal decline, James Mowatt returned to London and the couple travelled to Malvern to take the waters, residing there some four months. It was around this time that it was discovered that the manager of the Marylebone and the Olympic had swindled the couple out of money they should have earned during Mowatt's long engagement at his theatres.[20] At the start of 1851, recovered of health, and needing to recuperate something financially from their time in London, Mowatt began an extensive tour of the British Isles. In February, as she was performing in Newcastle, James Mowatt died in London. She undertook a farewell tour of the provinces before sailing for New York in July. Almost immediately she began an American tour at Niblo's Garden.

During this tour, which essentially continued until 1853, Mowatt met William Foushee Ritchie, of the *Richmond Enquirer*, who wooed her determinedly. Exhaustion finally forced her to withdraw from the stage during the summer of 1853, however she continued to write, completing her autobiography before returning to the stage for a farewell tour at the close of the year. Her final performance, on 3 June 1854, again at Niblo's Garden, was as Pauline, the role in which she had made her debut. On 6 June she married Ritchie and retired to Richmond society.

Her life in Richmond seemed settled enough but strains, already appearing in the marriage, were thrown into relief with the outbreak of Civil War in 1861. Anna Cora Mowatt Ritchie, her father's daughter and denizen of New York liberality, left the Southern environment to live with her family in the north. Later that same year she left America and spent the rest of her life abroad, first in Florence and later in England. Financial difficulties dogged these later years and, once gain motivated by economic necessity, she continued to write, mainly for American journals. She died of tuberculosis on 29 July 1870 at Twickenham, near London, and is buried, with her first husband, James Mowatt, at Kensal Green.

Mrs Mowatt's *Fashion* has endured, at least within American theatre scholarship, as one of the most important plays of the mid-century. It is generally regarded as the first play written by a native-American woman to win prominent stage success, and is certainly one of the most sophisticated plays of its time, a clever and enjoyable reflection on contemporary society by one who knew.

Mrs Henry Wood

Mrs Henry Wood did not write the line '. . . dead! dead! and . . . never called me mother.' The author of one of the most popular of Victorian morality tales never adapted her own work for the stage. However, there were many who were willing and, more or less, able to do it for her. This most infamous line from the nineteenth-century popular stage was the work of T. A. Palmer, who adapted the play for the Nottingham Theatre Royal in the 1870s.

Born in Worcester on 17 January 1814, Ellen Price was a daughter of the mercantile middle-class: her father a prosperous and cultured glove manufacturer, her mother associated with charitable deeds and local-history groups, although Ellen was brought up chiefly by her maternal grandmother, Mrs Evans. During her adolescence a serious spinal condition forced her to be bedridden for some four years and left her a semi-invalid, short, slightly hunched and physically weak throughout her life. In 1836, when she was twenty-two, she married Henry Wood, about whom rather little is known. He may have been the manager of a family-owned banking and shipping firm, he may have performed some consular services, certainly the couple lived in France, at Dauphiné, until 1856, when 'something occurred' which precipitated his retirement from business and a return to inexpensive lodgings and straightened circumstances in Norwood.

One may be inclined to the view that with *East Lynne* Mrs Henry Wood was something of an overnight sensation, an author thrust into celebrity by this one remarkable and fortuitously popular work. Nothing could be farther from the truth. Even whilst in France, Mrs Henry Wood had been writing and publishing, albeit anonymously, for several years. The earliest identified piece appears in the February 1851 edition of William Harrison Ainsworth's *New Monthly Magazine* and throughout the next decade hardly a month went by without one or more of her short stories or essays appearing in this magazine or in *Bentley's Miscellany*, which Ainsworth edited from December 1854. It seems certain, particularly with the dubious denouement in France, that her literary output was motivated more by financial need than by a mere desire for domestic diversion. However, her writing career shifted gear in 1860 when her novella *Danesbury House* won £100 in a competition run under the auspices of the Scottish Temperance League. During the next year (by which time she had reached the age of forty-seven), her most famous work, *East Lynne*, was serialised in the *New Monthly Magazine*. Ainsworth encouraged her to publish it as a novel but, two houses rejected it (one reader calling it 'foul') before Richard Bentley paid her £600 (well over the odds for the work of a relatively little-known writer) and issued it in the autumn of that year. An enthusiastic review in the *Times* encouraged the melodrama's success but could not predict the sheer magnitude of its celebrity – sales of 2.5 million by 1900[21], spawning some twenty pirated editions in North America alone, and achieving the status of the age's paradigmatic stage melodrama.

Although she never repeated the phenomenal success achieved with *East Lynne*, Mrs Henry Wood began her literary career in earnest in the 1860s and her output was remarkable. Sally Mitchell determines that 'In 1862 and 1863 she had two serials in *The Quiver*, one in *Once a Week*, and one in the *New Monthly Magazine*' and notes that 'In the seven years after *East Lynne* she wrote fifteen novels, often working on two at a time and producing instalments of both month by month under the pressure of serialization.'[22] Indeed, by the end of her life Mrs Wood had published more than thirty novels: a substantial output for one in full and robust health, let alone Mrs Wood whose frailty necessitated that she write propped in a reclining chair, with her manuscript rested on her knees.

In 1866 her husband died and Mrs Henry Wood moved from Kensington to St John's Wood where she passed the remainder of her life, not in peaceful retirement but, from 1867, as proprietor and editor of the *Argosy*, through which she published most of her subsequent work, including the 'Johnny Ludlow' stories, which appeared, anonymously, from 1868. Under her management the failing *Argosy* recovered to the point that it achieved monthly sales of around 20,000, and it was both popular and profitable when she handed it over to the stewardship of her son, Charles.

Mrs Henry Wood died in London on 10 February 1887, a popular and successful writer whose remarkable career as a storyteller and editor is all but eclipsed by the phenomenal success of one title.

Almost immediately upon its publication the theatre saw the drama and sentiment of Mrs Wood's narrative as fine fare for stage adaptation. Consequently, its stage history is remarkably and spectacularly successful, and, being international from the very beginning, is both extraordinary and labyrinthine.

East Lynne first appeared on stage at the close of 1862 at the Academy of Music in Brooklyn. In the same year American actress Lucille Western had commissioned Clifton W. Tayleur to dramatise the novel so that she might play Lady Isabel. Western's company premiered their version at the Winter Gardens in New York a few months later on 28 March 1863. Reviewers can be cruel, but the *Albion*'s 'Mercution' (William Winter) was vitriolic:

> In [*East Lynne*], a flimsy and stupid novel has been resuscitated into a flimsy unnatural, incongruous, and feverishly sentimental play. Miss Heron, it will be remembered, treated us to this picture of conjugal fidelity, in December last [. . .] Her version of the novel was called *Edith*. It adhered less closely even to the original story than that now presented at 'the Winter Garden,' introducing Miss Lucille Western as a 'popular young American Artiste.' But close adherence to the original is merely close adherence to trash, and *East Lynne* has acquired no new charm from its present dress, or from lapse of time since we were last afflicted with it [. . .] Many persons, I am assured, have wept over this sickly nonsense, as intepreted by Miss Heron; but it would seem that the most tender and gushing sensibilities might encounter with perfect safety the comparatively tame interpretation of Miss Western.[23]

Lucille Western's career was, however, unhurt by such a damning review. During this New York engagement her contract assured her a fee of half the gross income of the house and the production's popular success was such that she earned $350 a night – having paid Tayleur a once-only fee of $100. Western continued to be associated with the role of Lady Isabel, playing *East Lynne* in New York annually for the next ten years and making the play a mainstay of her repertoire for her extensive national tours.

Thereafter, adaptations of *East Lynne* were remarkably thick on the ground. A version by W. Archer was produced in London as *The Marriage Bells; or, The Cottage on the Cliff* in 1864, and John Oxenford's adaptation achieved significant success at the Surrey Theatre in 1866, being revived in 1867 at the Lyceum, in 1869 at Sadler's Wells, in 1875 at the Globe, and in 1878 at the Standard. In 1879 and in London alone, different versions of the novel ran at the Olympic, Astley's, the Adelphi and the Standard. Furthermore, there are at least nine stage versions by unknown authors from 1866 to the turn of the century, and it is impossible to judge how many productions were in the repertoire of provincial touring companies during the same period.

The version of *East Lynne* included here was the most successful of the contemporary adaptations and was made by T. A. Palmer. It was first produced at the Nottingham Theatre Royal on 19 November 1874 with a fine company which included Madge Robertson (later Kendal) as Lady Isabel, W. H. Kendal as Carlyle, Palmer himself as Mount Severn, with his wife as the servant, Joyce. Although relatively little is known about Palmer, he certainly had a successful, if predominantly provincial, career as both a performer and a writer. From 1861 to 1882 some seventeen plays were produced that are attributed to him, several of which were published as acting editions by French and by Lacy. His adaptation of *East Lynne* is particularly assured, suggesting the experienced eye of a stage professional. The play is a melodramatic roller-coaster of emotions (jealousy, betrayal, murderous hate, revenge, infidelity, despair, love) for performers and audience alike: Lady Isabel offers the leading lady a role of dizzying emotional extremes; Levison is the archetypal Victorian villain, murderer, seducer, ambitious ne'er-do-well; Cornelia a delightfully comic role tinged with sensitivity and some degree of hurt; and the pathos of Little Willie's death is legendary.

Florence Bell and Elizabeth Robins

The theatre of the 1890s was one of remarkable and revoluntionary praxis, developing a strong alternative tradition to the mainstream and commercial theatre that had been predominant and exclusive. The Court Theatre was the centre of the 'new drama' movement in Britain between 1904 and 1907, but two decades before that the foundations were laid for the radical modernisation of drama and theatre in Britain that the Court would champion. The key players in these changes were a number of actresses (Janet Achurch, Lillah McCarthy, Elizabeth Robins and Mrs Patrick Campbell), writers (Henry Arthur Jones, Arthur Wing Pinero and Bernard Shaw), producers and directors (William Archer, J. T. Grein and Harley Granville Barker).

Alan's Wife was written by two women at the centre of the theatrical, social and political ferment of the *fin de siècle*. Elizabeth Robins was an actress, producer and writer at the forefront of the movement for radical changes initiated by the new theatre ventures (the Independent Theatre Society and later the Court itself), who worked with and for the age's leading practitioners and producers, principally Archer, Grein and Barker. One of the 1890s' most celebrated actresses, a committed political activist and a capable and trenchant playwright and novelist, Robins developed a career that reflected the new attitudes of the public to the theatre and to the working woman. The life of Florence Bell was less celebrated, but she, too, was intimately involved with the cultural life of the *fin de siècle*, supporting (sometimes financially) the more public activities of Robins.

Florence Eveleen Eleanore Olliffe was born on 9 September 1851 in Paris. Her father, Sir Joseph Olliffe, was an eminent physician and her mother, Lady Laura, a member of a wealthy family of London builders, the Cubitts. Florence was brought up in Parisian diplomatic circles, as her father was the British Embassy's physician. The luxury of the Second Empire ended with the advance of the Prussian Army in 1870, and escape to London. Denied the opportunity to follow her musical ambitions through study at the Royal College in London, she instead turned to the more private activity of writing. She married Hugh Bell, a highly respected, soon to be knighted, ironmaster, in 1876. Florence Bell was prominent within London society and within the social circles of Yorkshire where she and her family lived. She had three children with Hugh Bell (Hugo, Elsa and Molly) and was stepmother to Maurice and Gertrude (the scholar, traveller, writer and eminent Arabist), children from her husband's first marriage. She wrote a sizeable number of plays and sketches for the professional stage as well as for domestic entertainments and charades. Her plays for children – in both English and French – were particularly popular. Being something of a linguist, she wrote beginners books in French and German and translated several stories from Swedish, including the source-text for *Alan's Wife*. Although by no means politically active, Lady Bell was a determined social improver whose activities included founding the Clarence Workingmen's Club, establishing the Winter Gardens for inexpensive recreation and leisure, and opening a tea garden in Albert Park. Today she is best remembered for her 1907 documentary record of the lives and lifestyles of the workers of her husband's factory and their families, *At the Works: a Study of a Manufacturing Town*. Florence Bell died on 16 May 1930, at the age of seventy-nine.

Of Elizabeth Robins very much more is known. Her emergence in the 1890s as one of the leading actresses of the age – one of the new breed of socially respectable, intellectually astute and politically aware performers – and her later career as writer and suffragist made her life highly visible and equally eventful. Nevertheless, some aspects of life, notably the details of her relationship with William Archer remain, deliberately, obscure.

Born in Louisville, Kentucky, on 6 August 1862 to Charles Ephraim Robins (an insurer and banker) and his second wife, Hannah Crowe, Elizabeth was the eldest of the couple's several children (although Charles did have an older son, Eugene, from his first marriage). Because of financial problems and the threat of Civil War the Robins family soon moved north to Statten Island. In all Hannah gave birth to six more children after Elizabeth, two dying as infants. The birth of her last child, Raymond, in the same year as the death of the adolescent Eugene, sent the young mother into severe post-natal depression and brought on the beginnings of the mental illness that ruined the rest of her life. This illness, combined with financial collapse, meant that the marriage soon split and the family began to disintegrate. In August 1872 Elizabeth and her sisters, along with the infant Raymond, were sent to live with their grandmother Jane Hussey Robins in Zanesville, Ohio, leaving her mother to descend into ever deeper madness and eventually confinement in an asylum in Louisville.

A keen and committed amateur performer, Robins saw in the stage the means to a fulfilling career away from the domestic responsibilities that restricted her home life. In 1881 the eighteen-year-old Elizabeth ran away to New York to become an actress. Despite initial difficulties, she gained employment with James O'Neill's company, featuring opposite him in a succession of melodramas, romances and other stock pieces. This apprenticeship led her to the highly respected Boston Museum Theatre where she enacted a sound apprenticeship, doubling and trebling her roles in melodramas, comedies, farces and other repertoire pieces.

On 12 January 1885 she secretly married fellow actor George Richmond Parks in Salem, Massachusetts. The disintegration of the match was almost immediate. Robins was a beautiful and vivacious rising young star, Parks a never more than adequate performer. After two years of marriage – much of which was spent apart, each working with different touring companies, and during which he became alcoholic – Parks walked to the Charles River in Boston, weighted himself down with a heavy suit of stage-armour and jumped into the water, quickly sinking to the bottom. A widow at twenty-three, Robins joined a coast-to-coast tour with a company led by Edwin Booth and Lawrence Barrett. For two seasons she played opposite these popular tragedians until the summer of 1888 when she became the travelling companion of her friend Sara Bull. Sara was the American widow of Norwegian musician Ole Bull, who had founded

Norwegian National Theatre at Bergen and given Henrik Ibsen his first job as writer-in-residence. Sara and her daughters were making a return journey to Norway and invited Robins to accompany them, and so in July 1888 the party arrived in Liverpool. Awaiting their onward journey to Oslo, Robins spent a week in London where she met an early supporter in the not insubstantial form of Oscar Wilde. In August she travelled on to Norway where, perhaps for the first time, she was introduced to the work of Ibsen. In September she returned to London, where Wilde had arranged a meeting with Beerbohm Tree. Assured of the possibility of work, Robins cancelled her return passage to New York and launched herself into the theatre world of London.

In October Elizabeth Robins made her London debut in a semi-private production of William Poel's *Chieromancy* at St George Hall, Langham Place, and in December played Portia to F. R. Benson's Shylock during a week's engagement at Exeter. Her first real breakthrough, however, came in January 1889 when she took over from Mary Rorke the role of Mrs Errol in *The Real Little Lord Fauntleroy* at Saturday matinées. She was seen by Pinero who immediately offered her a position as understudy in *The Profligate*. Gradually building her experience and reputation within the competitive world of London theatres, she became particularly interested in new work and in work of high quality and demanding nature. This led her to the burgeoning experimental sector and on 5 July she appeared in a trial matinée of Moore's *Forgotten* at the Islington Grand Theatre where she was seen by William Archer for the first time. (However, they were not to meet for almost another year when, on 10 June 1890, Robins consulted him during the planning of a proposed, but soon abandoned, production of *Ghosts*.) On 17 July 1889 Robins performed in an Ibsen play for the first time, taking the role of Martha Bernick in a matinée performance of *The Pillars of Society* at the Opera Comique. Thereafter her enthusiasm for Ibsen's plays grew and she was increasingly associated with their London stagings. On 27 January 1891 she appeared as Mrs Linde in a matinée production of *A Doll's House* at Terry's, and on 20 April 1891 her performance in the title role of *Hedda Gabler* assured her reputation as one of the most active exponents of the new European drama. The *Sunday Times* described her performance as 'one of the notable events in the history of the modern stage: it marks an epoch and clinches an influence'.[24]

Unlike the writers of the other plays in this volume Robins's reputation was made, not in the popular or commercial theatre but in a new, challenging, experimental theatre and was marked by a commitment to new forms of drama, new writers and new writing. Her primary interest during the 1890s was Ibsen – staging, translating, producing and championing his radical new dramas in London and even in America. Her reputation as an actress is inseparable from the import of Ibsen to the British stage. The 1890s was also the decade during which she most closely associated with William Archer – Britain's leading proponent of Ibsen, translator, director and critic. Robins's relationship with Archer was always important (they each respected and admired the work of the other) and, for a time at least, was intense and, despite Archer's marriage, physical. The affair, however, was scrupulously private and even when it was no longer sexual the two remained close – a remarkable meeting of equals.

Of her other significant relationships, it seems likely that none was sexual in any physical way. She maintained a devoted, if draining, relationship with her brother Raymond which led her to 'rescue' him from the wastelands of Alaska and later to invest in his own Florida estate. In 1910 she had an intense series of encounters with John Masefield that produced a remarkable and sexually explicit correspondence from the young poet, but scanty evidence of a consummated affair. Her final and closest relationship was a particularly rewarding and sustaining one with Octavia Wilberforce, whom she had encouraged and supported as a young medical student and who later ran Backsettown, for many years Robins's home, as a sanatorium and convalescent home for women.

Elizabeth Robins was a committed feminist, an early and prominent member of the Actresses' Franchise League – the theatre-world's branch of the Women's Suffrage movement – and several of her novels are direct commentaries on the theme of women's rights. Her identification of herself as a 'suffragette' was the one point of serious disagreement in her relationship with Florence Bell, who, along with her step-daughter Gertrude, declared herself to be anti-suffrage. Despite contemporary success, none of her novels (not even the remarkably popular volume based on her experiences in Alaska, *The Magnetic North*) achieved the lasting prominence of her 1906 suffrage play, *Votes for Women*, produced by Granville Barker and John Vedrenne at the Court. A rallying-cry for supporters of female suffrage, the play is a fervent and deeply felt call for women's rights, skilfully tempered with witty dialogue and a taut dramatic core.

Alan's Wife is a less successful piece of drama (the three scenes offer just snapshots of Jean Creyke's tragedy) but is equally committed to women's lives and women's stories, and it caused a sensation when it was produced in 1893 because it so violently countered any idealised image of the Victorian mother. It was first performed by the Independent Theatre at Terry's on 28 April 1893 and was immediately considered both scandalous and shocking (this, no doubt, a factor in the two authors' decision to produce it anonymously). Its theme – a young mother smothers her physically disabled infant and is condemned to death but refuses to repent – remains both topical and challenging. Although critics were universal in their condemnation of the play (generally blinded by their moral indignation), Robins received praise for her interpretation of the role of Jean and at least one critic noted that this was just the type of production that the Independent Theatre Society could and should be producing. It is certainly a remarkable achievement and is a useful counter to the tendency to see the 'problem' plays of the late 1800s as the sole province of male dramatists. The play is a forerunner of the 'new woman' dramas of Cicely Hamilton, Elizabeth Baker and Githa Sowerby. Elizabeth Robins died in Brighton on 8 May 1952. Her reputation continues to grow.

Pearl Craigie

Pearl Richards (later Mrs Pearl Mary Teresa Craigie and 'John Oliver Hobbes') is almost definitely an English playwright despite the fact that she was born on 3 November 1867, near Boston, Massachusetts. She made her career in English letters and is to be considered a notable beneficiary of the social climate of the *fin de siècle* and London's contemporary literati. When she was but months old her family moved to London, where her father, John Morgan Richards, a successful businessman and an innovative force in modern advertising techniques, made a vast fortune marketing American cigarettes. Expensively educated at boarding and day schools in England and Paris, she was particularly encouraged in this, and in her later literary pursuits, by her father to whom she was especially close. With her mother, Laura Hortense, she had a more strained relationship, which became particularly tense with regard to issues of religion and marriage.

She married a successful young banker, Reginald Walpole Craigie, in February 1887 but the match floundered almost immediately, and Craigie would often flee in despair to the familiarity of her parents' Lancaster Gate home. Like Anna Cora Mowatt and Mrs Henry Wood, she began to write professionally early in her married life, contributing to magazines and journals. She entered University College, London, to study classics with Professors Alfred Goodwin and W. P. Ker, the former emerging as an important and early influence upon her intellectual and, indeed, psychological development. Goodwin was the first of many (generally older) men who contributed significantly to her life with whom she developed close friendships and would study, collaborate and confide. This relationship with Goodwin, which Craigie enjoyed so much, was a cause of great jealousy for her husband and contributed to the early disintegration of her marriage. A son was born on 15 August 1890, some eight months before her final separation from her husband and during which time arguments would reach such proportions that she would taunt her husband with the claim that the child was, in fact, Goodwin's. In the same year as she separated from Reginald Craigie (1891) she published her first book, *Some Emotions and a Moral*, an engaging novel of characters caught in a tangle of loveless marriages, social expectations and romantic illusions.

In 1892 Craigie's mentor Goodwin died, and to rally herself she travelled with her father to New York. There she found an American publisher for her second novel, *The Sinner's Comedy*, which was published in New York and London in May of that year. The novel achieved satisfactory success in both markets and Craigie seemed relatively secure in her burgeoning career. In July she unexpectedly converted to Roman Catholicism. Although a few of her contemporaries were making a similar choice (influenced by the high-profile conversion in 1845 of John Henry Newman and his subsequent theological writings which were particularly potent), Craigie's conversion was initially dismissed as bold foolishness by her family (determined Nonconformists) and as a passing whim by her friends. Nevertheless, she explained her choice as founded on research and intellectual rigour and was determined to develop her new identity with similarly focussed scholarship.

In 1895, after a short but invasive and public hearing, she divorced her husband, winning exclusive custody of her son.[25] There is a strong suggestion that her husband, certainly a womaniser and certainly a drinker, may have already been ill with a venereal disease; in any case Craigie never wished to repeat the experience of married life, even if her new Catholic identity could have allowed such a step. It is perhaps significant that in her many subsequent friendships with men she never allowed the relationships to become sexual. Indeed, this was one of the causes of the split with the critic and author George Moore.

Craigie's first experience of writing for the theatre was, in fact, a collaboration with Moore. *Journey's End in Lovers Meeting* (1894) was a short comic piece first produced at Daly's and then at the Lyceum with significant success and enthusiasm. The two began to cooperate on a second piece, *The Fool's Hour*, which was abandoned when they rather rancorously split – Craigie finding the process of writing and the whole relationship tiresome, Moore frustrated that his infatuation was unrequited. In a letter to Barrett H. Clark Moore wrote that 'She was horrible. We saw each other every day for six months [. . .] We were very intimate but she would never allow me to become her lover. I was frantic.'[26] The stakes were very publicly raised when Moore kicked her 'squarely in the bottom' during a walk in Hyde Park; Craigie responded by withdrawing from *The Yellow Book*, which she described as 'a vulgar production', reserving enough venom to paint Moore as a 'vicious old lady – not a man at all'. Moore, however, felt wronged, his ire festered and he began to depict her in his fiction. In 1895 he published 'Mildred Lawson' in his rather pointedly entitled collection, *Celibates*. Mildred is a grotesque. She is an extravagant and ostentatious follower of society. She 'didn't want to marry but she would like to have all the nicest young men in love with her'. She is fashionable, with a particular penchant for the lavishly trimmed hats so favoured by Craigie. She is prone to deep introspection and flirtations with suicide and, like Craigie, is a convert to Newmanite Catholicism. Mildred is painted as a trivial figure to be teased and despised for her falsity, her flirtatiousness, her capriciousness. Craigie, and her circle of friends and acquaintances, knew exactly who 'Mildred' was.[27]

Although several of her plays had been staged before, the comedy *The Ambassador* was her most successful, opening at the St James's on 2 June 1898. It is rather similar in plot to Oscar Wilde's *Lady Windermere's Fan* (1892) and although Craigie's wit falls far short of the remarkable linguistic dexterity and socio-political astuteness of Wilde, her play is perhaps more typical of the general temper of the society comedies popular at the turn of the century in London's more fashionable West End theatres. The play revolves around a group of characters at the very centre of stylish society. Its slightest of plots involves wedding plans, secret love and gambling debts. However, such doings are merely a backdrop to the important business of *talking about* wedding plans, secret love and the good or bad reputations of the characters. It was a society that Craigie knew intimately and the characters are drawn well enough to allow actors to develop strong characterisation: in particular, St Orbyn and Lady Beauvedere offer the actor the potential for depth in their work. Despite the similarity of locus, Craigie can never muster the irony and critical detachment that marks Wilde's social comedies as the soaring pinnacle of the genre. Craigie's plays have none of the political edge that sets Wilde's apart, being essentially softer on the mores of the same class. She observes the escapades of the class around her, but observation never slips into criticism. Craigie was nonetheless keen to suggest parallels with Wilde: '*He* took some of *my* epigrams [. . .] Without vanity I may say that I am the one writer in England who could sign a Wilde comedy and pass unchallenged.'[28] However, as delightful as the play may have been in performance, it ultimately suffers from a lack of narrative drive, dramatic substance and psychological depth in the secondary characters. It is a highly disposable entertainment, promising a perfectly amusing night at the theatre, but little more.

Craigie's life was empowered by the era's acceptance of the active life of women: her divorce, her enrolment at University College, London, her role as single parent, her work as a journalist, public speaker and cultural commentator, all were possible due to the political and social advances of feminism and socialism. At the forefront of 'blue stocking' culture of professional women, she was President of the Society of Women Journalists in 1895/6. However, unlike her loose contemporaries – Elizabeth Robins, Mrs Patrick Campbell or Beatrice Webb – her work cannot easily fit into the framework of the politicised identity these performers and writers helped fashion. Despite her highly independent lifestyle, her return to education and her notable professional writing career, she is generally excluded from accounts of the women who were socially and culturally active in the 1890s. This may be explained by several factors. Craigie was neither a Socialist, a Fabian nor an active Suffragist. As far as it is possible her work is determinedly apolitical. Her interest and engagement with the theatre was relatively short-lived and was very much within the world of the commercial theatre, not part of the cutting-edge activity of the Independent Theatre Society or the new drama. Her conversion to Catholicism in a period when Humanist-Socialism was at the heart of cultural politics marks her as out of step with the period's general ideological trends. And her social life, at the very centre of Imperial Britain, is very different from the cultural milieu of the 'new women'.

Pearl Craigie died on 13 August 1906 and is buried at Kensal Green. Her popularity waned almost immediately and her reputation, never secure during her lifetime, diminished to such an extent that her work (ranging impressively across so many genres) is all but forgotten.

The Ambassador, like the other plays in this volume, is a response to its contemporary theatre environment. It achieved success during a period when the popular West End theatre could afford lavish stagings, was peopled by highly professional, assured actors with the skills to breathe life into the slightest of characterisations, and played to an audience that relished wit, enjoyed spectacle, and was tantalised and flattered by seeing a version of themselves on stage. It was an audience that expected entertainment and Craigie had ample skills, experience and intellect to be able to respond with some style to the demands of the marketplace.

ADRIENNE SCULLION

References

1. See his *Victorian Spectacular Theatre, 1850–1910* (London: Routledge and Kegan Paul, 1981) and Michael Baker's *The Rise of the Victorian Actor* (London: Croom Helm, 1978).

2. See her *Actresses as Working Women: their Social Identity in Victorian Britain* (London: Routledge, 1991).

3. Gwenn Davis and Beverly A. Joyce, *Drama by Women to 1900: A Bibliography of American and British Writers* (London: Mansell, 1992): xiii.

4. The production is catalogued, with Scott's account of the opening night, in James C. Dibdin's *The Annals of the Edinburgh Stage* (Edinburgh: Cameron, 1888): 261–2.

5. Alasdair Cameron, 'Scottish drama in the nineteenth century', *The History of Scottish Literature: volume 4, The Nineteenth Century*, edited by Douglas Gifford (Aberdeen: Aberdeen University Press, 1988): 430.

6. Quoted by Margaret S. Carhart, *The Life and Work of Joanna Baillie* (New Haven: Yale University Press and London: Humphrey Milford and Oxford University Press, 1923): 1.

7. Letters quoted by Carhart, *ibid*: 38–9.

8. Marie-Thérèse De Camp wrote as 'Mrs Charles Kemble'. However, to avoid confusion with her daughter, Fanny Kemble, I have throughout referred to her as 'Marie-Thérèse De Camp'.

9. *Times*, 28 January 1795: 1.

10. The benefit night was a traditional method of supplementing the income of the performer or, in the case of a new play, the author. Under this system on a given night the house's box-office profits would go

directly to the beneficiary – a risky arrangement that, in any case, did little to support the income of anyone but the star performers.

11. De Camp no doubt considered the benefit a success, however, for she made £447.8s, less £211 for the House, from the performance. See 'Mrs Charles Kemble', *A Biographical Dictionary of Actors, Actresses, Musicians, Dancers, Managers and other Stage Personnel in London, 1660–1800*, volume 8 (Carbondale and Edwardsville: Southern Illinois University Press, 1982): 321–9, 325.

12. Several weeks after the opening success of this comedy, on 24 May 1808, she appeared in *Matchmaking; or, 'Tis a Wise Child Knows His Own Father*, a play which is often attributed to her. Again it was neither revived nor printed.

13. In an advertisement included in some copies of the first edition De Camp makes this clear:

> To Mrs Opie's beautiful Tale of *Father and Daughter*, I am indebted for the serious interests of the Play; upon a French Piece in one Act, entitled *La Suite d'un Bal Masqué, some* of the lighter scenes were founded.

Smiles and Tears; or, The Widow's Stratagem by Mrs C. Kemble (London: John Miller, 1815): i.

14. The 1823 play *Nigel; or, The Crown Jewels* is variously attributed to Marie-Thérèse De Camp and to Isaac Pocock. Despite its source in Walter Scott's tale of chivalrous daring-dos (a genre very much associated with Pocock), and the fact that it is written in verse (a register that Kemble had never previously used), the *National Union Catalog* and Davis and Joyce's bibliographical guide, *Drama by Women to 1990*, ascribe the play to De Camp. The manuscript of the play lodged with the Lord Chamberlain throws no light on the matter and the printed version's title page credits no author.

15. Frances Ann Kemble, *Records of a Girlhood*, volume 2 (London: Richard Bentley, 1878): 131.

16. *ibid*: 164. Later (on 15 September) she was one of the guests at the formal opening of his first commercial railway line. Her journals also vividly record the dramatic events of the opening, with the death of William Huskisson, MP. *ibid*: 187–91.

17. See Tamara Follini, 'The Friendship of Fanny Kemble and Henry James', *Cambridge Quarterly* v19 n3 (1990): 230–42.

18. Sandra Richards, *The Rise of the English Actress* (London: Macmillan, 1993): 110.

19. Biographers are divided as to the exact date of her birth with various dates being proposed including 5, 12 and 15 March.

20. There is also a suggestion that Mowatt's London manager was in love with the actress and that he committed suicide at this time. See 'Anna Cora Mowatt', by Stern in *The Dictionary of Literary Biography: Antebellum Writers in New York and the South* (Detroit, Michigan: Gale Research, 1979): 304.

21. According to *The Bloomsbury Guide to Women's Literature*, edited by Claire Buck (New York, et al: Prentice Hall General Reference, 1992): 1149.

22. Sally Mitchell, 'Introduction', Mrs Henry Wood, *East Lynne* (New Brunswick, New Jersey: Rutgers University Press, 1984): ix.

23. 'Mercution', *New York Albion*, 28 March, 1863: quoted by Barnard Hewitt, *Theatre USA: 1665 to 1957* (New York, et al: McGraw-Hill, 1959): 187–8.

24. *Sunday Times*, 26 April 1891.

25. Readers can find a report of the proceeding in the *Times* 4 July 1895.

26. Barrett H. Clark, *Intimate Portraits* (New York: Dramatists Play Service, [1951]): 145.

27. The affair is described in detail by Margaret Maison in *John Oliver Hobbes: Her Life and Work* (London: The Eighteen Nineties Society, 1976).

28. Letter to Rev. William Brown, 23 February 1905: quoted by Maison, *ibid*: 39.

NOTE ON THE TEXTS

The student of the nineteenth-century stage has access to a wide range of source material from playbills, musical scores and engravings to newspaper reviews, magazine articles, theatre accounts and parliamentary papers, autobiographies and reminiscences. But even this wealth of information offers only a partial view of the theatre activity of the period. Nevertheless, play texts remain an important part of the documentary evidence that must be gathered and reconsidered before any understanding of the theatre culture might be achieved. This anthology makes use of the following texts:

The Family Legend, by Joanna Baillie, was first published in 1810 and appears in the 1851 and 1853 editions of the *Collected Works*. There is little difference between the editions (minor typographical changes at most) but the text given here is based on the first edition.

Smiles and Tears, by Marie Thérèse De Camp, was published in London in 1815 by John Miller and the version included here is based on this edition.

The first edition of Fanny Kemble's play *Francis the First* was published in 1832 in London by John Murray. Some nine editions followed that same year, with a tenth the next. Although these are virtually identical, the version published here is taken from the first edition.

Fashion, by Anna Cora Mowatt, was published first in London by Newbery in 1850, and was reprinted with *Armand* in Boston in 1855 by Ticknor and Fields. These two editions vary only slightly and so whilst the version given here is founded on the 1850 edition, the amendments of the later Boston edition are incorporated.

The text of *East Lynne* included here is based on T. A. Palmer's adaptation of Mrs Henry Wood's novel. It was published as a French's acting edition and, although undated, it is generally placed at 1874, the year of its premiere.

The text of *The Ambassador* by Pearl Craigie given here is that of the first edition published in London by T. Fisher Unwin in 1898. Some copies of this play include an erratum slip indicating minor typographical errors: these changes have been incorporated into the version given here.

In all plays (and later in 'The Playwrights and their Critics') I have silently corrected obvious misprints, including punctuation and spelling. In addition archaic spelling has been modernised. However, where the vernacular is suggested (for example, in Baillie's use of idiomatic Scots and Mowatt's denotation of Zeke's Southern patois and Millinette's schoolroom French) the author's spellings are maintained.

THE PLAYS

THE FAMILY LEGEND

a tragedy, in five acts
BY JOANNA BAILLIE
(1810)

DRAMATIS PERSONAE

Women

HELEN	daughter of Argyll, and wife of Maclean
ROSA	Helen's maid
FISHERMAN'S WIFE	

Men

MACLEAN	Chief of the clan of that name
EARL OF ARGYLL	father of Helen, Chief of his clan
JOHN OF LORNE	son to Argyll
SIR HUBERT DE GREY	friend to Lorne, in love with Helen
BENLORA	
LOCHTARISH	the kinsmen and chief vassals of Maclean
GLENFADDEN	
DUNCAN	a fisherman
MORTON	Helen's servant
DUGALD	Argyll's servant
PIPER	at Argyll's castle
MESSENGER	
VASSALS, SERVANTS	

Act I

SCENE i

Before the gate of MACLEAN's *castle, in the Isle of Mull: several Highlanders discovered crossing the stage, carrying loads of fuel; whilst* BENLORA *is seen on one side, in the background, pacing to and fro, and frequently stopping and muttering to himself*

1ST HIGH. This heavy load, I hope, will be the last:
My back is almost broken.
2ND HIGH.   Sure am I,
Were every beeve[1] in Mull slain for the feast,
Fuel enough already has been stowed
To roast them all: and must we still with our burdens
Our weary shoulders gall?
                    Enter MORTON
MORTON: Ye lazy lubbards![2]
Grumble ye thus? – Ye would prefer, I trow,
To sun your easy sides, like household curs,
Each on his dung-hill stretched, in drowsy sloth.
Fy onit! to grumble on a day like this,
When to the clan a rousing feast is given,
In honour of an heir born to the chief—
A brave Maclean, still to maintain the honours
Of this your ancient race!
1ST HIGH. A brave Maclean indeed! – vile mongrel hound!
Come from the south, where all strange mixtures be
Of base and feeble! sprung of varlet's blood![3]
What is our race to thee?
2ND HIGH. (*to* MORTON) Thou'lt chew, I doubt not,
Thy morsel in the hall with right good relish,
Whether Maclean or Campbell be our lord.
MORTON: Ungracious surly lubbards! in, I say,
And bring your burdens quicker. And, besides,
Where are the heath and hare-bells,[4] from the glen,
To deck my lady's chamber?
2ND HIGH. To deck my lady's chamber!

MORTON: Heartless hounds!
  Is she not kind and gentle? spares she aught
  Her generous stores afford, when you or yours
  Are sick, or lack relief? Hoards she in chests,
  When shipwrecked strangers shiver on our coast,
  Or robe or costly mantle?⁵ – All comes forth!
  And when the piercing shriek of drowning mariners
  Breaks through the night, up-starting from her couch,
  To snatch, with eager haste, the flaming torch,
  And from the tower give notice of relief,
  Who comes so swiftly as her noble self?
  And yet ye grumble.
1ST HIGH.   Ay, we needs must own,
  That, were she not a Campbell, fit she were
  To be a queen, or even the thing she is—
  Our very chieftain's dame. But, in these towers,
  The daughter of Argyll to be our lady!
MORTON: Out! mountain savages! is this your spite?
  Go to!
2ND HIGH. Speakst thou to us? thou Lowland loon!⁶
  Thou wandering pedlar's son, or base mechanic!
  Com'st thou to lord it here over brave Macleans?
  We'll carry loads at leisure, or forbear,
  As suits our fancy best, nor wait thy bidding.
    [*Exeunt* HIGHLANDERS *grumbling, and followed by* MORTON]
    (BENLORA *now comes forward, and after remaining some
    time on the front of the stage, wrapt in thought, not observing*
          LOCHTARISH, *who enters behind him*)
  Heigh ho! heigh ho, the day!
LOCHTARISH: How so? What makes Benlora sigh so deeply?
BENLORA: (*turning round*) And does Lochtarish ask? Full well thou
      knowst,
  The battles of our clan I've boldly fought,
  And well maintained its honour.
LOCHTARISH: Yes, we know it.
BENLORA: Who dared, unpunished, a Maclean to injure?
  Yea; he who dared but with a scornful lip
  Our name insult, I thought it feeble vengeance
  If steed or beast within his walls were left,
  Or of his holds one tower unruined stood.
LOCHTARISH: Ay; who dared then to brave us?
BENLORA: Thus dealt Benlora even with common foes;

But in the warfare of our deadly feud,
When rang the earth beneath our bloody strife,
And brave Macleans brave Campbells boldly fronted,
(Fiends as they are, I still must call them brave,)
What sword more deeply drank the hated blood
Than this which now I grasp – but idly grasp!

LOCHTARISH: There's never a man of us that knows it not,
That swears not by thy valour.

BENLORA: Until that fatal day, by ambush taken,
And in a dungeon kept, where, two long years,
Nor light of day, nor human voice ever cheered
My loneliness, when did I ever yield,
To even the bravest of that hateful name,
One step of ground upon the embattled field—
One step of honour in the bannered hall?

LOCHTARISH: Indeed thou hast our noble champion been;
Deserving well the trust our chief deceased,
This chieftain's father, did to thee consign.
But when thou was a captive, none to head us,
But he, our youthful lord, yet green in arms,
We fought not like Macleans; or else our foe,
By fiends assisted, fought with fiend-like power,
Far – far beyond the Campbells' wonted pitch.
Even so it did befall – we lost the day –
That fatal day! – Then came this shameful peace.

BENLORA: Ay, and this wedding; when, in form of honour
Conferred upon us, Helen of Argyll
Our sovereign dame was made, a bosom worm,
Nursed in that viper's nest, to infuse its venom
Through all our after race.
                              This is my welcome!
From dungeons freed, to find my once-loved home
With such vile change disgraced; to me more hateful
Than thraldom's murkiest den.[7] But to be loosened
From captive's chains to find my hands thus bound!

LOCHTARISH: It is, indeed, a vile and irksome peace.

BENLORA: Peace, say they! who will bonds of friendship sign
Between the teeming ocean's finny broods,
And say, 'Sport these upon the hither waves,
And leave to those that farther billowy reach?'
A Campbell here to queen it o'er our heads,
The potent dame o'er quelled and beaten men,

Rousing or soothing us, as proud Argyll
Shall send her secret counsel! – hold, my heart!
This, base degenerate men! – this, call ye peace?
Forgive my weakness: with dry eyes I laid
My mother in her grave, but now my cheeks
Are, like a child's, with scalding drops disgraced.

LOCHTARISH: What I shall look upon, ere in the dust
My weary head be laid to rest, heaven knows,
Since I have lived to see Benlora weep.

BENLORA: One thing, at least, thou never shalt live to see—
Benlora crouching, where he has commanded.
Go ye, who will, and crowd the chieftain's hall,
And deal the feast, and nod your grizzled heads
To martial pibrochs,[8] played, in better days,
To those who conquered, not who wooed their foes;
My soul abhors it. On the sea-beaten rock,
Removed from every form and sound of man;
In proud communion with the fitful winds
Which speak, with many tongues, the fancied words
Of those who long in silent dust have slept;
While eagles scream, and sullen surges roar—
The boding sounds of ill – I'll hold my feast –
My moody revelry.

LOCHTARISH: Nay, why so fierce?
Thinkst thou we are a tame and mongrel pack?
Dogs of true breed we are, though for a time
Our master-hound forsakes us. Rouse him forth
The noble chase to lead: his deep-toned yell
Full well we know; and for the opening sport
Pant keenly.

BENLORA: Ha! is there amongst you still
Spirit enough for this?

LOCHTARISH: Yes, when good opportunity shall favour.
Of this, my friend, I'll speak to thee more fully
When time shall better serve.

                        Maclean, thou knowst,
Is of a soft, unsteady, yielding nature;
And this, too, well, the crafty Campbell knew,
When to our isle he sent this wily witch
To mould, and govern, and besot his wits,
As suits his crafty ends. I know the youth:
This dame or we must hold his will in thraldom:

Which of the two. But softly: steps approach.
Of this again.
BENLORA: As early as thou wilt.
LOCHTARISH: Then be it so: some staunch determined spirits
This night in Irka's rocky cavern meet;
There must thou join us. Wear thou here the while
A brow less cloudy, suited to the times.

                Enter GLENFADDEN

See, here comes one who wears a merry face;
Yet, nevertheless, a clans-man staunch he is,
Who hates a Campbell, worse than Ileom's monks
The horned fiend.
BENLORA: Ha! does he so?
            (*Turning graciously to* GLENFADDEN)
How goes it with thee? – Joyous days are these –
These days of peace.
GLENFADDEN: These days of foul disgrace!
Com'st thou to cheer the piper in our hall,
And goblets quaff to the young chieftain's health,
From proud Argyll descended?
BENLORA: (*smiling grimly*)   Yes, Glenfadden,
If ye will have it so; not else.
GLENFADDEN: Thy hand—
Thy noble hand! – thou art Benlora still.
            (*Shaking* BENLORA *warmly by the hand, and then
                    turning to* LOCHTARISH)
Know ye that banished Allen is returned—
Allen of Dura?
LOCHTARISH: No; I knew it not.
But in good time he comes. A daring knave!
He will be useful. (*After considering*)
                    Of Maclean we'll crave
His banishment to cancel; marking well
How he receives it. This will serve to show
The present bent and bearing of his mind.
                    (*After considering again*)
Were it not also well, that to our council
He were invited, at a later hour,
When of our purpose we shall be assured?
GLENFADDEN: Methinks it were.
LOCHTARISH: In, then; now is our time.
BENLORA: I'll follow thee when I awhile have paced

Yon lonely path, and thought upon thy counsel.

[*Exeunt* LOCHTARISH *and* GLENFADDEN *into the castle, and*
                    BENLORA *by the opposite side*]

SCENE ii

An apartment in the castle

Enter MORTON *and* ROSA, *speaking as they enter*

ROSA: Speak with my lady privately?
MORTON: Ay, please you:
  Something I have to say, regards her nearly.
  And though I doubt not, madam, your attachment—
ROSA: Good Morton, no apology: thy caution
  Is prudent; trust me not till thou hast proved me.
  But oh! watch over thy lady and with an eye
  Of keen and guarded zeal! she is surrounded—
                    (*Looking round the room*)
  Does no one hear us? – O those baleful looks
  That, from beneath dark surly brows, by stealth,
  Are darted on her by those stern Macleans!
  Ay; and the gestures of those fearful men,
  As on the shore in savage groups they meet,
  Sending their loosened tartans to the wind,
  And tossing high their brawny arms where oft
  In vehement discourse, I have, of late,
  At distance marked them. Yes; thou shakest thy head:
  Thou hast observed them too.
MORTON: I have observed them oft. That calm Lochtarish,
  Calm as he is, the growing rancour fosters:
  For, fail the offspring of their chief, his sons
  Next in succession are. He hath his ends,
  For which he stirs their ancient hatred up;
  And all too well his devilish pains succeed.
ROSA: Too well indeed! The very bed-rid crones[9]
  To whom my lady sends, with kindly care,
  Her cheering cordials – couldst thou have believed it?
  Do mutter spells to fence from things unholy,
  And grumble, in a hollow smothered voice,
  The name of Campbell, as unwillingly

They stretch their withered hands to take her bounty.
The wizards are in pay to rouse their fears
With dismal tales of future ills foreseen,
From Campbell and Maclean together joined,
In hateful union. – Even the very children,
Sporting the heath among, when they discover
A loathsome toad or adder on their path,
Crush it with stones, and, grinding wickedly
Their teeth, in puny spite, call it a Campbell.
Benlora, too, that savage gloomy man—

MORTON: Ay, evil is the day that brings him back,
Unjustly by a Campbell hath he been,
The peaceful treaty of the clans unheeded,
In thraldom kept; from which but now escaped,
He like a furious tiger is enchafed,[10]
And thinks Argyll was privy to the wrong
His vassal put upon him. Well I know
His bloody vengeful nature: and Maclean,
Weak and unsteady, moved by every counsel,
Brave in the field, but still in purpose timid,
Ofttimes the instrument in wicked hands
Of wrongs he would abhor – alas, I fear,
Will ill defend the lovely spouse he swore
To love and cherish.

ROSA: Heavy steps approach:
Hush! see who comes upon us! – sly Lochtarish,
And his dark colleagues. – Wherefore come they hither?

> (MORTON *retires to the bottom of the stage, and*
> *enter* LOCHTARISH, BENLORA, *and* GLENFADDEN)

LOCHTARISH: We thought, fair maid, to find the chieftain here.

ROSA: He is in these apartments.

LOCHTARISH: Would it greatly
Annoy your gentleness to tell his honour,
We wait to speak with him upon affairs
Of much concernment?

ROSA: My service is not wanted; to your wish,
See, there he comes unwarned, and with him too
His noble lady. (*Retiring to the bottom of the stage*)

LOCHTARISH: Ha! there they come! see how he hangs upon her
With boyish fondness!

GLENFADDEN: Ah, the goodly creature!
How fair she is! how winning! – See that form;

Those limbs beneath their foldy vestments moving,
As though in mountain clouds they robed were,
And music of the air their motion measured.

LOCHTARISH: Ay, shrewd and crafty earl! 'tis not for nought
Thou hither sent this jewel of thy race.
A host of Campbells, each a chosen man,
Could not enthral us, as, too soon I fear,
This single Campbell will. Shrewd crafty foe!

BENLORA: Hell lend me aid, if heaven deny its grace,
But I will thwart him, crafty though he be!

LOCHTARISH: But now for your petition: see we now
How he receives your suit.

Enter MACLEAN *and* HELEN

BENLORA: (*eyeing her attentively as she enters*) A potent foe it is: ay,
    by my faith,
    A fair and goodly creature!

MACLEAN: Again, good morrow to you, gallant kinsmen:
Come ye to say I can with any favour
The right good liking prove, and high regard
I bear to you, who are my chiefest strength,—
The pillars of my clan?

BENLORA: Yes, we are come, Maclean, a boon[11] to beg.

LOCHTARISH: A boon that, granted, will yourself enrich.

MACLEAN: Myself enrich?

LOCHTARISH: Yes; thereby wilt thou be
One gallant man the richer. Hear us out.
Allen of Dura, from his banishment—

MACLEAN: False reiver![12] name him not. Is he returned?
Dares he again set foot upon this isle?

BENLORA: Yes, chief; upon this isle set foot he hath:
And on nor isle nor mainland doth there step
A braver man than he. – Lady, forgive me:
The boldest Campbell never saw his back.

HELEN: Nay, good Benlora, ask not my forgiveness:
I love to hear thee praise, with honest warmth,
The valiant of thy name, which now is mine.

BENLORA: (*aside*) Ha! good Benlora! – this is queenly pride.
(*Aloud*) Madam, you honour us.

HELEN: If so, small thanks be to my courtesy,
Sharing myself with pride the honest fame
Of every brave Maclean.— I'll henceforth keep
A proud account of all my gallant friends:

And every valiant Campbell therein noted,
On the opposing leaf, in letters fair,
Shall with a brave Maclean be proudly matched.
          (BENLORA *and* GLENFADDEN *bow in silence*)
LOCHTARISH: Madam, our grateful duty waits upon you.
(*Aside to* BENLORA) What thinkst thou of her, friend?
BENLORA: (*aside to* LOCHTARISH) What think I of her?
  Incomparable hypocrite!
LOCHTARISH: (*aloud*) But to our suit: for words of courtesy
  It must not be forgotten.— Chief, vouchsafe:
  Benlora here, who from his loathly prison,
  Which for your sake two years he hath endured,
  Begs earnestly this grace for him we mentioned.
  Allen of Dura. (*Aside to* BENLORA)
              Kneel, man; be more pressing.
BENLORA: (*aside to* LOCHTARISH) Nay, by my fay! if crouching
  pleases thee,
  Do it thyself. (*Going up proudly to* MACLEAN)
  Maclean; thy father put into these hands
  The government and guidance of thy nonage.[13]
  How I the trust fulfilled, this castle strengthened
  With walls and added towers, and stored, besides,
  With arms and trophies in rough warfare won
  From even the bravest of our western clans,
  Will testify. What I in recompense
  Have for my service earned, these galled wrists[14]
          (*Pushing up the sleeve from his arm*)
  Do also testify. – Such as I am,
  For an old friend I plainly beg this grace:
  Say if my boon be granted or denied.
MACLEAN: The man for whom thou pleadst is most unworthy;
  Yet let him safely from my shores depart:
  I harm him not.
BENLORA: (*turning from him indignantly*) My suit is then denied.
        (*To* LOCHTARISH *and* GLENFADDEN)
  Go ye to Dura's Allen; near the shore
  He harbours in his aged mother's cot;
  Bid him upon the ocean drift again
  His shattered boat, and be a wanderer still.
HELEN: (*coming forward eagerly*) His aged mother!
  (*To* MACLEAN) Oh! and shall he go?
  No, no, he shall not! On this day of joy,

Wilt thou to me refuse it?
>   (*Hanging upon him with looks of entreaty, till, seeing
>   him relent, she then turns joyfully to* BENLORA)
>   Bid your wanderer
Safe with his aged mother still remain—
A banished man no more.
MACLEAN: This is not well: but be it as thou wilt;
Thou hast prevailed, my Helen.
LOCHTARISH *and* GLENFADDEN: (*bowing low*) We thank thee, lady.
>   (BENLORA *bows slightly, in sullen silence*)
MACLEAN: (to BENLORA) Then let thy friend remain; he has my
>   pardon.
>   (BENLORA *bows again in silence*)
Clear up thy brow, Benlora; he is pardoned.
>   (*Pauses, but* BENLORA *is still silent*)
We trust to meet you shortly in the hall;
And there, my friends, shall think our happy feast
More happy for your presence.
>   (*Going up again, with anxious courtesy, to* BENLORA)
>   Thy past services,
Which great and many are, my brave Benlora,
Shall be remembered well. Thou hast my honour,
And high regard.
HELEN: And mine to boot, good kinsman, if the value
You put upon them makes them worth the having.
BENLORA: (*bows sullenly and retires; then muttering aside to
>   himself as he goes out*) Good kinsman! good Benlora! gracious
>   words
From this most high and potent dame, vouchsafed
To one so poor and humble as myself.   [*Exit*]
LOCHTARISH: (*aside to* GLENFADDEN) But thou forget—
GLENFADDEN: (*aside to* LOCHTARISH) No. I'll stay behind,
And move Maclean to join our nightly meeting.
Midnight the hour when you desire his presence?
LOCHTARISH: Yes, even so; then will we be prepared.
>   [*Exit*]
GLENFADDEN: (*returning to* MACLEAN) Chieftain, I would some
>   words of privacy
Speak with you, should your leisure now permit.
MACLEAN: Come to my closet, then, I'll hear thee gladly.
>   [*Exeunt* MACLEAN *and* GLENFADDEN]
HELEN: (*to* ROSA, *who now comes forward*) Where hast thou been,

    my Rosa, with my boy,
Have they with wild flowers decked his cradle round?
And peeps he through them like a little nestling—
A little heath-cock[15] broken from its shell,
That through the bloom puts forth its tender beak,
As steals some rustling footstep on its nest?
Come, let me go and look upon him. Soon,
Ere two months more go by, he'll look again
In answer to my looks, as though he knew
The wistful face that looks so oft upon him,
And smiles so dearly, is his mother's.
                          Thinkst thou
He'll soon give heed and notice to my love?
ROSA: I doubt it not: he is a lively infant,
And moves his little limbs with vigour, spreading
His fingers forth, as if in time they would
A good claymore[16] clench bravely.
HELEN: A good claymore clench bravely! – O! to see him
A man ! – a valiant youth! – a noble chieftain!
And laying on his plaided shoulder, thus,
A mother's hand, say proudly, 'This is mine!'
I shall not then a lonely stranger be
'Mid those who bless me not: I shall not then—
But silent be my tongue. (*Weeps*)
ROSA: Dear madam, still in hope look forward cheerily.
      (MORTON *comes from the bottom of the stage*)
And here is Morton, with some tidings for you:
God grant they comfort you! – I must withdraw:
His wary faithfulness mistrusts my love,
But I am not offended. (*Offering to retire*)
HELEN: Nay, remain. (*Beckoning her back*)
Say what thou hast to say, my worthy Morton,
For Rosa is as faithful as thyself.
MORTON: This morning, lady, amongst the farther cliffs,
Dressed like a fisher peasant, did I see
The Lord of Lorne, your brother.
HELEN: Ha! sayst thou,
The Lord of Lorne, my brother? – Thou'rt deceived.
MORTON: No, no: in vain his sordid garb concealed him!
His noble form and stately step I knew
Before he spoke.
HELEN: He spoke to thee?

MORTON: He did.
HELEN: Was he alone?
MORTON: He was; but, near at hand,
  Another stranger, noble as himself,
  And in like garb disguised, amongst the rocks
  I marked, though he advanced not.
HELEN: Alas, alas, my brother! why is this?
  He spoke to thee, thou sayst – I mean my brother.
  What did he say?
MORTON: He earnestly entreats
  To see you privately; and bids you say
  When this may be. Meantime he lies concealed
  Where I may call him forth at your command.
HELEN: O, why disguised? – Thinkst thou he is not safe?
MORTON: Safe in his hiding-place he is: but yet
  The sooner he shall leave this coast, the better.
HELEN: To see him thus! O, how I am beset!
  Tell him at twilight, in my nurse's chamber,
  I will receive him. But be sure thou add,
  Himself alone will I receive – alone –
  With no companion must he come. Forget not
  To say, that I entreat it earnestly.
MORTON: I will remember this.
HELEN: Go to him quickly then: and, till the hour,
  Still do thou hover near him. Watch his haunt,
  Lest some rude fisherman or surly hind[17]
  Surprise him. Go thou quickly. O, be prudent!
  And be not for a moment off the watch.
MORTON: Madam, I will obey you: trust me well.

                                                    [*Exit*]

HELEN: (*much disturbed*) My brother on the coast; and with him
    too,
  As well I guess, the man I must not see!
ROSA: Mean you the brave Sir Hubert?
HELEN: Yes, my Rosa.
  My noble brother in his powerful self
  So strong in virtue stands, he thinks full surely
  The daughter of his sire no weakness hath;
  And wists not how a simple heart must struggle
  To be what it would be – what it must be –
  Ay, and so aid me, heaven! what it shall be.
ROSA: And heaven will aid you, madam, doubt it not.

Though on this subject still you have repressed
All communing, yet, nevertheless, I well
Have marked your noble striving and revered
Your silent inward warfare, bravely held;
In this more pressing combat firm and valiant,
As is your noble brother in the field.

HELEN: I thank thee, gentle Rosa; thou art kind—
I should be franker with thee; but I know not—
Something restrains me here.

               (*Laying her hand on her heart*)

I love and trust thee;
And on thy breast I'll weep when I am sad;
But ask not why I weep.   [*Exeunt*]

Act II

An apartment in twilight, almost dark; the door of an inner chamber, standing a little ajar, at the bottom of the stage

Enter JOHN OF LORNE *and* SIR HUBERT DE GREY,
disguised as peasants

DE GREY: Nay, stop, I pray; advance we not too far?
LORNE: Morton hath bid us in this place to wait.
   The nurse's chamber is adjoining to it;
   And, till her light within give notice, here
   Thou mayst remain; when I am called, thou'lt leave me.
DE GREY: Till thou art called! and may I stay to hear
   The sweetness of her voice – her footstep's sound;
   Perhaps snatch in the torch's hasty light
   One momentary vision of that form—
   The form that hath to me of earthly make
   No fellow? May it be without transgression?
LORNE: Why shouldst thou not? De Grey, thou art too fearful;
   Here art thou come with no dishonest will;
   And well she knows thine honour. Her commands,
   Though we must yield to them, capricious seem;
   Seeing thou art with me, too nicely scrupulous;
   And therefore need no farther be obeyed
   Than needs must be. She puts thee not on honour.
   Were I so used—
DE GREY: 'Spite of thy pride, wouldst thou
   Revere her still the more. – O, no, brave Lorne,
   I blame her not. When she, a willing victim,
   To spare the blood of two contending clans,
   Against my faithful love her suffrage gave,
   I blessed her; and the deep, but chastened sorrow
   With which she bade me. – Oh! that word! farewell,
   Is treasured in my bosom as its share
   Of all that earthly love hath power to give.
   It came from Helen, and, from her received,
   Shall not be worn with thankless dull repining.

LORNE: A noble heart thou hast: such manly meekness
Becomes thy generous nature. But for me,
More fierce and wilful, sorely was I chafed
To see thy faithful heart robbed of its hope,
All for the propping up a hollow peace
Between two warlike clans, who will, as long
As bagpipes sound, and blades flash to the sun,
Delighting in the noble sport of war,
Some fierce opponents find. What doth it boot,[18]
If men in fields must fight, and blood be shed,
What clans are in the ceaseless strife opposed?
DE GREY: Ah, John of Lorne! too keenly is thy soul
To war inclined – to wasteful, ruthless war.
LORNE: The warlike minstrel's rousing lay[19] thou lov'st:
Shall bards in the hall sing of our fathers' deeds
To lull their sons to sleep? Vain simple wish!
I love to hear the sound of holy bell,
And peaceful men their praises lift to heaven:
I love to see around their blazing fire
The peasant and his cheerful family set,
Eating their fearless meal. But, when the roar
Of battle rises, and the closing clans,
Darkening the sun-gleamed heath, in dread affray
Are mingled; blade with blade, and limb with limb,
Nerve-strained, in terrible strength; yea, soul with soul
Nobly contending; who would raise aloft
The interdicting hand, and say, 'Be stilled?'
If this in me be sin, may heaven forgive me!
That being am not I.
DE GREY: In very deed
This is thy sin; and of thy manly nature
The only blemish worthy of that name.
More peaceful be, and thou wilt be more noble.
LORNE: Well, here we will not wrangle for the point.
None in the embattled field who have beheld
Hubert de Grey in mailed hauberk[20] fight,
Will guess how much that knight in peace delights.
Still burns my heart that such a man as thou
Wast for this weak, unsteady, poor Maclean—
DE GREY: Nay, with contempt, I pray thee, name him not.
Her husband, and despised! O, no, no, no!
All that pertains to her, even from that hour,

Honoured and sacred is.

LORNE: Thou generous heart! more noble than myself!
I will not grieve thee. – I'll to Helen go,
With every look and word that might betray
Indignant thoughts, or wound her gentle spirit,
Strictly suppressed: and to her ear will give
Thy generous greetings, and thy manly words
Of cheering comfort – all most faithfully
Shall be remembered.

DE GREY: Ay, and my request.

LORNE: To see the child?

DE GREY: Even so: to look upon it—
Upon the thing that is of her; this bud—
This seedling of a flower so exquisite.

                (*Light is seen in the inner chamber*)
Ha! light is in the chamber! moves the door?
Someone approaches. O! but for a moment
Let me behind thy friendly tartans be,
And snatch one glance of what that light will give.

                (*Conceals himself behind* LORNE, *who steps some
paces back, setting his hand to his side, and tilting his plaid over his
arms to favour him; while the door of the inner chamber
opens, and* HELEN *appears, bearing a lamp, which she afterwards sets
upon a stone slab as she advances*)
Her form – her motion – yea, that mantled arm,
Pressed closely to her breast, as she was wont
When chilly winds assailed. – The face – O, woe is me!
It was not then so pale.

LORNE: (*to him, in a low voice*) Begone: begone.

DE GREY: Blest vision, I have seen thee! Fare thee well!

                                        [*Exit in haste*]

HELEN: (*coming forward, alarmed*) What sound is that of steps that
      hasten from us?
Is Morton on the watch.

LORNE: Fear nothing; faithful Morton is at hand:
The steps thou heardst were friendly.

HELEN: (*embracing* LORNE) My brother! meet we thus – disguised,
      by stealth?
Is this like peace? How is my noble father?
Hath any ill befallen?

LORNE: Argyll is well;
And nothing ill, my sister, hath befallen,

If thou art well and happy.

HELEN: Speakst thou truly?
  Why art thou come? Why thus upon our coast?
  O take it not unkindly that I say,
  'Why art thou come?'

LORNE: Near to the opposite shore,
  With no design, but on a lengthened chase,
  A lusty deer pursuing from the hills
  Of Morven, where Sir Hubert and myself
  Guests of the social lord two days had been,
  We found us; when a sudden strong desire
  To look upon the castle of Maclean,
  Seen from the coast, our eager fancy seized,
  And that indulged, forthwith we did agree
  The frith[21] to cross, and to its chief and dame
  A hasty visit make. But as our boat
  Lay waiting to receive us, warned by one
  Whom well I knew (the vassal of a friend
  Whose word I could not doubt), that jealous rancour,
  Stirred up amongst the vassals of Maclean,
  Who, in their savage fury, had been heard
  To utter threats against thy innocent self,
  Made it unsafe in open guise to venture,
  Here in this garb we are to learn in secret
  The state in which thou art. – How is it then?
  Morton's report has added to my fears:
  All is not well with thee.

HELEN: No, all is well.

LORNE: A cold constrained voice that answer gave:
  All is not well. – Maclean – dares he neglect thee?

HELEN: Nay, wrong him not; kind and affectionate
  He still remains.

LORNE: But it is said, his vassals with vile names
  Have dared to name thee, even in open clan:
  And have remained unpunished. Is it so?
        (*Pauses for an answer, but she is silent*)
  All is not well.

HELEN: Have I not said it is?

LORNE: Ah! dost thou thus return a brother's love
  With cold reserve? – O speak to me, my Helen!
  Speak as a sister should. – Have they insulted thee?
  Has any wrong – my heart within me burns

If I but think upon it. – Answer truly.
HELEN: What, am I questioned then? Thinkst thou to find me
   Like the spoiled heiress of some Lowland lord,
   Peevish and dainty; who, with scorn regarding
   The ruder home she is by marriage placed in,
   Still holds herself an alien from its interest,
   With poor repining, losing every sense
   Of what she is, in what she has been? No.—
   I love thee, Lorne; I love my father's house:
   The meanest cur that round his threshold barks
   Is in my memory as some kindred thing:
   Yet take it not unkindly when I say,
   The lady of Maclean no grievance hath
   To tell the Lord of Lorne.
LORNE: And has the vow,
   Constrained, unblest, and joyless as it was,
   Which gave thee to a lord unworthy of thee,
   Placed thee beyond the reach of kindred ties—
   The warmth of blood to blood – the sure affection
   That nature gives to all – a brother's love?
   No, by all sacred things! here is thy hold:
   Here is thy true, unshaken, native stay:
   One that shall fail thee never, though the while,
   A faithless, wavering, intervening band
   Seems to divide thee from it.
     (*Grasping her hand vehemently, as if he would lead her away*)
HELEN: What dost thou mean? What violent grasp is this?
   Com'st thou to lead me from my husband's house,
   Beneath the shade of night, with culprit stealth?
LORNE: No, daughter of Argyll; when John of Lorne
   Shall come to lead thee from these hated walls
   Back to thy native home – with culprit stealth,
   Beneath the shades of night, it shall not be.
   With half our western warriors at his back,
   He'll proudly come. Thy listening timid chief
   Shall hear our martial steps upon his heath,
   With heavy measured fall, send, beat by beat,
   From the far-smitten earth, a sullen sound,
   Like deep-delled forests groaning to the strokes
   Of lusty woodmen. On the watch-tower's height,
   His straining eye shall mark our sheathless swords
   From rank to rank their lengthened blaze emit,

Like streams of shivering light, in hasty change,
Upon the northern firmament. – By stealth!
No! not by stealth! – believe me, not by stealth
Shalt thou these portals pass.

HELEN: Them have I entered,
The pledge of peace: and here my place I'll hold
As dame and mistress of the warlike clan
Who yield obedience to their chief, my lord;
And whatsoever their will to me may bear,
Of good or ill, so will I hold me ever.
Yea, did the Lord of Lorne, dear as he is,
With all the warlike Campbells at his back
Here hostile entrance threaten; on these walls,
Failing the strength that might defend them better,
I would myself, while by my side in arms
One valiant clan's-man stood, against his powers,
To the last push, with desperate opposition,
This castle hold.

LORNE: And wouldst thou so? so firm and valiant art thou?
Forgive me, noble creature! – Oh! the fate—
The wayward fate that binds thy generous soul
To poor unsteady weakness!

HELEN: Speakst thou thus?
Thus pressing still upon the galled spot?
Thou dealst unkindly with me. Yes, my brother,
Unkindly and unwisely. Wherefore hast thou
Brought to this coast the man thou knowest well
I ought not in mysterious guise to see?
And he himself – seeks he again to move
The hapless weakness I have striven to conquer?
I thought him generous.

LORNE: So think him still.
His wishes tend not to disturb thy peace:
Far other are his thoughts. – He bids me tell thee
To cheer thy gentle heart, nor think of him,
As one who will in vain and stubborn grief
His ruined bliss lament – he bids me say
That he will even strive, if it be possible,
Amongst the maidens of his land to seek
Some faint resemblance of the good he lost,
That thou mayst hear of him with less regret,
As one by holy bands linked to his kind.

He bids me say, should ever child of his
And child of thine – but here his quivering lip
And starting tears spoke what he could not speak.
HELEN: O noble, generous heart; and does he offer
Such cheering manly comfort? Heaven protect,
And guide, and bless him! On his noble head
Such prosperous bliss be poured, that hearing of it
Shall, through the gloom of my untoward state,
Like gleams of sunshine break, that from afar
Look over the dull dun heath.[22]
LORNE: But one request—
HELEN: Ha! makes he one?
LORNE: It is to see thy child.
HELEN: To see my child! Will he indeed regard it?
Shall it be blessed by him?
                    Enter MORTON *in haste*
MORTON: Conceal yourself, my lord, or by this passage
                    (*Pointing off the stage*)
The nearest postern[23] gain: I hear the sound
Of heavy steps at hand, and voices stern.
HELEN: O fly, my brother! Morton will conduct thee
(*To* MORTON) Where is Sir Hubert?
MORTON: Safe he is without.
HELEN: Heaven keep him so!
(*To* LORNE)   O leave me! I, the while,
Will in, and, with mine infant in mine arms,
Meet thee again, ere thou depart. – Fly! fly!
[*Exeunt;* HELEN *into the inner chamber, putting out the lamp as she
                    goes, and* LORNE *and* MORTON *by a side passage*]

SCENE ii

*A cave, lighted by flaming brands fixed aloft on its rugged sides,
and shedding a fierce glaring light down upon the objects below.*
LOCHTARISH, BENLORA, GLENFADDEN, *with several of the
chief* VASSALS OF MACLEAN, *are discovered in a recess, formed
by projecting rocks, at the bottom of the stage, engaged in
earnest discourse, from which they move forward slowly,
speaking as they advance*

LOCHTARISH: And thus ye see, by strong necessity,
  We are compelled to this.
1ST VASSAL: Perhaps thou art right.
LOCHTARISH: Sayst thou *perhaps?* Dost thou not plainly see
  That never a man amongst us can securely
  His lands possess, or say, 'My house is mine,'
  While, under tutorage of proud Argyll,
  This beauteous sourceress our besotted chief
  By soft enchantment holds?
            (*Laying his hand on the* 1ST VASSAL)
                    My brave Glenore,
  What are thy good deserts, that may uphold thee
  In favour with a Campbell? – Duncan's blood,
  Slain in his boat, with all its dashing oars
  Skirting our shore, while that his vaunting piper[24]
  The Campbell's triumph played? Will this speak for thee?
            (*Turning to* 2ND VASSAL)
  And, Thona, what good merit pleadest thou?
  The coal-black steed of Clone, thy moonlight plunder,
  Taken from the spiteful laird, will he, good sooth!
  Neigh favour on thee? (*To* 3RD VASSAL)
                And my valiant Fallen,
  Bethink thee well if fair-haired Flora's cries
  Whom from her native bower by force thou tookst,
  Will plead for thee. – And say ye still *perhaps*—
  Perhaps there is necessity?
1ST VASSAL: Strong should it be, Lochtarish; for the act
  Is fell and cruel thou wouldst push us to.
GLENFADDEN: (*to* 1ST VASSAL) Ha, man of mercy! are thy lily hands
  From bloody taint unstained? What sights were those
  Thou lookedst upon in Brunock's burning tower,
  When infants through the flames their wailings sent,
  And yet unaided perished?
LOCHTARISH: (*soothingly*)   Tush, Glenfadden!
  Too hasty art thou.
  (*To the* VASSALS) Ye will say, belike,
  'Our safety – our existence did demand
  Utter extinction of that hold of foes.'
  And well ye may. – A like necessity
  Compels us now, and yet ye hesitate.
GLENFADDEN: Our sighted seers the funeral lights have seen,
  Not moving onward in the wonted path

On which by friends the peaceful dead are borne,
But hovering over the heath like countless stars,
Spent and extinguished on the very spot
Where first they twinkled. This too well foreshows
Interment of the slain, whose bloody graves
Of the same mould are made on which they fell.
2ND VASSAL: Ha! so indeed! some awful tempest gathers.
1ST VASSAL: What sighted man hath seen it?
GLENFADDEN: He whose eye
Can see on northern waves the foundering bark,
With all her shrieking crew, sink to the deep,
While yet, with gentle winds, on dimpling surge
She sails from port in all her gallant trim:
John of the Isle hath seen it.
OMNES: (*starting back*) Then hangs some evil over us.
GLENFADDEN: Know ye not
The mermaid hath been heard upon our rocks?
OMNES: (*still more alarmed*) Ha! when?
GLENFADDEN: Last night, upon the rugged crag
That lifts its dark head through the cloudy smoke
Of dashing billows, near the western cliff.
Sweetly, but sadly, o'er the stilly deep
The passing sound was borne. I need not say
How fatal to our clan that boding sound
Hath ever been.
3RD VASSAL: In faith thou makest me quake.
2ND VASSAL: Some fearful thing hangs o'er us.
1ST VASSAL: If 'tis fated
Our clan before our ancient foe shall fall,
Can we heaven's will prevent? Why should we then
The Campbells' wrath provoke?
BENLORA: (*stepping up fiercely to* 1ST VASSAL) Heaven's will prevent
    – the Campbells' ire provoke!
Is such base tameness uttered by the son
Of one, who would into the fiery pit
Of damned fiends have leapt, so that his grasp
Might pull a Campbell with him?
                              Bastard blood!
Thy father spoke not thus.
LOCHTARISH: (*soothingly*)   Nay, brave Benlora,
He means not as thou thinkst.
BENLORA: If heaven decree

Slaughter and ruin for us, come it then!
But let our enemies, close grappled to us,
In deadly strife, their ruin join with ours.
Let corse to corse,[25] upon the bloody heath,
Maclean and Campbell, stiffening side by side,
With all the gnashing ecstasy of hate
Upon their ghastly visages impressed,
Lie horribly! – For every widow's tear
Shed in our clan, let matron Campbells howl!

LOCHTARISH: Indeed, my friends, although too much in ire,
Benlora, wisely speaks. – Shall we in truth
Wait for our ruin from a crafty foe,
Who here maintains this keenly watchful spy
In gentle kindness masked?

GLENFADDEN: Nor need we fear,
As good Lochtarish hath already urged,
Her death will rouse Argyll. It will be deemed,
As we shall grace it with all good respect
Of funeral pomp, a natural visitation.

LOCHTARISH: Ay, and besides, we'll swear upon the book,
And truly swear, if we are called upon,
We have not shed her blood.

BENLORA: I like not this.
If ye her life will take, in open day
Let her a public sacrifice be made.
Let the loud trumpet far and near proclaim
Our bloody feast, and at the rousing sound,
Let every clans-man of the hated name
His vengeful weapon clench.—
I like it not, Lochtarish. What we do,
Let it be boldly done. – Why should we slay her?
Let her in shame be from the castle sent;
Which, to her haughty sire, will do, I ween,
Far more despite than taking of her life.—
A feeble woman's life! – I like it not.
(*Turning on his heel angrily, and striding to the bottom of the stage*)

LOCHTARISH: (*aside to* GLENFADDEN) Go to him, friend, and
    soothe him to our purpose.
The fiery fool! how madly wild he is!
        (GLENFADDEN *goes to the bottom of the stage, and is seen
            remonstrating, in dumb-show, with* BENLORA, *while*
            LOCHTARISH *speaks to the vassals on the front*)

LOCHTARISH: My friends, why on each other look ye thus
    In gloomy silence? freely speak your thoughts.
    Mine have I freely spoken: that advising
    Which for the good – nay, I must say existence,
    Of this our ancient clan most needful is.
    When did Lochtarish ever for himself
    A separate 'vantage seek, in which the clan
    At large partook not? Am I doubted now?
2ND VASSAL: No, nothing do we doubt thy public zeal.
LOCHTARISH: Then is my long experience of the sudden
    To childish folly turned?
                            Thinkst thou, good Thona,
    We should beneath this artful mistress live,
    Hushed in deceitful peace, till John of Lorne,
    For whom the office of a treacherous spy
    She doth right slyly manage, with his powers
    Shall come upon us? Once ye would have spurned
    At thoughts so base; but now, when forth I stand
    To do what vengeance, safety, nay, existence,
    All loudly call for; even as though already
    The enemy's baleful influence hung o'er you,
    Like quelled and passive men ye silent stand.
1ST VASSAL: (roused) Nay, cease, Loctarish! quelled and passive
    men
    Thou knowst we are not.
LOCHTARISH: Yet a woman's life,
    And that a treacherous woman, moves you thus.
    Bold as your threats of dark revenge have been,
    A strong decisive deed appals you now.
    Our chieftain's feeble undetermined spirit
    Infects you all: ye dare not stand by me.
OMNES: We dare not, sayst thou?
LOCHTARISH: Dare not, will I say!
    Well spoke the jeering Camerons, I trow,
    As past their fishing boats our vessel steered,
    When with pushed lip, and finger pointing thus,
    They called our crew the Campbell-cowed Macleans.
OMNES: (roused fiercely) The Campbell-cowed Macleans!
2ND VASSAL: Infernal devils!
    Dare they to call us so?
LOCHTARISH: Ay, by my truth!
    Nor think that from the Camerons alone

Ye will such greeting have, if back ye shrink,
And stand not by me now.
OMNES: (*eagerly*) We'll stand! – We'll stand!
2ND VASSAL: Tempt us no more. There's never a man of us
    That will not back thee boldly.
LOCHTARISH: Ay, indeed?
    Now are ye men! Give me your hands to this.
              (*They all give him their hands*)
    Now am I satisfied. (*Looking off the stage*)
              The chief approaches.
    Ye know full well the spirit of the man
    That we must deal withal; therefore be bold.
OMNES: Mistrust us not.
    Enter MACLEAN, *who advances to the middle of the stage, while*
LOCHTARISH, BENLORA, GLENFADDEN, *and all the other vassals*
gather round him with stern determined looks. A pause; MACLEAN
      eyeing them all round with inquisitive anxiety
MACLEAN: A goodly meeting at this hour convened.
            (*A sullen pause*)
    Benlora; Thona; Allen of Glenore;
    And all of you, our first and bravest kinsmen;
    What mystery in this sullen silence is?
    Hangs any threatened evil over the clan?
BENLORA: Yes, chieftain; evil, that doth make the blood
    Within your grey-haired warriors' veins to burn,
    And their brogued feet to spurn the ground that bears them.
LOCHTARISH: Evil, that soon will wrap your tower in flames,
    Your ditches fill with blood, and carrion birds
    Glut with the butchered corses of your slain.
GLENFADDEN: Ay; evil, that doth make the hoary locks[26]
    Of sighted men around their age-worn scalps
    Like quickened points of crackling flame to rise;
    Their teeth to grind, and strained eye-balls roll
    In fitful frenzy, at the horrid things,
    In terrible array before them raised.
1ST VASSAL: The mermaid hath been heard upon our rocks:
    The fatal song of waves.
GLENFADDEN: The northern deep
    Is heard with distant moanings from our coast,
    Uttering the dismal bodeful sounds of death.
2ND VASSAL: The funeral lights have shone upon our heath,
    Marking in countless groups the graves of thousands.

BENLORA: Yea, chief; and sounds like to thy father's voice
Have from the sacred mould wherein he lies,
At dead of night, by wakeful men been heard
Three times distinctly. (*Turning to* GLENFADDEN)
Saidst thou not thrice?

GLENFADDEN: Yes; three times heard distinctly.

MACLEAN: Ye much amaze me, friends. – Such things have been?

LOCHTARISH: Yea, chief; and thinkst thou we may lightly deem
Of coming ills, by signs like these forewarned?

MACLEAN: Then an it be, high heaven have mercy on us!

LOCHTARISH: (*in a loud solemn voice*) Thyself have mercy on us!

MACLEAN: How is this?
Your words confuse and stun me. – Have I power
To ward this evil off?

OMNES: Thou hast! thou hast!

MACLEAN: Then God to me show mercy in my need,
As I will do for you and for my clan
Whatever my slender power enables me.

OMNES: Amen! and swear to it.

MACLEAN: (*starting back*) What words are these,
With such wild fierceness uttered? Name the thing
That ye would have me do.

BENLORA: (*stepping out from the rest*) Ay, we will name it.
Helen the Campbell, fostered in your bosom,
A serpent is, who wears a hidden sting
For thee and all thy name; the oath-bound spy
Of dark Argyll, our foe; the baleful plague
To which ill-omened sounds and warnings point,
As that on which existence or extinction—
The name and being of our clan depend—
A witch of deep seduction. – Cast her forth.
The strange, unnatural union of two bloods,
Adverse and hostile, most abhorred is.
The heart of every warrior of your name
Rises against it. Yea, the grave calls out,
And says it may not be. – Nay, shrink not, chief,
When I again repeat it – cast her off.

MACLEAN: Art thou a man? and bidst me cast her off,
Bound as I am by sacred holy ties?

LOCHTARISH: Bound as thou art by that which thou regardest
As sacred holy ties; what tie so sacred
As those that to his name and kindred vassals

The noble chieftain bind? If ties there be
To these opposed, although a saint from heaven
Had blessed them o'er the crossed and holy things,
They are anulled and broken.

BENLORA: Ay, Lochtarish;
Sound doctrine hast thou uttered. Such the creed
Of ancient warriors was, and such the creed
That we their sons will with our swords maintain.
(*Drawing his sword fiercely, whilst the rest follow his example*)

MACLEAN: Ye much confound me with your violent words.
I can in battle strive, as well ye know:
But how to strive with you, ye violent men,
My spirit knows not.

LOCHTARISH: Decide – decide, Maclean: the choice is thine
To be our chieftain, leading forth thy bands,
As heretofore thy valiant father did,
Against our ancient foe, or be the husband,
Despised, forsaken, cursed, of her thou prizest
More than thy clan and kindred.

GLENFADDEN: Make thy choice.
Benlora, wont in better times to lead us
Against the Campbells, with a chieftain's power,
Shall, with the first blast of his warlike horn,
If so he will it, round his standard gather
Thy roused and valiant vassals to a man.

MACLEAN: (*greatly startled*) Ha! go your thoughts to this? Desert me
    so?
My vassals so desert me?

LOCHTARISH: Ay, by my faith, our very women too:
And in your hall remain, to serve your state,
Nor child nor aged crone.

MACLEAN: (*after great agitation*) Decide, and cast her off! – How far
    the thoughts
To which these words ye yoke may go, I guess not.
(*Eagerly*) They reach not to her life?
        (*Pauses and looks at them anxiously, but they are silent*)
Oh, oh! oh, oh! that stern and dreadful silence!

LOCHTARISH: We will not shed her blood.

MACLEAN: Then ye will spare her?

LOCHTARISH: Commit her to our keeping: ask us not
How we shall deal with her.

MACLEAN: Some fearful mystery is in your words,

Which covers cruel things. O woe the day,
That I on this astounding ridge am poised!
On every side a fearful ruin yawns.
    (*A voice heard without, uttering wild incoherent words,*
        mixed with shrieks of horror)
What frenzied voice is that?
        Enter 4TH VASSAL, *as if terribly frightened*
LOCHTARISH: (*to* 4TH VASSAL) What brings thee hither?
4TH VASSAL: He fixes wildly on the gloomy void
  His starting eyeballs, bent on fearful sights,
  That make the sinews of his aged limbs
  In agony to quiver.
LOCHTARISH: Who didst thou say?
4TH VASSAL: John of the Isle, the sighted awful man.
  Go, see yourselves: in the outer cave he is.
  Entranced he stands; arrested on his way
  By horrid visions, as he hurried hither
  Enquiring for the chief.
        (*Voice heard without, as before*)
LOCHTARISH: Hark! hark, again! dread powers are dealing with
    him.
  Come, chieftain – come and see the awful man.
  If heaven or hell hath power to move thy will,
  Thou canst not now withstand us.
  (*Pausing for him to go*) Hearst thou not?
  And motionless?
MACLEAN: I am beset and stunned,
  And every sense bewildered. Violent men!
  If ye unto this fearful pitch are bent,—
  When such necessity is pressed upon me,
  What doth avail resistance? Woe the day!
  Even lead me where ye will.
[*Exit* MACLEAN, *exhausted and trembling, leaning on* LOCHTARISH,
    and followed by BENLORA *and* GLENFADDEN *and vassals; two*
                inferior VASSALS *alone left upon the stage*]
1ST VASSAL: (*looking after* MACLEAN) Ay, there he goes; so spent,
    and scared, and feeble!
  Without a prophet's skill, we may foretell,
  John of the Isle, by sly Lochtarish taught,
  Will work him soon to be an oath-bound wretch
  To this their fell design. – Are all things ready?
2ND VASSAL: All is in readiness.

1ST VASSAL: When ebbs the tide?
2ND VASSAL: At early dawn, when in the narrow creek
  Near to the castle, with our trusty mates,
  Our boat must be in waiting to receive her.
1ST VASSAL: The time so soon! alas, so young and fair!
  That slow and dismal death! To be at once
  Plunged in the closing deep many have suffered,
  But to sit waiting on a lonely rock
  For the approaching tide to throttle her—
  But that she is a Campbell, I could weep.
2ND VASSAL: Weep, fool! think soon how we'll to war again
  With our old enemy; and, in the field,
  Our good claymores die with their hated blood:
  Think upon this, and change thy tears to joy.

                              [Exeunt]

SCENE iii

The bed-chamber of MACLEAN

Enter MACLEAN, *followed by* HELEN

HELEN: Ah! wherefore art thou so disturbed? the night
  Is almost spent: the morn will break ere long,
  And rest hast thou had none. Go to thy bed:
  I pray thee, go.
MACLEAN: I cannot: urge me not.
HELEN: Nay, try to rest: I'll sit and watch by thee.
MACLEAN: Thou'lt sit and watch! O woe betide the hour!
  And who will watch for thee?
HELEN: And why for me?
  Can any harm approach? When thou art near,
  Or sleeping or awake, I am secure.
MACLEAN: (*pacing to and fro distractedly*) O God! O God!
HELEN: Those exclamations!
        (*Going up to him, while he avoids her*)
                Turnst thou from me thus?
  Have I offended? dost thou doubt my faith?
  Hath any jealous thought – I freely own
  Love did not make me thine: but, being thine,
  To no love-wedded dame, bound in the ties

Of dearest sympathy, will I in duty—
In steady, willing, cheerful duty yield.
Yea, and though here no thrilling rapture be,
I look to spend with thee, my habit fostered,
The evening of my days in true affection.
MACLEAN: The evening of thy days! alas, alas!
Would heaven had so decreed it!
                    (*Pulling away his hand from hers*)
Grasp me not!
It is a fiend thou clingst to. (*A knock at the door*)
Power of heaven!
Are they already at the chamber door!
HELEN: Are those who knock without unwelcome?—hush!
Withdraw thyself, and I will open to them.
                    (*Goes to the door*)
MACLEAN: O go not! go not!
    (*Runs after her to draw her back, when a* VASSAL, *rushing from
                behind the bed, lays hold of him*)
VASSAL: Art thou not sworn to us? Where is thy faith?
MACLEAN: I know, I know! the bands of hell have bound me.
O fiends! ye've made of me – what words can speak
The hateful wretch I am!
                            Hark! hark! she cries!
She shrieks and calls on me!
        (HELEN's *cries heard without, first near and distinct,
    afterwards more and more distant as they bear her away; while
    the* VASSAL *leads* MACLEAN *forcibly off the stage by the opposite
        side, he breaks from him, and hastens towards that by
                    which* HELEN *went out*)
VASSAL: Thou art too strong for me. Do as thou wilt;
But if thou bringst her back, even from that moment
Benlora is our leader, and thyself,
The Campbell's husband, chieftain and Maclean
No more shalt be. We've sworn as well as thou.
        [MACLEAN *stops irresolutely, and then suffers the* VASSAL *to
                    lead him off by the opposite side*]

Act III

SCENE i

A small island, composed of a rugged craggy rock, on the front of the stage, and the sea in the background

Enter two VASSALS *dragging in* HELEN, *as if just come out of their boat*

HELEN: O why is this? Speak, gloomy, ruthless men!
  Our voyage ends not here?

1ST VASSAL: It does: and now,
  Helen the Campbell, fare thee – fare thee well!

2ND VASSAL: Helen the Campbell, thy last greeting take
  From mortal thing.

HELEN: What! leave me on this rock,
  This sea-girt rock,[27] to solitude and famine?

1ST VASSAL: Next rising tide will bring a sure relief
  To all the ills we leave thee.

HELEN: (*starting*)   I understand you.
         (*Raising her clasped hands to heaven*)
                   Lord of heaven and earth;
  Of storms and tempests, and the unfathomed deep;
  Is this thy righteous will?
        (*Grasping the hands of the men imploringly*)
                   Ye cannot mean it!
  Ye cannot leave a human creature thus
  To perish by a slow approaching end,
  So awful and so terrible! Instant death
  Were merciful to this.

1ST VASSAL: If thou prefer it, we can shorten well
  Thy term of pain and terror: from this crag,
  Full fourteen fathom deep thou mayst be plunged.
  In shorter time than three strokes of an oar
  Thy pains will cease.

2ND VASSAL: Come, that were better for thee.
    (*Both of them take her hands, and are going to hurry her
       to the brink of the rock, when she shrinks back*)

HELEN: O no! the soul recoils from swift destruction!

Pause ye awhile. (*Considering for a moment*)
                    The downward terrible plunge!
The coil of whelming waves! – O fearful nature!
            (*Catching hold of a part of the rock near her*)
To the rough rock I'll cling: it still is something
Of firm and desperate hold – Depart and leave me.
        (*Waving her hand for the* VASSALS *to go, whilst she keeps
                close hold of the rock with the other*)

1ST VASSAL: Thou still mayst live within a prison pent,
    If life be dear to thee

HELEN: (*eagerly*) If life be dear! – Alas, it is not dear!
    Although the passing fearful act of death
    So very fearful is. – Say how, even in a prison,
    I still may wait my quiet natural end.

1ST VASSAL: Whatever thou art, such has thy conduct been,
    Thy wedded faith, even with thy fellest foes,
    Sure and undoubted stands. – Sign thou this scroll,
    Owning the child, thy son, of bastard birth;
    And this made sure, Lochtarish bade me say
    Thy life shall yet be spared.

HELEN: (*pushing him away with indignation as he offers her the
    scroll*) Off, off, vile agent of a wretch so devilish!
    Now do I see from whence my ruin comes:
    I and my infant foil his wicked hopes.
    O harmless babe! will heaven abandon thee?
    It will not! – No; it will not!
                (*Assuming firmness and dignity*)
    Depart and leave me. In my rising breast
    I feel returning strength. Heaven aids my weakness:
    I'll meet its awful will.
                (*Waving them off with her hand*)

1ST VASSAL: Well, in its keeping rest thee: fare thee well,
    Helen the Campbell!

2ND VASSAL: Be thy sufferings short!
    (*Aside to the other*) Come, quickly let us go, nor look behind.
    Fell is the service we are put upon:
    Would we had never taken that cruel oath!
                                    [*Exeunt* VASSALS]

HELEN (*alone, after standing some time gazing round her, paces
    backwards and forward with agitated steps, then, stopping
    suddenly, bends her ear to the ground as if she listened
    earnestly to something*) It is the sound; the heaving hollow

swell
That notes the turning tide. – Tremendous agent!
Mine executioner, that, step by step,
Advances to the awful work of death.—
Onward it wears: a little space removed
The dreadful conflict is.
    (*Raising her eyes to heaven, and moving her lips, as in the
        act of devotion, before she again speaks aloud*)
Thou art in the blue coped sky[28] – the expanse immeasurable;
In the dark rolled clouds, the thunder's awful home:
Thou art in the wide-shored earth – the pathless desert;
And in the dread immensity of waters—
In the fathomless deep Thou art.
Awful but excellent! beneath Thy hand,
With trembling confidence, I bow me low,
And wait Thy will in peace.
    (*Sits down on a crag of the rock, with her arms crossed
    over her breast in silent resignation; then, after a pause of
        some length, raises her head hastily*)
Is it a sound of voices in the wind?
The breeze is on the rock: a gleam of sunshine
Breaks through those farther clouds. It is like hope
Upon hopeless state.
      (*Starting up, and gazing eagerly around her*)
I'll to that highest crag and take my stand:
Some little speck upon the distant wave
May to my eager gaze a vessel grow—
Some onward wearing thing – some boat – some raft—
Some drifted plank. – O hope! thou quit us never!
    [*Exit, disappearing amongst the rugged divisions of the rock*]

SCENE ii

*A small island, from which the former is seen in the distance, like a
little pointed rock standing out of the sea*

Enter SIR HUBERT DE GREY, *followed by two*
FISHERMEN

DE GREY: This little swarded spot,[29] that over the waves,
  Clothed in its green light, seemed to beckon to us,

Right pleasant is: until our comrades join,
Here will we rest. I marvel much they stand
So far behind. In truth, such lusty rowers
Put shame upon their skill.

1ST FISHERMAN: A cross-set current bore them from the track,
    But see, they now bear on us rapidly. (*Voices without*)
        Holla!

2ND FISHERMAN: They call to us. – Holla! holla!
                   How fast they wear! they
    are at hand already.

DE GREY: Right glad I am: the Lord of Lorne, I fear,
Will wait impatiently: he has already
With rapid oars the nearer mainland gained,
Where he appointed us to join him. – Ho!
        (*Calling off the stage*)
Make to that point, my lads.
(*To those near him*) Here, for a little while, upon the turf
We'll snatch a hasty meal, and, so refreshed,
Take to our boats again.

    Enter three other FISHERMEN, *as from their boat, on*
        the other side of the stage

Well met, my friends! I'm glad you're here at last.
How was it that you took that distant track?

3RD FISHERMAN: The current bore us wide of what we wished;
And, were it not your honour is impatient
Mainland to make, we had not come so soon.

DE GREY: What had detained you?

3RD FISHERMAN: As near yon rock we bore, that o'er the waves
Just shows its jetty point, and will, ere long,
Beneath the tide be hidden, we heard the sound
Of feeble lamentation.

DE GREY: A human voice?

3RD FISHERMAN: I cannot think it was;
For on that rock, sea-girt, and at high tide
Sea-covered, human thing there cannot be;
Though, at the first, it sounded in our ears
Like a faint woman's voice.

DE GREY: Perceived ye aught?

3RD FISHERMAN: Yes; something white that moved, and, as we
    think,
Some wounded bird that there hath dropped its wing,
And cannot make its way.

4TH FISHERMAN: Perhaps some dog,
   Whose master, at low water, there hath been,
   And left him.

3RD FISHERMAN: Something 'tis in woeful case,
   Whatever it be. Right fain I would have gone
   To bear it off.

DE GREY: (*eagerly*) And wherefore didst thou not?
   Return and save it. Be it what it may;
   Something it is, lone and in jeopardy,
   Which hath a feeling of its desperate state,
   And therefore doth to woe-worn, fearful man,
   A kindred nature bear. – Return, good friend—
   Quickly return and save it, ere the tide
   Shall wash it from its hold. I to the coast
   Will steer the while, and wait your coming there.

3RD FISHERMAN: Right gladly, noble sir.

4TH FISHERMAN: We'll gladly go:
   For, by my faith! at night I had not slept
   For thinking of that sound.

DE GREY: Heaven speed you then! whatever ye bring to me
   Of living kind, I will reward you for it.
   Our different tracks we hold; nor longer here
   Will I remain. Soon may we meet:
   God speed you! [*Exeunt severally*]

SCENE iii

A fisherman's house on the mainland

Enter JOHN OF LORNE *and* SIR HUBERT DE GREY

LORNE: Then wait thou for thy boat; I and my men
   Will onward to the town, where, as I hope,
   My trusty vassals and our steeds are stationed.
   But lose not time.

DE GREY: Fear not; I'll follow quickly.

LORNE: I must unto the castle of Argyll
   Without delay proceed; therefore, whatever
   Of living kind, bird, beast, or creeping thing,
   This boat of thine produces, bring it with thee;
   And, were it eaglet fierce, or wolf, or fox,

On with us shall it travel, mounted bravely,
Our homeward cavalcade to grace. Farewell!
DE GREY: Farewell, my friend! I shall not long delay
   Thy homeward journey.
LORNE (*calling off the stage*) But ho! good host and hostess! (*To* DE
   GREY) Ere I go
I must take leave of honest Duncan here,
And of his rosy wife. – Ay, here they come.
                    Enter the host and his wife
(*To host*) Farewell, my friends, and thanks be to you both!
Good cheer, and kindly given, of you we've had.
Thy hand, good host. May all the fish of the ocean
Come crowding to thy nets! – And healthy brats,
Fair dame, have thou! with such round rosy cheeks
As brats of thine befit: and, by your leave,

                                        [*Kissing her*]

So be they kissed by all kind comers too!
Good luck betide you both!
DUNCAN: And, sir, to you the same. Whoever you be,
   A brave man art thou, that I will be sworn.
WIFE: Come you this way again, I hope, good sir,
   You will not pass our door.
LORNE: Fear not, good hostess;
   It is a pleasant, sunny, open door,
   And bids me enter of its own accord;
   I cannot pass it by. – Good luck betide you!
                [*Exit, followed to the door by* SIR HUBERT]
DUNCAN: I will be sworn it is some noble chieftain,
   Though homely be his garb.
WIFE: Ay, so will I: the Lord of Lorne himself
   Could not more courteous be.
DUNCAN: Hush! hush! be quiet!
   We live not now amongst the Campbells, wife.
   Should some Maclean overhear thee – hush, I say.
            (*Eyeing* DE GREY, *who returns from the door*)
   And this man, too; right noble is his mien;
   He is no common rambler.
(*To* DE GREY)   By your leave,
   If I may be so bold without offending,
   Your speech, methinks, smacks of a southern race;
   I guess at least of Lowland kin ye be.
   But think no shame of this; we'll nevertheless

Regard thee: thieves and cowards be not all
Who from the Lowlands come.
WIFE: No; no, in sooth! I knew a Lowlander,
Some years gone by, who was as true and honest—
Ay, and I do believe well nigh as brave,
As though, with brogued feet, he never else
Had all his days than muir[30] or mountain trodden.
DE GREY: Thanks for your gentle thoughts!— It has indeed
Been my misluck to draw my earliest breath
Where meadows flower, and corn fields wave in the sun.
But let us still be friends! Heaven gives us not
To choose our birth-place, else these wilds, no doubt,
Would be more thickly peopled.
DUNCAN: Ay, true it is, indeed.
WIFE: And hard it were
To quarrel with him too for his misfortune.
                    (*Noise heard without*)
DE GREY: Ha! 'tis my boat returned.
                Enter 1ST FISHERMAN
1ST FISHERMAN: Ay, here we are.
DE GREY: And aught saved from the rock?
1ST FISHERMAN: Yes, by my faith! but neither bird nor beast.
Look there, my master. (*Pointing to the door*)
Enter HELEN, *extremely exhausted, and almost senseless, wrapped*
closely up in one of their plaids, and supported by the other two
FISHERMEN
DE GREY: A woman! Heaven in mercy! was it then
A human creature there exposed to perish?
1ST FISHERMAN: (*opening the plaid to show her face*). Ay, look; and
such a creature!
DE GREY: (*starting back*) Helen of Argyll!
O God! was this the feeble wailing voice?
(*Clasping his arms about her knees, as she stands almost senseless,*
supported by the fishermen, and bursting into tears)
Could heart of man so leave thee? thou, of all
That lovely is, most lovely. – Woe is me!
Some aid, I pray you. (*To host and his wife*)
                    Bear her softly in,
And wrap warm garments round her. Breathes she freely?
Her eyes half open are, but life, alas!
Is almost spent, and holds within her breast
A weak uncertain seat. (HELEN *moves her hand*)

                        She moves her hand.
  She knows my voice. – O heaven, in mercy save her!
  Bear her more gently, pray you. Softly, softly!
  How weak and spent she is!
1ST FISHERMAN: No marvel she is weak: we reached her not
  Until the swelling waters laved her girdle.[31]
  And then to see her—
DE GREY: Cease, I pray thee, friend,
  And tell me not—
2ND FISHERMAN: Nay, faith, he tells you true:
  She stood above the water, with stretched arms
  Clung to the dripping rock, like the white pinions—[32]
DE GREY: Peace, peace, I say! thy words are agony—
  Give to my mind no image of the thing!
          [*Exeunt, bearing* HELEN *into an inner part of the house*]

Act IV

SCENE i

A small Gothic hall, or ante-room, in ARGYLL's *castle, a door at the bottom of the stage, leading to the apartment of the Earl, before which is discovered the piper pacing backwards and forwards, playing on his bagpipe*

Enter DUGALD

DUGALD: Now, pray thee, piper, cease! That stunning din[33]
 Might do good service by the ears to set
 Two angry clans; but for a morning's rouse,
 Here at an old man's door, it does, good sooth,
 Exceed all reasonable use. The Earl
 Has passed a sleepless night: I pray thee now
 Give o'er, and spare thy pains.
PIPER: And spare my pains, sayst thou? I'll do mine office,
 As long as breath within my body is.
DUGALD: Then mercy on us all! if wind thou meanst,
 There is within that sturdy trunk of thine,
 Old as it is, a still exhaustless store.
 A Lapland, witch's bag could scarcely match it.
 Thou couldst, I doubt not, belly out the sails
 Of a three-masted vessel with thy mouth:
 But be thy mercy equal to thy might!
 I pray thee now give o'er: in faith the Earl
 Has passed a sleepless night.
PIPER: Thinkst thou I am a Lowland, day-hired minstrel,
 To play or stop at bidding? Is Argyll
 The lord and chieftain of our ancient clan,
 More certainly, than I to him, as such,
 The high hereditary piper am?
 A sleepless night, forsooth! He's slept full oft
 On the hard heath, with fifty harnessed steeds
 Champing their fodder round him – soundly too.
 I'll do mine office, loon, chafe as thou wilt.
   (*Continuing to pace up and down, and play as before*)
DUGALD: Nay, thou the chafer art, red-crested cock!

The Lord of Lorne has spoilt thee with indulging
Thy wilful humours. Cease thy cursed din!
See; here the Earl himself comes forth to chide thee.   [*Exit*]

    Enter ARGYLL, *attended, from the chamber*

ARGYLL: Good morrow, piper! thou hast roused me bravely:
A younger man might gird his tartans on
With lightsome heart to martial sounds like these,
But I am old.

PIPER: O no, my noble chieftain!
It is not age subdues you.

ARGYLL: No; what else?

PIPER: Alack! the flower and blossom of your house
The wind hath blown away to other towers.
When she was here, and gladsome faces brightened
With looking on her, and around your board
Sweet lays were sung, and gallants in the hall
Footed it trimly to our varied measures,
There might, indeed, be found beneath your roof
Those who might reckon years fourscore and odds,
But of old folks, I warrant, never a soul.
No; we were all young then.

ARGYLL: (*sighing deeply*)   'Tis true, indeed,
It was even as thou sayst. Our earthly joys
Fly like the blossoms scattered by the wind.

    Enter a Servant

SERVANT: Please you, my lord,
Some score of vassals in the hall attend
To bid good morrow to you, and the hour
Wears late: the chamberlain hath bid me say
He will dismiss them, if it please your honour.

ARGYLL: Nay, many a mile have some of them, I know,
With suit or purpose lurking in their minds,
Ridden over rough paths to see me; disappointed
Shall none of them return. I'm better now.
I have been rather weary than unwell.
Say, I will see them presently.   [*Exit servant*]

    Re-enter DUGALD *in haste*

(*To* DUGALD) Thou comest with a busy face: what tidings?

DUGALD: The Lord of Lorne's arrived, and please your honour:
Sir Hubert too, and all their jolly train;
And with them have they brought a lady, closely
In hood and mantle muffled: never a glimpse

May of her face be seen.

ARGYLL: A lady, sayst thou?

DUGALD: Yes; closely muffled up.

ARGYLL: (*pacing up and down, somewhat disturbed*) I like not this.
 – It cannot surely be –
>> (*Stopping short, and looking hard at* DUGALD)
Whence comes he?

DUGALD: He a-hunting went, I know,
To Cromack's ancient laird, whose youthful dame
So famed for beauty is; but whence he comes,
I cannot tell, my lord.

ARGYLL: (*pacing up and down, as he speaks to himself in broken
 sentences, very much disturbed*) To Cromack's ancient laird – If
 that indeed –
Beshrew me, if it be! – I'd rather lose
Half of my lands, than son of mine such wrong,
Such shameful wrong, should do. This sword I've drawn
Like robbery to revenge, never to abet it:
And shall I now with hoary locks – No, no!—
My noble Lorne! he cannot be so base.

>> *Enter* LORNE, *going up to* ARGYLL *with agitation*

ARGYLL: (*eyeing him suspiciously*) Well, John, how is it? Welcome
 art thou home,
If thou returnst, as well I would believe,
Deserving of a welcome.

LORNE: Doubts my lord
That I am so returned?
>> (*Aside to* ARGYLL, *endeavouring to draw him apart
 from his attendants*)
>> Your ear, my father.
Let these withdraw: I have a thing to tell you.

ARGYLL: (*looking still more suspiciously upon* LORNE, *from seeing the
 eagerness and agitation with which he speaks, and turning from
 him indignantly*) No, by this honest blade! if wrong thou'st done.
Thou hast no shelter here. In open day,
Before the assembled vassals shalt thou tell it;
And he whom thou hast injured be redressed,
While I have power to bid my Campbells fight
In the fair and honoured cause.

LORNE: I pray, my lord—
Will you vouchsafe to hear me?

ARGYLL: Thoughtless boy!

How far unlike the noble Lorne I thought thee!—
Proud as I am, far rather would I see thee
Joined to the daughter of my meanest vassal,
Than see thy manly, noble worth engaged
In such foul raid as this.
LORNE: Nay, nay! be pacified!
I'd rather take, in faith, the tawny hand
Of homeliest maid, that doth, of holidays,
Her sun-burnt locks with worsted ribbon bind,
Fairly and freely won, than brightest dame
That ever in stately bower or regal hall
In graceful beauty shone, gained by such wrong—
By such base treachery as you have glanced at.
These are plain words: then treat me like a man,
Who hath been wont the manly truth to speak.
ARGYLL: Ha! now thy countenance and tone again
Are John of Lorne's. That look, and whispering voice,
So strange appeared, in truth I liked it not.
Give me thy hand. – Where is the stranger dame?
If she in trouble be—
LORNE: *(aside)*   Make these withdraw,
And I will lead her hither.
     [*Exit, while the* EARL *waves his hand, and* DUGALD *and attendants,*
                                              etc. go out]
          Presently re-enter LORNE, *leading in* HELEN, *covered*
                         closely up in a mantle
LORNE: This is the dame, who, houseless and deserted,
Seeks shelter here, nor fears to be rejected.
HELEN: (*sinking down, and clasping* ARGYLL's *knees*) My father!
ARGYLL: That voice! – O God! – unveil – unveil, for mercy!
          [*Tearing off the mantle that conceals her*]
My child! my Helen!
          (*Clasping her to his heart, and holding her there for*
                    some time, unable to speak)
My child! my dearest child! – my soul! my pride!
Deserted! – houseless! – comst thou to me thus?
Here is thy house – thy home: this aged bosom
Thy shelter is, which thou shalt quit no more.
My child! my child!
               (*Embracing her again;* HELEN *and he weeping*
                         upon one another's necks)
Houseless! deserted – 'neath the cope of heaven

Breathes there a wretch who could desert thee?— Speak,
If he hath so abused his precious trust,
If he – it makes me tear these hoary locks
To think what I have done! – Oh thoughtless father!
Thoughtless and selfish too!
          (*Tearing his hair, beating his forehead with all the
                    violent gestures of rage and grief*)
HELEN: Oh, oh! forbear! It was not you, my father;
I gave myself away: I did it willingly:
We acted both for good; and now your love
Repays me richly – stands to me instead
Of many blessings. – Noble Lorne, besides—
O, he hath been to me so kind – so tender!
(*Taking her brother's hand, and pressing it to her breast; then joining
    her father's to it and pressing them both ardently to her lips*)
Say not I am deserted: heaven hath chid me—
Hath chid me sorely: but hath blessed me too,—
O, dearly blessed me!
ARGYLL: Hath chid thee sorely! – how I burn to hear it!
What hast thou suffered?
LORNE: We will not tell thee now. Go to thy chamber,
And be awhile composed. We have, my father,
A tale to tell that will demand of thee
Recruited strength to hear. – We'll follow thee.
[*Exeunt:* LORNE *supporting his father and* HELEN *into the chamber*]

SCENE ii

The garden of the castle

Enter ARGYLL, LORNE, *and* SIR HUBERT DE GREY,
speaking as they enter

LORNE: A month! – A week or two! – No, not an hour
Would I suspend our vengeance. Such atrocity
Makes even the little term between our summons,
And the dark crowding round our martial pipes
Of plumed bonnets nodding to the wind,
Most tedious seem; yea, makes the impatient foot
To smite the very earth beneath its tread,
For being fixed and inert.

ARGYLL: Be less impatient, John: thou canst not doubt
 A father's keen resentment of such wrong:
 But let us still be wise; this short delay
 Will make revenge the surer; to its aim
 A just direction give.
DE GREY: The Earl is right:
 We shall but work in the dark, impatient Lorne,
 If we too soon begin.
ARGYLL: How far Maclean
 Hath to this horrible attempt consented,
 Or privy been, we may be certified,
 By waiting silently to learn the tale
 That he will tell us of his lady's loss,
 When he shall send to give us notice of it,
 As doubtless soon he will.
DE GREY: If he, beset and threatened, to those fiends,
 Unknowing of their purpose, hath unwillingly
 Committed her, he will himself, belike,
 If pride prevent him not, your aid solicit
 To set him free from his disgraceful thraldom.
LORNE: And if he should, shrunk be this sinewed arm,
 If it unsheath a weapon in his cause!
 Let every ragged stripling[34] on his lands
 In wanton mockery mouth him with contempt;
 Benlora head his vassals; and Lochtarish—
 That serpent, full of every devilish wile,
 His prison-keeper and his master be!
DE GREY: Ay; and the keeper also of his son,
 The infant heir.
LORNE: (*starting*) I did not think of this.
ARGYLL: Then let thy headstrong fury pause upon it.
 Thanks to Sir Hubert's prudence! thou as yet
 Before thy followers hast restrained been;
 And who this lady is, whom to the castle,
 Like a mysterious stranger, ye have brought,
 From them remains concealed. – My brave De Grey!
 This thy considerate foresight, joined to all
 Thy other service in this woeful matter,
 Hath made us much thy debtor.
DE GREY: I have indeed, my lord, considered only
 What I believed would Helen's wishes be,
 Ere she herself could utter them; if this

Hath proved equivalent to wiser foresight,
Let it direct us still; let Helen's wishes
Your measures guide.
ARGYLL: Ah, brave De Grey! would they had ever done so!
I had not now—
(*Taking* SIR HUBERT's *hand with emotion*)
Forgive me, noble youth
Alas, alas! the father's tenderness
Before the chieftain's policy gave way,
And all this wreck hath been.
LORNE: 'Tis even so.
That cursed peace; that coward's shadeless face
Of smiles and promises, to all things yielding
With weak, unmanly pliancy, so gained you—
Even you, the wise Argyll! – it made me mad!
Who hath no point that he maintains against you,
No firmness hath to hold him of your side:
Who cannot sturdily against me stand,
And say, 'Encroach no farther,' friend of mine
Shall never be.
DE GREY: Nay, Lorne, forbear! – forbear!
Thine own impetuous wilfulness did make
The other's pliant mind more specious seem;
And thou thyself didst to that luckless union,
Although unwittingly, assistance lend.
Make now amends for it, and curb thy spirit,
While that the Earl with calmer judgment waits
His time for action.
LORNE: Beshrew me, but thy counsel strangely smacks
Of cautious timid age! In faith, De Grey,
But that I know thy noble nature well,
I could believe thee—
ARGYLL: Peace, unruly spirit!
Bold as thou art, methinks, with locks like these,
Thy father still may say to thee, 'Be silent!'
LORNE: (*checking himself, and bowing very low to* ARGYLL) And be
obeyed devoutly. – O forgive me!
Those locks are to your brows a kingly fillet
Of strong authority, to which my heart
No rebel is, though rude may be my words.
(*Taking* SIR HUBERT's *hand with an assured countenance*)
I ask not thee, De Grey, to pardon me.

Resistance here with gentleness is joined:
Therefore I've loved thee, and have laid upon thee
The hand of sure possession! claiming still
A friend's endurance of my froward temper,
Which, froward as it is, from thee hath borne
What never human being but thyself
Had dared to goad it with.

DE GREY: It is indeed
Thy well-earned right thou askest, noble Lorne,
And it is yielded to thee cheerfully.

ARGYLL: My aged limbs are tired with pacing here;
Some one approaches: within that grove
We'll find a shady seat, and there conclude
This well-debated point.   [*Exeunt*]

SCENE iii

A court within the castle, surrounded with buildings

Enter DUGALD *and a* VASSAL, *two servants at the same time
crossing the stage, with covered dishes in their hands*

VASSAL: I'd wait until the Earl shall be at leisure;
My business presses not. Where do they carry
Those covered meats? Have ye within the castle
Some noble prisoner?

DUGALD: Would so it were! but these are days of peace.
They bear them to the stranger dame's apartment,
Whom they have told thee of. There, at her door,
An ancient faithful handmaid of the house,
Whatever they bring receives; for none beside
Of all the household is admitted.

VASSAL: Now, by my fay! my purse and dirk[35] I'd give
To know who this may be. – Some chieftain's lady
Whom John of Lorne—

DUGALD: Nay, there, I must believe,
Thou guess erringly. – I grant, indeed,
He doffs his bonnet to each tacks-man's wife,[36]
And is with every coif[37] amongst them all,
Both young and old, in such high favour held,
Nor maiden, wife, nor beldame of the clan

But to the Earl doth her petition bring
Through intercession of the Lord of Lorne;
But never yet did husband, sire, or brother,
Of wrong from him complain.

VASSAL: I know it well.

DUGALD: But be she who she may,
This stranger here; I doubt not, friend, ere long,
We shall have bickering for her in the field
With some fierce foe or other.

VASSAL: So I trust:
And by my honest faith! this peace of ours
Right long and tiresome is. – I thought, ere now,
Some of our restless neighbours would have trespassed
And inroads made: but no; Argyll and Lorne
Have grown a terror to them: all is quiet;
And we ourselves must the aggressors be,
Or still this dull and slothful life endure,
Which makes our men of three-score years and ten
To fret and murmur.

Enter ROSA, *with a servant conducting her*

SERVANT: (*to* DUGALD). A lady here, would see my Lord of Lorne.

DUGALD: Yes, still to him they come.

(*Looking at* ROSA)
Ha! see I rightly?
Rosa from Mull?

ROSA: Yes, Dugald; here thou seest
A woeful bearer of unwelcome tidings.

DUGALD: What, hath thy lady sent thee?

ROSA: Alas, alas! I have no lady now.

DUGALD: Ha! is she dead? not many days ago
She was alive and well. – Hast thou so soon
The castle quitted – left thy lady's corse?

ROSA: Thinkst thou I would have left her? – On the night
When, as they say, she died, I from the castle
By force was taken, and to mainland conveyed;
Where in confinement I remained, till chance
Gave me the means of breaking from my prison;
And hither am I come, in woeful plight,
The dismal tale to tell.

DUGALD: A tale, indeed,
Most dismal, strange, and sudden.

ROSA: How she died

God knows; but much I fear foul play she had.
Where is the Lord of Lorne? for first to him
I wish to speak.
DUGALD: Come, I will lead thee to him. – Had foul play!
VASSAL: Fell fiends they are could shed her blood! If this
Indeed hath been, 'twill make good cause, I wot;[38]
The warlike pipe will sound our summons soon.

                                    [*Exeunt* DUGALD *and* ROSA, *etc.*]

                ARGYLL *and* SIR HUBERT *enter by the opposite side*
ARGYLL: And wilt thou leave us then, my noble friend?
May we not still for some few days retain thee?
DE GREY: Wherever I go, I carry in my heart
A warm remembrance of the friendly home
That still within these hospitable walls
I've found: but longer urge me not to stay.
In Helen's presence now, constrained and strange,
With painful caution, chasing from my lips
The ready thought, half-quivered into utterance,
For cold corrected words, expressive only
Of culprit consciousness – I sit; nor even
May look upon her face but as a thing
On which I may not look; so painful now
The mingled feeling is, since dark despair
With one faint ray of hope hath tempered been.
I can no more endure it. She herself
Perceives it, and it pains her. – Let me then
Bid you farewell, my lord. When evening comes,
I'll, under favour of the rising moon,
Set forth.
ARGYLL: Indeed! so soon? and must it be?
DE GREY: Yes; to Northumberland without delay
I fain would take my road. My aged father
Looks now impatiently for my return.
ARGYLL: Then I'll no longer urge thee. To thy father,
The noble baron, once, in better days,
My camp-mate and my friend, I must resign thee.
Bear to him every kind and cordial wish
An ancient friend can send, and—
                    (*A horn heard without*)
                                        Hark! that horn!
Some messenger of moment is arrived.—
We'll speak of this again. – The moon tonight

Is near the full, and at an early hour—
   Enter a messenger, bearing a letter
Whose messenger art thou, who in thy hand
That letter bearst with broad and sable seal,
Which seems to bring to me some dismal tidings?
MESSENGER: From Mull, my lord, I come; and the Maclean,
 Our chief, commissioned me to give you this,
 Which is indeed with dismal tidings fraught.
 (ARGYLL *opens the letter, and reads it with affected surprise and*
      sorrow)
ARGYLL: Heavy, indeed, and sudden is the loss—
 The sad calamity that hath befallen.
 The will of heaven be done!
 (*Putting a handkerchief to his eyes, and leaning, as if for support,*
 upon SIR HUBERT; *then, after a pause, turning to the messenger*)
 How didst thou leave the chieftain? He, I hope,
 Permits not too much sorrow to o'ercome
 His manhood. Doth he bear his grief composedly?
MESSENGER: O no, it is most violent! At the funeral,
 Had not the good Lochtarish, by his side,
 Supported him, he had with very grief
 Sunk to the earth. – And good Lochtarish too
 Was in right great affliction.
ARGYLL: Ay, good man;
 I doubt it not. – Ye've had a splendid funeral?
MESSENGER: O yes, my lord! that have we had. Good truth!
 A grand and stately burial has it been.
 Three busy days and nights through all the isle
 Have bagpipes played, and sparkling beakers flowed;
 And never corse, I trow, in the earth was laid
 With louder lamentations.
ARGYLL: Ay, I doubt not,
 Their grief was loud enough. – Pray pass ye in.
 (*To attendants at a distance*) Conduct him there; and see that he
  be treated,
 After his tedious journey, as befits
 A way-tired stranger.
    (*Exeunt all but* ARGYLL *and* SIR HUBERT)
 This doth all hope and all belief exceed.
 Maclean will shortly follow this his notice,
     (*Giving* SIR HUBERT *the letter*)
 To make me here a visit of condolence;

And thus within our power they put themselves
With most assured blindness.
DE GREY: (*after reading it*) 'Tis Lochtarish,
In all the arts of dark hypocrisy
So deeply skilled, who doth o'ershoot his mark,
As such full often do.
ARGYLL: And let him come!
At his own arts we trust to match him well.—
Their force, I guess, is not in readiness;
Therefore, meantime, to stifle all suspicion,
This specious mummery[39] he hath devised;
And his most wretched chief, led by his will,
Most wretchedly submits. – Well, let us go
And tell to Lorne the news, lest too unguardedly
He should receive it.   [*Exeunt*]

SCENE iv

An apartment in the castle

Enter SIR HUBERT DE GREY, *beckoning to* ROSA,
who appears on the opposite side

DE GREY: Rosa; I pray thee, spare me of thy leisure
Some precious moments: something would I say:
Wilt thou now favour me?
ROSA: Most willingly.
DE GREY: As yet thy mistress knows not of the letter
Sent by Maclean, announcing his design
Of paying to the Earl this sudden visit—
This mockery of condolence?
ROSA: No; the Earl
Forbade me to inform her.
DE GREY: This is well;
Her mind must be prepared. Meantime I go,
And thou art here to comfort and attend her:
O do it gently, Rosa! do it wisely!
ROSA: You need not doubt my will. – Go ye so soon;
And to Northumberland?
DE GREY: So I intended.
And so Argyll and John of Lorne believe:

But since this messenger from Mull arrived,
Another thought has struck me. – Saidst thou not
The child – thy lady's child, taken from the castle,
Is to the keeping of Lochtarish's mother
Committed, whose lone house is on the shore?
ROSA: Yes, whilst in prison pent, so did I hear
My keeper say, and much it troubled me.
DE GREY: Canst thou to some good islander commend me,
Within whose house I might upon the watch
Concealed remain? – It is to Mull I go,
And not to England. While Maclean is here,
Attended by his vassals, the occasion
I'll seize to save the infant.
ROSA: Bless thee for it!
Heaven bless thee for the thought! – I know a man—
An aged fisherman, who will receive you;
Uncle to Morton: and if he himself
Still in the island be, there will you find him,
Most willing to assist you.
DE GREY: Hush, I pray
I hear thy lady's steps.
ROSA: Near to the castle gate, ere you depart,
I'll be in waiting to inform you farther
Of what may aid your purpose.
DE GREY: Do, good Rosa,
And make me much thy debtor. But be secret.
ROSA: You need not doubt me.
        Enter HELEN, *and* DE GREY *goes up to her as if he would
        speak, but the words falter on his lips, and he is silent*
HELEN: Alas! I see it is thy parting visit;
Thou comst to say 'farewell!'
DE GREY: Yes, Helen: I am come to leave with thee
A friend's dear benison – a parting wish—
A last – rest every blessing on thy head!
Be this permitted to me:
            (*Kissing her hand with profound respect*)
                    Fare thee well!
Heaven aid and comfort thee! Farewell! farewell!
(*Is about to retire hastily, whilst* HELEN *follows to prevent him*)
HELEN: O go not from me with that mournful look!
Alas! thy generous heart, depressed and sunk,
Looks on my state too sadly.—

I am not, as thou thinkst, a thing so lost
In woe and wretchedness. – Believe not so!
All whom misfortune with her rudest blasts
Hath buffeted, to gloomy wretchedness
Are not therefore abandoned. Many souls
From cloistered cells, from hermits' caves, from holds
Of lonely banishment, and from the dark
And dreary prison-house, do raise their thoughts
With humble cheerfulness to heaven, and feel
A hallowed quiet, almost akin to joy;
And may not I, by heaven's kind mercy aided,
Weak as I am, with some good courage bear
What is appointed for me? – O be cheered!
And let not sad and mournful thoughts of me
Depress thee thus. – When thou art far away,
Thou'lt hear, the while, that in my father's house
I spend my peaceful days, and let it cheer thee.
I too shall every southern stranger question,
Whom chance may to these regions bring, and learn
Thy fame and prosperous state.
DE GREY: My fame and prosperous state, while thou art thus!
    If thou in calm retirement livst contented,
    Lifting thy soul to heaven, what lack I more?
    My sword and spear, changed to a pilgrim's staff,
    Will be a prosperous state; and for my fame,—
    A feeble sound that after death remains,
    The echo of an unrepeated stroke
    That fades away to silence – surely this
    Thou dost not covet for me.
HELEN: Ah, I do!
    Yet, granting here I err, didst thou not promise
    To seek in wedded love and active duties
    Thy share of cheerful weal? – and dost thou now
    Shrink from thy generous promise? – No, thou shalt not.
    I hold thee bound – I claim it of thee boldly.
    It is my right. If thou, in sad seclusion,
    A lonely wanderer art, thou dost extinguish
    The ray that should have cheered my gloom: thou makest
    What else had been a calm and tempered sorrow,
    A state of wretchedness. – O no! thou wilt not!
    Take to thy generous heart some virtuous maid,
    And doubt not thou a kindred heart wilt find.

The cheerful tenderness of woman's nature
To thine is suited, and when joined to thee,
Will grow in virtue. – Take thou then this ring,
If thou wilt honour so my humble gift,
And put it on her hand; and be assured
She who shall wear it – she whose happy fate
Is linked with thine, will prove a noble mate.
DE GREY: O there I am assured! she whose fate
Is linked with mine, if fixed be such decree,
Most rich in every soft and noble trait
Of female virtue is: in this full well
Assured I am – I would – I thought – forgive—
I speak but raving words – a hasty spark,
Blown and extinguished, makes me waver thus.
Permit me then again. (*Kissing her hand*)
                    High heaven protect thee!
Farewell!
HELEN: Farewell! and heaven's good charge be thou!
   (*They part, and both turn away to opposite sides of the stage,*
     when SIR HUBERT, *looking round just as he is about to*
       go off, and seeing HELEN *also looking after him*
          sorrowfully, eagerly returns)
DE GREY: Ah! are those looks—
   (*Going to kneel at her feet, but immediately checking*
      himself with much embarrassment)
                Alas! why come I back?
Something there was – thou gavest me a ring;
I have not dropped it?
ROSA: (*coming forward*) No, 'tis on your finger.
DE GREY: Ay, true, good Rosa; but my wits are wildered;
I knew not what I sought.—
              Farewell! farewell!
   [*Exit* DE GREY *hastily, while* HELEN *and* ROSA *go off by the*
                      opposite side]

Act V

SCENE i

ARGYLL's castle, the vestibule, or grand entrance; a noise of bustle and voices heard without, and servants seen crossing the stage, as the scene opens

Enter DUGALD, *meeting* 1ST SERVANT

DUGALD: They are arrived, Maclean and all his train;
    Run quickly, man, and give our chieftains notice.
1ST SERVANT: They know already: from the tower we spied
    The mournful cavalcade: the Earl and Lorne
    Are down the staircase hasting to receive them.
DUGALD: I've seen them light, a sooty-coated train,
    With lank and woeful faces, and their eyes
    Bent to the ground, as though our castle gate
    Had been the scutcheoned portal of a tomb,[40]
    Set open to receive them.
2ND SERVANT: Ay, on the pavement fall their heavy steps
    Measured and slow, as if her palled coffin
    They followed still.
DUGALD: Hush, man! Here comes the Earl,
    With face composed and stern; but look behind him
    How John of Lorne doth gnaw his nether lip,
    And beat his clenched hand against his thigh,
    Like one who tampers with half-bridled ire!
2ND SERVANT: Has any one offended him?
DUGALD: Be silent,
    For they will overhear thee. – Yonder too
          (*Pointing to the opposite side of the stage*)
    Come the Macleans: let us our stations keep,
    And see them meet.
            [*Retiring with the other to the bottom of the stage*]
Enter ARGYLL *and* LORNE, *attended, and in deep mourning;
while, at the same time, by the opposite side of the stage, enter*
MACLEAN, BENLORA, LOCHTARISH, *and* GLENFADDEN, *with
attendants, also in deep mourning:* ARGYLL *and* MACLEAN
go up to one another, and formally embrace

ARGYLL: Welcome! if such a cheerful word as this
  May with our deep affliction suited be.
  Lochtarish too, and brave Benlora, ay,
  And good Glenfadden also – be ye all
  With due respect received, as claims your worth.
(Taking them severally but the hand as he names them. MACLEAN
then advances to embrace LORNE, *who shrinks back from him, but
immediately correcting himself, bends his body another way, as if
suddenly seized with some violent pain)*
ARGYLL: *(to* MACLEAN*)* Regard him not: he hath imprudently
  A recent wound exposed to chilling air,
  And oft the pain with sudden pang attacks him.
LOCHTARISH: Ay, what is shrewder? we have felt the like,
  And know it well, my lord.
ARGYLL: *(bowing to* LOCHTARISH, *but continuing to speak to*
  MACLEAN*)* Yet, nevertheless; good son-in-law and chieftain,
  Believe thou well that with a brother's feelings,
  Proportioned to the dire and dismal case
  That hath befallen, he now receives you; also
  Receiving these your friends with equal favour.
  This is indeed to us a woeful meeting,
  Chieftain of Mull.
    (Looking keenly in his face, while the other shuns his eye)
        I see full well the change
  Which violent grief upon that harrowed visage
  So deeply hath impressed.
MACLEAN: *(still embarrassed, and shrinking from* ARGYLL'S
  observation) Ah! ah! the woeful day! – I cannot speak.
  Alas, alas!
ARGYLL: Alas, in truth,
  Too much the woeful widower's altered looks,
  Upon thy face I see.
LOCHTARISH: *(to* ARGYLL*)* You see, my lord, his eyes with too much
    weeping
  Are weak, and shun the light. Nor should we marvel:
  What must to him the sudden loss have been,
  When even to us, who were more distantly
  Connected with her rare and matchless virtue,
  It brought such keen affliction?
ARGYLL: Yes, good Lochtarish, I did give her to you—
  To your right worthy chief, a noble creature,
  With every kindly virtue – every grace

That might become a noble chieftain's wife:
And that ye have so well esteeemed – so well
Regarded, cherished, and respected her,
As your excessive sorrow now declares,
Receive from me a grateful father's thanks.
Lochtarish, most of all to thy good love
I am beholden.

LOCHTARISH: Ah! small was the merit
Such goodness to respect.

ARGYLL: And thou, Benlora;
A woman, and a stranger, on the brave
Still potent claims maintain; and little doubt I
They were by thee regarded.
     (BENLORA *steps back, frowning sternly, and remains silent*)
                         And, Glenfadden,
Be not thy merits overlooked.

GLENFADDEN: Alas!
You overrate, my lord, such slender service.

ARGYLL: Wrong not, I pray, thy modest worth.—
     But here, (*Turning again to* MACLEAN)
Here most of all, from whom her gentle virtues,
(And so indeed it right and fitting was.)
Their best and dearest recompense received,
To thee, most generous chieftain, let me pay
The thanks that are thy due.

MACLEAN: Oh, oh! alas!

ARGYLL: Ay, in good sooth! I see thy grief-worn eyes
Do shun the light.
But grief is ever sparing of its words.
In brief, I thank you all: and for the love
Ye have so dearly shown to me and mine,
I trust, before we part, to recompense you
As suits your merit and my gratitude.

LORNE: (*aside to* ARGYLL) Ay, father; now ye speak to them shrewd
     words;
And now I'm in the mood to back you well.

ARGYLL: (*aside to* LORNE) 'Tis well thou art; but check those eager
     looks;
Lochtarish eyes thee keenly.
     (*Directing a hasty glance to* LOCHTARISH, *who is whispering to*
          GLENFADDEN, *and looking suspiciously at* LORNE)

LORNE: (*stepping forward to* MACLEAN, *etc.*) Chieftain, and

honoured gentlemen, I pray
The sullen, stern necessity excuse
Which pain imposed upon me, and receive,
Joined with my noble father's, such poor thanks
As I may offer to your loving worth.

ARGYLL: Pass on, I pray you; till the feast be ready,
Rest ye above, where all things are prepared
For your refreshment.   [*Exeunt*]

SCENE ii

A narrow arched room or closet, adjoining to a gallery

Enter LOCHTARISH *and* GLENFADDEN

LOCHTARISH: How likest thou this, Glenfadden? Doth the face
Argyll assumes, of studied courtesy,
Raise no suspicion?

GLENFADDEN: Faith, I know not well!—
The speech, indeed, with which he welcomed us,
Too wordy, and too articificial seemed
To be the native growth of what he felt.

LOCHTARISH: It so to me appeared: and John of Lorne,
First shrinking from Maclean, with sudden pain,
As he pretended, struck; then stern and silent;
Till presently assuming, like his father,
A courtesy minute and over-studied,
He glozed[41] us with his thanks:—
Didst thou not mark his keenly flashing eye,
When spoke Argyll of recompensing us
Before we part?

GLENFADDEN: I did indeed observe it.

LOCHTARISH: This hath a meaning.

GLENFADDEN: Faith, I do suspect
Some rumour must have reached their ear; and yet
Our agents faithful are; it cannot be.

LOCHTARISH: Or can, or can it not, beneath this roof
A night I will not sleep. When evening comes
Meet we again. If at this banquet, aught
Shall happen to confirm our fears, forthwith
Let us our safety seek in speedy flight.

GLENFADDEN: And leave Maclean behind us?
LOCHTARISH: Ay, and Benlora too. Affairs the better
  At Mull will thrive, when we have rid our hands
  Of both these hinderances, who in our way
  Much longer may not be. (*Listening*)
                              We're interrupted.
  Let us into the gallery return,
  And join the company with careless face,
  Like those who have from curiosity
  But stepped aside to view the house. – Make haste!
  It is Argyll and Lorne.
     [*Exeunt, looking at the opposite side, alarmed, at which enter*
                                    ARGYLL *and* LORNE]
LORNE: Are you not now convinced? his conscious guilt
  Is in his downcast and embarrassed looks,
  And careful shunning of all private converse
  Whenever aside you've drawn him from his train,
  Too plainly seen: you cannot now, my lord,
  Doubt of his share in this atrocious deed.
ARGYLL: Yet, Lorne, I would, ere further we proceed,
  Prove it more fully still. The dinner hour
  Is now at hand. (*Listening*)
                          What steps are those,
  That in the gallery, close to this door,
  Like some lone straggler from the company
  Withdrawn, sound quickly pacing to and fro?
  Look out and see.
LORNE: (*going to the door, and calling back to* ARGYLL *in a low
  voice*) It is Maclean himself.
ARGYLL: Beckon him hither then. – Thank heaven for this!
  Now opportunity is fairly given,
  If that constrainedly he cloaks their guilt,
  To free him from their toils.
               Enter MACLEAN, *conducted by* LORNE
ARGYLL: (*to* MACLEAN) My son, still in restraint before our vassals
  Have we conversed; but now in privacy—
  Start not, I pray thee – sit thee down, Maclean:
  I would have close and private words of thee:
  Sit down, I pray; my aged limbs are tired.
     (ARGYLL *and* MACLEAN *sit down, whilst* LORNE *stands behind
       them, with his ear bent eagerly to listen, and his eyes fixed
                  with a side-glance on* MACLEAN)

Chieftain, I need not say to thee, who deeply
Lamentst with us our sad untimely loss,
How keenly I have felt it.—
And now indulge a father in his sorrow.
And say how died my child. – Was her disease
Painful as it was sudden?

MACLEAN: It was – alas! I know not how it was.
A fell disease! – Her end was so appointed.

LORNE: (*behind*) Ay, that I doubt not.

MACLEAN: A fearful malady! though it received
All good assistance.

LORNE: (*behind*) That I doubt not either.

MACLEAN: A cruel ill! – but how it dealt with her,
My grief overwhelmed me so, I could not tell.

ARGYLL: Say – wast thou present? didst thou see her die?

MACLEAN: Oh, oh! the woeful sight, that I should see it!

ARGYLL: Thou didst not see it then?

MACLEAN: Alack! alack!
O would that I had seen – O woe is me!
Her pain – her agony was short to mine!

LORNE: (*behind, impatiently*) Is this an answer, chieftain, to the question
Argyll hath plainly asked thee – wast thou present
When Helen died? didst thou behold her death?

MACLEAN: O yes; indeed I caught your meaning lamely;
I meant – I thought – I know not certainly
The very time and moment of her death,
Although within my arms she breathed her last.

LORNE: (*rushing forward eagerly*) Now are we answered.
        (ARGYLL, *covering his face with his hands, throws himself
            back in his chair for some time without speaking*)

MACLEAN: (*to* ARGYLL) I fear my lord, too much I have distressed you.

ARGYLL: Somewhat you have indeed. – And further now
I will not press your keen and recent sorrow
With questions that so much renew its anguish.

MACLEAN: You did, belike, doubt of my tenderness.

ARGYLL: O no! I have no doubts. Within your arms
She breathed her last?

MACLEAN: Within my arms she died.

ARGYLL: (*looking hard at* MACLEAN, *and then turning away*) His
father was a brave and honest chief!

MACLEAN: What says my lord?

ARGYLL: A foolish exclamation,
   Of no determined meaning. (*Bell sounds without*)
                              Dry our tears:
   The hall-bell warns us to the ready feast;
   And through the gallery I hear the sound
   Of many footsteps hastening to the call.
   Chieftain, I follow thee.

                              [*Exeunt* ARGYLL *and* MACLEAN]

LORNE: (*alone, stopping to listen*) The castle, thronged throughout
      with moving life,
   From every winding stair, and arched aisle,
   A mingled echo sends.
   Ay; light of foot, I hear their sounding steps
   A-trooping to the feast, who never more
   At feast shall sit, or social meal partake.
   O wretch! O fiend of vile hypocrisy!
   How fiercely burns my blood within my veins
   Till I am matched with thee!   [*Exit*]

SCENE iii

*The great hall of the castle, with a feast set out, and the company
already placed at table, with servants and attendants in waiting,
who fill the stage in every part:* ARGYLL *is seated at the head of
the table, with* MACLEAN *on his left hand, and a chair left empty
on his right*

ARGYLL: (*to* MACLEAN, *etc.*) Most worthy chief, and honoured
      guests and kinsmen,
   I crave your pardon for this short delay:
   One of our company is wanting still,
   For whom we have reserved this empty place;
   Nor will the chief of Mull unkindly take it
   That on our better hand this chair of honour
   Is for a lady kept.

OMNES: A lady!
      (*A general murmur of surprise is heard through the hall*)

ARGYLL: Yes;
   Who henceforth of this house the mistress is;

And were it palace of our Scottish king,
Would so deserve to be.
OMNES: We give you joy, my lord.
                    (*A confused murmur heard again*)
MACLEAN: We give you joy, my lord: your age is blessed.
    We little thought, in these our funeral weeds,
    A bridal feast to darken.
LORNE: No, belike.
    Many who don their coat at break of day,
    Know not what shall befall them, therein girt,
    Ere evening close. (*Assuming a gay tone*)
    The Earl hath set a step-dame over my head
    To cow my pride[42] – What think you, brave Maclean?
    This world so fleeting is and full of change,
    Some lose their wives, I trow, and others find them.
    Bridegrooms and widowers do, side by side,
    Their beakers quaff; and which of them at heart
    Most glad or sorry is, the subtle fiend,
    Who in men's hollow hearts his council holds,
    He wotteth best, though each good man will swear,
    His, *lost* or *found*, all other dames excelled.
ARGYLL: Curb, Lorne, thy saucy tongue: Maclean himself
    Shall judge if she – the lady I have found,
    Equal in beauty her whom he hath lost,
    In worth I'm sure she does. But hush! she comes.
    (*A great commotion through the hall amongst the attendants, etc.*)
OMNES: It is the lady.
ARGYLL: (*rising from his seat, and making signs to the attendants
        nearest the door*) Ho there! make room, and let the lady pass.
    (*The servants, etc. stand apart, ranging themselves on every side
        to let the lady pass; and enter* HELEN, *magnificently dressed,
    with a deep white veil over her face; while* LORNE, *going forward
    to meet her, conducts her to her chair on* ARGYLL's *right hand*)
ARGYLL: (*to the* CAMPBELLS) Now, fill a cup of welcome to our
        friends!
LOCHTARISH: (*to* MACLEAN) Chieftain, forgettest thou to greet the
        lady?
MACLEAN: (*turning to* ARGYLL) Nay, rather give, my lord, might I
        presume,
    Our firstling cup to this fair lady's health,
    The noble dame of this right princely house.
    And though close veiled she be, her beauty's lustre

I little question.
(*Fills up a goblet, while* LOCHTARISH, BENLORA, *etc. follow his*
        example, and standing up, bow to the lady)
Your health, most noble dame!
        (HELEN, *rising also, bows to him, and throws back her veil:*
the cup falls from his hands; all the company start up from table;
screams and exclamations of surprise are heard from all
corners of the hall, and confused commotion seen everywhere.
MACLEAN, LOCHTARISH, *and* GLENFADDEN, *stand appalled*
and motionless; but BENLORA, *looking fiercely round him,*
                draws his sword)
BENLORA: What! are we here like deer bayed in a nook?[43]
And think ye so to slay us, crafty foe?
No, by my faith! like such we will not fall,
Arms in our hands, though by a thousand foes
Encompassed. Cruel, murderous, ruthless men,
Too good a warrant have you now to think us,
But cowards never!
                Rouse ye, base Macleans!
(*To* LOCHTARISH) And thou, whose subtlety around us thus
With wreckful skill these cursed toils hast wound,
Sinks thy base spirit now?
ARGYLL: (*holding up his hand*) Be silence in the hall!
Macleans, ye are my guests; but if the feast
Delight you not, free leave ye have to quit it.
Lorne, see them all, with right due courtesy,
Safely protected to the castle gate.
                (*Turning to* MACLEAN)
Here, other name than chieftain or Maclean
He may not give thee; but, without our walls,
If he should call thee murderer, traitor, coward,
Weapon to weapon, let your fierce contention
Be fairly held, and he, who first shall yield,
The liar be.—
                Campbells! I charge you there,
Free passage for the chieftain and his train.
(MACLEAN *and* LOCHTARISH, *etc., without speaking, quit the*
hall through the crowd of attendants, who divide, and form a
line to let them pass. HELEN, *who had sunk down almost*
senseless upon her seat, seeing the hall cleared of the crowd, who
go out after the MACLEANS, *now starts up, and catches hold of*
ARGYLL with an imploring look of strong distress)

HELEN: O father! well I know foul are his crimes,
But what – O what, am I, that for my sake
This bloody strife should be? O think, my lord!
He gave consent and sanction to my death,
But thereon could not look: and at your gate—
E'en on your threshold, must his life be taken?
For well I know the wrath of Lorne is deadly.
And gallant Lorne himself, if scathed should be,[44]
O pity! pity! – O for pity stay them!
ARGYLL: Let go thy hold, weak woman: pity now!
Rosa. Support her hence.
   (*Committing her to* ROSA, *who now comes forward,*
      and tearing himself away)
HELEN: (*endeavouring to run after him, and catch hold of him*
 again) O be not stern! beneath the ocean rather
Would I had sunk to rest, than been the cause
Of horrid strife like this! O pity! pity!
   [*Exeunt, she running out after him distractedly*]

SCENE iv

Before the gate of the castle: a confused noise of an approaching crowd heard within, and presently enter, from the gate, MACLEAN, BENLORA, LOCHTARISH, *and* GLENFADDEN, *with their attendants, conducted by* LORNE, *and followed by a crowd of* CAMPBELLS, *who range themselves on both sides of the stage*

LORNE: (*to* MACLEAN) Now, chieftain, we the gate have passed, –
 the bound
That did restrain us. Host and guest no more,
But deadly foes we stand, who from this spot
Shall never both with life depart. Now, turn,
And boldly say to him, if so thou darest,
Who calls thee villain, murderer, traitor, coward,
That he belies thee. Turn then, chief of Mull!
Here, man to man, my single arm to thine,
I give thee battle; or, refusing this,
Our captive here retain thee to be tried
Before the summoned vassals of our clans,
As suits thy rank and thine atrocious deeds.

Take thou thy choice.
MACLEAN: Yes, John of Lorne, I turn.
This turf on which we tread my death-bed is;
This hour my latest term; this sky of light
The last that I shall look on. Draw thy sword:
The guilt of many crimes overwhelms my spirit
But never will I shame my brave Macleans,
By dying, as their chief, a coward's death.
BENLORA: What! shalt thou fight alone, and we stand by
Idly to look upon it? (*Going up fiercely to* LORNE)
                    Turn me out
The boldest, brawniest Campbell of your bands;
Ay, more than one, as many as you will;
And I the while, albeit these locks be grey,
Leaning my aged back against this tree,
Will show your youngsters how, in other days,
Macleans did fight, when baited round with foes.
LORNE: Be still, Benlora; other sword than these,
Thy chief's and mine, shall not this day be drawn.
If I prevail against him, here with us
Our captives you remain. If I be conquered,
Upon the faith and honour of a chieftain,
Ye shall again to Mull in safety go.
BENLORA: Spoken like a noble chieftain!
LORNE: Ye shall, I say, to Mull in safety go.
But there prepare ye to defend your coast
Against a host of many thousand Campbells.
In which, be well assured, swords as good
As John of Lorne's, to better fortune joined,
Shall of your crimes a noble vengeance take.
        (LORNE *and* MACLEAN *fight; and, after a combat of some
        length,* MACLEAN *is mortally wounded, and the* CAMPBELLS
                    give a loud shout)
MACLEAN: It is enough, brave Lorne; this wound is death:
And better deed thou couldst not do upon me,
Than rid me of a life disgraced and wretched.
But guilty though I be, thou seest full well,
That to the brave opposed, arms in hand,
I am no coward. – Oh! could I as bravely,
In home-raised broils, with violent men have striven,
It had been well: but there, alas! I proved
A poor, irresolute, and nerveless wretch.

(*After a pause, and struggling for breath*)
To live, alas! in good men's memories
Detested and contemned – to be with her
For whom I thought to be – Come, gloomy grave!
Thou coverest all!

(*After another painful struggle, every one standing in deep silence round him, and* LORNE *bending over him compassionately*)
Pardon of man I ask not,
And merit not. – Brave Lorne, I ask it not;
Though in thy piteous eye a look I see
That might embolden me. – There is above
One who doth know the weakness of our nature,—
Our thoughts and conflicts – all that ever have breathed,
The banned and blessed must pass to Him – my soul
Into His hands, in humble penitence,
I do commit. [*Dies*]

LORNE: And may Heaven pardon thee, unhappy man!

Enter ARGYLL, *and* HELEN *following him, attended by* ROSA

LORNE: (*to attendants*) Alas, prevent her!
(*Endeavouring to keep her back*)
Helen, come not hither:
This is no sight for thee.

HELEN: (*pressing forward, and seeing the body*). Oh! oh! and hast thou dealt with him so quickly,
Thou fell and ruthless Lorne? – No time allowed?
(*Kneeling by the body*)
O that within that form sense still were lodged!
To hear my voice – to know that in my heart
No thought of thee – Let others scan thy deeds,
Pitied and pardoned art thou here.
(*Her hand on her breast*)
Alas!
So quickly fell on thee the avenging stroke,
No sound of peace came to thy dying ear,
No look of pity to thy closing eyes!
Pitied and pardoned art thou in this breast,
But canst not know it now. – Alas! alas!

ARGYLL: (*to attendants*) Prepare ye speedily to move the body.
Mean time, our prisoners within the castle
Secure ye well.

(*To other attendants, who lay hold of* LOCHTARISH *and* GLENFADDEN, *while* BENLORA, *drawing his sword, attacks*

furiously those who attempt to seize and disarm him, and they,
closing round and endeavouring to overpower him, he is
mortally wounded in the scuffle)

BENLORA: Ay, bear me now within your prison walls;
    Alive indeed, thought ye to bind me? No.
    Two years within your dungeons have I lived,
    But lived for vengeance: closed that hope, the earth
    Close o'er me too! – Alive to bind Benlora!
                (*Falls*)
LORNE: (*running up to him*) Ha! have ye slain him! – Fierce and
    warlike spirit!
    I'm glad that thou hast had a soldier's death,
    Arms in thy hands, all savage as thou art.
       (*Turning to* LOCHTARISH *and* GLENFADDEN)
    But thou, the artful, base, contriving villain,
    Who hast of an atrocious, devilish act
    The mover been, and this thy vile associate,
    Prepare ye for the villains' shameful end,
    Ye have so dearly earned.
    (*Waving his hand for the attendants to lead them off*)
LOCHTARISH: Be not so hasty, Lorne. – Thinkst thou indeed
    Ye have us here within your grasp, and nought
    Of hostage or security retained
    For our protection?
LORNE: What dost thou mean?
LOCHTARISH: Deal with us as ye will:
    But if within a week, returned to Mull,
    In safety I appear not, with this blood,
    The helpless heir, thy sister's infant son,
    Who in my mother's house our pledge is kept,
    Must pay the forfeit.
HELEN: (*starting up from the body in an agony of alarm*) O horrible!
    ye will not murder him?
    Murder a harmless infant!
LOCHTARISH: My aged mother, lady, loves her son
    As thou dost thine; and she has sworn to do it.
HELEN: Has sworn to do it! Oh! her ruthless nature
    Too well I know.
    (*To* LORNE *eagerly*) Loose them, and let them go!
LORNE: Let fiends like these escape?
ARGYLL: (*to* HELEN)   He does but threaten
    To move our fears: they dare not slay the child.

HELEN: They dare! they will! – O if thou art my father!
  If Nature's hand ever twined me to thy heart
  As this poor child to mine, have pity on me!
  Loose them and let them go! – Nay, do it quickly.
  O what is vengeance? Spare my infant's life!
  Unpitying Lorne! – art thou a brother too?
  The hapless father's blood is on thy sword,
  And wilt thou slay the child? O spare him! spare him!
      (*Kneeling to* ARGYLL *and* LORNE, *who stand irresolute,*
  when enter SIR HUBERT DE GREY, *carrying something in his arms,*
      wrapped up in a mantle, and followed by MORTON.
      On seeing SIR HUBERT, *she springs from the ground, and
              rushes forward to him*)
  Ha! art thou here? in blessed hour returned
  To join thy prayers with mine – to move their hearts—
  Their flinty hearts – to bid them spare my child!
DE GREY: (*lifting up the mantle, and showing a sleeping child*) The
  prayer is heard already: look thou here
  Beneath this mantle where he soundly sleeps.
      (HELEN *utters a cry of joy, and holds out her arms for the
      child, but at the same time sinks to the ground, embracing
  the knees of* SIR HUBERT. ARGYLL *and* LORNE *run up to him, and all
      their vassals, etc., crowding round close them about on every
      side, while a general murmur of exultation is heard through
          the whole.* LOCHTARISH *and* GLENFADDEN, *remaining on
  the side of the stage with those who guard them, are struck with
              astonishment and consternation*)
ARGYLL: (*to those who guard* LOCHTARISH, *etc., stepping forward
      from the crowd*) Lead to the grated keep your prisoners,
  There to abide their doom. Upon the guilty
  Our vengeance falls, and only on the guilty.
  To all their clan beside, in which I know
  Full many a gallant heart included is,
  I still extend a hand of amity.
  If they reject it, fair and open war
  Between us be: and trust we still to find them
  The noble, brave Macleans, the valiant foes,
  That, ere the dark ambition of a villain,
  For wicked ends, their gallant minds had warped,
  We heretofore had found them.
                          O that men
  In blood so near, in country, and in valour,

Should spend in petty broils their manly strength,
That might, united for the public weal,
On foreign foes such noble service do!
O that the day were come when gazing southron,
Whilst these our mountain warriors, marshalled forth
To meet in foreign climes their country's foes,
Along their crowded cities slowly march,
To sound of warlike pipe, their plaided bands,
Shall say, with eager fingers pointing thus,
'Behold those men! – their sunned but thoughtful brows:
Their sinewy limbs; their broad and portly chests,
Lapped in their native vestments, rude but graceful!—
Those be our hardy brothers of the north;—
The bold and generous race, who have, beneath
The frozen circle and the burning line,
The rights and freedom of our native land
Undauntedly maintained.'
　　　　　　　　　　That day will come,
When in the grave this hoary head of mine,
And many after heads, in death are laid;
And happier men, our sons, shall live to see it.
O may they prize it too with grateful hearts;
And, looking back on these our stormy days
Of other years, pity, admire, and pardon
The fierce, contentious, ill-directed valour
Of gallant fathers, born in darker times!

　　　　　　　　　　　　　　[The curtain drops]

NOTES

1   **beeve:** cattle, especially those fattened for slaughter.

2   **lubbards:** seemingly a form of lubber – clumsy, stupid fellows, louts or an inferior servant, a scullion.

3   **varlet:** a male servant, menial, sometimes a groom.

4   **heath and hare-bells:** blue-bells and wild hyacinth.

5   **mantle:** loose, sleeveless cloak.

6   **loon:** a fellow, a lad, sometimes a rascally servant or menial.

7   **thraldom's murkiest den:** meanest and darkest bondage or servitude.

8   **pibrochs:** themes played on the bagpipes.

9   **crones:** withered old women.

10   **enchafed:** angered, excited.

11   **boon:** favour.

12   **reiver:** raider, plunderer.

13   **nonage:** being under age, minor, immature.

14   **galled wrists:** wrists rubbed sore by chafing.

15   **heath-cock:** grouse.

16   **claymore:** Scottish, two-edged broadsword.

17   **surly hind:** uncivil farm servant.

18   **what doth it boot:** what good is it?, what does it matter?

19   **lay:** narrative poem, generally to be sung.

20   **hauberk:** a coat of mail.

21   **frith:** alternative spelling for firth on estuary.

22 **the dull dun heath:** the dull grey-brown heath, the monotonous heath.

23 **postern:** back door – here, escape route.

24 **vaunting piper:** arrogant piper.

25 **corse:** corpse.

26 **hoary locks:** hair grey with age.

27 **sea-girt rock:** a rock encircled or surrounded by the sea.

28 **blue coped sky:** blue vault of heaven.

29 **swarded spot:** a place covered with short grass.

30 **muir:** variant of moor.

31 **laved her girdle:** here – had risen to her waist.

32 **pinions:** wings.

33 **din:** stunning or distracting noise.

34 **stripling:** youth.

35 **dirk:** dagger.

36 **He doffs his bonnet to each tacks-man's wife:** He shows respect to everyone – the tacks-man being the tenant of a small-holding.

37 **coif:** close cap covering the top, back and sides of the head.

38 **I wot:** I know.

39 **specious mummery:** plausible deception.

40 **the scutcheoned portal of a tomb:** a gravestone or tomb marked with an heraldic device.

41 **glozed:** fawned.

42 **to cow my pride:** to temper, control, my pride.

43 **like deer bayed in a nook:** like a deer backed into a corner.

44 **if scathed should be:** if he is at all injured.

SMILES AND TEARS;

or,

THE WIDOW'S STRATAGEM

———————

a comedy, in five acts
BY MARIE-THÉRÈSE DE CAMP
(1815)

DRAMATIS PERSONAE

Women

LADY EMILY GERALD	a beautiful and rich young widow in love with O'Donolan, but courted by Delaval
MRS BELMORE	an equally beautiful young widow engaged in a protracted and increasingly expensive lawsuit with Sir Henry Chomley
CECIL FITZHARDING	seduced by Delaval
MRS JEFFERIES	housekeeper at Stanly's Richmond home
FANNY	Cecil's maid

Men

MR FITZHARDING	Cecil's father, fallen into madness after her seduction, the former owner of Stanly's home
SIR HENRY CHOMLEY	friend of Delaval and O'Donolan, in love with a mysterious beauty, engaged in a protracted lawsuit with Mrs Belmore
COLONEL O'DONOLAN	in love with Lady Emily, but hot-headed and jealous
MR STANLY	Emily's older uncle, a good man
MR DELAVAL	a seemingly cold-blooded libertine, who has seduced and abandoned Cecil

JEFFERIES   Delaval's valet, husband of Mrs Jefferies

ROBERTS   a servant at Stanly's house

KEEPER   employee of the asylum where Fitzharding is restrained

GROOM   Sir Henry's groom

Scene   London and Richmond

Act I

SCENE i

DELAVAL's *apartments*

DELAVAL *and* JEFFERIES, *discovered*

JEFFERIES: (*shutting a secretary*) I don't see the letter anywhere, Sir.

DELAVAL: Have you looked over all the papers?

JEFFERIES: I have, Sir; and there is certainly no letter with your father's seal upon it: I think, Sir, you must have dropped it out of doors, for I have searched every place within, in vain.

DELAVAL: Heaven forbid! – (*Aside*) there are some secrets contained in that letter, which, published, would prove neither creditable to my fame or beneficial to my interests. (*Aside*) – Let a more diligent search be made after it, d'ye hear? I would not have it lost for the world.

[*Exit* JEFFERIES]

—'Tis very odd that I have not heard from old Stanly yet! – without encouragement from that quarter, I know not what will become of me! Lord Glenthorn, like a kind father, obstinately refuses to advance me one shilling – my creditors are already informed that I have lost my election, and they grow clamorous upon it: when I could not be *compelled* to pay, they were glad enough to be civil.[1]

Re-enter JEFFERIES, *with letters*

JEFFERIES: The post is just come in, Sir, and has brought half a dozen letters from the old borough. (*Significantly*)

DELAVAL: The privilege of escaping the persecution of duns,[2] makes a seat in Parliament a desideratum of no mean value; but to lose the election, and yet be obliged to disburse, neither suits my humour nor my finances – 'tis cursedly provoking, to be sure. (*Opening one of the letters*) What have we here?

'SIR,

As a free and independent burgess,[3] I insist upon my agreement: I am an Englishman, Sir, and always act according to my conscience; and if I had thought you would have quitted the borough without paying me the price of my vote, I should have felt it my duty to support the Ministerial Candidate. Your humble Servant, when you pay him,   PETER PLUMPER!

—Well said, Independence! Here, Jefferies, put Peter Plumper, and the rest of this incorruptible fraternity, behind the fire. Any more duns?

JEFFERIES: No, Sir; none but our constituents this morning. I beg pardon, Sir, but I forgot to give you this letter, which came last night from Mr Stanly.

DELAVAL: And why the devil, Sir, did you forget? when I told you over and over again of what consequence it was to me to hear from that quarter. (*Takes the letter from him and reads it*)

JEFFERIES: (*aside*) I wish I could have kept it from you altogether; I fear it bodes little comfort to poor Miss Fitzharding.[4]

DELAVAL: Have you found my father's letter yet?

JEFFERIES: No, indeed, Sir; I have searched all your pockets – emptied every drawer and closet, but all to no purpose.

DELAVAL: It must be found; I would not lose it for the universe. Go, go, and look for it again.

[*Exit* JEFFERIES]

—This brings some consolation, however, and deserves a more attentive perusal. (*Reads it aloud*)—

'My dear Delaval, I have felt the ground, as I promised, with Lady Emily, and find her by no means averse to the thoughts of a second marriage. I shall return to Richmond tomorrow, whither I have prevailed upon her to accompany me: the sooner, therefore, you make your appearance there, the better. My long intimacy with your father, induces me to use every endeavour to be serviceable to you; and in my niece, though perhaps I ought not to be her panegyrist, I dare assert you will find wealth without ostentation, beauty without pride.'

—Ay, ay, and what I prize above them all, an unincumbered income of four thousand a year. I'm beholden to you, however, old Stanly; and sincerely hope your endeavours may prosper; but I have no relish for revisiting Richmond. My adventure there, is still too recent; and my being seen about Lady Emily, will revive among the gossips of the place, every circumstance relative to Cecil's elopement; but yet, the deranged state of my affairs requires that I should take this step.[5] At any rate, a marriage with Lady Emily will enable me to make a settlement upon poor Cecil and her child – to place her above the fear of want, shall be the first use to which I will apply my newly acquired wealth. – Let me see what says the 'Fashionable World' – (*Takes up the newspaper*) 'Richmond – We have authority to contradict the report of Mr Fitzharding's marriage; that unhappy gentleman having, in consequence of the seduction of his only daughter, been deprived of reason, is at this moment, an inmate of the lunatic asylum.' – How! Cecil's father a maniac? what have I to answer for? I had the article respecting his marriage inserted, to persuade Cecil that her father had ceased to lament her – should this refutation meet her eye, I know not to what fatal extremity her feelings may impel her!

Enter JEFFERIES

JEFFERIES: Sir Henry Chomley, Sir.

DELAVAL: Why did you say I was at home?

JEFFERIES: I did not know you wished to be out, Sir.

DELAVAL: Order my horse to be saddled immediately – should any message come from my father, bring it after me to Blackheath.

[*Exit* JEFFERIES]

Enter SIR HENRY CHOMLEY

SIR HENRY: Did I hear you say you were going out, so early too? I thought no one had been restless but myself – I want half an hour's conversation with you.

DELAVAL: It must be some other time then, my dear Chomley; for at present a very particular engagement carries me from home.

SIR HENRY: Don't let me prevent you. I heard you say something about Blackheath, as I came in; and as my horses are at the door, I'll ride with you, and we can talk as we go.

DELAVAL: You must excuse me, Chomley; I am under very peculiar circumstances, and for the present, must decline the pleasure of your company.

SIR HENRY: Why then 'tis clear, you are going to meet your man or your woman; in both cases, you may confide in me; for I'll neither send the Bow-Street officers[6] after you, if it prove an affair of honour, or elope with your mistress, should it be an assignation – for Oh! I am already so desperately in love.

DELAVAL: In love? ha ha! you? and with whom?

SIR HENRY: I don't know.

DELAVAL: What's her name?

SIR HENRY: I can't tell.

DELAVAL: Where does she live?

SIR HENRY: Can you inform me?

DELAVAL: What are her connections?

SIR HENRY: Men and women, I suppose.

DELAVAL: Where did you see her?

SIR HENRY: Nowhere, my good fellow; that's a happiness I'd give the world for.

DELAVAL: Psha! this is your last night's dream, and I am by no means certain that you are awake now.

SIR HENRY: Yes, but I am; and awake to the reality of being the wretchedest dog alive, too, unless I can gain some account of my charming incognita. I met her at Lady Brellington's masquerade; where, in the most tantalizing manner, she persisted in concealing from me both her name and rank – I enquired of every body; every body had admired, but nobody knew her. Last night, however, I learned that you were the favoured mortal who waited upon her to her carriage; and unable any longer to restrain my curiosity, I have flown upon the wings of impatience for the complete and instant gratification of it.

DELAVAL: Lady Brellington's masquerade! let me see, whom did I take that night to a carriage? Oh! the old Dowager of—

SIR HENRY: Dowager be damned! do you think I would fall in love with a Dowager?

DELAVAL: The case is by no means uncommon, now-a-days, but stay – perhaps it was crooked little Mrs—

SIR HENRY: No, no; it was no crooked Mrs— but a divinely proportioned figure, that might have lent additional charms to one of Titian's graces.[7]

DELAVAL: Oh, that was my mother.

SIR HENRY: The devil it was!

DELAVAL: Yes, all in black.

SIR HENRY: Black! no; the woman I mean, had a sort of a thing – that is, it looked like a kind of a – faith I never knew how to describe a woman's dress in my life – but I know she had something on—

DELAVAL: Probably; though what, by your description, it is not very easy to define – but now I recollect, I led Lady Emily Gerald to her carriage; who, by the way, was so inimitably well disguised, that even I, though I am perfectly well acquainted with her person, should have been as much puzzled to discover her, as yourself, had not her Uncle, old Stanly, let me into the secret.

SIR HENRY: Lady Emily Gerald! and you are acquainted with her? then you can tell me – nothing of her wit and person, I have already *felt* the power of those – but her face, my dear fellow, her face—

DELAVAL: An angel's!

SIR HENRY: I know it, I know it – but detail, detail—

DELAVAL: Forehead, white as alabaster, smooth as ivory, eyes beaming with sweetness and expression; an aquiline nose, teeth like pearls, with a bewitching dimple on each side of her ruby lips, that—

SIR HENRY: Say no more; I'll have her, whether she be maid, wife, or widow – tell me, is there a husband to poison?

DELAVAL: No, nor to cuckold; which is the more fashionable practice of the two – she is a widow, with a noble fortune too, I can tell you.

SIR HENRY: Curse fortune! I have enough for both.

DELAVAL: (*aside*) What an absurd idiot am I! to tell him all this, and raise an obstacle to my own views on Lady Emily – this must be remedied.

SIR HENRY: My horses are at the door, I'll go and call on her directly – where does she live?

DELAVAL: In Ireland.

SIR HENRY: That's rather too far, for a morning visit.

DELAVAL: I should think so.

SIR HENRY: When does she return?

DELAVAL: I don't know.

SIR HENRY: I'll tell you what, Delaval, it is quite clear that you don't choose to know; and the reason is obvious; you are in love with her yourself – but though you don't think proper to answer my enquiries, I shall soon find those who will, I warrant me!

DELAVAL: (*constrained*) You totally mistake my motive, my dear Chomley; 'tis my regard for your happiness, that keeps me silent. Lady Emily's beauty is undisputed, but I should be sorry, be very sorry, my dear friend, to see you fall a sacrifice to so artful a character – she is the arrantest coquette – why she broke her husband's heart.

SIR HENRY: So much the better! If he hadn't died, she couldn't have been a widow, and I shouldn't now be the happiest dog in the universe,

DELAVAL: If you have such a passion for widows, why don't you close with Mrs Belmore, and reversing the natural order of things, put an end to all disputes by marriage?

SIR HENRY: (*rings the bell*) Weugh! you have given me a surfeit, which even the thoughts of my beloved Lady Emily will hardly enable me to overcome – give me leave to write a short note to Counsellor Pother (*Sits down*) – But for these cursed consultations with my lawyers, I might have followed her all the world over – what should a man in love do with a lawsuit? Now, more than ever, do I detest this Mrs Belmore, for preventing the pursuit of my enchantress.

Enter JEFFERIES

JEFFERIES: (*to* DELAVAL) Did you ring, Sir?

SIR HENRY: (*writing*) Send my horse up— Psha! I mean, my groom.

JEFFERIES: I will, Sir – *your* horses are at the door too, Sir.

[*Exit* JEFFERIES]

DELAVAL: Very well; I am sorry to leave you, Chomley, but, as the case is urgent, I know your good nature will excuse me: so fare you well; and if you should make a trip to the sister kingdom, I wish you a prosperous voyage! but if you will take a friend's advice, you will stay where you are, and put the fair widow, Lady Emily, entirely out of your head.

[*Exit* DELAVAL]

SIR HENRY: (*seals the note, and rises*) That you wish me to do so, I am fully persuaded – but advice and physic are equally disagreeable to me, and I never take either, if I can possibly avoid it. It is evident, Delaval wants to mislead me – she is no more in Ireland, than I am.

Enter SIR HENRY'S GROOM

—Here, put this note into the first two-penny post-office you come to – Do you know Lady Emily Gerald?

GROOM: Can't say as how I does, Sir Henry.

SIR HENRY: Do you remember where she lives?

GROOM: No, I don't Sir Henry, 'cause I never know'd.

SIR HENRY: You are a stupid blockhead! Go, knock at every door from St James's to Whitechapel, till you find it out; and as you go, Sir, if you chance to meet a beautiful figure, with an alabaster forehead, an aquiline nose, a piercing eye, with lovely dimples on each side her ruby lips, that's she – follow her home, bring me word directly where she lives, or I'll kick you to the devil!   [*Exit* SIR HENRY]

SCENE ii

A room in Lady Emily's house

Enter LADY EMILY, *and* MR STANLY

STANLY: (*as he enters*) That's not the point, Lady Emily; that's not the point.

LADY EMILY: But, my dear Uncle, there need be no argument upon a subject upon which we are already agreed. I have told you twenty times, that I have no objection whatever to marrying again.

STANLY: Then, why won't you accept of Delaval?

LADY EMILY: Because, I have told you as often, that I have great objections to him.

STANLY: But your objections are not founded in reason, Emily; upon his father's, Lord Glenthorn's death, he will enjoy both title and fortune.

LADY EMILY: Then, let him bestow both upon one possessing neither, Uncle.

STANLY: (*growing warm*) That's as you mean to do, Emily; that's as you mean to do – I can see as far into a mill-stone as most folks; you have a preference elsewhere.

LADY EMILY: Well, Sir, if that really be the case – join that preference upon one side, to my aversion upon the other, and then calculate how insuperable an obstacle it raises to the accomplishment of your wishes.

STANLY: This Colonel O'Donolan, who is on the Staff in our neighbourhood, has done the business, 'tis plain; but you'll repent it Emily – a hot-headed Irishman—

LADY EMILY: You will not surely make that a *reproach* to him! till time shall have obliterated the records of our days, while any trace remains of the bright achievements destined to adorn the future pages of our history, gratitude will endear the name of Irishman to every lover of his country's glory!

STANLY: O'Donolan is a spendthrift for all that – over head and ears in debt!

LADY EMILY: A proof of credit, Sir!

STANLY: So is the National Debt, I have heard; but I wish it was paid for all that!

LADY EMILY: Well, at any rate Sir, a hot-headed spendthrift, is better than a cold-hearted libertine – but I never believed that Colonel O'Donolan had anything to throw away.

STANLY: No, no; everybody knows that – yet, beggar as he is, he no doubt endeavours to make you believe, that his passion for you is entirely disinterested – but he is a deep one, though he makes no show of it; now Delaval is an honest fellow—

LADY EMILY: Though *he* makes no show of it – everybody, my dear Uncle, yourself excepted, does justice to Mr Delaval's total carelessness of even appearing to possess any principle.

STANLY: Hey, hey! Emily – I never heard—

LADY EMILY: No, my dear Sir; because, being the simplest, most upright character yourself, your ears are shut against the report of villainies, of which your heart can scarcely credit the existence – do not confound me with those scandal-mongers, who are never so happy as when they can relate a tale of slander, at every word of which, 'a reputation dies,' or with those wretched beings, who, having themselves infringed the laws of morality and religion, are delighted to find a fellowship in vice; but there are circumstances – I do not wish to detail them – which render it impossible that I should ever marry Mr Delaval – as your friend, I shall receive, and show him every attention, which respect for you can suggest – but it must be distinctly understood, and I hope you will take particular care that it is so by Mr Delaval, that his visits here, can only be sanctioned under that character.

[Exit]

STANLY: I can't comprehend what this means – there's something in it; for Emily is not apt to be ill-natured – and yet, I never heard – but then I have been a long time in India, and as she says, never enquire into these things, and upon principle; for if there were fewer listeners to detraction, there would not be so many detractors – O, here comes Mrs Jefferies; I wonder whether she has at any time heard Emily speak of Delaval: when I was a youngster, the Lady Abigail⁹ was a very important agent in a family, but since ladies can write their own love-letters, I fancy the office is fallen into disrepute.

Enter MRS JEFFERIES

—Good morning, Mrs Jefferies, good morning! your Lady and I have just had a bit of a squabble – you must know, I think it a shame she should remain a widow any longer.

MRS JEFFERIES: There's many gentlemen of your mind for that, I fancy, Sir; but if my mistress takes my advice, she'll keep as she is – I would have every woman marry once, because it's as well to know the nature of things; but she's a fool that tries it a second time.

STANLY: What! if things have answered, Mrs Jefferies? now I should think that a good husband—

MRS JEFFERIES: Law, Sir; bad's the best; but whether good, bad or indifferent, a husband is still a master; and give me freedom I say.

STANLY: I am sorry to find you are of that opinion; for I wanted you to second me in persuading Lady Emily to accept Mr Delaval.

MRS JEFFERIES: Who? Lord Glenthorn's son, Sir? not I indeed: and he can be no friend of my Lady's, who would recommend such a match.

STANLY: Do you know him then, that you speak so decidedly?

MRS JEFFERIES: I know more than's good of him – why, Sir, are you one of the Governors of the Lunatic Assylum at Richmond, and never heard the story of Mr Fitzharding? Poor old soul! he little thought when he laid the foundation of that building, that it was, one day to become his own wretched residence! and who has he to thank for it but that vile wretch, Delaval?

STANLY: (*warmly*) Don't judge too hastily; I hate scandal, Mrs Jefferies – a slanderer's tongue is like a raging fire, that withers everything it touches – most active when it seems extinct, it undermines the structure of the fairest reputation, blackening even that which it has not power to destroy. You may have been misinformed.

MRS JEFFERIES: That's very likely indeed; when my own husband is valet to Mr Delaval, and when I have been constantly living in the midst of it all.

STANLY: That alters the case, to be sure; but I had always understood that the failure in his circumstances, had deprived Mr Fitzharding of his senses.

MRS JEFFERIES: No such thing, Sir; 'twas his daugahter's elopement that drove the poor gentleman mad; and then, and not till then, the bank went all to smash! Everything was seized and sold; even the very mansion which you live in at Richmond, fell into the creditor's hands.

STANLY: What! did my house belong to Mr Fitzharding?

MRS JEFFERIES: O yes; for many years, Sir.

STANLY: Poor fellow! the last time I saw him, he was very differently lodged – his habitation was a cell, a truss of straw its only furniture. How came his daughter to forsake him?

MRS JEFFERIES: O, Sir, it never could have happened, had she remained under her father's care, for she doated upon *him* even more, if possible, than he did upon her; but being compelled to take a long journey, he placed her under the care of an old crabbed maiden-sister of his, who (when she first discovered Miss Fitzharding's attachment to this Delaval, with whom she had frequently danced at our Richmond balls), instead of giving her good advice and mild treatment, had recourse to every kind of harsh usage; confined her to her own room, and denied her the company of her friends, the use of pen, ink, and paper.

STANLY: The stupid old fool! not to know that difficulties are the food of love, and opposition the whetstone of disobedience. I always hated old maids, and now I know the reason why.

MRS JEFFERIES: Delaval was but too well pleased at this restraint; it put him upon stratagems and contrivances, and he very soon contrived to get her out of the window, under pretence of carrying her off to Gretna-Green; but before he had got fifty miles on his way, he found, poor man! that he had forgotten his pocket-book; and consequently, not having money enough to proceed to Scotland, he must bring her to London, and place her in a quiet lodging till a licence could be procured.

STANLY: But that, I imagine, was dispensed with?[10]

MRS JEFFERIES: It was, Sir; and Miss Fitzharding is now a mother at eighteen years of age, without a friend, and probably destitute of common necessaries; for Delaval's a beggar, solely dependent on his father's bounty, who, informed of this connection, hopes to break it off, by depriving him of all means of supporting her and her child.

STANLY: (very angrily) So, so, so! and this is the fellow who has dared to solicit my good offices with Lady Emily. Why, the scoundrel should be hunted out of society! O that the Legislature, which has so well protected the honour of our English husbands, would take the English father's case into consideration too, and brand the heartless wretch with infamy, who in the wantonness of vanity could rob a doating parent of his child, the blossom of his hope, the only stay and comfort of his age. I thank you, Mrs Jefferies, for your story – it will save your lady some persecution, but it has given me a sad awkward feeling towards human nature.

MRS JEFFERIES: Law, Sir, I wonder your own experience has not taught you, that human nature is as good for nothing as it can be; for instance now, was there ever any thing so abominable as Sir Henry Chomley's endeavouring to deprive that sweet woman, Mrs Belmore, of her estate, and make an absolute beggar of her?

STANLY: Ah, Jefferies! she is a sweet woman indeed; and I'll tell you what I have been meditating – if she should lose her cause, and unfortunately be reduced to beggary, as you say, I have some idea of offering myself, as a trifling compensation.

MRS JEFFERIES: (laughs) A very trifling compensation, I'm afraid, Sir.

STANLY: Indeed! you think, then, she would not have me?

MRS JEFFERIES: Why, she has had one old husband already, and that's rather against her trying another; don't you think so, Sir?

STANLY: (laughing) That depends upon circumstances – but I see you are a wag, Mrs Jefferies.

MRS JEFFERIES: No, upon my word, Sir; I'm a plain matter-of-fact person, and from what I see, I judge it would not answer.

STANLY: Mrs Jefferies, let me give you a bit of advice; never judge of anything but upon your own experience – for many a man besides the Prince of Denmark, 'has that within which passeth show.'

[Exit STANLY]

MRS JEFFERIES: Well said, old gentleman – he is as kind-hearted an oddity as ever lived!

Enter LADY EMILY

LADY EMILY: Did not I hear Mrs Belmore come in a little while ago?

MRS JEFFERIES: No, my Lady; and her maid Mrs Simkison is sadly afraid she won't come home in time enough to accompany you to Richmond; but she left word that she would follow you as soon as the consultation was over.

LADY EMILY: Poor soul! how she is tormented by this vexatious lawsuit; though she has been nearly six weeks in my house, I declare I have not enjoyed her society for as many hours, so entirely are her time and attention engrossed by it.

MRS JEFFERIES: Ah, my Lady, he must be a tasteless, ugly old fellow, that could find in his heart to persecute such a charming creature.

LADY EMILY: No, Jefferies, not old, or ugly; neither do I think the man entirely devoid of taste, for he is one of my most ardent admirers: what think you of his being my masquerade enamorato?

MRS JEFFERIES: No, sure, my Lady! and does Mrs Belmore know this?

LADY EMILY: She knows that a *somebody* has followed me from masquerade to masquerade; but she has such a horror of the name of Chomley, he being her opponent in this lawsuit, that I have never told her it was he; though I have drawn him on for the express purpose of bringing them together if I can.

MRS JEFFERIES: Lau! my Lady; to what end? if he is so desperately in love with *you?*

LADY EMILY: Oh, he cannot be incurable; for he has never even beheld my face.

MRS JEFFERIES: But if you made a conquest of him under a mask, my Lady, your attraction is not likely to be weakened by showing him your face; but poor Colonel O'Donolan! how he'll fret and fume when he hears of this!

LADY EMILY: The Colonel will be very silly if he fret or fume about any such thing – he ought to be perfectly assured by this time, that I have the sincerest regard for him.

MRS JEFFERIES: If he isn't, everybody else is, my Lady: to be sure he thinks your Ladyship has no objection to a little admiration.

LADY EMILY: A great objection to a *little;* I like an abundance of admiration; it is the privilege of our sex – if the love of conquest were not inherent in our natures, common prudence would prescribe it as a necessary policy – *to please all men*, is the sure way to fix *the man who pleases us* – there's nothing like uncertainty – it quickens attention – a lover soon grows weary of an intercourse into which his mistress does not contrive to throw a little occasional mortification.

MRS JEFFERIES: Why then, Colonel O'Donolan will long remain

attached to your Ladyship; for to be sure, you do plague him most handsomely sometimes – he will never get over your having concealed from him that you were going to the masquerade.

LADY EMILY: I concealed it, because I had a point to carry, which his presence would have marred; and when he knows the motive upon which I acted, I have no doubt even his jealous scruples will be appeased.

Enter a SERVANT, *with a letter*

SERVANT: The servant waits for an answer, my Lady.

LADY EMILY: Very well, Jefferies shall bring it to you.

[*Exit* SERVANT]

—I don't know the hand. (*Opens it*) 'Chomley!' So then he has found me out! but what says he?

'Can you, Madam, forgive me, for having, contrary to your strict commands, sought to discover the enchantress whose spells have rivetted me so entirely within her power? and were you not convinced, while you imposed the cruel restriction, how impossible it was to have seen and heard, and not hazard every thing to hear and see you again? it was not in human effort to resist the impulse, and I have learnt in whom my happiness must henceforth centre – but alas! how little will this knowledge advance my felicity, if you deny me the hope of being admitted to your presence – no, you will not be so obdurate as to force me upon expedients, which, though they may serve to multiply my perplexities, will never alter my determination of remaining eternally yours.'

Admitted to my presence! a modest request, upon my word; yet if I refuse, what will become of my plan? it will be impossible to persuade Mrs Belmore to let me present Sir Henry Chomley to her. (*Ruminates*)

MRS JEFFERIES: Is there any answer, my Lady?

LADY EMILY: Presently; it is the very thing – I protest it will do admirably, and yet, I fear she will never believe – but why not? I was masked, and if the worst come to the worst, we'll say it was a masking frolic – I'll venture it – the grand point is to get them to meet – the rest I leave to chance – (*Writes an answer*)

MRS JEFFERIES: (*aside*) She seems delighted – she may say as she pleases, but I'll be hanged if the pleasure of the flirtation here, does not outweigh the desire to serve Mrs Belmore, and it certainly is no small stretch of disinterestedness to give up a lover to forward the views of a friend.

[*Exit*]

(LADY EMILY reads the answer)

'For reasons, which I am not, now, at liberty to divulge, I cannot receive you as Sir Henry Chomley; but if you will consent to present yourself at my Uncle Stanly's at Richmond, under the assumed name of Grenville, I shall be happy in the honour of receiving you. – I am, etc. etc.'

(Folds it)

This is rather a strong measure – (*Re-enter* MRS JEFFERIES *with a candle*) – but I think I am justified in hazarding a stratagem, which may be productive of the happiest consequences, not only to my friend, but to Sir Henry himself. There, give this to the servant.

[*Exit* MRS JEFFERIES]

I must let Jefferies into my plans, or she may set her wits to work and defeat my intentions.

Re-enter MRS JEFFERIES

MRS JEFFERIES: Sir Henry's man has got the note, my Lady.[11]

LADY EMILY: I have appointed Sir Henry to come to Richmond, but as he will probably present himself under a feigned name, you will be so good as not to speak of it.

MRS JEFFERIES: Lau! my Lady; what, in disguise?

LADY EMILY: (*aside*) That's an interpretation I was not prepared for: if I don't take care, I shall have the credit of being engaged in an intrigue – I have already hinted to you, Jefferies, that I have a scheme, by which I hope to put a stop to the lawsuit between Mrs Belmore and Sir Henry Chomley – he never saw me but under a mask, and as he evidently did not know me, I mean, if I can, to pass Mrs Belmore upon him for myself; and, in order that she may not be compromised, I have contrived, that he shall appear before her under the name of Grenville – I have but one fear, which is, that O'Donolan should stumble upon him, which would at once put an end to the whole plot.

MRS JEFFERIES: Then quarrel with him, my Lady: he is of the true spaniel breed, and may be whistled back at any time.

Enter a SERVANT

SERVANT: The carriage is at the door, and Mr Stanly is waiting for your Ladyship.

LADY EMILY: Very well; – My shawl, Jefferies.

MRS JEFFERIES: Here it is, my Lady; but I did not think your Ladyship would wear it any more – it is not good enough for *you*, Ma'am.

LADY EMILY: Is not it? Well – is it good enough for you, Jefferies?

MRS JEFFERIES: Lau! my Lady. (*Curtseying*)

LADY EMILY: There, there; you may take it – and remember, Jefferies, that upon your discretion I implicitly rely.   [*Exit*]

MRS JEFFERIES: 'Tis a pity to lose any thing for want of a hint – and my Lady, to do her justice, takes one as readily as it is given – an Indian shawl! very handsome too! – Well, I'm sure I deserve it; for if one is denied the satisfaction of talking, one ought at least to be placed upon the secret service list, and handsomely rewarded for one's silence.

[*Exit* MRS JEFFERIES]

Act II

A room in a neat cottage

FANNY, *discovered looking through the window*

FANNY: Dear, dear; what can keep Mr Delaval so long today? He didn't use to be so late – I've looked, and looked till I've cried my eyes blind – My mother too not returned! why I could have gone there and back again, twice in the time; but she would have the pleasure of telling Mr Delaval the doleful tidings herself. If some of 'em don't come soon, I shall go beside myself – Hark! sure I heard the trampling of horses (*Goes to the window*) – The powers be praised! its Mr Delaval come at last – but, Lord, Lord! how shall I ever be able to tell him what has happened?

Enter DELAVAL

DELAVAL: I am late to day, Fanny; I was overtaken on my way hither, by an express from my father; who, I fear, is on the point of death. I have, therefore, but a few moments to command – is Miss Fitzharding in her own room?

FANNY: (*crying*) Oh, Sir!

DELAVAL: What is the matter? Cecil is not ill, I hope, has anything happened to the child? Let me know the worst at once. Miss Fitzharding—

FANNY: Is gone away, Sir!—

DELAVAL: Gone! Whither?

FANNY: Heaven only knows, Sir; she was very low after you went away last night, and had two of those frightful fits; from which, my mother and I could scarce recover her – however, we did get her about again – and, after a time, she seemed tolerably composed; so much so, indeed, that, upon her insisting I should go to bed, I left her; but I shall never forgive myself for it – had I stayed by her bedside, she couldn't have got away, as she did, in the middle of the night. (*Crying*)

DELAVAL: In the middle of the night, do you say?

FANNY: Ay, that it must have been; – I thought I heard a noise in the house, like somebody walking about, and I listened; but as I'm very

timorous, and apt to take fancies into my head, and as the great dog
didn't bark, I thought, to be sure, I had been dreaming. – Little did I
fancy that, when I should go into Madam's room in the morning, I
should find both her and baby vanished: such a stormy night, too!
she must have been perished before she got half way across the
heath; for she took nothing with her but a shawl.[12]

DELAVAL: And did she drop no hint of her design? Say nothing, from
which you might gather what she purposed doing?

FANNY: Not a word, Sir; she cried a good deal over the baby, and
kissed it very often as she put it to bed; which, for all we could say to
her, she always did herself – but that we were not surprised at; for
she would often taken it in her arms and say, 'and will you break *my*
heart? will you desert *me*, as *I* deserted my poor father?' And then,
the tears would roll one after another, down her cheeks, in such big
drops, that we that stood by could not help crying too.

DELAVAL: (*wiping away a tear*) Poor Cecil! where is your mother,
Fanny?

FANNY: Gone after you, Sir; I can't think how you happen'd to miss of
one another – she has got a letter for you.

DELAVAL: From Miss Fitzharding? Oh! why didn't she wait my
arrival? It may afford some clue to her retreat – how long has she
been gone?

FANNY: Since ten o'clock this morning: as Miss hadn't rung her bell at
seven, I thought she was in a comfortable sleep – I wondered too,
that I didn't hear the child; but at nine, hearing neither of 'em stir, a
chill, somehow, came all over me; and I thought I would go and see
if they were getting up – finding the door open, I went up to the bedside; but mother and babe were both gone, – without money too; for
here's her purse, and the ring which she always wore upon her
wedding finger, left behind.

Enter JEFFERIES

JEFFERIES: I beg pardon, Sir; I've brought poor Mrs Jennings home.
Your mother, Fanny, is very unwell – you had better step to her.

[*Exit* FANNY]

—The poor old woman is seriously indisposed, Sir, and I thought you
wouldn't be displeased at my accompanying her home – she was on
her way to our house with this letter, when she was taken ill, and
forced to turn back again. (*Gives him the letter*)

DELAVAL: Heaven be praised! it is her hand and seal. (*Opens the
cover, and finds his father's letter, which he enquired so anxiously
after in the first scene of the play. Reads*)

'Your ready acquiescence, my dear son, with my desire to see you
married'—

Confusion! my father's lost letter! the letter I was so anxious to find
– this explains the motive of her flight: my poor, poor Cecil! what is
become of her? overwhelmed by the conviction of being deserted by
the father of her child, may she not have devoted herself and her
innocent offspring to an untimely death! and am I not accountable
for this double crime of murder and of suicide? I am, I am! –
Barbarous father! it is you, who have heaped this load of guilt upon
me; it is you, who have plunged me into this abyss of horror and
despair!

JEFFERIES: O, Sir, spare yourself the regret of having reproached your
father's memory – Lord Glenthorn is no more!

DELAVAL: What do you say, dead?

JEFFERIES: You had scarcely quitted his chamber, this morning, when
turning to Lady Glenthorn, he uttered in a feeble tone, 'I am happy –
Delaval has proved himself a son, and may the blessing of a dying
parent communicate to his heart, that peace and comfort which his
filial duty now imparts to mine' – he wished to add something more,
but the words expired upon his lips, and he breathed his last – and
now, my Lord—

DELAVAL: I cannot weep for him! No, Cecil is lost, and what is all the
world to me? a void – dreary and cheerless as my own bosom! what
have I to do with rank and splendour? I, who ought to crawl upon
the earth, shunned and detested by the human race – I, the betrayer,
the destroyer – the thought is frenzy – oh! that it were! come
madness! and with your hottest fires consume the worm that gnaws
my tainted soul! O come and free me from this conflict of the brain,
this agonizing torture of reflection!

[*Exeunt* DELAVAL *and* JEFFERIES]

SCENE ii

Stanly's house at Richmond

LADY EMILY *and* MRS BELMORE, *meeting*

LADY EMILY: Bless me, Mrs Belmore! why you are here almost as soon
as we are – but how jaded you look, my dear creature!

MRS BELMORE: I am indeed fagged out[13] of all spirits.

LADY EMILY: But have you done anything; are you satisfied as you proceed?

MRS BELMORE: How is it possible to be satisfied in the midst of so many contradictory opinions? you know it is a question which involves not merely affluence, but the very means of my existence – that hateful Sir Henry Chomley!

LADY EMILY: I did not understand that he had been so much to blame; it was his father who commenced the action against Mr Belmore, wasn't it? mine is mere hear-say information, though, which, nine times out of ten is erroneous; and, as you never thought proper to speak upon the subject—

MRS BELMORE: I had so firm a reliance upon Mr Belmore's judgment, that I never interfered in matters of business.

LADY EMILY: There, my dear, in my opinion, you were to blame; I am far from thinking a wife should have the sole direction of them; but a voice, in all that are of importance, no reasonable husband can deny her – your interference might perhaps have prevented this lawsuit.

MRS BELMORE: I doubt not; my husband was positive as to his right; old Chomley, equally convinced of the legality of his pretensions; the lawyers were interested in persuading their clients that each had a good cause – obstinacy is the infirmity of age, so they found no difficulty in cutting out work for themselves; and, as very soon after, I lost my husband, and Sir Henry his father, I unexpectedly found myself involved in a lawsuit, the event of which may be my utter ruin.

LADY EMILY: I wonder you never endeavoured to settle the matter amicably, with young Chomley – I hear, he is a very good sort of man, though now I recollect, I have heard you say you don't know him at all.

MRS BELMORE: No; I never even saw him, and very sincerely hope I never shall. That meddling old man, General Harding, on his return to England, took it into his head that a marriage would be the shortest way of ending our disputes, and without consulting me, wrote to Sir Henry to propose the match – now, as the General is a relation of mine, Sir Henry will never believe that I did not know of, and even authorize the measure – I declare, I never think of it, but I am in a perfect fever!

LADY EMILY: Poor General! he meant it well, no doubt.

MRS BELMORE: But you will acknowledge, my dear Lady Emily, that without much pretension, it is not very flattering to one's vanity, to be rejected; which has certainly been my case; and probably in no very delicate terms – for the General, with all his zeal in my behalf, never ventured to show me Sir Henry's answer. O! here's Colonel O'Donolan!

LADY EMILY: (*aside*) How unlucky! if Sir Henry should walk in now, I shall be in a fine scrape.

Enter O'DONOLAN

O'DONOLAN: Are you visible, Lady Emily? I fear I'm breaking in upon you.

MRS BELMORE: No, indeed; we were upon that eternal subject, my lawsuit; and it will be quite a relief to talk of something else.

LADY EMILY: (*to* O'DONOLAN) Are you engagead *this evening*, Colonel O'Donolan?

O'DONOLAN: That's as much as to say, that *you* are this morning: and had rather I went away.

LADY EMILY: How suspicious you always are! (*Aside*) He's quite right, though. What I meant was, that we shall have some very good music, and I thought you might like to hear it.

O'DONOLAN: I had rather hear the music of your voice with Mrs Belmore, all three in a *tête-à-tête* – Oh! Lady Emily, that you had my taste for the quiet enjoyments of life!

LADY EMILY: I'm much obliged to you; but I hate anything so dull; I like society, it amuses me – doesn't it you?

O'DONOLAN: Indeed it does not, Lady Emily; I'm not an April-day, to laugh and cry at the same time – I can't be amused, while I'm upon the rack!

LADY EMILY: But, my good friend, why will you be upon the rack?

O'DONOLAN: Why will I? O! and is it myself that wishes it? now here's Mrs Belmore, who knows what a fool I am, and how distractedly I am devoted to you – she shall judge between us – Lady Emily asks why I am upon the rack; can I be otherwise, when a whole week will sometimes elapse, without my being able to obtain so much as a word or a look – I have been at her door every hour in the day – I have not gone away from it, before I have come back again; and yet, I have not been able to catch a glimpse of her – my only chance of seeing her now, is in public places, or assemblies, where the devil a bit can I see her at all; for she is so everlastingly surrounded by a herd of coxcombs,[14] pouring flattery into her ears, that 'tis impossible to get near her.

LADY EMILY: Why not you, as well as the rest of the coxcombs? if you won't come, I can't drag you by the sleeve.

O'DONOLAN: Ah, now! and did I ever expect it? No, upon my honour! – But a look, – if you would only give me a look, just to say, O, you're there, are you! I should be satisfied: but no such luck for *me!* – it's a nod to one, a shake of the hand with another, a whisper to a third! and while I am kicking my heels in a corner, I have the mortification of seeing her led off in triumph to her carriage by some stupid fellow, who would be deemed too great an ass to stand behind it – then do I return home to pass a sleepless night, and dream of the miseries I've endured through the day.

LADY EMILY: Poor O'Donolan, jealous even in his dreams! Why, that's working double tides! – and how can you, with all this barbarous usage, persist in wishing to marry me?

O'DONOLAN: Because I'm a madman, I believe.

MRS BELMORE: Not so; but because you yet hope that time and your entreaties—

LADY EMILY: Or the commands of a lord and master, when we are linked together, may work a wonderful reformation – but I foresee your jealousy will—

O'DONOLAN: Jealousy! O give me but an assurance that you will be mine, and I shall be forever cured of jealousy.

LADY EMILY: How little do you know the extent of your malady! – it is but two days ago that you displayed it in a paroxysm of frenzy, merely on account of my rencontre at the masquerade—

O'DONOLAN: No, Lady Emily, no; it was your concealing from me that you were going thither.

LADY EMILY: Why, doesn't one always keep it a secret? What amusement can there be, but in the mystery?

O'DONOLAN: Besides, who could with common temper hear you commend the wit and person of a man, whose name you did not even know?

LADY EMILY: O! didn't I tell you his name? – 'tis Grenville.

O'DONOLAN: Some adventurer, I suppose.

LADY EMILY: You suppose very wrongly – I am particularly well acquainted with all his connections – his father's estate is close to my uncle Stanly's.

O'DONOLAN: A mighty weak reason, for following him from masquerade to masquerade, for all that.

LADY EMILY: Following him? You have a delicate manner of expressing yourself, Colonel O'Donolan!

O'DONOLAN: Well, then, for letting him follow you – 'tis the same thing, I hope – isn't it?

LADY EMILY: Not exactly, I apprehend; at least in this country.

O'DONOLAN: That's a reflection upon Ireland, Lady Emily, and I only wish you were a man!

LADY EMILY: A very flattering wish from a lover to his mistress!

O'DONOLAN: Only for half an hour, I mean; that I might have the satisfaction of calling you out.

LADY EMILY: (*aside*) I wish to heaven somebody would call you out; for 'tis plain you'll not go of your own accord.

O'DONOLAN: You should not dare to speak of Ireland in black or in white, without answering it to me – I'd have you to know, Lady Emily, that the women of Ireland are beautiful without art, free without impropriety, and virtuous without ostentation.

LADY EMILY: Charming creatures!

O'DONOLAN: O! you may say that, and tell no story – for they've the heads of men, the forms of women, and the hearts of angels!

LADY EMILY: What a pretty description! why you talk like a book; a review, elegantly bound in calf.

O'DONOLAN: And when I speak of the men, I shall talk like an extraordinary gazette, I believe; for that has published more than once to the world, how neatly they can fight – or like the parliamentary debates, when I tell you that they are eloquent orators, sound politicians, and incorruptible patriots.

LADY EMILY: Bravo! St Patrick for Ireland! They have their merits; and I am free to confess, that, bating one solitary instance, I have generally found them extremely agreeable.

O'DONOLAN: And your exception is myself, I suppose – I knew it: but whatever *your* opinion of me may be, I think tolerably well of myself.

LADY EMILY: That's modest, at any rate!

O'DONOLAN: I didn't mean what I said – I only meant, that as long as I did nothing to forfeit my own good opinion, I ought not to forfeit that of others, nor be considered by any means so exceptional as your Mr Grenville, a fellow that nobody knows!

LADY EMILY: Whom *you* don't know, you mean.

O'DONOLAN: One meets him, nowhere.

LADY EMILY: I beg your pardon; I meet him everywhere.

O'DONOLAN: O! I dare be bound you do; I shouldn't wonder if he came here.

LADY EMILY: He does? for once, you are right in your conjecture, and you may probably meet him here.

O'DONOLAN: Here! when?

LADY EMILY: Tonight.

O'DONOLAN: No – you are joking, sure.

LADY EMILY: Not I, upon my word; I expect him.

O'DONOLAN: You do? and pray, who introduced him?

LADY EMILY: He introduced himself.

O'DONOLAN: Talk of Irish impudence! what, he has been here already?

LADY EMILY: No; but we have corresponded.

O'DONOLAN: Corresponded! now, I ask, I only ask, Mrs Belmore, if this is not the sort of thing to drive a man wild?

LADY EMILY: What sort of thing?

O'DONOLAN: To be clandestinely carrying on—

LADY EMILY: Clandestinely? I beg, Sir, you'll govern your expressions.

MRS BELMORE: Nay – nay now—

O'DONOLAN: Excuse me, Lady Emily; but if in order to please you, it be necessary to banish all sense of right and wrong—

LADY EMILY: It is, at least, indispensible, in order to be *endured* by me, to possess good manners.

MRS BELMORE: Now, my good friends—

O'DONOLAN: O! my dear Madam, no allowances are to be made for disappointed attachment!

LADY EMILY: Your attachment is oppressive.

O'DONOLAN: Very well, Madam, it shan't oppress you much longer.

LADY EMILY: I'm rejoiced to hear it – 'twill be a great relief.

O'DONOLAN: O then! and you shall have it – in this disagreement, at least, we are of one way of thinking – 'tis high time to make up my mind—

LADY EMILY: I only wish you had done so long ago.

O'DONOLAN: It's not too late, Ma'am; I can shake off my bonds and live free – live happily, Ma'am!

LADY EMILY: I'm glad to hear it.

MRS BELMORE: How can you both be so inconsiderate? my dear Emily, say but a word to him.

LADY EMILY: Wherefore? I think Colonel O'Donolan quite right – I have often told him that our dispositions did not accord.

O'DONOLAN: You'll not deny at least, that there is some cause for jealousy, now?

LADY EMILY: No, indeed; I will deny nothing.

O'DONOLAN: A jealous man deserves pity, at any rate.

LADY EMILY: (*contemptuously*) You do excite my pity.

O'DONOLAN: And a coquette contempt – she ought to be shunned—

LADY EMILY: Why don't you go?

O'DONOLAN: I will, Ma'am, I will; this last stroke has unsealed my eyes; I now see see clearly – I will leave the field open for Mr Grenville; and that he may meet no obstruction from me, I this moment bid you eternally farewell. (*Goes off, and returns*) And after that, you need not expect to see me again.

[*Exit* O'DONOLAN]

MRS BELMORE: (*calling after him*) Mr O'Donolan! Mr O'Donolan! He is really gone.

LADY EMILY: Well, let him go.

MRS BELMORE: Indeed, you are to blame; why did you consent to receive this young man?

LADY EMILY: And why not? am I to bury myself alive, to gratify Colonel O'Donolan's jealous whims?

MRS BELMORE: No; but where a man is so devotedly attached as he appears to be, I think he merits some consideration – unless, indeed, you feel an interest for Mr Grenville.

LADY EMILY: Not the slightest; and I would put him off, but that O'Donolan's jealousies are so perfectly well known in the world, that my motive would at once be divined, and we should become the ridicule of all our acquaintance.

MRS BELMORE: You would rather have him suppose then, that this Grenville is a favoured lover?[15]

LADY EMILY: On the contrary, I very much wish he were undeceived upon that point – But how? his reason is so perverted, that – Yet stay – there might be a way – but then I don't like to place you in so awkward a predicament.

MRS BELMORE: My dear Emily, you know I would do anything to reconcile you.

LADY EMILY: I will fairly confess to you, that I did not think of driving things to such an extremity.

MRS BELMORE: Then, at once proceed to the remedy – what can I do?

LADY EMILY: Why then, it has occurred to me, that all difficulties would be overcome, if you would but consent to be my representative, and receive Mr Grenville under my name.

MRS BELMORE: What an extravagant idea!

LADY EMILY: Not at all; Mr Grenville cannot possibly be offended at it; for we shall laugh it off as a masquerade frolic: O'Donolan himself will view it in the same light, and will then be so ashamed of his unjust suspicions, that it may cure him of his jealousies for ever.

MRS BELMORE: If I thought that – but Mr Grenville, I am certain, must at once detect the imposture.

LADY EMILY: Impossible! I disguised my voice, never took off my mask, and my dress was so contrived, that I defy my most intimate friend to have recognized me – it will afford us all a hearty laugh, and what I know will have great weight with you, *it will serve me*, by setting poor O'Donolan's mind effectually at ease.

MRS BELMORE: I will hazard any thing to accomplish that; but I know, I shall commit every sort of blunder, so pray be near to assist me; and if I should fail—

LADY EMILY: I'll answer for it, you will not fail; for the motive which prompts the endeavour will supply you with confidence for the execution of it.

She who can boldly dare in friendship's cause,
Though unsuccessful, fails with all the world's applause.

[*Exeunt*]

Act III

SCENE i

STANLY's *house at Richmond*

LADY EMILY, *and* MRS BELMORE

MRS BELMORE: I begin to think Mr Grenville does not intend to favour us to day. It grows late.

LADY EMILY: I am glad to see this impatience; it looks as if you entered into the spirit of the plot – but you forget that days at this time of the year are not remarkable for length, and the fashion of making morning calls by moonlight, very much in favour of his arriving yet.[16]

Enter a SERVANT

SERVANT: Mr Grenville is at the door, my Lady, and wishes to know if you are at home.

LADY EMILY: (*aside*) Thank heaven! he has remembered his assumed name – I have been in an agony lest he should walk in as Chomley. Say I shall be happy to see Mr Grenville.

[*Exit* SERVANT]

MRS BELMORE: I declare I am quite in a tremble – you are not leaving me – no; Emily, that's not the agreement – (*To* LADY EMILY, *who is going*).

LADY EMILY: But for a moment – I must set Jefferies to keep my uncle out of the way – if he should walk in, it will entirely spoil the joke: I'll return instantly to second you. [*Exit* LADY EMILY]

MRS BELMORE: How extremely awkward is this situation! I don't know what to say or do: there certainly is a great deal of levity in the proceeding, and I ought not to have lent myself to it.

Enter SIR HENRY CHOMLEY

SIR HENRY: Shall I not incur your displeasure, Lady Emily, in thus early presuming to avail myself of your permission? The happy are seldom discreet: if I have been too precipitate, attribute my intrusion to its true cause, the impossibility of checking the ardour of my gratitude.

MRS BELMORE: (*aside*) He has fallen into the deception to her very wish.

SIR HENRY: I have, as you perceive, observed your Ladyship's commands.

MRS BELMORE: (*aside*) Dear! what commands have I laid upon him? O! you are very good! (*Pretending to understand him*)

SIR HENRY: Would there had been some difficulty in them, Madam, that I might have proved how far above all other considerations, I prize an opportunity of obeying you.

MRS BELMORE: I can perfectly understand your desire to see a person who has so successfully evaded your discovery in the support of an assumed character – there's always a certain charm attached to mystery – imagination, no doubt, had pictured to you—

SIR HENRY: Nothing, which the reality has not far exceeded – the first moment I beheld you, I was enraptured by the symmetry of your person, by the exquisite grace of all your movements, and the sweetness of your accents. However you endeavored to disguise your voice, I now perfectly recognize to be the same which thrilled to my heart at Lady Brellington's masquerade.

MRS BELMORE: (*smiling*) And you really know my voice again?

SIR HENRY: I should have distinguished it amongst a thousand; and though concealed by an envious mask, you will perhaps scarcely believe, that my fancy had pictured your *features* just what they are. But, in my warmest moments, I must acknowledge, that I failed of imparting to them that irresistible charm of expression which they possess in so eminent a degree.

MRS BELMORE: So you think, that if chance had thrown me in your way, you should have known me?

SIR HENRY: So entirely am I convinced of it, that ever since I had the happiness of meeting you, I have gone to every assembly, every public place; paraded every street, visited every shop, in hopes of seeing you – if I saw a fine arm across the room, I instantly darted to the spot, full of breathless expectation, till some uncouth defect in the rest of the person, painfully proved to me how much I was mistaken. A small foot has led me to Kensington – to Hampstead have I trotted after a well-turned ankle; in short, Lady Emily, I have left no place in London or its environs unvisited, in pursuit of your separate perfections.

MRS BELMORE: I am quite at a loss how to answer so many civilities – I can only say, that one reason, and a very sufficient one I think it, for your not having met me in your perambulations about London, is, that I very rarely go thither.

SIR HENRY: Formed in every way to constitute its chief ornament, permit me to say, you are unjust in secluding yourself – 'tis a public loss – besides, you wrong yourself as well as others, for surely there is no existence out of London.

MRS BELMORE: That very much depends upon circumstances – the best years of my life, were passed in a remote county, in an ancient castle, with a husband, old enough to be my father; and yet, I can with truth declare, that I never knew what it was to experience a moment's tedium.

SIR HENRY: And friendship, the only feeling of your breast? O! Lady Emily, had love been of the party—

MRS BELMORE: It would have ruined all – when two people are so utterly dependent upon each other for their enjoyments, 'tis fortunate when their sentiments are of a calm, enduring nature – passion is seldom long-lived; and what painful regrets take place of those feelings which are too ardent to be lasting!

SIR HENRY: Then you don't believe that love can endure for ever?

MRS BELMORE: I'm not certain that I believe in the existence of the passion at all.

SIR HENRY: And can it be possible that you have never felt its power?

MRS BELMORE: That is a question which—

SIR HENRY: I fear may appear presumptuous – but did you know how deeply I am interested in it – you would say—

Enter LADY EMILY

(*Aside*)—The devil take this woman, for interrupting us!

LADY EMILY: (*with music in her hand, aside*) He seems confounded at my approach – that's a good sign (*Aside*) My dear! I shall never be able to accomplish this duet for tonight.

MRS BELMORE: Allow me to present Mr Grenville.

LADY EMILY: Mr Grenville of Gloucestershire?

SIR HENRY: (*aside*) Upon my soul I don't know – but I suppose so. (*Bows very low*)

LADY EMILY: I shall be happy in the honour of your acquaintance, Sir; I formerly knew your sister, and a sweet creature she was – she's quite well, I hope? Your poor dear father too, is he still alive?

SIR HENRY: (*aside*) Curse me if I can tell; but I had better kill him, lest she should ask more questions – No, Ma'am, he is dead.

LADY EMILY: I beg pardon – I'm quite shocked that – Do you understand music?

SIR HENRY: No, I do not.

LADY EMILY: Then, I'm afraid you can't sing?

SIR HENRY: Not in the least.

LADY EMILY: That's very unlucky; for I meant to have asked you to help me out in this duet, this evening.

SIR HENRY: (*aside*) What an opportunity had I nearly lost! Sing? sing, did you say? O, to be sure; everybody sings (*aside*) devil a tune can I turn, – that is, I – in a sort of a manner–

LADY EMILY: Yes, yes; that's just in my own way; so, if you'll step into the next room, we can amuse ourselves with trying it over.

SIR HENRY: (*aside*) Confound you and your duet too! – (*Affects to cough*) – Bless my soul, Ma'am, the worst cold I ever had in my life!

LADY EMILY: Ay, it seems very bad, indeed; I think you had better not venture into the night air – I must insist upon your not coming here this evening – we'll positively have the doors shut against you.

SIR HENRY: My dear Madam, I shall mend surprisingly by that time. After dinner, I always sing like a nightingale; my notes would quite astonish you – (*Aside*) there's no lie in that, at any rate.

LADY EMILY: But the fogs, at this time of the year–

SIR HENRY: Are a sovereign remedy for coughs like mine – you see 'tis not a common sort of cold; 'tis only a – Hum! – (*Coughs*)

LADY EMILY: So I perceive, Sir.

SIR HENRY: An asthma, or spasmodic affection that – in short – the fouler the air, the better I feel myself.

LADY EMILY: (*to* MRS BELMORE) How do you find him?

MRS BELMORE: O, very agreeable.

LADY EMILY: (*aside*) That's as much as to say, quite charming. Well, since you won't sing with me, I must give it up for the present. – I have two calls to make across the Green, and I'll take this opportunity.

SIR HENRY: (*eagerly*) Do people let one another in at Richmond?

LADY EMILY: Oh yes; but I shall be so anxious to return, that I will merely slide in my card. There never was anything so tormenting as this tax upon society; visiting people one hardly knows by sight, and that one shou'dn't care, if one never saw again. I'm sure you must have experienced how annoying it is, to be compelled to be civil to a person one wishes a hundred miles off – one, that won't be driven away by a hint, however broadly given, but that will run on from one thing to another – talk, talk, talk, till one's spirits are worn out, and one's patience quite exhausted! Don't you detest such beings?

MRS BELMORE: I do indeed.

LADY EMILY: I am sure you must. Well, as I hope to be back again in a very few minutes, I won't take my leave – *sans adieu*?

[*Exit* LADY EMILY]

SIR HENRY: (*aside*) Thank heaven! you are gone, at any rate.

MRS BELMORE: How do you like my friend?

SIR HENRY: I hardly looked at her, and I shall not easily forgive her having interrupted a conversation which was so replete with interest to me. – I remember I was asking a question of Lady Emily—

MRS BELMORE: Which, I remember, I had no intention of answering.

SIR HENRY: I am aware it was a very delicate one, but recollect, Lady Emily, this is not the first time of our meeting – you cannot have misunderstood my declarations at the masquerade; though it is evident, by the reserve and total change in your manner, that they have not been so favourably received as I then flattered myself they would be.

MRS BELMORE: You would not have me all my life in masquerade—

SIR HENRY: Ah! believe me, I do not regret the absence of your vivacity! How many women attract by their brilliancy – how few, by the ineffable charm of unaffected sensibility! Till this moment, I had judged of your wit only; but now I think I know how to appreciate your heart also – before, I could find words to express my admiration; but now, the utterance of my feelings is impossible. Oh! but for a moment, resume your mask, that, unawed by the dignity of your expression, I may tell you with what fervour I adore you!

Enter MRS JEFFERIES

—Another interruption, by Jove!

MRS JEFFERIES: My mistress has been prevented going out, Ma'am; Mr Stanly has just been brought in rather ill, and very much agitated.

MRS BELMORE: Good heavens! what has happened?

MRS JEFFERIES: Returning home, it seems, he was met by an unfortunate maniac, who had just broken from his confinement. – Having seen Mr Stanly at the Asylum, he probably mistook him for one of the keepers; and, with all the strength which madness gives, dragged him to the ground; but, luckily, somebody was within hearing, and came to his assistance – upon which the maniac fled, and the keepers are already in pursuit of him. [*Exit*]

MRS BELMORE: (*retiring*) You must excuse me, Sir—

SIR HENRY: But wherefore, Madam? You hear that Mr Stanly is more frightened than hurt – now, *I* am more hurt than frightened, and of the two, a much fitter object for your compassion.

MRS BELMORE: You must, notwithstanding, allow me to retire – my situation was rather embarrassing; and, but for this accident, I might have found it difficult to extricate myself.

[*Exit* MRS BELMORE][17]

SIR HENRY: The devil take the keepers, for not securing their madmen better, I say. I had just arrived at the critical juncture! When such a

favourable opportunity may occur again, heaven only knows –
however, I shall certainly return this evening. – Charming, charming Lady Emily! what manners! what sentiments! that rogue,
Delaval, too! to slander her perfections! – Oh! 'twas blasphemy!
(*Takes out his watch*) – Let me see; at five, I am to meet the lawyers
however, I can be back by eight but will she be ready to receive me?
they'll probably sit down to dine at seven – Soup – she'll be five
minutes, at least, eating that – she can't be less; it is generally so
confoundedly hot! I wish she would eat fish in its stead; but there,
there again! the bones are a great drawback – Psha! she's a divinity;
and far above the vulgar prejudice of eating and drinking as coarse
mortals do! Lady Emily, I adore you! Mrs Belmore, I detest you! and
heartily wish the lawyers and you were all at the bottom of the Red
Sea!   [*Exit*]

SCENE ii

*A gloomy part of Richmond Park – several trunks
of trees lying here and there – twilight*

Enter CECIL, *with an infant wrapped in a shawl*

CECIL: Your cries, at length, are hushed in sleep, my precious infant!
and cold and hunger are, for awhile, forgotten! How awful is this
silence! no sound falls on my ear, but the tumultuous beating of my
frightened heart – lie still, lie still; your throbbings will awake my
babe – how comes this mist before my eyes? I'm very faint – My
child, my child! I can no longer bear your weight: (*She sinks, placing
the infant upon the trunk of one of the trees*) – What agony is this?
numbed as my limbs are by the stiffening blast, a scorching fire
consumes my brain! – Can this be fear? It is, the terror of a guilty
conscience: there was a time, when neither solitude nor night had
power to terrify me – but I was innocent then; then I had not
offended Heaven, whose protection I dare not now implore. – Ha! I
hear a voice – Oh! welcome, welcome sound! – Yet, should it be any
one whom I have known in other days – an idle fear; for if it should,
night's friendly shadows will conceal the features of the guilty Cecil
– I'll follow his footsteps – in common charity, he'll not deny that
comfort to a wretched, houseless wanderer!

MR FITZHARDING: (*without*) Ha, ha! have I escaped you, ruffians?
here I shall be safe from their pursuit.

(*He is seen climbing the wall, and with the assistance of the arm of a tree, lets himself down upon the stage; in this effort he breaks one of the smaller branches, and uses it as a weapon of defence*)
—Here will I lie concealed – they shall not again imprison me!

CECIL: Some miscreant escaped from justice! What will become of us?

MR FITZHARDING: There, there they go! – One, two, three, four! – So, so; lie close; they are gone, they are gone, and now I breathe again.

CECIL: Alas! a maniac! what's to be done? shall I conceal myself? No; I'll make for the gate, and endeavour to regain the public road.

(FITZHARDING *turns suddenly round*)

MR FITZHARDING: What are you? one lying in ambush to entrap me? Wretch! advance one hair's breadth, and I'll fell you to the ground! (*Raising the broken branch*) – Ah! a woman!

CECIL: Yes; one without the power or wish to harm you.

MR FITZHARDING: That's false – you are a woman, born only to betray – I know you are leagued against me – but thus – (*Threateningly*)

CECIL: O! for my child's sake, do not harm me.

MR FITZHARDING: A child! – have you a child? give it me – let me strangle it, before the little serpent turns to sting the breast that nourished it – pity is folly – if she live, she lives to blast your comfort. I had a child, a child more precious to me than my own heart's blood – but she betrayed me – made a gay festival to welcome me upon my return from a long, tedious journey – invited guests too – three hideous guests! Seduction, Penury, and Despair – With the first she fled, and left me victim to the other two.

CECIL: What do I hear? what horrid vision darts across my brain! Can it be? No, no! and yet, although destruction follow, I must, I will be satisfied. (*She throws off* FITZHARDING's *hat, recognises, and falls at his feet*) – Great God! my father!

MR FITZHARDING: (*raising her, looks wistfully in her face, and laughs wildly – pause*) They are coming – you will not give me up to my pursuers – you will have more compassion than my unnatural daughter.

CECIL: Can I hear this, and yet not curse thee, Delaval?

MR FITZHARDING: Ha! does that damned name again assail my ears? Does *he* pursue me still? What new torment can he inflict upon me? Yes, yes, I see him now – where is my daughter, villain? Give her back – restore her to me, polluted as she is, and I will bless you – but you have murdered her – your barbarous hand has nipped my pretty rose-bud ere it was blown, and now she lies, scorned, pale, and lifeless – monster! no longer shall your poisonous breath infect the

air – an injured father strikes this poniard to your faithless heart –
no struggling – down – down – Oh, oh! (CECIL *supports him*)

CECIL: (*weeping*) O, sight of horror! will all the agony I feel restore
your peace, beloved, much injured father!

MR FITZHARDING: (*recovering – feels her cheeks*) How! weeping!
tears, real tears! poor thing, poor thing! don't cry – I cannot be a
partner in your grief – since my poor Cecil died (for she is dead, is
she not?) I have not shed a tear.

CECIL: Oh, Heaven! too much, too much to bear!

MR FITZHARDING: Poor thing! poor thing! (*Pause*) You will not leave
me, will you? (*Draws her close to his bosom*)

CECIL: Leave you! O never, never; I will serve you, live for you, die for
you.

MR FITZHARDING: Come then, come with me; and I will shew you
Cecil's grave; and we will strew fresh yew and cypress over it –
Come, come!

(*As he is leading her away, voices of the* KEEPERS *are heard without –*
1ST KEEPER. '*This way, this way; I'll follow him over the wall – do
you secure the gate.*' *– He leaps from the wall, two more come on at
the gate*)

MR FITZHARDING: I hear them, they are coming – don't let them tear
me from you – save, O, save me!

CECIL: Kind people, hear me! he is my father – leave him to my tender
care!

1ST KEEPER: O yes, you'll do much good; I wish we had more hands
with us – step across to the cottage, and see if you can get any body
to assist.   [*Exit* 2ND KEEPER]

CECIL: You call in vain for assistance – no power on earth shall part us
– once again, I tell you he is my father.

1ST KEEPER: That may be – but what can you do for him? you had
better stand aside, young woman; you'll only get yourself hurt.

CECIL: You shall tear me limb from limb, rather than separate me from
him.

Re-enter 2ND KEEPER, *with cottager*

1ST KEEPER: (*to cottager*) There, do you take charge of the young
woman and keep her off – Now, now! – (*They rush forward to seize
him*)

MR FITZHARDING: The first who approaches, I will lay dead at my
foot – folded in your arms I fear them not.

(*A scuffle ensues, on which they are separated –* FITZHARDING
disarmed, and dragged away)

—Save me from these butchers! O save me, save me!

[*Exeunt* FITZHARDING *and* KEEPERS]

CECIL: O, for the love of mercy! let me follow him.

1ST KEEPER: (*without*) Bind his hands!

CECIL: No, no; for the love of Heaven, no! Inhuman men! I must, I will go to him. O cruel! cruel! O my poor deceived, unhappy father!

(*She breaks from the cottager, and endeavours to follow her father, but her strength fails her, and she sinks upon her knees; the cottager supports her, and the curtain falls*)

Act IV

SCENE i

A library in STANLY's *house*

Enter STANLY, *followed by a* SERVANT

STANLY: Who wants me, whom did you say?

SERVANT: The young woman, herself, wouldn't send any name, but Mrs Jefferies, who happened to come into the hall at the time, cried 'Bless me! is that you, Miss Fitzharding?'

STANLY: Miss Fitzharding! at this door? are you certain of it?

SERVANT: I only know what Mrs Jefferies said— the young woman made no answer, but drew her bonnet over her face. When I told her that you couldn't see her (for as it was so near dinner, I thought you would not choose to be disturbed), she seemed greatly distressed, and talked something about the Asylum.

STANLY: Ay, that's a subject that may well distress her – Worthless minx! is there any body in the carriage with her?

SERVANT: Carriage, Sir?

STANLY: Carriage, Sir! ay; don't you know what a carriage is?

SERVANT: Yes, Sir; but there's no carriage, nor anything like one, that I saw – I think you must mistake the person, Sir, altogether; for the young woman in the hall said she had heard that a servant was wanted at the Asylum, and that she had been directed to apply to you, as one of the Governors.

STANLY: Ah! this is another of your blessed blunders!

SERVANT: Upon my word, Sir—

STANLY: Poh! poh! did not you yesterday say there was an old woman in the parlour, who wanted to see Mrs Belmore, and when she went in, did not it turn out to be a Master in Chancery?[18]

SERVANT: Well, Sir, what message shall I take?

STANLY: Take, Sir! do you take me for a walking Therapolegia, that you bring your maid-servants to me for places?

SERVANT: I took you for no such thing, Sir; but the poor creature seemed in a deal of trouble, and you don't usually send away such as apply in distress: so, I thought—

STANLY: Thought, blockhead! why didn't you bring her in at once then?

SERVANT: (*aside*) That's as good as a five pound note in her pocket.

[*Exit* SERVANT]

Enter LADY EMILY

LADY EMILY: O! my dear Uncle; what an extraordinary circumstance! Who, do you think is here? Miss Fitzharding: the daughter of the unfortunate gentleman—

STANLY: Who had nearly made worms-meat of me – the fellow, was right, then; William, said she wanted to see me. Why does not she come? I desired she might be sent in.

LADY EMILY: She will come, no doubt, as soon as she is sufficiently recovered, for she appears very urgent to speak with you: Jefferies, who had known her, it seems, asked some unguarded question, which threw her into a dreadful agitation, and she fainted – I ran to entreat that you would see her, Sir; for her mind is burdened with a grief which, she says, no body but yourself can relieve.

STANLY: I am no conscience-doctor, Emily, and though I am willing to see Miss Fitzharding, and to do all in my power to alleviate her sorrow, since you say she suffers; yet, it will never be in my ability to relieve her from the burden of remorse, which her unfeeling conduct towards her father, must needs have laid upon her soul.

LADY EMILY: I am sincerely sorry for her – she is so interesting—

STANLY: Interesting! Psha! don't prostitute the epithet, Emily; the virtuous only should be interesting – but now-a-days, everything is interesting – let a lady abandon a worthy husband, and half a dozen lovely children, for the arms of a paramour, and the cry directly is, 'but she's so interesting!' – Here's a girl, who has driven a doating father into madness, by her profligacy, then *you* come and tell me, 'she's so interesting.'

LADY EMILY: Well, my dear Uncle, if I have used an expression which offends you, I will retract it – only tell me into what words I shall put an entreaty that may induce you, not only to see Miss Fitzharding, but dispose you, if possible, to serve her.

STANLY: As to serving her, I have already told you that I mean to do so, if it be within my power; and in order to understand how that may best be done, I am willing to admit Miss Fitzharding; but, I must make it a particular request, that you do not so far forget what is due to your rank, as to converse a second time with so degraded a being.

LADY EMILY: Is there any situation, my dear Sir, that puts one person above the obligation of succouring another in distress? 'tis the best privilege of superior rank, and in my opinion, the sole condition upon which Providence intended that we should possess it.

STANLY: True, Emily, charity is undoubtedly the greatest of all virtues;

but beware of indiscriminate compassion; and remember, that to *tolerate* vice, is to *encourage* it.

Enter a SERVANT

SERVANT: Miss Fitzharding waits to know if you are disengaged, Sir.

STANLY: Desire her to walk in – Emily – (*Signs to her to retire*)

LADY EMILY: Well, Sir, you wish it, and I will leave you, but don't be harsh with her; consider the cause she has for *self*-condemnation, and do not, by your reproaches, add to the load of her affliction; which even now seems greater than she can bear.

[*Exit* LADY EMILY *on one side*]
Enter SERVANT *and* CECIL *on the other*

STANLY: (*with constrained civility*) A chair! (SERVANT *sets chairs*) Sit down, Miss Fitzharding; let dinner be served, and desire the ladies not to wait. [*Exit* SERVANT] I am sorry you have been indisposed – Sit down, Ma'am, sit down; and inform me what are your commands with me – pray compose yourself: you seem greatly agitated.

CECIL: Agitated! Ah, Sir, when every surrounding object reminds me of happier days, of days passed in innocence and peace, I may well seem agitated, and sink with conscious shame and agony. Many a time has my poor father, while seated in that chair, placed his beloved hands upon my head, and with tears of fondness glistening in his eyes, implored of Providence to bless his darling child! Little did he then know what a serpent he cherished in his bosom! little did I then anticipate the deep, deep anguish which has been since my portion.

STANLY: Be comforted, Madam; there is no state, however wretched, which does not admit of hope.

CECIL: True, true; I have yet a hope, and in you that hope is centered; on my knees, let me implore your kind interposition, Sir; you may be the blessed means of restoring a father to reason, and his repentant daughter to tranquillity, though not to happiness.

STANLY: Let me know in what manner you think I can relieve you, Miss Fitzharding – the inclination, be assured, will not be wanting.

CECIL: The particulars of my unhappy story, I fear, are but too generally known; spare me the shame of repeating what, I wish I could for ever blot from recollection.

STANLY: We will remember nothing but that which may at present forward your views – speak, Madam.

CECIL: Flying from the man, who (after having seduced me to the dereliction of every sacred duty) was on the point of sacrificing, not only me, but his innocent child, to worldly selfish views, I chanced to meet my father – Good Heaven! in what a state! bereft of recollection, driven to fiercest madness, by the dishonour of his thankless child.

STANLY: He did not recognize you then?

CECIL: O that he had! though it had been to curse me – but no – 'twas nearly dark, and I am sadly changed since he last saw me – yet, I fondly think, that he was pleased to hear my voice – he implored me not to forsake him – O! that I never had! (*Weeps bitterly*) – from this circumstance, I feel a certain conviction, that were I constantly about his person, my dutiful attentions might at last restore that precious reason, of which my guilt so fatally deprived him. (*Weeps*)

STANLY: Madam! Miss Fitzharding!—

CECIL: Let me become a servant in the Asylum, by a thousand little assiduities, I may, at least ameliorate his condition; and, Oh! should it please Heaven to smile on my endeavours, and crown my penitent design with favour, intelligence once more shall beam from his bright eyes and he again may bless me ere I die.

STANLY: (*aside*) O Delaval! what have you to answer for in labouring to corrupt a heart like this – Your request is granted, Madam; you shall be near your father, you shall watch over and console him – every facility shall be afforded you, to put your virtuous resolution into practice: should your efforts prove successful, there are still many of your father's friends residing here; we will consult together, and see what may be done towards his support, and the alleviation of your sorrows.

CECIL: (*nobly*) His support? Sir, I shall provide for that – I will not eat the bread of idleness or shame; and the best alleviation of my griefs, will be to toil incessantly for him and my poor infant – too blest, if, in fulfilling the duties of a mother, I may make some atonement for the errors of a daughter.

STANLY: Accept, at least, a temporary assistance, till you possess the means so honourably acquired.

CECIL: O! Sir, I have not a proud or an ungrateful heart. Your generous compassion towards a poor degraded creature, has sunk deeply into my soul; but, from the misery into which my own guilt has plunged me, I am resolved that nothing but my own unwearied industry shall ever extricate me.

STANLY: I will not again attempt to shake a resolution pregnant at once with sensibility and honour; but though you refuse my offer of assistance, Madam, I trust you will allow me to present you to my niece, whose soothing cares and prudent councils will support and aid you in the virtuous task you have imposed upon yourself – may reformation so sincere, and filial piety so exemplary, draw down a blessing on you from above, and crown your efforts with complete success!   [*Exeunt*]

SCENE ii

A drawing room in STANLY's *house*

Enter O'DONOLAN

O'DONOLAN: Isn't it past all belief now, that a man possessing, upon most points, as clear a conception of things as any Irishman in the world, shall, upon the subject of his passion, be an absolute idiot? Though I know I am deceived, laughed at, and condemned by this perfidious woman, I can't help hovering about her, if possible, with increased infatuation – wretched as she makes me, I feel a delight in being tormented by such an angelic creature, that I would not exchange for the quiet possession of any other woman upon earth! if I could but contrive to see her before the company assembles, I might—

      Enter SIR HENRY CHOMLEY, *and a* SERVANT

—somebody arrived already – ever frustrated in all that regards her! (*Turns up*)

SIR HENRY: Why, 'tis eight o'clock, Sir; past eight; I heard it strike: 'tis past eight by my watch too.

SERVANT: I don't say it is not, Sir, but dinner was later than usual today, and the Ladies have not yet left table – I can let them know you are here; Mr Stanly is the only gentleman, and I dare say will be very glad if you will take your wine with him.

SIR HENRY: By no means; I wouldn't have them disturbed for the world – say nothing about it, if you please; I'd rather wait. [*Exit* SERVANT] No, no; it would have been rather too good a joke to have been fixed with old Stanly swallowing glass after glass of his London particular, instead of quaffing love's inebriating draught from the fascinating eyes of the adorable Lady Emily – for the last half hour I have been walking backwards and forwards opposite the windows, in hopes of seeing the fellow walk into the drawing-room with a long stick to light the candles – but my impatience could endure it no longer. There's an uneasy restlessness about me, which I never felt before – the fidgets, I think they call it – since I left this house, I have done nothing but wander up and down with my hands in my pockets, as if I had lost something – I have, I have lost my heart to this enchanting siren, and come what may, my fate this very night shall be decided, – What, O'Donolan!

O'DONOLAN: Chomley!

SIR HENRY: Hush!

O'DONOLAN: How long have you been returned from the continent?

SIR HENRY: Above a fortnight.

O'DONOLAN: My dear Chomley!

SIR HENRY: Hush, I tell you, for the love of mystery! I am no longer Chomley, I have changed my name.

O'DONOLAN: For an estate? I give you joy, my dear fellow!

SIR HENRY: No – for a better thing – a devilish handsome woman, my boy: Lady Emily Gerald! a most extraordinary adventure; and so you'll think it.

O'DONOLAN: O, I dare say I shall.

SIR HENRY: Her reasons, I don't know; but, as she thought proper to *desire* that I would change my name, I have done so, in compliance with her wishes. – I know you can be discreet, so I'll let you into the whole affair – The very day after my return, I met Lady Emily at a masquerade – you know her figure; and may guess what the effect of it was upon a fellow, who for many months had not feasted his eyes upon the gratifying sight of a well-dressed Englishwoman of fashion! She seemed pleased with *my* attentions; I was charmed with her conversation; and, though she persisted in concealing from me who she was, yet she so far encouraged me, as to say, she should be at the subscription masquerade on the Thursday; and again, at Lady Brellington's on the Saturday: at each of these we met, we talked, and liked – this very morning only I discovered who she was, wrote to solicit her permission to present myself; and here, you rogue, is the angel's answer – (*Gives* O'DONOLAN *the letter – he reads, and returns it*) – Very satisfactory – don't you think so?

O'DONOLAN: O, very! – (*Aside*) Damn her for a jilt! – But why this change of name?

SIR HENRY: That's what I don't understand myself; I was too happy, you may be sure, to be admitted upon any terms, and of course never stopped to make enquiries – my interview with her this morning has rivetted my chains; and I am now here, under a fixed determination of proposing to her—

O'DONOLAN: And do you expect to be accepted?

SIR HENRY: Why, without any extraordinary portion of vanity, I flatter myself that the thing is possible – I am delighted to have met you here; are you intimate in the family?

O'DONOLAN: Faith, you may say that.

SIR HENRY: Better and better! What a lucky dog I am!

O'DONOLAN: How so, pray?

SIR HENRY: You may assist me, by speaking to Lady Emily in my favour.

O'DONOLAN: I! No, curse me if I do.

SIR HENRY: How, O'Donolan? I thought I could have depended upon your friendship; but perhaps you think the match objectionable.

O'DONOLAN: Indeed and I do, Sir; very objectionable.

SIR HENRY: Hey day! what can this mean?

O'DONOLAN: It means, Sir, that you are damnably mistaken, if you imagine that I shall plead your cause in this affair – Lady Emily has received me, avowedly admitted me as her lover, for the last fifteen months, Sir; and although I think her the vilest of coquettes, I shall not relinquish my claim to you, or any man in England, or Ireland, Sir. Now, do you understand what it means, Sir?

SIR HENRY: Why, yes, I begin to apprehend – then you suppose that she has a regard for you?

O'DONOLAN: (*imitating him*) Why, without any extraordinary portion of vanity, I had a pretty good right to think so, Sir.

SIR HENRY: (*playing carelessly with the letter*) – Ay, fifteen months ago – but, possibly, she may have changed her mind since that time.

O'DONOLAN: Possibly; but I have not changed mine; so you will be pleased to release your pretensions, whether 'tis agreeable to you or not.

SIR HENRY: But, my dear O'Donolan, as the Lady ought unquestionably to have a voice in this affair, don't you think we may as well refer the matter to her – if she decide in your favour, I swear, it shall make no difference in my feelings towards you: if she declare in mine—

O'DONOLAN: I'll cut your throat, my dear friend!

SIR HENRY: I hope not; at any rate, let all be fair and open between us. (*Aside*) By Jove! I have just recollected, that I have ordered the carriage, without apprizing my servants of my new appellation of Grenville; and I shall have some fellow bawling out, Sir Henry Chomley's carriage stops the way! that would ruin me with Lady Emily – I must continue the name of Grenville, 'till I have my charmer's leave to throw it off. I am compelled to return to the hotel, O'Donolan, for ten minutes, and all I require at your hands, is, not to betray that I have let you into my confidence.

O'DONOLAN: And did I ask for it Sir Henry? No, indeed; you *foisted* it upon me.

SIR HENRY: That's very true; but since chance, or I will rather say, a reliance on your friendship, has helped you to my secret, I trust to your *honour*, not to obtain any unfair advantage, by representing what I have said, under false colours to Lady Emily; but wait my return, before you enter into an explanation with her.

O'DONOLAN: Upon this subject, you have no right to prescribe any conditions, Sir Henry; but for old friendship's sake, I *do* agree to postpone this explanation till your return; and then, I shall have the double satisfaction of telling her, all I think of you, all I think of her, and all I think of myself, for being such a damned ass, as still to waste one thought upon her!

SIR HENRY: Ha! ha! ha! *au revoir*! I rely upon your *honour*, O'Donolan, and hope, upon my return, to find you as entertaining as I now leave you.   [*Exit* SIR HENRY]

O'DONOLAN: How shall I contain myself? The jilt! I'll not speak to her before he comes back – I'll have the gratification of confounding her, in the presence of her new lover – I will expose her perfidy, lay bare her arts, tell her how I love her, how I hate her, and put an end to my torments, by blowing out my brains.

Enter MRS BELMORE

MRS BELMORE: Colonel O'Donolan! now this *is* kind of you; and I am sure Lady Emily will –

O'DONOLAN: Don't name her, Madam; a perfidious – O! Mrs Belmore, Mrs Belmore! ain't I the most miserable of human creatures?

MRS BELMORE: What do you mean? – nothing new, I hope, has happened!

O'DONOLAN: Yes, Ma'am; an unequivocal confirmation of all my suspicions – no longer, treacherous as she is, can she deny the justice of my accusation – my doubts have been cleared, all cleared, and by Sir Henry Chomley himself.

MRS BELMORE: Whom do you say, by Sir Henry Chomley?

O'DONOLAN: Yes, Madam; I met him here not five minutes ago, and, upon the strength of former friendship, he made me his confidante – told me of their *rencontres* at the masquerade, of his request to see her – showed me her answer to it, in which, no doubt, the better to impose upon me, she desires him to *assume the name of Grenville*. – False, false woman! to fix her affections upon such a profligate! – such an ugly fellow too!

MRS BELMORE: (*eagerly*) Heavens! what do you tell me?

O'DONOLAN: You are amazed, astonished at her perfidy – no wonder.

MRS BELMORE: Sir Henry Chomley, under the name of Grenville?

O'DONOLAN: 'Tis too true, Madam – What deceit! what falsehood!

MRS BELMORE: To dupe her friend!

O'DONOLAN: To betray her lover!

MRS BELMORE: To involve me, so unwarrantably!

O'DONOLAN: To pretend a quarrel with me, that she might have more liberty to receive him!

MRS BELMORE: I did not think her capable of such an action!

O'DONOLAN: Nor I either, Ma'am.

MRS BELMORE: I never will forgive her!

O'DONOLAN: Nor I either, Ma'am: I have thought her light, capricious, sometimes even unfeeling; but never, never could I have imagined this! I'll see her once again – but it shall be to tell her that I know the extent of her unworthiness – to make her feel that I despise and hate her! Pardon me, Mrs Belmore, you know how tenderly I loved her, and the concern you show, calls for my warmest thanks.

MRS BELMORE: You will not wonder at the interest I take in this affair, when I inform you, Colonel O'Donolan, that I am the only person entitled to resent the conduct of Lady Emily.

O'DONOLAN: You, Madam?

MRS BELMORE: If Mr Grenville and Sir Henry Chomley are one person, Lady Emily must be absolved from all intention of offence towards you; but she has exposed, committed *me*, past all retrieving.

O'DONOLAN: Would you please to explain your meaning, Ma'am?

MRS BELMORE: Have you forgotten that I am engaged in a lawsuit with Sir Henry? 'Tis evident that Lady Emily has wished to reconcile us, and, hurried on by the warmth of her affections, has never stopped to weigh the consequences in which her conduct might involve me: she saw Sir Henry at a masquerade, permitted his visits here, and under a well-feigned apprehension of exciting your suspicions, prevailed upon me to assume her name, and receive the supposed Mr Grenville in her place.

O'DONOLAN: (*wild with joy*) Eh! How! What do you say? Am I in my senses? You, you, Mrs Belmore, as Lady Emily?

MRS BELMORE: 'Tis too true; you may readily believe I should not have lent myself to such an imposition, had I known it was Sir Henry whom I was to meet: this too, perfectly explains his being brought here, under the name of Grenville.

O'DONOLAN: So, after all, Mrs Belmore, it turns out that it's yourself that is the goddess of his idolatry!

MRS BELMORE: I, Colonel O'Donolan?

O'DONOLAN: O! and you may believe me, you; he raves about you – doats upon you from the crown of your head to the tip of your toe: marry, marry, Mrs Belmore, and make him and me the happiest man in the world.

MRS BELMORE: Don't you think that would be rather a rash measure, Colonel O'Donolan?

O'DONOLAN: Not in the least – do it, do it, if it be only for the pleasure of non-suiting the lawyers. O! 'twill be the prettiest match that ever was heard of – a match, where prudence and inclination are both of one mind.

MRS BELMORE: Colonel O'Donolan! have I ever professed a liking for Sir Henry?

O'DONOLAN: Not yet; but I'll engage you will; you must; he's very handsome, everybody must allow that; I have known him intimately for years, and upon my soul, a worthier fellow does not breathe.

MRS BELMORE: He has risen very rapidly in your good opinion, Sir; 'tis but a few minutes, since he was a profligate, a—

O'DONOLAN: O! that was while I thought Lady Emily was in love with him; but I know you will forgive me – indeed, we all have need of your indulgence.

MRS BELMORE: Lady Emily has the least right to expect my forgiveness; for at the time she put this imposture upon me, she was acquainted with a circumstance which makes my situation much more embarrassing than it appears.

O'DONOLAN: The friendly motive, I am sure, will weigh with you in her behalf. The angel! but why do I continue prating here, when I should be upon my knees before her, soliciting for pardon – I will confess my fault, renounce my jealousy, and by a life of adoration, make amends for all my suspicions past, present, and to come!

[Going]

MRS BELMORE: Stay, Colonel O'Donolan; with your permission, I had rather Lady Emily knew nothing of what has just occurred.

O'DONOLAN: Your reason, Madam? if you please.

MRS BELMORE: Why, at present, she is firmly persuaded that I am her dupe; now, I own, it would be no small pleasure to me, to turn the tables upon her, and make her mine – besides, 'twould be as well, I think, to know a little more of Sir Henry Chomley, before we venture to confess the trick that we have played him.

O'DONOLAN: Ha! ha! ha! yes, my dear Mrs Belmore, perhaps it would be as well, that you should see a little more of him.

MRS BELMORE: (*confused*) You are quite mistaken, I don't mean that, at all.

O'DONOLAN: O! by my soul then, if you didn't mean it, your tongue should teach your eyes not to make bulls, Mrs Belmore; but Chomley will be back again presently, and though I can't comprehend your meaning, I hope, at least, that you'll come to a right understanding with him.

MRS BELMORE: I see you are bent upon being amused at my expense, so I will say no more upon this silly subject; only give me your faithful promise not to betray me to Lady Emily.

O'DONOLAN: Ah now! and haven't I promised?

MRS BELMORE: But swear it; for if you do not, you will no more be able to resist the bright twinkle of her enquiring eye, than –

O'DONOLAN: (*kneels*) Why there, then; upon my knees I solemnly declare, that by you, and you only, shall Lady Emily be undeceived.—

Enter LADY EMILY, *behind, and unperceived*

—You have made me the happiest man in the universe, and have a right to impose upon me what conditions you please.

MRS BELMORE: Only abstain from seeing Lady Emily, till my explanation is over, and I shall be satisfied.

[*Exit* MRS BELMORE]

O'DONOLAN: (*kneeling*) That is a promise—

LADY EMILY: Which it will not be in your power to keep – I am here, Colonel O'Donolan, and delighted in the opportunity of congratulating you upon being the happiest man in the universe – I lament that Mrs Belmore has withdrawn; because it deprives me of the pleasure of congratulating her too, upon having been the fortunate mortal who has made you so.

O'DONOLAN: Hey! what! you surely can't believe that – Upon my soul!

LADY EMILY: No explanation, Colonel O'Donolan; you have brought this affair to a most satisfactory conclusion, and I have now only to request that you will leave this house immediately – some other place will more honorably suit your declarations to Mrs Belmore.

O'DONOLAN: O! and is it Mrs Belmore that you mean? the sweetest creature, sure—

LADY EMILY: How!

O'DONOLAN: No, I don't mean that – the most amiable—

LADY EMILY: Intolerable!

O'DONOLAN: I don't mean that, either.

LADY EMILY: Didn't I find you upon your knees before her?

O'DONOLAN: Yes.

LADY EMILY: Weren't you making declarations of love to her?

O'DONOLAN: No.

LADY EMILY: How! did not you say, she had made you the happiest man in the universe?

O'DONOLAN: Yes, – no, – most certainly I did; but that was – Oh, botheration! how will I ever get out of this?

LADY EMILY: 'Tis all in vain, Sir, you are a faithless lover! Mrs Belmore a false friend! and I am the silliest dupe that was ever cheated by either.

O'DONOLAN: Wait a while, Lady Emily, only wait a while – don't turn me away unheard, till I've told you all I have to say – your Mr Grenville is at the bottom of all this – only wait till I fetch him – he has just stepped to the hotel, but I'll run after him immediately, that I may be sure of meeting him – patience, my dear Lady Emily, patience for five minutes only, and I'll be with you again in less than a quarter of an hour.

[Exit O'DONOLAN]

Act V

SCENE i

A room in STANLY's *house*

Enter STANLY, *and* LADY EMILY

LADY EMILY: Well, Sir, what tidings? has the meeting taken place? did Mr Fitzharding recognize his daughter?

STANLY: I fear not; but one so lovely in resignation as that poor suffering girl, I never saw – wholly absorbed in the pious purpose to which she has devoted herself, she watches every look, every turn of countenance, lending herself to all his childish fancies, and smiling, even in agony, to please him.

LADY EMILY: And may I not call that creature interesting? but what were his sensations when he first beheld her?

STANLY: When we first entered his cell, we found him seated with his back to the door, drawing upon the wall.

LADY EMILY: Drawing! what?

STANLY: A tomb – over the entrance of which, he had inscribed the name of Cecil.

LADY EMILY: Unhappy man!

STANLY: Startled by an involuntary groan, which burst from the overcharged heart of his afflicted daughter, he suddenly turned – he was much agitated at the sight of her – gazed wildly upon her features for an instant, then shook his head, and sighing deeply, again resumed his occupation: still, from time to time, as if he could not chase the idea of her from his mind, he would cast enquiring glances at her; and when he saw the tears piteously chasing one another down her pale cheeks, in a tone of deep commiseration, he exclaimed, 'Poor thing! Poor thing!' – looked in her face again with eager curiosity, and snatching his hand away, which she was fondly pressing to her lips, muttered, with disappointment, to himself, 'but she is dead for all that.'

LADY EMILY: (*with great vivacity*) Then, be assured, my dear Uncle, he does recollect her – his present habitation, Cecil's appearance, so altered by misfortune, and the menial dress she has assumed, joined to a strong impression of her death, all, all combine to puzzle his bewildered mind – some strong effect, must be produced upon him, and if my heart deceive me not, I am the doctor destined to restore him.

STANLY: What stronger effect than that we have already tried, can—

LADY EMILY: One that has just flashed across my mind – Will you grant me a diploma? am I at liberty to practise?

STANLY: Provided you call in the physician of the Asylum.

LADY EMILY: By all means; as I am but a young practitioner, I shan't object to a consultation.

Enter a SERVANT

SERVANT: Lord Glenthorn, Sir, is at the door, and begs to know if he can speak with you upon particular business.

STANLY: Come to support the pretensions of his worthless son, I suppose – the moment is not auspicious – what can I do?

LADY EMILY: Of course you will admit him, Sir; but let me see you as soon as possible, for I'm impatient till I put a scheme in execution, which I foresee will translate me to the skies – the world shall acknowledge the genuine offspring of Æsculapius,[19] and raise altars to me under the appellation of the modern Hygeia.[20] [*Exit*]

STANLY: Desire Lord Glenthorn to walk in. [*Exit* SERVANT]

—How perplexing is my present position! My old friend is, no doubt, come to ascertain the result of my promised endeavours on behalf of his son Delaval, at a time too, when my heart is swelling with indignation at his barbarity! I would not wantonly wound the feelings of a father; but I know it will be impossible for me to conceal the abhorrence that I feel of his unprincipled son! What do I see! Delaval himself?

Enter LORD GLENTHORN

GLENTHORN: I read in your countenance, Mr Stanly, that I am an unwelcome visitor; but the assurance I beg to offer, that my stay will not be protracted beyond the time necessary for a few enquiries, will, I trust, ensure me the favour of a patient hearing.

STANLY: Ask all you wish to know, Sir; take your own time; for I mean to claim the same privilege to tell you, more perhaps than you may wish to hear.

GLENTHORN: As I am convinced that Mr Stanly cannot say anything which I ought not to listen to, I accede to his proposal.

STANLY: Sir, how far you may flatter yourself that you are safe under the shelter of my forbearance, I cannot tell; but that you may not deceive yourself upon that point, I beg, as a preliminary, to inform you, that I hold your conduct in utter detestation; and that nothing could have added to the disgust it has excited, but the mean subterfuge under which you have presumed to gain admittance here.

GLENTHORN: Sir! I am unconscious of having resorted to any artifice – 'tis evident you are not yet informed of your late friend, my father's death; by which, unfortunately, I am privileged to announce myself under the title of Lord Glenthorn – your mistake is excusable; but this language, Mr Stanly—

STANLY: You must hear from me, and every man who has a grain of honest feeling in his breast – your heartless conduct has given every upright character a *right* to express the just abhorrence which he entertains of your unpardonable profligacy – Crimes like yours—

GLENTHORN: Crimes! Mr Stanly—

STANLY: Crimes, my Lord; by what title would you dignify the seduction of an innocent girl? By what specious argument gloss over the subsequent desertion of her and of her infant? Can the ingenious sophistry of vice supply a single palliative for actions such as these? or are you so presumptuous as to believe that Heaven will leave the libertine unpunished, whose arts betrayed a virtuous child to shame, and drove a doating father into madness?

GLENTHORN: I am not here to palliate or defend my actions – whatever they have been, I am not accountable at this tribunal, although my future life may prove, I hold them in as much abhorrence as yourself. The object of my visit here, was to gain some intelligence of Miss Fitzharding; I have traced her hither, and if I have trespassed upon your patience, tell me but where she is, and I'll obtrude no longer.

STANLY: She is under my protection, now, my Lord; and whatever you may have to say to her, must be communicated through me.

GLENTHORN: Until I know upon what authority you arrogate this power to yourself, I can't acknowledge it – and I must add, her having sought protection of a person so entirely unknown to her, as you are, savours as little of prudence, as it does of delicacy.

STANLY: And what must you be, who have forced her to seek refuge at the hands of strangers? Prudence and delicacy! whither would your insinuations tend?

GLENTHORN: No farther than your own declaration – you have acknowledged that Miss Fitzharding is now under *your protection*.

STANLY: And what of that, Sir? Have you anything to offer upon that?

GLENTHORN: (*sneeringly*) Congratulations only: to you, upon your good fortune – to Miss Fitzharding, upon her well-directed preference.

STANLY: O spare your irony, my Lord; sarcasm is a *blunt* weapon in the hands of guilt: the authority which I possess over her, springs solely from a pure desire to serve an injured woman; to heal the wounds of an afflicted heart, and restore a fallen, but repentant angel, to health, tranquillity, and self-respect.

GLENTHORN: Pardon me, Mr Stanly – although I scorn to whine, I am not ashamed to display my feelings, when I am conscious they originate in truth and virtue; and though I own, my former conduct gives me little claim to your consideration, yet, from the patience which I have evinced while smarting under the lash of your deserved reproach, you may perhaps form some opinion of the sincerity of my contrition. For Cecil's sake, for her dear infant's, I entreat you will allow me once more to see her, though but for a few moments. I fear I have no longer any influence over her; but should it happily prove otherwise, I pledge my honour to make no unworthy use of it: you may yourself be witness to our interview – but let me, let me see her!

STANLY: (*after reflection*) It shall be so – your request, my Lord, is granted – order the carriage!

GLENTHORN: Mine is at the door – O, let us not lose a moment!

STANLY: Proceed, my Lord: I have one word to say to Lady Emily before I go, and I will follow you immediately.

[*Exit* LORD GLENTHORN *on one side*]

—If you *have* a heart, I will yet probe it to the core.

[*Exit* STANLY *on the other*]

Enter SIR HENRY CHOMLEY

SIR HENRY: Then I was right, and it *was* Delaval's carriage that I saw at the door – In what a hurry he brushed by me! – he seemed as little inclined to be seen by me, as I could be to be recognized by him – but for this name of Grenville, though, which I am forced to assume, I should have had some pleasure in shewing him, that in spite of his efforts to mislead me, I had not only found Lady Emily out, but was already established here, upon a tolerable footing of intimacy. But where's O'Donolan? should he have given Lady Emily an impression that I have boasted of the distinction with which she has honoured me, 'twould ruin me for ever! – but she is here! I don't read any marks of hostility in her looks – then, O'Donolan, thou art a noble fellow!

Enter MRS BELMORE

—I hardly hoped to have the good fortune of finding you alone, Madam; I thought the Colonel had been with you – he is often here, he tells me.

MRS BELMORE: O, yes; almost every day.

SIR HENRY: (*aside*) So far accounts agree – He is a very good sort of fellow!

MRS BELMORE: Excellent, I think; his feelings are so warm, his understanding so good, his manners so amiable, I have the greatest possible esteem for Colonel O'Donolan.

SIR HENRY: (*aside*) So it appears; and 'tis as well to know it from the fountain head –

MRS BELMORE: You seem a little discomposed this evening.

SIR HENRY: I do feel a little awkwardly, I own, Madam; I have a most earnest desire to be informed upon a particular point, and yet I fear you may deem my question impertinent.

MRS BELMORE: I dare say not – what is it?

SIR HENRY: Believe me, I don't propose it from idle curiosity, but from a feeling in which my happiness is deeply involved. – O'Donolan is young; prepossessing in person; unexceptionable in character; – with all these advantages, (pardon the enquiry), has he not been fortunate enough to inspire you with a sentiment of preference?

MRS BELMORE: Colonel O'Donolan? No; nor did he ever dream of such a thing.

SIR HENRY: O, you must pardon me; he loves you tenderly, most ardently; for, by the oddest accident in the world, we communicated to each other—

MRS BELMORE: I have no wish to enquire into the subject of his confidences; but, whatever the Colonel may have asserted, I owe it to myself to say, the only sentiments he ever inspired in me, were those of friendship.

SIR HENRY: You will, at least, allow that I had cause for apprehension – widowhood is not the natural state of youth and beauty.

MRS BELMORE: Be that as it may, 'tis a state which I shall never change.

SIR HENRY: And what motive can have determined you in so selfish a resolution?

MRS BELMORE: The hazard I should run of not being happy under a second engagement; besides, 'tis not unlikely that, by a lawsuit which is now pending, my whole fortune may be forfeited, and I reduced to absolute penury.

SIR HENRY: Happy, thrice happy the man, who is permitted to avert the wrongs of fortune from you! Were I so blessed! Oh, Lady Emily, I can no longer struggle with my passion, and though a declaration may for ever drive me from your presence, yet, I must hazard all, to ease a heart overflowing with the purest adoration – my character is known to all the world, my fortune, already ample, will shortly be considerably increased, by a favourable decree in Chancery.

MRS BELMORE: And are you, too, so unfortunate as to be involved in law?

SIR HENRY: Nay, call me rather fortunate; for my lawyers assure me positively of success – it was once proposed that I should terminate the difference by a marriage with the hateful woman with whom I am at issue, one Mrs Belmore.

MRS BELMORE: Mrs Belmore! – And she is very disagreeable?

SIR HENRY: Yes, I dare say she is; I never saw her though – a fat, ruddy dame, with a fine broad provincial dialect, I'll be sworn, whose accomplishments are making punch, preserves and pickles, whose virtue is prudery, whose conversation is scandal, and whose code of morality consists in a zealous intolerance towards all the weaknesses of frail humanity.

MRS BELMORE: What a portrait! but I can assure you, Mrs Belmore, in no one point, resembles the description you have given of her.

SIR HENRY: You know her then, Madam?

MRS BELMORE: Intimately; I know too, that she possesses many estimable qualities: Her husband, Mr Belmore, was a man of cultivated taste and polished manners; can it then be believed that he would be content to live, and in retirement too, with such a being as you have just depicted? Come, let us do her justice, and suppose she may possess some virtues, which entitled her to the esteem and love of so wise and honourable a man: she is prouder, too, than you imagine; and, if you have received an offer of her hand, be assured, it was without her knowledge, and the proposal has entailed upon its author the strongest marks of her resentment.

SIR HENRY: As I have never seen the lady, what I have said, were she even informed of it, ought not to wound her self-love in the least. But, can *you* pardon this attack upon your friend, for, by your warmth in her defence, I perceive she is so?

MRS BELMORE: What inconsiderate creatures are you men! hating and loving, as prejudice or prepossession governs! For instance, now, you think me pleasing, at least you have told me so; yet scarcely know me, and judge as superficially of me as you have done of Mrs Belmore; but she shall take her own revenge, for I am determined you shall see her.

SIR HENRY: My dear Lady Emily, you cannot mean to—

MRS BELMORE: How do you know that you may not think her agreeable?

SIR HENRY: As your friend, I may, just that; but nothing more.

MRS BELMORE: I have a strong idea that you would fall in love with *her* as suddenly as you have done with me, and in that case, a marriage—

SIR HENRY: Never, never! Were I to lose my cause, and my whole estate to it, I would save neither by an union with her. – No, no; 'tis you, and only you.

MRS BELMORE: But I have already told you, I may shortly be a beggar; should I *lose* my lawsuit—

SIR HENRY: I shall gain mine – the chances are, we cannot both be cast.

MRS BELMORE: Probably not; but what would you say, now, if, without knowing it, you had already met Mrs Belmore? Suppose she were the lady whom you saw here this morning, and with whom you are engaged to sing tonight?

SIR HENRY: You are not in earnest, surely – What! that lady Mrs Belmore?

MRS BELMORE: The same.

SIR HENRY: Now isn't this extraordinary! the very instant I saw that woman, I took an aversion to her.

MRS BELMORE: And yet, she is extremely beautiful!

SIR HENRY: I don't think so.

MRS BELMORE: And remarkably clever.

SIR HENRY: If you desire it, I will subscribe to all her perfections; and to prove that she does not in vain possess the title of your friend, I here drop all proceedings against her, and to your arbitration submit my cause.

MRS BELMORE: Why then – but here she comes.

Enter LADY EMILY *and* O'DONOLAN

LADY EMILY: (*as she enters, to* O'DONOLAN) Well, since you so solemnly assert it, I, like an upright judge, am bound to believe you innocent till you are proved guilty.

MRS BELMORE: You could not, my dear friend, have arrived at a more propitious moment; Sir Henry Chomley, for I must now give him his real appellation, informed of my friendship to Mrs Belmore, generously agrees to drop all further proceedings, and is desirous of terminating the dispute by an amicable arrangement.

O'DONOLAN: O! then, I'm delighted to hear it; and by what method do you propose—

SIR HENRY: Faith, 'tis a matter of indifference to me – the simplest and shortest way, however, I think best.

O'DONOLAN: The simplest way, would be by marriage; Oh! I give you joy, with all my heart!

SIR HENRY: The simplest, indeed; I understand it, Sir; you would be happy to get rid of a rival.

LADY EMILY: But Mrs Belmore may think her cause better than Sir Henry's, and not easily be induced to relinquish—

SIR HENRY: You'll see, now, this confounded woman will force me to marry her whether I will or not.

LADY EMILY: To be sure, as Colonel O'Donolan observes, a marriage would—

SIR HENRY: There, there! I told you so – (*Aside*) – a bold push for a husband, that, by Jupiter! Madam, it would be vain to use any ceremony upon the present occasion; you may be, and I dare say are, everything that is charming – but, we are not the masters of our affections, and I must inform you, that mine are irrevocably devoted to your amiable friend.

LADY EMILY: I don't comprehend you, Sir Henry; for whom do you take me?

SIR HENRY: For whom, but Mrs Belmore?

LADY EMILY: (*to* MRS BELMORE) So then, it seems I pass for you now?

MRS BELMORE: And why not, my dear Lady Emily, since you so lately contrived to make me pass for you?

SIR HENRY: What do I hear? Lady Emily! and you then, after all, are—

MRS BELMORE: The hateful Mrs Belmore.

SIR HENRY: (*kneeling*) O! how shall I ever atone for the injuries which I have done to you?

LADY EMILY: Rise, rise, Sir Henry; for I read in her looks, that you have gained your cause.

SIR HENRY: (*to* MRS BELMORE) Will you not deign to confirm the—

LADY EMILY: Why will you force her to look more silly than she does already? The thing is settled; say no more about it; and now, having ended a case in *law*, to the satisfaction, I hope, of all parties, I have one in that claims our immediate attention; and may the cause of poor Fitzharding terminate as happily as that of Belmore *versus* Chomley!   [*Exeunt*]

SCENE ii

A ward in the asylum

FITZHARDING *and* CECIL

FITZHARDING: She used to sing it, and it thrilled my very soul!

CECIL: Shall I sing it to you?

FITZHARDING: No, no; not you, not you: I could not bear it – yet let me hear the words; repeat them!

CECIL:

> 'Tears, such as tender fathers shed,
> Warm from my aged eyes descend,
> For joy – to think when I am dead,
> My son will have mankind his friend.'

FITZHARDING: No, no, no, not so;

> 'For joy – to think when I am dead,
> Cecil will have mankind her friend.'

—She used to sing it so, when I desired her – and Oh! so well – but she can sing it no more now; she is dead, she is dead! and we will go and weep upon her tomb – you will not leave me?

CECIL: (*weeping*) O, never, never, never!

FITZHARDING: (*looking wistfully in her face*) Poor thing! poor thing! pale, very pale; and *she* had such a bloom! you have promised not to leave me? The ruffians will, perhaps, attempt to drive you hence; but do not go, Oh! no; stay here, and talk with me the live-long day of Cecil.

CECIL: (*eagerly*) You love her still, then?

FITZHARDING: Ah! can a father cease to love his child? Assassins have stabbed, and vultures gnawed my flesh, morsel by morsel; but they have not yet reached the seat of life – feel, feel my heart is whole, still (*She lets her head sink upon his breast*) very, very pale!

CECIL: If you were to see your Cecil, should you – should you know her again?

FITZHARDING: (*recollecting*) Should I know her? O yes, yes; were she to appear before me with her golden ringlets playing luxuriantly about her face, her ethereal form all clad in virgin white, and her soft voice breathing these heavenly sounds which still vibrate in my heart, Oh! then, I could not be mistaken in her – but she is gone! she is there (*Pointing to the drawing of the tomb in his cell*) cold, cold and lifeless!

CECIL: But were she living, now to clasp your knees, as I do now, confess her fault, and with a penitent and humble heart solicit your forgiveness, what would you do?

FITZHARDING: (*furiously*) Do? I would strike the wanton lifeless to my feet!

CECIL: Oh horrible!

FITZHARDING: No, no; not if it give you pain – no, no; if she *could* come again, the only vengeance I would take, should be to clasp her to my heart, and ratify the pardon she implored—

Enter STANLY

STANLY: (*to* CECIL) Your presence is immediately required in the adjoining chamber.

FITZHARDING: Ah! whither are you going? And can *you* leave me too?

CECIL: I will soon return, my Father.

FITZHARDING: Father! Father! Ha, ha, ha! 'tis long, 'tis very long, since I have heard that appellation, and in such a tone – repeat it – O! repeat it!

CECIL: Farewell, my Father!

FITZHARDING: Ha! ha! ha! but you'll return; O! say you will – you have been too long away – I cannot longer live without you.

CECIL: (*delighted*) O! heard you that?

STANLY: Come, come; but a few hours, and with Heaven's assistance, all your distress will vanish. (STANLY *forces* CECIL *gently off*)

FITZHARDING: She's gone; again she has abandoned me – is this another dream? once before, I thought I saw a form resembling Cecil: I pressed her to my heart: this very day, she sheltered me from ruffians – but, for all that, she is dead; she's there! – (*Points to the tomb*) – There, and my own for ever! O Cecil! Cecil! Cecil!—

[*Exit into his cell*]

SCENE iii

An apartment in the asylum

Enter LORD GLENTHORN

GLENTHORN: What have I heard! am I myself infected, or have I really beheld my Cecil and her frantic father? and could I view the frightful spectacle occasioned by my crime, and not expire upon the spot! Inhuman Stanly! were not the agonies of remorse sufficiently acute, but you must superadd[21] this scene of horror? should Cecil scorn my unfeigned repentance, I have no remedy, no hope for this world or the next.

Enter STANLY *and* CECIL

STANLY: Grieve not, that you must leave him now – the impression given to his mind, will be a powerful auxiliary in Lady Emily's plan; while you remain here, I will give orders for his immediate conveyance to my house, and trust to providence, to crown our efforts with success.   [*Exit* STANLY]

CECIL: Success! alas! I have not deserved it – at my Father, whose life has been one scene of pure unsullied goodness, for his sake, Heaven may extend its mercy, and change our present misery, to joy unutterable – (LORD GLENTHORN *timidly advances*) – What do I see? Delaval, here! this shock at least might have been spared me.

GLENTHORN: Cecil!

CECIL: Ah! leave me – 'tis not my wish to upraid you, Delaval, therefore leave me – lest suffering under anguish, great, sure, as ever human breast endured, I vent my feelings in reproach and bitterness.

GLENTHORN: Spare me not, Cecil; pour deepest curses on my head – I have deserved them all.

CECIL: No, Delaval; in my acutest moments of affliction, when scarcely mistress of my desperate thoughts, I have recollected that you were the father of my infant, and all my maledictions have been changed to fervent prayers for your repentance.

GLENTHORN: Those prayers were heard, my Cecil: truer contrition never touched a sinner's heart, than that which Heaven has awakened here – by that remorse, and for our tender infant's sake, let me conjure you—

CECIL: Delaval, desist! nor, by appealing to a mother's weakness, strive to shake a resolution which is now irrevocable.

GLENTHORN: At your suspicions of my sincerity, Cecil, I have no right to feel offended – your worst reproaches cannot wound more keenly than those of my own self-accusing conscience! but by my regenerated heart I swear, that every future hour of my life shall prove my truth, every faculty of my soul be bent to repair the wrongs that I have done you, and bring back peace and comfort to your heart.

CECIL: Peace! O, cast a look within yon cell, behold my father, driven to madness by my guilt, then tell me where a wretch like me should look for peace! That your sentiments have undergone a change so conducive to your future welfare, Heaven knows how truly I rejoice! – for me, I have imposed a sacred duty upon myself, to which every instant, every thought, must be assiduously dedicated – to your protection I dare now assign our child; it would have eased my afflicted heart to have wept over him sometimes; but to comfort I have no claim, and even that sorrowful consolation I will forego for his advantage – receive him, Delaval! teach him to shun the vices

which have destroyed our happiness, and never, Oh! never let him
know the wretched being to whom he owes existence!

GLENTHORN: (*striking his forehead*) Fool! Fool! what a treasure hast
thou cast away!   [*Exeunt severally*]

SCENE iv

A room in STANLY's *house*

Enter O'DONOLAN *and* SIR HENRY CHOMLEY

O'DONOLAN: Had I not sworn to renounce all jealousy for the future, I
should feel inclined to give way to something like ill-humour,
during this separation from Lady Emily; and how you can be so
composed under your privation, is to me marvellous! I'm sure I
shan't be able to keep my temper long.

SIR HENRY: I tell you what, my friend, 'tis a devilish bad one, and the
sooner you get rid of it the better; but the truth is, I am too happy to
be out of humour at anything that can happen – and had you
employed yourself as I have done, you would have had no leisure for
irritability – the secret of happiness, is occupation, and the true art
of attaching man or woman, the constant endeavour to make
yourself useful – take my word for it, a woman of spirit soon grows
tired of a fellow who can do nothing but languish and look soft –
there's too little variety in sighs and groans; for, when you have
breathed your longest Oh! you have reached your climax, and
there's an end of you.

O'DONOLAN: And how the devil can I help looking soft! Well, that you
should choose to walk into a dirty lumber-room and tumble over
fusty old pictures and broken china, when you ought to have been
elevated to the seventh heaven with delight, is past my comprehen-
sion.

SIR HENRY: I think it good policy to be concerned as far as possible in
everything which gives pleasure to others; and trifling as the
circumstance may appear, my having assisted in hunting out the
family pictures, if they should contribute to Mr Fitzharding's
recovery, will not only ensure me Lady Emily's good wishes, but I
shall have the satisfaction also of knowing, that I had some little
share in producing so desirable an event; and I hope that's better
than being, like you, happy till you are quite miserable.

Enter LADY EMILY

LADY EMILY: Come, come; everything is in readiness – Fitzharding is arrived, and though hitherto kept in total darkness, has been perfectly tranquil – the room that we have selected for our scene of action, is, in every particular, restored to the same state it was in when he himself inhabited this house. My own agitation is scarcely less than that of Cecil; who, flushed with anxiety and wild with hope, is looking more animatedly beautiful than she could have done even in her days of happiness – pray come, for the moment of trial is at hand.

O'DONOLAN: Are there no more tables and chairs to move then? Ah, now, can't *I* make myself useful by making some sort of trouble?

LADY EMILY: I am afraid not, Colonel; so for the present, you must content yourself with being merely ornamental.

O'DONOLAN: O then, that will suit me to a hair; for sure I can be that without any trouble at all.   [*Exeunt*]

SCENE V

A room in STANLY'*s house, hung with pictures; a full length portrait of* CECIL, *playing upon the harp occupies the centre: it is covered by a green curtain.* FITZHARDING, STANLY, LADY EMILY, SIR HENRY CHOMLEY, MRS BELMORE, *and* O'DONOLAN, *discovered*

FITZHARDING: Yes, I remember now, 'twas there, on summer evenings I used to sit with one, too dearly loved, and watch the sunbeams sparkling in the stream.

SIR HENRY: And shall again, I hope, Sir.

FITZHARDING: Never, never; she was snatched from me by the damned artifices of a human fiend – Oh! never, never!

STANLY: Stung by remorse, and eager to repair the wrongs that he has done you – he comes to give her to your arms again, and crave your blessing on their union.

FITZHARDING: For shame, for shame! falsehood but ill becomes that silvered head.

STANLY: By Heaven—

FITZHARDING: You mock me, Sir; I tell you she is dead – Poor Cecil! Cold! cold! cold!

LADY EMILY: (*drawing back the curtain*) Has not this portrait some resemblance to her?

FITZHARDING: Ha! hide her, hide her! she has shot lightning through my veins! – and see, see, see, at her command, the spirits of departed joys flit quickly by, pointing and grinning at me as they pass – Oh! let me fly – (*As he is rushing off, she plays and sings 'Tears such as,' etc.*) – Why, yes, that voice! and yet, O, tell me, art thou real, or sent by Hell to tantalize and torture me?

CECIL: (*rising in the frame*) – Oh! my beloved father!

FITZHARDING: (*in ecstasy.*) – Ha! 'tis not illusion -- for by the thick pulsation of my heart, I feel 'tis she, my long-lost child, my much-loved, erring, and forgiven Cecil! (*They rush into each other's arms, then* CECIL *falls at his feet, and embraces his knees*)

LADY EMILY: This is a spectacle, on which even Heaven smiles – repentance, kneeling at the feet of Mercy!

[*The curtain falls, and the play concludes*]

NOTES

1 ... **glad enough to be civil**: In a manuscript of the play held in Lord Chamberlain's Collection the phrase continues: '... they were glad enough to be civil. Tradesmen are either the most abject or insolent beings in existence. Obsequious and grovelling till they have got you in their books; rude, pertinacious and unmerciful when your necessities oblige you to remain in them.'

2 **duns**: creditors.

3 **burgess**: citizen, particularly the inhabitant of a borough with full municipal rights.

4 **'bodes little comfort ... Miss Fitzharding'**: in manuscript held in Lord Chamberlain's Collection Jefferies adds the aside: '... I fear it bodes little comfort to Miss Fitzharding. Ah! he's as hard as nails.'

5 **this step**: in manuscript Delaval further comments that: '... the deranged state of my affairs requires that I should take this step and Cecil lives so much secluded and is so absolutely in ignorance of what is passing in the world that she will not have the remotest suspicion of changes in my situation.'

6 **the Bow-street officers**: policemen.

7 **Titian's graces**: Titian's painting of *Cupid Blindfolded* (dating from around 1565) is often referred to as 'The Three Graces':

> The Graces at the right hold Cupid's bow and arrows, while his mother, Venus (also regarded as one of the graces) binds his eyes so that he may not regain his weapons and stir up amorous misadventures in the world. The very nature of the blindfolding is associated with evil. Here the concept of the two Cupids (Eros and Anteros) is clearly presented. Anteros, the god of sensual love, receives the blindfold, while Eros, the god of mutual love, whispers in his mother's ear, as he urges her to make his brother harmless.

Harold E. Wetley, *The Paintings of Titian: volume three, The Mythological and Historical Paintings* (London: Phaidon, 1975: 131). Generally, in Greek mythology the three graces were the sisters Aglaia, Thalia and Euphrosyne, who bestowed beauty and charm, and were themselves, the embodiments of both.

8 *Exit Sir Henry*: in manuscript the groom has an additional speech: 'That's cool now – in master. I should like to know how I'm to find out this lady – Umph! 'twas Lady Something I'll take my oath; but if I remember what I wish I may be shot! I've forgot the name, that's certain; but I think I've got her description. – Plastered forehead, glass nose, one piercing eye, and lovely dimples on each side of her mouth, that's it, ha! ha! ha! Master said she was a fine figure, and egod, I'm of his mind for that.'

9 the Lady Abigail: a lady's maid – from a character in Beaumont and Fletcher's 1613 play, *The Scornful Lover*.

10 '. . . was dispensed with: in manuscript the text is slightly amended: 'MRS JEFFERIES: . . . and placed her in a quiet lodging till a licence could be procured.
STANLY: Oh! – I see – a common house with green blinds and a back door: the licence, I imagine, was dispensed with?'

11 '. . . has got the note, my Lady': in manuscript the text includes the following exchange:
'MRS JEFFERIES: Sir Henry's man has got the note, my Lady.
LADY EMILY: How did you know it was Sir Henry's servant? Mrs Jefferies: Why, I thought it was, so I determined to ask him. Lady Emily: (aside) How absolutely are we at the mercy of our servants. I have appointed Sir Henry to come . . .'

12 'I should find . . . but a shawl': in manuscript the scene is all the more melodramatic: '. . . I should find both her and the baby vanished. Such a bitter night too. She must have been perish'd before she got half way across the heath; for she took nothing with her but a shawl; and the snow was two feet deep under my window when I got up this morning.'

13 fagged out: exhausted, drained.

14 coxcombs: raffish, but conceited, persons.

15 '. . . favoured lover?': in manuscript the scene continues:
'LADY EMILY: . . . we should become the ridicule of all our acquaintances.

MRS BELMORE: Shall I write to Mr O'Donolan?

LADY EMILY: By no means; he would at once consider it as an acknowledgement that I thought myself in the wrong, which is a triumph I will not afford him.

MRS BELMORE: You would rather have him suppose then, that this Grenville is a favour'd lover?'

16 '. . . his arriving yet.': in manuscript Lady Emily comments: 'I am glad to see his impatience; it looks as if you entered into the spirit of the plot – but you forget that days at this time of year are not remarkable for length, and the fashion for making morning calls by moonlight, very much in favour his arriving yet. However, I must own, I don't find his ardour quite so raging as I expected; to be sure, the weather is against it, 'tis hardly reasonable to require a man to burn in a har frost.'

17 *Exit* MRS BELMORE: in manuscript Mrs Jefferies has an aside, wherein, after Mrs Belmore's exit, she comments: 'Well, this Chomley is a good looking fellow enough; and I think Lady Emily deserves some credit for turning him over to Mrs Belmore.'

18 Chancery: division of the High Court.

19 Æsculapius: the Greek god of medicine.

20 Hygeia: the Greek goddess of health.

21 superadd: add over and above, also take into consideration.

FRANCIS THE FIRST

an historical drama
BY FANNY KEMBLE
(1832)

DRAMATIS PERSONAE

Women

LOUISA OF SAVOY	the King's mother
MARGARET OF VALOIS	her daughter
FRANÇOISE DE FOIX	Lautrec's sister
FLORISE	her attendant
VARIOUS LADIES OF THE COURT	

Men

FRANCIS THE FIRST	King of France
CHARLES OF BOURBON CHARLES OF ALENÇON	Princes of the Blood
HENRI D'ALBRET CHABANNES VENDÔME	King of Navarre old generals
LAVAL LAUTREC BONNIVET VARENNES	French nobles
CLEMENT MAROT	a poet
TRIBOULET	the King's jester
GONZALES	a monk
PESCARA	a Spanish general
LAYVA	Governor of Pavia
NOBLES, PAGES, GUARDS, HERALDS, SOLDIERS	

Scene　At the Court of Francis I,
Paris; at the Chateau de
Foix; and on the battlefield
at Pavia, Italy.

Act I

A court of the Louvre

Enter VENDÔME *and* CHABANNES, *meeting the* DUKE
OF ALENÇON

VENDÔME: Good morrow to my lord of Alençon!
ALENÇON: Good morrow, noble sir. My lord Chabannes,
  You are right welcome back to court again:
  I pray you, Vendôme, is the King returned
  From tennis yet?
VENDÔME: My lord, as I passed through
  The gallery, I saw the royal train
  Dismount, and now the King holds private converse
  With the Queen's confessor: a moment since,
  I saw them both enter the Queen's apartment,
  In very earnest and impassioned talk;
  And, as I think, the Duke de Bourbon's name
  Full many a time escaped their anxious lips.
CHABANNES: The Queen's confessor! – what! old Father Jerôme?
ALENÇON: Oh no! old Father Jerôme, rest his soul,
  Is dead. This man (between ourselves I speak it),
  To me, seems rather a mysterious minister,
  And secret instrument, than a confessor.
VENDÔME: Strange to say, he is a Spaniard,
  And, stranger yet, he hath not been at court
  But a brief space, which renders his estate
  (Being so trusted by the Queen) a riddle,
  Whereat we guess in vain. She is not wont
  To doff her wariness[1] on slight acquaintance;
  Yet is this monk for ever with her; holding
  In full possession her most secret counsels.
CHABANNES: To me, my lords, who newly am returned
  To court, all this seems passing strange indeed:
  With greater wonder though, Vendôme, I learn
  De Bourbon is recalled from Italy.
ALENÇON: 'Tis not the absent only are amazed,

You do but share the wonder of the town;
All note the strange event, none know the cause
And we have yet to learn what fault or folly—
VENDÔME: Your pardon, sir, but 'tis not very like
That the young hero, who at Marignan
Did deeds of war and wisdom so combine,
That nothing short a kingdom could reward
His merit, now should fail in either point.
ALENÇON: This problem, sir,
Surpasses my poor wit; and all I know
Is, that the duke is coming home again;
And that an eager expectation runs
Before his path, to see how he will bear
This sudden mandate, and how be received
At court.
CHABANNES: Look, here comes one in haste, methinks,
That should be my old friend and comrade
Triboulet.

Enter TRIBOULET

TRIBOULET: Gentles, beseech ye leave me passing room;
Most worshipful sir, I am right glad to see you!
CHABANNES: That is a joy reciprocal.
Good fool, how hast thou fared, since last we parted?
TRIBOULET: Indifferent well, my lord; I thank ye, though very
indifferent; but still as well as may be considering tides and times,
and things as they were, and things as they are, and sundry other
things – heigh ho!
CHABANNES: What! melancholy, eh! poor fellow?
TRIBOULET: Oh! sir, very melancholy. I should think I was dying in
right earnest, an it were not—
ALENÇON: That he eats like a pig, and sleeps like a dormouse.
TRIBOULET: Sir, your comparisons are very beastly, and that's the best
that can be said of them.
ALENÇON: The best is bad, and far from civil, then.
TRIBOULET: The farther from civil, the nearer to your speech.
CHABANNES: There, never anger thee at truth, good fool:—
But tell me where that foul fiend Melancholy
Hath driven the damask of thy rosy cheeks?
VENDÔME: Marry, it needs no search into his nose:
Which juts from out the main land of his face,
Like some peaked promontory, on whose verge
The beacon light its warning blaze advances.

ALENÇON: Well, but what makes thee sad?

TRIBOULET: E'en that which makes you glad.

ALENÇON: And what is that, sir Fool?

TRIBOULET: The Lord High Constable's return, sir Duke.

(D'ALENÇON turns on his heel, and walks up
the stage with VENDÔME)

CHABANNES: My lord of Alençon, you have your answer—
And why doth that affect thee?

TRIBOULET: Why, sir, thus:
The Duke de Bourbon is a worthy gentleman,
Fine fighter, wise statesman, and great fool—

CHABANNES: How now, sir Triboulet, a fool! – a man who gives
His blood—

TRIBOULET   To the earth.

CHABANNES: And his counsel—

TRIBOULET   To the air.

CHABANNES: For his country—

TRIBOULET: No, for that; (Snaps his fingers) why how ye stare, is it not
so? – And doth not the event prove that he was a fool?

CHABANNES: (aside) O wisdom! thou hast kissed the lips of idiots,
And gemmed the motley[2] with thy precious pearls!

(ALENÇON and VENDÔME appear to be observing
someone in the distance – they come forward)

ALENÇON: Oh yes, 'tis he! now, by this living light,
There is no nauseous reptile crawls the earth
That I so loathe at this same Bonnivet!

CHABANNES: Is that de Bonnivet, that plumed thing!
So sparkling and so brave in his attire.
Who treads disdainfully the upholding earth?

TRIBOULET: Oh, that he hath done long on all his upholders.

CHABANNES: Is that the brother of King Francis' tutor,
Whom I remember well a page at court?

ALENÇON: Sir, he is now the King's prime minister.

CHABANNES: Sir! – tut – impossible!

TRIBOULET: He means the Queen's prime minister.

VENDÔME: Why, aye, that's something nearer to the mark.

Enter DE BONNIVET – he bows haughtily to them – they
return his salute in the same manner

TRIBOULET: (staring in his face) He hath a very bright eye, and a very
high brow, and very handsome teeth – (While he says this, DE
BONNIVET threateningly obliges him to retreat step by step, until he

gets behind VENDÔME, *when he adds*) – By reason of all which, no
woman need miscarry that looks at him.

DE BONNIVET: (*aiming a blow at* TRIBOULET: *with his glove*)
Hold thy fool's tongue!

TRIBOULET (*showing himself from behind* ALENÇON) That we may
listen to thine? Now, for aught I know, thou mayst be the most
learned of the two, seeing thy brother was a pedagogue.

(DE BONNIVET *draws his sword, and rushes upon*
TRIBOULET; VENDÔME *and* CHABANNES *hold him back.*
D'ALENÇON *places himself before* TRIBOULET)

VENDÔME: For manhood, sir, put up your sword: he knows not what
he says.

CHABANNES: He is a fool! an idiot!

TRIBOULET: The King's fool, sir, the King's fool, and no idiot!

BONNIVET: King's fool or not, he shall not fool it with me,
Or, by the Lord! I'll make him find his brains.

TRIBOULET: Sir, if you knock them out, I bequeath them to you; you're
poor in such commodities.

BONNIVET: Unhand me, lords!

Enter MARGARET DE VALOIS *followed by* CLEMENT

MARGARET: How now, what coil is here! My lords, I thought not
To meet foul discord in such company.
Gentlemen, if a lady's voice hath power
To win your hands from their ungentle purpose,
Pray you, put up your swords. Why so, I thank ye.
And now, what, may I ask, in this assembly
Was cause of such affray?

TRIBOULET: My wit, sweet mistress.

CLEMENT: Then drew thy wit more points than ever it uttered.

MARGARET: Truly such origin doth honour to your quarrel.
And if whole nations fought for ten long years
For no more cause than a light woman's love,
We well may pardon, nay approve, four heroes
Who fall to fighting on a jester's words.

ALENÇON: Madam, *your* words are sharp, and came they not
From lips, where soft sweet smiles have made their home,
They would, indeed, be terrible: but now,
We even bless reproachful oracles
That breathe from such a shrine.

TRIBOULET: (*aside to him*) Oh, excellent!
Where didst thou con that dainty speech, I pray thee?

(ALENÇON *pushes him angrily away*, MARGARET *bows*

to VENDÔME, *and extends her hand to* CHABANNES)

MARGARET: Most worthy sir, you're welcome back again
  To our fair court.

CHABANNES: Lady, can you rejoice
  To see grey hairs come bowing in your train?
  Doth spring cry welcome to the hoary winter?

MARGARET: Oh, sir, your winter so hath crowned itself
  With bays and laurels – glorious evergreens,
  Still smiling in the sunshine of fair fame,
  That 'tis but like a second, longer spring,
  Born of the growth of years destined to flourish
  As bright and fresh for ever. – Who is that,
  Standing behind my Lord of Alençon?
  I pray you, sir, come forth into the light.
  Unless the shame of your encounter—

BONNIVET: (*kneeling to kiss her hand*)
  It was not shame, but the broad dazzling sun,
  That shone so fully in my sight, fair lady,
  That I was fain to shade my eyes.

MARGARET: Indeed!
  You said the same last night, if you remember,
  After the sun had set.

BONNIVET: Oh, when
  Do those bright orbs, his rivals, cease to shed
  Such floods of light? – when will those beaming eyes
  Grant respite, which the sunset gives us not?

CLEMENT: (*aside to* TRIBOULET)
  He understands the business, doth he not?

MARGARET: These eyes, I trust, are far less powerful—
  Their sphere is bounded, happily for you;
  And if their light be so insufferable,
  It hath a narrow compass, you may find
  Relief from such a radiance easily.

TRIBOULET: (*aside to* CLEMENT)
  I'faith, and she understands it, too – see how she waves him off.

MARGARET: Chabannes,
  Will not the tourney[3] that my brother holds
  Today, in honour of the Duke's return,
  Be favoured by your presence?

CHABANNES: Gracious Madam,
  We all intend, as I believe, to be there:
  I to look on, and criticise as age

Ever will do, drawing comparisons,
'Twixt that which is, and that which hath been once.

MARGARET: Envious comparisons! say, are they not?
Surely the world alters not every day,
That those, who played their parts but some score years
Gone by, should cry out, 'How the times are altered!'—
I do appeal to thy philosophy;
Say, is it so, Chabannes?

CHABANNES: In sober truth, then, in philosophy,
Since thus your Grace commands, I do believe
That at our feet the tide of time flows on
In strong and rapid course; nor is one current
Or rippling eddy liker to the rest,
Than is one age unto its predecessor:
Men still are men, the stream is still a stream,
Through every change of changeful tide and time;
And 'tis, I fear, only one partial eye
That lends a brighter sunbeam to the wave
On which we launched our own adventurous bark.

MARGARET: Oh fair confession! thou art but half a soldier—

CHABANNES: But half a soldier, and no more, fair madam.

TRIBOULET: Listen: one quarter of a good soldier is valour, the second
quarter prudence, and the remaining half (the biggest half by far)
wrong-headedness – now, lacking the latter half, thou art, as the
princess saith, but half a soldier.

MARGARET: Why so; I am content my meaning thus
Should be interpreted, although 'twas not
My thought. Come thou with me, sir Fool,
I've business for thee in the Banquet-hall:
You, gentlemen, farewell, until the tourney;
'Till then, all good attend you, and I pray
Keep the king's peace, an it be possible.

[*Exeunt* MARGARET, CLEMENT, *and* TRIBOULET
on one side; the rest on the other]

SCENE ii

The QUEEN MOTHER'S *apartment*

The QUEEN *enters precipitately*

QUEEN: So – I am glad Gonzales is not here;
   I would not even he should see me thus.
   Now out upon this beating heart, these temples,
   That throb and burn so; and this crimson glow
   That rushes o'er my brow: now, by this light,
   I had not dreamed so much weak womanhood
   Still slumbered in my breast! – I must remember me—
   Mother of France, and well nigh Queen of it,
   I'll even bear my love as royally,
   As I have borne my power – the time is near,
   Oh very near, when he will kneel again
   Before my feet – the conqueror to the conquered!—
   I am ashamed of this ill timed relapse—
   This soft unnerving power which thus enthrals me.
               Enter GONZALES
   Thou art right welcome, by my word, Gonzales!
   Where be those parchments?
GONZALES: Noble madam, here.
QUEEN: Hast thou drawn out the plan of the possessions?
GONZALES: So please your grace, I have. Pardon me, madam,
   I fear you are not well; your cheek is pale,
   And your lip quivers – is your highness ill?
QUEEN: Hush! *'twas* a trumpet, was it not? – and now—
   Surely it is the tramp of horses' hoofs
   That beat the ground thus hurriedly and loud—
   I pray thee, father, throw the casement wide—
   The air is stifling.
GONZALES: I do entreat your highness to be seated;
   I never saw you thus o'ercome before:
   You tremble, madam.
QUEEN: (*rising*)
   Do I so, indeed?
   I thank thee for that word – it hath revived me:
   I'm very well – I do not tremble now—

By heaven I never heard that word before:
It hath a wondrous virtue! Pray thee, father,
What think the people of Bourbon's return?
GONZALES: Madam, the summer clouds
   That flit across the heavens are not more various,
   More strange, and different in shape and colour,
   Than are the opinions born from his recall.
QUEEN: But thou – but thou—
   Accustomed as thou art to thread the mazes
   Of dark intriguing policy – how thinkst *thou*?
GONZALES: Accustomed, as your highness should have said,
   To read the will and wisdom of your eyes,
   And watch, for your commands, each meaning look,
   If I might say it, madam – I should think
   That much indeed lay in this mystery;
   For your eye speaks strange things.
QUEEN: How sayest thou—
   This hand is passing fair, is it not, Gonzales?
GONZALES: Madam! – 'tis not for me to estimate
   The hand that kings have prized above their kingdom.
QUEEN: Psha! fool! Oh, rather say the hand that held
   The sovereign rule over their kingdoms. Now,
   Mark me attentively. This woman's hand,
   That but this moment trembled with alarm—
   This fair, frail hand, hath firmly held the reins
   Of this vast empire for full many a year:
   This hand hath given peace and war to Europe—
   This hand hath placed my son upon his throne—
   This hand hath held him there – this hand it was
   That signed the warrant for Bourbon's recall.
GONZALES: Amazement!
QUEEN: Ay! this woman's hand, led by a woman's heart.
   Now hear me, thou; for to thy secrecy
   I will confide what none, save only thou,
   Have known – *must* know. Note well the latter word!
   It is because I love the Duke de Bourbon
   With the strong love of such a soul as mine,
   That I have called him from his government,
   To lift him to the dizziest height of power
   This hand can grant, or kingdom can confer.
GONZALES: (*aside*) Perdition on her! this will ruin all!
   (*Aloud*) – And will you tell him of your love?

QUEEN: I will.
 Nay, answer not – I have resolved on it—
 Thou wouldst but waste thy words, and anger me.
 I never yet knew friend or minister,
 But they were ever readier to advise
 Than act.
GONZALES: Now, madam, by the holy mass,
 You shall not find it so. I've not forgot
 My fame and honours were bestowed by you;
 And rather take them back – nay, life itself—
 Than taunt me with unwillingness to serve you.
QUEEN: Why, so! I did but jest. In sooth, Gonzales,
 I know thou art as good, in a bad way,
 As any faithful son of the Holy Church
 Need be.
GONZALES: But does the King—
QUEEN: Out, bungler! out!
 The King was very dutiful, and well
 Believed what I strenuously assured.
 I told him that the Duke de Bourbon's power
 Was growing strongly in the Milanese;
 Urged his return; and showed him how, when distant,
 The high ambition of the Bourbon's mind
 Was far less checked than here, beneath the shadow
 Of the throne, and so he was recalled—
   (*Trumpets without – shouts of* 'DE BOURBON!')
 And now he is arrived – hark how the trumpets
 Bray themselves hoarse with sounding welcome to him!
 Oh, could I join my voice to yonder cry,
 By heavens I think its tones would rend the welkin[4]
 With repetition of the hero's name,
 Who's dearer far to me than life or fame.

              [*Exit*]

GONZALES: In love with Bourbon! by this living light,
 My mission here is well nigh bootless, then.
 Now might I back to Spain, since Charles' objects
 Are all defeated by this woman's passion,
 Were there not yet another task, the dearest,
 The labour that is life – mine own revenge!
 Till I have reached that goal, my foot shall never
 Tread its own soil; or, freed from its disguise—
 This noiseless sandal of slow-gaited priesthood—

Resume its manly garb. Oh, very long
Is the accomplishment; but it is sure—
Sure as the night that curtains up each day—
Sure as that death which is the end of life.
Lie still, thou thirsty spirit, that within
Callst for the blood that *shall* allay thy craving!
Down, down with thee, until the hour be come
When I can fling this monkish treachery by,
Rush on my prey, and let my soul's hot flame
Lick up his blood, and quench it in his life!
Time, and the all-enduring soul that never
Shrinks from the trial, be my speed! and nought
My hope, my spur, my instrument, my end,
Save hate – eternal hate – immeasurable hate!

                                                              [*Exit*]

SCENE iii

The PRINCESS MARGARET'S *chamber*

Enter MARGARET *and* TRIBOULET

MARGARET: It is the hour of tourney. Triboulet,
     Go thou unto the Queen, and tell her grace,
     That, if it please her, I'll attend her thither.

                                              [*Exit* TRIBOULET]

He is returned! he will be there! and yet
Though meeting, after long eventful absence—
We shall not in our meeting be half blest:
A dizzy, whirling throng will be around us,
'Mid whose loud jar the still small voice of love,
Whose accents breathe their soft enchantment best
In whispered sighs, or but half-whispered words,
Will die unheard. Oh that we thus should meet!
But, then, there is love's eye to flash his thought
Into a language, whose rich eloquence
Beggars all voice; our eyes at least may meet,
And change, like messengers, the loving freight
That either heart sends forth.
                         Enter CLEMENT MARÔT
CLEMENT: So please you, madam,

The Queen hath bid me say that she will not
Grace with her sight the tournament today;
And as I came from her apartment hither,
I met the King, who bade me bear you word
He cannot yet unto the lists, but you,
And your fair train, had best ride quickly there,
And let the tilt commence; he will not tarry,
But join ye ere the first three blows be struck.

                                    [*Exit* CLEMENT]

MARGARET: 'Tis well, I will obey – 'Tis very strange
How much I fear my mother should perceive
De Bourbon's love for me – I know not why—
I dare not tell it her – she is a fearful spirit,
And stands so proudly over all her sex,
She surely ne'er hath known what 'tis to love.

                                            [*Exit*]

SCENE iv

The lists

Enter LAUTREC *and* LAVAL, *meeting*

LAUTREC: Well met, by this glad light, Laval! Will not
The Queen attend this tournament today?
LAVAL: No, sir, she's closeted with that grim holiness!
LAUTREC: That Spanish monk!
LAVAL: That walking mystery!
That man, to my mind, hath a villainous look.
I never met his eyes but they were glaring
Like some hyena's, or the devil's own;
And when I've spoken to him, I have seen
His lip, which as you know is ever pursed up
Into an humble simper of devotion,
Grow pale as death, and quiver, and instead
Of that same *sneaking* smile, it wore a sneer
That looked like ghastly and convulsive agony.
Once, I remember me, the Queen had sent
By me some mission to this confessor—
By chance, the Princess Margaret, by whose side
He stood, let fall a jewel from her finger;

Both stooped, and as we did, our hands encountered—
He started back as though a serpent stung him—
By'r Lady, but I would not be the man
To wrong that surly monk: is it not strange,
That when I gaze on him it seems as though
I knew him, and had seen him oft before?
LAUTREC: Nay, in thy dreams it must have been, Laval;
But leave this theme, and tell me what it is
Thou wouldst with me?
LAVAL: This is no fitting place
To speak what I would say at greater length;
But love prompts me, once more, to urge my suit—
My unanswered suit.
LAUTREC: Once more I tell thee, then,
My sister shall be thine, I have said it—
Alençon!
Enter ALENÇON
LAVAL: Thoust tarried long at tennis.
ALENÇON: Why, the King
Still loitered on with racket in his hand;
And Bonnivet vaunting their mutual prowess.
LAUTREC: 'Tis much past noon.
ALENÇON: He will be here anon.
For as I rode, I passed him with his train,
The gathering crowd thronging and clamouring
Around him, stunning him with benedictions
And stifling him with love and fumes of garlic!
He, with the air he knows so well to don,
With cap in hand, and his thick chestnut hair
Fanned from his forehead, bowing to his saddle,
Smiling and nodding, cursing at them too
For hindering his progress – while his eye,
His eagle eye, well versed in such discernment,
Roved through the crowd; and ever lighted, where
Some pretty ankle, clad in woollen hose,
Peeped from beneath a short round petticoat,
Or where some wealthy burgher's buxom dame,
Decked out in all her high-day splendour, stood
Showing her gossips the gold chain, which lay
Cradled upon a bosom, whiter far
Than the pure lawn that kerchieft it.
But how is not the joust begun? – his Majesty—

LAUTREC: Nay, it began when first his order reached us;
  Already hath one combat been decided
  'Twixt Jouy and de Varennes; and the latter,
  Proving the conqueror, in yonder tent
  Now rests him for awhile: he will come forth
  When next the trumpets sound. Wilt thou, Laval,
  Try fortune in the lists?
LAVAL: Oh, not today,—
  Not before her, beneath whose eyes defeat
  Were worse than death – no, not today.
LAUTREC: Nay, then, de Varennes shall not loiter there
  Longer in proud expectance of a rival—
  I will encounter him. Herald! what ho!
  There is my gauntlet – bear to Count de Varennes
  A fair defiance! Bid my page lead round
  My charger, let your trumpets sound a blast,
  And raise the escutcheon[5] of our ancient house
  Before the tent.

> [*Exit into the lists. Shouts and acclamations
> without, and trumpets*]

> *Enter* FRANCIS, CHABANNES, VENDÔME, BONNIVET,
> CLEMENT MARÔT, TRIBOULET, *and Courtiers*

OMNES: Long live the King! Long live great Francis!
FRANCIS: Now are we heartily ashamed to think
  That we have robbed our excellent good people
  Of any portion of the day's rejoicing!
  We fear we're somewhat past the appointed time.
TRIBOULET: An hour or so, not more.
FRANCIS: Curse on that ceaseless clock – thy tongue!
TRIBOULET: It goes right, though, for once.
FRANCIS: If we have caused the joust to be retarded,
  Which we sent word should not be so, we trust
  Our faithful subjects will forgive the offence
  In favour of the cause – their own dear interests
  Having withheld us in deep council from
  Their well-beloved presence, which to us
  Is like the sunshine of a summer's day—
  We were detained by weighty matters.
TRIBOULET: Ay,
  A tennis-ball, was it not? There, never frown,
  I'll spare thee – I'll be silent.
FRANCIS: On with the combats!

Chabannes, 'tis long since such a joust has been
Honoured by your good presence.
CHABANNES: True, my liege;
   Since I left France, though, many a time and oft
   We've run a charge against Colonna's knights,
   Had not disgraced the fair eyes that look down
   Upon this bloodless mimicry of war. (*Shouts*)
   But, see! the gates unclose – Lautrec is conqueror
         (*Shouts and trumpets.* FRANÇOISE DE FOIX *rises,
         and leans forward with every mark of intense interest*)
FRANCIS: De Bonnivet, who is yon lady? look—
   In front of the Princess's balcony?
   Is she not passing fair?
BONNIVET: Indeed, my liege,
   She's very fair. I do not know her, though.
   (*To* LAVAL) Who is yon lady, leaning forth, Laval?
LAVAL: Count Lautrec's sister.
FRANCIS: Had a limner's[6] hand
   Traced such a heavenly brow, and such a lip,
   I would have sworn the knave had dreamt it all
   In some fair vision of some fairer world.
   See how she stands, all shrined in loveliness;
   Her white hands clasped; her clustering locks thrown back
   From her high forehead; and in those bright eyes
   Tears! radiant emanations! drops of light!
   That fall from those surpassing orbs as though
   The starry eyes of heaven wept silver dew.
   (*To* LAVAL) Is yonder lady married, sir?
LAVAL: My liege,
   Not yet; but still her hand is bound in promise—
   She is affianced.
FRANCIS: And to whom?
LAVAL: To me, sire.
FRANCIS: Indeed! (*Aside to* BONNIVET)
   Methinks I was too passionate in my praise,
   Eh? Bonnivet – and yet how fair she is!
                  (*Trumpets and shouts*)
         Enter LAUTREC *and* DE VARENNES *from the lists*
BONNIVET: The time is well nigh spent,
   And yet no stir of arms in token yet
   Of any other knight, whose envious prowess
   Disputes the prize which Lautrec else may claim.

FRANCIS: Let him not claim it, though, for 'tis not his;
  And, by this light, *shall* not be his, while I
  Can strike one blow for it. Behold, Count Lautrec,
  Another combatant awaits thee, here!
  Another bids thee halt on triumph's threshold,
  And strive once more for victory. What, ho!
  Unfurl our royal standard to the wind,
  And let our *fleur-de-lys*, that oft have shadowed
  The bloody battle-field, bloom over the tourney.
LAUTREC: The King! I yield!
FRANCIS: Not so, sir, if you please;
  We'd show that we can run a lance as well
  As any other gentlemen: come on!

                   [*Exeunt* LAUTREC *and the* KING]

FRANÇOISE: How bravely does war's plumed majesty
  Become him, as he vaults upon his steed!
  His crimson crest waving upon the air
  Like Victory's ruddy favours! on they go—
  Now quakes the earth beneath their chargers' hoofs,
  That whirl around, taking their vantage space;
  Now each fierce steed bends on his haunches down,
  Ready to rush his headlong course; each knight
  Springs from his seat, and rising in the stirrups,
  Directs his rested lance; on, on, they go,
  Flashing and thundering! Ah! the King's unhorsed.

      (*Shouts within the lists* – '*Long live the King!*')

BONNIVET: Madam, your loyal fears outran your eyes,
  Count Lautrec fell, but he received no hurt:
  The King is conqueror!
TRIBOULET: Ay, so I thought:
  Fortune's a true courtier.
CLEMENT: Now out on thee, unmannerly—
TRIBOULET: I meant to say courtiers are—
LAVAL: How now, jackanapes?[7]
TRIBOULET: Well, well, what I meant to say is, that I never yet saw the
  King worsted in a fight.
BONNIVET: Surely not because—
TRIBOULET: Umph! because broken pates[8] are better than broken
  fortunes, and ye know it full well!

               (*Shouts and trumpets*)
     Enter FRANCIS, *followed by* LAUTREC, *heralds, pages,*
  and squires: MARGARET, FRANÇOISE, *and* LADIES, *descend*

and advance; the KING *kneels to* MARGARET, *who throws a gold chain round his neck*

Act II

SCENE i

An apartment of the PRINCESS MARGARET'S

Enter DE BOURBON, *followed by* MARGARET

BOURBON: A plague upon their tournaments, I say!
MARGARET: Nay then, de Bourbon, by my woman's word,
This must not be; oh, say it shall not be!
Say, thou wilt rein this hot, impatient mood,
For thy sake – no, for mine, for mine I meant:
Are we not twined together in our love?
What wonder then, if, speaking of myself,
Thy name was on my lips? – for my sake, Bourbon.
BOURBON: If thou wilt bid me journey to the moon
Upon a moth's wing, or wilt send me forth,
Belted and spurred, to fight some score of devils—
Or worse, wilt bid me with some twenty men
Turn out Colonna from the Milanese,
Say so; and by this light I'll *do* it too!
But, to submit to *this* – to bear all this –
To let a woman tear my laurels off—
And trample them – Hell! when I think on it!
Pshaw! never fix those dangerous eyes on me,
And clasp thy hands – I say –
MARGARET: She is my mother!
BOURBON: I'faith I've often doubted of that truth;
Thou art not like her, for the which thank heaven!
MARGARET: I *can* be like her though, my lord, in this:
Not to endure the licence of your tongue.
If headlong passion urge you, sir, beyond
The bounds of prudence, look that you control it,
Nor vent bold thoughts in bolder words to me;
Else you may chance to find—
BOURBON: She *is* thy mother?
Nay, smooth that brow, thou art too like the Queen;
And in those soft blue eyes, whose orbs reflect
Heaven's light with heaven's own purity, let not

The stormy gleam of anger e'er flash forth!
I had thought, Margaret, that love forgot
All ranks and all distinctions?

MARGARET: Ay, so it doth.

All ties, the world, its wealth, its fame, or fortune,
Can twine; but never those of nature, Bourbon.
So mine can give up all, save the first bond
My heart e'er knew – the love of those who gave
Life, and the power to love; those early links
Lie wreathed like close-knit fibres round my heart,
Never to sever thence till my heart break.

BOURBON: Lo! at thy feet I sue for pardon, sweet!

By thine own purity, thou virgin lily!
Thou flower of France! forgive the word that broke
Too hastily from my rash lips; which thus,
Having offended, will do penance now
Upon this marble shrine, my lady-love.

                                        (Kisses her hand)

MARGARET: A goodly penitent! Nay, never kneel,

And look so pitiful – there, I forgive thee.
But, Bourbon, by the faith of our sworn love,
I do implore thee to bear with my mother.

BOURBON: Pshaw!—

MARGARET: Why, look now, there's your brow dark and con-
tracted—

I see the passion flashing in your eyes;
You will *not* think of me, and bear with her?

BOURBON: If I could think of thee, and not see her—

Or think of thee, and not hear her, why, then—
Well, patience, and kind thoughts of thee befriend me!
And I will do my best to second them.

MARGARET: Go you to meet my mother now?

BOURBON: This hour

Love stole from duty to bestow on thee;
And now I must attend upon the Queen.

MARGARET: See you observe my lesson.

BOURBON: Fear me not;

Oh! I'll be wonderfully calm and patient.

MARGARET: (aside) Methinks I'll try thee. (Aloud) – How if she
should ask
Some question of your late left government?
I see you're very calm already! How

If she should speak of a fit successor?
Most patient! Lautrec now, or Bonnivet?
BOURBON: Confusion light upon them! Bonnivet?
And Lautrec? Beardless boys! whose maiden swords
Have not yet blushed with one red drop of blood;
Whose only march hath been a midnight measure,
Whose only field hath been a midnight masque;
Is it for these, and their advancement, I
Have watched, have toiled, have fought, have bled, have conquered;
Rushed over fields strewed with the dead and dying,
Swam streams that ran all curdled with the blood
Of friend and foe, stood in the bristling breach,
And in the hour of death and desolation
Won never fading victories for France?
Shall the Queen's minions – by this living light—
MARGARET: Oh, patient gentleman! how calm he is!
Now in those flaming eyes, and scornful lips,
I read how well my lesson profits thee.
Thou shalt not to the Queen in this hot mood.
BOURBON: I'faith I must; the storm is over now;
And having burst, why, I shall be the calmer.
Farewell, sweet monitress! I'll not forget.
MARGARET: Oh, but I fear—
BOURBON: Fear not – she is thy mother!

[*Exeunt severally*]

SCENE ii

An apartment of the QUEEN MOTHER's

The QUEEN *is discovered writing. Enter* GONZALES

GONZALES: So please your highness, the Duke de Bourbon
Attends your grace.
QUEEN: Give him admittance straight.   [*Exit* GONZALES]
Now then to try the mettle of his soul,
And tempt him with the glitter of a crown.
                    Enter BOURBON
BOURBON: Madam, I humbly kiss your highness's hands.
QUEEN: I thank you, sir; and though last night's blithe close
Was hardly rest to one o'er marched before,

I trust you are recovered from the weariness
Of your long journey.

BOURBON (*aside*) Pray heaven, she go no further with that theme!
(*Aloud*) I thank your grace, but owing to the speed
Enjoined by those who penned my – my recall—
My journey was a short one.

QUEEN: Did ye not rest at Chantelle?

BOURBON: Ay, good madam.

QUEEN: Short as you hold your march, my lord, and lightly
As you think fit to speak of it, I trow
It was swift riding to reach Paris yesterday.

BOURBON: (*aside*) Hell! – how she hangs upon the cursed subject.
(*Aloud*) To me both time and road seem short, indeed,
From a proud kingdom back to a poor dukedom.

QUEEN: My lord, there is much bitterness in that!

BOURBON: Bitterness! madam – oh, I do not doubt
There were high, weighty reasons warranted
My being thus recalled from Italy:
And those same weighty reasons will, no doubt,
Point out a fit successor to me also.

QUEEN: There is much bitterness in *that*, my lord—
Your mind is apt to start at fancied wrongs,
And makes a shadow where no substance is.

BOURBON: Your grace will pardon me; but hitherto
We have not seen such payment given to service;
Can governments be wrested from a man
Unheard – nay, unaccused, without a cause?

QUEEN: No, sir, they cannot – but might not the cause
Have been your future profit and advancement,
Instead of your disgrace?

BOURBON: Oh! we all know
The government of our Italian states
Must henceforth be a post for beardless soldiers,
Lacking wit wherewithal to win their honours,
Or courtiers lacking valour to deserve them.

QUEEN: I see the bent and mark of this discourse;
And though, be well assured, no other man
That breathes had thus far ventured in his speech—
Your daring I have borne with patiently.

BOURBON: Borne with me! Borne with me, forsooth!

QUEEN: Ay, sir,
Borne with you: further still – for in that sorrow

Hath fallen on your mind too bitterly,
And well nigh changed its bright and polished metal
With its corrosive touch – I've pitied you.
BOURBON: Wronged! borne with! pitied! By our Lady, madam—
This is too much.
QUEEN: Oh, sir, the King's advisers—
BOURBON: The King should hearken less to false advice,
And more to honest service, madam.
QUEEN: (aside) – Ha!
Now is the bridle thrown upon the steed;
That word, that one unguarded word, shall make
My victory, or thy perdition sure!
(Aloud) – I pass you that, my lord, you are too hot—
And now that I have curbed all proud respects
In kind indulgence of your hasty spleen,
Hear me: what if (I will repeat the question),
'Stead of ingratitude or envy, motives
With which you seem full well contented,
Being the spring of this your swift return,
Your quick preferment, and increase of glory
Had been alone consulted?
BOURBON: How so, madam?
QUEEN: Ever too rash in your belief, my lord,
You run before the truth – you've followers,
Eager and zealous partisans you have;
Think you it is impossible some friend
May haply have contrived this prompt recall,
To bring you nearer to a court, where you
May find paths unexplored as yet, in which
Ambition might discover such a prize,
As were worth winning?
BOURBON: I would have you know
De Bourbon storms, and does not steal his honours
And though your highness thinks I am ambitious,
(And rightly thinks) I am not so ambitious
Ever to beg rewards that I can win—
No man shall call me debtor to his tongue.
QUEEN: (rising) 'Tis proudly spoken; nobly too – but what,
What if a woman's hand were to bestow
Upon the Duke de Bourbon such high honours,
To raise him to such state, that grasping man,
Even in his wildest thoughts of mad ambition,

Never dreamt of a more glorious pinnacle?
BOURBON: I'd kiss the lady's hand, an she were fair.
　But if this world filled up the universe—
　If it could gather all the light that lives
　In every other star or sun, or world;
　If kings could be my subjects, and that I
　Could call such power and such a world my own,
　I would not take it from a woman's hand.
　Fame is my mistress, madam, and my sword
　The only friend I ever wooed her with.
　I hate all honours smelling of the distaff,
　And, by this light, would as lief wear a spindle[9]
　Hung round my neck, as thank a lady's hand
　For any favour greater than a kiss.
QUEEN: And how, if such a woman loved you – how
　If, while she crowned your proud ambition, she
　Could crown her own ungovernable passion,
　And felt that all this earth possessed, and she
　Could give, were all too little for your love?
　Oh good, my lord! there may be such a woman.
BOURBON: (aside) Amazement! can it be, sweet Margaret—
　That she has read our love? – impossible! – and yet –
　That lip never wore so sweet a smile! – it is,
　That look is pardon and acceptance! (aloud) – speak.
　　　　　　　(He falls at the QUEEN's feet)
　Madam, in pity speak but one word more,—
　Who is that woman?
QUEEN (throwing off her veil) I am that woman!
BOURBON (starting up) You, by the holy mass! I scorn your proffers—
　Is there no crimson blush to tell of fame
　And shrinking womanhood! Oh shame! shame! shame!
　　(The QUEEN remains clasping her hands to her temples, while
　　DE BOURBON walks hastily up and down: after a long pause
　　　　　　　the QUEEN speaks)
QUEEN: What ho! Marlon! St Evreux!
　　　　　　　Enter two gentlemen
　Summon my confessor!　　　　　　　　　　　　　　[Exeunt]
　– And now, my lord,
　I know not how your memory serves you;
　Mine fails not me – If I remember well,
　You made some mention of the King but now—
　No matter – we will speak of that anon.

Enter GONZALES

Sir, we have business with this holy father;
You may retire.
BOURBON: Confusion!
QUEEN: Are we obeyed?
BOURBON (*aside*)
Oh Margaret! – for thee! for thy dear sake!

[*Rushes out.*]

(*The* QUEEN *sinks into a chair*)
QUEEN: Refused and scorned! Infamy! – the word chokes me!
How now! why standst thou gazing at me thus?
GONZALES: I wait your highness' pleasure. – (*Aside*) So, all is well –
A crown hath failed to tempt him – as I see
In yonder lady's eyes.
QUEEN: Oh sweet revenge!
Thou art my only hope, my only dower,
And I will make thee worthy of a Queen.
Proud noble, I will weave thee such a web—
I will so spoil and trample on thy pride,
That thou shalt wish the woman's distaff were
Ten thousand lances rather than itself.
Ha! waiting still, sir Priest! Well, as thou seest
Our venture hath been somewhat baulked – 'tis not
Each arrow reaches swift and true the aim—
Love having failed, we'll try the best expedient,
That offers next – what sayst thou to revenge?
'Tis not so soft, but then 'tis very sure;
Say, shall we wring this haughty soul a little?
Tame this proud spirit, curb this untrained charger?
We will not weigh too heavily, nor grind
Too hard, but, having bowed him to the earth,
Leave the pursuit to others – carrion birds,
Who stoop, but not until the falcon's gorged
Upon the prey he leaves to their base talons.
GONZALES: It rests but with your grace to point the means.
QUEEN: Where be the plans of those possessions
Of Bourbon's house? – see that thou find them straight:
His mother was my kinswoman, and I
Could aptly once trace characters like those
She used to write – enough – Guienne – Auvergne –
And all Provence that lies beneath his claim—
That claim disproved, of right belong to me.

The path is clear, do thou fetch me those parchments.

[*Exit* GONZALES]

Not dearer to my heart will be the day
When first the crown of France decked my son's forehead,
Than that when I can compass thy perdition—
When I can strip the halo of thy fame
From off thy brow, seize on the wide domains,
That make thy hated house akin to empire,
And give thy name to deathless infamy.

[*Exit*]

SCENE iii

A gallery in the palace

Enter FRANÇOISE DE FOIX *and* LAUTREC

LAUTREC: Nay, nay, my pretty sister, be not sad!
And that thou better mayst endure this parting,
I'll give thee hope, shall make thee think of nought
Save my return – what sayst thou to a husband?
One feared in battle-field, and no less full
Of courtesy, and other noble virtues,
Than high in birth, and rank, and fortune – eh?
FRANÇOISE: I could be well content that such a man
Had sought a meeter bride.[10] Oh there be many
Maidens, of nobler parentage than mine,
Who would receive so brave a gentleman
With more of joy than I.
LAUTREC: Why, my sweet sister!
This is a strange unnatural coldness hangs
Upon thy brow, and in thy measured speech.
I know not much of maiden state and pride,
But, by the mass! thy words seem less in coyness
Than in indifference.
FRANÇOISE: Oh say in love,
In true and tender love to thee, my brother:
Trust me, I'm not ambitious, and would rather
Live ever by thy side unwooed, unwon—
With nought to think or live for, but for thee—
On whom, since earliest infancy, my heart

Hath spent its hopes and fears, its love and pride.
Oh do not give me to another; do not,
Dear Lautrec, send me from thee, and at once
Sever the ties of sweet and holy love
That live between us!

LAUTREC: To the man, whom best
On earth I value, I resign thee, Françoise.
My word was plighted to thy glad consent,
And unless thou wilt break the faith I gave,
And cancel thus one of my fondest hopes,
Thou wilt be his.

FRANÇOISE: I thank him for the honour
He doth our house, and my unworthy hand;
I thank thee, too, in that thy love hath made
So proud a choice for me. Oh, do not think
That, by one word, I will unknit the friendship
Of so long years. Wherever it seemeth thee
Best to bestow me, there will I endeavour
Humbly to bend my heart's untried affections—
There love, if it be possible – at least
There willingly obey.

LAUTREC: Then, dearest love,
If that, indeed, this offer please thee well,
Think on it as the fondest wish I have,
And look to see me come from Italy,
Bringing thee home a bridegroom, proudly crowned
With war's victorious wreaths; and who shall woo
The better, that he previously hath won
Fortune's hard favours, who, if I guess right,
Is coyer even than thou, my pretty sister.
Farewell awhile, I go to meet Laval.

[*Exit*]

FRANÇOISE: Farewell! Oh, heaven be praised that thou art blind
To that which, could thine unsuspecting heart
Once dream, would blast and wither it for ever.
I must not dwell on this sad theme; and though
I have read rightly in those dangerous eyes
Which gazed so passionately on me, I
Must even forget love's first and fondest lesson,
And write another in my lone heart's core.
What though the King – oh, very full of danger
Is solitude like this – and dangerous

These thoughts that flock around me, melting down
Each sterner purpose. By thy thrusting love,
My brother! by thy hopes, that all in me
Centre their warmth and energy, I swear,
That while one throb of strength remains, I'll bear
This torture patiently, and in my heart
Lock love and misery until life depart.   [*Exit*]

SCENE iv

An anteroom in the palace

Enter, at opposite sides, the KING *and* CLEMENT

FRANCIS: The very man I seek! – well met, Clement
  I have a boon to ask of thee.
CLEMENT: My liege,
  Speak but your will, it is my law.
FRANCIS: I thank thee.
  But first answer me this – didst thou not mark,
  This morning at the tournament, a lady
  Who sat beside my sister?
CLEMENT: That did all
  Who were there – 'twas the young Countess de Foix,
  Lautrec's fair sister.
FRANCIS: Ay, the very same.
  Dost know her, good Clement?
CLEMENT: My liege, I do;
  And even will say, that her surpassing beauty
  Surpasseth not her wit, which is, indeed,
  So perfect, and withal so gentle, too,
  That her fair form is but a priceless casket,
  Wherein lie precious treasures.
FRANCIS: By my fay,
  The lady's praise falls freely from thy tongue,
  Indeed, Clement! Methinks she must be perfect,
  Else art thou very mad!
CLEMENT: My gracious liege!
FRANCIS: Come, come, Sieur Clement, thou dost love the lady!
CLEMENT: All saints defend me from it! as I see
  Your grace would hold such love insanity.

FRANCIS: Hast known her long?

CLEMENT: Ay, long enough, my lord,
  To have o'ercome that sudden love which springs
  To life from the first glance of beauteous eyes.

FRANCIS: Do thou mine errand then, and bear to her
  This letter and this ring; but see thou name not
  Whence they are sent; be silent, and be swift,
  And to my chamber bring me her reply.
  How, now! I thought thee gone; why dost thou stop,
  And turn your letter o'er and o'er, and look
  So sad and doubting?

CLEMENT: May it please your grace,
  I had a sister once – my thoughts were of
  This lady's brother.

FRANCIS: Well, sir! what of him?

CLEMENT: I pray you, pardon me, my noble lord,
  But if—

FRANCIS: I will arrest the treason hanging
  Upon thy lip; for, by my knightly word,
  Yon scroll is such as any gentleman
  Might bear to any lady.

CLEMENT: For that word
  I thank your majesty with all my heart—
  I'll bear your message trustily.

FRANCIS: And quickly;
  And meet me in my chamber with thine answer.
  Good speed – farewell! – be swift! I wait for thee.

  [Exeunt severally]

SCENE V

Council Chamber

Under a canopy is placed the throne; on either side a vacant seat.
Seats are placed on either side of a long table

Enter the QUEEN-MOTHER

QUEEN: What, dazzled and ensnared, ere the black eyes
  That blinded can have flashed three glances on him!
  The last that should have won his yielding heart, too!
  She hath a brother, young and proud – ambitious,

Or else he comes not of the haughty stock
Whose name he bears. Ambitious! ay, and if
This black-eyed girl have the de Foix' high blood
Within her veins, she'll forward his ambition.
I fear this government of Italy
No longer lies at my disposal now.
I would that blindness had put out the beauty
That lies in every woman's eyes! – I would
A foul deformity alone had been
The portion of all women, ere this thing
Had come to pass! – Beset on every side –
Hemmed in – and forced to guard – even more than life –
My power; and let revenge meantime go sleep:
No matter! in the storm the pilot's skill
Shows best. – The King approaches to the council.

> (*Flourish of trumpets*)
> *Enter the* KING *and all the Court,* ALENÇON, BONNIVET,
> VENDÔME, CHABANNES, LAUTREC, LAVAL, *etc.*

FRANCIS: The Duke de Bourbon's absence we might deem
Strange and uncourteous; but we'll rather hope
That some event of unforeseen importance
Hath stood between his duty and ourselves:
Time wears—

> (*The* KING *leads his Mother to the throne –* ALENÇON
> *seats himself on the left of it; the rest of the nobles place themselves
> according to their rank*)

On to the business of the day.

QUEEN: Sire, will it not seem also strange in us,
And all uncourteous, if we should discuss
This matter, ere the first prince of the blood
Be here to give his voice in this decision?

> *Enter* BOURBON

Said I not so? We know my lord of Bourbon
Is ever at the post where duty points.

> (BOURBON *seats himself on the right of the throne*)

FRANCIS: Cousin of Bourbon, you are welcome here.

BOURBON: I thank your majesty who bids me so,
And crave the assembly's pardon: on my way
A man withheld me, unto whom I owed
Some gratitude.

FRANCIS: Indeed! his name, I pray?
He that hath served those whom we love, serves us.

I prithee, coz,[11] what was it thou owdst to him?
I'll be his debtor too.
BOURBON: Your majesty
  (As we have seen in battle oft) holds life
  At too unworthy price: unto that man,
  I owed my life at Marignan.
FRANCIS: Indeed!
QUEEN: Shall we not to the point – our time grows short?
FRANCIS: Ay, marry; thus, then, noble lords, it is.
  But now a messenger from Italy
  Hath reached our court, with tidings from Milan—
  Prosper Colonna is in arms again;
  And Charles of Spain hath sent his swarthy bands
  To ravage the fair tributary states
  Our fathers won of yore, and ever deemed
  The brightest flower of foreign growth that wreathed
  Their coronet: now, in this urgency,
  We lack some trusty arm to wield our brand
  In the defence of Italy. Already,
  Two have been named to us – de Bonnivet,
  And Lautrec.
QUEEN (*aside to* BOURBON)
  Bourbon, you look wondrous pale;
  I fear me you are ill.
BOURBON (*aside*) Oh gracious madam!
  Fear's pallid tint must live within your eye,
  And lend whatever you look on its own hue.
FRANCIS: Stand forth, Count Lautrec; for de Bonnivet,
  Methinks, his youth may follow yet the wars
  Before he lead them on; how says our mother?
QUEEN: How should she say when that the royal choice
  Lights on such valour? how but well? but you,
  My lord of Bourbon, we would have your voice;
  Does silence, disapproving, seal your lips?
  Or takes your wisdom no exception here?
BOURBON: None, madam; and the only wish I have
  Is, that you ever had been served in Italy,
  As I foresee Count Lautrec's arm will serve you.
LAUTREC: My liege! beseech you, hold; and you, my lords!
  The honour now conferred sits blushingly
  On my unworthy brow: oh! not on me
  Bestow a prize, which years of bloody service,

And hairs bleached in your camps, alone should wear.
FRANCIS: Now, by my fay,[12] Lautrec, thy speech but shows
  As brave and gallant soldier's speech should show,
  Shrinking from praise and guerdon[13] duly won:
  With our own royal hand we'll buckle on
  The sword, that in thy grasp must be the bulwark
  And lode-star[14] of our host. Approach!
QUEEN: Not so.
  Your pardon, sir; but it hath ever been
  The pride and privilege of woman's hand
  To arm the valour that she loves so well:
  We would not, for your crown's best jewel, bate
  One jot of our accustomed state today:
  Count Lautrec, we will arm thee, at our feet:
  Take thou the brand which wins thy country's wars,—
  Thy monarch's trust, and thy fair lady's favour.
  Why, how now! – how is this! – my lord of Bourbon!
  If we mistake not, 'tis the sword of office
  Which graces still your baldric[15] – with your leave,
  We'll borrow it of you.
BOURBON (*starting up*)
  Ay, madam! 'tis the sword
  You buckled on with your own hand, the day
  You sent me forth to conquer in your cause;
  And there it is! – (*Breaks the sword*) – take it – and with it all
  The allegiance that I owe to France! ay, take it;
  And with it, take the hope I breathe over it:
  That so, before Colonna's host, your arms
  Lie crushed and sullied with dishonour's stain;
  So, reft in sunder[16] by contending factions,
  Be your Italian provinces; so torn
  By discord and dissension this vast empire;
  So broken and disjoined your subjects' loves;
  So fallen your son's ambition, and your pride!
QUEEN (*rising*)
  What ho! a guard within there! Charles of Bourbon,
  I do arrest thee, traitor to the crown!
                Enter guard
  Away with yonder wide-mouthed thunderer!
  We'll try if gyves[17] and strait confinement cannot
  Check this high eloquence, and cool the brain
  Which harbours such unmannered hopes.

[BOURBON *is forced out*]

Dream ye, my lords! that thus with open ears,
And gaping mouths and eyes, ye sit and drink
This curbless torrent of rebellious madness!
And you, sir! are you slumbering on your throne!
Or has all majesty fled from the earth,
That women must start up, and in your council
Speak, think, and act for ye; and, lest your vassals,
The very dirt beneath your feet, rise up
And cast ye off, must women, too, defend ye?
For shame, my lords! all, all of ye, for shame!
Off, off with sword and sceptre, for there is
No loyalty in subjects; and in kings,
No king-like terror to enforce their rights.

FRANCIS: Our mother speaks warmly in the cause:
Though we must own we hold it somewhat shame,
That we forestalled her not in her just wrath;
But verily, surprise had chained up motion;
And hand and eye, and tongue, alike were bound
In wonder, at yon rebel noble's daring.
Now unto thee once more we turn, Count Lautrec—
Tomorrow's sun must find you on your march:
Already hath Colonna dared too much,
'Tis time we check his hopes of future progress,
And rescue back our torn Italian states.
Well speed ye all! and victory be with you!
Farewell; be faithful, and heaven send ye back
With no more danger than may serve to be
The plea for praise and honourable guerdon.
Mother, thy hand! we'll speak awhile with thee.

[*Exeunt all but* LAUTREC *and* LAVAL]

LAUTREC: I cry thy mercy, friend! but I'm so amazed,
So thunderstruck, so lost in wonderment!
Bourbon arrested! Bourbon prisoner!
And, by the Queen!

LAVAL: I shall not soon forget
That woman's look, and voice.

LAUTREC: Come, come, Laval,
Let us shake off this dream that haunts us thus;
The Queen's a woman, who, upon emergency,
Can don the devil – which of them cannot?

'Tis time we think of our departure – hark!
Footsteps!
LAVAL: Ay, light, though hurried – 'tis thy sister –
                    Enter FRANÇOISE
LAVAL: Lady, you're welcome as the joyous sun,
    And gentle summer airs, that, after storms,
    Come wafting all the sweets of fallen blossoms
    Through the thick foliage; whose green arms shake off,
    In gratitude, their showers of diamond drops,
    And bow to the reviving freshness.
FRANÇOISE: Oh, my dear brother, have I found thee here?
    Here will I lock my arms, and rest for ever.
LAUTREC: My dearest love! what means this passionate grief;
    These straining arms and gushing tears? for shame!
    Look up and smile; for honour crowns our house.
    Dost know that I am governor of Milan?
FRANÇOISE: They told me so; but oh! they told me, too,
    That ere tonight be come, thou wilt go hence;
    And the anticipated grief let forth
    The torrent of my tears to sweep away
    All thoughts of thy promotion. Is it so—
    Dost thou, indeed, forsake me?
LAUTREC: Maiden, no;
    'Tis true we march for Italy tonight;
    'Tis true that this embrace must be the last
    For many a day. But for forsaking thee
    I leave thee with the Princess Margaret;
    I leave thee here at court – nay, silly girl –
LAVAL: Oh, peace!
    Prithee upbraid her not: see where she stands,
    Bowed with the weight of mourning loveliness:
    Canst thou, with sharp reproving words, wound one
    Who gems the lustre of thy new made honours,
    With such rare drops of love!
LAUTREC: My gentle sister!
FRANÇOISE: Oh, Lautrec! blame me not; we twain have been
    Even from our birth together and alone;
    Two healthful scions,[18] of a goodly stock,
    Whose other shoots have withered all – we've grown,
    Still side by side; I like some fragile aspen[19]—
    And thou a sturdy oak, 'neath whose broad shelter
    I reared my head: then frown not, that the wind

Doth weigh the trembling aspen to the earth,
While the stout oak scarce owns the powerless breeze.
LAUTREC: Oh, churl![21] to say one unkind word to thee;
Look up, sweet sister; smile once more on me,
That I may carry hence one gleam of sunshine:
Come, dearest, come; unlock thy hands, Laval!
Take her, in pity, from my arms: for sense
Is well nigh drowned in sorrow.
FRANÇOISE: Yet one word;
I do beseech thee, leave me not at court;
But let me back to our old castle walls—
Let me not stay at court!
LAUTREC: Even as thou wilt:
But, dearest love, methinks such solitude
Will make of grief a custom; whilst at court—
No matter; use thine own discretion; do
Even as it seemeth unto thee most fitting.
Once more, farewell! Laval, thou'lt follow?

[*Exit* LAUTREC]

LAVAL: Ay.
But ere I go, perchance for ever, lady,
Unto the land, whose dismal tales of battles,
Where thousands strewed the earth, have christened it
The Frenchman's grave; I'd speak of such a theme
As chimes with this sad hour, more fitly than
Its name gives promise. There's a love, which, born
In early days, lives on through silent years,
Nor ever shines, but in the hour of sorrow,
When it shows brightest – like the trembling light
Of a pale sunbeam, breaking over the face
Of the wild waters in their hour of warfare.
Thus much forgive! and trust, in such an hour,
I had not said even this, but for the hope
That when the voice of victory is heard
From the far Tuscan valleys, in its swell
Should mournful dirges mingle for the dead,
And I be one of those who are at rest,
You may chance recollect this word, and say,
That day, upon the bloody field, there fell
One who had loved thee long, and loved thee well.
FRANÇOISE: Beseech you, speak not thus: we soon, I trust,
Shall meet again – till then, farewell, and prosper;

And if you love me – which I will not doubt,
Sith[11] your sad looks bear witness to your truth—
This do for me – never forsake my brother!
And for my brother's sake, since you and he
Are but one soul, be mindful of yourself.

                                                        [*Exit* LAVAL]

Defenceless, and alone! ay, go thou forth,
For hope sits sunnily upon thy brow,
My brother! but, to me, this parting seems
Full of ill-omened dread, woe's sure forerunner.
I could have told thee how seduction's arts,
Even 'neath the bulwark of thy fond protection,
Have striven to overthrow my virtue – ay,
That letter and that ring – they were the king's.
Oh! let me quickly from this fatal court,
Beneath whose smiling surface chasms lie yawning,
To gulp alike the unwary and the wise.
I'll bid farewell to the Princess Margaret,
And then take shelter in my ancient home;
There brood on my vain love, till grief become
Love's substitute – till foolish hope be dead,
And heaven shall grant me patience in its stead.

                                                        [*Exit*]

Act III

The Royal Chamber

FRANCIS *discovered*

FRANCIS: By Jupiter! he must have made an errand
    Unto the antipodes, or this new world,
    Which, it should seem, our grandsire Adam's will
    Did leave to Charles of Spain, else doth he wear
    Dull lead for Mercury's air-cutting pinions.[22]
              Enter CLEMENT
    Why, how now, slow foot! art thou lame, I prithee?
    Hath she the ring – hath she perused the letter—
    What does she – says she – answers she? Be quick,
    Man; thy reply. Come, come, the devil speed thee.
CLEMENT: My liege! I found the lady beaming all
    With smiles of hope her brother should be chosen:
    Then to her hand delivered I your scroll.
FRANCIS: Ha!
CLEMENT: The which she, with a doubting look, did open;
    And, for a moment, her fixed eye did seem
    To drink the characters, but not the sense
    Of your epistle: like some traveller,
    Who, lacking understanding, passes over
    Wide tracts and foreign countries, yet brings back
    No fruit of his own observation: thus
    Stood the fair lady, till her eye was fain
    Begin the scroll again; and then, as though
    That moment comprehension woke in her,
    The blood forsook her cheeks; and straight, ashamed
    Of its unnatural desertion, drew
    A crimson veil over her marble brows.
FRANCIS: I would I'd borne the scroll myself, thy words
    Image her forth so fair!
CLEMENT: Do they, indeed?
    Then sorrow seize my tongue! for, look you, sir,
    I will not speak of your own fame or honour,

Nor of your word to me: king's words, I find,
Are drafts on our credulity, not pledges
Of their own truth. You have been often pleased
To shower your royal favours on my head;
And fruitful honours from your kindly will
Have raised me far beyond my fondest hopes;
But had I known such service was to be
The nearest way my gratitude might take
To solve the debt, I'd even have given back
All that I hold of you: and, now, not even
Your crown and kingdom could requite to me
The cutting sense of shame that I endured
When on me fell the sad reproachful glance
Which told me how I stood in the esteem
Of yonder lady. Let me tell you, sir,
You've borrowed for a moment what whole years
Cannot bestow – an honourable name!
Now fare you well; I've sorrow at my heart,
To think your majesty hath reckoned thus
Upon my nature. I was poor before,
Therefore I can be poor again without
Regret, so I lose not mine own esteem.

FRANCIS: Skip me thy spleen, and onward with thy tale.
What said the lady then?

CLEMENT: With trembling hands
She folded up your scroll; and more in sorrow,
As I believe, than anger, letting fall
Unheeded from her hand the sparkling jewel,
She left me.

FRANCIS: Thou, I warrant, sore abashed,
And durst not urge her further. Excellent!
Oh, ye are precious wooers, all of ye!
I marvel how ye ever ope your lips
Unto, or look upon that fearful thing,
A lovely woman.

CLEMENT: And I marvel, sir,
At those who do not feel the majesty—
By heaven! I'd almost said the holiness—
That circles round a fair and virtuous woman
There is a gentle purity that breathes
In such a one, mingled with chaste respect,
And modest pride of her own excellence—

A shrinking nature, that is so adverse
To aught unseemly, that I could as soon
Forget the sacred love I owe to heaven,
As dare, with impure thoughts, to taint the air
Inhaled by such a being: than whom, my liege,
Heaven cannot look on anything more holy,
Or earth be proud of anything more fair.   [*Exit*]
FRANCIS: Good! 'tis his god stirs in him now, I trow;
The poet is inspired, and doubtless, too,
With his own muse; whose heavenly perfections,
He fain would think belong to Eve's frail daughters.
Well: I will find occasions for myself—
With my own ardent love I'll take the field,
And woo this pretty saint until she yield.   [*Exit*]

SCENE ii

A small apartment in the Louvre

Enter GONZALES, *with papers in his hand*

GONZALES: Bourbon arrested! oh sweet mistress Fortune,
Who rails at thee, doth wrong thee, on my soul!
Thy blindness steads me well; for thou hast thrown,
All time, and place, and opportunity
To boot, into my path – these documents,
That, but this moment, seemed foul witnesses
To my suspicious fears, must now become
The charts of my new born, though late dead purpose.
(*Reading*) So! now I know my task, how far I may
Promise with truth; and how far with false promises
Garnish my snare – I'll straight unto the Queen,
And strive to win access to Bourbon's prison;
It shall fare ill, if I cannot outwit
Even this lynx-eyed[23] woman.
                          Enter the QUEEN
QUEEN: Save you, father!
Throw by those papers now, and hearken to me:
De Bourbon is arrested; 'tis of that
I came to speak – you must straight to his prison.
GONZALES (*aside*)

I cannot, for my life, remember me
That ever I made bargain with the devil;
Yet do all things fall out so strangely well
For me, and for my purpose, as though fate
Served an apprenticeship unto my will.

QUEEN: How now, what counsel hold you with yourself?

GONZALES: Debate of marvel, only, please your grace;
Is then the Duke so near his verge of life,
That he hath need of spiritual aid,
To improve this brief and waning tenure?

QUEEN: Good!
Oh excellent! I laugh; yet, by my fay,
This whined quotation from thy monkish part
Hath lent a clue to my unfixed purpose,
Which had not yet resolved by what pretext
Thou mightst unto his prison with best seeming.
Most reverend sir, and holy confessor!
Get thee unto the prison of this lord;
There, see thou do exhort him unto death;—
And, mark me – for all warriors hold acquaintance
With the grim monarch: when he rides abroad
The battle-skirts, they crown him with proud crests;
In human blood dye they his purple robes;
They place a flashing sword in his right hand,
And call him Glory! – therefore be thou sure
To speak of nought but scaffolds robed in black;
Grim executioners, and the vile mob
Staring, and jeering; 'neath whose clouted shoes,
Unhonoured, shall the noble stream of life
That flows through his proud veins soak in the earth.

GONZALES: Madam, I will.

QUEEN: Then, when thou hast overcome
The haughty spirit, mould it to thy will,
And tutor him so well, that presently
Bid them strike off his chains; and to the palace
Lead him in secret: above all, be sure
To lard thy speech, but chiefly at the first,
With sober strains of fitting holiness,
Quote me the saints, the fathers – bring the church
With all its lumber, into active service.
Briefly, dissemble well – But pshaw! I prate!24
I had forgot again – thou art a priest:

Tarry not, and conduct thy prisoner
Unto my chamber, where I wait for thee.   [*Exit*]
GONZALES: Dissemble well! witness, deep hell, how well
I have, and will dissemble! Now, then, to seek
De Bourbon's prison; by my holidame!
Lady, you'll wait till doomsday ere he come.
He shall be free within this hour – and yet—
But ere I pour my proffer in his ear,
I'll work upon his hot and violent nature,
And make him sure, ere I attempt to win him.
But come, time tarries not – sweet Fortune! prithee
Still let me woo thee, till I have achieved
The task another's proud ambition sets me;
Then frown or smile, I care not; for thou hast
No power to stem the headlong tide of will
That bears me onward to my own revenge.

SCENE iii

A prison

BOURBON *and* MARGARET *discovered*

BOURBON: Lady, you speak in vain.
MARGARET: I do beseech thee!
Oh Bourbon! Bourbon! 'twas but yesterday
That thou didst vow eternal love to me;
Now, hither have I wended to your prison,
And, spite of maiden pride and fearfulness,
Held parley with thy guards to win my way.
I've moved their iron natures with my tears;
Which seemed as they would melt the very stones
Whereon they fell so fast. I do implore thee,
Speak to me, Bourbon! – but a word – one word!
I never bowed my knee to aught of earth,
Ere this; but I have ever seen around me,
Others who knelt, and worshipped princes' favours:
From them, or rather from my love, I learn
The humble seeming of a suppliant;—
Upon my bended knees, I do implore thee,—

Look not, or speak not, if thou so hast sworn,—
But take the freedom that my gold hath bought thee:
Away! nor let these eyes behold thy death!

BOURBON: You are deceived, lady, they will not dare
To take my life.

MARGARET: 'Tis thou that art deceived!
What! talkst thou of not daring – dost thou see
Yon sun that flames above the earth? I tell thee,
That if my mother had but bent her will
To win that sun, she would accomplish it.

BOURBON: My life is little worth to any now,
Nor have I any, who shall after me
Inherit my proud name.

MARGARET: Hold, there, my lord!
Posterity, to whom great men and their
Fair names belong, is your inheritor.
Your country, from whose kings your house had birth,
Claims of you, sir, your high and spotless name!
Fame craves it of you; for when there be none
Bearing the blood of mighty men, to bear
Their virtues also – Fame emblazons them
Upon her flag, which over the world she waves,
Persuading others to like glorious deeds.
Oh! will you die upon a public scaffold?
Beneath the hands of the executioner!
Shall the vile rabble bait you to your death!
Shall they applaud and make your fate a tale
For taverns, and the busy city streets?
And in the wide hereafter – for the which
All warriors hope to live – shall your proud name
Be bandied to and fro by foul tradition—
Branded and curst, as rebel's name should be?

BOURBON: No! light that curse on those who made me such—
Who stole my well-earned honours from my brow,
And gave such guerdon to whole years of service!
Light the foul curse of black ingratitude—
Of shame and bitter sorrow – and the sharp
Reproving voice of after times and men—
Upon the heartless boy, who knew not how
To prize his subject's love! A tenfold curse
Light on that royal harlot—

MARGARET: Oh! no more—

BOURBON: Nay, maiden, 'tis in vain! for thou shalt hear me!
Drink to the dregs the knowledge thou hast forced,
And dare upbraid me, even with a look:
Had I but loved thy mother more – thee less,
I might this hour have stood upon a throne!
Ay, start! I tell thee, that the Queen thy mother
Hath loved – doth love me with the fierce desires
Of her unbridled nature; she hath thrown
Her crown, her kingdom, and herself before me;
And but I loved thee more than all the world,
I might have wed Louisa of Savoy!
Now stare, and shudder – freeze thyself to marble –
Now say where best the meed of shame is due—
Now look upon these prison walls – these chains –
And bid me rein my anger!
MARGARET: Oh, be silent!
For you have rent in twain the sacredest veil
That ever hung upon the eyes of innocence.
GONZALES: (*without*) God bless the inmates of this prison-house!
BOURBON: Who calls without?

        Enter GONZALES

MARGARET: The pulse of life stands still
Within my veins, and horror hath o'ercome
My strength! Oh! holy father, to thy care
Do I commend this wayward man.

                            [*Exit* MARGARET]

BOURBON: How, now?
A priest! what means this most unwelcome visit?
GONZALES: Who questions thus a son of the holy church
In tones so rude?
BOURBON: One who has known
Much of the church – more of her worthy sons;
Therefore, sir monk, be brief – thy business here?
GONZALES: Look on these walls, whose stern time-stained brows
Frown like relentless justice on their inmates.
Listen! – that voice is Echo's[25] dull reply
Unto the rattling of your chains, my lord—
What *should* a priest do here?
BOURBON: Ay, what, indeed!
Unless you come to soften down these stones
With your discourse, and teach the tedious echo
A newer lesson: trust me, that is all
Your presence, father, will accomplish here.

GONZALES: Oh sinful man! and is thy heart so hard,
    That I might easier move thy prison stones?
    Know, then, my mission – death is near at hand!
    The warrant hath gone forth – the seal is set;
    Thou art already numbered with those
    Who leave their names to lasting infamy,
    And their remains to be trod under foot
    Of the base rabble.
BOURBON: Hark thee, in thine ear—
    Shall I hear when I'm dead what men say of me?
    Or will my body blench and quiver 'neath
    The stamp of one foot rather than another?
    Go to – go to! I have fought battles, father,
    Where death and I have met in full close contact,
    And parted, knowing we should meet again;
    Therefore, come when he may, we've looked upon
    Each other far too narrowly, for me
    To fear the hour when we shall be so joined,
    That all eternity shall never sunder us.
    Go prate to others about skulls and graves;
    Thou never didst in heat of combat stand,
    Or know what good acquaintance soldiers have
    With the pale scarecrow – Death!
GONZALES: (aside)
    Ah, thinkst thou so?
    And thou didst never lie wrapped round so long
    With death's cold arms, upon the gory field,
    As I have lain. (Aloud) – Hear me, thou hard of heart!
    They who go forth to battle are led on
    With sprightly trumpets and shrill clamorous clarions;
    The drum doth roll its double notes along,
    Echoing the horses' tramp; and the sweet fife[26]
    Runs through the yielding air in dulcet measure,
    That makes the heart leap in its case of steel!
    Thou, shalt be knelled unto thy death by bells,
    Ponderous and brazen-tongued, whose sullen toll
    Shall cleave thine aching brain, and on thy soul
    Fall with a leaden weight: the muffled drum
    Shall mutter round thy path like distant thunder:
    Stead of the war-cry, and wild battle-roar—
    That swells upon the tide of victory,
    And seems unto the conqueror's eager ear

Triumphant harmony of glorious discords!
There shall be voices cry foul shame on thee!
And the infuriate populace shall clamour
To heaven for lightnings on thy rebel head!
BOURBON: Monks love not bells, which call them up to prayers
In the dead noon of night, when they would snore
Rather than watch: but, father, I care not,
Even if the ugliest sound I ever did hear—
Thy raven voice – croak curses over my grave.
GONZALES: What! death and shame! alike you heed them not!
Then, Mercy, use thy soft, persuasive arts,
And melt this stubborn spirit! Be it known
To you, my lord, the Queen hath sent me hither.
BOURBON: Then get thee hence again, foul, pandering priest!
By heaven! I knew that cowl did cover over
Some filthy secret, that the day dared not
To pry into. I know your holy church,
Together with its brood of sandalled fiends!
Ambition is your God; and all the offering
Ye bring him, are your vile compliances
With the bad wills of vicious men in power,
Whose monstrous passions ye do nurse and cherish,
That from the evil harvest which they yield,
A plenteous gleaning may reward your toils.
Out, thou unholy thing!
GONZALES: Hold, madman! hear me!
If for thy fame, if for thy warm heart's blood
Thou wilt not hear me, listen in the name
Of France thy country.
BOURBON: Tempter, get thee gone!
I have no land, I have no home – no country –
I am a traitor, cast from out the arms
Of my ungrateful country! I disown it!
Withered be all its glories, and its pride!
May it become the slave of foreign power!
May foreign princes grind its thankless children!
And make all those, who are such fools, as yet
To spill their blood for it, or for its cause,
Dig it like dogs! and when they die, like dogs,
Rot on its surface, and make fat the soil,
Whose produce shall be seized by foreign hands!
GONZALES (*aside*) Now, then, to burst the last frail thread that checks

His headlong course – another step, and then
He topples over the brink! – he's won – he's ours.
(*Aloud*) – You beat the air with idle words; no man
Doth know how deep his country's love lies grained
In his heart's core, until the hour of trial!
Fierce though you hurl your curse upon the land,
Whose monarchs cast ye from its bosom; yet,
Let but one blast of war come echoing
From where the Ebro and the Douro[27] roll;
Let but the Pyrenees reflect the gleam
Of twenty of Spain's lances, and your sword
Shall leap from out its scabbard to your hand!
BOURBON: Ay, priest it shall! eternal heaven, it shall!
And its far flash shall lighten o'er the land,
The leading star of Spain's victorious host!
But flaming, like some dire portentous comet,
In the eyes of France, and her proud governors!
Oh, vengeance! 'tis for thee I value life:
Be merciful, my fate, nor cut me off,
Ere I have wreaked my fell desire, and made
Infamy glorious, and dishonour fame!
But, if my wayward destiny hath willed
That I should here be butchered shamefully,
By the immortal soul, that is man's portion,
His hope, and his inheritance, I swear,
That on the day Spain overflows its bounds,
And rolls the tide of war upon these plains,
My spirit on the battle's edge shall ride;
And louder than death's music, and the roar
Of combat, shall my voice be heard to shout,
On – on – to victory and carnage.
GONZALES: Now,
That day is come, ay, and that very hour;
Now shout your war-cry; now unsheath your sword!
I'll join the din, and make these tottering walls
Tremble and nod to hear our fierce defiance!
Nay, never start, and look upon my cowl[28]—
You love not priests, de Bourbon, more than I.
Off! vile denial of my manhood's pride!
Off, off to hell! where thou wast first invented—
Now once again I stand and breathe a knight.
Nay, stay not gazing thus: it is Garcia,

Whose name hath reached thee long ere now, I trow:
Whom thou hast met in deadly fight full oft,
When France and Spain joined in the battle-field!
Beyond the Pyrenean boundary
That guards thy land, are forty thousand men:
Their unfurled pennons[29] flout fair France's sun,
And wanton in the breezes of her sky:
Impatient halt they there; their foaming steeds,
Pawing the huge and rock-built barrier,
That bars their further course: they wait for thee;
For thee whom France hath injured and cast off;
For thee, whose blood it pays with shameful chains,
More shameful death; for thee, whom Charles of Spain
Summons to head his host, and lead them on
                    (*Gives him a parchment*)
To conquest and to glory!
BOURBON: To revenge!
    What tells he here of lands, and honours! Pshaw!
    I've had my fill of such. Revenge! Revenge!
    That is the boon my unslaked anger craves,
    That is the bribe that wins me to thy cause,
    And that shall be my battle cry! Ha! ha!
    Why, how we dream! why look, Garcia; canst thou
    With mumbled priestcraft file away these chains,
    Or must I bear them into Spain with me,
    That Charles may learn what guerdon valour wins
    This side the Pyrenees?
GONZALES: It shall not need—
    What ho! but hold – together with this garb,
    Methinks I have thrown off my prudence!
                    (*Resumes the monk's dress*)
BOURBON: What!
    Wilt thou to Spain with me in frock and cowl,
    That men shall say De Bourbon is turned driveller,
    And rides to war in company with monks?
GONZALES: Listen. The Queen for her own purposes
    Confided to my hand her signet-ring,
    Bidding me strike your fetters off, and lead you
    By secret passes to her private chamber:
    But being free, so use thy freedom, that
    Before the morning's dawn all search be fruitless.
    What, ho! within.

Enter Gaoler

Behold this signet-ring!
Strike off those chains, and get thee gone.

[*Exit Gaoler*]

And now
Follow. How now – dost doubt me, Bourbon?
BOURBON: Ay,
  First for thy habit's sake; and next, because
  Thou rather, in a craven priest's disguise,
  Tarriest in danger in a foreign court,
  Than seekest that danger in thy country's wars.
GONZALES: Thou art unarmed: there is my dagger; 'tis
  The only weapon that I bear, lest fate
  Should play me false: take it, and use it, too,
  If in the dark and lonely path I lead thee,
  Thou markst me halt, or turn, or make a sign
  Of treachery! – and now, tell me, dost know
  John Count Laval?
BOURBON: What! Lautrec's loving friend—
  Who journeys now to Italy with him?
GONZALES: How! gone to Italy! he surely went
  But a short space from Paris, to conduct
  Count Lautrec on his way.
BOURBON: I tell thee, no!
  He's bound for Italy, along with him.
GONZALES: Then the foul fiend hath mingled in my plot,
  And marred it too! my life's sole aim and purpose!
  Didst thou but know what damned injuries,
  What foul, unknightly shame and obloquy,[30]
  His sire – whose name is wormwood to my mouth –
  Did heap upon our house – didst thou but know –
  No matter – get thee gone – I tarry here.
  And if three lingering years, ay, three times three,
  Must pass ere I obtain what three short days
  Had well nigh given me, even be it so—
  Life is revenge! revenge is life! Follow;
  And, though we never meet again, when thou
  Shalt hear of the most fearful deed of daring,
  Of the most horrible and bloody tale,
  That ever graced a beldame's midnight legend,
  Or froze her gaping listeners, think of me

And my revenge! Now, Bourbon, heaven speed thee!

[Exeunt]

SCENE iv

The Royal apartment

FRANCIS *seated: two gentlemen attending*

Enter the QUEEN

QUEEN: Hear you these tidings, son? – Milan is lost!
  A messenger, who rode the live-long night,
  Hath brought the news, and faints for weariness.
  Prosper Colonna hath dissolved our host
  Like icicles in the sun's beams: and Count Lautrec,
  Maddened with his defeat and shame, fled from it
  The night Colonna entered Milan.

FRANCIS (*starting up*)
  Coward!
  But he shall answer dearly for his flight
  And for fair Milan's loss. Say they not whither
  He fled to?

QUEEN: Oh, he doubtless is concealed
  In some dark corner of the Milanese,
  Where heaven can scarcely look upon his shame.
                          (*Shouts without*)

FRANCIS: What din without?

QUEEN: It is the people, who
  Throng round the palace gates, with gaping mouths,
  To hear the confirmation of the tidings.

FRANCIS: There's some commotion, for their ceaseless shouts
  Shake our imperial dwelling to its base. (*Shouts without*)
                  Enter a MESSENGER
  How now! what more?

MESSENGER: So please you, my dread liege,
  News are this hour arrived that the Count Lautrec,
  Passing disguised from Italy towards Paris,
  Hath been arrested by stout Lord St Pol:
  Who, in his castle, holds him a strait prisoner
  Until your royal pleasure be made known,

Whether he there sojourn in longer durance,
Or be sent hither to abide his trial.

FRANCIS: Confessed he the betraying of our Milan?

MESSENGER: He holds an unmoved silence on the point,
    Still craving of your majesty a hearing,
    And, after that, stern and impartial justice.

FRANCIS: And, by the soul of Charlemagne, we swear
    He shall have justice, such as he demands.

                                     [*Exit* MESSENGER]

His deeds, upon the swift wings of the wind,
Have reached the high tribunal of our throne,
And, ere himself arrive, have there condemned him.
But, for the well-remembered services
Done by his sire to France and to our house,
As a dear mercy's boon, we leave him life.
Mother, how is't with thee? thou art drowned in thought.

QUEEN: Can it be otherwise, when wave over wave
    Of fortune's adverse tide comes whelming us
    With most resistless ruin? Hast thou heard,
    Or did this loss of Milan stop thine ears
    With its ill-fated din – Bourbon's escaped?

FRANCIS: Bourbon escaped! then fortune loves Colonna!
    For, if he once set foot in Italy,
    Our injured subject and our haughty foe
    Shall prove an overmatch for France himself!
    How fell this evil chance?

QUEEN: Another time
    Shall fit us better for long argument:
    We tell of his escape, while he improves it.
    Deeds, and not words, suit best this exigency;
    Our task is vigilant and swift pursuit.   [*Exit*]

FRANCIS: My task is vigilant though slow pursuit;
    I have small care for even this event,
    Which seems as though it shook my very throne:
    One thought alone hath room within my breast—
    How I may win this maid, whose fearful charms
    Have deemed themselves secure in absence only:
    Forgetting how fond memory, young love's shadow,
    Laughs at such hope. I'll win her, though the stars
    Link hands, and make a fiery rampart round her:
    Though she be ice, steel, rock, or adamant,[31]
    Or anything that is more hard and stubborn.

Love, lend me aid, this victory must be thine;
Win thou this peerless votary to thy shrine!   [*Exit*]

SCENE V

An apartment in the Chateau-de-Foix

FRANÇOISE *discovered seated*

Enter FLORISE

FLORISE: How fare you, madam?
FRANÇOISE: Well, Florise. Why, girl—
  Why dost thou gaze on me? Do hollow cheeks
  And tear-stained eyes belie me?
FLORISE: Lady, no;
  But something in your voice and in your look—
  Something that is all sorrow's, only hers—
  Is grafted on the roses of your cheek,
  And burns in the sad lustre of your eye.
  Pardon me, sweet my mistress! but, indeed,
  Since your return from court—
                    (*A horn is heard without*)
FRANÇOISE: Hark! from without
  A horn is winded: hasten, prating girl,
  And fetch me tidings of this sudden summons!

                                    [*Exit* FLORISE]

  I tremble! yet I scarce know wherefore – how
  If it should be my brother? – heaven forefend!
  He brings with him Laval, my promised husband!
  Oh! grief hath wedded me for ever more;
  Our bridal vow was all made up of sighs,
  And tears have sealed it!
                    Re-enter FLORISE
FLORISE: Please you, madam, one,
  A messenger from court, hath just arrived
  With this despatch.

                                    [*Exit* FLORISE]

FRANÇOISE: From court? – oh give it me!
  Hold! should it be the King! pshaw, trembling fool!
  I long, yet fear to look upon it – thus (*Breaks the seal*)

Evil or good come of it, I will read—
(*Reads*) – 'This, from my most doleful prison-house—
If half the love thou oft has sworn to me,
But half be true, read, and deliver me!
This I indite in such a darksome cell
As fancy shrinks from – where the blessed light
And genial air do never visit me—
Where chains bow down my limbs to the damp earth,
And darkness compasseth me like a veil,
I do beseech thee, by the tender love
That I have borne thee from thine infancy—
I do beseech thee, by all strongest ties
Of kin, and of compassion – let me not
Lie like a cursed and a forgotten thing,
Thrust down beneath the earth – let not the blood
That bounds in youth's swift current through my veins
Be chilled by dungeon dews before its time;
Or thickened by the weight of galling fetters!'
Oh misery! my brother – my dear brother!
(*Reads*) – 'If this doth move the spirit of thy love,
Hie thee to court, and there, at the King's feet,
Kneel and implore my pardon – do not fear
To let thy tears plead for me – to thy prayers
Do I commit my fate; and on thy lips,
Whose moving eloquence must touch his soul,
Hang all my hopes! – Sweet sister, think upon me!'
What, back to court! – what, sue at the King's feet!
Oh, God! but just escaped from the wild wave,
Must I plunge headlong back again! My brain
Is dizzy with the flocking ills that gather
All numberless and indistinct around me.
Alas! poor scroll; how his hand shook in tracing
Thy sad appeal! Oh my unhappy brother!
Why didst thou not at price of my own blood
Rate thy deliverance! but with heart still throbbing
With most unnerving and resistless love,
Shall I encounter the King's eyes, and feel
That winning is but loss; and life, and liberty,
Given to thee, the warrants of my ruin?
(*Reads*) – 'I do beseech thee, by the tender love
That I have borne thee from thine infancy!'—
I can no more! thou shalt be rescued! yet—

Enter FLORISE

FLORISE: Madam, the messenger awaits your answer.

FRANÇOISE: Oh maiden, read! my brother is in prison;
    His fond arms that so oft have clasped around me,
    Strait bound with gyves. Oh heaven! my dear, dear brother.

FLORISE: Why, madam, how now? are ye lost in grief?
    Are tears his ransom? – Up! for shame! for shame!
    You must to court, and straight procure his pardon.
    Nay, never wring your hands; they say the King
    Is gentle-hearted, and did never refuse
    Bright eyes, whose prayers were tearful rosaries,
    Told with devotion at his royal feet.

FRANÇOISE: Kind heaven be with me! I will do this deed.
    Oh, Lautrec! there is sorrow at my heart,
    Heavy and boding! – Florise is't not strange—
    I fear – alas! alas! I am undone!

FLORISE: Why this is madness! and your brother lies,
    Meantime, in darkness, and deep silence – winging
    In fancy hither – hoping, with the hope
    That is but intense agony – so deep,
    That hope which anchors on so frail a stay!
    Now, at this hour, he calls imploringly;
    His fettered arms are stretched abroad to you.

FRANÇOISE: No more! no more! I will this hour away—
    Nay, come not with me; ere the night be fallen,
    I shall return, successful and most blest;
    Or thou wilt hear, that at the obdurate feet
    Of him, whom I am sent to supplicate,
    I poured my life in prayers for my dear brother.

[*Exeunt severally*]

SCENE vi

A room in the palace

Enter FRANCIS *and* BONNIVET

FRANCIS: No tidings of de Bourbon; search is vain.
    The storm is gathering, and 'tis time we spread
    Due shelter over us. De Bonnivet!

How say'st thou? here be more despatches – see
Young John de Laval hath supplied the place
Of this same Lautrec, and Colonna's host
Reeling with victory, which thought to trample
The last poor remnant of our broken troops,
Has been repulsed by him, and overthrown.
Yet fear I much, this vantage will be lost
For lack of power to keep or to improve it.
BONNIVET: The messenger brought word, that Count Laval
   Had, in that very fray, been so sore wounded,
   That long he lay upon the field of death,
   As he'd taken there his everlasting rest.

                    Enter a GENTLEMAN

FRANCIS: In this despatch – How now?
GENTLEMAN: So please your grace,
   One stands without, and earnestly entreats
   To see your majesty.
FRANCIS: Hath he no name?
GENTLEMAN: My liege, it is a woman; but her veil
   So curtains all her form, that even eyes
   Which knew, and oft had gazed on her, might guess
   In vain.
FRANCIS: A woman, and a suppliant!
   Let her have entrance.
BONNIVET: At some other time
   Your majesty, perhaps will deign to inform me
   Further concerning Italy.
FRANCIS: Ay, ay,
   At some more fitting time.   [*Exit* BONNIVET]

                    Enter FRANÇOISE

FRANÇOISE (*aside*)
   Oh, heaven! be merciful!
   My eyes are dim, and icy fear doth send
   My blood all shuddering back upon my heart.
FRANCIS: Close veiled, indeed: mysterious visitant!
   Whom curious thought doth strive to look upon,
   Despite the cloud that now enshrines you; pardon,
   If failing in its hope, the eager eye
   Doth light on every point, that, unconcealed,
   Tells of the secret it so fain would pierce:
   That heavenly gait, whose slow majestic motion
   Discloses all the bearing of command;

That noiseless foot, that falling on the earth,
Wakes not an echo; leaves not even a print—
So jealous seeming of its favours; and
This small white hand, I might deem born of marble,
But for the throbbing life that trembles in it.
Why, how is this? 'tis cold as marble's self;
And by your drooping form! – this is too much –
Youth breathes around you; beauty is youth's kin:
I must withdraw this envious veil—

FRANÇOISE: Hold, sir!
Your highness need but speak to be obeyed;
Thus then – (*Unveils*) –

FRANCIS: Amazement! oh, thou peerless light!
Why thus deny thy radiance, and enfold,
Like the coy moon, thy charms in envious clouds?

FRANÇOISE: Such clouds best suit, whose sun is set for ever;
And veils should curtain over those eyes, whose light
Is all put out with tears: oh, good my liege!
I come a suitor to your pardoning mercy.

FRANCIS (*aside*)
Sue on, so thou do after hear my suit.

FRANÇOISE: My brother! Out, alas! – your brow grows dark,
And threateningly doth fright my scarce-breathed prayer
Back to its hold of silence.

FRANCIS: Lady, aye,
Your brother hath offended against the state,
And must abide the state's most lawful vengeance;
Nor canst thou in thy sorrow even say
Such sentence is unjust.

FRANÇOISE: I do, I do;
Oh, vengeance! what hast thou to do with justice?
Most merciful, and most vindictive, who
Hath called ye sisters; who hath made ye kin?
My liege, my liege, if you do take such vengeance
Upon my brother's fault, yourself do sin,
By calling your's that which is heaven's alone:
But if 'tis justice that hath sentenced him,
Hear me; for he, unheard, hath been condemned,
Against all justice, without any mercy.

FRANCIS: Maiden, thou pleadst in vain.

FRANÇOISE: Oh, say not so:
Oh, merciful, my lord! you are a soldier;

You have won war's red favours in the field,
And victory hath been your handmaiden:
Oh! think, if you were thrust away for ever
From fame and glory, warrior's light and air;
And left to feel time's creeping fingers chill
Your blood; and from fame's blazonry efface
Your youthful deeds, which, like a faithless promise,
Bloomed fair, but bore no after-fruit—

FRANCIS: Away!
Thou speakst of that no woman ever knew.
Thy prayer is cold: hast thou no nearer theme,
Which, having felt thyself, thou mayst address
More movingly unto my heart?

FRANÇOISE: None, none,
But what that heart itself might whisper you.
Where is the Princess Margaret? my liege!
As she loves you, so have I loved my brother:
Oh, think how she would be overcome with woe,
Were you in hopeless dungeon pent? Oh, think!
If iron-handed power had so decreed
That you should never clasp her, or behold
Her face again!

FRANCIS: Farewell, fair maid, thy suit
Is bootless[32] all – perchance – but no, 'tis vain:
Yet had'st thou pleaded more, and not so coldly—

FRANÇOISE: Oh, good my liege! turn not away from me!
See, on the earth I kneel; by these swift tears
That witness my affliction; by each throb
Of my sad heart; by all you love!—

FRANCIS: Ah, tempter!
Say rather by these orient pearls, whose price
Would bribe the very soul of justice; say,
By these luxuriant tresses, which have thrown
Eternal chains around my heart—
                    (FRANÇOISE *starts up*)
Nay, start not;
If thou, so soon, art weary of beseeching,
Hearken to me, and I will frame a suit
Which thou must hear.   (*Kneels*)   By the resistless love
Thou hast inspired me with! – by thy perfections –
Thy matchless beauty! – Nay, it is in vain,
Thou shalt not free thyself, till thou hast heard;

Thou shalt not free thy brother, till—
FRANÇOISE: Unhand me!
  Sir, as you are a man—

Enter the QUEEN

QUEEN: Oh, excellent!
FRANCIS (*starts up*)
  Confusion seize yon woman's watchfulness!
QUEEN: I fear me I have marred a wise discourse;
  Which, if I read aright, yon lady's looks,
  Was argued most persuasively; fair madam,
  My son hath had the happiness already
  To welcome you to court; 'twould seem remiss
  In me to be so backward, were it not
  That ignorance of your return hath robbed
  Me of joy's better half – anticipation;
  Which, as it seems, you have been pleased to grant
  His Majesty: what, not one little word!
  Nay, then, your conference is doubtless ended;
  If so – I have some business with the King—

(*She waves* FRANÇOISE *off*)

FRANCIS: Then, madam, you must let that business rest;
  For, look you, I have matters, which, though long
  I've pondered over them, I've reserved till now,
  Unto your private ear. How many years
  Longer am I to live in tutelage?
  When will it please your wisdom to resign
  The office, which, self-arrogated, seems
  Daily to grow beyond that wisdom's compass,
  Though strained unto its utmost? Hark you, madam!
  'Tis time you lay aside the glittering bauble,
  Which, hourly, in your hands grows more respectless.
  I speak of power – I'm weary of these visions;
  In which, you've nursed and pampered your ambition
  Until it dreams its dream is true. How long
  Am I to wear the yoke, which every day
  Grows heavier, but less firm? – if longer yet,
  Take this good counsel – lighten it, or else
  'Twill break and crush you: nay, never gaze on me
  With that fixed haughty stare; I do not sleep—
  'Tis you that dream – full time you were awakened.
QUEEN: What, thankless boy! whose greatness is the work
  Of my own hands – this, to your mother, sir?

FRANCIS: I am your King, madam – your King – your King!—
　　Ay, start and boil with passion, and turn pale
　　With rage, whose powerless effort wakes but scorn:
　　Who made you Queen of France? my father's wife
　　Was Duchess of Savoy and Angoulême:
　　These, are your only titles – and the rest,
　　A boon, which courtesy hath lent, not given,
　　Unto the mother of the King of France.
　　And, for the boast you make, of having made me
　　All that I am, 'tis false; my open right,
　　Strong in its truth, and in the world's approval,
　　Both called me to the throne, and held me there.
　　'Tis you who shine from a reflected light—
　　'Tis you, whose greatest honour is my crown—
　　'Tis you, who owe me, and my royal state,
　　All that you have of state and of observance.
　　Think on it well; henceforth you'll find it so:
　　And, as you value the faint shade of power
　　Which clings to you, beware how it is used.
　　Curb your unbounded pride and haughty spirit;
　　Which, brooking no control itself, would make
　　Slaves of all else that breathe; and, mark me well,
　　Slacken your leading strings or ere they break.　　　　[*Exit*]
QUEEN: The hour is come at last – so long foreseen –
　　So long averted by my anxious efforts,
　　My overgrown power is toppling from its base—
　　And, like a ruined tower, whose huge supporters
　　At length decay, it nods unto its ruin.
　　I am undone! But, if I needs must fall,
　　No rising foot shall tread upon my neck,
　　And say I paved the way for its ascension.
　　Proud spirit! thou who in the darkest hours
　　Of danger and defeat hast steaded me—
　　Thou dauntless, uncontrolled, and daring soul!
　　Who hast but seen in all the world a throne—
　　In all mankind, thine instruments; rejoice!
　　I'll do a deed, which, prospering, shall place me
　　At once upon the summit of my hopes—
　　Beyond all power of future storm or wreck;
　　Or, if I fail, my fall shall be like his,
　　That wondrous mighty man, who overthrew
　　The whole Philistian host – when revelry

Was turned to mourning – and the ponderous ruin,
That he drew down on his own head, overwhelmed
The power of Gath, when Gaza shook for fear.[33]

Enter GONZALES

Come hither, sirrah, now the day is done—
And night, with swarthy hands, is sowing stars
In yonder sky. De Bourbon is escaped:
Thy days are forfeit; but thy life is now
More needful to my present purposes,
Than was thy purposed death, to appease my rage.
Thou art free! – I've need of thee; live and obey.

GONZALES (*aside*)

Revenge! I clutch thee still, since still I live.
(*Aloud*) Madam, obedience ever was my life's
Sole study and attainment.

QUEEN: Hark thee, father!

I have a deed for thee, which may, perhaps,
For a short moment, freeze thy startled blood;
And fright thy firmly-seated heart, to beat
Hurried and trembling summons in thy breast.
Didst ever look upon the dead?

GONZALES: Ay, madam,

Full oft; and in each calm or frightful guise
Death comes in – on the bloody battle-field;
When with each gush of black and curdling life
A curse was uttered – when the prayers I've poured,
Have been all drowned with din of clashing arms;
And shrieks, and shouts, and loud artillery,
That shook the slippery earth, all drunk with gore;
I've seen it, swollen with subtle poison, black
And staring with concentrate agony;
When every vein hath started from its bed,
And wreathed like knotted snakes, around the brows
That, frantic, dashed themselves in tortures down
Upon the earth. I've seen life float away
On the faint sound of a far tolling bell;
Leaving its late warm tenement as fair,
As though 'twere the incorruptible that lay
Before me; and all earthly taint had vanished
With the departed spirit.

QUEEN: Father, hold!

Return to the other – to that second death,

Most fearful in its ghastly agony.
Come nearer to me; didst thou ever – nay.
Put back thy cowl – I fain would see thy face:
So – didst thou ever – thou lookst very pale—
Art feared?
GONZALES: Who, I? Your highness surely jests!
QUEEN: Did ever thine own hand – thou understandst me.
GONZALES: I begin to understand you, madam; aye,
It has been red with blood, with reeking life.
QUEEN: Father! so steep that hand for me once more,
And, by my soul I swear, I will reward thee
With the cardinal's hat when next Rome's princes meet.
GONZALES: The cardinal's hat! go on, I pray you, madam,
I know but half my task.
QUEEN: True, father, true,
I had forgot: and now methinks I feel
Lightened of a huge burden, now thou knowst
My settled purpose. Listen! there is one,
Whose envious beauty doth pluck down my power,
Day after day, with more audacious hand—
That woman!
GONZALES: Ha! a woman!
QUEEN: Well, how now!
Blood is but blood, and life no more than life,
Be it cradled in however fair a form!
Dost shrink, thou vaunting caitiff, from the test
Thine own avowal drew upon thee? Mark me!
If, ere two suns have risen and have set,
Françoise de Foix—
GONZALES: How?
QUEEN: The young Lautrec's sister,
Count Laval's bride.
GONZALES: What! John de Laval's bride!
Hell! what a flash of light bursts in on me!
Revenge! revenge! thou art mine own at last!
QUEEN: Why dost thou start, and look so wide and wild,
And clench thy hands?
GONZALES: So please your grace – O pardon me! –
'Twas pity – sorrow – I – Oh! how has she
Provoked your dreadful wrath, that such a doom
Should cut her young days off thus suddenly?
QUEEN: Content thee, that it falls not on thy head,

And do my bidding, as thou valuest
That head of thine. I tell thee she must die;
By subtle poison, or by sudden knife,
I care not – so those eyes be closed for ever.
Look, priest! thou art free; but if, in two more days,
The grave hide not that woman from my hate,
She shall not die the less: and, by high heaven!
Be thou in the farthest corner of the earth,
Thou shalt be dragged from thence; and drop by drop,
Shall thy base blood assuage my full revenge!
Think on it, and resolve – and so farewell!

[*Exit*]

GONZALES: Rejoice, my soul! thy far-off goal is won!
  His bride – all that he most doth love and live for –
  His heart's best hope – she shall be foul corruption
  When next his eager arms are spread to clasp her!
  I'll do this deed, ere I go mad for joy:
  And when her husband shall mourn over her
  In blight and bitterness, I'll drink his tears;
  And when his voice shall call upon his bride,
  I'll answer him with taunts and scorning gibes,
  And torture him to madness: and, at length,
  When he shall deem some persecuting fiend
  Hath escaped from hell to curse and ruin him,
  I'll rend the veil, that for so long hath shrouded me,
  And, bursting on him from my long disguise,
  Reveal the hand that hath overshadowed him
  With such a deadly and eternal hate!

[*Exit*]

SCENE vii

A gallery in the palace

Enter TRIBOULET, *followed by* FRANÇOISE DE FOIX

FRANÇOISE: Hold, hold! I do beseech thee, ere my brain
  Whirl with this agony – show me the letter.
TRIBOULET: Nay, but you did refuse it some time gone;
  I'll to the King, and give it back again.
FRANÇOISE: Perchance 'tis of my brother! – oh! for mercy,

Give it me now; I do repent me – give it!
TRIBOULET: Give it? – no, take it; give it back again!
Which way doth the wind blow?
FRANÇOISE: I shall go mad
With this most dread suspense! Oh! if that letter
Tell of my brother's fate, as chance it doth!
Give it me once again or ere I die!
TRIBOULET: Listen. I'll read it thee.
FRANÇOISE: Oh! no, no, no!
(*Aside*) – For if the King doth plead his love in it—
No, tear, but do not open it, good fool!
TRIBOULET: I cannot read unless I open it. Listen: (*Reads*)
'If thou do not follow his footsteps, who shall bring thee this, not
only shall thy brother's liberty, but even his life'—
FRANÇOISE: Oh gracious heaven! it is impossible!
His life! his precious days! Give me that scroll.
                    (*She reads, and faints*)
TRIBOULET: Let me spell over this letter; for the lady, she'll be the
better for a little rest. (*Reads*) – 'If thou do not follow his footsteps,
who shall bring thee this.' – Marry, that means my footsteps; and
whither tend my footsteps?— Even to the King's chamber. What,
shall her brother die, unless she meet the King alone at this dead
hour of night? I would I had lost the letter! my back and the whip
had been acquainted of a surety; but that were better than – poor
maiden! By my wisdom, then, I will not lead her to the King! I'll run
away, and then, if I be questioned, I can swear she fell into a swoon
by the way, and could not come!
                    (*Going,* FRANÇOISE *revives*)
FRANÇOISE: Oh, no – not death! mercy! oh, mercy! spare him!
Where am I! have I slept! – oh, heaven be praised,
Here's one will be my guide! Good Triboulet,
If thou have aught of reason, lend it me.
TRIBOULET: Alack! poor thing, how wide she talks! – she's come
To borrow wisdom of a fool! Poor lady!
FRANÇOISE: Nay, gaze not on me, for dear charity!
But lead, and I will follow to the King—
Fall on my knees – once more implore his mercy!
I do beseech thee – Life is on our haste!
TRIBOULET: How say you, pretty lady – life, and no more?
FRANÇOISE: Oh! I shall go distraught with this delay.
See, to thine eyes I will address my speech—
For what thou lookst on that thou understandst.

TRIBOULET: Ay, marry, and more, as I think, than either of us look on,
do I understand.

FRANÇOISE: These jewels are of a surpassing value—
Take them, and lead me to the king.

TRIBOULET: What, at this hour?

FRANÇOISE: If not, my brother dies.

TRIBOULET: Alone?

FRANÇOISE: The night grows pale, and the stars seem
To melt away, before the burning breath
Of fiery morn. If thou art born of woman—
If thou hast but one drop of natural blood
That folly hath not frozen – I beseech thee
Lead to the king, whiles I have strength to follow!

TRIBOULET: Then heaven be with thee, lady! for I can no more.
Follow! and may I in this hour have been a greater fool than ere I
was before.

[*Exeunt*]

Act IV

SCENE i

An apartment in the Chateau-de-Foix

FRANÇOISE *is discovered sitting, pale and motionless, by*
a table – FLORISE *is kneeling by her*

FRANÇOISE: How heavily the sun hangs in the clouds—
The day will never be done.
FLORISE: Oh, lady, thou hast sat
And watched the western clouds, day after day,
Grow crimson with the sun's farewell, and said,
Each day, the night will never come: yet night
Hath come at last, and so it will again.
FRANÇOISE: Will it, indeed! will the night come at last,
And hide that burning sun, and shade my eyes,
Which ache with this red light – will darkness come
At last?
FLORISE: Sweet madam, yes; and sleep will come:
Nay, shake not mournfully your head at me—
Your eyes are heavy; sleep is brooding in them.
FRANÇOISE: Hot tears have lain in them, and made them heavy;
But sleep – oh, no! no, no! they will not close:
I have a gnawing pain, here, at my heart:
Guilt, thou liest heavy, and art hard to bear.
FLORISE: What say you, madam, guilt!
FRANÇOISE: Who dare say so!
(*Starting up*) 'Twas pity – mercy – 'twas not guilt! and though
The world's fierce scorn shall call it infamy, I say 'twas not!
Speak – speak – dost thou? Oh? answer me!
Say, was it infamy?
FLORISE: Dear lady, you are ill!
Some strange distemper fevers thus your brain.
Come, madam, suffer me at least to bind
These tresses that have fallen over your brow,
Making your temples throb with added weight:
Let me bind up these golden locks that hang
Dishevelled thus upon your neck.

FRANÇOISE: Out, viper!
  Nor twine, nor braid, again shall ever bind
  These locks! Oh! rather tear them off, and cast them
  Upon the common earth, and trample them—
  Heap dust and ashes on them – tear them thus,
  And thus, and thus! Oh, Florise, I am mad!
  Distracted! – out alas! alas! poor head!
  Thou achest for thy pillow in the grave—
  Thy darksome couch – thy dreamless, quiet bed!
FLORISE: These frantic passions do destroy themselves
  With their excess, and well it is they do so:
  But, madam, now the tempest is overlaid,
  And you are calmer, better, as I trust,
  Let me entreat you send for that same monk
  I told you of this morn: he is a leech,
  Learned in theory, and of wondrous skill
  To heal all maladies of soul or body.
FRANÇOISE: Of soul – of soul – ay, so they'd have us think:
  Dost thou believe that the hard coin we pour
  Into their outstretched hands, indeed, buys pardon
  For all, or any sin, we may commit?
  Dost thou believe forgiveness may he had
  Thus easy cheap, for crimes as black in hue
  As – as –
FLORISE: As what? I know no sin whatever
  The church's minister may not remit:
  As – what were you about to say?
FRANÇOISE: Come hither;
  Thinkst thou a heap of gold as high as Etna
  Could cover from the piercing eye of heaven
  So foul a crime as – as – adultery?
  Why dost thou stare thus strangely at my words,
  And answerest not?
FLORISE: I do believe, indeed,
  Not all the treasury of the wide world,
  Not all the wealth hid in the womb of ocean,
  Can ransom sin – nothing but deep repentance—
  Austere and lengthened penance – frequent tears.
FRANÇOISE: 'Tis false! I know it – these do nought avail:
  To move relentless heaven it must be bribed.
  And yet – go, call thy priest; I'll speak with him.
  I will cast off the burthen of my shame,

Or ere it press me down into the grave!   [*Exit*]
FLORISE: Alas, poor flower, the canker's in thy core!
                    Enter GONZALES
Good morrow to my reverend confessor!
GONZALES: Good morrow, maiden;
    Where's thy lady, Florise?
FLORISE: This moment, as I think, gone to her chamber.
GONZALES: To sleep, perchance!
FLORISE: Oh, father, would she could!
    But there's a sleepless sorrow at her heart—
    She hath not closed her eyes for many a night.
GONZALES: Her brother, Lautrec, for the loss of Milan,
    Was lately thrust in prison.
FLORISE: Even so:
    And at that very time a messenger
    Arrived with news of that most dire mischance,
    Which quite overcame my mistress' drooping heart:
    She often read a scroll Count Lautrec sent her,
    And wept, and read it over and over again;
    And then, as though determined by its arguments,
    She sought the king, to move him to forgiveness:
    Short space elapsed ere home she came again,
    Thus broken-hearted, and, as I do think,
    Bowed to the grave by some overmastering sorrow.
GONZALES: 'Tis a strange tale: but tell me now, Florise,
    Where's her young lord, John de Laval? methought
    It was agreed on with her brother, who
    Disposes of his sister's hand and fortune,
    That, soon as this Italian war permitted,
    Laval should hasten back again to France,
    And claim the lady Françoise as his bride.
    Was it not so?
FLORISE: Ay; and I've sometimes thought
    That the Count's absence was my lady's grief.
    I fear this last campaign hath ended him,
    And that he'll never come back to wed his bride,
    Who mourns his loss, and fades a virgin widow.
    Out on my prating tongue! I had forgot—
    The lady Françoise straight would speak with you.
GONZALES: With me – with me! What, Florise, dost thou think
    That she hath aught she would confess? – no matter.
    Tell her I'll wait upon her instantly.   [*Exit* FLORISE]

Strange! passing strange! I guess at it in vain.
Lautrec forgiven, and herself broken-hearted!
This simple maid knows nothing – can the king!
'Tis sure he loved her – oh, that it were so!
Oh, that his passion had forestalled my vengeance!
That love in him had done the deed my hate
Most covets! – An I had not worn so long
This monkish garb, and all uncourtly seeming,
Methinks for such an end I could have done
All that disuse hath made unnatural
And strange to me: acted the fool again;
Conned over youth's love tale; sued, implored, entreated,
And won her, but that I might give her back
Defiled unto Laval! – would it were so!
I'll to her straight, and from her wring confession
By such keen torture, as designless looks
And careless words inflict on secret guilt.   [*Exit*]

SCENE ii

An inner court in the Chateau-de-Foix

Enter FRANCIS, *wrapped in a cloak, and* FLORISE

FLORISE: Then be it even as you will, sir stranger,
    Since you bring joyful tidings to my lady,
    Good heart! who sorely stands in need of such.
    At sunset meet me here, when I will bring you
    Where you shall see and speak with her, fair sir.
FRANCIS: At sunset I'll not fail: farewell, fair maiden!

[*Exit* FLORISE]

They tell me she is sunk in sorrow,
Lets a consuming grief destroy her beauty;
Therefore, in this disguise, leave I the court,
To follow and to claim her; for though overthrown,
If shame and woe have followed her defeat,
I hold myself no lawful conqueror;
But one whose love, like the fierce eastern wind,
Hath withered that it hung upon. But, pshaw!
'Tis idle all; if that her hand be promised,
It is not bound; and, were it so, kings' wills

Melt compacts into air. She must be mine—
Mine only – mine for ever! and, for Laval,
Another and a wealthier bride, I trow,
Shall well repay him for the one I've stolen.   [*Exit*]

Enter GONZALES

GONZALES: 'Tis true, by heaven! 'tis as my hope presaged,—
Her lips avowed it. Oh! then there is torture
Far worse than death in store for thee, Laval.

Enter a PAGE

PAGE: Save you. From court a letter, reverend sir.
GONZALES: Give it, and get thee gone.   [*Exit* PAGE]
'Tis from the queen!
Further injunctions to be sudden, doubtless – so:
                 (*Opens the letter, and reads*)
'That which thou hast in hand, quickly dispatch; else opportunity
will play thee false. Laval is now in France, and by tomorrow will
have reached Chateau-de-Foix; therefore, if it is not done, do it as
soon as thou shalt have received this letter.—LOUISA.'
Tomorrow! how! why that should be today:
Today – today – ah! say you so, indeed:
He could not come at a more welcome hour.
                 (*Horns without*)
Hark! even now the horn proclaims my triumph!
The gates swing wide, the outer courtyard rings
With neighing steeds and jingling spurs, and steps
Whose haste doth tell of hot, impatient love:
He stands upon the threshold of his home
Reeling with joy. Now, now—
             Enter LAVAL *and attendants*
Hail, noble sir!
LAVAL: I joy to see thee, yet I cannot now
Even stay to say as much. Where is my love?
GONZALES: The lady Françoise, sir, is in her chamber.
                 (LAVAL *is going*)
I pray you tarry, good my lord, I've much
To say to you.
LAVAL: Ay, so have I to her:
Another time, another time, good father.
GONZALES: No time so fitting as the present, sir.
LAVAL: 'Sdeath! wouldst thou have me listen, and not hear?
Look on thee, and not see thee? stand aside!
Till ears and eyes have had their fill of her.

I'm blind, and deaf, and well nigh mad.
GONZALES: My lord,
  What I would say will bear no tarrying.
LAVAL: A plague on thee! come with me, then, and thus—
  While I do gaze on her I'll hear thy tale.
GONZALES: What I've to say you'd rather hear alone.
LAVAL: I tell thee, no, thou most vexatious priest!
  That which I hear shall she hear too; my heart,
  And all it owes or wishes, is her own;
  Knowledge, hopes, fears, desires – all, all are hers.
GONZALES: Then be it so – follow unto her chamber!
LAVAL: Follow! I could not follow the swift wind!
  Thou dost not love, sir priest; follow thyself!
GONZALES: Even as you will I do: lead on, my lord!   [*Exeunt*]

SCENE iii

An apartment in the Chateau-de-Foix

Enter FRANCIS *and* FLORISE

FRANCIS: I tell thee, ere she see the Count Laval,
  I must inform her of mine errand.
FLORISE: Well—
  I had forgot, in all this sudden joy:
  But see, behind the tapestry, here, you may
  Wait for, and speak with her.
FRANCIS: I thank thee, maiden.
FLORISE: Farewel, and good success attend you, sir.

                                        [*Exit* FLORISE]
            FRANCIS *conceals himself behind the tapestry*
                      Enter FRANÇOISE
FRANÇOISE: Now, ye paternal halls, that frown on me,
  Down, down, and hide me in your ruins – ha!
        (*As* LAVAL *and* GONZALES *enter*, FRANÇOISE *shrieks*)
LAVAL: My bride! – my beautiful!
GONZALES: Stand back, young sir!
LAVAL: Who dares extend his arms 'twixt those whom love
  Hath bound? whom holy wedlock shall, ere long.
GONZALES: The stern decree of the most holy church,
  Whose garb I bear; and whose authority

I interpose between you; until I
Interpret to your ears the fearful shriek
That greeted you, upon your entrance here:
Look on that lady, Count Laval – who stands
Pale as a virgin rose, whose early bloom
Hath not been gazed on yet by the hot sun;
And fair—

LAVAL: Oh, how unutterably fair!

GONZALES: Seems not that shrinking flower the soul of all
That is most pure, as well as beautiful?

LAVAL: Peace, thou vain babbler! Is it unto me
That thou art prating? – unto me, who have
Worshipped her, with a wild idolatry,
Liker to madness than to love?

GONZALES: Indeed!
Say, then, if such a show of chastity
Ere sat on lips that have been hot with passion?
Or such a pale cold hue did ever rest
On cheeks, where burning kisses have called up
The crimson blood, in blushes all as warm?
Look on her yet; and say, if ever form
Showed half so like a breathing piece of marble.
Off with thy specious seeming, thou deceiver!
And don a look that better suits thy state.
Oh, well-dissembled sin! say, was it thus,
Shrinking, and pale, thou stoodst, when the King's arms
Did clasp thee, and his hot lip seared from thine
Their oath to wed thy brother's friend?

LAVAL: Damnation
Alight upon thee, thou audacious monk!
The blight thou breath'st recoil on thine own head;
It hath no power to touch the spotless fame
Of one, from whom thy cursed calumnies
Fly like rebounding shafts. Ha! ha! ha! ha!
The king! a merry tale forsooth!

GONZALES: Then we
Will laugh at it, ha! ha! – why, what care I?
We will be merry; since thou art content
To laugh and be a—

LAVAL: Françoise – I – I pray thee
Speak to me – smile – speak – look on me, I say –
What, tears! what, wring thine hands! what, pale as death!—

And not one word – not one!

FRANÇOISE: (*to* GONZALES)

Oh deadly fiend!

Thou hast but hastened that which was foredoomed.

(*To* LAVAL) My lord, ere I make answer to this charge,

I have a boon to crave of you – my brother –

LAVAL: How wildly thine eye rolls; thy hand is cold

As death, my fairest love.

FRANÇOISE: Beseech you, sir,

Unclasp your arm. Where is my brother?

LAVAL: Lautrec?

In Italy; ere now is well and happy.

FRANÇOISE: Thanks, gentle heaven! all is not bitterness,

In this most bitter hour. My Lord Laval,

To you my faith was plighted, by my brother;

That faith I ratified by mine own vow.

LAVAL: The oath was registered in highest heaven.

Thou art mine!

FRANÇOISE: To all eternity, Laval,

If blood cannot efface that damning bond.

(*Snatches his dagger and stabs herself*)

'Tis cancelled, I've struck home – my dear, dear brother.

[*Dies*]

GONZALES (*aside*)

It works, it works!

LAVAL: Oh horrible! – she's dead!

(FRANCIS *rushes from his concealment at the word*)

FRANCIS: Dead!

(LAVAL *draws his sword, and turns upon the*
KING, *who draws to defend himself*)

LAVAL: Ha! what fiend hath sent thee here?

Down! down to hell with thee, thou damned seducer!

Enter QUEEN, *followed by attendants*

QUEEN: Secure that madman!

(*Part of the attendants surround and disarm* LAVAL)

QUEEN (*aside to* GONZALES)

Bravely done, indeed!

I shall remember. – (*Aloud*) – How now, wayward boy?

How is't I find thee here in private broils,

Whilst proud rebellion triumphs over the land?

Bourbon's in France again! and strong Marseilles

Beleaguered round by Spanish soldiery.

These tidings brought young Henry of Navarre,
Whom Bourbon, and Colonna, joining arms,
Have stripped and spoiled of his paternal crown.

FRANCIS: Peace, mother, prithee peace; look here! look here!
Here is a sight, that hath more sorrow in it,
Than loss of kingdoms, empires, or the world!
There lies the fairest lily of the land,
Untimely broken from its stem, to wither!
                    (*Going towards the body*)

LAVAL (*breaks from attendants*)
Stand back, King Francis! lay not even a finger
On this poor wreck, that death hath sanctified!
This soulless frame of what was once my love!
Oh! thou pale flower, that in death's icy grasp
Dost lie, making the dissolution that we dread
Look fair. Farewell! for ever, and for ever!
Thou shouldst have been the glad crown of my youth,
Maturer life's fruitful and fond companion—
Dreary old age's shelter.

GONZALES: Tears, my Lord?

LAVAL: Ay, tears, thou busy mischief; get thee hence!
Away! who sent for thee? – who bade thee pour
The venom of thy tongue into my wounds?
What seekst thou here?

GONZALES: To see thee weep, Laval!
And I am satisfied! Look on me, boy!
Dost know Garcia – first scion of a house
Whose kindred shoots by thine were all cut down?

LAVAL: For dead I left thee on Marignan plain!
Art thou from thence arisen! or from hell!
To wreak such ruin on me?

GONZALES: They die not
Who have the work I had on hand unfinished;
The spirit would not from its fleshly house,
In which thy sword so many outlets made,
Ere it had seen its fell revenge fulfilled.

LAVAL: Revenge! – for what? – wherefore dost thou pursue me?

GONZALES: Look on thy bride! look on that faded thing,
That even the tears thy manhood showers so fast,
And bravely, cannot wake to life again!
I call all nature to bear witness here—
As fair a flower once grew within my home,

As young, as lovely, and as dearly loved.
I had a sister once, a gentle maid—
The only daughter of my father's house,
Round whom our ruder loves did all entwine,
As round the dearest treasure that we owned.
She was the centre of our souls' affections—
She was the bud, that underneath our strong
And sheltering arms, spread over her, did blow.
So grew this fair, fair girl, till envious fate
Brought on the hour when she was withered.
Thy father, sir – now mark! – for 'tis the point
And moral of my tale – thy father, then,
Was, by my sire, in war taken prisoner—
Wounded almost to death, he brought him home—
Sheltered him – cherished him – and, with a care,
Most like a brother's, watched his bed of sickness,
Till ruddy health, once more through all his veins,
Sent life's warm stream in strong returning tide.
How think ye he repaid my father's love?
From her dear home he lured my sister forth,
And, having robbed her of her treasured honour,
Cast her away, defiled – despoiled – forsaken!—
The daughter of a high and ancient line—
The child of so much love! – she died! – she died! –
Upon the threshold of that home, from which
My father spurned her! – over whose pale corse
I swore to hunt, through life, her ravisher;
Nor ever from my bloodhound track desist,
Till due and deep atonement had been made—
Honour for honour given – blood for blood.

LAVAL: These were my father's injuries – not mine,
Remorseless fiend!

GONZALES: Thy father died in battle;
And as his lands, and titles, at his death,
Devolved on thee, on thee devolved the treasure
Of my dear hate. I have had such revenge!
Such horrible revenge! – thy life, thy honour,
We're all too little – I have had thy tears!
I've wrung a woman's sorrow from thine eyes,
And drunk each bitter drop of agony,
As heavenly nectar, worthy of the gods!
Kings, the earth's mightiest potentates, have been

My tools and instruments: you, haughty madam,
And your ambition – yonder headstrong boy,
And his mad love – all, all beneath my feet,
All slaves unto my will and deadly purpose.

QUEEN: Such glorious triumphs should be short-lived. Ho!
Lead out that man to instant death.

GONZALES: Without confession, madam, shall I go?
Shall not the world know on what services
Louisa of Savoy bestows such guerdon?

QUEEN: Am I obeyed! away with him!

FRANCIS: Your pardon—
If he have aught to speak before he dies,
Let him unfold, it is our pleasure so!

GONZALES: You did not deal so hardly with the soul
Of Bourbon, when you sent me to his cell,
Love's frocked and hooded messenger, I trow.
But let that pass. King Francis, mark we well—
I was, by yonder lady, made the bearer
Of amorous overtures unto de Bourbon,
Which he with scorn flung back; else trust me, sir,
You had not stood so safely on your throne
As now you stand. 'Twas I who set him free:
Empowered by Charles of Spain to buy his arm
At any cost: so much for Bourbon! Now,
Look on the prostrate form of this fair creature!
Why, how now, madam, do you blench and start?
You're somewhat pale! fie, fie! what matters it—
   'Blood is but blood, and life no more than life,
   Be't cradled in however fair a form.'
Is it not well done! ha! well and sudddenly?
Are you not satisfied?

QUEEN: Thou lying devil!

GONZALES: Darest thou deny the part thou hast in this?

QUEEN: Darest thou to me? Ay, reptile!

GONZALES: Here! look here! – (*Shows her letter*)

QUEEN: Ha!

GONZALES: Hast thou found thy master spirit, Queen!
Our wits have grappled hard for many a day.
What! mute at last? or hast some quaint device?

QUEEN: No! hell has conquered me!

FRANCIS: Give me that scroll – hast thou said all, Garcia?

GONZALES: Ay, all! Fair madam, fare ye well awhile;

And for my death, I thank you from my soul.
For after the rich cup I've drained this hour,
The rest were tasteless, stale, and wearisome.
Life had no aim, or joy, or end, save vengeance—
Vengeance is satisfied, so farewell life!

[*Exit, guarded*]

FRANCIS (*reads the letter*)
Oh, mother! guilt hath taken from thy lips
All proud repelling answer. Give me that ring—
Strip me that diadem from off thy brows—
And bid a long farewell to vanity!
For in a holy nunnery immured,
Thou shalt have leisure to make peace with heaven,
And mourn in the shade of solitude thy errors.
It is our sovereign pleasure. (*To the body*) – And for thee,
Thou lovely dust, all pomp and circumstance
That can gild death shall wait thee to thy grave:
Thou shalt lie with the royal and the proud;
And marble, by the dexterous chisel taught,
Shall learn to mourn thy hapless fortunes.

LAVAL: No!
Ye shall not bear her to your receptacles;
Nor raise a monument, for busy eyes
To stare upon: no hand, in future days,
Shall point to her last home; no voice shall cry
'There lies King Francis' paramour!' In life,
Thou didst despoil me of her; but in death,
She's mine! I that did love her so,
Will give her that, my love doth tell me best
Fits with her fate – an honourable grave:
She shall among my ancestral tombs repose,
Without an epitaph, except my tears.

FRANCIS: Then now for war, oh! ill to end, I fear,
Ushered with such dark deeds and fell disasters.

[*Exeunt* FRANCIS, *followed by the* QUEEN *and
Attendants on one side, and* LAVAL, *with the
others, bearing the body*][34]

Act V

SCENE i

A wide encampment

Alarums

Enter BOURBON, PESCARA, *and troops*

BOURBON: Command them halt, and draw their lines along
    The forest skirts.

PESCARA: Perez, how goes the hour?

FIRST SOLDIER: By our march, an't please you, I should guess it late
    In the afternoon.

BOURBON: Ay, see the sun, that gorgeous conqueror,
    Upon the western gate of heaven doth halt.

PESCARA: A conqueror call you him, Bourbon?

BOURBON: Ay, marry.
    Hath he not ridden forth, as though to battle,
    Armed with ten thousand darts of living flame?
    Hath he not, in his journey 'thwart the sky
    Encountered and overcome each gloomy cloud,
    Each fog, or noisome vapour, that in the air
    Hovered, like foul rebellion, to put out
    His glorious light; and having conquered them,
    Hath he not forced them don his livery –
    The amber glow – that all he looks on wears?
    And now, behold, he stands on the last verge
    Of his career, and looks back over his path,
    Marked with a ruddy hue, how like a conqueror!
    Now sinks he in that glowing mass of light,
    Which he hath fired; and look, Pescara, yonder
    Comes on the night, who draws her sable veil
    Over the whole; and this bright pageantry,
    This gorgeous sunset, and this glorious sun,
    Shall be forgotten in tomorrow's dawning!
    So comes in death, and so oblivion falls
    Over the mighty of the earth! How far
    Is it to the beleaguered Pavia?

PESCARA: By
   The open road, some twelve hours' weary march;
   But here is one, a sturdy labourer,
   Who, in his hard vocation toiling, hath
   Discovered paths, through these wide woodlands, which,
   Before the dawn, would bring us into sight
   Of Pavia, and King Francis' host.
BOURBON: 'Tis well:
   That path we choose; and trust to bring, at once,
   Daylight and death into his camp. Do thou,
   Pescara, bid them form, and march again;
   Speak to them cheeringly and cheerily;
   Give them good hope, by showing them thine own,
   And tell them we must march another night:
   Yet but one more, and that, tomorrow, all
   Shall rest in the glad arms of victory,

                      [Exeunt PESCARA *and soldiers]*
   Or sleep in those of death – a most rare slumber!
   And one for which I long right wearily!
   For I am sorely burthened, and the sleep
   Of every night hath no more power on me
   To quicken or refresh my numbed senses.
   A very dream hath been my life to me!
   Full of fair disappointments and mischances
   Dressed in fantastic trappings by my hopes.
   The fairest parted first. Oh, Margaret!
   Thou star! that all alone, in this thick darkness,
   Still shinest upon my troubled destinies
   With an eternal constancy; to thee
   How often veers my soul! But 'tis no more,
   With the fond looks of hope, but with the gaze
   Of one to whom despair is grown familiar;
   And who, in death, still fixes his strained eye
   On what he hoped, and sickened, and then died for!
   What quick and incoherent footsteps beat
   The ground? Why, this should seem some distraught wretch
   Reft of his reason! – what! it cannot be!
   Count Lautrec!

     Enter, precipitately, LAUTREC, *with a letter in his hand*
LAUTREC: Hear me, oh thou injured man;
   And, by thine injuries, be moved to aid me!
BOURBON: Lautrec in Italy! in our encampment!

A suitor to the man who was overthrown,
To make a step to raise him into greatness!
LAUTREC: Oh read, read here! He that did ruin thee—
That raised me but to cast me down again—
That lustful tyrant, Francis of Valois,
Hath brought dishonour on our ancient house!
I thank the gods she did not long outlive
Such deadly shame!
BOURBON (*reads the letter*)
The fair Françoise, alas!
LAUTREC: More, more than this – Laval, my childhood's brother –
He who in years, in arms, in love, and honour,
Did so resemble me, that nature seemed
To have intended, from our birth, our friendship—
Is dead, by the slow hand of his despair,
Which, ever since my sister's fatal end,
Had seized upon him; dead by lingering pain,
Slow but consuming fever, and that hopelessness
Of the sad heart which is the surest end
Life hath. But, here, he hath bequeathed to me
Such an inheritance as mocks all price—
His vengeance! Oh, thou shalt be satisfied,
Departed friend! and when, from thine abode,
Thou seest my keen sword glittering over the head
Of him, thy murderer – when his life's blood,
Spilt on the earth, shall reek to heaven, remember
I struck the blow – 'tis I that did avenge thee!
BOURBON: That I do sorrow for thee, Lautrec, credit me;
For I have loved – but that mine aid in this
Can aught avail thee, I discover not.
LAUTREC: Desire doth sharpen my perception, Bourbon,
And shapes all circumstances to its purposes.
Grant me but forty – nay, but twenty men;
And let me join my arm unto thy host,
Whose every weapon shall, ere day dawn, point
At the foul tyrant – mine alone must strike.
What, cautious grown, and doubtful art, on sudden!
Thou who didst never, to the weightiest matter,
Lend even a moment's thinking space, dost now
Ponder on such a suit as this, forsooth!
BOURBON: Fair sir, Care and her sister, Thought, have been
Companions of my dreary days and nights

Of late, and they have left their cautious traces.
I should be loth to tell, since last we parted,
How sorrow hath, in envy of my youth,
Sown age's silver tokens on my head,
And furrowed over my brow. But I have thought,
Even in this moment's space, enough to tell thee
I cannot grant thy suit. Men's hearts have cooled,
Lautrec, since I was driven forth from France;
And now their busy tongues begin to scan,
With a misprising[35] censure, my revenge.
My fame – my last, best-guarded treasure – is
Melting beneath the fiery touch of slander:
And, when men speak of Bourbon, it is now,
Bourbon the traitor – the revolted Bourbon—
But let that pass! – 'tis undeserved; and, therefore,
Again I say it, let it pass! But yet
There is, among the scornful eyes, that look
Upon my venturous career, one eye,
That, like the guarding gaze of Providence,
Keeps me from all offence. Therefore, if I
Do make my army a retreat and welcome
For rebels – for so injured men are deemed –
To one, moreover, who hath sworn to plunge
His sword, up to the hilt, in the king's heart,—
I shall do sorrow to the one I love,
And therein merit all the rest do say.

LAUTREC: Thou art become too wise, de Bourbon; I
Am all too eager for revenge to think.
Farewell: and if thou wouldst not the king's life
Be perilled, see that he and I meet not.   [*Exit*]

Enter PESCARA

PESCARA: I've done my mission, and successfully.
I've given them new hearts and freshened courage;
Already stand they eager to depart,
Their lances glittering in this crimson light,
And all the banners spreading their huge wings,
As though they meant to fly upon the gale
That flutters laughing round them. Come, de Bourbon,
They only halt for you; do but appear,
And they shall be tenfold invigorate
With the dear sight of him they love so well!

[*Exeunt*]

SCENE ii

Night – a lamp burning: on one couch HENRY
OF NAVARRE *sleeping, on the other,* FRANCIS

FRANCIS (*in his sleep*)
  Down! down! help ho! the traitor's stabbed me! – help!
  (*Wakes*) What all alone! and night! – an idle dream!
  (*Rising*) Yet sure methought we did together fight,
  Bourbon and I; and ever as I struck him,
  Laval did come between us – but 'tis nought.
  A very fantasy, born of my thoughts,
  Which have been straining on tomorrow's issue.
  (*To* NAVARRE) – How well thou sleepst, thou disinherited King!
  Thou hast no dream of empire or dominion;
  Thine being lost, no longer are a care.
  And all the event tomorrow brings to thee,
  Is life, or death, a paltry stake at best!
  Taken by itself, and without added value
  Of crown, or kingdom, fame, or name to lose.
  Sleep on – youth's healthful current keeps its course
  Within thy veins; and thy unwrinkled brow
  Shows like the glassy wave, when sunset smiles on it.
  Oh, would that I were eased of power too!—
  Then might I rest, perchance, as thou dost now.
      (*He walks to the end of the tent, and draws back the curtains*
        at the entrance of it; which, being opened, discover the
      camp by moonlight, the Tesino, and distant walls of Pavia)
  How many are there, sleeping on yon field,
  Who shall tomorrow lay them down for ever.
  How many heads, whose dreams are all of conquest,
  Lie pillowed on their graves. – Where shall they be
  After the dawn, awakened by our trumpets,
  Has drawn away night's curtain? Then shall come
  War's horrid din – then shall these slumberers,
  All drenched in gore, all gashed, and mangled, roll
  Together in the thirsty dust; and some

Shall pray to heaven for mercy, and for years
Of future life – and some shall yell for pain,
And curse the hour that they were born, and cry
For water to allay their dying drought.
There shall the proud lie writhing, in the herd
Of common soldiers; there the brave shall lie,
Bleeding beside the coward; – there, perchance,
I shall be stretched, stark, ere the evening fall—
A fearful thought! – Now through the silent air,
And the dark night, might fancy dream she saw
Death stalking in the midst of yonder field,
Marking the prey that shall be his tomorrow.
Why, how is this? – my blood chills in my veins!
A shadow passes over me! – shall I?—
Oh conscience! lie thou still; it is thy hand
That strikes so cold upon my sense, and turns
The rapid current of my blood athwart,
With these slow shivering fears.— I'll wake D'Albret;
For now already through the twilight breaks
The dappled hue of morn, chasing away
Night's shadows, and these gloomy fantasies.
There is a freshness in the early air,
That quickens every faculty, and makes
A keen enjoyment of existence only.
Now falls the grey veil from fair Nature's face,
And streaks of light shoot through the amber sky.
What ho! awake, D'Albret! the day hath dawned,
And the young morning, clad in saffron robes
Of glorious light, opens heaven's eastern gate,
And bids the sun good morrow. – (*Trumpet*) – Hark! the trumpet,
Clear, as the lark's shrill matin note, doth sound
Through the blue vault – the hum of multitudes
Rises in the still air – the clash of steel –
The tramp of trained feet doth beat the ground,
In even measure – steeds neigh long and loud –
And voices of command, whoop and halloo,
Ring through the tented lines; – arouse thee! slumberer!
The day is broke – the camp is all awake –
Shake off this sleep, and fit thyself for—

Enter TRIBOULET *at the back*

TRIBOULET: Death, master! I've ended thy period with a rare grace
for thee!

FRANCIS: Thou here? I deemed thee safe in Paris.

TRIBOULET: Thou deemedst wrong, then; for I am sound before Pavia.

FRANCIS: When camst thou hither?

TRIBOULET: With the last reinforcement: men, there are no more that can come, and fools, there being so many already, I thought thou couldst not take exception at one more of the order.

FRANCIS: But what wilt thou do here?

TRIBOULET: That which thou wilt: fight, I conceive.

FRANCIS: Go to, with thy lath!

TRIBOULET: No, with my faulchion, master.

(*He draws his faulchion*)

FRANCIS: Why, my poor fool, what shall they do at court if thou art slain?

TRIBOULET: Resolve me this, master – what shall they do if thou art slain?

FRANCIS: Marry, even get them another King.

TRIBOULET: What! kings in such abundance, and fools so rare— royalty in such plenty, and folly scarce in the market! But I'll tell thee; if I am slain, dear master, do thou console my mourners; they will be many, doubtless – I'll bequeath thee my cap and bells – and let poor Clement write my epitaph.

FRANCIS: Out weather-brain![36] but see, here come the heads
Of our grave council; get thee gone awhile
Into the further tent, and tarry there
Until I send for thee.

[*Exit* TRIBOULET]

I'll have him kept
Safely throughout the day – for worlds I would not
That the poor knave should come to any harm

(*During this scene* HENRY D'ALBRET *has
arisen, buckled on his sword and spurs, etc.*)

Enter VENDÔME, CHABANNES, DE VARENNES, *and pages*

FRANCIS: Now, good my lords, your voices, and perchance
Some short hour hence we'll ask you for your swords;
Speak forth, speak freely. (*To a page*) – Bid a herald sound
Summons through all the camp, to all the chiefs
And leaders of our host, that straightaway here
They do convene to counsel or consult
How best our conduct may be ordered,
In this emergency and strait of war.
Despatch, despatch! we suffer no delay;
All must be quickly said and done today:

Sit, gentle lords – good cousin D'Albret, sit.
                    (*They seat themselves*)   [*Exeunt pages*]
                    Enter CHARLES OF ALENÇON
ALENÇON: Sir,
    The morning blushes, that she lay asleep,
    Pillowed on the grey clouds, long after you
    Had left your couch, in busy thought preparing
    To meet the venture of this perilous day.
FRANCIS: We'll make the noon blush redder yet, good cousin,
    If thou and all these nobles here assembled
    Are half as willing for the siege as I!
    But, Vendôme, thou art riper in thy years,
    And of a judgement more mature than any,
    Than all, that sit in council round us here.
    Speak, therefore; say, shall we attempt the assault,
    And lay this rebel city in the dust?
    Or back to France, there to recruit and raise
    Our wearied troops, who, through their weariness,
    Find strength to talk of marching home again?
VENDÔME: My gracious liege, brief words do best befit
    The brief allotment time hath portioned us:
    Therefore, unprefaced be my say, and short.
    Pavia hath not yet given sign of yielding,
    Though now a lengthened siege hath tried her force;
    Resistance in the city, and without
    (At least, so rumour saith) a mighty band,
    Marching to aid her worst extremity,
    In numbers countless—
FRANCIS: Ay, so rumour saith,
    But rumour's best arithmetic we know;
    Multiplication, Vendôme, is it not?
D'ALBRET: I do entreat your Majesty's excuse
    For that I break my lord of Vendôme's speech,
    In seeming hotness of impatient youth.
    But had he said, fresh, full of strength and life,
    And courage, such as untried armies feel,
    Before grim war hath pricked a single vein,
    Or drained one drop of blood, or drank one breath,
    Methinks his argument had stronger proved.
CHABANNES: We, good my liege, have poured forth crimson floods
    Around the walls of Pavia, mingling with
    The silver Tesino another stream,

All full of warmth, and but just robbed of life.
FRANCIS: Hark! for methinks, without, we hear the stir
   Of hasty footsteps drawing near our tent:
   Who comes?

Enter BONNIVET

   De Bonnivet! ah, is it thou?
   Welcome, thou King of Tennis! thou art wanted,
   Thou giver of hard blows and unwise counsels:
   Here be these lords, advising us to raise
   This weary siege, and back to France again.
BONNIVET: Out on such counsel! How, sirs, raise the siege
   And fly?
D'ALBRET: Ay, even so, sir, raise the siege!
   I marvel that your eyes serve not thus far,
   To see that on a combat hangs the venture
   Of life and death, freedom and slavery.
   Do you not see 'tis all the foe doth seek?
   What stake is this, where, failing, they lose nought;
   And where, if they should win, we must lose all?
   This battle will be double victory
   To them, for 'tis their only confidence—
   'Tis the last effort of their desperate hope—
   The straining of the nerve before it cracks;
   The issue that must crown, or crush, for ever.
ALENÇON: Besides all this, another point remains—
   Men are not fed with words, and well we know,
   Would Bourbon give his heart's best blood for it,
   He hath no other coin. Thus following
   Through lands, laid waste by our victorious arms,
   Without a hope of combat, and with fear
   Of mutiny among their starving thousands—
   Think ye they will not rue this hasty march?
   And curse the hour they quitted Germany,
   To hold that rebel Bourbon's cause for food,
   And page our heels through Italy for rest.
   But, an we wait them here, and give them fight,
   And let them weigh the fearful odds that all
   Spur them to battle, even to the death—
   Why they may chance, my liege, to find a strength
   From out their very weakness, and a hope,
   Born in the moment of extreme despair—
   And should we be defeated—

FRANCIS: Defeated! sayst thou? by my soul, Alençon
　　Thou speakst as thou hadst never worn a sword!
　　Defeated by a set of German clods!
　　What though the traitor Bourbon lead them on!
　　Methinks ye have forgotten, all of ye,
　　That in our camp his deeds of arms were learnt.
　　The masters of his infancy are here,
　　And though that youthful age hath budded forth
　　Into most powerful and vigorous manhood,
　　Here are the men who trained the haughty spirit,
　　That having broken through all curb of duty,
　　Threats its instructors; here the very men,
　　Who first put weapons in those grasping hands,
　　That now, forsooth, ye deem invincible.
　　By heavens! ye are bewildered all by fear!
　　Or else your eyes have taken some other taint,
　　That makes ye shake so at this scarecrow, Bourbon.
　　What though he hath heart, head, and hand, the which
　　Are merits that I freely own and praise?
　　Yet hath he not ten thousand hearts and heads,
　　To move this mass of thick-brained, half-trained savages
　　Whereat, oh, valiant chevaliers! ye tremble.
　　Nay, cousin D'Albret, we are poor, indeed,
　　If in this very presence be not some,
　　Ay, many, that could match with yonder rebel;
　　Thyself art proof against thy argument.
BONNIVET: Nor is this all: did not the King of France
　　Swear by his knighthood's sword, he would exalt
　　Leyva's head on conquered Pavia's walls?
　　The vow was spoke like thunder in our ears;
　　The sword flashed brightly in the king's right hand;
　　And now shall Pavia triumph in our flight?
　　And bathe its ramparts in Tesino's flood,
　　All curdled with the red libations poured
　　By us, as tributes to the unconquered town?
　　Shall Leyva, that haughty Spaniard, smile,
　　To think, that with his single bilboa
　　He held at bay the chivalry of France
　　More, more than all, shall Europe, 'neath whose eyes
　　The fearful hazard of our game we play,
　　Point to the plains of Italy, and cry,
　　There was a gallant king and knight forsworn?

There France's lilies swept the dusty field,
Not blushing with the hue of deadly fight,
But pale with shame at this most foul retreat!
Oh shame upon ye, lords!

ALENÇON: Now, by this light,
I did but urge the measure, that we might
Survive to fight and bleed in France's quarrel
Nor all be slaughtered here by rebel hands.

FRANCIS: Cousin D'Albret, thou hast forgot thine own
Immediate cause and quarrel in this fray.
Thy lost inheritance, Navarre, doth lie
Within the compass of today's engagement.
If we are conquerors, why then thy crown—

D'ALBRET: Perish my crown – and with it all my hopes –
If that the dear desire of righting me,
Hath made your majesty so long to waver
'Twixt your host's safety, and my interest!
By heaven! 'ere I behold this fair array,
And all its gallant leaders, perilled thus,
My crown and kingdom shall remain unclaimed,
And my good sword be my inheritance!

VENDÔME: But see, who comes in haste; his tidings seem—
If one may read them in his dusty trappings—
Sudden.

Enter a MESSENGER

MESSENGER: My liege, tidings have reached our post,
Within this hour, the city must surrender,
If we attack. The Spaniard Leyva's troops,
Too harshly disciplined by want and weariness,
Have broke all discipline, and will not raise
An arm to save their town.

BONNIVET: Now, now, my liege!
To horse; and bid the trumpets sound the assault.

Enter another MESSENGER

2ND MESSENGER
Arm! arm! my liege! the Spaniard is upon us!
De Bourbon and his army are at hand!
Over the westward plains, the clouds of dust
Rise thickly from the vanguard of his host;
From whose dense canopy full oft flash forth
Helmet, and crest, and lance, and pennon bright,
Giving dread promise of the coming fight!

(*They all start up*)

FRANCIS: Up, and away! to horse, to horse, my lords!
'Twill be the battle then, and not the assault!
Or if our cousin D'Albret be not wearied,
We'll have the battle first, and then the siege.

D'ALBRET: I pray to heaven your majesty may find
No rest he seeks not!

FRANCIS: Nay now, gentle coz,
Thy hand, and ere we part, we'll have thy word,
To meet us in our tent, after the battle;
Where we will fill a health to our fair ladies—
Amongst whose number, Victory is not
The most unkind. Now, all unto your posts!
It may so chance we may meet here again;
But if fate wills it other, farewell all,
Whom one short hour shall cause to stand or fall.

[*Exeunt all but* BONNIVET]

De Bonnivet, do thou draw out thy men
Close by the Tesino, but keep them back;
Nor let thy bloodhounds slip the leash, till I
Send signal for the onset.

[*Exit* BONNIVET]

(FRANCIS *draws his sword*)

Now, all ye powers that rule the tide of war,
Whose voice is in the belching cannon's roar –
Whose wing is in its flashing light – who spread
Its smoky canopy along the plain –
Making death doubly hideous by disguise:
Come! sit upon my brow! and be my eyes
The heralds of your sentences to Spain;
That at each glance the rebel host may read
The terrors waiting on incensed kings.
Now, Bourbon, traitor! we shall meet once more,
And proud shall be the prize of thy revolt;
For I'll encounter thee, and sword to sword,
I'll pay thy heavy debt of injuries,
With such a glorious death, that men shall say
Thou wert more honoured, dying by this hand,
Than hadst thou lived, and conquered all the world!

(*Trumpets*)

Hark! hark! they sound the onset! to the field!

Confusion light on him who first shall yield!

[*Rushes out*]

SCENE iii

Battle-field

Alarums – Enter BOURBON *and* PESCARA

PESCARA: Oh, what a glorious conflict rages there!
Our breaking of their lines, and swift pursuit,
Have taken the breath from off my lips, but more
With joy than weariness.
BOURBON: Oh, brave, my lions!
Hark! how they roar! see how their bristling line
Drives back King Francis and his chevaliers!
Come, come, Pescara, come, my blood's on fire!
PESCARA: Art sure that Leyva will keep his word,
And sallying from the city, fall upon
Their rear guard?
BOURBON: I've his oath; and art thou sure,
That thou didst to the troops enjoin to spare
King Francis' life?
PESCARA: Certain: they'd sooner turn
Their swords on thee or me, than upon him.
BOURBON: Then follow, follow back into the fight!
Follow! and shout Bourbon! for Spain and vengeance!

[*Exeunt*]

Alarums – Enter, in great disorder, ALENÇON,
CHABANNES, *and some troops*

ALENÇON: No power on earth can rally them again!
They fly, they fly! Oh, miserable day!
Where is the king?
CHABANNES: Yonder, in the mêlèe.
Seest not his white plume, dabbled all with gore,
Floating upon the tide of battle? Hell
Rides on the sulphurous clouds that shroud the field,
And death riots beneath!
ALENÇON: Where's Bonnivet?
CHABANNES: Cut down, with his whole troop. The accursed
Spaniard,
Leyva, did, as he rushed on to the charge,

Open his city gates, which belched forth
The enraged and hungry garrison that we
So long have pent within their city walls;
These fell upon De Bonnivet's small band,
And made such havoc as wild beasts alone,
Or starving savages, should make.

ALENÇON: But, come—
Once more into the field; and, if all hope
Be lost of rallying our broken host,
Let us, around our gallant king, make stand,
And fight ourselves to death!   [*Exeunt*]

SCENE iv

Another part of the battle-field

Alarums – Enter FRANCIS, *supported by* D'ALBRET *and*
TRIBOULET; *his sword broken, and his whole dress
very much disordered*

FRANCIS: Oh, coward traitors, to forsake me thus!
Thrice did I lead them on, and thrice again
That fiend incarnate, Bourbon, routed them.
D'Albret, leave me, and get thee to the brow
Of yonder hill, and look upon the field,
And come and tell me how the battle fares.
                    [*Exit* D'ALBRET. FRANCIS *seats himself on the ground*]
FRANCIS: So thou didst break thy prison, Triboulet?
TRIBOULET: Ay, and I would have broken my neck to have got to you;
but, master mine, you bleed – you are sore wounded.
FRANCIS: A score of scratches, nothing more, kind friend.
Take off my helmet – so – I thirst, good fool:
I pray thee fetch me, from yon spring, some water,
To lay this fever in my throat.
                    (TRIBOULET *takes the King's helmet and goes for water*)
Oh, mother!
Ill shall it fare with thee if the day's lost,
As I do fear it will be.
                    Re-enter TRIBOULET
Thank thee, friend.
Pah! there is blood! blood! in the curdled stream!

I cannot, for my life, dip even my lip
Into it.
LAUTREC (*without*)
Where, where is the tyrant?
                              (*Enters*)   Ha!
Take this, thou ravisher! Laval doth send it thee!
          (*He rushes on the* KING; TRIBOULET *throws himself before
          him, but is felled by* LAUTREC – FRANCIS *starts up, and, with
          his broken sword, defends himself. Enter* PESCARA *and
          Spanish troops –* HENRI D'ALBRET *is brought in prisoner
          –* PESCARA *strikes down* LAUTREC'S *sword*)
PESCARA: Down with thy sword for very shame, Lautrec!
    Wouldst strike an unarmed and a wounded man?
FRANCIS: Pescara! thou hast saved a worthless life;
    Worthless to all but him unto whose vengeance
    It was most rightly due. Alas, poor fool!
    Wounded, I fear, to death!
TRIBOULET: For thee, master – dear master, 'tis for thee!
FRANCIS: My crown! – I had forgot – but my heart's thanks,
    And all my fallen fortunes may have spared me,
    To him that shall restore thee!
TRIBOULET: Oh master mine! thou canst not buy me a new heart;
    mine is unseamed, and life hath played the truant – forgive poor
    Clement, master, for my sake – and hark thee – hark thee in thine
    ear – thou hast been called a wise King hitherto, and I now ratify the
    sentence; – henceforth thou shalt be wise—
FRANCIS: Why so?
TRIBOULET: Because thy folly is departing, master! – alack, poor
    cap and bells!
                              (*Dies*)
FRANCIS: Curse on these smarting wounds, whose pain doth bring
    Unmanly tears! – Pescara, I beseech thee,
    Let this kind fellow sleep in honored grave!
    His head was light; for it did lack the weight
    Of evil thought – but for his faithful heart,
    Oh! how it shamed all sense and intellect,
    That was so passing excellent without them!
PESCARA: It shall be looked to, sir, right heedfully.
    But, sir, you bleed; there is a convent near
    If you can mount—
FRANCIS: Faith – I feel somewhat faint –
    Lead on, sir, so our haven be not far.

D'Albret, thine arm; thou art something of a prophet—
Fortune has cheated us of all save patience.

> [*Exeunt – Soldiers follow them, bearing the*
> *body of* TRIBOULET]

SCENE V

The inside of a church

Monks in the background, singing the service for the dead
Enter PESCARA *and* D'ALBRET, *supporting* FRANCIS. *Soldiers*
follow them

MONKS *chaunt* 'De profundis clamavi ad te, Domine. Domine,
exaudi vocem meam.'

FRANCIS: Why, this is fit! Peace, do not break their chaunt!

MONKS *chaunt* 'Fiant aures tuæ intendentes in vocem deprecationis
meæ.'

D'ALBRET: Oh it chimes truly with our dismal fortunes.

MONKS *chaunt* 'Si iniquitates observaveris, Domine: Domine, quis
sustinebit.

FRANCIS (*speaking the response*) 'Quia apud te propitiatio est et
propter legem tuam sustinui te, Domine.'

> (*Shouts without*)
> *Enter* LEYVA *and Spanish troops*

LEYVA: What drowsy dirge is this? Be we not conquerors?
Shout a *Te Deum* for our victory,
And leave these doleful dumps to Frenchmen!

PESCARA: Leyva, this boisterous triumph shows not well
Before the fallen—

FRANCIS: Oh, sir, take no heed,
For I take none of this – to be overcome
May be the lot of base and brave alike,—
But, to be moderate in conquest makes
A great man greater than his victory.

SOLDIERS: Come, baldpates,[37] come, a merry psalm!

LEYVA: Pescara, it is fitting thou shouldst talk,
Who hast but marched some leagues thy lusty troops
Through fruitful lands, levying all plenteousness,
To satisfy their need or their desire:
These wretches have been pent within their walls

With nought to stay their stomachs for three weeks,
Save scraps thy dogs would loathe – I cannot curb them—
They're mad with hunger and excess.
>   *Enter, shouting, a body of drunken soldiers; they seize*
>   *the ornaments on the priests, and begin stripping the altar.*

FRANCIS: Do ye stand by, and see this sacrilege?
Oh Spanish nobles! – Christian gentlemen!
>   (FRANCIS *snatches a sword from one of the Soldiers*
>   *– shouts without*)
>   *Enter* BOURBON, *followed by Spanish officers*
>   *and soldiers*

BOURBON: (*striking down a soldier at the foot of the altar*)
Down, dog! How now, whence this unholy outrage?
Pescara, Leyva – (*Seeing* FRANCIS) – The King!

FRANCIS: Bourbon!

BOURBON: Wounded – alone – a prisoner! – Oh, sir!
Had you but harkened timely to true counsel,
This never had come to pass – you had not fallen
To this estate – nor Italy been drenched
With the best blood of your best chivalry.

FRANCIS: This is a strange encounter for us two,
My lord – full of deep thoughts that need no comment.
That thou wert wronged, the world will bear thee witness;
That wrong endured hath made thee commit wrong;
The world and all its aftertimes will judge thee:
For my own part, though fate has played me false,
I will not wrangle with the lot she throws me,
Nor hold this day the darkest of my life,
Though thou hast won, and I lost all save honour.
(*To* PESCARA) – Sir, take my sword, I am *your* prisoner.

BOURBON (*to an officer*)
Go, bid our trumpets sound to the recall.
All slaughter, and despoiling of the dead, forbear.
And for our royal prisoners, their fate
Hangs at the mastery of Charles of Spain.
From us all courtesy their rank doth claim,
And admiration for their noble valour.
Now sheathe your bloody swords, and all prepare
To march to Spain this very hour, that there,
By well-improved victory, we may
Crown the strange tale of this eventful day.

NOTES

1 **doff her wariness:** lower her guard.

2 **gemmed the motley:** literally, adorned the jester's costume.

3 **tourney:** tournament.

4 **rend the welkin:** split the sky.

5 **escutcheon:** shield with heraldic, armorial bearings.

6 **limner:** painter.

7 **jackanapes:** a pert fellow, a coxcomb.

8 **broken pates:** broken heads, fractured skulls.

9 **lief wear a spindle:** gladly, preferably wear a spindle.

10 **a meeter bride:** a better more appropriate, literally, more tolerable, bride.

11 **coz:** archaic form of cousin.

12 **by my fay:** by my faith, in truth.

13 **guerdon:** reward, recompense.

14 **bulwark and lode-star:** metal and principle.

15 **baldric:** a belt for a sword.

16 **reft in sunder:** forcibly cut apart, divided.

17 **gyves:** shackles, fetters.

18 **scions:** descendants, or younger members of a noble family.

19 **aspen:** a kind of poplar with especially tremulous leaves.

20 **churl:** literally, a peasant or person of low birth, but also an ill-bred fellow, a niggardly or surly person.

21 **sith**: since.

22 **pinions**: wings, more precisely wing-feathers.

23 **lynx-eyed**: keen-sighted, sharp.

24 **I prate**: I chatter, talk too much.

25 **Echo**: in classical mythology Echo was a nymph in love with Narcissus; her love not being returned, she pined away until only her voice remained.

26 **fife**: a small, shrill flute associated with military music.

27 **the Ebro and the Douro**: two of the longest rivers in the Iberian peninsula – the Ebro the longest river to run entirely in Spain, the Douro running through both Spain and Portugal.

28 **cowl**: hood.

29 **pennons**: pennant, a long narrow triangular or swallow-tailed flag.

30 **obloquy**: abuse, dishonour.

31 **adamant**: diamond, or other hard substance.

32 **bootless**: unavailing.

33 **'. . . when Gaza shook for fear.'**: the Queen refers to the biblical story of Samson. Gath and Gaza were two of the five principle cities of the Philistines: Gath inland, Gaza coastal. Gath was said to be the home of Goliath, while Gaza is the city in which Samson was imprisoned.

34 **Exeunt . . . bearing the body**: in the manuscript of the play held in Lord Chamberlain's Collection and in at least the early performances of its production in 1832 the play stops here at the end of Act IV.

35 **misprising**: hateful despising.

36 **weather-brain**: foolish, fickle fellow.

37 **baldpates**: tonsured monks.

FASHION;

or,

LIFE IN NEW YORK

———————

a comedy, in five acts

BY ANNA CORA MOWATT
(1845)

DRAMATIS PERSONAE

Women

MRS TIFFANY	a lady who imagines herself fashionable
PRUDENCE	a maiden lady of a certain age, sister to Mrs Tiffany
MILLINETTE	a French lady's maid
GERTRUDE	a governess to Seraphina
SERAPHINA TIFFANY	a belle

Men

ADAM TRUEMAN	a farmer from Catteraugus
COUNT JOLIMAITRE	a fashionable European importation
COLONEL HOWARD	an officer in the US army
MR TIFFANY	a New York merchant
T. TENNYSON TWINKLE	a modern poet
AUGUSTUS FOGG	a drawing room appendage
SNOBSON	a rare species of confidential clerk
ZEKE	a coloured servant
LADIES AND GENTLEMEN OF THE BALL ROOM	

Act I

SCENE i

A splendid drawing room in the house of MRS TIFFANY. *Open folding doors, discovering a conservatory. On either side glass windows down to the ground. Doors on right and left. Mirror, couches, ottomans, a table with albums, beside it an armchair.* MILLINETTE *dusting furniture.* ZEKE *in a dashing livery, scarlet coat*

ZEKE: Dere's a coat to take de eyes ob all Broadway! Ah! Missy, it am de fixins dat make de natural *born* gemman. A libery for ever! Dere's a pair ob insuppressibles to 'stonish de coloured population.

MILLINETTE: *(aside)* Oh, *oui*, Monsieur Zeke. *(Very politely)* I not *comprend* one word he say!

ZEKE: I tell 'ee what, Missy, I'm 'stordinary glad to find dis a bery 'spectabul like situation! Now, as you've made de acquaintance ob dis here family, and dere you've had a supernumerary advantage ob me – seeing dat I only receibed my appointment dis morning. What I wants to know is your publicated opinion, privately expressed, ob de domestic circle.

MILLINETTE: You mean vat *espèce*, vat kind of *personnes* are Monsieur and Madame Tiffany? Ah! Monsieur is not de same ting as Madame – not at all.

ZEKE: Well, I s'pose he ain't altogether.

MILLINETTE: Monsieur is man of business – Madame is lady of fashion. Monsieur make de money – Madame spend it. Monsieur nobody at all! – Madame everybody altogether. Ah! Monsieur Zeke, de money is all dat is *necessaire* in dis country to make one lady of fashion. Oh! it is quite another ting in *la belle France*!

ZEKE: A bery lucifer explanation. Well, now we've disposed ob de heads ob de family, who come next?

MILLINETTE: First, dere is Mademoiselle Seraphina Tiffany. Mademoiselle is not at all one proper *personne*. Mademoiselle Seraphina is one coquette. Dat is not de mode in *la belle France*; de ladies dere never learn *la coquetrie* until dey do get one husband.

ZEKE: I tell 'ee what, Missy, I disreprobate dat proceeding altogether!

MILLINETTE: Vait! I have not tell you all *la famille* yet. Dere is

Ma'mselle Prudence – Madame's sister, one very *bizarre personne*. Den dere is Ma'mselle Gertrude, but she not anybody at all; she only teach Mademoiselle Seraphina *la musique*.

ZEKE: Well now, Missy, what's your own special defunctions?

MILLINETTE: I not understand, Monsieur Zeke.

ZEKE: Den I'll amplify. What's de nature ob your exclusive services?

MILLINETTE: *Ah, oui! je comprend.* I am Madame's *femme de chambre* – her lady's maid, Monsieur Zeke. I teach Madame *les modes de Paris*, and Madame set de fashion for all New York. You see, Monsieur Zeke, dat it is me, *moi-même*, dat do lead de fashion for all de American *beau monde!*

ZEKE: Yah! yah! yah! I hab de idea by de heel. Well now, p'raps you can 'lustrify my officials?

MILLINETTE: Vat you will have to do? Oh! much tings, much tings. You vait on de table – you tend de door – you clean de boots – you run de errands – you drive de carriage – you rub de horses – you take care of de flowers – you carry de water – you help cook de dinner – you wash de dishes – and den you always remember to do everyting I tell you to!

ZEKE: Wheugh, am dat *all*?

MILLINETTE: All I can tink of now. Today is Madame's day of reception, and all her grand friends do make her one *petite* visit. You mind run fast ven de bell do ring.

ZEKE: Run? If it wasn't for dese superfluminous trimmings, I tell 'ee what, Missy, I'd run—

MRS TIFFANY: (*outside*) Millinette!

MILLINETTE: Here comes Madame! You better go, Monsieur Zeke.

ZEKE: (*aside*) Look ahea, Massa Zeke, doesn't dis open rich!

[*Exit Zeke*]

Enter MRS TIFFANY, *dressed in the most extravagant height of fashion*

MRS TIFFANY: Is everything in order, Millinette? Ah! very elegant, very elegant, indeed! There is a *jenny-says-quoi* look about this furniture – an air of fashion and gentility perfectly bewitching. Is there not, Millinette?

MILLINETTE: Oh, *oui*, Madame!

MRS TIFFANY: But where is Miss Seraphina? It is twelve o'clock; our visitors will be pouring in, and she has not made her appearance. But I hear that nothing is more fashionable than to keep people waiting. – None but vulgar persons pay any attention to punctuality. Is it not so, Millinette?

MILLINETTE: Quite *comme il faut*. – Great *personnes* always do make little *personnes* wait, Madame.

MRS TIFFANY: This mode of receiving visitors only upon one specified day of the week is a most convenient custom! It saves the trouble of keeping the house continually in order and of being always dressed. I flatter myself that *I* was the first to introduce it amongst the New York *ee-light*. You are quite sure that it is strictly a Parisian mode, Millinette?

MILLINETTE: Oh, *oui*, Madame; entirely *mode de Paris*.

MRS TIFFANY: (*aside*) This girl is worth her weight in gold. Millinette, how do you say *armchair* in French?

MILLINETTE: *Fauteuil*, Madame.

MRS TIFFANY: *Fo-tool!* That has a foreign – an out-of-the-wayish sound that is perfectly charming – and so genteel! There is something about our American words decidedly vulgar. *Fowtool!* how refined. *Fowtool! Arm-chair!* what a difference!

MILLINETTE: Madame have one charmante pronunciation. *Fowtool* (*Mimicking aside*) charmante, Madame!

MRS TIFFANY: Do you think so, Millinette? Well, I believe I have. But a woman of refinement and of fashion can always accommodate herself to everything foreign! And a week's study of that invaluable work – *French without a Master*, has made me quite at home in the court language of Europe! But where is the new valet? I'm rather sorry that he is black, but to obtain a white American for a domestic is almost impossible; and they call this a free country! What did you say was the name of this new servant, Millinette?

MILLINETTE: He do say his name is Monsieur Zeke.

MRS TIFFANY: Ezekiel, I suppose. Zeke! Dear me, such a vulgar name will compromise the dignity of the whole family. Can you not suggest something more aristocratic, Millinette? Something *French!*

MILLINETTE: *Oh, oui*, Madame; *Adolph* is one very fine name.

MRS TIFFANY: A-dolph! Charming! Ring the bell, Millinette! (MILLI- NETTE *rings the bell*) I will change his name immediately, besides giving him a few directions.

Enter ZEKE. MRS TIFFANY *addresses him with great dignity*
Your name, I hear, is *Ezekiel*. – I consider it too plebeian an appellation to be uttered in my presence. In future you are called A-dolph. Don't reply – never interrupt me when I am speaking. A-dolph, as my guests arrive, I desire that you will inquire the name of every person, and then announce it in a loud, clear tone. That is the fashion in Paris.

[MILLINETTE *retires up in the stage*]
ZEKE: Consider de office discharged, Missus. (*Speaking very loudly*)

MRS TIFFANY: Silence! Your business is to obey and not to talk.

ZEKE: I'm dumb, Missus!

MRS TIFFANY: (*pointing up stage*) A-dolph, place that *fowtool* behind me.

ZEKE: (*looking about him*) I habn't got dat far in de dictionary yet. No matter, a genus gets his learning by nature.

(*Takes up the table and places it behind* MRS TIFFANY, *then expresses in dumb show great satisfaction.* MRS TIFFANY, *as she goes to sit, discovers the mistake*)

MRS TIFFANY: You dolt! Where have you lived not to know that *fowtool* is the French for *armchair*? What ignorance! Leave the room this instant.

(MRS TIFFANY *draws forward an armchair and sits.* MILLINETTE *comes forward suppressing her merriment at* ZEKE's *mistake and removes the table*)

ZEKE: Dem's de defects ob not having a libery education.   [*Exit*]

(PRUDENCE *peeps in*)

PRUDENCE: I wonder if any of the fine folks have come yet. Not a soul – I knew they hadn't. There's Betsy all alone. (*Walks in*) Sister Betsy!

MRS TIFFANY: Prudence! how many times have I desired you to call me *Elizabeth*? *Betsy* is the height of vulgarity.

PRUDENCE: Oh! I forgot. Dear me, how spruce we do look here, to be sure – everything in first rate style now, Betsy. (MRS TIFFANY *looks at her angrily*) *Elizabeth*, I mean. Who would have thought, when you and I were sitting behind that little mahogany-colored counter, in Canal Street[1] making up flashy hats and caps—

MRS TIFFANY: Prudence, *what do* you mean? Millinette, leave the room.

MILLINETTE: *Oui*, Madame.

(MILLINETTE *pretends to arrange the books upon a side table, but lingers to listen*)

PRUDENCE: But I always predicted it – I always told you so, Betsy – I always said you were destined to rise above your station!

MRS TIFFANY: Prudence! Prudence! have I not told you that—

PRUDENCE: No, Betsy, it was *I* that told *you*, when we used to buy our silks and ribbons of Mr Antony Tiffany – '*talking Tony*', you know we used to call him, and when you always put on the finest bonnet in our shop to go to his – and when you stayed so long smiling and chattering with him, I always told you that *something* would grow out of it – and didn't it?

MRS TIFFANY: Millinette, send Seraphina here instantly. Leave the room.

MILLINETTE: *Oui*, Madame. (*Aside*) So dis Americaine lady of fashion vas one *milliner*? Oh, vat a fine country for *les marchandes des modes!* I shall send for all my relation by de next packet!

[*Exit* MILLINETTE]

MRS TIFFANY: Prudence! never let me hear you mention this subject again. Forget what we *have* been, it is enough to remember that we *are* of the *upper ten thousand!*[2]

(PRUDENCE *goes up and sits down*)

Enter SERAPHINA, *very extravagantly dressed*

MRS TIFFANY: How bewitchingly you look, my dear! Does Millinette say that that head dress is strictly Parisian?

SERAPHINA: Oh, yes, Mamma, all the rage! They call it a *lady's tarpaulin,* and it is the exact pattern of one worn by the Princess Clementina at the last court ball.

MRS TIFFANY: Now, Seraphina, my dear, don't be too particular in your attentions to gentlemen not eligible. There is Count Jolimaitre, decidedly the most fashionable foreigner in town – and so refined, – so much accustomed to associate with the first nobility in his own country that he can hardly tolerate the vulgarity of Americans in general. You may devote yourself to him. Mrs Proudacre is dying to become acquainted with him. By the by, if she or her daughters should happen to drop in, be sure you don't introduce them to the Count. It is not the fashion in Paris to introduce – Millinette told me so.

Enter ZEKE

ZEKE: (*in a very loud voice*) Mister T. Tennyson Twinkle!

MRS TIFFANY: Show him up. [*Exit* ZEKE]

PRUDENCE: I must be running away! (*Going.*)

MRS TIFFANY: Mr T. Tennyson Twinkle – a very literary young man and a sweet poet! It is all the rage to patronize poets! Quick, Seraphina, hand me that magazine. – Mr Twinkle writes for it.

(SERAPHINA *hands the magazine to* MRS TIFFANY *who seats herself in an armchair and opens the book*)

PRUDENCE: (*returning*) There's Betsy trying to make out that reading without her spectacles.

(*Takes a pair of spectacles out of her pocket and hands them to* MRS TIFFANY)

There, Betsy, I knew you were going to ask for them. Ah! they're a blessing when one is growing old!

MRS TIFFANY: What do you mean, Prudence? A woman of fashion *never* grows old! Age is always out of fashion.

PRUDENCE: Oh, dear! what a delightful thing it is to be fashionable.

[*Exit* PRUDENCE. MRS TIFFANY *resumes her seat*]
Enter TWINKLE. *He salutes* SERAPHINA

TWINKLE: Fair Seraphina! the sun itself grows dim,
Unless you aid his light and shine on him!

SERAPHINA: Ah! Mr Twinkle, there is no such thing as answering you.

TWINKLE: (*looks around and perceives* MRS TIFFANY) (*Aside*) The 'New Monthly Vernal Galaxy'. Reading my verses by all that's charming! Sensible woman! I won't interrupt her.

MRS TIFFANY: (*rising and coming forward*) Ah! Mr Twinkle, is that you? I was perfectly *abimé* at the perusal of your very *distingué* verses.

TWINKLE: I am overwhelmed, Madam. Permit me. (*Taking the magazine*) Yes, they do read tolerably. And you must take into consideration, ladies, the rapidity with which they were written. Four minutes and a half by the stop watch! The true test of a poet is the *velocity* with which he composes. Really they do look very prettily, and they read tolerably – *quite* tolerably – *very* tolerably – especially the first verse. (*Reads*) 'To Seraphina T—.'

SERAPHINA: Oh! Mr Twinkle!

TWINKLE: (*reads*) 'Around my heart'—

MRS TIFFANY: How touching! Really, Mr Twinkle, quite tender!

TWINKLE: (*recommencing*) 'Around my heart—'

MRS TIFFANY: Oh, I must tell you, Mr Twinkle! I heard the other day that poets were the aristocrats of literature. That's one reason I like them, for I do dote on all aristocracy!

TWINKLE: Oh, Madam, how flattering! Now pray lend me your ears! (*Reads*) 'Around my heart thou weavest'—

SERAPHINA: That is such a *sweet* commencement, Mr Twinkle!

TWINKLE: (*aside*) I wish she wouldn't interrupt me! (*Reads*) 'Around my heart thou weavest a spell'—

MRS TIFFANY: Beautiful! But excuse me one moment, while I say a word to Seraphina! (*Aside to* SERAPHINA) Don't be too affable, my dear! Poets are very ornamental appendages to the drawing room, but they are always as poor as their own verses. They don't make eligible husbands!

TWINKLE: (*aside*) Confound their interruptions! My dear Madam, unless you pay the utmost attention you cannot catch the ideas. Are you ready? Well, now you shall hear it to the end! (*Reads*)
'Around my heart thou weavest a spell
Whose'—

Enter ZEKE

ZEKE: Mister Augustus Fogg! (*Aside*) A bery misty lookin young gemman?

MRS TIFFANY: Show him up, Adolph!

[*Exit* ZEKE]

TWINKLE: This is too much!

SERAPHINA: Exquisite verses, Mr Twinkle,— exquisite!

TWINKLE: Ah, lovely Seraphina! your smile of approval transports me to the summit of Olympus.

SERAPHINA: Then I must frown, for I would not send you so far away.

TWINKLE: Enchantress! (*Aside*) It's all over with her.

(*Retire up and converse*)

MRS TIFFANY: Mr Fogg belongs to one of our oldest families – to be sure he is the most difficult person in the world to entertain, for he never takes the trouble to talk, and never notices anything or anybody – but then I hear that nothing is considered so vulgar as to betray any emotion, or to attempt to render oneself agreeable!

Enter MR FOGG, *fashionably attired but in very dark clothes*

FOGG: (*bowing stiffly*) Mrs Tiffany, your most obedient. Miss Seraphina, yours. How d'ye do, Twinkle?

MRS TIFFANY: Mr Fogg, how do you do? Fine weather, – delightful, isn't it?

FOGG: I am indifferent to weather, Madam.

MRS TIFFANY: Been to the opera, Mr Fogg? I hear that the *bow monde* make their *debutt* there every evening.

FOGG: I consider operas a bore, Madam.

SERAPHINA: (*advancing*) You must hear Mr Twinkle's verses, Mr Fogg!

FOGG: I am indifferent to verses, Miss Seraphina.

SERAPHINA: But Mr Twinkle's verses are addressed to me!

TWINKLE: Now pay attention, Fogg! (*Reads*)—
'Around my heart thou weavest a spell
Whose magic I'—

Enter ZEKE

ZEKE: Mister – No, he say he ain't no Mister—

TWINKLE: 'Around my heart thou weavest a spell
Whose magic I can never tell!'

MRS TIFFANY: Speak in a loud, clear tone, A-dolph!

TWINKLE: This is terrible!

ZEKE: Mister Count Jolly-made-her!

MRS TIFFANY: Count Jolimaitre! Good gracious! Zeke, Zeke – A-dolph I mean. – (*Aside*) Dear me, what a mistake! Set that chair out of the way, – put that table back. Seraphina, my dear, are you all in order? Dear me! dear me! Your dress is so tumbled! (*Arranges her dress*) What are you grinning at? (*To* ZEKE) Beg the Count to *honour* us by walking up!   [*Exit* ZEKE]

Seraphina, my dear (*Aside to her*), remember now what I told you about the Count. He is a man of the highest, – good gracious! I am so flurried; and nothing is so ungenteel as agitation! what will the Count think! Mr Twinkle, pray stand out of the way! Seraphina, my dear, place yourself on my right! Mr Fogg, the conservatory – beautiful flowers – pray amuse yourself in the conservatory.

FOGG: I am indifferent to flowers, Madam.

MRS TIFFANY: (*aside*) Dear me! the man stands right in the way – just where the Count must make his *entray!* Mr Fogg, – pray—

Enter COUNT JOLIMAITRE *very dashingly dressed, wears a moustache*

MRS TIFFANY: Oh, Count, this unexpected honour—

SERAPHINA: Count, this inexpressible pleasure—

COUNT: Beg you won't mention it, Madam! Miss Seraphina, your most devoted! (*Crosses*)

MRS TIFFANY: (*aside*) What condescension! Count, may I take the liberty to introduce – (*Aside*) Good gracious! I forgot. Count, I was about to remark that we never introduce in America. All our fashions are foreign, Count.

(TWINKLE, *who has stepped forward to be introduced, shows great indignation*)

COUNT: Excuse me, Madam, our fashions have grows antediluvian before you Americans discover their existence. You are lamentably behind the age – lamentably! 'Pon my honour, a foreigner of refinement finds great difficulty in existing in this provincial atmosphere.

MRS TIFFANY: How dreadful, Count! I am very much concerned. If there is anything which I can do, Count—

SERAPHINA: Or I, Count, to render your situation less deplorable—

COUNT: Ah! I find but one redeeming charm in America – the superlative loveliness of the feminine portion of creation – (*Aside*) and the wealth of their obliging papas.

MRS TIFFANY: How flattering! Ah! Count, I am afraid you will turn the head of my simple girl here. She is a perfect child of nature, Count.

COUNT: Very possibly, for though you American women are quite charming, yet, demme, there's a deal of native rust to rub off!

MRS TIFFANY: *Rust?* Good gracious, Count! where do you find any rust? (*Looking about the room*)

COUNT: How very unsophisticated!

MRS TIFFANY: Count, I am so much ashamed, – pray excuse me! Althought a lady of large fortune, and one, Count, who can boast of the highest connections, I blush to confess that I have never travelled – while you, Count, I presume are at home in all the courts of Europe.

COUNT: *Courts?* Eh? Oh, yes, Madam, very true. I believe I am pretty well known in some of the courts of Europe – *police courts.* (*Aside, crossing*) In a word, Madam, I had seen enough of civilized life – wanted to refresh myself by a sight of barbarous countries and customs – had my choice between the Sandwich Islands and New York – chose New York!

MRS TIFFANY: How complimentary to our country! And, Count, I have no doubt you speak every conceivable language? You talk English like a native.

COUNT: Eh, what? Like a native? Oh, ah, demme, yes. I am something of an Englishman. Passed one year and eight months with the Duke of Wellington, six months with Lord Brougham, two and a half with Count d'Orsay – knew them all more intimately than their best friends – no heroes to me – hadn't a secret from me, I assure you – (*Aside*) *especially of the toilet.*

MRS TIFFANY: (*aside to* SERAPHINA) Think of that, my dear! Lord Wellington and Duke Broom!

SERAPHINA: (*aside to* MRS TIFFANY) And only think of Count d'Orsay, Mamma! I am so wild to see Count d'Orsay!

COUNT: Oh! a mere man milliner. Very little refinement out of Paris! Why, at the very last dinner given at Lord – Lord Knowswho, would you believe it, Madam, there was an individual present who wore a *black* cravat and took *soup twice*!

MRS TIFFANY: How shocking! the sight of him would have spoilt my appetite! (*Aside to* SERAPHINA) Think what a great man he must be, my dear, to despise lords and counts in that way. (*Aside*) I must leave them together. Mr Twinkle, your arm. I have some really very *foreign exotics* to show you.

TWINKLE: I fly at your command. (*Aside, and glancing at the* COUNT) I wish all her exotics were blooming in their native soil!

MRS TIFFANY: Mr Fogg, will you accompany us? My conservatory is well worthy a visit. It cost an immense sum of money.

FOGG: I am indifferent to conservatories, Madam; flowers are such a bore!

MRS TIFFANY: I shall take no refusal. Conservatories are all the rage – I could not exist without mine! Let me show you, – let me show you.

[*Places her arm through* MR FOGG'S *without his consent.*

Exeunt MRS TIFFANY, FOGG, *and* TWINKLE *into the*
conservatory, where they are seen walking about]

SERAPHINA: America, then, has no charms for you, Count?

COUNT: Excuse me – some exceptions. I find you, for instance,
particularly charming! Can't say I admire your country. Ah! if you
had ever breathed the exhilarating air of Paris, ate creams at
Tortoni's, dined at the Café Royale, or if you had lived in London –
felt at home at St James's, and every afternoon driven a couple of
Lords and a Duchess through Hyde Park, you would find America –
where you have no kings, queens, lords, nor ladies – insupportable!

SERAPHINA: Not while there was a Count in it?

Enter ZEKE, *very indignant*

ZEKE: Where's de Missus?

Enter MRS TIFFANY, FOGG *and* TWINKLE, *from the conservatory*

MRS TIFFANY: Whom do you come to announce, A-dolph?

ZEKE: He said he wouldn't trust me – no, not eben wid so much as his
name; so I woundn't trust him up stairs, den he ups wid *his stick* and
I *cuts mine.*

MRS TIFFANY: (*aside*) Some of Mr Tiffany's vulgar acquaintances. I
shall die with shame. A-dolph, inform him that I am *not at home.*

(*Exit* ZEKE]

My nerves are so shattered, I am ready to sink. Mr Twinkle, that
fow tool, if you please!

TWINKLE: What? What do you wish, Madam?

MRS TIFFANY: (*aside*) The ignorance of these Americans! Count, may
I trouble you? That *fow tool*, if you please!

COUNT: (*aside*) She's not talking English, nor French, but I suppose it's
American.

TRUEMAN: (*outside*) Not at home!

ZEKE: No, Sar – Missus say she's not at home.

TRUEMAN: Out of the way, you grinning nigger!

Enter ADAM TRUEMAN, *dressed as farmer, a stout cane*
in his hand, his boots covered with dust. ZEKE *jumps out of*
his way as he enters

[*Exit* ZEKE]

TRUEMAN: Where's this woman that's not *at home* in her own house?
May I be shot! if I wonder at it! I shoudn't think she'd ever feel *at*
home in such a showbox as this! (*Looking round*)

MRS TIFFANY: (*aside*) What a plebeian looking old farmer! I wonder
who he is? Sir – (*Advancing very agitatedly*) what do you mean, Sir,
by this *ow*dacious conduct? How dare you intrude yourself into my

parlor? Do you know who I am, Sir? (*With great dignity*) You are in the presence of Mrs Tiffany, Sir!

TRUEMAN: Antony's wife, eh? Well now, I might have guessed that – ha! ha! ha! for I see you make it a point to carry half your husband's shop upon your back! No matter; that's being a good helpmate – for he carried the whole of it once in a pack on his own shoulders – now you bear a share!

MRS TIFFANY: How dare you, you impertinent, *ow*dacious, ignorant old man! It's all an invention. You're talking of somebody else. (*Aside*) What will the Count think!

TRUEMAN: Why, I thought folks had better manners in the city! This is a civil welcome for your husband's old friend, and after my coming all the way from Catteraugus to see you and yours! First a grinning nigger tricked out in scarlet regimentals—

MRS TIFFANY: Let me tell you, Sir, that liveries are all the fashion!

TRUEMAN: The fashion, are they? To make men wear the *badge of servitude* in a free land – that's the fashion, is it? Hurrah, for republican simplicity! I will venture to say now, that you have your coat of arms too!

MRS TIFFANY: Certainly, Sir; you can see it on the panels of my *voyture*.

TRUEMAN: Oh! no need of that. I know what your escutcheon must be! A bandbox *rampant* with a bonnet *couchant*, and a peddlar's pack *passant*! Ha, ha, ha! that shows both houses united!

MRS TIFFANY: Sir! you are most profoundly ignorant – what do you mean by this insolence, Sir? (*Aside*) How shall I get rid of him?

TRUEMAN: (*Looking at* SERAPHINA) (*Aside*) I hope that is not Gertrude!

MRS TIFFANY: Sir, I'd have you know that – Seraphina, my child, walk with the gentlemen into the conservatory.

[*Exeunt* SERAPHINA, TWINKLE, FOGG *into conservatory*]
Count Jolimaitre, pray make due allowances for the errors of this rustic! I do assure you, Count— (*Whispers to him*)

TRUEMAN: (*aside*) Count! She calls that critter with a shoe brush over his mouth, Count! To look at him, I should have thought he was a tailor's walking advertisement!

COUNT: (*addressing* TRUEMAN *whom he has been inspecting through his eye-glass*) Where did you say you belonged, my friend? Dug out of the ruins of Pompeii, eh?

TRUEMAN: I belong to a land in which I rejoice to find that you are a foreigner.

COUNT: What a barbarian. He doesn't see the honour I'm doing his

country! Pray, Madam, is it one of the aboriginal inhabitants of the
soil? To what tribe of Indians does he belong – the Pawnee or
Choctaw? Does he carry a tomahawk?

TRUEMAN: Something quite as useful – do you see that? (*Shaking his
stick*)

     (COUNT *runs behind* MRS TIFFANY)

MRS TIFFANY: Oh, dear! I shall faint! Millinette! (*Approaching*)
Millinette!

  Enter MILLINETTE, *without advancing into the room*

MILLINETTE: *Oui*, Madame.

MRS TIFFANY: A glass of water!

            [*Exit* MILLINETTE]

Sir, (*Crossing to* TRUEMAN) I am shocked at your plebeian
conduct! This is a gentleman of the highest standing, Sir! He is a
Count, Sir!

  Enter MILLINETTE, *bearing a salver with a glass of water.*
  In advancing towards MRS TIFFANY, *she passes in front*
 of the COUNT, *starts and screams. The* COUNT, *after a start of*
 surprise, regains his composure, plays with his eye glass, and
      looks perfectly unconcerned

MRS TIFFANY: What is the matter? What *is* the matter:

MILLINETTE: Noting, noting – only – (*Looks at* COUNT *and turns
away her eyes again*) only – noting at all!

TRUEMAN: Don't be afraid, girl! Why, did you never see a live Count
before? He's tame, – I dare say your mistress there leads him about
by the ears.

MRS TIFFANY: This is too much! Millinette, send for Mr Tiffany
intantly!

   (*Crosses to* MILLINETTE, *who is going*)

MILLINETTE: He just come in, Madame!

TRUEMAN: My old friend! Where is he? Take me to him – I long to
have one more hearty shake of the hand!

MRS TIFFANY: (*Crosses to him*) Count, honour me by joining my
daughter in the conservatory, I will return immediately.

(COUNT *bows and walks towards conservatory,* MRS TIFFANY
following part of the way and then returning to TRUEMAN)

TRUEMAN: What a Jezebel! These women always play the very devil
with a man, and yet I don't believe such a damaged bale of goods as
that (*Looking at* MRS TIFFANY) has smoothed the heart of little
Antony!

MRS TIFFANY: This way, Sir, *sal vous plait*.

         [*Exit with great dignity*]

TRUEMAN: *Sal vous plait*. Ha, ha, ha! We'll see what Fashion has done for him. [*Exit*]

Act II

SCENE i

Inner apartment of MR TIFFANY's *counting house.* MR TIFFANY, *seated at a desk looking over papers.* MR SNOBSON, *on a high stool at another desk, with a pen behind his ear*

SNOBSON: (*rising, advances to the front of the stage, regards* TIFFANY *and shrugs his shoulders*) (*Aside*) How the old boy frets and fumes over those papers, to be sure! He's working himself into a perfect fever – ex-actly – therefore *bleeding's* the prescription! So here goes! Mr Tiffany, a word with you, if you please, Sir?

TIFFANY: (*sitting still*) Speak on, Mr Snobson, I attend.

SNOBSON: What I have to say, Sir, is a matter of the first importance to the credit of the concern – the *credit* of the concern, Mr Tiffany!

TIFFANY: Proceed, Mr Snobson.

SNOBSON: Sir, you've a handsome house – fine carriage – nigger in livery – feed on the fat of the land – everything first rate—

TIFFANY: Well, Sir?

SNOBSON: My salary, Mr Tiffany!

TIFFANY: It has been raised three times within the last year.

SNOBSON: Still it is insufficient for the necessities of an honest man – mark me, an *honest* man, Mr Tiffany.

TIFFANY: (*crossing, aside*) What a weapon he has made of that word! Enough – another hundred shall be added. Does that content you?

SNOBSON: There is one other subject, which I have before mentioned, Mr Tiffany – your daughter – what's the reason you can't let the folks at home know at once that I'm to be *the man*?

TIFFANY: (*aside*) Villain! And must the only seal upon this scoundrel's lips be placed there by the hand of my daughter? Well, Sir, it shall be as you desire.

SNOBSON: And Mrs Tiffany shall be informed of your resolution?

TIFFANY: Yes.

SNOBSON: Enough said! That's the ticket! The CREDIT *of the concern's safe,* Sir!

(*Returns to his seat*)

TIFFANY: (*aside*) How low have I bowed to this insolent rascal! To rise himself he mounts upon my shoulders, and unless I can shake him off he must crush me!

Enter TRUEMAN

TRUEMAN: Here I am, Antony, man! I told you I'd pay you a visit in your money-making quarters. (*Looks around*) But it looks as dismal here as a cell in the States' prison!

TIFFANY: (*forcing a laugh*) Ha, ha, ha! States' prison! You are so facetious! Ha, ha, ha!

TRUEMAN: Well, for the life of me I can't see anything so amusing in that! I should think the States' prison plaguy uncomfortable lodgings. And you laugh, man, as though you fancied yourself there already.

TIFFANY: Ha, ha, ha!

TRUEMAN: (*imitating him*) Ha, ha, ha! What on earth do you mean by that ill-sounding laugh, that has nothing of a laugh about it! This *fashion*-worship has made heathens and hypocrites of you all! *Deception* is your household God! A man laughs as if he were crying, and cries as if he were laughing in his sleeve. Everything is something else from what it seems to be. I have lived in your house only three days, and I've heard more lies than were ever invented during a Presidential election! First your fine lady of a wife sends me word that she's not at home – I walk up stairs, and she takes good care that *I* shall not be *at home* – wants to turn me out of doors. Then *you* come in – take your old friend by the hand – whisper, the deuce knows what, in your wife's ear, and the tables are turned in a tangent! Madam curtsies – says she's enchanted to see me – and orders her grinning nigger to show me a room.

TIFFANY: We were exceedingly happy to welcome you as our guest!

TRUEMAN: Happy? *You* happy? Ah, Antony! Antony! that hatchet face of yours, and those criss-cross furrows tell quite another story! It's many a long day since you were *happy* at anything! You look as if you'd melted down your flesh into dollars, and mortgaged your soul in the bargain! Your warm heart has grown cold over your ledger – your light spirits heavy with calculation! You have traded away your youth – your hopes – your tastes, for wealth! and now you *have* the wealth you coveted, what does it profit you? Pleasure it cannot buy; for you have lost your *capacity* for enjoyment – Ease it will not bring; for the love of gain is never satisfied! It has made your counting-house a penitentiary, and your home a fashionable *museum* where there is no niche for you! You have spent so much time *ciphering* in the one, that you find yourself at last a very *cipher* in the other! See me, man! seventy-two last August! – strong as a hickory and every whit as sound!

TIFFANY: I take the greatest pleasure in remarking your superiority, Sir.

TRUEMAN: Bah! no man takes pleasure in remarking the superiority of another. Why the deuce, can't you speak the truth, man? But it's not the *fashion* I suppose! I have not seen one frank, open face since – no, no, I can't say that either, though lying *is* catching! There's that girl, Gertrude, who is trying to teach your daughter music – but Gertrude was bred in the country!

TIFFANY: A good girl; my wife and daughter find her very useful.

TRUEMAN: Useful? Well, I must say you have queer notions of *use!* – But come, cheer up, man! I'd rather see one of your old smiles, than know you'd realized another thousand! I hear you are making money on the true, American, high pressure system – better go slow and sure – the more steam, the greater danger of the boiler's bursting! All sound, I hope? Nothing rotten at the core?

TIFFANY: Oh, sound – quite sound!

TRUEMAN: Well, that's pleasant – though I must say you don't look very pleasant about it!

TIFFANY: My good friend, although I am solvent, I may say, perfectly solvent – yet you – the fact is, you can be of some assistance to me!

TRUEMAN: That's the *fact* is it? I'm glad we've hit upon one *fact* at last! Well—

> (SNOBSON, *who during this conversation has been
> employed in writing, but stops occasionally to listen, now
> gives vent to a dry chuckling laugh*)

TRUEMAN: Hey? What's that? Another of those deuced ill-sounding, city laughs! (*Sees* SNOBSON) Who's that perched up on the stool of repentance – eh, Antony?

SNOBSON: (*aside and looking at* TIFFANY'S *seat*) The old boy has missed his text there – *that's* the stool of repentance!

TIFFANY: One of my clerks – my confidential clerk!

TRUEMAN: Confidential? Why he looks for all the world like a spy – the most inquisitorial, hang-dog face – ugh! the sight of it makes my blood run cold! Come, (*Crosses*) let us talk over matters where this critter can't give us the benefit of his opinion! Antony, the next time you choose a confidential clerk, take one that carries his credentials in his face – those in his pocket are not worth much without!

> [*Exeunt* TRUEMAN *and* TIFFANY]

SNOBSON: (*jumping from his stool and advancing*) The old prig has got the tin, or Tiff would never be so civil! All right – Tiff will work every shiner into the concern – all the better for me! Now I'll go and make love to Seraphina. The old woman needn't try to knock me down with any of her French lingo! Six months from today if I ain't driving my two footmen tandem, down Broadway – and as fashionable as Mrs Tiffany herself, then I ain't the trump I thought I was! that's all. (*Looks at his watch*) Bless me! eleven o'clock and I haven't had my julep[3] yet! Snobson, I'm ashamed of you!   [*Exit*]

SCENE ii

The interior of a beautiful conservatory; walk through the centre; stands of flower pots in bloom; a couple of rustic seats. GERTRUDE, *attired in white, with a white rose in her hair; watering the flowers.* COLONEL HOWARD *regarding her*

HOWARD: I am afraid you lead a sad life here, Miss Gertrude?

GERTRUDE: (*turning round gaily*) What! amongst the flowers?
                          (*Continues her occupation*)

HOWARD: No, amongst the thistles, with which Mrs Tiffany surrounds you; the tempests, which her temper raises!

GERTRUDE: They never harm me. Flowers and herbs are excellent tutors. I learn prudence from the reed, and bend until the storm has swept over me!

HOWARD: Admirable philosophy! But still this frigid atmosphere of fashion must be uncongenial to you? Accustomed to the pleasant companionship of your kind friends in Geneva, surely you must regret this cold exchange?

GERTRUDE: Do you think so? Can you suppose that I could possibly prefer a ramble in the woods to a promenade in Broadway? A wreath of scented wild flowers to a bouquet of these sickly exotics? The odour of new-mown hay to the heated air of this crowded conservatory? Or can you imagine that I could enjoy the quiet conversation of my Geneva friends, more than the edifying chit-chat of a fashionable drawing room? But I see you think me totally destitute of taste?

HOWARD: You have a merry spirit to jest thus at your grievances!

GERTRUDE: I have my *mania* – as some wise person declares that all mankind have – and mine is a love of independence! In Geneva, my wants were supplied by two kind old maiden ladies, upon whom I know not that I have any claim. I had abilities, and desired to use them. I came here at my own request; for here I am no longer *dependent! Voila tout,* as Mrs Tiffany would say.

HOWARD: Believe me, I appreciate the confidence you repose in me!

GERTRUDE: Confidence! Truly, Colonel Howard, the *confidence* is entirely on your part, in supposing that I confide that which I have no reason to conceal! I think I informed you that Mrs Tiffany only received visitors on her reception day – she is therefore not prepared to see you. Zeke – Oh! I beg his pardon – Adolph, made some mistake in admitting you.

HOWARD: Nay, Gertrude, it was not Mrs Tiffany, nor Miss Tiffany, whom I came to see; it – it was—

GERTRUDE: The conservatory perhaps? I will leave you to examine the flowers at leisure! (*Crosses*)

HOWARD: Gertrude – listen to me. (*Aside*) If I only dared to give utterance to what is hovering upon my lips! Gertrude!

GERTRUDE: Colonel Howard!

HOWARD: Gertrude, I must – must –

GERTRUDE: Yes, indeed you *must*, must leave me! I think I hear somebody coming – Mrs Tiffany would not be well pleased to find you here – pray, pray leave me – that door will lead you into the street.

(*Hurries him out through door; takes up her watering pot, and commences watering flowers, tying up branches*)

What a strange being is man! Why should he hesitate to say – nay, why should I prevent his saying, what I would most delight to hear? Truly man *is* strange – but woman is quite as incomprehensible!

(*Walks about gathering flowers*)

Enter COUNT JOLIMAITRE

COUNT: There she is – the bewitching little creature! Mrs Tiffany and her daughter are out of ear-shot. I caught a glimpse of their feathers floating down Broadway, not ten minutes ago. Just the opportunity I have been looking for! Now for an engagement with this captivating little piece of prudery! 'Pon honour, I am almost afraid she will not resist a *Count* long enough to give value to the conquest. (*Approaching her*) Ma belle petite, were you gathering roses for me?

GERTRUDE: (*starts on first perceiving him, but instantly regains her self-possession*) The roses here, Sir, are carefully guarded with thorns – if you have the right to gather, pluck for yourself!

COUNT: Sharp as ever, little Gertrude! But now that we are alone, throw off this frigidity, and be at your ease.

GERTRUDE: Permit me to *be alone*, Sir, that I *may* be at my ease!

COUNT: Very good, *ma belle*, well said! (*Applauding her with his hands*) Never yield too soon, even to a *title*! But as the old girl may find her way back before long, we may as well come to particulars at once. I love you; but that you know already. (*rubbing his eye-glass unconcernedly with his handkerchief*) Before long I shall make Mademoiselle Seraphina my wife, and, of course, you shall remain in the family!

GERTRUDE: (*indignantly*) Sir—

COUNT: 'Pon my honour you shall! In France we arrange these little matters without difficulty!

GERTRUDE: But I am an *American!* Your conduct proves that you are not one!

(*Going, crosses*)

COUNT: (*preventing her*) Don't run away, my immaculate *petite Americaine!* Demme, you've quite overlooked my condescension – the difference of our stations – you a species of upper servant – an orphan – no friends.

Enter TRUEMAN *unperceived*

GERTRUDE: And therefore more entitled to the respect, and protection of every *true gentleman!* Had you been one, you would not have insulted me!

COUNT: My charming little orator, patriotism and declamation become you particularly! (*Approaches her*) I feel quite tempted to taste—

TRUEMAN: (*thrusting him aside*) An American hickory-switch! (*Strikes him*) Well, how do you like it?

COUNT: (*aside*) Old matter-of-fact! Sir, how dare you?

TRUEMAN: My stick has answered that question!

GERTRUDE: Oh! now I am quite safe!

TRUEMAN: Safe! not a bit safer than before! All women would be safe, if they knew how virtue became them! As for you, Mr Count, what have you to say for yourself! Come, speak out!

COUNT: Sir – aw – aw – you don't understand these matters!

TRUEMAN: That's a fact! Not having had *your* experience, I don't believe I *do* understand them!

COUNT: A piece of pleasantry – a mere joke—

TRUEMAN: A joke was it? I'll show you a joke worth two of that! I'll teach you the way we natives joke with a puppy who don't respect an honest woman! (*Seizing him*)

COUNT: Oh! oh! demme – you old ruffian! let me go. What do you mean?

TRUEMAN: Oh! a piece of pleasantry – a mere joke – very pleasant isn't it?

(*Attempts to strike him again;* COUNT *struggles with him*)
Enter MRS TIFFANY *hastily, in her bonnet and shawl*

MRS TIFFANY: What is the matter? I am perfectly *abimé* with terror. Mr Trueman, what has happened?

TRUEMAN: Oh! we have been *joking!*

MRS TIFFANY: (*to* COUNT, *who is re-arranging his dress*) My dear Count, I did not expect to find you here – how kind of you!

TRUEMAN: Your *dear* Count has been showing his *kindness* in a very *foreign* manner. Too *foreign* I think, he found it to be relished by an *unfashionable native!* What do you think of a puppy, who insults an innocent girl all in the way of *kindness*? This Count of yours – this importation of—

COUNT: My dear Madam, demme, permit me to explain. It would be unbecoming – demme – particular unbecoming of you – aw – aw – to pay any attention to this ignorant person. (*Crosses to* TRUEMAN) Anything that he says concerning a man of my standing – aw – the truth is, Madam—

TRUEMAN: Let us have the truth by all means, – if it is only for the novelty's sake!

COUNT: (*turning his back to* TRUEMAN) You see, Madam, hoping to obtain a few moments private conversation with Miss Seraphina – with *Miss Seraphina* I say and – aw – and knowing her passion for flowers, I found my way to your very tasteful and *recherché* conservatory. (*Looks about him approvingly*) *Very* beautifully arranged – does you great credit, madam! Here I encountered this young person. She was inclined to be talkative; and I indulged her with – with a – aw – demme – a few *common places!* What passed between us was mere *harmless badinage* – on *my* part. You, madam, you – so conversant with our European manners – you are aware that when a man of fashion – that is, when a woman – a man is bound – amongst noblemen, you know—

MRS TIFFANY: I comprehend you perfectly – *parfittement*, my dear Count.

COUNT: (*aside*) 'Pon my honour, that's very obliging of her.

MRS TIFFANY: I am shocked at the plebeian forwardness of this conceited girl!

TRUEMAN: (*walking up to* COUNT) Did you ever keep a reckoning of the lies you tell in an hour?

MRS TIFFANY: Mr Trueman, I blush for you!
                    (*Crosses to* TRUEMAN)

TRUEMAN: Don't do that – you have no blushes to spare!

MRS TIFFANY: It is a man of rank whom you are addressing, Sir!

TRUEMAN: A rank villain, Mrs Antony Tiffany! A *rich one* he would be, had he as much *gold* as *brass!*

MRS TIFFANY: Pray pardon him, Count; he knows nothing of *how ton!*

COUNT: Demme, he's beneath my notice. I tell you what, old fellow – (TRUEMAN *raises his stick as* COUNT *approaches, the latter starts back*) the sight of him discomposes me – aw – I feel quite uncomfortable – aw – let us join your charming daughter? I can't do you the honour to shoot, you, Sir – (*To* TRUEMAN) you are beneath me – a nobleman can't fight a commoner; Good bye, old Truepenny! I – aw – I'm insensible to your insolence!

[*Exeunt* COUNT *and* MRS TIFFANY]

TRUEMAN: You won't be insensible to a cow hide in spite of your nobility! The next time he practises any of his foreign fashions on you, Gertrude, you'll see how I'll wake up his sensibilities!

GERTRUDE: I do not know what I should have done without you, sir.

TRUEMAN: Yes, you do – you know that you would have done well enough! Never tell a lie, girl! not even for the sake of pleasing an old man! When you open your lips let your heart speak! Never tell a lie! Let your face be the looking-glass of your soul – your heart its clock – while your tongue rings the hours! But the glass must be clear, the clock true, and then there's no fear but the tongue will do its duty in a woman's head!

GERTRUDE: You are very good, Sir!

TRUEMAN: That's as it may be! – (*Aside*) How my heart warms towards her! Gertrude, I hear that you have no mother?

GERTRUDE: Ah! no, Sir; I wish I had.

TRUEMAN: So do I! Heaven knows, so do I! (*Aside, and with emotion*) And you have no father, Gertrude?

GERTRUDE: No, Sir – I often wish I had!

TRUEMAN: (*hurriedly*) Don't do that, girl! don't do that! Wish you had a mother – but never wish that you had a father again! Perhaps the one you had did not deserve such a child!

Enter PRUDENCE

PRUDENCE: Seraphina is looking for you, Gertrude.

GERTRUDE: I will go to her. (*Crosses*) Mr Trueman, you will not permit me to thank you, but you cannot prevent my gratitude!

[*Exit*]

TRUEMAN: (*looking after her*) If falsehood harbours there, I'll give up searching after truth!

(*Crosses, retires up the stage musingly, and commences examining the flowers*)

PRUDENCE: (*aside*) What a nice old man he is to be sure! I wish he would say something!

(*Crosses, walks after him, turning when he turns – after a pause*)
Don't mind *me*, Mr Trueman!

TRUEMAN: Mind you? Oh! no, don't be afraid (*Crosses*) – I wasn't minding you. Nobody seems to mind you much!
(*Continues walking and examining the flowers
– PRUDENCE follows*)

PRUDENCE: Very pretty flowers, ain't they? Gertrude takes care of them.

TRUEMAN: Gertrude? So I hear – (*Advancing*) I suppose you can tell me now who this Gertrude—

PRUDENCE: Who she's in love with? I *knew* you were going to say that! I'll tell you all about it! Gertrude, she's in love with – Mr Twinkle! and he's in love with her. And Seraphina she's in love with Count Jolly – what-d' ye-call-it: but Count Jolly don't take to her at all – but Colonel Howard – he's the man – he's desperate about her!

TRUEMAN: Why you feminine newspaper! Howard in love with that quintessence of affectation! Howard – the only, frank, straightforward fellow that I've met since – I'll tell him my mind on the subject! And Gertrude hunting for happiness in a rhyming dictionary! The girl's a greater fool than I took her for!
(*Crosses*)

PRUDENCE: So she is – you see I know all about them!

TRUEMAN: I see you do! You've a wonderful knowledge – wonderful – of *other people's concerns!* It may do here, but take my word for it, in the county of Catteraugus you'd get the name of a great *busybody*. But perhaps you know that too?

PRUDENCE: Oh! I always know what's coming. I feel it beforehand all over me. I knew something was going to happen the day you came here – and what's more I can always tell a married man from a single – I felt right off that you were a bachelor!

TRUEMAN: Felt right off I was a bachelor did you? you were sure of it – sure? – quite sure? (PRUDENCE *assents delightedly*) Then you felt wrong! – a bachelor and a widower are not the same thing!

PRUDENCE: Oh! but it all comes to the same thing – a widower's as good as a bachelor any day! And besides I knew that you were a farmer *right off*.

TRUEMAN: On the spot, eh? I suppose you saw cabbages and green peas growing out of my hat?

PRUDENCE: No, I didn't – but I knew all about you. And I knew – (*Looking down and fidgeting with her apron*) I knew you were for getting married soon! For last night I dream't I saw your funeral going along the streets, and the mourners all dressed in white. And a funeral is a sure sign of a wedding, you know! (*Nudging him with her elbow*)

TRUEMAN: (*imitating her voice*) Well I can't say that I *know* any such thing! you know! (*Nudging her back*)

PRUDENCE: Oh! it does, and there's no getting over it! For my part, I like farmers – and I know all about setting hens and turkeys, and feeding chickens, and laying eggs, and all that sort of thing!

TRUEMAN: (*aside*) May I be shot! if mistress newspaper is not putting in an advertisement for herself! This is your city mode of courting I suppose, ha, ha, ha!

PRUDENCE: I've been west, a little; but I never was in the county of Catteraugus, myself.

TRUEMAN: Oh! you were not? And you have taken a particular fancy to go there, eh?

PRUDENCE: Perhaps I shouldn't object—

TRUEMAN: Oh! – ah! – so I suppose. Now pay attention to what I am going to say, for it is a matter of great importance to yourself.

PRUDENCE: (*aside*) Now it's coming – I know what he's going to say!

TRUEMAN: The next time you want to tie a man for life to your apron-strings, pick out one that don't come from the county of Catteraugus – for greenhorns[4] are scarce in those parts, and modest women plenty!

[*Exit*]

PRUDENCE: Now who'd have thought he was going to say that! But I won't give him up yet – I won't give him up.

[*Exit*]

Act III

SCENE i

MRS TIFFANY's *parlour. Enter* MRS TIFFANY *followed by* MR TIFFANY

TIFFANY: Your extravagance will ruin me, Mrs Tiffany!

MRS TIFFANY: And your stinginess will ruin me, Mr Tiffany! It is totally and *toot a fate* impossible to convince you of the necessity of *keeping up appearances.* There is a certain display which every woman of fashion is forced to make!

TIFFANY: And pray who made *you* a woman of fashion?

MRS TIFFANY: What a vulgar question! All women of fashion Mr Tiffany—

TIFFANY: In this land are *self-constituted*, like you, Madam – and *fashion* is the cloak for more sins than charity ever covered! It was for *fashion's* sake that you insisted upon my purchasing this expensive house – it was for *fashion's* sake that you ran me in debt at every exorbitant upholsterer's and extravagant furniture warehouse in the city – it was for *fashion's* sake that you built that ruinous conservatory – hired more servants than they have persons to wait upon – and dressed your footman like a harlequin!

MRS TIFFANY: Mr Tiffany, you are thoroughly plebeian, and insufferably *American*, in your grovelling ideas! And, pray, what was the occasion of these very *mal-ap-pro-pos* remarks? Merely because I requested a paltry fifty dollars to purchase a new style of head-dress – a *bijou* of an article just introduced in France.

TIFFANY: Time was, Mrs Tiffany, when you manufactured your own French head-dresses – took off their first gloss at the public balls, and then sold them to your shortest-sighted customers. And all you knew about France, or French either, was what you spelt out at the bottom of your fashion plates – but now you have grown so fashionable, forsooth, that you have forgotten how to speak your mother tongue!

MRS TIFFANY: Mr Tiffany, Mr Tiffany! Nothing is more positively vulgarian – more *unaristocratic* than any allusion to the past!

TIFFANY: Why I thought, my dear, that *aristocrats* lived principally upon the past – and traded in the market of fashion with the bones of their ancestors for capital?

MRS TIFFANY: Mr Tiffany, such vulgar remarks are only suitable to the counting house, in my drawing room you should—

TIFFANY: Vary my sentiments with my locality, as you change your *manners* with your *dress!*

MRS TIFFANY: Mr Tiffany, I desire that you will purchase Count d'Orsay's 'Science of Etiquette', and learn how to conduct yourself – especially before you appear at the grand ball, which I shall give on Friday!

TIFFANY: Confound your balls, Madam; they make *footballs* of my money, while you dance away all that I am worth! A pretty time to give a ball when you know that I am on the very brink of bankruptcy!

MRS TIFFANY: So much the greater reason that nobody should suspect your circumstances, or you would lose your credit at once. Just at this crisis a ball is absolutely *necessary* to save your reputation! There is Mrs Adolphus Dashaway – she gave the most splendid fête of the season – and I hear on very good authority that her husband has not paid his baker's bill in three months. Then there was Mrs Honeywood—

TIFFANY: Gave a ball the night before her husband shot himself – perhaps you wish to drive me to follow his example?

(*Crosses*)

MRS TIFFANY: Good gracious! Mr Tiffany, how you talk! I beg you won't mention anything of the kind. I consider black the most unbecoming colour. I'm sure I've done all that I could to gratify you. There is that vulgar old torment, Trueman, who gives one the lie fifty times a day – haven't I been very civil to him?

TIFFANY: Civil to his *wealth*, Mrs Tiffany! I told you that he was a rich, old farmer – the early friend of my father – my own benefactor – and that I had reason to think he might assist me in my present embarrassments. Your civility was *bought* – and like most of your *own* purchases has yet to be *paid* for. (*Crosses*)

MRS TIFFANY: And will be, no doubt! The condescension of a woman of fashion should command any price. Mr Trueman is insupportably indecorous – he has insulted Count Jolimaitre in the most outrageous manner. If the Count was not so deeply interested – so *abimé* with Seraphina, I am sure he would never honour us by his visits again!

TIFFANY: So much the better – he shall never marry my daughter! – I am resolved on that. Why, Madam, I am told there is in Paris a regular matrimonial stock company, who fit out indigent dandies for this market. How do I know but this fellow is one of its creatures, and that he has come here to increase its dividends by marrying a fortune?

MRS TIFFANY: Nonsense, Mr Tiffany. The Count, the most fashionable young man in all New York – the intimate friend of all the dukes and lords in Europe – not marry my daughter? Not permit Seraphina to become a Countess? Mr Tiffany, you are out of your senses!

TIFFANY: That would not be very wonderful, considering how many years I have been united to you, my dear. Modern physicians pronounce lunacy infectious!

MRS TIFFANY: Mr Tiffany, he is a man of fashion—

TIFFANY: Fashion makes fools, but cannot *feed* them. By the by, I have a request, – since you are bent upon ruining me by this ball, and there is no help for it, – I desire that you will send an invitation to my confidential clerk, Mr Snobson.

MRS TIFFANY: Mr Snobson! Was there ever such an *you-nick* demand! Mr Snobson would cut a pretty figure amongst my fashionable friends! I shall do no such thing, Mr Tiffany.

TIFFANY: Then, Madam, the ball shall not take place. Have I not told you that I am in the power of this man? That there are circumstances which it is happy for you that you do not know – which you cannot comprehend – but which render it essential that you should be civil to Mr Snobson? Not you merely, but Seraphina also? He is a more appropriate match for her than your foreign favourite.

MR TIFFANY: A match for Seraphina, indeed! (*Crosses*) Mr Tiffany, you are determined to make a *fow pas*.

TIFFANY: Mr Snobson intends calling this morning. (*Crosses*)

MRS TIFFANY: But, Mr Tiffany, this is not reception day – my drawing-rooms are in the most terrible disorder—

TIFFANY: Mr Snobson is not particular – he must be admitted.

Enter ZEKE

ZEKE: Mr Snobson.

Enter SNOBSON, *exit* ZEKE

SNOBSON: How dye do, Marm? (*Crosses*) How are you? Mr Tiffany, your most!—

MRS TIFFANY: (*formally*) Bung jure. Comment vow portè vow, Monsur Snobson?

SNOBSON: Oh, to be sure – very good of you – fine day.

MRS TIFFANY: (*pointing to a chair with great dignity*) Sassoyez vow, Monsur Snobson.

SNOBSON: (*aside*) I wonder what she's driving at? I ain't up to the fashionable lingo yet! Eh? what? Speak a little louder, Marm?

MRS TIFFANY: (*aside*) What ignorance!

TIFFANY: I presume Mrs Tiffany means that you are to take a seat.

SNOBSON: Ex-actly – very obliging of her – so I will. (*Sits*) No ceremony amongst friends, you know – and likely to be nearer – you understand? *OK*, all correct. How *is* Seraphina?

MRS TIFFANY: Miss Tiffany is not visible this morning. (*Retires up*)

SNOBSON: Not visible? (*Jumping up*) I suppose that's the English for can't see her? Mr Tiffany, Sir – (*Walking up to him*) what am I to understand by this *de-fal-ca-tion*, Sir? I expected your word to be as good as your bond – beg pardon. Sir – I mean *better* – considerably better – no humbug about it, Sir.

TIFFANY: Have patience, Mr Snobson.

(*Rings bell*)
Enter ZEKE

Zeke, desire my daughter to come here.

MRS TIFFANY: (*coming down*) Adolph – I say, Adolph—

(ZEKE *straightens himself and assumes foppish airs, as he turns to* MRS TIFFANY)

TIFFANY: Zeke

ZEKE: Don't know any such nigga, Boss.

TIFFANY: Do as I bid you instantly, or off with your livery and quit the house!

ZEKE: Wheugh! I 'se all dismission! [*Exit*]

MRS TIFFANY: A-dolph, A-dolph! (*Calling after him*)

SNOBSON: (*aside*) I brought the old boy to his bearings, didn't I though! Pull that string, and he is sure to work right. Don't make any stranger of me, Marm – I'm quite at home. If you've got any odd jobs about the house to do up, I sha'n't miss you. I'll amuse myself with Seraphina when she comes – we'll get along very cosily by ourselves.

MRS TIFFANY: Permit me to inform you, Mr Snobson, that a French mother never leaves her daughter alone with a young man – she knows your sex too well for that!

SNOBSON: Very *dis*-obliging of her – but as we're none French—

MRS TIFFANY: You have yet to learn, Mr Snobson, that the American *ee-light* – the aristocracy – the *how-ton* – as a matter of conscience, scrupulously follow the foreign fashions.

SNOBSON: Not when they are foreign to their interests, Marm – for instance – (*Enter* SERAPHINA). There you are at last, eh, Miss? How d'ye do? Ma said you weren't visible. Managed to get a peep at her, eh, Mr Tiffany?

SERAPHINA: I heard you were here, Mr Snobson, and came without even arranging my toilette; you will excuse my negligence?

SNOBSON: Of everything but *me*, Miss.

SERAPHINA: I shall never have to ask your pardon for *that*, Mr Snobson.

MRS TIFFANY: Seraphina – child – really—

(*As she is approaching* SERAPHINA, MR TIFFANY *plants himself in front of his wife*)

TIFFANY: Walk this way, Madam, if you please. (*aside*) To see that she fancies the surly fellow takes a weight from my heart.

MRS TIFFANY: Mr Tiffany, it is highly improper and not at all *distingué* to leave a young girl—

Enter ZEKE

ZEKE: Mr Count Jolly-made-her!

MRS TIFFANY: Good gracious! The Count—Oh, dear! – Seraphina, run and change your dress – no there's not time! A-dolph, admit him. (*Exit* ZEKE) Mr Snobson, get out of the way, will you? Mr Tiffany, what are you doing at home at this hour?

Enter COUNT JOLIMAITRE, *ushered by* ZEKE

ZEKE: (*aside*) Dat's de genuine article ob a gemman.   [*Exit*]

MRS TIFFANY: My dear Count, I am overjoyed at the very sight of you.

COUNT: Flattered myself you'd be glad to see me, Madam – knew it was not your *jour de reception*.

MRS TIFFANY: But for you, Count, all days—

COUNT: I thought so. Ah, Miss Tiffany, on my honour, you're looking beautiful.

(*Crosses*)

SERAPHINA: Count, flattery from you—

SNOBSON: What? Eh? What's that you say?

SERAPHINA: (*aside to him*) Nothing but what etiquette requires.

COUNT: (*regarding* MR TIFFANY *through his eye glass*) Your worthy Papa, I believe? Sir, your most obedient.

(MR TIFFANY *bows coldly*; COUNT *regards* SNOBSON *through his glass, shrugs his shoulders and turns away*)

SNOBSON: (*to* MRS TIFFANY) Introduce me, will you? I never knew a Count in all my life – what a strange-looking animal!

MRS TIFFANY: Mr Snobson, it is not the fashion to introduce in France!

SNOBSON: But, Marm, we're in America. (MRS TIFFANY *crosses to*

COUNT, *aside*) The woman thinks she's somewhere else than where she is – she wants to make an *alibi*?

MRS TIFFANY: I hope that we shall have the pleasure of seeing you on Friday evening, Count?

COUNT: Really, madam, my invitations – my engagements – so numerous – I can hardly answer for myself: and you Americans take offence so easily—

MRS TIFFANY: But, Count, everybody expects you at our ball – you are the principal attraction—

SERAPHINA: Count, you *must* come!

COUNT: Since you insist – aw – aw – there's no resisting you, Miss Tiffany.

MRS TIFFANY: I am so thankful. How can I repay your condescension! (COUNT *and* SERAPHINA *converse*) Mr Snobson, will you walk this way? – I have *such* a cactus in full bloom – remarkable flower! Mr Tiffany, pray come here – I have something particular to say.

TIFFANY: Then speak out, my dear – (*Aside to her*) I thought it was highly improper just now to leave a girl with a young man?

MRS TIFFANY: Oh, but the Count – that is different!

TIFFANY: I suppose you mean to say there's nothing of *the man* about him?

Enter MILLINETTE *with a scarf in her hand*

MILLINETTE: (*aside*) Adolph tell me he vas here. Pardon, Madame, I bring dis scarf for Mademoiselle.

MRS TIFFANY: Very well, Millinette; you know best what is proper for her to wear.

(MR *and* MRS TIFFANY *and* SNOBSON *retire up; she engages the attention of both gentlemen*)

(MILLINETTE *crosses towards* SERAPHINA, *gives the* COUNT *a threatening look, and commences arranging the scarf over* SERAPHINA'S *shoulders*)

MILLINETTE: Mademoiselle, *permettez-moi*. (*Aside to* COUNT) Per-*fide*! If Mademoiselle vil stand *tranquille* one *petit moment*. (*turns* SERAPHINA'S *back to the* COUNT, *and pretends to arrange the scarf*.) (Aside to COUNT) I must speak vid you today, or I tell all – you find me at de foot of de stair ven you go. *Prends garde!*

SERAPHINA: What is that you say, Millinette?

MILLINETTE: Dis scarf make you so very beautiful, Mademoiselle – *Je vous salue, mes dames*. (*Curtsies*)   [*Exit*]

COUNT: (*aside*) Not a moment to lose! Miss Tiffany, I have an unpleasant – a particularly unpleasant piece of intelligence – you see, I have just received a letter from my friend – the – aw – the Earl of Airshire,⁵ the truth is, the Earl's daughter – beg you won't mention it – has distinguished me by a tender *penchant*.

SERAPHINA: I understand – and they wish you to return and marry the young lady; but surely you will not leave us, Count?

COUNT: If *you* bid me stay – I shouldn't have the conscience – I couldn't *afford* to tear myself away. (*Aside*) I'm sure that's honest.

SERAPHINA: Oh, Count!

COUNT: Say but one word – say that you shouldn't mind being made a Countess – and I'll break with the Earl tomorrow.

SERAPHINA: Count, this surprise – but don't think of leaving the country, Count – we could not pass the time without you! – yes – yes, Count – I do consent!

COUNT: (*aside, while he embraces her*) I thought she would! Enchanted rapture, bliss, ecstacy, and all that sort of thing – words can't express it, but you understand. But it must be kept a secret – postively it *must!* If the rumour of our engagement were whispered abroad – the Earl's daughter – the delicacy of my situation, aw – you comprehend? It is even possible that our nuptials, my charming Miss Tiffany, *our nuptials* must take place in private!

SERAPHINA: Oh, that is quite impossible!

COUNT: It's the latest fashion abroad – the very latest. Ah, I knew that would determine you. Can I depend on your secrecy?

SERAPHINA: Oh, yes! Believe me.

SNOBSON: (*coming forward in spite of* MRS TIFFANY's *efforts to detain him*) Why Seraphina, haven't you a word to throw to a dog?

TIFFANY: (*aside*) I shouldn't think she had after wasting so many upon a puppy.

Enter ZEKE, *wearing a three-cornered hat*

ZEKE: Missus, de bran new carriage am below.

MRS TIFFANY: Show it up – I mean, Very well, A-dolph.

[*Exit* ZEKE]

Count, my daughter and I are about to take an airing in our new *voyture* – will you honour us with your company?

COUNT: Madam, I – I have a most *pressing* engagement. A letter to write to the *Earl of Airshire* – who is at present residing in the *Isle of Skye*. I must bid you good morning.

MRS TIFFANY: Good morning, Count.   [*Exit* COUNT]

SNOBSON: *I'm* quite at leisure, (*Crosses to* MRS TIFFANY) Marm. Books balanced – ledger closed – nothing to do all the afternoon – I'm for you.

MRS TIFFANY: (*without noticing him*) Come, Seraphina, come!

(*As they are going* SNOBSON *follows them*)

SNOBSON: But, Marm – I was saying, Marm, I am quite at leisure – not a thing to do; have I, Mr Tiffany?

MRS TIFFANY: Seraphina, child – your red shawl – remember – Mr Snobson, *bon swear!*

[*Exit, leading* SERAPHINA]

SNOBSON: Swear! Mr Tiffany, Sir, am I to be fobbed off with a *bon swear*? Damn it, I will swear!

TIFFANY: Have patience, Mr Snobson, if you will accompany me to the counting house—

SNOBSON: Don't count too much on me, Sir. I'll make up no more accounts until these are settled! I'll run down and jump into the carriage in spite of her *bon swear*.   [*Exit*]

TIFFANY: You'll jump into a hornet's nest, if you do! Mr Snobson, Mr Snobson!   [*Exit after him*]

SCENE ii

Housekeeper's room

Enter MILLINETTE

MILLINETTE: I have set dat bête, Adolph, to vatch for him. He say he would come back so soon as Madame's *voiture* drive from de door. If he not come – but he vill – he vill – he *bien etourdi*, but he have *bon cœur*

Enter COUNT

COUNT: Ah! Millinette, my dear, you see what a good-natured dog I am to fly at your bidding—

MILLINETTE: Fly? Ah! *trompeur*! Vat for you fly from Paris? Vat for you leave me – and I love you so much? Ven you sick – you almost die – did I not stay by you – take care of you – and you have no else friend? Vat for you leave Paris?

COUNT: Never allude to disagreeable subjects, *mon enfant*! I was forced by uncontrollable circumstances to fly to the land of liberty—

MILLINETTE: Vat you do vid all de money I give you? The last sou I had – did I not give you?

COUNT: I dare say you did, ma petite—(*Aside*) wish you'd been better supplied! Don't ask any questions here – can't explain now – the next time we meet—

MILLINETTE: But, ah! ven shall ve meet – ven? You not deceive me, not any more.

COUNT: Deceive you! I'd rather deceive myself – (*Aside*) I wish I could! I'd persuade myself you were once more washing linen in the Seine!

MILLINETTE: I vil tell you ven ve shall meet – On Friday night Madame give one grand ball – you come *sans doute* – den ven de supper is served – de Americans tink of noting else ven de supper come – den you steal out of de room, and you find me here – and you give me one grand *explanation!*

Enter GERTRUDE, *unperceived*

COUNT: Friday night – while supper is serving – *parole d'honneur* I will be here – I will explain everything – my sudden departure from Paris – my – demme, my countship – everything! Now let me go – if any of the family should discover us—

GERTRUDE: (*who during the last speech has gradually advanced*) They might discover more than you think it advisable for them to know!

COUNT: The devil!

MILLINETTE: *Mon Dieu!* Mademoiselle Gertrude!

COUNT: (*recovering himself*) My dear Miss Gertrude, let me explain – aw – aw – nothing is more natural than the situation in which you find me—

GERTRUDE: I am inclined to believe that, Sir.

COUNT: Now – 'pon my honour, that's not fair. Here is Millinette will bear witness to what I am about to say—

GERTRUDE: Oh, I have not the slightest doubt of that, Sir.

COUNT: You see, Millinette happened to be lady's-maid in the family of – of – the Duchess Chateau D'Espagne – and I chanced to be a particular friend of the Duchess – *very particular* I assure you! Of course I saw Millinette, and she, demme, she saw me! Didn't you, Millinette?

MILLINETTE: Oh! *oui* – Mademoiselle, I knew him ver vell.

COUNT: Well, it is a remarkable fact that – being in correspondence with this very Duchess – at this very time—

GERTRUDE: That is sufficient, Sir – I am already so well acquainted with your extraordinary talents for improvisation, that I will not further tax your invention—

MILLINETTE: Ah! Mademoiselle Gertrude do not betray us – have pity!

COUNT: (*assuming an air of dignity*) Silence, Millinette! My word has been doubted – the word of a nobleman! I will inform my friend, Mrs Tiffany, of this young person's audacity. (*Going.*)

GERTRUDE: (*aside*) His own weapons alone can foil this villain! Sir –

Sir – Count! (*at the last word the* COUNT *turns*) Perhaps, Sir, the least said about this matter the better!

COUNT: (*delightedly*). The least said? We won't say anything at all. (*Aside*) She's coming round – couldn't resist me. Charming Gertrude—

MILLINETTE: *Quoi?* Vat that you say?

COUNT: (*aside to her*) My sweet, adorable Millinette, hold your tongue, will you?

MILLINETTE: (*aloud*) No, I vill not! If you do look so from out your eyes at her again, I vill tell all!

COUNT: (*aside*) Oh, I never could manage two women at once, – jealousy makes the dear creatures so spiteful. The only valor is in flight! Miss Gertrude, I wish you good morning. Millinette, *mon enfant*, adieu. [*Exit*]

MILLINETTE: But I have one word more to say. Stop, Stop!

[*Exit after him*]

GERTRUDE: (*musingly*) Friday night, while supper is serving, he is to meet Millinette here and explain – what? This man is an impostor! His insulting me – his familiarity with Millinette – his whole conduct – prove it. If I tell Mrs Tiffany this she will disbelieve me, and one word may place this so-called Count on his guard. To convince Seraphina would be equally difficult, and her rashness and infatuation may render her miserable for life. No – she shall be saved! I must devise some plan for opening their eyes. Truly, if I *cannot* invent one, I shall be the first woman who was ever at a loss for a stratagem – especially to punish a villain or to shield a friend.

[*Exit*]

Act IV

SCENE i

A ball room splendidly illuminated. A curtain hung at the further end. MR *and* MRS TIFFANY, SERAPHINA, GERTRUDE, FOGG, TWINKLE, COUNT, SNOBSON, COLONEL HOWARD, *a number of guests – some seated, some standing. As the curtain rises, a cotillion is danced;* GERTRUDE *dancing with* HOWARD, SERAPHINA *with* COUNT

(COUNT: (*advancing with* SERAPHINA *to the front of the stage*) Tomorrow then – tomorrow – I may salute you as my bride – demme, my Countess!
                    Enter ZEKE, *with refreshments*
SERAPHINA: Yes, tomorrow.
          (*As the* COUNT *is about to reply* SNOBSON *thrusts himself in front of* SERAPHINA)
SNOBSON: You said you'd dance with me, Miss – now take my fin, and we'll walk about and see what's going on.
          (COUNT *raises his eye-glass, regards* SNOBSON *and leads* SERAPHINA *away;* SNOBSON *follows, endeavouring to attract her attention, but encountering* ZEKE, *bearing a tray of refreshments; stops him, helps himself, and puts some in his pockets*)
Here's the treat! get my tomorrow's luncheon out of Tiff.
          Enter TRUEMAN, *yawning and rubbing his eyes*
TRUEMAN: What a nap I've had, to be sure! (*Looks at his watch*) Eleven o'clock, as I'm alive! Just the time when country folks are comfortably *turned in*, and here your grand *turn-out* has hardly begun yet. (*To* TIFFANY, *who approaches*)
GERTRUDE: (*advancing*) I was just coming to look for you, Mr Trueman. I began to fancy that you were paying a visit to dreamland.
TRUEMAN: So I was, child – so I was – and I saw a face – like yours – but brighter! – even brighter. (*To* TIFFANY) There's a smile for you, man! It makes one feel that the world has something worth living for in it yet! Do you remember a smile like that, Antony? Ah! I see you don't – but I do – I do! (*Much moved*)

HOWARD: (*advancing*) Good evening, Mr Trueman.
(*Offers his hand*)

TRUEMAN: That's right, man; give me your whole hand! When a man offers me the tips of his fingers, I know at once there's nothing in him worth seeking beyond his fingers ends.

(TRUEMAN *and* HOWARD, GERTRUDE *and* TIFFANY *converse*)

MRS TIFFANY: (*advancing*) I'm in such a fidget lest that vulgar old fellow should disgrace us by some of his plebeian remarks! What it is to give a ball, when one is forced to invite vulgar people!

(MRS TIFFANY *advances towards* TRUEMAN: SERAPHINA *stands conversing flippantly with the gentlemen who surround her; amongst them is* TWINKLE, *who having taken a magazine from his pocket, is reading to her, much to the undisguised annoyance of* SNOBSON)

Dear me, Mr Trueman, you are very late – quite in the fashion, I declare!

TRUEMAN: Fashion! And pray what is *fashion*, madam? An agreement between certain persons to live without using their souls! to substitute etiquette for virtue – decorum for purity – manners for morals! to affect a shame for the works of their Creator! and expend all their rapture upon the works of their tailors and dressmakers!

MRS TIFFANY: You have the most *ow-tray* ideas, Mr Trueman – quite rustic, and deplorably *American!* But pray walk this way.

(MRS TIFFANY *and* TRUEMAN *go up*)

COUNT: (*advancing to* GERTRUDE, HOWARD *a short distance behind her*) Miss Gertrude – no opportunity of speaking to you before – in demand you know!

GERTRUDE: (*aside*) I have no choice, I must be civil to him. What were you remarking, Sir?

COUNT: Miss Gertrude – charming Ger – aw – aw – (*Aside*) I never found it so difficult to speak to a woman before.

GERTRUDE: Yes, a very charming ball – many beautiful faces here.

COUNT: Only one! – aw – aw – one – the fact is—
(*Talks to her in dumb show*)

HOWARD: What could old Trueman have meant by saying she fancied that puppy of a Count – that paste jewel thrust upon the little finger of society.

COUNT: Miss Gertrude – aw – 'pon my honour – you don't understand – really – aw – aw – will you dance the polka with me?

(GERTRUDE *bows and gives him her hand; he leads her to the set forming;* HOWARD *remains looking after them*)

HOWARD: Going to dance with him too! A few days ago she would hardly bow to him civilly – could old Trueman have had reasons for what he said? (*Retires up*)

> (*Dance, the polka;* SERAPHINA, *after having distributed her bouquet, vinaigrette and fan amongst the gentlemen, dances with* SNOBSON)

PRUDENCE: (*peeping in as dance concludes*) I don't like dancing on Friday; something strange is always sure to happen! I'll be on the look out.

> (*Remains peeping and concealing herself when any of the company approach*)

GERTRUDE: (*advancing hastily*) They are preparing the supper – now if I can only dispose of Millinette while I unmask this insolent pretender! [*Exit*]

PRUDENCE: (*peeping*) What's that she said? It's coming!

> (*Re-enter* GERTRUDE, *bearing a small basket filled with bouquets; approaches* MRS TIFFANY; *they walk to the front of the stage*)

GERTRUDE: Excuse me, Madam – I believe this is just the hour at which you ordered supper?

MRS TIFFANY: Well, what's that to you! So you've been dancing with the Count—how dare you dance with a nobleman—*you*?

GERTRUDE: I will answer that question half an hour hence. At present I have something to propose, which I think will gratify you and please your guests. I have heard that at the most elegant balls in Paris, it is customary—

MRS TIFFANY: What? What?

GERTRUDE: To station a servant at the door with a basket of flowers. A bouquet is then presented to every lady as she passes in – I prepared this basket a short time ago. As the company walk in to supper, might not the flowers be distributed to advantage?

MRS TIFFANY: How *distingué!* You are a good creature, Gertrude – there, run and hand the *bokettes* to them yourself! You shall have the whole credit of the thing.

GERTRUDE: (*aside*) Caught in my own net! But, Madam, I know so little of fashions – Millinette, being French herself, will do it with so much more grace. I am sure Millinette—

MRS TIFFANY: So am I. She will do it a thousand times better than you – there go call her.

GERTRUDE: (*giving basket*) But, Madam, pray order Millinette not to leave her station till supper is ended – as the company pass out of the supper room she may find that some of the ladies have been overlooked.

MRS TIFFANY: That is true – very thoughtful of you, Gertrude.

[Exit GERTRUDE]

What a *recherché* idea!

Enter MILLINETTE

Here, Millinette, take this basket. Place yourself there, and distribute these *bokettes* as the company pass in to supper; but remember not to stir from the spot until supper is over. It is a French fashion you know, Millinette. I am so delighted to be the first to introduce it – it will be all the rage in the *bow-monde!*

MILLINETTE: (*aside*) Mon Dieu! dis vill ruin all! Madame, Madame, let me tell you, Madame, dat in France, in Paris, it is de custom to present *les* bouquets ven everybody first come – long before de supper. Dis vould be *outré! barbare!* not at all la mode! Ven dey do come in – dat is de fashion in Paris!

MRS TIFFANY: Dear me! Millinette, what is the difference? besides I'd have you to know that Americans always improve upon French fashions! here, take the basket, and let me see that you do it in the most *you-nick* and genteel manner.

MILLINETTE poutingly takes the basket and retires up stage.
A march. Curtain hung at the further end of the room is drawn
back, and discloses a room, in the centre of which stands a supper
table, beautifully decorated and illuminated; the company
promenade two by two into the supper room; MILLINETTE
presents bouquets as they pass; COUNT leads MRS TIFFANY)

TRUEMAN: (*encountering* FOGG, *who is hurrying alone to the supper room*) Mr Fogg, never mind the supper, man! Ha, ha, ha! Of course you are indifferent to suppers!

FOGG: Indifferent! suppers – oh, ah – no, Sir – suppers? no – no – I'm not indifferent to suppers!

(Hurries away towards table)

TRUEMAN: Ha, ha, ha! Here's a new discovery I've made in the fashionable world! Fashion don't permit the critters to have *heads* or *hearts*, but it allows them stomachs! (*To* TIFFANY, *who advances*) So it's not fashionable to *feel*, but it's fashionable to *feed*, eh, Antony? ha, ha, ha!

(TRUEMAN and TIFFANY retire towards supper room.
Enter GERTRUDE, followed by ZEKE)

GERTRUDE: Zeke, go to the supper room instantly – whisper to Count Jolimaitre that all is ready, and that he must keep his appointment without delay – then watch him, and as he passes out of the room, place yourself in front of Millinette in such a manner, that the Count cannot see her nor she him. Be sure that they do not see each other – everything depends upon that. (*Crosses*)

ZEKE: Missey, consider dat business brought to a scientific conclusion.
　　　　　　　[*Exit* ZEKE *into supper room. Exit* GERTRUDE]
PRUDENCE: (*who has been listening*) What can she want of the Count?
　I always suspected that Gertrude, because she is so merry and busy!
　Mr Trueman thinks so much of her too – I'll tell him this! There's
　something wrong – but it all comes of giving a ball on a Friday! How
　astonished the dear old man will be when he finds out how much I
　know!
　　　　　(*Advances timidly towards the supper room*)

SCENE ii

Housekeeper's room; dark stage; table, two chairs

Enter GERTRUDE, *with a lighted candle in her hand*

GERTRUDE: So far the scheme prospers! and yet this imprudence – if I
　fail? Fail! to lack courage in a difficulty, or ingenuity in a dilemma,
　are not woman's failings!
　　　Enter ZEKE, *with a napkin over his arm, and a bottle of*
　　　　　　　　champagne in his hand
　Well, Zeke – Adolph!
ZEKE: Dat's right, Missey; I feels just now as if dat was my legitimate
　title; dis here's de stuff to make a nigger feel like a gemman!
GERTRUDE: But he is coming?
ZEKE: He's coming! (*Sound of a champagne cork heard*) Do you hear
　dat, Missey? Don't it put you all in a froth, and make you feel as
　light as a cork? Dere's nothing like the *union brand*, to wake up de
　harmonies ob de heart.
　　　　　　　(*Drinks from bottle*)
GERTRUDE: Remember to keep watch upon the outside – do not stir
　from the spot; when I call you, come in quickly with a light – now,
　will you be gone!
ZEKE: I'm off, Missey, like a champagne cork wid de strings cut.
　　　　　　　　　　　　　　　　　　　　　　[*Exit*]
GERTRUDE: I think I hear the Count's step. (*Crosses, stage dark; she
　blows out candle*) Now if I can but disguise my voice, and make the
　best of my French.
　　　　　　　　Enter COUNT
COUNT: Millinette, where are you? How am I to see you in the dark?

GERTRUDE: (*imitating* MILLINETTE's *voice in a whisper*) Hush! *parle bas.*

COUNT: Come here and give me a kiss.

GERTRUDE: Non – non – (*Retreating alarmed,* COUNT *follows*) make haste, I must know all.

COUNT: You did not use to be so deuced particular.

ZEKE: (*without*) No admission, gemman! Box office closed, tickets stopped!

TRUEMAN: (*without*) Out of my way; do you want me to try if your head is as hard as my stick?

GERTRUDE: What shall I do? Ruined, ruined! (*She stands with her hands clasped in speechless despair*)

COUNT: Halloa! they are coming here, Millinette! Millinette, why don't you speak? Where can I hide myself? (*Running about stage, feeling for a door*) Where are all your closets? If I could only get out – or get in somewhere; may I be smothered in a clothes' basket, if you ever catch me in such a scrape again! (*His hand accidentally touches the knob of a door opening into a closet*) Fortune's favourite yet! I'm safe!

(Gets into closet and closes door. Enter PRUDENCE, TRUEMAN, MRS TIFFANY, *and* COLONEL HOWARD, *followed by* ZEKE, *bearing a light; lights up*)

PRUDENCE: Here they are, the Count and Gertrude! I told you so!

(Stops in surprise on seeing only GERTRUDE*)*

TRUEMAN: And you see what a lie you told!

MRS TIFFANY: Prudence, how dare you create this disturbance in my house? To suspect the Count too – a nobleman!

HOWARD: My sweet Gertrude, this foolish old woman would—

PRUDENCE: Oh! you needn't talk – I heard her make the appointment – I know he's here – or he's been here. I wonder if she hasn't hid him away! (*Runs peeping about the room*)

TRUEMAN: (*following her angrily*) You're what I call a confounded – troublesome – meddling – old – prying – (*As he says the last word,* PRUDENCE *opens closet where the* COUNT *is concealed*) Thunder and lightning!

PRUDENCE: I told you so!

(They all stand aghast; MRS TIFFANY, *with her hands lifted in surprise and anger;* TRUEMAN, *clutching his stick;* HOWARD, *looking with an expression of bewildered horror from the* COUNT *to* GERTRUDE*)*

MRS TIFFANY: (*shaking her fist at* GERTRUDE) You depraved little minx! this is the meaning of your dancing with the Count!

COUNT: (*stepping from the closet and advancing, aside*) I don't know what to make of it! Millinette not here! Miss Gertrude – oh! I see – a disguise – the girl's desperate about me – the way with them all.

TRUEMAN: I'm choking – I can't speak – Gertrude – no – no – it is some horrid mistake! (*Partly aside, changes his tone suddenly*) The villain! I'll hunt the truth out of him, if there's any in – (*Crosses, approaches* COUNT *threateningly*) do you see this stick? You made its first acquaintance a few days ago; it is time you were better known to each other.

(*As* TRUEMAN *attempts to seize him,* COUNT *escapes, and shields himself behind* MRS TIFFANY, TRUEMAN *following*)

COUNT: You ruffian! would you strike a woman? – Madam – my dear Madam – keep off that barbarous old man, and I will explain! Madam, with – aw – your natural *bon gout* – aw – your fashionable refinement – aw – your – aw – your knowledge of *foreign customs*—

MRS TIFFANY: Oh! Count, I hope it ain't a *foreign custom* for the nobility to shut themselves up in the dark with young women? We think such things *dreadful* in *America*.

COUNT: Demme – aw – hear what I have to say, Madam – I'll satisfy all sides – I am perfectly innocent in this affair – 'pon my honour I am! That young lady shall inform you that I am so herself! – can't help it, sorry for her. (*Aside*) Old matter-of-fact won't be convinced any other way, – that club of his is so particularly unpleasant! Madam, I was summoned here *malgré moi*, and not knowing whom I was to meet – Miss Gertrude, favour the company by saying whether or not you directed – that – aw – aw – that coloured individual to conduct me here?

GERTRUDE: Sir, you well know—

COUNT: A simple yes or no will suffice.

MRS TIFFANY: Answer the Count's question instantly, Miss.

GERTRUDE: I did – but—

COUNT: You hear, Madam—

TRUEMAN: I won't believe it – I can't! Here, you nigger, stop rolling up your eyes, and let us know whether she told you to bring that critter here?

ZEKE: I'se refuse to gib ebidence; dat's de device ob de skilfullest counsels ob de day! Can't answer, Boss – neber git a word out ob dis child – Yah! yah!   [*Exit*]

GERTRUDE: Mrs Tiffany – Mr Trueman, if you will but have patience—

TRUEMAN: Patience! Oh, Gertrude, you've taken from an old man

something better and dearer than his patience – the one bright hope of nineteen years of self-denial – of nineteen years of—
 (*Throws himself upon a chair, his head leaning on table*)
MRS TIFFANY: Get out of my house, you *ow*-dacious – you ruined – you *abimé* young woman! You will corrupt all my family. Good gracious! don't touch me, – don't come near me. Never let me see your face after tomorrow. Pack.
 (*Goes up*)
HOWARD: Gertrude, I have striven to find some excuse for you – to doubt – to disbelieve – but this is beyond all endurance!
 [*Exit*]

Enter MILLINETTE *in haste*

MILLINETTE: I could not come before— (*Stops in surprise at seeing the persons assembled*) Mon Dieu! vat does dis mean?
COUNT: (*aside to her*) Hold your tongue, fool! You will ruin everything, I will explain tomorrow. Mrs Tiffany – Madam – my dear Madam, let me conduct you back to the ball-room. (*She takes his arm*) You see I am quite innocent in this matter; a man of my standing, you know – aw, aw – you comprehend the whole affair.
 [*Exit* COUNT *leading* MRS TIFFANY]
MILLINETTE: I will say to him von vord, I will!   [*Exit*]
GERTRUDE: Mr Trueman, I beseech you – I insist upon being heard – I claim it as a right!
TRUEMAN: Right? How dare you have the face, girl, to talk of rights? (*Comes down*) You had more rights than you thought for, but you have forfeited them all! All right to love, respect, protection, and to not a little else that you don't dream of. Go, go! I'll start for Catteraugus tomorrow – I've seen enough of what fashion can do!
 [*Exit*]
PRUDENCE: (*wiping her eyes.*) Dear old man, how he takes on! I'll go and console him!   [*Exit*]
GERTRUDE: This is too much! How heavy a penalty has my imprudence cost me! – his esteem, and that of one dearer – my home – my— (*Burst of lively music from ball-room*) They are dancing, and I – I should be weeping, if pride had not, sealed up my tears.
 (*She sinks into a chair. Band plays the polka behind till curtain falls*)

Act V

SCENE i

MRS TIFFANY's *drawing room – same scene as Act I*. GERTRUDE *seated at a table, with her head leaning on her hand; in the other hand she holds a pen. A sheet of paper and an ink-stand before her*

GERTRUDE: How shall I write to them? What shall I say? Prevaricate I cannot – (*rises and comes forward*) and yet if I write the truth – simple souls! how can they comprehend the motives for my conduct? Nay – the truly pure see no imaginary evil in others! It is only vice, that reflecting its own image, suspects even the innocent. I have no time to lose – I must prepare them for my return. (*Resumes her seat and writes*) What a true pleasure there is in daring to be frank! (*After writing a few lines more pauses*) Not so frank either, – there is one name that I cannot mention. Ah! that he should suspect – should despise me.

(Writes)
Enter TRUEMAN

TRUEMAN: There she is! If this girl's soul had only been as fair as her face – yet she dared to speak the truth – I'll not forget that! A woman who refuses to tell a lie has one spark of heaven in her still. (*Approaches her*) Gertrude,

(GERTRUDE *starts and looks up*)
What are you writing there? Plotting more mischief, eh, girl?

GERTRUDE: I was writing a few lines to some friends in Geneva.

TRUEMAN: The Wilsons, eh?

GERTRUDE: (*surprised, rising*) Are you acquainted with them, Sir?

TRUEMAN: I shouldn't wonder if I was. I suppose you have taken good care not to mention the dark room – that foreign puppy in the closet – the pleasant surprise – and all that sort of thing, eh?

GERTRUDE: I have no reason for concealment, Sir! for I have done nothing of which I am ashamed!

TRUEMAN: Then I can't say much for your modesty.

GERTRUDE: I should not wish you to say more than I deserve.

TRUEMAN: (*aside*) There's a bold minx!

GERTRUDE: Since my affairs seem to have excited your interest – I will not say *curiosity*, perhaps you even feel a desire to inspect my correspondence? There, (*Handing the letter*) I pride myself upon my good nature, – you may like to take advantage of it?

TRUEMAN: (*aside*) With what an air she carries it off! Take advantage of it? So I will. (*Reads*) What's this? 'French chambermaid – Count – impostor – infatuation – Seraphina – Millinette – disguised myself – expose him.' Thunder and lightning! I see it all! Come and kiss me, girl! (GERTRUDE *evinces surprise*) No, no – I forgot – it won't do to come to that yet! She's a rare girl! I'm out of my senses with joy! I don't know what to do with myself! Tol, de rol, de rol, de ra. (*Capers and sings*)

GERTRUDE: (*aside*) What a remarkable old man! Then you do me justice, Mr Trueman?

TRUEMAN: I say I don't! Justice? You're above all dependence upon justice! Hurrah! I've found one true woman at last! *True?* (*Pauses thoughtfully*) Humph! I didn't think of that flaw! Plotting and manoeuvring – not much truth in that? An honest girl should be above stratagems!

GERTRUDE: But my *motive*, Sir, was good.

TRUEMAN: That's not enough – your *actions* must be *good* as well as your *motives!* Why could you not tell the silly girl that man was an impostor?

GERTRUDE: I did inform her of my suspicions – she ridiculed them; the plan I chose was an imprudent one, but I could not devise—

TRUEMAN: I hate devising! Give me a woman with the *firmness* to be *frank*! But no matter – I had no right to look for an angel out of Paradise; and I am as happy – as happy as a Lord! that is, ten times happier than any Lord ever was! Tol, de rol, de rol! Oh! you – you – I'll thrash every fellow that says a word against you!

GERTRUDE: You will have plenty of employment then, Sir, for I do not know of one just now who would speak in my favour!

TRUEMAN: Not *one*, eh? Why, where's your dear Mr Twinkle? I know all about it – can't say that I admire your choice of a husband! But there's no accounting for a girl's taste.

GERTRUDE: Mr Twinkle! Indeed you are quite mistaken!

TRUEMAN: No – really? Then you're not taken with him, eh?

GERTRUDE: Not even with his rhymes.

TRUEMAN: Hang that old mother meddle-much! What a fool she has made of me. And so you're quite free, and I may choose a husband for you myself? Heart-whole, eh?

GERTRUDE: I – I – I trust there is nothing *unsound* about my heart.

TRUEMAN: There it is again. Don't prevaricate, girl! I tell you an *evasion* is a *lie in contemplation*, and I hate lying! Out with the truth! Is your heart *free* or not?

GERTRUDE: Nay, Sir, since you *demand* an answer, permit *me* to demand by what right you ask the question?

Enter HOWARD

Colonel Howard here!

TRUEMAN: I'm out again! What's the Colonel to her? (*Retires up*)

HOWARD: (*crosses to her*) I have come, Gertrude, to bid you farewell. Tomorrow I resign my commission and leave this city, perhaps for ever. You, Gertrude, it is you who have exiled me! After last evening—

TRUEMAN: (*coming forward to* HOWARD) What the plague have you got to say about last evening?

HOWARD: Mr Trueman!

TRUEMAN: What have you got to say about last evening? and what have you to say to that little girl at all? It's Tiffany's precious daughter you're in love with.

HOWARD: Miss Tiffany? Never! I never had the slightest pretension—

TRUEMAN: That lying old woman! But I'm glad of it! Oh! Ah! Um! (*Looking significantly at* GERTRUDE *and then at* HOWARD) I see how it is. So you don't choose to marry Seraphina, eh? Well now, whom do you choose to marry? (*Glancing at* GERTRUDE)

HOWARD: I shall not marry at all!

TRUEMAN: You won't? (*Looking at them both again*) Why you don't mean to say that you don't like—

(*Points with his thumb to* GERTRUDE)

GERTRUDE: Mr Trueman, I may have been wrong to boast of my good nature, but do not presume too far upon it.

HOWARD: You like frankness, Mr Trueman, therefore I will speak plainly. I have long cherished a dream from which I was last night rudely awakened.

TRUEMAN: And that's what you call speaking plainly? Well, I differ with you! But I can guess what you mean. Last night you suspected Gertrude there of – (*Angrily*) of what no man shall ever suspect her again while I'm above ground! You did her injustice – it was a mistake! There, now that matter's settled. Go, and ask her to forgive you – she's woman enough to do it! Go, go!

HOWARD: Mr Trueman, you have forgotten to whom you dictate.

TRUEMAN: Then you won't do it? you won't ask her pardon?

HOWARD: Most undoubtedly I will not – not at any man's bidding. I must first know—

TRUEMAN: You won't do it? Then if I don't give you a lesson in politeness—

HOWARD: It will be because you find me your *tutor* in the same science. I am not a man to brook an insult, Mr Trueman! but we'll not quarrel in presence of the lady.

TRUEMAN: Won't we? I don't know that— (*Crosses*)

GERTRUDE: Pray, Mr Trueman – Colonel Howard, pray desist, Mr Trueman, for my sake! (*taking hold of his arm to hold him back*) Colonel Howard, if you will read this letter it will explain everything.

(*Hands letter to* HOWARD, *who reads*)

TRUEMAN: He don't deserve an explanation! Didn't I tell him that it was a mistake? Refuse to beg your pardon! I'll teach him. I'll teach him!

HOWARD: (*after reading*) Gertrude, how have I wronged you!

TRUEMAN: Oh, you'll beg her pardon now?

(*Between them*)

HOWARD: Hers, Sir, and yours! Gertrude, I fear—

TRUEMAN: You needn't – she'll forgive you. You don't know these women as well as I do – they're always ready to pardon; it's their nature, and they can't help it. Come along, I left Antony and his wife in the dining room; we'll go and find them. I've a story of my own to tell! As for you, Colonel, you may follow. Come along. Come along!

(*Leads out* GERTRUDE, *followed by* HOWARD)
Enter MR *and* MRS TIFFANY, MR TIFFANY *with a bundle of bills in his hand*

MRS TIFFANY: I beg you won't mention the subject again, Mr Tiffany. Nothing is more plebeian than a discussion upon economy – nothing more *ungenteel* than looking over and fretting over one's bills!

TIFFANY: Then I suppose, my dear, it is quite as ungenteel to *pay* one's bills?

MRS TIFFANY: Certainly! I hear the *ee-light* never condescend to do anything of the kind. The honour of their invaluable patronage is sufficient for the persons they employ!

TIFFANY: *Patronage* then is a newly invented food upon which the working classes fatten? What convenient appetites poor people must have! Now listen to what I am going to say. As soon as my daughter marries Mr Snobson—

Enter PRUDENCE, *a three-cornered note in her hand*

PRUDENCE: Oh, dear! oh, dear! what shall we do! Such a misfortune! Such a disaster! Oh, dear! oh, hear!

MRS TIFFANY: Prudence, you are the most tiresome creature! What *is* the matter?

PRUDENCE: (*pacing up and down the stage*) Such a disgrace to the whole family! But I always expected it. Oh, dear! Oh, dear!

MRS TIFFANY: (*following her up and down the stage*) What are you talking about, Prudence? Will you tell me what has happened?

PRUDENCE: (*still pacing,* MRS TIFFANY *following*) Oh! I can't, I can't! You'll feel so dreadfully! How could she do such a thing! But I expected nothing else! I never did, I never did!

MRS TIFFANY: (*still following*) Good gracious! what do you mean, Prudence? Tell me, will you tell me? I shall get into such a passion! What *is* the matter?

PRUDENCE: (*still pacing*) Oh, Betsy, Betsy! That your daughter should have come to that! Dear me, dear me!

TIFFANY: Seraphina? Did you say Seraphina? What has happened to her? what has she done?

(*Following* PRUDENCE *up and down the stage on the opposite side from* MRS TIFFANY)

MRS TIFFANY: (*still following*) What *has* she done? what *has* she done?

PRUDENCE: Oh! something dreadful – dreadful – shocking!

TIFFANY: (*still following*) Speak quickly and plainly – you torture me by this delay – Prudence, be calm, and speak! What is it?

PRUDENCE: (*stopping*) Zeke just told me – he carried her travelling trunk himself – she gave him a whole dollar! Oh, my!

TIFFANY: Her trunk? where? where?

PRUDENCE: Round the corner!

TIFFANY: What did she want with her trunk? You are the most vexatious creature, Prudence! There is no bearing your ridiculous conduct!

PRUDENCE: Oh, you will have worse to bear – worse! Seraphina's gone!

TIFFANY: Gone! where?

PRUDENCE: Off! – eloped – eloped with the Count! Dear me, dear me! I always told you she would!

TIFFANY: Then I am ruined!

(*Stands with his face buried in his hands*)

MRS TIFFANY: Oh, what a ridiculous girl! And she might have had such a splendid wedding! What could have possessed her?

TIFFANY: The devil himself possessed her, for she has ruined me past all redemption! Gone, Prudence, did you say gone? Are you *sure* they are gone?

PRUDENCE: Didn't I tell you so! Just look at this note – one might know by the very fold of it—

TIFFANY: (*snatching the note*) Let me see it! (*Opens the note and reads*) 'My dear Ma, – When you receive this I shall be a *countess!* Isn't it a sweet title? The Count and I were forced to be married privately, for reasons which I will explain in my next. You must pacify Pa, and put him in a good humour before I come back, though now I'm to be a countess I suppose I shouldn't care!' Undutiful huzzy! 'We are going to make a little excursion and will be back in a week. Your dutiful daughter – Seraphina.'

A man's curse is sure to spring up at his own hearth – here is mine! The sole curb upon that villain gone, I am wholly in his power! Oh! the first downward step from honour – he who takes it cannot pause in his mad descent and is sure to be hurried on to ruin!

MRS TIFFANY: Why, Mr Tiffany, how you do take on! And I dare say to elope was the most fashionable way after all!

Enter TRUEMAN, *leading* GERTRUDE, *and followed by* HOWARD

TRUEMAN: Where are all the folks? Here, Antony, you are the man I want. We've been hunting for you all over the house. Why – what's the matter? There's a face for a thriving city merchant! Ah! Antony, you never wore such a hang-dog look as that when you trotted about the country with your pack upon your back! Your shoulders are no broader now – but they've a heavier load to carry – that's plain!

MRS TIFFANY: Mr Trueman, such allusions are highly improper! What would my daughter, *the Countess*, say!

GERTRUDE: The Countess? Oh! Madam!

MRS TIFFANY: Yes, the Countess! My daughter Seraphina, the Countess *dee* Jolimaitre! What have you to say to that? No wonder you are surprised after your *recherché, abimé* conduct! I have told you already, Miss Gertrude, that you were not a proper person to enjoy the inestimable advantages of my patronage. You are dismissed – do you understand? Discharged!

TRUEMAN: Have you done? Very well, it's my turn now. Antony, perhaps what I have to say don't concern you as much as some others – but I want you to listen to me. You remember, Antony, (*His tone becomes serious*), a blue-eyed, smiling girl—

TIFFANY: Your daughter, Sir? I remember her well.

TRUEMAN: None ever saw her to forget her! Give me your hand, man. There – that will do! Now let me go on. I never coveted wealth – yet twenty years ago I found myself the richest farmer in Catteraugus. This cursed money made my girl an object of speculation. Every idle fellow that wanted to feather his nest was sure to come courting Ruth. There was one – my heart misgave me the instant I laid eyes upon him – for he was a city chap, and not over fond of the truth. But Ruth – ah! she was too pure herself to look for guile! His fine words and his fair looks – the old story – she was taken with him – I said, 'no' – but the girl liked her own way better than her old father's – girls always do! and one morning – the rascal robbed me – not of my money, he would have been welcome to that – but of the only treasure I cherished – my daughter!

TIFFANY: But you forgave her!

TRUEMAN: I did! I knew she would never forgive herself – that was punishment enough! The scoundrel thought he was marrying my gold with my daughter – he was mistaken! I took care that they should never want; but that was all. She loved him – what will not woman love? The villain broke her heart – mine was tougher, or it wouldn't have stood what it did. A year after they were married, he forsook her! She came back to her old home – her old father! It couldn't last long – she pined – and pined – and – then – she died! Don't think me an old fool – though I am one – for grieving won't bring her back.

(*Bursts into tears*)

TIFFANY: It was a heavy loss!

TRUEMAN: So heavy, that I should not have cared how soon I followed her, but for the child she left! As I pressed that child in my arms, I swore that my unlucky wealth should never curse it, as it had cursed its mother! It was all I had to love – but I sent it away – and the neigbours thought it was dead. The girl was brought up tenderly but humbly by my wife's relatives in Geneva. I had her taught true independence – she had hands – capacities – and should use them! Money should never buy her a husband! for I resolved not to claim her until she had made her choice, and found the man who was willing to take her for herself alone. She turned out a rare girl! and it's time her old grandfather claimed her. Here he is to do it! And there stands Ruth's child! Old Adam's heiress! Gertrude, Gertrude! – my child!

(GERTRUDE *rushes into his arms*)

PRUDENCE: (*after a pause*) Do tell; I want to know! But I knew it! I always said Gertrude would turn out somebody, after all!

MRS TIFFANY: (*aside*) Dear me! Gertrude an heiress! My dear Gertrude, I always thought you a very charming girl – quite *you-*

nick – an heiress! I must give her a ball! I'll introduce her into society myself – of course an heiress must make a *senation!*

HOWARD: (*aside*) I am too bewildered even to wish her joy. Ah! there will be plenty to do that now – but the gulf between us is wider than ever.

TRUEMAN: Step forward, young man, and let us know what you are muttering about, I said I would never claim her until she had found the man who loved her for herself. I *have* claimed her – yet I never break my word – I think I *have* found that man! and here he is. (*Strikes* HOWARD *on the shoulder*) Gertrude's yours! There – never say a word, man – don't bore me with your thanks – you can cancel all obligations by making that child happy! There – take her! – Well, girl, and what do you say?

GERTRUDE: That I rejoice too much at having found a parent for my first act to be one of disobedience!

(*Gives her hand to* HOWARD)

TRUEMAN: How very dutiful! and how disinterested!

(TIFFANY *retires up – and paces the stage, exhibiting great agitation*)

PRUDENCE: (*to* TRUEMAN) All the *single folks* are getting married!

TRUEMAN: No they are not. You and I are single folks, and we're not likely to get married.

MRS TIFFANY: My dear Mr Trueman – my sweet Gertrude, when my daughter, the Countess, returns, she will be delighted to hear of this *deenooment!* I assure you that the Countess will be quite charmed!

GERTRUDE: The Countess? Pray, Madam, where *is* Seraphina?

MRS TIFFANY: The Countess *dee* Jolimaitre, my dear, is at this moment on her way to – to Washington! Where after visiting all the fashionable curiosities of the day – including the President – she will return to grace her native city!

GERTRUDE: I hope you are only jesting, Madam? Seraphina is not married?

MRS TIFFANY: Excuse me, my dear, my daughter had this morning the honour of being united to the Count *dee* Jolimaitre!

GERTRUDE: Madam! He is an impostor!

MRS TIFFANY: Good gracious! Gertrude, how can you talk in that disrespectful way of a man of rank? An heiress, my dear, should have better manners! The Count—

Enter MILLINETTE, *crying*

MILLINETTE: Oh! Madame! I will tell everything – oh! dat monstre! He break my heart.

MRS TIFFANY: Millinette, what is the matter?

MILLINETTE: Oh! he promise to marry me – I love him much – and now Zeke say he run away vid Mademoiselle Seraphina!

MRS TIFFANY: What insolence! The girl is mad! Count Jolimaitre marry my *femmy de chamber!*

MILLINETTE: Oh! Madame, he is not one Count, not at all! Dat is only de title he go by in dis country. De foreigners always take de large title ven dey do come here. His name *à Paris* vas Gustave Treadmill. But he not one Frenchman at all, but he do live one long time *à Paris.* First he live vid Monsieur Vermicelle – dere he vas de head cook! Den he live vid Monsieur Tire-nez, de barber! After dat he live wid Monsieur le Comte Frippon-fin – and dere he vas le Comte's valet! Dere, now I tell everyting I feel one great deal better!

MRS TIFFANY: Oh! good gracious! I shall faint! Not a Count! What will everybody say? It's no such thing! I say he *is* a Count! One can see the foreign *jenny says quoi* in his face! Don't you think I can tell a Count when I see one? I say he *is* a Count!

> *Enter* SNOBSON, *his hat on – his hands thrust in his pocket*
> *– evidently a little intoxicated*

SNOBSON: I won't stand it! I say I won't!

TIFFANY: (*rushing up to him*) (*Aside*) Mr Snobson, for heaven's sake—

SNOBSON: Keep off! I'm a hard customer to get the better of! You'll see if I don't come out strong!

TRUEMAN: (*quietly knocking off* SNOBSON's *hat with his stick*) Where are your manners, man?

SNOBSON: My business ain't with you, Catteraugus; you've waked up the wrong passenger! – (*Aside*) Now the way I'll put it into Tiff will be a caution. I'll make him wince! That extra mint julep has put the true pluck in me. Now for it! Mr Tiffany, Sir – you neen't think to come over me, Sir – you'll have to get up a little earlier in the morning before you do *that*, Sir! I'd like to know, Sir, how you came to assist your daughter in running away with that foreign loafer? It was a downright swindle, Sir. After the conversation I and you had on that subject she wasn't your property, Sir.

TRUEMAN: What, Antony, is that the way your city clerk bullies his boss?

SNOBSON: You're drunk, Catteraugus – don't expose yourself – you're drunk! Taken a little too much toddy, my old boy! Be quiet! I'll look after you, and they won't find it out. If you want to be busy, you may take care of my *hat* – I feel so deuced weak in the chest, I don't think I *could* pick it up myself. (*Aside*) Now to put the screws to Tiff. Mr Tiffany, Sir – you have broken your word, Sir – you have

broken your word, as no virtuous individual – no honourable
member – of – the – com – mu – ni – ty—

TIFFANY: (*aside to him*) Have some pity, Mr Snobson, I beseech you! I
had nothing to do with my daughter's elopement! I will agree to
anything you desire – your salary shall be doubled – trebled—

SNOBSON: (*aloud*) No you don't. No bribery and corruption.

TIFFANY: (*aside to him*) I implore you to be silent. You shall become
partner of the concern, if you please – only do not speak. You are
not yourself at this moment.

SNOBSON: Ain't I, though? I feel *twice* myself. I feel like two Snobsons
rolled into one, and I'm chock full of the spunk of a dozen! Now Mr
Tiffany, Sir—

TIFFANY: (*aside to him*) I shall go distracted! Mr Snobson, if you have
one spark of manly feeling—

TRUEMAN: Antony, why do you stand disputing with that drunken
jackass? Where's your nigger? Let him kick the critter out, and be of
use for once in his life.

SNOBSON: Better be quiet, Catteraugus. This ain't your hash, so keep
your spoon out of the dish. Don't expose yourself, old boy.

TRUEMAN: Turn him out, Antony!

SNOBSON: He daren't do it! Ain't I up to him? Ain't he in my power?
Can't I knock him into a cocked hat with a word? And now he's got
my steam up – I *will* do it!

TIFFANY: (*beseechingly*) Mr Snobson – my friend—

SNOBSON: It's no go – steam's up – and I don't stand at anything!

TRUEMAN: You won't *stand* here long unless you mend your manners
– you're not the first man I've *upset* because he didn't know his
place.

SNOBSON: I know where Tiff's place is, and that's in the *States' Prison!*
It's bespoke already. He would have it! He wouldn't take pattern of
me, and behave like a gentleman! He's a *forger*, Sir! (TIFFANY
*throws himself into a chair in an attitude of despair; the others stand
transfixed with astonishment*) He's been forging Dick Anderson's
endorsements of his notes these ten months. He's got a couple in the
bank that will send him to the wall anyhow – if he can't make a
raise. I took them there myself! Now you know what he's worth. I
said I'd expose him, and I have done it!

MRS TIFFANY: Get him out of the house! You ugly, little, drunken
brute, get out! It's not true. Mr Trueman, put him out; you have got
a stick – put him out!

Enter SERAPHINA, *in her bonnet and shawl – a parasol in her hand*

SERAPHINA: I hope Zeke hasn't delivered my note.

(*Stops in surprise at seeing the persons assembled*)

MRS TIFFANY: Oh, here is the Countess!

(*Advances to embrace her*)

TIFFANY: (*starting from his seat, and seizing* SERAPHINA *violently by the arm*) Are – you – married?

SERAPHINA: Goodness, Pa, how you frighten me! No, I'm not married, *quite*.

TIFFANY: Thank heavens.

MRS TIFFANY: (*drawing* SERAPHINA *aside*) What's the matter? Why did you come back?

SERAPHINA: The clergyman wasn't at home – I came back for my jewels – the Count said nobility couldn't get on without them.

TIFFANY: I may be saved yet! Seraphina, my child, you will not see me disgraced – ruined! I have been a kind father to you – at least I have tried to be one – although your mother's extravagance made a *madman* of me! The Count is an impostor – you seemed to like him – (*Pointing to* SNOBSON, *aside*) Heaven forgive me! Marry *him* and save me. You, Mr Trueman, you will be my friend in this hour, of extreme need – you will advance the sum which I require – I pledge myself to return it. My wife – my child – who will support them were I – the thought makes me frantic! You will aid me? You had a child yourself.

TRUEMAN: But I did not *sell* her – it was her own doings. Shame on you, Antony! Put a price on your own flesh and blood! Shame on such foul traffic!

TIFFANY: Save me – I conjure you – for my father's sake.

TRUEMAN: For your *father's* SON's sake I will *not* aid you in becoming a greater villain than you are!

GERTRUDE: Mr Trueman – Father, I should say – save him – do not embitter our happiness by permitting this calamity to fall upon another—

TRUEMAN: Enough – I did not need your voice, child. I am going to settle this matter my own way.

(*Goes up to* SNOBSON – *who has seated himself and fallen asleep – tilts him out of the chair.*)

SNOBSON: (*waking up*) Eh? Where's the fire? Oh! it's you, Catteraugus.

TRUEMAN: If I comprehend aright, you have been for some time aware of your principal's forgeries?

(*As he says this, he beckons to* HOWARD, *who advances as witness*)

SNOBSON: You've hit the nail, Catteraugus! Old chap saw that I was up to him six months ago; left off throwing dust into my eyes—

TRUEMAN: Oh, he did!

SNOBSON: Made no bones of forging Anderson's name at my elbow.

TRUEMAN: Forged at your elbow? You saw him do it?

SNOBSON: I did.

TRUEMAN: Repeatedly.

SNOBSON: Re-pea-ted-ly.

TRUEMAN: Then you, Rattlesnake, if he goes to the States' Prison, you'll take up your quarters there too. You are an accomplice, an *accessory!*

(TRUEMAN *walks away and seats himself,* HOWARD *rejoins* GERTRUDE, SNOBSON *stands for some time bewildered*)

SNOBSON: The deuce, so I am! I never thought of that! I must make myself scarce. I'll be off! Tif, I say, Tif! (*Going up to him and speaking confidentially*) that drunken old rip has got us in his power. Let's give him the ship and be off. They want men of genius at the West – we're sure to get on! You – you can set up for a writing master, and teach copying *signatures*; and I – I'll give lectures on *temperance!* You won't come, eh? Then I'm off without you. Good bye, Catteraugus! Which is the way to California?   [*Steals off*]

TRUEMAN: There's one debt your city owes me. And now let us see what other nuisances we can abate. Antony, I'm not given to preaching, therefore I shall not say much about what you have done. Your face speaks for itself – the crime has brought its punishment along with it.

TIFFANY: Indeed it has, Sir! In *one year* I have lived a *century* of misery.

TRUEMAN: I believe you, and upon one condition I will assist you—

TIFFANY: My friend – my first, ever kind friend – only name it!

TRUEMAN: You must sell your house and all these gew gaws, and bundle your wife and daughter off to the country. There let them learn economy, true independence, and home virtues, instead of foreign follies. As for yourself, continue your business – but let moderation, in future, be your counsellor, and let *honesty* be your confidential clerk.

TIFFANY: Mr Trueman, you have made existence once more precious to me! My wife and daughter shall quit the city tomorrow, and—

PRUDENCE: It's all coming right! Its all coming right! We'll go to the country of Catteraugus.

(*Walking up to* TRUEMAN)

TRUEMAN: No, you won't – I make that a stipulation, Antony; keep clear of Catteraugus. None of your fashionable examples there!

(JOLIMAITRE *appears in the conservatory and peeps*

into the room unperceived)

COUNT: What can detain Seraphina? We ought to be off!

MILLINETTE: (*turns round, perceives him, runs and forces him into the room*) Here he is! Ah, Gustave, *mon cher* Gustave! I have you now and we never part no more. Don't frown, Gustave, don't frown—

TRUEMAN: Come forward, Mr Count! and for the edification of fashionable society confess that you're an impostor.

COUNT: An impostor? Why, you abominable old—

TRUEMAN: Oh, your feminine friend has told us all about it, the cook – the valet – barber and all that sort of thing. Come, confess, and something may be done for you.

COUNT: Well, then, I do confess I am no count; but really, ladies and gentlemen, I may recommend myself as the most capital cook.

MRS TIFFANY: Oh, Seraphina!

SERAPHINA: Oh, Ma!

(*They embrace and retire up*)

TRUEMAN: Promise me to call upon the whole circle of your fashionable acquaintances with your own advertisements and in your cook's attire, and I will set you up in business tomorrow. Better turn stomachs than heads!

MILLINETTE: But you will marry me?

COUNT: Give us your hand, Millinette! Sir, command me for the most delicate *paté* – the daintiest *croquette à la royale* – the most transcendent *omelette soufflée* that ever issued from a French pastry-cook's oven. I hope you will pardon my conduct, but I heard that in America, where you pay homage to titles while you profess to scorn them – where *Fashion* makes the basest coin current – where you have no kings, no princes, no *nobility*—

TRUEMAN: Stop there! I object to your use of that word. When justice is found only among lawyers – health among physicians – and patriotism among politicians, *then* may you say that there is no *nobility* where there are no titles! But we *have* kings, princes, and nobles in abundance – of *Nature's stamp*, if not of *Fashion's* – we have honest men, warm hearted and brave, and we have women – gentle, fair, and true, to whom no *title* could add *nobility*.

EPILOGUE

PRUDENCE: I told you so! And now you hear and see.
 I told you *Fashion* would the fashion be!
TRUEMAN: Then both its point and moral I distrust.
COUNT: Sir, is that liberal?
HOWARD: Or is it just?
TRUEMAN: The guilty have escaped!
TIFFANY: Is, therefore, sin
 Made charming? Ah! there's punishment within!
 Guilt ever carries his own scourge along.
GERTRUDE: Virtue her own reward!
TRUEMAN: You're right, I'm wrong.
MRS TIFFANY: How we have been deceived!
PRUDENCE: I told you so.
SERAPHINA: To lose at once a title and a beau!
COUNT: A count no more, I'm no more of *account*.
TRUEMAN: But to a nobler title you may mount,
 And be in time – who knows? – an honest man!
COUNT: Eh, Millinette?
MILLINETTE: Oh, *oui* – I know you can!
GERTRUDE: (*to audience*) But ere we close the scene, a word with
 you,—
 We charge you answer – Is this picture true?
 Some little mercy to our efforts show,
 Then let the world your honest verdict know.
 Here let it see portrayed its ruling passion,
 And learn to prize at its just value – *Fashion*.

NOTES

1 **Canal Street:** a street in lower Manhattan that runs almost all the way across the island through the Lower East Side, Chinatown, Soho and Tribeca.

2 **the upper ten thousand:** the upper classes, the aristocracy. The term, 'the upper ten', or 'the upper ten thousand', was first used by N. P. Willis (1806–61) an American journalist, in speaking of the fashionable society of New York.

3 **julep:** a sweet drink consisting of iced and flavoured spirit and water, especially mint julep.

4 **greenhorns:** newcomers, raw recruits.

5 **Earl of Airshire:** clearly an imagined acquaintance but also a misspelling of 'Ayrshire', a county in the south west of Scotland.

EAST LYNNE

a domestic drama, in a prologue and four acts
Adapted from Mrs Henry Wood's novel
BY T. A. PALMER
(1874)

DRAMATIS PERSONAE

Women

LADY ISABEL	dependent on Mount Severn since the death of her father, wooed by Archibald Carlyle
BARBARA HARE	in love with Archibald Carlyle, jealous of Isabel
CORNELIA CARLYLE	Archibald's older unmarried sister
AFY HALLIJOHN	Richard Hare's duplicitous lover
WILSON JOYCE SUSANNE	} maids

Men

LORD MOUNT SEVERN	cousin to Isabel's father, her guardian
CAPTAIN LEVISON, later SIR FRANCIS LEVISON, BARONET	an ambitious and scheming rake
ARCHIBALD CARLYLE	lawyer, in love with Isabel
MR HARE	Justice of the Peace, father to Richard and Barbara

RICHARD HARE	a young man
MR DILL	Archibald Carlyle's law clerk
GEORGE HALLIJOHN	Afy's father
COLONEL OTWAY BETHELL	a passer-by and witness to a crime
LOCKSLEY	a poacher
VILLAGERS AND TOWNSPEOPLE	

Prologue

SCENE i

Library at Castle Marling, with long window, and door, LORD
MOUNT SEVERN *discovered at a table looking over papers*

MOUNT SEVERN: Well, well; there's no help for it, I must go to town at
once and see Warburton about those mortages. I would my
unfortunate cousin had not died in the prime of life, leaving that
poor girl Isabel penniless, through his reckless extravagance, and
burdening me with the accession to title and estates so hopelessly
involved that I hardly know what is mine and what belongs to his
numerous creditors. (*Rings bell.*)
Enter SERVANT
Tell Barton to put the horses to directly, I wish to catch the express
to London.
[*Exit* SERVANT. MOUNT SEVERN *goes to window, looks off*]
Ah! there's Isabel with Levison again. I hope she will not lose her
heart to him, he's a bad man, vain, idle, and unprincipled, and were
he not my wife's cousin, should not be suffered here, to trifle with
Isabel. I wish my lady could be made to see his faults and behave more
kindly to that gentle girl, fatherless as she is, with no home but ours.
SERVANT *enters*
SERVANT: The carriage, sir.   [*Exit* SERVANT]
MOUNT SEVERN: (*gathers letters on table*) I very much fear that my
wife's dislike to Isabel arises from jealously of the poor girl's youth
and beauty; however, I shall insist on her showing more kindness
and consideration for one who has every claim to our care and
affection.   [*Exit*]
LEVISON *and* ISABEL VANE *enter from garden by window*
LEVISON: No, Isabel, I can never forget those happy hours – happy at
least to me when first we met at East Lynne. *I had hopes then* –
hopes that to cherish now would be folly, broken down and fettered
with debts, surrounded by difficulties as I am. Ah, Isabel, if I had a
home to offer you, a home worthy of your grace and bounty.
ISABEL: Love and contentment can make the humblest home happy.
LEVISON: (*aside*) Humph! Love in a cottage frame of mind. I am
beyond the pale of such happiness myself and dare not think of

entering the happy state; like other men I *have* sometimes indulged in dreams, but a poor gentleman, with no property, no prospects can only play the butterfly to his life's end.

ISABEL: (*aside*) He does not love me, or he—

SERVANT: (*enters with card*) A gentleman wished to see you, my lady.

ISABEL: (*looking at card*) Mr Carlyle! oh, how that name recalls the sad days at Lynne. (*Aside*)

LEVISON: (*looks at watch*) Umph! time I started on my ten mile ride to West Lynne, poor little Afy Hallijohn will be anxiously awaiting me.

ISABEL: (*abstractedly, aside*) When I was so overwhelmed with grief how generous and noble he was in his – (*Suddenly recollecting the* SERVANT *is waiting, turns to* SERVANT) Show him in.

[*Exit* SERVANT]

LEVISON: Au revoir, dear Isabel, Mr Carlyle may wish to see you alone on business.   [*Exit through window*]

ISABEL: (*goes to window, looks after him*) When *he* leaves me, it seems as though the sunshine had faded from my life.

SERVANT *shows in* MR CARLYLE

CARLYLE: Lady Isabel, having some business in the neighbourhood, I could not resist the impulse which prompted me to call and see you, but how is this, you look pale, sad, and there are tears in your eyes. I claim the privilege of one, whom you honour by calling friend, to ask why you are so distressed; I hope this a happy home to you?

ISABEL: No, Mr Carlyle, it is not, it is a miserable home, and I cannot remain here, I have lain awake night after night thinking of what is to become of me, I have no friend in the world (CARLYLE *looks surprised*), but you, *you* have indeed been a true friend; but I cannot stay here with Lady Mount Severn, she insults me daily, taunts me with my helplessness and poverty, my dependence on her bounty, she hates me (I know not why), I have never given her any cause; Lord Mount Severn is most kind, but she, she would break my heart, as she has already wellnigh broken my spirit.

CARLYLE: Indeed, I am grieved to hear that, what can I do to serve you?

ISABEL: Nothing – what can *any* one do to serve me – oh Carlyle, if I could but awake and find that the last few years had been past only in a hideous dream – awake, to see dear papa alive again; ah! were *he* alive East Lynne (with all the trouble we had to encounter there) would be a very Eden to me now.

CARLYLE: There is but one way by which you could return to East Lynne; may I be permitted to point out that way? If my words should offend you Lady Isabel, check them, as my presumption deserves. May I dare to offer you a welcome to your old home, as – as – its mistress.

ISABEL: As its mistress?

CARLYLE: As my wife.

ISABEL: Mr Carlyle! (*Surprised*)

CARLYLE: I know how presumptuous it must seem to you that *I*, a mere lawyer, in an obscure country town, should venture on such a proposal to the daughter of the late Earl Mount Severn, but my excuse is, that your father was good enough to call me friend, to confide in me when trouble was hastening him to an early grave. (ISABEL *affected*) Forgive me for awakening memories which must be so full of pain; my dearest hope is to soften the anguish of those recollections in a future of such tenderness and care on my part, that you might, in time, feel less keenly the loss of that love which died with him to whom you were so dear, my life-long study would be your happiness.

ISABEL: Mr Carlyle, I esteem and respect you very, very much knowing your noble nature as I do from past experience of your kindness, but I do not feel that I could love you yet, as *you should* be loved.

CARLYLE: I do not dare to hope so, but will you let me try to be deserving of that priceless treasure, *your love*.

ISABEL: You are more than '*deserving*' of the truest love which the best of women could bestow, but I – (*She rises and goes to window. Looking off through window*) (*aside*) His wife, and I fear that I love, or almost love another, ah! if *he* would ask me to be his wife, or that I had never seen him. (*abstracted*)

CARLYLE: (*after pause*) You do not answer me, you turn from me! Oh, say that I have not offended you by—

ISABEL: (*recovering herself*) Oh, no – no! But will you give me a few days for consideration, your – your proposal is so sudden!

CARLYLE: I am only too happy to find that you are willing to give my proposal your consideration, for that emboldens me to hope!

(*Close in*)

Room in HARE's *house*

BARBARA: (*comes to window and looks off*) East Lynne is tenantless. Lady Isabel is no longer there to act as a magnet for Archibald Carlyle. She has gone, and he will be free from the memory of her beauty!

(MR HARE *through window.*)

HARE: Well, that cobs all. I can hardly believe it.

BARBARA: Believe what, papa?

HARE: Why, the report that Carlyle has bought East Lynne!

BARBARA: Can it be true?

HARE: As likely as not; he's rich enough. His father, Mr Carlyle, had the finest practice in the three counties. I have just been over to see him, but he's away; gone over to Castle Marling!

BARBARA: (*aside*) To Castle Marling! *She* is there!

HARE: I put the question to old Dill, his clerk; but he's close – very close. However, he didn't deny it, so you may depend there's some truth in the rumour.

BARBARA: He has lost no time in making the purchase!

HARE: Let lawyers alone for despatching business when they are their own clients, and their friends are as embarrassed as that prodigal spend-thrift, the late Lord Mount Severn.

BARBARA: I heard there was not enough money left, even for Lady Isabel to buy her mourning with. The Smiths told the Herberts, and the Herberts told me!

HARE: Ah, gossips all. 'Mrs Grundy'[1] has as many relatives in the Lynnes as everywhere else. Where's Dick?

BARBARA: He took his gun and said he was going over to the woods this evening.

HARE: What business has he there – in the evening? Is the young scamp going to poach? A pretty thing it would be if he were had up for dropping some of Carlyle's game. [HARE *goes off*]

BARBARA: Castle Marling – has he gone there to – to – see *her*? Oh, Archibald, if you did but know that a heart nearer home was aching for your love. But it must come some day – I feel it must, and when I am your wife you will know how dear you are to me.

[*Exit through gate*]

SCENE iii

Lynne wood. Cottage to back of stage; moonlight

(RICHARD HARE, *with gun enters, goes to door of cottage: knocks*)

RICHARD: Afy, Afy! Afy, Afy! (*softly*)
      (AFY *comes to door, which she closes.*)

AFY: Oh, Richard, why have you come? What are you doing with your gun?

RICHARD: I promised to lend your father one, while his own is being repaired. Why do you hold the door fast behind you?

AFY: You must not stay now, I'm busy!

RICHARD: Yes, with that fellow Thorne! he is there. It is not the first time you have made excuses for sending me away after you have appointed to meet me; I know the reason – that man is there!

AFY: No, no, he is not, indeed!

RICHARD: Then you expect him. Afy, he means you no good! Why does he always come at dusk, and take by-roads, so that no one shall see him as he comes here to dazzle you with his glittering diamond rings? Ah, I don't believe his name is Thorne; none of the Swainson Thornes are like him. Oh, Afy, why do you deceive me in this way?

AFY: I am not deceiving you; but do go, now!

RICHARD: Why do you wish me to 'go – now?'

AFY: Because my father has heard the gossips of West Lynne talking about you and me in a bad way. He says you must not come here any more, for when gentlemen come after poor girls in secret they haven't marriage in their thoughts.

RICHARD: But *you* know mine is as honourable a love as I could feel for any woman in my own station of life. I cannot marry you in opposition to my father's will; but if you are content to wait, and believe me true, I—

AFY: Well, dear Richard, I do believe that; but I expect father home every minute, so do – do go!

RICHARD: Then you will not let me come in and wait for him?

AFY: I dare not.

RICHARD: Then come out with me for a stroll!

AFY: No, no! Father would be so angry if he comes home and finds me out, he'll be sure I'm with you.

RICHARD: Oh, very well, give him the gun, but mind how you handle

it, for it's loaded. (*Gives her the gun, she goes in*) I know that man is
there. I'll watch and confound her with the proofs of her treachery!

[*Goes off*]

OTWAY BETHELL *enters from wood at back*

BETHELL: Ha, ha, Miss Hallijohn, mind you don't come to grief
between your two lovers. Young Hare is suspicious, and is watching
the cottage from yonder trees; a young fool, to be hoodwinked by
that cunning young Circé.[2] Ah! (*Turns as though at the sound of
some movement of game in the wood; goes off cautiously*)

(LEVISON *and* AFY *come from cottage*)

AFY: And must you go so soon?

LEVISON: My dear Afy, I must be back at Swainson by ten, I have an
appointment.

AFY: Oh, yes, to meet some other lady, I suppose?

LEVISON: Now, Afy, have you so little trust in me as to harbour such
suspicions. Now don't pout, my pretty one, but walk with me to the
hollow, where I have tethered my horse and as we walk along I hope
I shall convince you that you have no rival in my affections!

(*They stroll up and through wood at back, as* OLD HALLIJOHN
enters and goes into cottage)

HALLIJOHN: Afy, Afy, where are you? (*Comes to door, looks out*)
Umph, out again with young Hare I s'pose, his gun is here.

LEVISON: (*at back*) I've left something in the cottage, I'll not be a
moment my dear Afy.

HALLIJOHN: Ah! who is this stranger with my girl?

(*Retires into cottage at* LEVISON *comes from wood towards door*)

LEVISON: That riding whip has my name on it, and mustn't be left
there. (*Goes into cottage*)

HALLIJOHN: (*in house*) Who are you, why is my girl with you—

LEVISON: (*in house*) Take your hands from me.

HALLIJOHN: You mean no good to her, or why have you come here,
like a thief in the night.

LEVISON: Let go your hold, let go man, or—

HALLIJOHN: No, not till you have—

(*Shot fired in house –* LEVISON, *the gun in his hand, rushes out,
pale and excited,* HALLIJOHN'S *staggers to door as though to
detain* LEVISON *who throws down gun, and rushing out is met
by* OTWAY BETHELL, *who catches his arm as he tries to pass*)

BETHELL: What have you been doing, that you look so wild, and
horrified – was it you fired that shot *Captain Levison*?

LEVISON: Hush! for heaven's sake, since you know me.

BETHELL: I know *Thorne* of *Swainson*, and I know *you are* not he.
(*Not seeing* HALLIJOHN's *body, which is masked by* LEVISON)

LEVISON: It was an accident, done in the heat of passion, what right
had the fellow to strike me, I will make it worth your while to keep
silent, your saying you saw me here can do no good, shall it be
silent? Though a *gentleman* you are a *needy man* – under a cloud –
here are two notes for £50, all I have about me at present – shall it be
silence?

BETHELL: Yes, yes! (LEVISON *gives notes and rushes off*) I know him,
and may bleed him again, when he becomes *Sir* Francis Levison,
Baronet.   [*Exit*]

(RICHARD HARE *looking off*)

RICHARD: The deceitful coquette, he *was* with her. That was Thorne
who passed me, looking so pale and terrified. (*Sees* HALLIJOHN)
Good heavens! what is this – Hallijohn (*Kneeling by body*)
bleeding! dead! (*Placing his hand on the heart of* HALLIJOHN) – my
gun by his side (*Takes gun*) and discharged.

(LOCKSLEY *a poacher, emerges from wood.* RICHARD *retreats,
throws down gun, surprised and alarmed, rushes off*)

LOCKSLEY: Why, that's young Hare. (*Looking after* RICHARD, *sees
body of* HALLIJOHN) Ah, Hallijohn, bleeding, 'dead', did young
Dick Hare fire the shot I heard! (*As he is stooping over body* AFY
returns.)

AFY: What can detain him so long? (*Sees* LOCKSLEY) Locksley, what
are you doing here? (*He points*) Ah! my father senseless, who has
done this?

LOCKSLEY: I don't know for sure, but I heard a shot and came up just
in time to see Dick Hare fling away the gun, and fly from the place
like mad, but I must go for help, there may yet be life in him.[*Exit*]

RICHARD: (*enters*). I must not leave my gun by his body or they may
suspect that I – (*Turns and sees* AFY) Ah, Afy!

AFY: Murderer! what had my poor father done to you that you should
take his life.

RICHARD: I! Afy, do you imagine *me* capable of such a foul deed?

AFY: *Yes*, who else could have done it, here is your gun – discharged –
still warm. 'Twas your wicked hand that killed him.

RICHARD: I swear that I am innocent, I was not here – till—

AFY: 'Twas *you* Richard Hare, do not think I'll spare you, no *I* will
avenge my poor father's death by *yours* – I swear it over the corpse
of him – *you* have slain – oh – my poor kind dear – dear father.

RICHARD: If *she* can think me guilty, who will believe in my
innocence! (*Voices*) *No one* – I dare not stay to be accused by her in

the face of all – (*Voices*) – nearer, and nearer yet. (*Bewildered he looks around, and rushes into wood at back*)

LOCKSLEY, JUSTICE HARE, *and* VILLAGERS *enter*

HARE: Hallijohn murdered! by whom?

AFY: By your son Richard.

HARE: No, do not say by him, by – by – my son.

AFY: *Yes*, he was here by the body not a moment since, but you see he has fled guilt stricken; he dared not wait to answer for his crime.

LOCKSLEY: And, this is his gun, sir. (*Murmurs*)

VILLAGERS: Poor Hallijohn, shame on the murderous villain, etc.

HARE: Hark ye all! if it can be *proved* that his hand is red with the blood of this poor man, justice shall be done, son of mine though he be – I – I will *myself* assist to bring him to the punishment his foul crime should meet – aye, as though he were a stranger to my blood and name. Till his innocence is made clear *my* doors shall not shelter him, nor shall his name be spoken in the house he has disgraced. This I swear before ye all.

(*Curtain*)

Act I

SCENE i

Garden in CARLYLE's *estate at East Lynne*

LEVISON *and* CARLYLE *enter*

LEVISON: 'Pon my soul, Carlyle, this game of hide and seek is infernally boring. I'm sick of Boulogne and all other places of refuge for the impecunious.

CARLYLE: Then stay here till I can see your uncle, Sir Peter, and arrange with him about your affairs. I may prevail on him to relieve you once more from your embarrassments, and make you a free man again.

LEVISON: Really now, that is very kind of you, I dread going abroad, away from all my friends; but I dread the bailiffs still more.

CARLYLE: You will be safe enough here. No one will think of looking for you in my house; you are my Isabel's cousin, and for *her* sake you are welcome, so keep close, don't show yourself beyond the grounds till—

Enter BARBARA HARE

BARBARA: Oh, Archibald! (*Seeing* LEVISON) Mr Carlyle, can I speak to — to you for one moment.

CARLYLE: Excuse, Mr Levison, I will join you presently.

BARBARA: I am so glad to have met you; I've actually been to your office, and not finding you—

LEVISON: (*aside*) Umph! his wife's *bête noir*; Isabel is jealous of her now, and if she should by chance walk this way and see them—

[*Exit*]

CARLYLE: But why does Richard venture here? a warrant for his arrest still—

BARBARA: But *you* do not believe him guilty of Hallijohn's murder?

CARLYLE: No, *I do* not! but as the jury at the coroner's inquest returned a verdict of wilful murder against him, and the warrant for his arrest is still out: it is most perilous for him to venture here where he's so well known.

BARBARA: He is not *here*, but at an obscure place, four miles away, disguised as a farm labourer!

CARLYLE: Why did he not come forward and state all he knew, instead of absconding, and for four years hiding away?

BARBARA: He said that he felt the proofs were so strong against him, and as even Afy Hallijohn denounced him he feared no one would believe in his innocence, and now poor mamma is dying to see him; she has never seen him since his flight; he dare not venture near the house while papa is at home; for you know the oath he took, and you also know his obdurate, unforgiving nature. Now I thought if you would kindly make an appointment with him to meet you at your office tonight on some justice business, you might detain him while poor Richard stole a meeting with mamma.

CARLYLE: Certainly, I was going with my wife to a dinner party at the Jeffersons, but for your mother's and Dick's sake, I will forgo the engagement.

BARBARA: Oh, that is kind of you.

CARLYLE: Dill shall go to your father and ask him to meet me.

Exits as ISABEL *enters on* LEVISON'S *arm*

ISABEL: 'Doubt him'! never! how *could* I doubt one so good and affectionate, as my dear husband, no! I am too happy in his love, to wrong him by suspicion.

LEVISON: Then he is indeed to be congratulated; few men are blessed with such blindly confiding wives. (LEVISON *starts and turns quickly*) Ah!

ISABEL: Why did you start, and turn so quickly?

LEVISON: We might disturb a pleasant *tête-a-tête* if we go that way. (*Points*)

ISABEL: Ah! again with her, what does this mean? (*Half aside*)

LEVISON: You seem surprised, you would be less so, if *you* had seen them together as often as *I* have, when I am strolling about in the evening (the only time I'm safe from my infernal creditors) I frequently see —

(ISABEL *turns on him sharply*)

ISABEL: And if you do, by what right dare you impugn Mr Carlyle's proceedings, if you have not quite forgotten your duty as a gentleman, you would scorn to play the part of a spy and informer, or even attempt to raise doubts in the mind of a wife who loves and honours the husband to whom she owes so much. [*Exit*]

LEVISON: (*lights cigar*) Ha! a splendid spasm of conjugal confidence, but you *have* your doubts, and the jealous fire that is now smouldering could easily be fanned into a flame that would consume you, *ma bella*. [*Exit*]

SCENE ii

*Apartment at East Lynne, long window, avenue at back,
set trees, folding doors, fireplace, door,* ISABEL *coming up avenue*

WILSON *and* JOYCE *discovered*

WILSON: Ah, – yes; she does look ill indeed, (ISABEL *is coming in, but
hearing* BARBARA HARE'S *name, stops*) I shouldn't wonder if she
dies young. Oh, wouldn't Barbara Hare's hopes be up again then, if
anything should happen she'd snap him up to a certainty, she
wouldn't let him escape her a second time. Why *now* she's as much
in love with him as ever.

JOYCE: Oh, nonsense. (ISABEL *listening, concealed by foliage*)

WILSON: Oh, you may say 'nonsense', but if *you'd* lived in the Hare
family as *I* did for seven years before I came here, and seen *and*
heard what *I* have. Why *he* gave her that locket and chain she wears,
with a lock of *his hair* in it, too.

JOYCE: What of that? they were children together and playfellows.

WILSON: Um – yes; 'playfellows'. *She* didn't regard him *only* as a
playfellow. Why, even now she'll watch at the gate for his passing,
and take every chance of speaking to him.

JOYCE: Well, well: I don't want to hear anything about her. She must
be a great fool to think so much of a man who didn't care for her.

WILSON: You don't know that he *didn't* care for her then, we don't
know how it was between 'em, and if anything *should* happen to
Lady Isabel—

JOYCE: Nothing is going to happen to her I hope, for the sake of the
dear children.

WILSON: I'm sure *I* hope so, too. Barbara Hare wouldn't make a very
kind stepmother, hating the *mother* as she does, the *children*
wouldn't be loved much.

JOYCE: If you wish to remain in your place here you'd better put a curb
on your tongue, Miss Cornelia says yours is the longest in Lynne,
and if my lady heard you—

WILSON: Well, I only say what, etc. *[Exeunt, talking]*

ISABEL: (*comes forward*) I begin to understand all now. There *is* a
calmness almost amounting to indifference compared to the
passionate ardour of his love in the early days of our married life.
What if she *were* the companion of his youth, he is *mine* now; but is
his *heart* all – *all* – mine. Or does she still cast a spell over him, good,

kind, tender, as he is. I cannot help the feeling that there is a change. (*In chair*)

Enter CARLYLE

CARLYLE: Isabel dearest! how's this – in tears. (ISABEL *rises and speaks with great emotion*)

ISABEL: Oh, Archy, Archy, you will never marry her, if anything should happen to me – never let *her* usurp my place – she would be unkind to my children, draw your love from them, and from *my* memory.

CARLYLE: Of whom are you speaking dearest, what is troubling you so sorely?

ISABEL: Did you love no one, before you – you married me – oh Archy – even now, perhaps you love her still.

CARLYLE: Her! of whom do you speak Isabel?

ISABEL: Barbara Hare.

CARLYLE: I *never* loved Barbara Hare but as a brother, never loved any woman but you; and to you I have never been false in word, deed, or thought; what proof of true and earnest love can man give, that have *I* not given to *you*?

ISABEL: None, none. Oh do not be angry with me, I think sometimes that I must be dreaming; wild, strange, feverish dreams; I mistrust myself, *you*, all the world; I feel how much I owe you, and knowing how little I have to repay you with, I grow sad, suspicious, miserable.

CARLYLE: Indulge no more in such wild fancies, they are mere illusions, as unfair to me, as they are distressing to you.

ISABEL: I will try – to – to—

CARLYLE: You will not be yourself my darling, nor recover your spirits till you have had change of air, the sea breezes will soon bring the roses to your cheeks again – and –

Enter CORNELIA *with* LEVISON

CORNELIA: Sea breezes indeed, and change of air! what do people want with them, a parcel of new fangled[3] notions that doctors put in people's heads – ugh! they'll recommend change of air for a scratched finger next, I never want change of air.

CARLYLE: (*not heeding* CORNELIA) Some quiet watering place on the French or Belgian coast – Trouville,[4] for instance.

CORNELIA: You'd better sit down and calculate the cost of gallivanting[5] over the water.

CARLYLE: Two or three months there will set you up.

CORNELIA: (*aside*) Set her up indeed! She wants setting down.

CARLYLE: And make you blooming as ever.

ISABEL: But cannot you stay there with me? I shall be so lonely without you.

CARLYLE: I shall run over as often as business will allow; I must not neglect business even for *you*, darling.

CORNELIA: I think you are neglecting it! What are you doing now, away from your office? (ISABEL *joins* LEVISON)

CARLYLE: There's Dill to represent me, and a staff of clerks under him.

CORNELIA: Ah! you never used to neglect your business *before* you were *married.*.

LEVISON: (*to* ISABEL *aside*) Your husband will miss you very much when you go to Trouville; he will have only his sister and Miss Hare to console him in your absence. (*Pointedly* – HARE *and* CORNELIA *talking aside*)

CORNELIA: (*aloud*) And pray what did Barbara Hare want with you this morning? (ISABEL *starts, hearing* BARBARA'S *name*)

CARLYLE: She came to see me on business.

CORNELIA: She seems to be always wanting to see you. What is the business? (*Aside*) Ah! surely that old affair is not being revived again?

CARLYLE: (*crosses, aside*) I may trust to you, sister. Richard Hare is –

CORNELIA: Richard Hare!

CARLYLE: Hush! (*Hurries her off*)

(*Enter* LEVISON, *talking earnestly to* ISABEL)

LEVISON: (*learning on mantel*) But you will believe me some day when the truth is forced upon you, *you* saw them in the garden – in earnest conversation.

ISABEL: Why remind me of that again? you make a poor return for Mr Carlyle's hospitality, in maligning him, to *me, his wife*. (ISABEL *sits*)

LEVISON: (*leaning over her chair*) His wife, ah, Isabel, there is the bitterness in reflection, that you *are his*; had we listened to our hearts in those days we might have been happier now, you and I were created to love each other, and (ISABEL *rises*) I would have declared the love that was consuming me, but—

ISABEL: I will not, dare not, listen to you. (LEVISON *takes her hand and presses her into chair*)

LEVISON: You must for a few moments. What I say now can do no harm; the time has gone by, the gulf between us is impassable; I know the fault was mine, I might then have won you and been happy.

ISABEL: You are talking to me – as – as you have no right to talk. (*Rising*)

LEVISON: Only the right of my deep, my undying love. (*Following her*)

ISABEL: Must I again remind you that you are here as the guest of *him* whose wife you insult by such language, the roof *which* shelters *you, should* be *my* protection – (*Turns from him*)

LEVISON: (*in a low tone*) Isabel, there are moments, when the sweet remembrances of earlier, happier, more *hopeful* years, make us forget reason, duty, even our *honour*, when our hearts beat wildly, and our feelings cry louder than our judgment or the voice of conscience, but say that you forgive me. (*Goes to her*)

ISABEL: I forgive you Captain Levison, but you must leave this house, you have lost all right to the name of friend.

LEVISON: Oh, my dear Isabel, do not say that you banish me for a few rash words spoken in the inconsiderate warmth of a disappointed spirit, that is now dead to hope for evermore. (*Very earnestly*)

ISABEL: Leave me now. I would be alone.

LEVISON: I obey. (*Aside*) The poison works; that last touch of emotion, combined with her growing jealousy, must have its effect in the end.

[*Exit*]

ISABEL: How can I succeed in my endeavours to forget him while he remains at East Lynne, and I am thrown daily, hourly, into his dangerous companionship. Dangerous! where should be the danger to *me*? (*Pacing the room*) The wife of such a man as Archibald Carlyle, the mother of his children, and yet these sinful throbbings of my heart when Levison is by me, speak only too plainly of the peril there is to my peace in his insidious sophistries. Oh, if I had but courage to tell my husband all – tell him that I once had a girl's passing fancy for my Cousin Francis, and that now *he* is here, my thoughts, in spite of myself, my duty, and my conscience will stray back to that time, when I was free to love, when there was no sin in – (CARLYLE *speaks off*) I *will* confide in him as a wife should. I will beg him to send Francis away, and – yes – Archibald shall tell me what is the secret between him and Barbara Hare.

CARLYLE *enters*

ISABEL: Archy, my dear Archy, I want you to listen to me so patiently and calmly. I have a – a – secret to confide – a secret that has long—
(LEVISON *strolls on*)

LEVISON: Oh, by the bye, Carlyle, you are going to dine with the Jefferson tonight, are you not?

CARLYLE: Yes! (*Speaks aside to* LEVISON)

ISABEL: What strange fatality thwarts me every time I resolve to confide my fears to him who *should* know how cruelly I am beset by them?

WILSON *enters,* CARLYLE *crosses to her*

WILSON: Mr Hare's servant brought this note, Sir!   [*Exit* WILSON]
(ISABEL *starts*)

LEVISON: (*aside*) Umph, Hare's servant.

CARLYLE: 'I fear that Richard is no longer safe where he has *hitherto been concealed,* he is now hiding in the fir copse behind your garden, and *will steal* out *after dark* to *see* mamma WHEN PAPA HAS LEFT HOME *if you* can, persuade him to *come out.* – Yours, Barbara.' Dear, dear, how incautious to venture here!
(*He crosses to* ISABEL, *the note in his hand. Throws note on fire, and brings her forward.* LEVISON *comes down and snatches it off fire, throws it in fender. Goes up again*)

CARLYLE: (*his back to* LEVISON) Oh, Isabel, my dear, I forgot to tell you that I shall not be able to go with you to the Jeffersons!

ISABEL: Not go too Archibald! Why not?

CARLYLE: I have an appointment on important business that may detain me till late. (*Aside*) Foolish boy, foolish boy! (*As he goes off*)

ISABEL: (*aloud*) Ah, that note!

LEVISON: The note cannot be of the same importance as the 'business' or he would (*Points to fender*) not have thrown it *there,* and as *Hare's servant* brought it – (ISABEL *looks at him sharply*) (*Aside*) She'll never resist the temptation to read it! (*Goes out on verandah, watching her from behind foliage*)

ISABEL: Hare's servant! (*Pause, snatches note from fender.*) Some of the words are obliterated by fire, but there may be enough to give me a clue to the purport. (*Reads*) '*I fear – the note is partially burnt – no* longer safe – *hitherto been concealed* in copse – garden – will – after dusk – see – you – when – has – left home. – Barb–' Yes, the word half calcined[6] was 'Barbara' – (*Looking at note*) – has left home – 'Has left home'! When *she* has left home, that is the word – missing. Yes, when *I* have left (*Passionately*) home! Oh, shameless woman! and *he, my husband!* The words scarce spoken that my grief had wrung from me – can leave me to be by *her* side! False friend, false love – all false alike – all! (*Sinks in chair sobbing*)
(LEVISON *comes down quickly*)

LEVISON: But *me* Isabel.

(*Close in quickly*)

Chamber

CARLYLE: (*Dragging* RICHARD HARE, *who is disguised in smock-frock, false beard*) Come in here till I can think what shall be done, no one will come here. My dear lad what folly – to – to – why have you come here to Lynne?

RICHARD: (*takes off hat and beard*) What could I do, I fear the officers are on my track – I've been followed by *one* I know. I met that villain Thorne in London, and from that hour I have been dogged: I came here because I felt I was not safe in my old hiding place at Dale's-end, a stranger has followed me even there. Oh, Mr Carlyle, the life I have led has been dreadful – many and many a time I have thought that if I had laid down in the snow on some door step, and have been found dead in the morning it would – (CORNELIA *outside*)

CORNELIA: Archibald, who's with you now?

RICHARD: Don't let her come in. (*Alarmed*)

CARLYLE: You remember what she *was*, and she's not a bit altered, if she has a *mind* to come in I cannot keep her out – you need not fear, *she* will be as anxious as I am to shield you. (*Opens door to* CORNELIA)

CORNELIA: (*to* RICHARD) Powers of mercy, what brought *you* here, you must be mad?

RICHARD: I am, almost, leading such a life as I have, I don't mind toil (though that's hard enough, after being brought up like a gentleman), but to be banned, hunted, afraid to show my face among my fellowmen, in dread every hour that the law may doom me to—

CORNELIA: Well, you've only yourself to thank, you would go dangling after that brazen hussy[7] Afy Hallijohn – its all through your—

RICHARD: No! it is all through that villain, Thorne, who killed her father, that I am hunted down like this.

CORNELIA: Well, it seems to me a most extraordinary thing that the real truth can't be brought to light. You tell a cock and bull story about some man, some Thorne, whom nobody ever saw, or heard of.

CARLYLE: Dick has seen him again, lately, and says that it is he who has set the officers on his track.

CORNELIA: Then why didn't you turn the tables on him, and *set* the *officers* on *him*?

RICHARD: I have no proof that he was the murderer, my bare word would not be taken, and he might swear my life away. He saw me in the wood that night.

CORNELIA: Ugh! you always were the biggest noodle that was ever let out of leading strings, and always will be.

CARLYLE: Well, well, Cornelia. (*Expostulating*)

CORNELIA: Ugh! I've no patience, and if he wasn't so miserably woe-begone, I'd treat him to a bit of my mind, you may depend on that.

CARLYLE: We must think of some way to dispose of him. After he has crept home tonight to see his mother he must return here, for *here* he must stop for the present.

CORNELIA: I'm sure I don't know how he's to get to a bedroom, without servants knowing he's here, the only safe room is the one beyond mine.

CARLYLE: How is he to get to that?

CORNELIA: How! why, through *mine*, to be sure.

CARLYLE: Well, if *you* don't mind.

CORNELIA: I! Do you suppose I mind young Dick Hare, whom I've so often spanked when a child, and I wish he was young enough to spank now; he richly deserves it, if ever anybody did. I shall be in bed, and his passing through won't alarm me. I shan't be frightened if *he* isn't. Stand on ceremony with young Dick Hare indeed! What next, I wonder? Archy, you go and see that the coast is clear.

[*Exit* CARLYLE]

(*Turns to* DICK, *kindly*) Poor hunted boy, I'll bring you some food up, you look as though you wanted it. Though you deserve a good thrashing before you get anything else. There, there! we won't talk of that now, but if ever you do get clear of this trouble I'll let you have a bit of mind, I promise you! [*Exeunt*]

SCENE iv

Same as scene ii

LEVISON: (*discovered by fireplace*) I think that partially calcined note has added fuel to the flame, jealousy will develop into resentment; then will arise a desire for revenge, next to love a woman's pet passion. I may venture to take a stroll beyond the sanctuary of East

Lynne; I shall surely be safe for this evening from those infernal
pests of society – the sheriff's officers.

[*Exit down avenue*]

Enter CARLYLE *and* ISABEL *dressed as for a party*

CARLYLE: I really am very sorry, my dear; you must make my excuses
to Mrs Jefferson.

ISABEL: You never before have had business, so mysterious and
important as to demand your attendance at your office at this hour.

CARLYLE: I regret that it should have so happened now, but it is too
momentous to be neglected; and it must be done by myself alone.

ISABEL: Shall you join us later in the evening. (*Coldly*)

CARLYLE: I much fear that I shall be unable to do so; I will put you in
the carriage, Isabel. (*She sweeps past him*)   [*Exeunt*]

LEVISON *enters hurriedly*

LEVISON: (*agitated, putting his hair off his brow*) What is Dick Hare
doing about here, is he dogging me, lucky that he was so much
astonished at my sudden appearance, that I had time to make off
and double back here, before he was able to decide on any course of
action. What is his errand here? Is it to denounce me as the *soi
disant*[8] Thorne? If so I must become a fugitive once more, but, *not
alone*, I will have a fair partner in my exile.

Enter CARLYLE

CARLYLE: Why, Levison, you look as agitated as though you had seen
a bailiff.

(LEVISON *having started on hearing his footsteps turns quickly*)

BARBARA *enters*

BARBARA: Oh Archibald. (*Seeing* LEVISON) Mr Carlyle, will you?
(*Retiring from window*, CARLYLE *goes to her*)

LEVISON: Do not let me drive you away Miss Hare. Umph! Isabel's
back hardly turned before her hated rival appears; the carriage
cannot have gone far on the road; by the fields I may overtake the
injured wife.   [*Exit*]

BARBARA: Yes, he was emerging from the clump of trees in Bean-lane,
and came upon Thorne face to face.

CARLYLE: Dick must have been mistaken.

BARBARA: He says he can swear to him. Thorne was walking fast with
his hat in one hand, while with the other he pushed back the hair
from his brow. Dick knew him by that action alone, as he was
always doing so in the old days. There was the hand adorned with
the flashing diamond ring.

CARLYLE: Why did your brother allow him to escape?

BARBARA: He was so surprised, he had not the presence of mind to spring on him and accuse him of the murder. When he had recovered from his astonishment Thorne was making off rapidly in the direction of East Lynne.

CARLYLE: Where is Dick now?

BARBARA: Hiding in the fir copse till he sees my signal that all is safe in doors, for papa is still at home, and he says, with his usual contrariety, that if you want to see him tonight you must come to him (to use his own words) he is not going over to your office to sit with Dill and you among dusty deed boxes and mouldy old parchments.

CARLYLE: Oh, indeed Mr Justice Hare, then we must bring you up here out of the way.

BARBARA: Will you come over with me now and entice him away on some pretence; poor mamma is waiting so anxiously to see her boy. I am sorry to give you all this trouble.

CARLYLE: (*takes up his hat from chair*) My dear Barbara, it is no trouble to me if I can make any one happy, if only for an hour. I'll coax your obstinate dad up here, and Cornelia shall find him a long pipe and some strong October[9] such as he delights in at the 'Buck's Head', and we'll talk parochial politics while Dick—

BARBARA: But papa must not know that I've been up here, or he'll think it a plan.

CARLYLE: O, no, we'll, etc.

    Talking as they go off. LEVISON *and* ISABEL *enter*

LEVISON: There, dear Isabel, will you believe your own eyes. (ISABEL *goes into verandah*)

ISABEL: With *her*? Then my fears were *not* unfounded.

LEVISON: You see now why he could not accompany you – you see now why he is so anxious for your retirement at Trouville, that with the seas between you he may have the opportunity daily, *hourly*, of enjoying her dear society.

ISABEL: Oh! you torture me.

LEVISON: You whom I have loved so constantly through all, through coldness and disdain on your part, through the helpless, hopeless misery I have endured in seeing you the wife of one who loves you as you see. (*Points off*)

ISABEL: Oh! why have you shown me this? (*Fiercely*)

LEVISON: To prove how grossly you are deceived. Be avenged on him. Leave this life of doubts and fears; come to happiness with one whose love for you will never change.

ISABEL: Tempt me not, leave me, I am almost mad! (*Comes into room*)

LEVISON: (*points*) Look there again. Even from here you may see how he whispers in her ear, how close his lips are to hers. (*She goes to window again*) Can you not in imagination hear the loving words that he should speak to none *but you*.

ISABEL: It is too plain he loves her, and I am—

LEVISON: Deceived. Can you endure the sight of that, and yet seek no revenge? Will you still spurn my true love? Will you – oh, say, dear Isabel – will you fly with me – fly from him who insults you thus? (*Pointing off*)

ISABEL: Yes, come weal, come woe. I will – I will be avenged on him for so cruelly wronging me.

LEVISON: Come then, swift horses shall be in readiness, and we—

ISABEL: Go, I will rejoin you in a few minutes. (*He goes off, she sits at table, and writes, reading as she writes*) 'When years have passed and my – my – children ask where is their mother and why she left her home, then tell them that you, their father, goaded her to the rash act. Tell them that you deceived, outraged her feelings and her pride, until driven to the verge of madness, she – she – quitted them for ever.' (*Rises from table*) Now, Francis Levison, I trust my future in your hands, and may heaven forgive me.

As she is looking despairingly around the room JOYCE *enters*

JOYCE: Oh, my lady, are you ill?

ISABEL: Aye! ill and wretched! Joyce once before, when I was near death, you promised me to stay with my children, whatever might happen; promise me that again, promise, that when I am gone, you will not leave them.

JOYCE: Never! my dear lady – never! but do, my dear mistress, tell me, are you ill? What is the matter? What can I do?

ISABEL: Nothing that can avail me now, I am beyond mortal aid. Remember your promise, dear Joyce! Leave me now! Remember your promise, as you hope for mercy! [*rushes off*]

JOYCE: What can she mean? – 'when I am gone' – 'once before near death'. Ah! I know what her wild looks, her sad, pale face, and broken-acted tones meant. Merciful heavens! where is Mr Carlyle?

(CARLYLE *and* HARE *enter*) Oh, sir! have you seen my lady?

CARLYLE: She has gone to Mrs Jeffersons!

JOYCE: She has returned, and gone – gone – to take the life that is not hers; to take—

CARLYLE: Joyce, what do you mean?

JOYCE: (*sobbing*) My lady made me promise to – to—

CORNELIA *enters*

JOYCE: (*to* CORNELIA) Ah, when my dear lady is laid before us dead, what will be your feeling for having driven her to it!

CARLYLE: Joyce, I am at a loss to understand your meaning.

JOYCE: I know, sir you have done your duty to her in love and kindness, but Miss Cornelia has made her life a misery; yes ma'am you have; I've seen her with tears in her eyes after enduring your reproach a gentle high-born lady like her to be – eh! you've driven her to desperation! I know it!

CARLYLE: Oh, Cornelia! if Joyce's fears are well founded, heaven forgive you! She may be in the grounds. (HARE *and* CORNELIA *go off to grounds, sees note on desk, hesitates to read it*) Ah! writing in her hand! Why do I fear to read? (*Reads note*)

JOYCE: What does it say, sir; does it say – that – she – is dead?

CARLYLE: Worse, far worse than death. Had she died, I could still have worshipped, honoured her memory while I mourned her loss, but now –

A little boy and girl enter

CHILD Where's mamma? They are saying that mamma has gone. Where is she?

JOYCE: Oh! my dear Miss Isabel, you must not—

CARLYLE: Joyce! that name no more – no more – My children motherless – my home dishonoured – oh! God! give me strength to bear this blow (*Sinks in chair*) my children – you will see her no – no more. In this world you will have but me and your little brother to love you – my darlings, we must be all in all to each other now. I have only you – only you – (*Embracing the children*)

(*Curtain*)

Act II

SCENE i

Chamber at JUSTICE HARE'*s*

BARBARA *and* CARLYLE *discovered*

CARLYLE: And what do they say of me, Barbara?

BARBARA: That you go over to Lynboro' so often, not to see Sir John Dobede, but his daughter Louisa.

CARLYLE: And do *you* believe that?

BARBARA: Well, I don't know, why should it not be true?

CARLYLE: Because I shall never marry again. How can I? *she* who *was* my wife still lives.

BARBARA: But the law has – (*Stops suddenly*)

CARLYLE: I know what you would say: *the law* has now pronounced me free; *I* cannot accept that decree as a dissolution of so sacred a compact, *I* cannot forget those solemn words 'Till *death* do us part'.

BARBARA: His heart still clings to *her*, how he must have loved her, how could she have forsaken such a man. *I* would have died for him, happy to give my life for his love.

Enter MR HARE *hastily*

CARLYLE: What's the matter, Justice, you seem excited.

HARE: (*wiping his brow*) Excited! yes, and so would you be *excited* if you were worried out of your senses as I am; why, there's Barbara, as if we were not scandalised enough by her scamp of a brother, *she* must give folks reason to say that no one will have her because of his misdeeds.

CARLYLE: More shame on those who say so.

(BARBARA *crosses as though to go*)

HARE: (*Stopping her*) No, no, you shan't escape that way; that's how you always try to evade me when I'm telling you of your conduct, any one would think that rather than be under such a stigma and allow the parish to say that of her she would marry the first man who offered, even if it was the parish beadle[10] just to stop their chattering tongues.

CARLYLE: I should hardly think you'd like to have a parish beadle for your son-in-law.

HARE: But she's had bushels of *good* offers, and says no to all of them.

There's Tom Herbert, he was the last one whom she refused, point blank.

CARLYLE: Indeed! and why, eh Barbara? I'm sure he's a very nice fellow.

BARBARA: Oh yes, he *is* a very 'pleasant fellow', to *some* people.

                                                              [*Exit*]

HARE: Ugh, she's one of the obstinate, contrary, self-willed ones.

CARLYLE: She may have an excuse for that.

HARE: Excuse! what excuse?

CARLYLE: She is your child.

HARE: Of course she is, whose should she be? and as she is *my child*, she ought to do as I bid her, and now, to add to my vexations, here's this infernal report about the place.

CARLYLE: What report?

HARE: What report! why, that *he* has been here, disguised as a labourer, has dared to show himself here, *here* where he may yet come to the gibbet.

CARLYLE: Of *whom* are you speaking?

HARE: Of *whom* should I be *speaking*, but of that scoundrel. Dick (*Spluttering*), *who else* is likely to come to a felon's death? If he has dared to come near, Lynne, I'll put the police on his track, oh! I was in such a passion that I was nearly knocking down the man who told me; however, I'll have no more of this worry.

CARLYLE: I'm inclined to think you bring all this worry on yourself.

HARE: Now, that cobs all![11] Bring it on myself; did *I* shoot Hallijohn? Did *I* fly from justice and hide the devil knows where? Did *I* come back to my native parish disguised as a – a – dirty labourer, to worry my *own father*, eh? Bring it on myself, ugh.

CARLYLE: It was just the same when you received that anonymous letter some days ago, you were in a passion then.

HARE: And enough to make any man in a passion, here, this says (*Takes a letter from his pocket*) he may come down, and warns me to put him on his guard, and hush it up, as if I would put him on his guard – If I drop on him, I'll—

CARLYLE: I daresay some one has circulated this report, and written anonymous letters, merely for the purpose of vexing you.

HARE: I'd like to find out who had.

CARLYLE: I daresay you would – now, you follow my advice, take no notice of *rumours*, and put all anonymous letters in the fire – a pretty laugh they'd have at you if they thought you'd been hoaxed by—

HARE: Laugh at *me*, – would they? If they dared to do that, I'd have the whole parish of Lynne up before me, and I'd – I'd – (*Spluttering, in a rage*)

CARLYLE: *What* would you do, eh?

HARE: Do? why commit them all for trial.

CARLYLE: You couldn't do that.

HARE: Couldn't I? But I would – I would.

CARLYLE: No you would not. Even 'great unpaids' cannot commit or fine people for laughing at them, or they would have to sign commitments every hour in the day.

HARE: What do you mean by that? However, I'll call at the police-station and tell them to keep a sharp look-out for the young villain.

CARLYLE: You'll do nothing of the kind.

HARE: Y–yes I – will. (*Blustering*)

CARLYLE: I say you will *not*. Every man would cry shame on you, and justly so, if you did such a monstrous act. Oh, you may look angry, but if others shrink from telling you the truth, I do not; your unnatural harshness, your blind obstinacy have become a bye word.

HARE: *My* obstinacy! (*As though astonished*)

CARLYLE: Yes! give your own son up to justice. You will never do so cruel an act. Or if you *do*, you may take leave of your friends, for you'll not find any man willing to own *you* for one.

HARE: (*awed by* CARLYLE'*s tone*) But I took an oath to do it.

CARLYLE: But you did not 'take an oath' to go open mouthed to the police-station on the strength of some paltry anonymous letter or lying rumour, and say 'My son will be in Lynne today or to-morrow, look out for him'. You let the police look after their own business, don't *you* set them on.

HARE: Then you think this rumour—

CARLYLE: Not worth listening to.

HARE: And this letter? (*Showing it*)

CARLYLE: Put it in the fire.

HARE: Eh?

CARLYLE: That's what *I* should do.

HARE: Would you – eh? would you? (*More calmly*)

CARLYLE: I certainly would.

HARE: Umph – ha! Well I think I will. I don't know how it is Carlyle, but you've got a way of talking people over that's – that's damned annoying. (*Takes out handkerchief*) You talk, and you gammon and palaver,[12] and twist them round your finger as easily – as easily – as – as I— (*Flourishing his pockethandkerchief as though at a loss for a word, blows his nose, and exits,* CARLYLE *follows*)

SCENE ii

Chamber. LADY ISABEL *discovered by fire*

ISABEL: He comes too late now, too late to save the poor child from the life-long reproach that must rest on him.

LEVISON enters

LEVISON: I'm sorry I could not get away from town before.

ISABEL: Why did you come now?

LEVISON: Why did I come! I thought you at least would have been glad to welcome me.

ISABEL: When you left me in May last, you gave me a sacred promise to come back in time for our marriage, you know what I mean when I say 'in time' but—

LEVISON: Of course I meant to be back – but business—

ISABEL: You cannot deceive me now, you *did not* mean to be back in time, or you would have arranged our marriage before you went away.

LEVISON: What fancies have you taken up now Isabel?

ISABEL: No fancies, but bitter truths. On the morning of your departure you received two letters – one announcing the death of your uncle, and your accession to the title and estates, the other contained the information that the divorce was decreed – thus enabling you to make the only reparation in your power.

LEVISON: Well, you know—

ISABEL: You left those letters on your table. It would have been better to have undeceived me before you left, better to have told me that the hopes I was cherishing (for the sake of the poor unborn child) were worse than vain.

LEVISON: The excited state you were then in would have precluded your listening to any sort of reason.

ISABEL: You think it would not be in reason, that I should aspire to be made the wife of Sir Francis Levison.

LEVISON: Well, Isabel, you must be aware that it would be an awful sacrifice for a man in my position to marry a divorced woman. I am now the representative of an ancient and honorable baronetcy, and to make you my wife would—

ISABEL: I understand you, you need not be at any trouble to invent or seek for excuses. The injury to the child can never be repaired now; and for myself, I cannot imagine any worse fate in life than being obliged to pass it with *you*. You have made me what I am, but all the reparation in your power to make now, cannot undo my sin – that – and its effect must lie upon me forever more.

LEVISON: The sin! ha, ha! you women should think of that beforehand.

ISABEL: Ah, yes. May heaven help all to think of it when you're tempted as I was.

LEVISON: If you mean that as a reproach to me it is rather out of place. The temptation to *sin* (as you call it) did not lie so much in *my* persuasion as in *your own* jealous anger towards your husband.

ISABEL: Alas! too true – too true.

LEVISON: And I believe you were so outrageously jealous of him without any cause; their secret meetings were on some business matters in which Mrs Hare was much interested.

ISABEL: You told a different tale to me then.

LEVISON: All stratagems are fair in love and war.

           (ISABEL *takes banknotes from desk on table*)

ISABEL: I received these from you by post a month ago – I return them.

LEVISON: Return them! – why?

ISABEL: I have no more to do with you; all is over between us. (*Haughtily*)

LEVISON: Oh, very well; if it be your wish that all relations between us should end, be it so. I must confess I think it better so, for the cat and dog life we should, as it seems to me, henceforth lead, would be far from agreeable. (*Waiting for her to make some reply*) Remember, it is your doing, not mine. A sum (we will fix the amount) shall be placed to your account, and – (ISABEL *turns vehemently*)

ISABEL: Not one farthing[13] will I receive from *you* Sir Francis Levison.

LEVISON: You have no fortune of your own, you must have assistance from some one.

ISABEL: Not from *you*! If all the world denied me help, and I could find none from strangers, I would *die* rather than touch one coin of *your* money.

LEVISON: In time you may wish to recall your words, in that case a line to my bankers—

ISABEL: Put away those notes if you please. And now I have said all, we part; henceforth we are strangers.

LEVISON: As you please; good-bye. Will you not give me your hand?

           (ISABEL *stands with her back towards him*)

ISABEL: I would prefer not.

LEVISON: Very well. An encumbrance well got rid of, and by her own wish, so my conscience is clear on that score.　　　　　　　　[*Exit*]

ISABEL: What am I now – an outcast, whom men pity, and from whom all good women will shrink. I have abandoned my husband, children, my home, cast away my good name, wrecked my happiness for evermore, and deliberately offended heaven, for him – for *him* – oh! my punishment is hard to bear – but I have deserved it, all my future life spent in repentant expiation can never atone for the past, never, never.

Enter SUSANNE

SUSANNE: An English nobleman to see my lady.

ISABEL: Who can wish to see me, it cannot be my hus— Mr Carlyle.

SUSANNE: Not a young gentleman – he is 50 if an hour – and his hair a fine grey.

Enter LORD MOUNT SEVERN

[*Exit* SUSANNE]

MOUNT SEVERN: Isabel, I have sought you, that I might afford you aid in your time of trouble. (ISABEL *covers her face with her hands*)

ISABEL: How did you find me?

MOUNT SEVERN: I sought Levison when he was in London, and demanded what he had done with *you*, as I heard he was going to marry Blanche Challoner.

ISABEL: (*aside*) Poor Blanche, poor Blanche.

MOUNT SEVERN: (*with intense feelings*) Had this occurred in my young days, when gentlemen wiped out dishonour in blood, he would have had a bullet in his black heart ere now. (*Vehemently*) The coward! the heartless villain! may all good men shun him from henceforth, and may every *pure* woman look on him with scorn and loathing – oh! Isabel my poor girl, what demon tempted you to sacrifice yourself to that bad, heartless man.

ISABEL: He *is* heartless.

MOUNT SEVERN: I warned you at the commencement of your married life, not to admit him to your home.

ISABEL: His coming to East Lynne was not my doing – Mr Carlyle invited him.

MOUNT SEVERN: Invited him in unsuspecting confidence, believing his wife to be a true woman, to whom honour was dear as life, a woman whom he trusted, as he loved.

ISABEL: I believed that his love was no longer mine, that he had deserted me for another.

MOUNT SEVERN: Deserted you, why he was never from—

ISABEL: There is desertion of the heart.

MOUNT SEVERN: Tut, tut! I read the note you left, and I put the question to him as between man and man, whether he had ever given you cause to write such words, and he answered me (as with heaven about us) that he had always been faithful to you in thought and deed; but that is beside the question now, and foreign to the purpose of my visit here. Your father is gone and there is no one to stand in his place but *me*. (*In a kind tone*)

ISABEL: My father! oh, my father! (*Weeping*)

MOUNT SEVERN: You have no means of your own, no fortune, how will you live?

ISABEL: I have some money yet.

MOUNT SEVERN: That man's money? (*Sharply*)

ISABEL: No; I have sold my trinkets, and I shall try to earn my living by teaching.

MOUNT SEVERN: You earn! Tut, tut, my dear child; as much as you need I will supply.

ISABEL: No, no! I do not deserve such kindness, I have forfeited all claim to assistance.

MOUNT SEVERN: Not to *mine*; I am acting as for your dead father. Do you suppose that he would have abandoned you to work or starve. I never willfully neglect a duty, and I look upon it as an imperative duty to settle on you an income sufficient for a modest competency, and these notes will, I hope, meet your present demands Isabel. (*Tenderly*)

ISABEL: No, no; you are too good to me, I do not deserve this kindness.

MOUNT SEVERN: I am resolved not to leave you to the mercy of the harsh world without some protection against its trials and temptations. Adieu for the present, I shall see you again before I return to England, and we will talk of your future. (*Going to door*)

ISABEL: My future? ah! what do they say of me at East Lynne?

MOUNT SEVERN: Your name is never mentioned there; you are thought of as one, who was once dearly loved, but now dead, no stop. To your husband and your children: you are mourned with gentle pity, but the name of Isabel is never heard in that deserted home, the happiness of which you have for ever blighted. Adieu.

(*Moved by her look of despairing anguish he kisses her on the brow and exits slowly*)

ISABEL: My name is never mentioned, I am mourned as one dead. Oh, would that I had died when I might have heard kind loving voices as my spirit passed away from earth to heaven! My husband, my children! – Oh, never again to hear *him* say 'Isabel, my wife!' Never again to hear *their* infant tongues murmur the holy name of *'mother!'* Lost, degraded, friendless, abandoned, and alone! Alone

– utterly alone – for evermore!
    (*Sinks on her knees despairingly as the curtain falls*)

Act III

SCENE i

LORD MOUNT SEVERN *and* CORNELIA *discovered*

CORNELIA: No! I reside now in my house at West Lynne; when my brother was such a simpleton as to get married again, he was good enough to say that two mistresses in one house would not answer; so, after being like a mother to him ever since he was a boy, I have to turn out – ugh! what did he want to get married for? I never did! Why couldn't he remain single as I have done?

MOUNT SEVERN: Well, ma'am, why should he? Marriage is a happy state – happy, honourable, and—

CORNELIA: (*bitterly*) Very happy, very honourable; his first marriage brought him all that; did it not? – oh, I beg your pardon, I forgot you were a relative of – of – by-the-bye, was it positively ascertained as a fact, that Lady Isabel did die after that dreadful railway accident at Canmeres, in France?

MOUNT SEVERN: She certainly did die, poor child! Did not Carlyle tell you of the letter she wrote to me on her death-bed?

CORNELIA: No! I never heard of any letter; may I ask the nature of it?

MOUNT SEVERN: The letter was to the effect that she was dying from injuries she had received; she said that she was glad to die, and so deliver all who had ever loved her from the shame she had brought on them. I cannot remember the exact words now, but I recollect the last few lines, for they were written in characters such as might be scrawled by some poor sufferer who had signed a confession, forced by the tortures of the rack; they were: 'Go to Mr Carlyle, say that I humbly beg him to forgive me; tell him that I repent, bitterly repent; (I have no words to express how bitterly) the wrong I have done him; I can write no more, my bodily pain is so great, but no greater than my mental agony and remorse – farewell – forgive – Isabel—'

CORNELIA: Poor, erring creature; heaven be merciful to her! (*Rises*)

MOUNT SEVERN: When I received that letter I made every possible inquiry as to its truth in all the details, and was told at Canmeres that she died the night following the day of the – the accident; but why do you ask; have you any doubts?

CORNELIA: A thought came over me today as to whether she really *was* dead!

MOUNT SEVERN: Alas, poor child, she has gone, beyond all doubt.

Enter BARBARA, LORD MOUNT SEVERN *goes to her*

BARBARA: What can detain Archibald so long? (*Rings*)

CORNELIA: (*aside*) Ugh, I've no patience with him, letting that Barbara Hare catch him at last, after angling for him so long. I'd have gone into the church and have forbidden the banns if it would have been any use!

JOYCE *enters, goes to* BARBARA

MOUNT SEVERN: (*looking off*) Your new governess, Madame Vine, seems very fond of the children, especially that delicate little fellow, Willie.

BARBARA: (JOYCE *going*). Yes, she is all we could wish. Our friend, Mrs Latimer, met her in Germany, and recommended her to us.

[*Exeunt by window talking*]

CORNELIA: Joyce, of whom does the governess remind you! (*As* JOYCE *is going*)

JOYCE: The governess? Do you mean Madame Vine?

CORNELIA: Do I mean *you* or *myself*? Are *we* governesses? Have you seen her without her glasses?

JOYCE: No, ma'am, never!

CORNELIA: Well, I have, today, and was astounded by the wonderful likeness, one would have thought it was the ghost of – of Lady Isabel!

JOYCE: Oh, ma'am, pray don't joke on such a subject please!

CORNELIA: Joyce! did you ever know *me* guilty of *joking*?

JOYCE: N – no ma'am.

CORNELIA: No, and I hope you never will!   [*Exit*]

JOYCE: (*aside*) Ah, there are times when, in voice and manner, she puts *me* in mind of poor dear Lady Isabel!

Enter BARBARA *and* MADAME VINE, *with* WILLIE

BARBARA: I must protest, Madame Vine, against your thus fatiguing yourself, you are not strong. It is very, *very* kind of you, but – Come, William, Joyce will take you to your room with Archie.

MADAME VINE: I will take him, if you please. He is not well, and I – I— (*Clinging to* WILLIE)

BARBARA: No, no, madame. You have quite enough trouble with them in school hours. If you will not think for yourself we must think for you.

Enter CARLYLE *and* HARE *and* LORD MOUNT SEVERN
from front garden, the latter two talk on verandah, while
CARLYLE *greets* BARBARA

WILLIE: Ah! here's papa. (*Runs to* CARLYLE)

CARLYLE: Well, my darling, I was detained by a deputation. (*To* BARBARA)

MADAME VINE: Oh! to witness his loving tenderness for *her*! It is part of the cross I have undertaken to bear, and I *must* endure the penance.

JOYCE: (*half aside*) Ah! poor little Willie, he's going to his grave fast.

MADAME VINE: Oh! Joyce, Joyce, don't say that.

JOYCE: Why, ma'am, I wonder *you* can't see it. Ah! it's plain that he has got *no mother*, poor boy, or there would have been an outcry over him long ago. Of course, Mrs Carlyle can't be expected to have the feelings of one for him – (MADAME VINE *talks to* JOYCE)

WILLIE: Papa, I want to ask you something. (*Dragging* CARLYLE)

CARLYLE: Well, my dear, what is it?

WILLIE: Why should Madame Vine cry so often?

CARLYLE: Cry, my boy, does she?

WILLIE: Oh, yes, papa, often, she wipes her eyes under her spectacles, and thinks I don't see her. I know I'm very ill, but why should *she* cry for that?

BARBARA: Nonsense, William, who told you that, you are ill?

WILLIE: I heard the doctor tell Madame Vine and papa so; now why should she cry about that? If Lucy or Joyce cried there'd be some reason, for they have known me all my life.

BARBARA: There, there, Joyce, take him away, and don't let him worry Madame Vine.   [JOYCE *takes* WILLIE *off*]

CARLYLE: (*to* ISABEL) You seem naturally fond of children, Madame, and I am very grateful to you for your great kindness to mine. (*He holds out his hand. She puts her shaking hand in his*)

MADAME VINE: I am but discharging a duty, and we cannot help loving those, whom we— (*Attracted by her voice, he looks at her earnestly. She avoids his gaze*)

CARLYLE: The tones of her voice remind me of – ah! (*Sighs heavily*)

MADAME VINE: (*aside*) Oh, how the pressure of that hand thrilled me to my heart—

CARLYLE: Barbara, my love, your papa, Mr Herbert, and the rest of the squirearchy[15] have been worrying me to be put in nomination for our borough member.[16]

HARE: Yes, and you must stand, who else is there fit to send to parliament, there's *Pinner*, would he do? his head's full of mangold wurzel[17] patent manure, and all such rubbish.

CARLYLE: Complimentary to Squire Pinner.

HARE: Well, who else is there?

CARLYLE: Colonel Bethell.

                    [*Exit* BARBARA *and* MADAME *conversing*]

HARE: Oh, he's got no money to throw away on the free and incorruptible electors of Lynne.

CARLYLE: Pobjoy, or Swindon.

HARE: Pretty fellows they'd be to send to parliament, one's always drunk and the other is never sober.

CARLYLE: Well there's Richard Hare, Esq., J.P.[18]

HARE: Me! no, no, thank you, I should want my own way too much for my constituents, and I should lose my temper listening to the damned nonsense which crotchetty members inflict on the house, to the interruption of important business.

MOUNT SEVERN: No, no, the only fit and proper person as member of parliament for East Lynne is Archibald Carlyle.

                         Enter CORNELIA

CORNELIA: Archibald Carlyle in parliament! what next?

MOUNT SEVERN: In the House of Peers, I hope

HARE: We're going to nominate him.

CORNELIA: You'd better nominate him for admission to the county lunatic asylum. The idea of his entering that idle do-nothing House of Commons, have you thought of the cost pray?

CARLYLE: Oh, that's a mere nothing, the expense is not worth naming, if there is no opposition.

CORNELIA: Not worth naming! oh, that ever I should live to hear money talked of as not worth naming, and your business going to rack and ruin while you are kicking up your heels in that wicked Babylon, London, night after night; where's my bonnet and umbrella? (*Going*) Let me get out of this; parliament indeed.

CARLYLE: You are not going Cornelia? Do – nay, you *must* stay to dinner. (*Piano overheard*)

CORNELIA: Ugh! this is dinner enough for one day. My brother, a chattering, humbugging, stuck-up parliament man.   [*Exit*]

              (LORD MOUNT SEVERN: *listening to piano*)

MOUNT SEVERN: How charmingly that Madame Vine plays.

CARLYLE: Yes she does. Come in, and Barbara shall sing for us. Come Justice, I know you'll be—

HARE: Not I, I'm thankful to say I've no ear for music, and all that rubbish. Barb used to drive me nearly mad with her howling when she was at home. I'll leave you and my lord to the enjoyment of it while I go and commence to canvass the electors.

[*Exit* HARE, CARLYLE *and* LORD MOUNT SEVERN]
(BARBARA *sings one verse of song, and during the symphony
that follows,* MADAME VINE *enters*)

MADAME VINE: I cannot stay by them to be reminded of the happiness
that I have lost. (*Piano and laughter overheard*) Laugh on, Barbara
Hare, laugh on; you've won him, I have sealed the forfeit of his
esteem and love by my own mad act. (*The little boy* ARCHIE *runs in,*
MADAME VINE *catches him in her arms and sits in a low chair, or on
a stool, and caresses him fondly*) You will learn to love me I hope. I
am very fond of – (WILSON *enters*) Ah! (*Confused*) You are
surprised no doubt to see me so overcome. But I once had a dear boy
so like him – oh! so like him! and this dear child made me think of
my – my irreparable loss.

WILSON: You naughty young monkey, how dare you run away in this
manner?

MADAME VINE Oh, pray do not scold him.

WILSON: Oh, ma'am, you've no idea what he is; he's getting too
audacious and rumbustical[19] for the nursery. Come here sir, I'll
speak to your mamma about you. (*Shakes boy away from* MADAME
VINE)

MADAME VINE: Oh! do not beat him, I cannot bear to see him beaten.

WILSON: Beaten! If he did get a good sound one it's no more than he
deserves. You come along, sir, do. (*Jerks him out of the room.*
MADAME VINE *with difficulty restraining her emotion*)

MADAME VINE: My own child! and I dare not say to a servant, you
shall not beat him.

(BARBARA *sings one verse of* 'You'll remember me'[20]
during the foregoing, so that the last three lines are heard after
MADAME VINE *has said* 'You shall not beat him')

BARBARA 'Some recollection be
        Of days that have as happy been.
        Then you'll remember me.'

MADAME VINE: Does he remember me? Does he give one thought to
me as those words fall on his ear? Does he think of the time when I
sat *there* and sang them to him? Oh, to love him as I do now, to
yearn for his affection with such jealous, passionate longing, and to
know that we are separated for ever and for ever! To see that I am
nothing – worse than nothing – to him now!

(*During this speech* BARBARA *has sung the second verse,
and the final symphony is played as the scene closes in on*
ISABEL, *leaning by door*)

SCENE ii

Garden

Enter HARE *and* LORD MOUNT SEVERN *and* DILL

HARE: Carlyle must know of this at once, *at once*. The – the beast must be mad to dare – to *da-are* – to – to come down here to oppose the man he has injured – (*Very excitedly*)

MOUNT SEVERN: I heard the rumour in town, and I hurried down here to find if it were true.

HARE: Oh, it's true enough. I saw the men placarding the walls with bills, '*Vote for Levison,*' as I'm a living sinner. I was so enraged that I was a great mind to knock the dirty wretches down with their own paste cans. It's scandalous! Phew!

Enter CARLYLE

CARLYLE: What's scandalous? What has put you in such a heat, Justice?

HARE: Heat, I don't believe I shall ever be cool again. There's an opposition – another man in the field!

CARLYLE: Very well, the more the merrier!

DILL: You don't know who it is.

HARE: I'll buy up every egg in the place and have him pelted till—

CARLYLE: Really gentlemen, this violence toward a candidate who has a right to oppose me if—

HARE: A right! do you know who the blackguard[21] is – (*Aside to* MOUNT SEVERN) you tell him, you're a relation.

MOUNT SEVERN: (*aside to* HARE) No really, Mr Hare, I hardly like to soil my lips with his name – you tell him.

CARLYLE: Well, and who is the opponent?

Enter CORNELIA *with bonnet and umbrella*

CORNELIA: Sir Francis Levison indeed! the sneaking, crawling, worm. Archibald, when I left you half an hour ago I was averse to your going into parliament, now I insist on your going on with the election; you'll be no brother of mine if you abandon the field to that sneaking reptile, Levison.

CARLYLE: Has he dared?

DILL: He has done this on purpose to insult Mr Carlyle.

HARE: Aye, and to insult you, me, *all* of us – oh! he shall have a bath in the horse pond.

MOUNT SEVERN: The hound ought to be gibbetted.

CORNELIA: And I'd turn him off with pleasure. I'll canvass for you brother. I'll spend £1000 on ale for electors.

DILL: Take care Miss Cornelia, you may cause him to be unseated for bribery and corruption, you'd better keep your money.

HARE: Leave it to me, I know how to work an election, patriotic speeches and promises, beer for the blackguards, blankets for the old women. Tell 'em they shall have no taxes, no laws, no masters, no work, no – no – anything.

MOUNT SEVERN: Do nothing every day in the week.

DILL: And have double wages for that!

MOUNT SEVERN: All be masters and nobody servants.

HARE: Yes, down with everybody and up with somebody else.

CORNELIA: Down with Levison and up with Carlyle.

HARE: Some of the free and independent electors are my tenants, I'll put the screw on, and bring them all to the poll in a body.

DILL: You forget, *that* will be intimidation.

HARE: I'll go and promise all my men 5 shillings a head to put that hound Levison in the horse pond.

CORNELIA: And I'll give them another 5 shillings a head to keep him there.   [*Exeunt* DILL, CORNELIA, *and* HARE]

(CARLYLE *stands, absorbed and heedless of their conversation.*
    LORD MOUNT SEVERN *goes to him, takes his hand kindly*)

MOUNT SEVERN: Carlyle, you will not be driven from the field by – by – him; You'll face him – and—

CARLYLE: Face him! yes, yes—

MOUNT SEVERN: That's right, I'll bring all my influence to bear – ugh! the treacherous scoundrel, if duelling had been legal I would have shot him like a dog!   [*Exit*]

CARLYLE: Levison here! Oh, how the bitter memory of my irreparable wrong makes heart and brain burn with a mad, wicked desire for vengeance on the head of that man, who brought shame and death on her whom I loved. And you O Isabel, when I think of your untimely fate, I feel that his life would be a just sacrifice to your dear shade, but I dare not break a holier law than any made by man. I dare not disobey the voice of the Omnipotent, who hath said, 'Vengeance is mine alone, I will repay.' To his eternal Justice I leave the punishment of the wretched man, who dishonoured my name, and betrayed my poor lost Isabel.   [*Exit*]

SCENE iii

Bed-chamber, moonlight streaming through window on to bed

WILLIE *on bed*, JOYCE *by side*

WILLIE: Joyce, where is papa?

JOYCE: He will soon be here; he has gone out with grandpapa Hare.
(MADAME VINE *at door*)

MADAME VINE: Is – is – he worse, Joyce?

JOYCE: I'm afraid he is, and will not last long. Ah! well, he'll be better off, poor child.

MADAME VINE: Yes – yes; though it is a sore trial to see those we love fading away; there are worse – more bitter partings on earth than death. I think he is dropping off to sleep again, poor dear. You need not wait, Joyce, I will stay with him, and ring if he requires anything.

JOYCE: Very well, Madam. [*Exit*]

MADAME VINE: And have I come back but to see him die? – my own bright, beautiful Willie!

WILLIE: Are you there, Joyce?

MADAME VINE: No, my darling; but one who loves you more than Joyce, or any one can love you!

WILLIE: It will not be very long to wait, will it, Madame Vine?

MADAME VINE: Wait for what, my own darling?

WILLIE: Before they all come – papa, and Lucy, and Archie, and we all meet, where papa says there is no more pain.

MADAME VINE: Not long, my darling; oh, not long!

WILLIE: Do you think we shall know everybody there, or only our own relations?

MADAME VINE: My child, we cannot tell that, we must trust to our Father in heaven, who knows what is best for us.

WILLIE: Do you think my mama will be there? I mean my own, my very own mama; she who is gone away.

MADAME VINE: I hope so – if – if she is forgiven!

WILLIE: And shall I know her, I have quite forgotten what she was like; shall I know her?

MADAME VINE: I hope so, I do hope so; but there – there, my darling, do not talk any more now, try and sleep. (*Pause*)

WILLIE: Where are you, Madame Vine?

MADAME VINE: Here, my sweet boy – here!

WILLIE: I cannot see you, I can only see a bright shining light like the sun on the waters, and beyond that, oh! such a beautiful garden full of flowers, and I seem to hear music and sweet singing, as I've heard papa say the angels in heaven sing. (*Pause*) Are you there now, Madame Vine?

MADAME VINE: Yes darling?

WILLIE: I cannot see you or hear your voice. I cannot hear the singing of those voices in the shining garden. There! – there! (*Points up and falls back, pause*)

MADAME VINE: Ah! the sweet young face is calm as – as – if – in death. His little heart has ceased to beat for ev—. Oh! no! not for ever! Speak to me, Willie! (*Throws off her disguise*) This cannot be death so soon; speak to me, your broken-hearted mother. Oh! Willie! my own darling! my own – my—

JOYCE *enters*

JOYCE: Oh, Madame Vine, what is this? (*She starts up and faces* JOYCE)

MADAME VINE: Oh! My child is dead! (JOYCE *starts back in amazement*)

JOYCE: My dear Lady Isabel! Not! – not dead?

ISABEL: No, Oh, would that I were dead. I recovered by a miracle, and returned, the shattered wreck you see me here prematurely aged, crippled, broken-hearted. Oh, that I had died and had been spared this agony. Oh! my boy! – my boy! (*Sobbing on body of child*)

JOYCE: Do – do come away lady! Mr Carlyle is coming with his wife, for the love of heaven come away! If they find you here, thus—

ISABEL: I care not now, oh, my Willie!

JOYCE: Oh, my dear lady, you ought not to have come here.

ISABEL: (*lifting up her haggard face*) I could not stay longer away from my children. Think you it has been no punishment to me being here, to see *him, my* husband, once, the – the – husband of another, it was killing me; and now to see my boy close his eyes for ever on this world and me.

JOYCE: Oh, come, my dear lady, I hear their voices. They will be here in a moment, and you will be discovered – (*Trying to drag her away*)

ISABEL: (*breaks from* JOYCE) Let them come! I care not for my life's sands will soon be run. Oh, Willie, my child dead, dead, dead! and he never knew me, never called me mother! (*Falls sobbing across the body as* CARLYLE *and* BARBARA *enter*)

(*Curtain*)

Act IV

SCENE i

A lane or street in the suburbs of East Lynne

CORNELIA: (*meeting* DILL) What's the news Mr Dill? And is it really true that young Dick is in town here, disguised as a sailor? Joyce tells me his disappearance is made clear.

DILL: We hope that it will soon be made remarkably clear, now the mysterious Thorne is found (here at West Lynne) in the person of the villain Levison.

CORNELIA: What! that wretch. And to think that he should have the barefaced assurance to come to Lynne, after the reception he met with on his previous visit.

DILL: Well, yes, one would think that the ducking in a stinking pond to which he was treated on that occasion would have cooled his courage.

CORNELIA: His what?

DILL: Well, his impudence.

CORNELIA: How could he think of being elected for the very place where his name is execrated, and his presence provokes the just indignation of the whole town.

DILL: Well, he is a government nominee, and that party has great influence down here you know.

CORNELIA: But surely the government would not allow such a villain as Levison to sit in Parliament.

DILL: I don't know; they care very little about the moral character of a man whose vote, and influence, may help to keep the party in office.

CORNELIA: And that brazenfaced young baggage, Afy Hallijohn, has come flaunting about here again, the young Jezebel!

DILL: Ah, yes; and from Richard's information I was forced to subpoena her to give evidence before the magistrates, and by a severe cross examination, elicited *from her* the important admission that Levison (under the *alias* of *Thorne*) *was in the cottage* the very night her father was shot.

CORNELIA: Oh, the young wretch! Why couldn't she say so before? Why, as I live, here comes Richard – What does he mean by parading himself in this imprudent way, with a – a warrant for his arrest still out?

DILL: He can now walk about in the broad light of day, for the proofs of his innocence are so overwhelming, that he can enter a court of justice without fear.

CORNELIA: Who is that fellow with him, that looks like a polar bear?

DILL: Otway Bethell, who has returned to England only within the last few days; on his evidence the magistrates have issued a warrant for the arrest of Sir Francis Levison, *alias* Thorne.

CORNELIA: *Jubilate!* Then there is some hope of the villain being hanged at last.

DILL: Well, it will go very hard with him; he will, at any rate suffer a lengthened term of imprisonment.

CORNELIA: Imprisonment! bah! hang him at once.   [*Exit with* DILL]

(*Groans outside* 'Duck him', 'Down with him', etc. 'Put him in the horsepond', etc. LEVISON *hurries on alarmed*)

LEVISON: They mean mischief, I must hasten back to London, *there* I shall be safe from their threatened vengeance. (*Met by* RICHARD HARE, *dressed as a sailor*)

RICHARD: But not from mine. Now villain I can meet you face to face, without fear, you have more than once escaped me, when I was powerless to *prove* your villainy, but *now* you escape me not. (*Seizes* LEVISON)

LEVISON: Madman! Take your hands from me, or I will denounce you to the offices of justice.

Enter DILL *and* OFFICERS[22]

RICHARD: They are here to take charge of you. Officers, do your duty.

LEVISON: Stand off fellows, dare you lay hands on me.

DILL: Come, come, resistance is useless, here is the necessary warrant for your arrest.

LEVISON: My arrest! for what?

DILL: For the murder of George Hallijohn in Lynne Wood. Your quondam mistress,[23] Afy, has confessed that you were there, and Mr Otway Bethell has deposed that he saw you come from the cottage just after the fatal shot was fired.

LEVISON: Bethell! He is in Norway – has been there – or somewhere abroad, for years.

DILL: He has returned to give evidence against you.

Enter BETHELL, *wearing a fur coat*

BETHELL: Yes, and I would have returned years ago, had I known another was suffering for your crime.

LEVISON: Ha, betrayed! and by *you*, whom I—

DILL: Had bribed! Don't have any hesitation to say the word; we know all.

BETHELL: With the money you paid me for my silence I left England the day after the murder, little thinking that an innocent man might be accused of the crime which you had committed; but hearing that poor Dick Hare has been allowed by you to lie under this terrible accusation, I hastened to make a tardy reparation by telling all I knew.

LEVISON: Scoundrel!

BETHELL: I should have been had I not spoken the truth, and so put justice on the track of one who is a scoundrel and a coward.

(LEVISON *appears terrified by his position*)

LEVISON: (*aside*) What devil prompted me to come down here to provoke my Nemesis – my destruction. (*Assumes an air of bravado, and turns to* RICHARD) Richard Hare, you are premature in your triumph; we have yet to see whether the liberty and life of an English baronet are to be endangered by the assertions of an outlawed bankrupt, like your friend, Mr Otway Bethell. [*Exit with officers*]

(AFY HALLIJOHN *enters, speaks to* RICHARD)

AFY: Ah, good day, Mr Richard; why surely you're not going to pass an old friend in that way.

RICHARD: I have so many friends I can scarcely find time for them all individually.

AFY: But you might for *me*. Have you forgotten old days?

RICHARD: I am not likely to forget them.

AFY: I feel sure you had not. My heart told me you—

RICHARD: Your *what*, Miss Hallijohn?

AFY: My heart; when you went away on that dreadful night, I thought I should have died.

RICHARD: It was not your fault that *I* didn't.

[DILL *and* BETHELL *exit*]

AFY: Oh, and now to meet you again! Oh! (*Gushing*)

RICHARD: Don't be a fool, Afy. I was young and foolish; but I am older and wiser now. How's Mr Jiffin?

AFY: Mr Jiffin! Oh, is it possible you think I could ever bemean[24] myself to a man who sells cheese and cuts up bacon. That's Lynne all over; nothing but scandal and invention from week's end to week's end. But to think that *you* should believe—

RICHARD: I was thinking how lucky you were to get a man so well off, and so respectable.

AFY: Would you – could you bear to see me stoop to Jiffin?

RICHARD: Could I? Certainly. Why not? I don't know what ridiculous notions you may have in your head, but the sooner you get rid of them the better. I was foolish once, but you cured me of my folly very effectually. Henceforth we are strangers.

AFY: Oh, can you speak such words to me? (*Sobs hysterically*)

RICHARD: It *won't do*, Afy, it *won't* do.

AFY: Oh, oh, o-oh! and is this my reward after waiting for you all these years, pining and breaking my heart for you. I'm so ill, I – I shall faint; I know I shall faint. Oh! (*Swoons*)

RICHARD: I'm sorry I can't stay to catch you. Had you not better faint nearer Mr Jiffin's shop door? he will be enchanted to bear so lovely a burden in his arms. Good day.

JUSTICE HARE *and* DILL *enter*, HARE *greets* DICK *warmly*

AFY: (*recovers immediately*) Oh, the brute! the unfeeling beast! I'll go and be overcome by the heat near Jiffin's door. I'll marry the old wretch out of spite, yes, that I will; he's as soft as one of his own cheeses, and will jump at the chance. He's an old fool, but he'll do for a husband.   [*Exit*]

HARE: Oh, Dick, my dear boy, can you forgive me for my unnatural cruelty towards you?

RICHARD: Freely, dear dad, freely. We will forget the miserable past in our newly-found happiness.

HARE: But I can never forgive myself. I – I might have hunted my own son to death.

DILL: (*advances*) I am loth to disturb a family greeting, but remember, Justice, there is a meeting of the magistrates at—

HARE: They must meet without me for the future. A man who undertakes the administration of justice should have more wisdom than I have, and less conceited obstinacy. I've been an old fool, Dill, I *have*, so don't contradict me, Dill.

DILL: I was not going to contradict you in *that* admission.

HARE: Come, my boy, come to the home from which you have too long been banished – unjustly banished, and where a fond mother is longing to embrace you. Ah, Dill, you'll find Old Dick Hare a changed man now, I'm so happy, so thankful, and so humble.

DILL: That will be a change, indeed, ha, ha.   [*Exit*]

SCENE ii

Bedroom, pale orange sunlight through window, casting a warm hue on Isabel's face as she reclines in large chair by bed. JOYCE *and* CORNELIA *discovered by* LADY ISABEL

ISABEL: Only for a minute I have prayed Joyce to bring him to me, and she will not, only for one little fleeting minute, to *hear him* say, 'I forgive you.'

CORNELIA: Go, Joyce, request your master to come to me.

JOYCE: Oh, ma'am! will it be well for him to see her?

CORNELIA: (*putting* JOYCE *to door*) Tell him I wish to see him.

[*Exit* JOYCE]

My poor child, had I any part in sending you away from your home?

ISABEL: Oh, no, no! I was not very happy with you; but that was not the cause of – of – Oh! forgive me, Miss Carlyle.

CORNELIA: Forgive me my poor girl. I might have made your home happier, and I wish – oh how I wish I had.

CARLYLE *enters with* JOYCE

CARLYLE: Is Madame Vine worse?

CORNELIA: She wishes to see you alone.

JOYCE: (*to* CORNELIA) Oh, ma'am! won't you tell him.

(CORNELIA *gently puts* JOYCE *off and exits. They shut him in alone with her; he walks gently to the bed*)

CARLYLE: I am grieved Madame Vine that you—

ISABEL: Archibald! oh, do not leave me; do not turn from me! (*She puts out her trembling hand*)

CARLYLE: Isabel! were – were – you – Madame Vine!

ISABEL: I did not die, I recovered as by a miracle; though when I wrote that letter, I was given up as past all hope of recovery. I was so changed, nobody knew me, and I came here as Madame Vine to see my children and you – I could not stay away, I could not die without your forgiveness – oh! do not turn from me – bear with me a little, only a *little* while!

CARLYLE: Oh, Isabel! why, oh why did you leave me?

ISABEL: I thought you were false to me; that your love was given to another, and in my mad jealousy I listened to the tempter who whispered to me of revenge!

CARLYLE: My poor, darling, how could you have been so deceived, knowing me as you should have known me; loving you so tenderly as I did. There was not a thought wherein falsehood to you ever

found a place. Oh! how could you deem me false to *you*, who were
my world?

ISABEL: I was mad! I must have been. I have not known one moment's
peace since I became a guilty creature, in the sin that wrecked me –
see, Archibald! see what it has done for me! (*Tossing up her grey
hair and holding out her attenuated wrists*[25]) My sin was great, but
my punishment has been still greater. Think what torture it has been
– what it has been for me to bear, living in the same house with –
with – your wife; seeing your love for her – love that once was *mine*.
Oh, think what agony to watch dear Willie, and see him fading day
by day, and not be able to say 'he is my child as well as yours!'

CARLYLE: Why did you come back to endure—

ISABEL: I could not live away from you and my children; the longing
for them was killing me. I never thought to stay here to die; but
death is coming on me now, as with a leap – and my life is ebbing
fast – (*The orange sunlight gradually fades out of the room, leaving
her face deathly white, when the warm hue of lime-light is off*) Oh!
say, in mercy, say that you forgive me, that you forget and forgive.

CARLYLE: I have already *forgiven*; but you were too dear for me ever,
to forget how happy I was in your love. I cannot forget the blow that
crushed me, and well-nigh killed me, then.

ISABEL: Try and forget the dreadful time; let your thoughts go back
only to those days when you first knew me – here – a happy innocent
girl, with my dear father. Ah, how gentle you were with me when *he*
died! Oh, that the past could be blotted out, that I might die with a
pure conscience, as I *might* have died then!

CARLYLE: For your sake, as for mine, *I* wish the dark past could be
blotted out.

ISABEL: Let what I *am* be erased from your memory, think of me (if
you can) as the innocent, trusting girl whom you made your wife.
Say one word of love to me before I pass away! Oh, Archibald, my
heart is breaking for one last word of love.

CARLYLE: As mine was when you left me!

ISABEL: You forgive me?

CARLYLE: May God bless you, and so deal with me, as I forgive you,
Isabel, dear Isabel, my first, *first* love, who once was as *light* and *life*
to me!

ISABEL: Be kind and loving to Lucy and little Archie. Do not let their
mother's sin be visited on them!

CARLYLE: Never, never! They are dear to me as you *once* were!

ISABEL: Aye, as I once was, and as I might – alas – I might have been,
even now. Ah, is this death? 'Tis hard to part! Farewell, dear

Archibald! my husband once, and loved now in death, as I never loved before! Farewell, until eternity! Think of me sometimes, keep one little corner in your heart for me – your poor – erring – lost Isabel! (*Dies*)

(*Slow curtain*)

NOTES

1 'Mrs Grundy': an imaginary personage who is proverbially referred to as a personification of the tyranny of social opinion in matters of conventional propriety. In Tom Morton's play *Speed the Plow* (1798) Dame Ashfield is represented as constantly fearing to give occasion to the sneers of her neighbour, Mrs Grundy. Her frequent question, 'What will Mrs Grundy say?' became proverbial as expressing the attitude of those who regard the dissapproval of society as the worst of evils.

2 Circé: enchantress, as in Greek mythology.

3 new fangled: different from the traditional thing, objectionably novel, here, faddish.

4 Trouville: a fashionable seaside resort in Normandy, the subject of some of Boudin's most popular paintings.

5 gallivanting: gadding about.

6 calcined: burned to ashes.

7 brazen hussy: bold and worthless strumpet.

8 *soi disant:* self-styled, pretended.

9 some strong October: some strong October-brewed beer.

10 parish beadle: parish officer appointed by vestry to keep order in church.

11 that cobs all: that beats all.

12 you gammon and palaver: you talk humbug.

13 farthing: quarter of a penny, the lowest valued coin, so she declines the least amount.

14 forbidden the banns: objected to the wedding.

15 squirearchy: the class of landed proprietors, especially those with

social or, here, political influence.

16 **our borough member:** that is, our Member of Parliament for a borough constituency.

17 **mangold wurzel:** a large kind of beet, generally used as cattle feed.

18 **J.P.:** Justice of the Peace, a lay magistrate.

19 **rumbustical:** rumbustious, boisterous

20 **'You'll remember me':** sentimental popular song.

21 **blackguard:** scoundrel.

22 **officers:** an author's note insists upon 'Officers in plain clothes, not comic policemen.'

23 **your quondam mistress:** your sometime mistress.

24 **bemean myself:** belittle or subordinate myself, sell myself short.

25 **attenuated wrists:** thin and emaciated wrists.

ALAN'S WIFE

a dramatic study, in three scenes
BY FLORENCE BELL AND ELIZABETH ROBINS
(1893)

DRAMATIS PERSONAE

Women

JEAN CREYKE	a young woman, married to and in love with Alan
MRS HOLROYD	her widowed mother
MRS RIDLEY	Jean's neighbour
FIRST WOMAN	
SECOND WOMAN	

Men

HUTTON	a workman
JAMIE WARREN	minister in the parish, formerly in love with Jean
COLONEL STUART	prison governor
ROBERTS	chief warder
FIRST WARDER	
SECOND WARDER	

Scenes

SCENE i:	outside a cottage in a village in the north of England
SCENE ii:	the interior of the cottage
SCENE iii:	a room in a prison

Scene i

A village street runs transversely from front to back. At right angles to it, starting from front corner the outside of a workman's cottage. Door leading to passage: a window on each side of it, through which glimpses can be obtained of cottage interior. The central portion of the stage, in the angle between the street and the cottage, represents the cottage garden, shut off from the street by a low fence with a gate in it. A bench runs along the cottage wall: by it a table, on which are piled up plates, knives, etc., ready for the table to be laid

MRS HOLROYD *discovered sitting on bench outside house to the right of door, knitting. People passing along the street. Two men pass with a little child between them, then a little girl, then a woman carrying a child*

WOMAN: (*as she passes to* MRS HOLROYD) A fine day!

MRS HOLROYD: (*nodding*) Ay, it's a fine day. (*The woman passes on*)

MRS RIDLEY: (*comes along with a basket on her arm – she stops*) Good morning, Mrs Holroyd!

MRS HOLROYD: Good morning to you, Mrs Ridley: it's a warm day!

MRS RIDLEY: And you look very comfortable there.

MRS HOLROYD: Yes, it's nice out here – sit you down and rest a bit; you'll be tired after your marketing.

MRS RIDLEY: (*sitting down by her on the seat*) Well, I don't say I won't be glad of a rest. It's fine to see you settled in your daughter's house for a bit, like this.

MRS HOLROYD: It's the only place I do feel settled in, now she's married. I just feel lost in my own house without her.

MRS RIDLEY: Ay, you will that. It's bad when lassies take up with their husbands and leave their mothers alone.

MRS HOLROYD: Ay, you may well say so! And Jean is all I have. I never had a lad of my own, or another lass either, and it's hard to be left when one is getting into years.

MRS RIDLEY: Still, you must be glad she has got a good husband, that can work hard and give her all she wants.

MRS HOLROYD: Ay, Alan Creyke's a fine fellow, no doubt, and they say he'll soon be foreman. But I did think my Jean would have looked higher. I always thought she would marry a schoolmaster, as I did, or even a minister – seeing all the book-learning she got from her poor father. She knows as much as any lady, I do believe.

MRS RIDLEY: Ay, it's wonderful what the books'll do. They say young Mr Warren, that's just come to the chapel here, has got more book-learning than the schoolmaster himself, and can talk about it so as no one can understand him. Eh, but it's fine to know as much as that!

MRS HOLROYD: (*with a sigh*) It is indeed! And, Mrs Ridley, as sure as you see me sitting here beside you, there was a time when that young man was after our Jean, and she might have been the mistress of yon pretty house near the chapel, instead of living in a cottage like this.

MRS RIDLEY: Dear, dear! To think of that! Ah well, it's no wonder you're put about at the way she chose.

MRS HOLROYD: I don't say that Alan isn't a good husband, mind you, and a good worker too – only I did hope to see my girl a bit grander than she is, as mothers will.

MRS RIDLEY: Ah well, young people will do their own way. You must just make up your mind to it, Mrs Holroyd. I fear the book-learning doesn't go for much with the lassies, where a fine fellow like Creyke is concerned – and after all, as to the cottage, it's a nice little place, and she keeps it beautiful!

MRS HOLROYD: She does that – and she wouldn't be her mother's daughter if she didn't. And the pleasure she takes in it, too! keeping it as bright and shining as if there were five or six pair of hands to do it! She and Alan are nobbut[1] two children about it, and their house is just like a new toy.

MRS RIDLEY: Well, that's right! let them be happy now, poor things; they'll leave it off soon enough.

MRS HOLROYD: Eh, yes, I doubt they will, like other folk.

MRS RIDLEY: Where is Jean? I should like to wish her good morning. Is she in?

MRS HOLROYD: Yes, she's in the kitchen, I believe. (*Calls*) Jean, Jean! What are you doing, honey? Here's a neighbour come to see you.

JEAN: (*from within room to the left*) I'll come directly. I'm getting Alan's dinner ready. I can't leave the saucepan.

MRS RIDLEY: (*smiling*) Ay, getting Alan's dinner ready! That's the way of it.

MRS HOLROYD: Yes, it's always Alan's dinner, or Alan's tea, or Alan's supper, or Alan's pipe. There isn't another man in the North gets waited on as he does.

MRS RIDLEY: Eh, but that's what he'll want to keep him in his home; they're bad to please, is the men, unless you spoil them. (*Bell begins to ring outside*) There's the midday bell from the works. Creyke'll soon be here now – I must be getting home too.

MRS HOLROYD: Eh, now, but Jean would have liked to shake hands with ye. (*Calls*) Jean! Jean! Be quick, child!

JEAN: (*from within*) Just ready, Mother – I'm lifting it off the fire.

MRS RIDLEY: (*looking along the street*) And in the nick of time too, for here are the men. (*Two or three men walk past*) Yes, hurry up, Jean, or your man will be here before his dinner's ready.

JEAN: (*from within*) No, no, he won't. (*Appears in doorway of cottage*) Here it is! (*Comes out carrying a large smoking dish in her hand, which she puts on the table*) There! How are you, Mrs Ridley? (*Shakes hands with her*)

MRS RIDLEY: Nicely, thank you. And are you going to get your dinner outside then?

JEAN: Yes, indeed; let's be in the air while we can – it's not often we have it as fine as this.

MRS HOLROYD: I never saw such a lass for fresh air! and Alan is just as bad.

MRS RIDLEY: Well, they'll take no harm with it, I daresay; fresh air is bad for nowt but cobwebs, as the saying is.

JEAN: (*laughs*) Ah, that's true enough! (*Arranging table*) Now then, if that isn't a dinner fit for a king!

MRS RIDLEY: And I'll be bound, if it is, you won't be thinking it too good for your husband.

JEAN: Too good! I should think not! Is anything too good for him? Is anything good enough?

MRS HOLROYD: (*smiling*) Ah, Jean, Jean!

JEAN: Well, Mother, you know quite well it's true! Isn't he the best husband a girl ever had? And the handsomest, and the strongest?

MRS HOLROYD: Ah, yes, he's all that, I daresay.

JEAN: (*vigorously wiping tumblers*) Well, what more do you want?

MRS HOLROYD: Ah, my dear, as I've often told you, I should like you to have looked higher.

JEAN: Looked higher! How could I have looked higher than Alan?

MRS HOLROYD: I wanted to see you marry a scholar.

JEAN: We can't all marry scholars, Mother dear – some of us prefer marrying men instead. (*Goes into house*)

MRS RIDLEY: The lass is right – there must be some of that sort that there may be some of all sorts, as the saying is; and, neighbour, you must just make the best of it, and be pleased with the man that's made her look so happy. (*Getting up*)

MRS HOLROYD: (*smiling*) Ay, she looks bright enough, in all conscience. (JEAN *comes back with cheese and butter on a dish*)

MRS RIDLEY: (*smiling at* JEAN) She does that, indeed! Well, you won't have to wait long for him now, honey. Here they come down the road, and I must get back to my two lads. Good day to you both.

> [*Exit through garden gate and up street, to the left, exchanging greetings with passing workmen*]

JEAN: (*cutting bread*) Scholar, indeed! Mother, how can you say such things before folks? I know what you mean when you say scholar – yon minister, poor little Jamie Warren.

MRS HOLROYD: Ah, Jean, how can you speak so! He's a man who is looked up to by everybody. Didn't he go to the big house last Christmastide, to dinner with the gentry, just like one of themselves?

JEAN: Well, that's right enough if it pleased him, but I shouldn't care to go among folk who thought themselves my betters. (*Look from* MRS HOLROYD) No, I shouldn't. I like Jamie, and have done ever since we were boy and girl together; but it's a far cry to think of taking him for my master! no, Mother, that's not my kind. (*Goes to tub under the window, wrings out tea cloths and hangs them on picket fence*)

MRS HOLROYD: Ah, Jean, what would your poor father have said! When you and Jamie used to play together on the village green and go to school together, and Jamie was minding his books and getting all the prizes, your father used to say, 'When that lad grows up, he'll be the husband for Jean – he's a good lad, he never gets into mischief; he's never without a book in his hand.'

JEAN: Ah, poor father! but what would *I* have done with a good boy who never got into mischief! (*Laughs*) No, I always knew it wasn't to be Jamie. Why, I remember as far back as when Jamie and I used to come from school, and I'd rush on before and go flying up on the moors, to find the stags-horn moss, with the heathery wind in my face, and hear the whirring summer sounds around us. I used to want to shout aloud, just for the pleasure of being alive – and Jamie, poor little creature, used to come toiling up after me, and call out, 'Not so fast, Jean, I'm out of breath, wait for me!' And *I* used to have to help *him* up!

MRS HOLROYD: Well, perhaps he couldn't run and jump as well as you, but he had read all about the flowers and plants in his book, and could tell you the names of every one of them.

JEAN: Ay, their names, perhaps; but he couldn't swing himself up to the steep places where they grew to pull them for me. He was afraid – afraid! while I, a girl, didn't know what it was like to be afraid. I don't know now.

MRS HOLROYD: Maybe – but he would have been a good husband for all that!

JEAN: Not for me. I want a husband who is brave and strong, a man who is my master as well as other folks'; who loves the hills and the heather, and loves to feel the strong wind blowing in his face and the blood rushing through his veins! Ah! to be happy – to be alive!

MRS HOLROYD: Oh, Jean, you always were a strange girl! (*Two men pass*)

JEAN: Ah, Mother, can't you see how fine it is to have life, and health, and strength! Jamie Warren, indeed! Think of the way he comes along, poor fellow, as though he were scared of coming into bits if he moved faster! And the way Alan comes striding and swinging down the street, with his head up, looking as if the world belonged to him! Ah! it's good to be as happy as I am!

MRS HOLROYD: Well, you silly fondy![2] In the meantime, I wonder what Alan is doing this morning? Yon fine dinner of his will be getting cold.

JEAN: Indeed it will. I wonder where he is! (*Men pass*) All the men seem to have passed. (*Stands just outside the door and looks down the street to the right, sheltering her eyes from the sun.* HUTTON, *a workman, passes, and stops to speak to her*)

HUTTON: Good morning, Mrs Creyke: a fine day again!

JEAN: It is indeed, Mr Hutton. What's got my husband this morning, do you know? Why is he so long after the rest?

HUTTON: He's stayed behind to see about something that's gone wrong with the machinery. It's the new saw, I believe – that's what happens when folks try to improve on the old ways. I don't believe in improvements myself, and in trying these new-fangled things no one can understand.

JEAN: No one? I'll be bound Alan understands them well enough.

HUTTON: Well, happen he does, more than most, and that's why the manager called him back to fettle it up[3] – but I doubt he won't be much longer now.

JEAN: Ah, well, that's all right, as long as I know what keeps him. Good morning. (HUTTON *moves on*) You see, Mother, how they turn to Alan before all the rest!

MRS HOLROYD: Ah, well, when a lass is in love she must needs know better than her mother, I suppose.

JEAN: Ah, Mother dear, wasn't there a time when you were a girl – when you knew better too?

MRS HOLROYD: (*shaking her head*) Eh, but that's a long time ago.

JEAN: But you remember it, I'll be bound! I think I'd best be setting that dish in the oven again; it will be getting cold.   [*Exit with dish*]

MRS HOLROYD: (*alone*) Well – (*Shakes her head with a little smile as she goes on knitting*) – there's nowt so queer as folk! (*Shakes her head again*)

JEAN: (*coming back*) I wonder what makes him bide so long?

MRS HOLROYD: You had far better give over tewing,[4] and sit quietly down with a bit of work in your hands till he comes.

JEAN: No, Mother, I can't! (*Smiling*) I'm too busy – watching for him! (*Leans over railing and looks along road to the right*)

MRS HOLROYD: That'll be Jamie coming along. (*Looking off to the left*)

JEAN: (*looking round*) So it is. (*Indifferently*) Well, Jamie, good morning.

> (WARREN, *a small delicate man, wearing a*
> *wide-awake hat and carrying a stick in his hand, comes along*
> *the road from the left*)

WARREN: Good morning, Jean. Well, Mrs Holroyd, how are you?

(JEAN *stands and leans against the railing to the right looking down the road and listening to what the others are saying*)

MRS HOLROYD: Good morning, my lad: sit down a bit. And what have you been doing the day? You look tired.

WARREN: (*takes off his hat wearily, passing his hand over his brow*) I've been doing my work – giving the Word to those who can hear it.

MRS HOLROYD: And you will have been edifying, that it will! And ye'll have done them good with it, for ye always were a beautiful speaker, Jamie!

JEAN: (*from the back*) Mother, I doubt you should call him Mr Warren now he's a minister.

MRS HOLROYD: Eh, not I! I mind him since he was a bit of a lad running barefoot about the village at home.

JEAN: And do you mind, Jamie, that when you had a book in your hand I'd snatch it from you and throw it over the hedge? (*Laughs*)

WARREN: Yes, you always pretended you didn't like books, Jean – but you used to learn quicker than anybody else when you chose.

MRS HOLROYD: And so she does still, I'm sure. She likes her book as well as any one, though she will have it that she doesn't. She'll sit and read to Alan, when he's smoking his pipe, for half an hour at a time.

WARREN: And what does he think of it?

MRS HOLROYD: (*smiling*) Between you and me, Jamie, I don't think he minds much for what she reads.

JEAN: (*hotly*) Indeed, but he does! Alan can understand what I read just as well as me.

MRS HOLROYD: Eh, lass, it isn't the strongest in the arm that's the best at the books!

WARREN: Yes, it's rather hard upon the rest of us poor fellows if a fellow like Creyke is to have everything – if we mayn't have a little more book-learning to make up for not being a Hercules, like him.

JEAN: Why, Jamie, you wouldn't care to be a Hercules, as you call it – you never did.

WARREN: That's what you say.

JEAN: (*lightly, still watching road to the right*) Well, I say what I think, as honest folk do! (*Sheltering her eyes with her hand*) Where can he be? His dinner will be burnt to a cinder directly.

MRS HOLROYD: I wish he'd come and be done with it. She can't mind for anything else but yon dinner while she's waiting for him.

WARREN: Well, well, that's how it should be, I daresay.

MRS HOLROYD: And have you got settled in your new house against the chapel?

WARREN: Pretty well, yes.

MRS HOLROYD: Ah, I doubt you find it hard. A man's a poor creature at siding up, and getting things straight.

WARREN: He is indeed!

MRS HOLROYD: (*sympathetically*) You'll be lonesome at times, my lad, isn't it so?

WARREN: (*shakes his head*) Indeed I am!

MRS HOLROYD: Come, you must get yourself a little wife, and she'll make it nice and homely for you.

WARREN: (*shakes his head*) No, I don't think I shall be taking a wife yet a bit, somehow. (*Gets up*) Well, I must be going. (*Looks at his watch*) I said I would look in at the school for a bit after dinner, and the children go in again at half-past one.

JEAN: Yes, I always see them bustling past – some of them so little that if they didn't take hold of each other's hands they'd be tumbling down! (*She laughs*)

WARREN: Yes, there are some very weeny ones in the infant school. Canny little bairns![5] Goodbye, Jean – goodbye, Mrs Creyke.

JEAN: Goodbye, Jamie!   [*Exit* WARREN *to the right*]

MRS HOLROYD: Eh, but he has a tender heart. I like a man that can speak about the little ones that way.

JEAN: So do I. Oh, Mother, I like to watch Alan with a child – the way he looks at it and the way he speaks to it! Do you know, with those strong arms of his he can hold a baby as well as you, Mother? He picked up a little mite that was sobbing on the road the other day, and carried it home, and before a minute was over the bairn had left off crying, and nestled itself to sleep on his shoulder.

MRS HOLROYD: Ah, yes, he'll make a good father some day!

JEAN: A good father and a happy one, too! Yes, we shall be happier then than we are now even. Oh, Mother, is that possible? – shall I be happier when I have my baby in my arms?

MRS HOLROYD: Ah, my child, yes, you will that, in truth. People talk of happiness and the things that bring it, and the young people talk about it and dream of it – but there's one happiness in the world that's better and bigger when it comes than one ever thinks for beforehand – and that is the moment when a woman's first child lies in her arms.

JEAN: Is it, is it really? Oh, Mother, to think that this is coming to me! I shall have that too, besides all the rest! Isn't it wonderful?

MRS HOLROYD: (*moved*) God keep you, honey!

JEAN: Yes, when I think of the moment when my child will lie in my arms, how he will look at me—

MRS HOLROYD: (*smiling*) He! It's going to be a boy then, is it?

JEAN: Of course it is! Like his father. He shall be called Alan, too, and he will be just like him. He will have the same honest blue eyes, that make you believe in them, and the same yellow hair and a straight nose, and a firm, sweet mouth. But that's what he'll be like when he grows up a little; at first he'll be nothing but a pink, soft, round, little baby, and we will sit before the fire – it will be the winter, you know, when he comes – and he'll lie across my knee, and stretch out his little pink feet to the blaze, and all the neighbours will come in and see his sturdy little limbs, and say, 'My word, what a fine boy!' He'll be just such another as his father. Oh, Mother, it's too good to be true!

MRS HOLROYD: No, no, honey, it isn't! It will all come true some day.

JEAN: Oh, Mother, Mother, what a good world it is! (*Kisses her*) Ah, I see some more people coming – he'll soon be here now! (*Goes in to right*)

MRS HOLROYD: (*looking along road*) Yes, there they come. (*Gets up, puts her knitting down, begins straightening table, then goes in as though to fetch something*)

    (*Gradual signs of commotion, two boys rush along stage, then return with two more, and go off. Two children rush past;*

*then two women enter at back and stand a little to the right
of cottage, shading their eyes.* MRS HOLROYD *comes out of
the door with a brown jug in her hand)*

MRS HOLROYD: What is it? Anything happened?

1ST WOMAN: Ay, it's an accident, they say, at the works.

MRS HOLROYD: *(alarmed)* An accident?

2ND WOMAN: Yes, yes, look there! *(She points off to the right)*

JEAN: *(leaning out of room with her arms crossed on window sill)*
And, Mother, I've been thinking we shall have to call him wee Alan,
to tell him from his father, you know. Mother! *(Looks)* Mother,
what has happened?

MRS HOLROYD: *(hurriedly)* Nothing, honey, nothing. *(JEAN comes
hurriedly out of room and down passage)*

JEAN: No, Mother, I am sure there is something! What is it? *(To
woman)* Do you know?

1ST WOMAN: It will be an accident, they say, at the works.

JEAN: At the works! Anyone hurt?

2ND WOMAN: Eh, with yon machines, ye never know but there'll be
something.

JEAN: With the machines? *(Sees* WARREN *coming hurriedly past)*
Jamie, Jamie, what is it? What has happened?

WARREN: Jean, dear Jean, you must be prepared.

JEAN: Prepared? For what?

WARREN: There has been an accident.

JEAN: Not to Alan? Ah, do you mean he has been hurt? *(WARREN is
silent)* But he's so strong it will be nothing! I'll make him well again.
Where is he? We must bring him back!

WARREN: No, no! *(He looks back at something approaching)*

JEAN: What is that? *(Pause)*

WARREN: God's will be done, Jean; His hand is heavy on ye.
(A moment of silence. JEAN *is seen to look aghast at something
coming.* HUTTON *and two more, carrying a covered litter, come to
the gate, followed by a little crowd of men, women and children)*

JEAN: Oh, they're coming here! *(Rushes to them)* Hutton, tell me what
has happened?

HUTTON: Best not look, missis – it's a sore sight!
(MRS HOLROYD holds JEAN back)

JEAN: Let me be, Mother – I *must* go to him!

1ST WOMAN: Na, na, my lass – best keep back!

MRS HOLROYD: Keep back, honey! you're not the one to bear the
sight!

JEAN: *I must* – let me go! *(Struggles, breaks away, and rushes forward*

– lifts up cover) Alan! (*She falls back with a cry into* MRS HOLROYD's *arms*)

(*Curtain*)

SCENE ii

A room in JEAN's *cottage. Fireplace to the right with chimney-piece on which are candlesticks, tapers, etc.; door at back. Window with curtains; kitchen dresser with plates, jugs, and a bowl with green spray in it. A mahogany bookcase on the back wall, a table, chairs, etc.; a cradle*

JEAN *discovered sitting listlessly by the fire. She is in a white gown with a black shawl over it.* MRS HOLROYD *and* MRS RIDLEY *are standing one on each side of the cradle,* MRS HOLROYD *bending over it, smoothing the clothes, etc.,* MRS RIDLEY *standing by admiringly*

MRS HOLROYD: (*at cradle, finishing tucking it up*) There now, he looks the picture of comfort, the dear! and so sound asleep, it's a pleasure to see him.

MRS RIDLEY: (*at cradle, looking at him*) It is indeed; but I doubt you've got him too hot, Mrs Holroyd.

MRS HOLROYD: (*doubtfully*) Too hot, do you think so? Well, perhaps we might put off this quilt. (*Takes it off and stands with it in her hand*) And yet, I don't know, I am all for weeny babies being kept warm enough. (*Puts the quilt on again*)

MRS RIDLEY: Warm enough! Yes, but not stifled – ye'll fair smother the bairn with all yon clothes! (*Takes off quilt*)

MRS HOLROYD: Ay, now, it's difficult to know what one should do for the best! (*Stands looking doubtfully at cradle*)

MRS RIDLEY: Well, I always say with a baby, you can't do better than take a neighbour's advice, and one that's had eleven too. My bairns used just to lie in the cot with a patchwork counterpane[6] over them – it's a grand thing for a baby is the patchwork – and they grew up fine, sturdy lads as you'd wish to see.

MRS HOLROYD: Ah, fine and sturdy – that's just it! But it's very different with this poor little mite.

MRS RIDLEY: (*her arms folded as she holds the quilt, shaking her head and looking compassionately at the baby*) Ay, poor wee thing, indeed! well, the Lord's will be done! He must have His own way with the bairns, as with everything else.

MRS HOLROYD: Do you know, I think I'll leave the quilt on. (*Takes it*) I am fearful of the draughts down the chimney coming to him.

MRS RIDLEY: Eh, yes – every chimney'll blow both hot and cold, as the saying is. I'm all for keeping the fresh air from a baby till he's turned the twelvemonth. Eh, but his mother should see him now, looking so fine and comfortable! (*Looking round at* JEAN: *who pays no attention*) Jean, he's looking as happy as a prince, the dear! (JEAN *is absorbed in thought*)

MRS HOLROYD: (*shakes her head. Half aside to* MRS RIDLEY) Ah, it's not much his mother wants to see him, I'm afraid. Jean!

JEAN: (*as though waking out of a reverie*) Yes, Mother, what is it? (*Sits up*)

MRS HOLROYD: The baby has gone to sleep – he's quite comfortable now.

JEAN: Asleep, is he? Yes. (*Leans forward, her head on her right hand, her elbow on her knee.* MRS HOLROYD *puts her hand down to the ground near the cradle*)

MRS HOLROYD: I thought I felt a bit of a draught here, near the cradle head.

MRS RIDLEY: (*putting her hand to the ground with an anxious look*) No, no! There's no draught; it's just yourself that's made it, whisking round with your petticoats.

MRS HOLROYD: Well, happen you're right. (*Holds her skirts carefully together, then feels for the draught again*) Na, na, there's no draught here. He'll sleep now, right enough.

MRS RIDLEY: If he does it'll be more by good luck than good management, with all yon clothes on the top of him!

MRS HOLROYD: He should – he's not had much sleep this day, nor last night either.

MRS RIDLEY: And you look tired with it, Mrs Holroyd.

MRS HOLROYD: We've had a restless day with him, haven't we, Jean?

JEAN: (*indifferently*) Yes, he's cried.

MRS RIDLEY: It's too much for you, Mrs Holroyd, to have been after that bairn ever since daylight.

MRS HOLROYD: Eh well! It's my Jean's bairn, you know.

MRS RIDLEY: Yes, that's just it! It's Jean's bairn, and it's Jean ought to be tewing with it – it would do her good, Mrs Holroyd.

MRS HOLROYD: Eh, I doubt she's not strong enough yet! But you are right: she should take an interest in it, all the same. I can't get her to seem as though she minded for it, do what I will.

MRS RIDLEY: You should rouse her a bit, and not let her sit mounging[7] that way. (*Cheerily*) Come, Jean, do you think the cradle is out of the draught there, or shall we get it moved a bit?

JEAN: (*half looking round, then subsides again*) Oh, I think it will do very well where it is.

MRS HOLROYD: Ah, honey, I don't like to see you sitting there as though you had nothing to do with the bairn.

JEAN: Nay, Mother, I know it's well cared for with you looking after it – and Mrs Ridley.

MRS HOLROYD: Ah, but that's not enough. Ah, Jean, how little I thought when you used to talk of your baby, and long to have it in your arms, that you would be so hard to the little fatherless child when it came, and not bear to look at it, just because it isn't the fine lusty lad you wanted! (JEAN *shudders as she sits and looks into the fire.* MRS HOLROYD *is bustling about, arranging the room as she talks*)

MRS RIDLEY: Yes, poor wee thing! He can't help being a cripple; you should care for him all the more because he won't walk and run like other boys. What's a mother for, if it's not to care for the bairn that needs it most?

JEAN: (*looks into the fire*) Yes, yes, I suppose so! that is what's left – there'll be nothing else in my life.

MRS HOLROYD: Nothing else! You ought to be thankful for having the child!

JEAN: (*bitterly*) Thankful!

MRS RIDLEY: Ah, Jean, I doubt you have a hard heart! You don't know the blessings you have.

JEAN: (*covers her face, then goes on after a minute*) No, maybe I don't. Do you remember, Mother, that last afternoon that we talked about the child that was to come? You told me how beautiful everything would be, and that I should be happier than ever I'd been before. Happier – ah!

MRS HOLROYD: It's not ours to tell the future, and it's very wicked to repine[8] when things are not as we hoped.

JEAN: (*half to herself – looking into the fire*) I used to hope, all those happy weeks before that day, and then afterwards, when my only hope was in the bairn – and now I have no hope left . . . only horrible certainty!

MRS HOLROYD: (*arranging room*) Eh, Jean, yours is sinful talk – you must just be a good mother to the bairn now that it is here.

MRS RIDLEY: (*kneeling in front of fire, takes up fire-irons in her hand, and sweeps hearth*) Ay, there's many a mother with a family of fine boys and girls has thought more of her one deformed child than all the rest!

JEAN: (*covering her face*) Deformed! Yes, that's what they'll call him. (*Pause*)

MRS RIDLEY: Why, there's Meg Dowden who used to live beside the Green at home – how she used to go about with that little Tommy of hers, who could only sling along the road instead of walking! and she was as proud of him as you please. Then there's Kate Lockerby, when one of her bairns wasn't right in her head—

JEAN: Don't! Don't! I can't bear it!

MRS RIDLEY: Ah well, child, you must try to bear it, and to put up with things that can't be mended.

MRS HOLROYD: Yes, honey, you must put off that hard, rebellious spirit, and put on a meek and submissive one, else you will be punished for your pride some day. (*Goes on dusting and arranging room*)

MRS RIDLEY: Ah, but a young thing like that will feel it! I mind when my Johnnie was born, that only lived a week—

JEAN: Don't tell me about it, I say, don't tell me about any other woman's child!

MRS RIDLEY: My word, Jean, but you've got your saucy tongue in your head still! I'll tell you what, Mrs Holroyd, you ought to have the minister to her when she speaks that way; he would bring her to a better way of thinking.

MRS HOLROYD: (*aside to* MRS RIDLEY) I've told him today just to step in and see her. Ye see, Mrs Ridley, when the lass has been about a bit longer, she'll be better; she hasn't got her strength yet.

MRS RIDLEY: Ay, that's true – anyone can see that to look at her. She's as white as a sheet tonight.

MRS HOLROYD: Indeed, she is that! Come, dearie, get to bed with you, and you'll feel better in the morning.

JEAN: (*wearily*) To bed – very well!

MRS HOLROYD: Everything is ready for you in the next room – and Mrs Ridley will sit here and be a bit of company for you while I go back home to see how things are going on.

MRS RIDLEY: Eh, that I will. I'll sit here as long as you please. (*Sits by table, gets out her knitting*)

JEAN: No, no! I don't want anyone to stay with me.

MRS RIDLEY: Eh, I can knit just as well here as at home. My boys are on the night shift this week, and won't be in for supper.

MRS HOLROYD: (*to* MRS RIDLEY) And if the baby cries you can just put it over again.

MRS RIDLEY: No need to tell me what to do with a baby, that's had eleven to look after; and I can do for Jean too, if she wants anything.

JEAN: No, no; I can quite well fend for myself. I shan't want anything.

MRS HOLROYD: (*anxiously*) But what about the baby? I doubt you won't be able to manage him, Jean?

JEAN: Yes, yes, I shall! Didn't you say that's what a mother's for? (MRS RIDLEY *gets up*)

MRS RIDLEY: (*to* MRS HOLROYD) Well, neighbour, I believe the lass is right; and if you take my advice, you'll do as she says, and leave her to tew with the baby; she'll soonest get to care for him that way.

MRS HOLROYD: Maybe you are right after all.

MRS HOLROYD: MRS RIDLEY: Well, if I'm not wanted then, I'd best be getting home. Good night to you! (*Shakes her head to herself as she goes out*) Eh, but some folks are bad to do with when they're in trouble! [*Exit*]

JEAN: You go too, Mother; I shall be all right.

MRS HOLROYD: Suppose you wanted anything, or the baby wasn't well?

JEAN: Well, if the worst came to the worst, I could step up so far and fetch you: it's only a few doors off.

MRS HOLROYD: Yes; you could do that after all. Good night, then, honey! Go to bed, say your prayers, and wake up stronger and better in the morning. All that comes to us is for the best, you know, if we can but see it.

JEAN: Good night! (*Her mother kisses her.* MRS HOLROYD *goes out, after giving a last look at the baby, and a general straightening touch to things as she passes*) At last! Oh, if they would only give over telling me it's for the best! (*Looks at cradle*) For the best! *That* for the best! (*Bends over cradle*) But he has got a darling little face all the same! Poor little bairn – my poor little bairn! They say I don't love you – I don't care for you at all! Yes, yes, I do, dear, yes, I do! (*Buries her face and sobs. Knock heard at the door. Gets up, drying her eyes, and stands at foot of cradle, looking at child.* JEAN *looks round, crosses to fire – another knock*) Yes? who is it? (WARREN *on the threshold*)

WARREN: Good evening, Jean! (*Pause* – JEAN *still looking into fire* – WARREN *stands hesitating, and a little embarrassed at her inhospitality*.) Your mother asked me to look in, and—

JEAN: And tell me of my sinful ways – yes, I know! Come in, Jamie!

WARREN: (*comes forward*) Jean, how ill you look! You're fretting; you mustn't rebel so against the visitation o' God! His laws are—

JEAN: Good and merciful. Yes, I've heard that!

WARREN: Eh! I hope you're not doubting His loving-kindness, Jean!

JEAN: I'm not thinking about God, nor about loving-kindness.

WARREN: But you must, child. It'll steady and strengthen ye. Ye'll find His mercy everywhere.

JEAN: Do you think I'll find it in the cradle, yon?

WARREN: Eh? (*Shaking his head*) Yes, I know what you mean. I've heard—

JEAN: (*with smothered anguish, breaking in*) Then you *forgot*, Jamie Warren, or you wouldn't talk of loving-kindness. You forgot God couldn't even take Alan away without – without – (*Covers her face and shudders*)

WARREN: Jean! You're tempting the Almighty!

JEAN: Ye hadn't heard, maybe, that a little child was sent, hideous and maimed, to stumble through this terrible world – eh?

WARREN: Hush, hush, my girl! You're ill, or you wouldn't talk that wild and wicked way! (*As* JEAN *is about to break in*) When you're stronger you'll see how the child'll comfort you.

JEAN: (*slowly*) But how shall I comfort the child?

WARREN: He'll grow up to be a scholar and a God-fearing man yet, Jean. It's no ill fate.

JEAN: He'll grow up, you think?

WARREN: (*cheerily*) Aye, why not? He may quite well live to be old.

JEAN: You don't think that? (*Seizes* WARREN *by the arm*)

WARREN: Of course. Why not? He's not rightly formed, poor bairn, else he's sturdy enough, they say. He may outlive us all, yet!

JEAN: (*hoarsely*) You think he'll live longer than any of us?

WARREN: Well, in the course of nature and if God wills it; (JEAN *turns away*) but if it's the will of God that the child should be taken, Jean, you must bow to His will.

JEAN: You're sure the bairn would go to heaven, Jamie?

WARREN: How can you doubt it? Ye'll be having him baptised?

JEAN: Baptised! (*Listlessly*) Yes, I suppose so.

WARREN: Ah, Jean, take care lest it be too late! The innocent bairn mustn't suffer for the sinful neglect of others. Unless he be baptised, who can be sure? Jean, see to it that the child is saved.

JEAN: Saved! Why was he not saved from *that*?

WARREN: We are not here to ask that. It is enough for us to know that it is the will of God.

JEAN: (*passionately*) The will of God! I won't believe it!

WARREN: Jean!

JEAN: Or if you're right, so much the worse, then! If God were full of mercy and loving-kindness as you say, how could He be so cruel to a little harmless child? (*Crosses to cradle, and drops on her knees beside it*)

WARREN: Jean, Jean, ye tempt the Almighty by your wicked words. But I doubt you're sore at heart. His mercy endureth for ever; He will forgive you, and He'll have pity on you.

JEAN: (*with a burst of agony*) Pity on *me*, man! It's the child! It's the *child*! Don't you think I'd be glad to give up my health and strength to my baby? If God was angry at *me*, why didn't He strike *me* down? If I'd been doing wrong, He should have cursed *me*, and not hurt Alan's little bairn! *I* could have borne it. This minute I could stand up and let them hack me all to pieces if they'd make my baby straight and strong. (JEAN *walks unsteadily back towards fireplace*)

WARREN: Hush! hush! You'll come to better reason as the time goes on (JEAN *absorbed in her grief*) if you'll but strive in prayer to be given a meek spirit, and strength to bear your burden bravely, Jean. There's many a one has had to go through the world before bearing a cross as heavy as yours.

JEAN: And does it make it any better for me to think of those other wretched women?

WARREN: Ah, Jean, seek for strength where alone it can be found – pray for it, only pray, and it shall be given you! (JEAN *stands looking at the fire trying to control herself*) (*Moved*) Jean, my poor Jean, goodbye! I'll pray for you and for the bairn – I'll pray that God may bring you peace.   [*Exit*]

JEAN: (*alone – wildly*) Pray for the bairn – pray, pray! (*She falls on her knees*) Oh God! If I've been wicked, don't make it worse for the child – punish me some other way – don't hurt him any more – he's so little, dear God – so helpless, and he never did any wrong! *He* hasn't been drunk with life and strength and love – he hasn't walked through the world exulting and fearless and forgetting You. That was I, oh, Father in heaven! Punish *me* – and take the baby away. This is a hard place – this world down here. Take him away! (*She staggers to her feet – listens*) He is stirring. (*Goes and looks in cradle – leans over it*) Ah, how little you must know to be smiling in your sleep! (*Drops on her knees by the cradle*) Dear little face! Ah! It's brave of you to smile when God has laid such heavy burdens on you! Do you think you will be able to smile later on when you see other boys running and leaping and being glad – when you're a man, dear, and see how good it is to be strong and fair? Can you bear it, little one? (*She rocks the cradle as if to hush him, though the child sleeps on – she croons drearily*) Never mind, never mind! Mother'll be

always at your side – always – always. (*She stops, horror-stricken*)
Always? Who can say so? I might die! It's natural I should go first
and leave him to the mercy of – Oh, I cannot, I cannot! I *dare* not!
(*Bows her head over the cradle's edge – then half recovering, and yet
with suppressed wildness, whispers*) Baby, I'm frightened! Listen, I
don't know what to do. Do you *want* to live? Tell me, shall you ever
hate me for this horrible gift of life? (*With wide vacant eyes*) Oh, I
seem to see you in some far-off time, your face distorted like your
body, but with bitterness and loathing, saying, 'Mother, how *could*
you be so cruel as to let me live and suffer? You could have eased my
pain; you could have saved me this long martydom; when I was little
and lay in your arms. Why didn't you save me? You were a coward –
a coward!' (*She bows her head over the cradle again, overcome –
then she lifts a drawn white face*) It would be quite easy – only to
cover the dear face for a little while – only to shut out the air and
light for a little while, and remember I'm fighting for his release.
Yes, it would be quite easy – if only one's heart didn't sink and one's
brain grow numb! (*Leans against the cradle, faint – her eyes fall on
the child*) Are your lips moving, dear? (*Pause*) Are you asking for
life? No, you don't want to live, do you? No, no, you cannot!
Darling, it will be so easy – you'll never know – it will only be that
you'll go on sleeping – sleeping, until you wake up in heaven!
(*Clutches quilt together quickly, then stops*) In heaven! No – what
did Jamie say? 'Unless he be baptised' – (*Stands a minute – repeats to
herself*) He said, 'See to it that the child is saved'. Yes, darling, that's
what I'm trying to do save you! (*Lets quilt fall – stands staring into
space – moves like a woman in a dream; brings two candles; returns,
brings a bowl of water, and a big book with silver clasps; puts all on
table by cradle – lights candles – lifts the great book, and goes to the
cradle and looks at the child – turns away with a sob, and, standing
by the candle-light, opens the book and tries to find the place –
passes her hand across her eyes*) Where is the place? I can't find it! I
can't find it! (*Tries again – then falls on her knees between the table
and the cradle – she closes the great book and whispers*) Have pity
on us, Lord – show us the way! (*Still on her knees, she lets the book
fall to the floor, dips her hand in the water and sprinkles the child*) I
baptise thee, Alan! (*Prays a moment – then stands looking
yearningly at him*) Alan, my little Alan! (*Rises – looks anxiously
over her shoulder to door and window, blows out the candles one
by one, and goes stealthily towards cradle with a long wailing cry,
the eider quilt hugged to her breast as the curtain falls.*)

SCENE iii

Room in the prison

COLONEL STUART *sitting at writing-table with papers.*
CHIEF WARDER *standing by him*

COLONEL STUART: You have nothing more to report, Roberts?

ROBERTS: No, sir; nothing.

COLONEL STUART: And Jean Creyke?

ROBERTS: Just the same, sir. Can get nothing out of her.

COLONEL STUART: (*shaking his head*) Ah! Well, you can take these.
(*Gives him papers.* ROBERTS *gathers up papers and is turning away*)

Enter a WARDER

WARDER: Please, sir, there is some one to see the woman Creyke.

COLONEL STUART: Who is it?

WARDER: An old woman, sir, of the name of Holroyd. She is Creyke's mother, I believe.

COLONEL STUART: Her mother? Bring her in here.   [*Exit* WARDER]
I can't help feeling that there must be some extenuating circumstance if only we could get at it.

ROBERTS: Well, sir, maybe there is. It's a bad business, anyway!
(*Salutes, and goes out with papers. Enter* MRS HOLROYD *with* WARDER. *Exit* WARDER)

COLONEL STUART: Mrs Holroyd?

MRS HOLROYD: (*with her handkerchief to her eyes*) Ay, yes, your worship, my name is Holroyd.

COLONEL STUART: (*kindly*) I am very sorry for you; it must be a hard trial.

MRS HOLROYD: Ah, it's hard indeed to think that a girl of mine should have taken her own child's life.

COLONEL STUART: Yes, it's a very terrible story. (*Pause*)

MRS HOLROYD: (*anxiously*) What will they do to her, your worship?
(COLONEL STUART *is silent*) They won't take her life, will they? There must be a chance for her yet.

COLONEL STUART: I fear not much; a reprieve has been asked for, but—

MRS HOLROYD: Yes, I know – Jamie Warren said he would bring the news this morning, the moment it was known.

COLONEL STUART: Jamie Warren?

MRS HOLROYD: Yes; he's the minister down at our place; he's always been a good friend to our Jean, and if she would have listened to him, and not taken up with Creyke, things would have been very different.

COLONEL STUART: Well, there seems to be very little here to found an appeal for mercy on. We know so little of the whole thing. What could have made her kill the child? Do you think her mind was at all affected at the time?

MRS HOLROYD: Her mind! My Jean's? No, indeed! Why did she kill the little baby? Well, it was a poor wreckling, the lamb, and it well-nigh broke her heart that it wasn't fine and sturdy like the father – she wanted a boy like the husband she lost – she never seemed to take to the baby, never from the first, and she never would tew with it as mothers do.

COLONEL STUART: Do you mean that that's why she killed the poor little helpless child – that she could find it it her heart to kill it because it wasn't strong and sturdy?

MRS HOLROYD: Ah, yes, your worship, it's hard my Jean should have done it. I well-nigh can't believe it of my own bairn.

COLONEL STUART: It's hard to believe of any mother.

MRS HOLROYD: And if they spare her life what will become of her? Can I have her back with me to her home again?

COLONEL STUART: No, my poor woman, she can't go back to you again. The best will be that her sentence will be commuted to penal servitude for life.

MRS HOLROYD: (*crying out*) For life! My Jean? Oh Lord, oh Lord, Your hand is heavy on us!

COLONEL STUART: You shall see her. (*Rings bell*) (*A* WARDER *comes in*) Jean Creyke is to come here. (*Exit* WARDER) (*To* MRS HOLROYD) Perhaps you can bring her to a better frame of mind. She seems strangely hardened.

MRS HOLROYD: Ah, your worship, I am afraid she won't mind for me; she always knew I hadn't the wits to be up to her, or find the words to say to her. Oh, my poor girl, she always was too proud, I always told her she was. The Lord has punished her.

(*Enter* JEAN *with two* WARDERS)

MRS HOLROYD: Oh, Jean, Jean!

(JEAN's *sentences are given as a stage direction of what she is silently to convey, but she does not speak until nearly the end of the act*)

JEAN: (*silent*) Mother!

MRS HOLROYD: Honey, tell his worship how you came to do it. Tell him you hadn't your wits right; that you didn't know what you were doing to the little bairn!

JEAN: (*silent*) I knew well enough.

MRS HOLROYD: Oh, my dear, if you could tell him something that would make them let you off – now think, Jean, think, honey! it may be you could tell them something that would save you.

JEAN: (*silent – stares vacantly into space*) I can tell him nothing.

COLONEL STUART: Nothing you can say, of course, will clear you now; but, for the sake of the memory you will leave behind you, can you give no sort of reason, no explanation of the impulse that led to your terrible crime? (JEAN *shakes her head*)

MRS HOLROYD: Oh, your worship, your worship!

COLONEL STUART: (*to* MRS HOLROYD) No, it is no use, I'm afraid; she hasn't opened her lips from the beginning. (*Looks at watch*) You have twenty minutes together.

[*Exit*]

(*The two* WARDERS *stand at the back, apparently not listening*)

MRS HOLROYD: (*in tears*) Oh, my Jean, my bonny Jean! That it should have come to this!

(JEAN *stands motionless.* MRS HOLROYD
turns away, distractedly wringing her hands)

MRS HOLROYD: (*coming back to the girl*) Jean, Jean, do you know they will have the life of ye?

JEAN: (*silent – makes motion of assent*) Yes, I know.

MRS HOLROYD: How could you do it, my lass? Can't you remember? If you could have told them all about it and asked for mercy you could have got it.

JEAN: (*silent – smiles strangely*) I don't want mercy.

MRS HOLROYD: You're not afraid to die with your sins about ye?

JEAN: (*silent – shakes her head*) No, I am not afraid.

MRS HOLROYD: Ah, Jean, but I am afraid for ye. No, I cannot bear it. Jean! (*With a fresh outburst*) Are ye not thinking of your mother at all?

JEAN: (*silent – puts out her hand to her mother*) Poor mother!

MRS HOLROYD: Oh, Jean, you're very hard. You don't think of those who are left when you won't ask for mercy. And Jamie Warren, poor lad – his heart is broken as well as mine. (*Pause –* JEAN *stands erect seeming not to hear*) But there is still a chance, Jean – honey – there is indeed. Maybe Jamie'll come back here this morning with the blessed news. He should be here soon, very soon. (*In an agony*) Jean, Jean, if only I could get you to speak! His worship's been asking me about you. What can I tell him? Try to recollect, lassie –

try to think on that night when I left ye with the baby – try to think just how it all was. I left ye sitting by the fire, just after Mrs Ridley had gone out; ye'll mind she was a bit vexed, poor body, at the way ye'd spoken – and the baby was asleep in the cradle, I'd just covered him up warm with the quilt. (JEAN *gives a sharp cry, and makes a motion to stop her mother*)

JEAN: (*silent*) Ah!

(*The door opens, and* JAMIE WARREN *comes in hastily with a* WARDER, *who points to* JEAN *and goes out again*)

MRS HOLROYD: Jamie! Well, Jamie – what news do you bring? Speak, lad, tell us!

WARREN: (*looks at* MRS HOLROYD *and shakes his head, and then looks at* JEAN) The news I bring is – bad.

JEAN: (*silent – unmoved*)

WARREN: No, Jean, they won't grant it; they say the sentence must be carried out.

(JEAN *clasps her hands with a look of relief, almost of gladness*)

MRS HOLROYD: Oh, Jean, honey, it will kill me too! (JEAN *seems not to hear*) Jamie, Jamie, she doesn't seem to mind for me one little bit! Speak to her, my lad, try to soften her hard heart!

Re-enter COLONEL STUART

COLONEL STUART: (*to* JEAN) You have heard the result of the appeal?

JEAN: (*silent – bows*) Yes.

MRS HOLROYD: Oh, your worship, is there no hope?

COLONEL STUART: None – absolutely none.

WARREN: Jean, your only hope is in Him who alone can pardon your sin: turn to Him before it is too late. Do not die unforgiven.

JEAN: (*silent*) I shall not die unforgiven.

COLONEL STUART: Take care, Jean Creyke; remember your time is running short – the end is very near.

JEAN (*aloud*) When?

COLONEL STUART: Tomorrow morning at eight.

JEAN: Tomorrow! (*Her lips form the word*)

MRS HOLROYD: (*crying out*) Tomorrow morning!

WARREN: Yes, the time is short, indeed! Jean, confess! Confess, and turn you to the Lord your God.

MRS HOLROYD: Tomorrow! Tomorrow! Ah, but it's too soon for her to die! Jean, Jean, my honey, my little lass! Oh, my Jean!

(JEAN, *as if in a dream, turns to go*)

COLONEL STUART: My poor woman, all you can do for her now is to pray for her, and say goodbye. You won't see her again.

MRS HOLROYD: (*horror-stricken and bewildered*) Not see her again!

What do you mean? You'll let me come tonight, and tomorrow? (*Looks round – reads answer in faces of bystanders*)

COLONEL STUART: No, this is the last time.

MRS HOLROYD: The last time! No, no! You can't take her from me like that! Your worship, she's the only child I've ever had – the only thing I have in the world! Eh, but ye'll let me bide with her the day, till tonight, only till tonight! Just these few hours longer! Think, your worship – I must do without her all the rest of my life!

COLONEL STUART: (*compassionately*) My poor woman! (*He makes a sign to the* WARDERS)

MRS HOLROYD: (*rushing forward as* WARDERS *are going to take* JEAN *out*) Oh, wait, only wait! Jamie, don't let her go! Tell them they mustn't take her to die yet. She isn't ready to die, ye know she isn't ready. (*To* JEAN) Oh, my honey! Speak, speak, before it is too late. Tell them why you did it. Put away your rebellious heart! (*To* STUART) You think she's bad and wicked, but she's not wicked – she's not indeed! Jean, Jean, why did ye kill the poor little bairn?

WARREN: Jean, listen to me – tomorrow you are to appear before your Maker. Confess your crime, and lay down your burden before the throne of God.

JEAN: (*aloud*) Crime!

COLONEL STUART: Not a crime, that you in cold blood took the life of a poor, helpless, little baby, because you hadn't the courage to bear the sight of its misfortunes?

JEAN: I hadn't courage? I've had courage just once in my life – just once in my life I've been strong and kind – and it was the night I killed my child! (*She turns away to door*)

WARREN: Jean!

> (MRS HOLROYD *cries something inarticulate as she tries in despair to hold* JEAN *back*)

JEAN: Don't, mother, don't! You don't think I could live after this, do you? I had to do what I did, and they have to take my life for it. I showed him the only true mercy, and that is what the law shows me! Maybe I shall find him up yonder made straight and fair and happy – find him in Alan's arms. Goodbye – Mother – goodbye!

> [*She goes out as the curtain falls*]

NOTES

1 **nobbut:** nothing but.

2 **you silly fondy:** you foolish child – a good-natured chastisement.

3 **to fettle it up:** to sort it out, clean it up.

4 **tewing:** fussing, constant work and bustling, a state of worry or excitement.

5 **weeny ones . . . Canny little bairns:** tiny ones – here, good little children.

6 **counterpane:** bedspread.

7 **mounging:** pining, grieving.

8 **to repine:** to fret, to be discontented.

THE AMBASSADOR

---

a comedy, in four acts
BY JOHN OLIVER HOBBES (PEARL CRAIGIE)
(1898)

DRAMATIS PERSONAE

Women

LADY BEAUVEDERE	a young widow, stepmother to Sir William Beauvedere, mother of Vivian
JULIET GAINSBOROUGH	an orphan, engaged to Sir William
ALICE GAINSBOROUGH	her sister, a nun
LADY GWENDOLENE MARLEAZE	a young lady
THE PRINCESS VENDRAMINI	friend and confidante of Lord St Orbyn
THE DUCHESS OF HAMPSHIRE LADY BASLER LADY VANRINGHAM LADY ULLWEATHER MRS DASNEY	visitors to Lady Beauvedere
MRS WHITCOMB J. TAYLORSON	a guest at Lascelles' party
MISS KATIE TAYLORSON MISS MAMIE TAYLORSON MISS YOLANDE TAYLORSON	her daughters, studying Grand Opera in Paris
MRS SPEARING	Lady Beauvedere's housekeeper
TOMKINS	a housemaid

Men

LORD ST ORBYN	British Ambasador at Madrid
SIR WILLIAM BEAUVEDERE	Second Attaché to the Brit

	ish Embassy at Berlin, engaged to Juliet
VIVIAN BEAUVEDERE	his younger step-brother
MAJOR HUGO LASCELLES	neighbour to Lady Beauvedere
SIR CHARLES DE LORME	guests at Lady Beauvedere's
LORD LAVENSTHORPE	birthday party
RORTER	
JENKINS	footmen
DUVAL	Lascelles' manservant
TOTO	
LORD REGGIE	guests at Lascelles' party

Scenes

ACT I	At Lady Beauvedere's residence in the Champs-Elysées, Paris.
(Four days elapse)	
ACT II	Conservatory at Lady Beauvedere's. Thursday morning.
ACT III	At Major Lascelles' residence in the Champs-Elysées. Same morning.
ACT IV	Garden at Lady Beauvedere's. Same morning.

Act I

At Lady Beauvedere's in the Champs-Elysées, Paris. It is about half-past two in the afternoon. A room luxuriously furnished; style: Louis Seize. Here and there a modern piece of furniture. Quantities of roses, tables covered with books, photographs, vases, objets d'art. Cards on table. Fancy work. Photo on piano. Newspapers. A marble bust of SIR WILLIAM BEAUVEDERE *between the two windows (at side). A large conservatory at back. A piano, sofa, writing table and chairs. As curtain rises,* JULIET GAINSBOROUGH, *a pretty girl about eighteen, well, but not gaudily dressed, and* ALICE GAINSBOROUGH, *a nun, evidently some years her senior, are talking earnestly together on a sofa*

ALICE: (*with anxiety*) Dearest Juliet, you have not yet told me why you accepted Sir William.

JULIET: (*who is opening letters and throwing them aside*) Why? Because I wanted to be married, and wear a black velvet dinner-gown with a long diamond chain. . . . 'Severe simplicity', as Mrs Dasney would say, 'and twenty thousand pound dangling from my neck!'

ALICE: (*distressed*) Fancy marrying for such a reason!

JULIET: Lots of girls do!

ALICE: But you wouldn't.

JULIET: Oh, well! I hope to make Bill happy. . . . (*Rising and going up to bust*) . . . Alice, do you think he looks like a 'Bill'? (*Points to bust*) He ought to be a polysyllable! (*After a pause*) Yes, I want to make him happy. (*All through this scene she is evidently labouring under despair and an assumption of cynicism*)

ALICE: And your own happiness?

JULIET: That will come. I'm so grateful to him.

ALICE: What has he done?

JULIET: He gives me his love, his name, his career, his home, his fortune. . . .

ALICE: And why shouldn't he?

JULIET: Look at me! I'm a girl without a penny, without influence, without a single great relative!

ALICE: Grandpapa is a duke.

JULIET: But he's only a duke because one of our ancestors in the eleventh century fought for God and his King! No one cares for that sort of thing now. Grandpapa is neither rich nor new; he hates politics; he won't even be a guinea-pig![1] He's just a fussy old country gentleman with a large family and a few rents. He's nobody!

ALICE: Oh, Juliet! how you have changed since you came out!

JULIET: (*stifling a sob*) No, dear; I haven't changed, But, from the Convent window, we used to watch the sea. And the sea – no matter how rough it may be – always reflects the sky. Now, I have left school. . . . I am watching the *earth* and that . . . (*Crosses*)

ALICE: Well? . . .

JULIET: That, so far, seems to reflect . . . the other place! (*Covers her face with her hands*) Oh, I am disillusioned!

ALICE: Ah no! (*Rises*) Disillusions all come from within . . . from the failure of some dear and secret hope. The *world* makes no promises; we only dream it does; and when we wake, we cry! . . . Is Lady Beauvedere kind to you? (*Puts letters on piano*)

JULIET: All kindness. She gave me this frock; her maid does my hair; her newest genius is painting my portrait; her dearest friends will soon be mine. But . . .

ALICE: What?

JULIET: In her soul she cannot bear me.

ALICE: (*moving towards* JULIET) Juliet!

JULIET: She thinks I am mercenary – I am not. She thinks I am frivolous – I am not. She thinks me vain, heartless, selfish – I am not . . . I am not! (*She bursts into tears*)

ALICE: (*seating herself*) She cannot be so unjust! Consider – she has invited you here to this beautiful place.

JULIET: It isn't hers. It all belongs to Bill. That's why I feel an intruder. I am turning her out of her own home. As though I wanted it! I'd rather be a sparrow alone on a housetop than lead the life of these women of the world!

ALICE: Are you so miserable?

JULIET: Can't you see that I am utterly wretched!

ALICE: Juliet, do you . . . do you love him?

JULIET: No! no! no! I don't. But what shall I do? He has been so good to me. I must love him in time. . . . Yet, that's not all. . . . There's more.

ALICE: What else?

JULIET: There *is* a girl . . . who *does* love him.

ALICE: Who's that?

JULIET: Gwen Marleaze. I have just made this discovery. She's not kind; she's proud, suspicious and cold; she's cruel, she's worldly, but . . . she loves him. She would sell her soul for him. She's suffering . . . she's breaking her heart . . . she's dying, I believe, of love.

ALICE: Poor girl!

JULIET: Then what . . . is to be done?

ALICE: (*rising*) Dearest, this engagement must be broken off. Misery . . . piercing misery will come of it. You will repent it – Oh, with what anguish! what desolation of heart!

JULIET: Of course! Who ever heard of a pleasant, easy, enjoyable repentance!

ALICE: Where is Sir William now?

JULIET: At Berlin.

ALICE: Then write to him. Write to him now, and let me post the letter. Tell him, that in your attempt to make him happy, you have made two people miserable already, and the third will be himself! Tell him it is impossible, and again impossible, and yet again, impossible!

JULIET: (*with a cry of relief*) Oh, Alice, that is just what I have been writing to him.

ALICE: You don't mean it?

JULIET: (*drawing letter from pocket*) See, I wrote this this morning. (*Gives letter to* ALICE) I daren't tell you at first, till I knew what you thought. (*With emotion*) I felt such a burden at home, and I knew it was my duty to feel grateful for Sir William's kindness! But I can't marry him – I cannot!

Enter JENKINS

JENKINS: The carriage is at the door, miss.

[*Exit* JENKINS]

JULIET: I'll come at once. (*Takes letter from* ALICE) We can post this as we pass. (*Looking at calendar*) This is Saturday. There *is* time – he will receive it (*Sealing and stamping the letter*) before he leaves Berlin on Tuesday morning for the ball.

ALICE: What ball?

JULIET: The ball on Lady Beauvedere's birthday. (*Rises*) She's only thirty-five; that isn't much, and then, she's beautiful.

ALICE: Perhaps she will marry again.

JULIET: I have heard that she is very fond of Lord St Orbyn.

ALICE: How do they know?

JULIET: Because Mrs Dasney says that he always tells people, when her name is mentioned, that he isn't a marrying man! But come, we shall be late.

ALICE: We can post the letter together, and then . . . (*Half smiling and looking round the room*) . . . mind, it means you renounce all this – all diamonds and all black velvet.

JULIET: (*passionately*) I wouldn't take a whole city of such houses for even the least of the dreams I brought with me and lost here!

ALICE: (*going to Juliet*) The dreams will all come back again!

JULIET: Do you think so?

ALICE: I know it. Come! [*Exeunt*]

MRS SPEARING, *the housekeeper, followed by*
RORTER *and* TOMPKINS, *with a number
of flower vases on a tray, enter*

MRS SPEARING: (*to* RORTER) Put the marguerites on that table. (*Points to table*). Put that on the mantelpiece (RORTER *puts marguerites on table and other flowers on mantelpiece*) – the poppies on the piano (TOMPKINS *puts poppies on piano*) and the lilies on the writing-table. (*To* RORTER) Look at that chair!

RORTER: I am looking.

MRS SPEARING: What's the matter with it?

RORTER: (*after a pause*) *One* of us must be squinting!

MRS SPEARING: O, Rorter! Go to the liberry and bring up Sir Charles de Lorme's 'History of Asia' – it is his day for calling.

[*Exit* RORTER]

(*To* TOMPKINS)

Why, bless my soul (*Looking on writing table for photograph*), where is Lord St Orbyn's photigraph? and him expected down every moment? There's management!

TOMPKINS: (*looking on piano*) Here 'e is – be'ind the vase.

MRS SPEARING: (*taking photograph*) Now, there's a man I could take to. Cold, 'aughty, you-keep-your-place-I'll-keep-mine; that's the style! That's a man to make 'ome happy. (*Hands it to* TOMPKINS) Don't put it on the writing-table – that's most conspicuous and indelicate! The pianner's the right place. Where are them cards? Ah, here they are. Her ladyship's wonderful fond of a game of Patience lately. It's so soothing when you're sitting with a sword, so to speak, over your head! (*Looks about the room*) . . . And, oh, my goodness! Tompkins!

TOMPKINS: Yes, Mrs Spearing?

MRS SPEARING: Who's been and dusted half the marble off Sir Williamses' bust?

TOMPKINS: It's Lady Gwendolene. Come in when I will she is a-dusting of it fit to break her 'eart!

MRS SPEARING: Poor young lady!

TOMPKINS: (*putting things straight on piano*) And 'as Sir William really be'aved so 'eartless to her, Mrs Spearing?

Re-enter RORTER *with book, and 'The Upper Ten'*

RORTER: (*who has evidently been listening at the door*) Something shameful!

MRS SPEARING: (*taking book from him and putting it on table*) Hold your tongue! What do you know about it?

RORTER: You can read it for yourself in *The Upper Ten*.[2] (TOMPKINS *looks at paper over* RORTER'*s shoulder*) 'Ere's the column. 'Things we should like to know.' (*Reads*) 'What will become of a certain peer's daughter now that a certain Bart. has engaged himself to the penniless Miss What's-her-name?' I call that pretty straight!

MRS SPEARING: I wouldn't read such low stuff. (*Approaching them*) Let me see it with my own eyes. Be off, – both of you!

[*Exeunt* RORTER *and* TOMPKINS]

MRS SPEARING: (*seating herself*) 'A much-talked-of match is not finding favour in the right quarters. It seems an occasion for half-mourning.' There's impudence and *radicalism!* 'Lady Beauvedere is receiving congratulations on her step-son's engagement to Miss Juliet Gainsborough.' Ah, poor thing, she is indeed!

Enter VIVIAN BEAUVEDERE, *a precocious, delicate-looking boy, about eighteen, through the conservatory*

VIVIAN: Oh, Speary, I am so depressed! (*Opens piano*)

MRS SPEARING: (*rising*) For pity's sake, Master Vivie, don't you go and fall in love too, and make us all unhappy!

VIVIAN: (*turning over music*) There's no danger. I see too much of women and their little ways. That's one advantage, after all, in being too delicate to go to school or Oxford. (*Begins to play a waltz*)

MRS SPEARING: I do hope that nice tune will liven up her poor ladyship. (*Goes out wiping her eyes*)

(*As* VIVIAN *plays*, LADY BEAUVEDERE, *a very handsome, young-looking woman, about thirty-five, enters, followed by* LADY GWENDOLENE, *a girl about twenty-two, very intense, silent and languishing*)

LADY BEAUVEDERE: (*crossing to* VIVIAN, *and placing her hands on his shoulder*) Darling boy, my mind is crowded with painful thoughts, yet, when you play, I can forget them all. You are my comfort. Never, never disappoint me. I could not bear it. (*Wipes her eyes*)

VIVIAN: (*rising from piano and arranging the cushions for her on the sofa where* LADY BEAUVEDERE *now sits*)
Why do you say that? It almost implies a doubt. You ought to feel sure of me.

GWENDOLENE: (*who has seated herself at fancy-work, mournfully*)
Disappointments – like fate and love – will not bear to be too much talked about.

VIVIAN: (*walking about*) Oh! I am so depressed. I do wish you would all smile again just as you used before Bill's engagement.

(LADY GWENDOLENE *stifles a sob, rises suddenly, and leaves the room*)

LADY BEAUVEDERE: (*looking after her*) Poor sweet girl! Her eyes were full of tears. Did you notice how pale she grew just at the mention of Bill's name? And yet your brother can forsake a heart like that for the sake of a little serpent in dove's feathers.

VIVIAN: Oh, hang it all! A fellow can't marry every girl who gets pale every time his name is mentioned. There would simply be no end to it.

Enter JENKINS, *bearing a salver of letters*
Ah, the post! (JENKINS *puts letters on writing table*)

LADY BEAUVEDERE: (*to* VIVIAN) One moment. (*To* JENKINS) Is Lord St Orbyn still in his room, Jenkins?

JENKINS: Yes, my lady. His lordship is still dressing, my lady. His lordship's servant led me to suppose that his lordship would not be down for a couple of hours.

LADY BEAUVEDERE: That will do.   [*Exit* JENKINS]

VIVIAN: (*turning over the letters*) What a heap! (*Seats himself*)

LADY BEAUVEDERE: (*covering her eyes with her handkerchief*) Read them for me; my head is too bad.

VIVIAN: (*opening the letters and reading*) The Savignys accept . . . . The de Traceys are in mourning. . . . Lady Agnes and her bony girls. Soames hopes to find time. . . . What an ass! . . . (*Opens letter containing cheque; looks at* LADY BEAUVEDERE, *and quietly places cheque in pocket*) . . . (*After a pause*) Mama!

LADY BEAUVEDERE: (*with her eyes still covered*) Yes, dear.

VIVIAN: May I send a card to Hugo Lascelles?

LADY BEAUVEDERE: (*with energy*) No! I have told you that I refuse to know him – a gambler – a horrid wretch who lives on other men's losses!

VIVIAN: How ridiculous! We all do that – more or less! He is a high-minded fellow as ever got up a baccarat table.

LADY BEAUVEDERE: Baccarat!

VIVIAN: Well, you can't expect me to sit playing loto with old Spearie in the housekeeper's room at my age!

LADY BEAUVEDERE: Major Lascelles is so shocking that he can even say witty things about his own bad character.

VIVIAN: You think all the world of St Orbyn, yet St Orbyn is one of his greatest friends.

LADY BEAUVEDERE: Lord St Orbyn has a great official position, and he has to know many odd characters – for various reasons. One attends an Ambassador's parties as one goes to church – one has to rub shoulders with all sorts of people and be civil, after a fashion, to all of 'em.

VIVIAN: But . . .

LADY BEAUVEDERE: Not another word, ...

Enter JENKINS

JENKINS: Lady Basler.

Enter LADY BASLER, *fashionably dressed*

[*Exit* JENKINS]

LADY BASLER: (*crossing the room and sitting on sofa near* LADY BEAUVEDERE, *who makes but a feeble attempt to rise. She plays the invalid all through the following scene*) Dearest Geraldine! Don't move. How *are* you? I am dying to hear about the engagement.

LADY BEAUVEDERE: Oh, that engagement!

LADY BASLER: Of course Bill is far too young – and fancy *you* a possible grandmother! Dear Geraldine, *how* trying!

LADY BEAUVEDERE: In the first place, dear, a *step*-grandmother, – it is not *quite* as though he were my own son, and then, I married very young myself.

LADY BASLER: But I want to know . . .

Enter JENKINS

JENKINS: Mrs Dasney.

MRS DASNEY, *in a very elaborate gown, trips in*

[*Exit* JENKINS]

MRS DASNEY: What luck! I was afraid you wouldn't be at home. I have just been to such a smart funeral this morning. I had barely time to get back and change into this. Everybody was there.

(VIVIAN *places chair from piano for* MRS DASNEY)

LADY BEAUVEDERE: Whose funeral was it?

MRS DASNEY: (*in a hushed voice*) Poor Milly's. (*Seats herself*) I am *so* sorry you missed it. You would have enjoyed . . . I mean, you would have been so *interested*. Now, you have your *own* excitement. Fancy that naughty boy getting engaged! I hear that Miss Gainsborough is *too* pretty. What a mercy, dear, that she isn't third-rate!

LADY BASLER: Third-rate women always to try to be second-rate!

MRS DASNEY: And what is worse than a second-rate manquée? (LADY BASLER *is crushed*) I suppose when Bill marries you'll have to give up all this? (*Looking round the room*)

LADY BEAUVEDERE: Of course, and go to my dower-house[3] in Wiltshire, among the Moon-rakers![4]

LADY BASLER: I'm afraid I'm rather out of this conversation. I'll move. (*Rises and goes up right*)

MRS DASNEY: (*taking her place*) Thanks so much. What I want to know is . . .

Enter JENKINS

JENKINS: Lady Vanringham.

Enter LADY VANRINGHAM; *pretty, thin, helpless*

[*Exit* JENKINS]

LADY VANRINGHAM: Oh . . . I was hoping you would be alone . . . I mean . . . don't get up. . . .

LADY BEAUVEDERE: (*pointing to chair by sofa*) Dear Harriet, do take this chair! So good of you.

LADY VANRINGHAM: (*seating herself*) Are you *awfully* upset?

LADY BEAUVEDERE: (*wearily*) Oh, no. Of course dear Bill is very young, but I married very young myself. . . .

LADY VANRINGHAM: If they love each other what does it matter? The great thing is the girl. Is she a nice girl?

LADY BEAUVEDERE: Oh, charming.

LADY BASLER: Where's her photo, G.?

VIVIAN: Bill has taken them all away with him to Berlin.

LADY BASLER: How sweet of him! But I'm rather sorry that the poor girl isn't plain.

LADY BEAUVEDERE: Why?

LADY BASLER: Because a plain woman can defy the three cruellest enemies of her sex – Time, Sorrow – and Men's Fickleness!

MRS DASNEY: You've forgotten the fourth – the worst of the lot.

LADY VANRINGHAM: What's that?

MRS DASNEY: The jealousy of rivals!

Enter JENKINS

JENKINS: (*announcing*) Sir Charles de Lorme.

Enter SIR CHARLES DE LORME

[*Exit* JENKINS]

LADY BEAUVEDERE: (*Rising and shaking hands with* SIR CHARLES) Dear Sir Charles, this is too nice.

>(MRS DASNEY *moves up on sofa till she is right of*
>LADY VANRINGHAM; LADY BASLER *sits left of right table.*
>VIVIAN *on stool below this table*)

SIR CHARLES: (*lugubriously*) I have called to offer my congratulations.

LADY BEAUVEDERE: Thanks so much. We are all so happy about the affair. Of course Bill is a little young, but I married very young myself, and it all seems so idyllic!

SIR CHARLES: (*relieved*) Really now. I am delighted, simply delighted! What a comfort that you are happy about it! (LADY BEAUVEDERE *sits on sofa where* MRS DASNEY *sat before*)

MRS DASNEY: She is not rich, but she is *quite* lovely, and he is *very* fond of her.

LADY VANRINGHAM: (*with sentiment*) And if the young people love each other, what *does* it matter?

SIR CHARLES: It seems an ideal match in every respect. (*Seats himself*) Miss Gainsborough is Bill's equal in birth, his superior in beauty, his junior in years. An ideal match!

LADY VANRINGHAM: Who brought them together, dear?

LADY BEAUVEDERE: The Duchess of Hampshire.

MRS DASNEY: She is so tactless.

LADY BASLER: Not at all. I believe she does it on purpose. She has a mania for marrying off poor orphans. I often wish my girls were orphans. They'd do so much better.

MRS DASNEY: I believe men like orphans . . . there's no mother-in-law! But I must be going. Goodbye, dear. (*Crosses the room, pauses, then returns to* SIR CHARLES) Oh, Sir Charles, *do* let me drop you somewhere.

SIR CHARLES: (*a little embarrassed, but not displeased*) That's very sweet of you, but . . .

MRS DASNEY: No, I insist! you know I *never* see you. (SIR CHARLES *tries not to look astonished at this remark*) You need a blow in the Bois. And we can see the blossoms in bloom. Really! my life is such a whirl, that I'm a stranger – a perfect stranger – to the real pleasures of existence. (*Puts one hand on his arm as if to keep him quiet*)

LADY BASLER: But you *do* so much, don't you?

LADY BEAUVEDERE: (*smiling, to save the situation*) And does it all so beautifully!

MRS DASNEY: (*quickly*) My husband is very hospitable; of course, entertainment for entertainment's sake is the most expensive form of death, and perhaps — (*Hesitating*)

LADY BASLER: Vulgar?

LADY BEAUVEDERE: (*Rising and addressing* MRS DASNEY) Do come to lunch on Saturday.

MRS DASNEY: Awfully sorry – can't. In the morning I have the Armenian Massacres Committee, and in the afternoon I *must* decide on my gown for the Glossop Fancy Ball, and I lunch with . . . let me think – who *do* I lunch with?

LADY BEAUVEDERE: What a bore! Come Sunday.

MRS DASNEY: Delighted.

LADY BEAUVEDERE: Bring your husband.

MRS DASNEY: Oh, no; ask him when you don't ask me. We are so dull together. Goodbye.

LADY BEAUVEDERE: (*to* SIR CHARLES) Dine with us on Sunday?

SIR CHARLES: Charmed.

MRS DASNEY: Sir Charles.

SIR CHARLES: Charmed. (*Follows* MRS DASNEY *out of the room*)

LADY VANRINGHAM: I must go too. Goodbye. But I *am* sorry to see you looking so poorly. But if the young people *love* each other, what *does* it matter! It will be all right; don't worry. (*Advancing and addressing* LADY BASLER) Goodbye, Edith. I'm sure we all married for love. Even Dolly Dasney married for love; and there's nothing the matter with us . . . we are happy enough. Goodbye.

[*Exit, followed by* VIVIAN]

LADY BASLER: (*looking after her*) Poor Harriet! she's dear, but such a bore; and that dreadful Dasney woman! How she does chase after Sir Charles de Lorme! I call her such a bounder!

LADY BEAUVEDERE: (*crossing to table*) But she can make anything 'go' . . . that's a rest! Everybody knows her – all Society. . . .

LADY BASLER: (*sneering a little*) Represented by the Duchess of Hampshire!

LADY BEAUVEDERE: All Propriety?

LADY BASLER: Represented by yourself!

LADY BEAUVEDERE: (*smiling a little*) And all Impropriety?

LADY BASLER: My dear! Now you *have* stumped me! (*After a pause*) Well, darling, has St Orbyn arrived?

LADY BEAUVEDERE: Yes, he arrived last night. I have not seen him yet. It was so late.

LADY BASLER: What a pity it is, dear, that St Orbyn is not a marrying man! What a comfort he would have been to you . . . now that Bill is settling in life!

LADY BEAUVEDERE: Oh, my dear! St Orbyn and I are such friends as we are, that the idea of marrying him would seem almost . . . almost a pity.

LADY BASLER: All the same he would have married you sixteen years ago!

LADY BEAUVEDERE: How can you say that – when you know my heart was buried with dear Basil?

LADY BASLER: That, my dear, was a case of premature burial!

LADY BEAUVEDERE: What *do* you mean?

LADY BASLER: Just what I say. St Orbyn was dying to marry you sixteen years ago, when you were a widow of nineteen!

LADY BEAUVEDERE: Yes . . . I was very young.

LADY BASLER: And now, of course, Gerry dear, you are still young – in a way – but ten to one now St Orbyn don't keep you for a friend because you are amusin', and marry some little noodle – because she's so fresh! That's the world! That's men! Take the case of Monty. How did Monty treat me?

LADY BEAUVEDERE: That's a certain type of man. St Orbyn is quite different!

LADY BASLER: They're all different, dear (*Rises and crosses to* LADY BEAUVEDERE), till it comes to a question of marriage, and then they're all the same! But I must be going. Goodbye, pet. Don't come. I shall meet Vivie on the stairs.

(LADY BASLER *goes out.* LADY BEAUVEDERE *moves to piano and looks at St Orbyn's photograph, then sits down and sings—*)

> 'Le doux printemps a bu dans le creux de sa main
> Le premier pleur qu'au bois laissa tomber l'aurore;
> Vous aimerez demain, vous qui n'aimiez encore,
> Et vous qui n'aimiez plus, vous aimerez demain!'[5]

ST ORBYN: (*heard outside*) Is Lady Beauvedere in the drawing-room? (LADY BEAUVEDERE *rises and crosses*) I will join her at once. What delicious roses! May I steal one?

GWENDOLENE: (*appearing in doorway*) Pray do. (*She disappears again*)

(ST ORBYN *enters through the conservatory. He is a distinguished, rather blasé-looking man of about forty-five*)

ST ORBYN: My dear Geraldine, what a pleasure this is! (*Kisses her hand*) I thought you so sensible not to sit up for me last night. My

train arrived at the most uncivil hour. Ah, to get away from my
work, and to come here to you – the enchantress – the irresistible! I
am a boy in my happiness – a boy!

LADY BEAUVEDERE: (*sitting*) Dear Bertie, I am too happy to see you.
To think that a whole year has passed since our last meeting!

ST ORBYN: (*lightly*) What is a year? A little hunting, a little shooting, a
little dancing, a little dining, a little racing, a little losing, a little
cursing, a little yawning, a little flirting, and – a little repenting!
Why, a year is no more than a well-ordered day!

LADY BEAUVEDERE: Can you keep a secret?

ST ORBYN: Give me several, and then, thank God! one will help me to
keep the others!

LADY BEAUVEDERE: Well, let me tell you this, the days seem long –
only when I neither see nor hear from you!

ST ORBYN: What charming things you say!

LADY BEAUVEDERE: That's because I'm in practice.

ST ORBYN: How so?

LADY BEAUVEDERE: I have just seen a lot of women callers. In a
minute I shall sing 'God save the Queen!' (*Rising*)

ST ORBYN: What a mood is this!

LADY BEAUVEDERE: (*reseating herself*) Oh, don't you know that every
dinner, every lunch, every call where women meet is a field of
Waterloo?

ST ORBYN: Why?

LADY BEAUVEDERE: Napoleon and Wellington settled their battle
once and for ever, but women . . .

ST ORBYN: Well . . . ?

LADY BEAUVEDERE: Waterloo begins, for a woman, from the moment
she disappoints her mother by not being a boy, and it ends – only
when her dearest friend drops a wreath on her coffin. (*Wipes her
eyes*)

ST ORBYN: (*approaching her*) Dearest G., what's the matter?

LADY BEAUVEDERE: Edith Basler is a cat, and yet she was my
bridesmaid. But they are all horrid!

ST ORBYN: (*watching her intently*) What about?

LADY BEAUVEDERE: About Bill's engagement.

ST ORBYN: But I hear Miss Gainsborough is a delightful creature.

LADY BEAUVEDERE: Ah, some woman told you that!

ST ORBYN: Several women have told me so. Some of 'em, too, had
daughters of their own!

LADY BEAUVEDERE: Spiteful things!

ST ORBYN: Well, isn't Miss Gainsborough a delightful creature?

LADY BEAUVEDERE: Yes, but they needn't go about *telling* everybody, as though I were the only one who *didn't* think so!

ST ORBYN: Whereas I gather you are really in the best of spirits over the affair!

LADY BEAUVEDERE: Well, I do like her – in a way – but dear Bertie, she has faults. . . .

ST ORBYN: Faults! I *adore* faults! I can never find too many in any creature. And I'm sure a man without faults never yet pleased the women!

LADY BEAUVEDERE: Ah, now we are coming to the point. That's my worry.

ST ORBYN: What?

LADY BEAUVEDERE: Bill is so good, and such a dear in every way. . . .

ST ORBYN: While the little Gainsborough has perhaps a failing or two. . . .

LADY BEAUVEDERE: (*eagerly*) Ah, then you *have* heard of some. . . .

ST ORBYN: Not at all. A mere guess on my part. I hear her praises sung in every quarter. Really, G., you ought to be delighted.

LADY BEAUVEDERE: I am . . . I am . . . !

ST ORBYN: The girl is pretty, her father was a distinguished soldier, her mother died before she could become distinguished. . . .

LADY BEAUVEDERE: Ah, then you have heard . . .

ST ORBYN: What?

LADY BEAUVEDERE: The story about her mother. You cannot deceive me. You have heard the story.

ST ORBYN: I have *nothing* to tell *you*, but you have *everything* to tell *me*.

LADY BEAUVEDERE: I could tell you a good deal . . . my heart is too full to go on.

ST ORBYN: I am an old friend – you can cry before me! Besides, I always think a woman is all the prettier for crying.

LADY BEAUVEDERE: (*absently*) Juliet's mother was a fool! Everyone says so.

ST ORBYN: No – no. There is only one fool in the whole of creation – and that is – an unmarried man! (LADY BEAUVEDERE *gives him a quick glance*) Why do I keep single? Perhaps I love too many women too well – or, possibly, too many too little!

LADY BEAUVEDERE: I wish you would be serious.

ST ORBYN: Believe me, I was never more serious.

LADY BEAUVEDERE: I feel a strong temptation to tell you the whole story from beginning to end. . . .

ST ORBYN: I do not see any reason why you should resist that temptation.

LADY BEAUVEDERE: You would think me ill-natured.

ST ORBYN: Never!

LADY BEAUVEDERE: Yes, you would.

ST ORBYN: Have your own way.

LADY BEAUVEDERE: You are so provoking today that . . . I forget half the things I wanted to speak of.

ST ORBYN: Then tell me how *Bill* speaks of his intended.

LADY BEAUVEDERE: He speaks of her as all young men going to be married do speak of their *fiancées*. One would think he had secured an angel of a girl!

ST ORBYN: Well, and hasn't he?

LADY BEAUVEDERE: Of course not. He is infatuated. Juliet is not the wife for a young man in official life. Bill needs some plain, earnest girl who would devote herself solely to his interests.

ST ORBYN: One, in fact, who would *please* the women by *boring* all the men!

LADY BEAUVEDERE: Well, that is not a bad sort of wife for a young fellow with a career before him.

ST ORBYN: The Powers of Europe are getting sick of these devoted wives who think that governments can be dissolved by inviting the right people to a dinner, or the wrong people to a crush!

LADY BEAUVEDERE: I know you are thinking of Sarah Hampshire!

ST ORBYN: No, I ain't. But, all the same, there is a tremendous demand now for simpletons – old school – white muslin – rose behind the ear – a bit of black velvet ribbon round the throat – nice throat – no past, no future – and Heaven our home! Bless 'em!

LADY BEAUVEDERE: I should like to see you with a wife like that!

ST ORBYN: How I should worship her!

LADY BEAUVEDERE: You know you like witty women.

ST ORBYN: I love 'em, the darlings! but not to marry. Why, I'm a wit myself, or used to be! Imagine it! Two wits with but a single epigram – two jokes that pass for one! Good Lord! (*Rises and crosses the room*) Let us talk about Bill.

LADY BEAUVEDERE: (*rising*) I want him to be happy. . . .

ST ORBYN: (*drily*) Quite so!

LADY BEAUVEDERE: My fear is – that Juliet does not love the poor boy.

ST ORBYN: Ah, that's cynical!

LADY BEAUVEDERE: I ask you, Bertie, would a pretty, young, lively girl care naturally for poor darling Bill? (*Points to bust*)

ST ORBYN: Is that considered a good likeness? I have not seen him lately.

LADY BEAUVEDERE: If it were Vivian I could understand it, but . . . Bill is . . . not taking, in fact, he's stodgy! (*Crosses and turns to him with a sentimental air*) Gwen Marleaze has loved him ever since they played together as children.

ST ORBYN: (*approaching her*) There's nothing like force of habit in these things! I knew a man who hated his wife when he married her, and after twenty-five years of wrangling, he would not have given her for Venus! That's a true story!

LADY BEAUVEDERE: (*sitting on stool*) But do you think dear Gwen is interesting enough to quarrel with?

ST ORBYN: No . . . I shouldn't call her a first-class fighting woman – and fighting certainly does appeal to the old Viking spirit of the Anglo-Saxon! (*Seating himself*)

LADY BEAUVEDERE: That's all very well, but this gives me no comfort about Juliet.

ST ORBYN: You are vexed because I have not attacked her. Remember, I have not yet laid eyes upon the poor thing.

LADY BEAUVEDERE: She is very deep – quite impenetrable.

ST ORBYN: Nevertheless, I may not condemn a girl I have never met, because her mother – whom I never knew – nearly ran away with a man – I never saw!

LADY BEAUVEDERE: *Nearly* ran away! Why, every one knows that if she hadn't been thrown from her horse and killed that very morning – on her way to meet him . . .

ST ORBYN: I never attend post-mortems on a conscience!

  Enter GWENDOLENE. ST ORBYN *rises and crosses room;*
    LADY BEAUVEDERE *approaches* ST ORBYN

GWENDOLENE: Dear Lady Beauvedere, the doctor is here. (*Advances to a sofa*)

ST ORBYN: Go at once, Geraldine. Don't let me keep you. I have one or two letters to write.

LADY BEAUVEDERE: (*preparing a seat at the table*) Write them here – at my table.

ST ORBYN: I make it a rule never to write letters at another person's desk.

LADY BEAUVEDERE: What a fancy! Why not?

ST ORBYN: Well, once, when I was younger and more experienced than I am now, I was staying in the country with Lord Glevering when he was Foreign Secretary.

LADY BEAUVEDERE: Dear Lord Glevering!

ST ORBYN: I sat at his table by his own invitation, and I wrote my letters. It happened, however, that without perceiving my mistake, I whipped up some of his private papers which happened to be on the desk. He sought them high and low, the servants were questioned, the guests were perplexed. Four days after I found them in my own portfolio!

(GWENDOLENE, *during this speech, moves down the room with 'The Upper Ten' paper, and sits on sofa*)

LADY BEAUVEDERE: How awkward!

ST ORBYN: Ingenuously, I returned them – with my explanation! To this day I do not know what the documents were, but I am tolerably convinced that, also to this day, his Lordship thinks I did a very neat thing in a confoundedly impudent way!

LADY BEAUVEDERE: (*laughing*) After this I must insist on your using the table.

ST ORBYN: Well, if you insist, I must obey, but – I have a presentiment – a strong presentiment – that history may repeat itself.

(*He crosses to door, to open it for* LADY BEAUVEDERE, *who goes out. He returns to the writing table, without perceiving* GWENDOLENE, *who is reading the paper*)

GWENDOLENE: (*reading aloud to herself*) 'A marriage is arranged and will shortly take place between Sir William Beauvedere, Baronet, and Juliet, youngest daughter of the late Colonel Gainsborough and the late Lady Georgina Gainsborough. All friends will join in wishing the young diplomatist and his beautiful young bride' . . . (*She bursts into tears*) Oh, I cannot wish them happiness – I cannot!

ST ORBYN: (*dropping his pen*) What is that? Is she crying? (*Advances towards her*) My dear child, do you often cry?

GWENDOLENE: (*apparently confused*) Oh, no . . . I am so sorry . . . it is nothing . . . really, nothing.

ST ORBYN: I knew it was nothing. I said to myself – why should she cry? A charming young girl with pretty eyes, devoted friends, and (*Pointing to a brooch she wears*) even the moon – set in diamonds!

GWENDOLENE: That was a present from Bill – on my coming of age. I always wear it.

ST ORBYN: He must feel flattered.

GWENDOLENE: I don't think he notices it.

ST ORBYN: Leave it off for a few days . . . and try the rogue – I know these puppies.

GWENDOLENE: I am sure he wouldn't notice it. He is so absorbed in Miss Gainsborough. Have you met her yet?

ST ORBYN: I have not yet had that pleasure. When does she come back from her drive?

GWENDOLENE: She went out with her sister.

ST ORBYN: Has she got a sister?

GWENDOLENE: Oh, yes, her sister, the nun. It is so droll to think that Juliet's own sister shold have chosen a life of piety and sick nursing.

ST ORBYN: Why droll?

GWENDOLENE: Juliet is so different.

ST ORBYN: And isn't she also a great deal younger!

GWENDOLENE: True, and perhaps the elder sister wanted to clear the way for Juliet! I heard that Colonel Gainsborough could not afford to give both his daughters a dowry – it was small enough, goodness knows! for one, so Alice, being the plainer of the two, became a nun. But people say such horrid things, don't they?

ST ORBYN: They do.

GWENDOLENE: But I am interrupting your letters. . . .

ST ORBYN: Not at all, but I asked Vivian to come to my room for a chat. . . . Remember my advice about the brooch, and, *when the puppy comes back . . . don't wear it.*

GWENDOLENE: I won't forget.

(ST ORBYN *goes out through conservatory.* GWENDOLÉNE
approaches bust, and is looking at it when JULIET *enters
and, without perceiving* GWENDOLENE, *runs across the room,
opens window and waves her handkerchief, laughing loudly*)

JULIET: (*speaking from window to some one outside*) Ah, you are first, after all! But that is as it should be. Thanks so much. I am all right. I am so grateful. . . . Nonsense! How very absurd! How *can* you!

GWENDOLENE: Juliet!

JULIET: It is too amusing. I met Major Lascelles just as I was getting out of the carriage. It seems he lives over the way . . . that is his window. . . . (*Waving again*)

GWENDOLENE: Major Lascelles! That dreadful man!

JULIET: What do you mean? He isn't dreadful. He's charming! He is one of papa's best friends. I have known him all my life and am devoted to him. (*Waves again, kisses her hand, and closes the window*)

(*The two girls look at each other defiantly.* GWENDOLENE
*is standing by the writing table. In her agitation she turns
a pack of cards. They all fall to the floor*)

JULIET: (*springing forward*) Don't touch them. I'll tell your fortune. (*She stoops and turns them over*) I see good news.

GWENDOLENE: (*bitterly*) For me?

JULIET: A great surprise.

GWENDOLENE: A sad one? . . .

JULIET: No . . . a strange one. And look . . . there's hope.

GWENDOLENE: Where?

JULIET: From the poor two of spades!

GWENDOLENE: That's the most trumpery card in the pack!

JULIET: All the same, she brings hope. Oh, Gwen, I see a marriage.

GWENDOLENE: That's your own!

JULIET: No, not mine.

GWENDOLENE: Whose marriage, then? (*Affecting not to care*) How silly!

JULIET: I think . . . it must be yours!

GWENDOLENE (*mechanically*) How silly!

JULIET: And the man is thin . . . tall. . . .

GWENDOLENE: Oh! (*Pretends indifference*)

JULIET: And good-looking . . . rather solemn. . . .

GWENDOLENE: What card is that?

JULIET: Oh, that . . . isn't on the card!

GWENDOLENE: You're making it up!

JULIET: I'm not. His hair is black; his eyes are dark; his nose is narrow; his chin is firm; he knows all the long words in every language!

GWENDOLENE: That's absurd. I don't know a man at all like that. . . .

JULIET: One always marries the most unlikely person! Now I must go . . . but, Gwen. . . .

GWENDOLENE: What?

JULIET: (*whispers in her ear*) You'll see him perhaps at the ball! (*Picks up her parasol and runs out*)

GWENDOLENE: (*following* JULIET *up, stops; then with sudden feeling, to bust*) Oh, did you hear that? Or, if you heard, would you care? (*Hurls the cards at* SIR WILLIAM'S *bust*) Would you care?

(*As she throws the cards, enter* JENKINS *to announce the* PRINCESS VENDRAMINI. *He hesitates a moment. Enter the* PRINCESS VENDRAMINI, *a handsome, worldly person, haughty in bearing, but well bred; emotional, rather affected; dressed in the height of fashion. She speaks with a slight Italian accent, expressing each syllable with care*)

JENKINS: (*announcing*) Madame the Princess Vendramini.

(GWENDOLENE *moves down looking away.* JENKINS *takes books off table and lays tea-cloth.* RORTER *enters with tea-tray, which he puts on table. Both men lift the table a little further down. Then exeunt.*)

VENDRAMINI: *Mon ange!*

GWENDOLENE: (*turning to the* PRINCESS) Oh, is that you, Princess? (*Advances in tears*)

VENDRAMINI: (*kissing her on both cheeks*) How pale! Did I startle you?

GWENDOLENE: (*laughs hysterically*) I was losing my temper. I do sometimes. . . .

VENDRAMINI: Incredible!

GWENDOLENE: I am but human.

VENDRAMINI: Then why quarrel with Nature? We live to love, to suffer, and to die!

GWENDOLENE: (*with passion*) I think I shall die soon – because I cannot die!

VENDRAMINI: (*waving her hand indefinitely toward the bust*) Why don't you go away from these associations?

GWENDOLENE: I *am* going – the day after the ball. I must see him once more – once more, at least!

VENDRAMINI: Then when you meet him – show your spirit. Reproach him, threaten him, sneer at him, laugh at him – exasperate him!

GWENDOLENE: That is not Lord St Orbyn's advice.

VENDRAMINI: (*biting her lip*) Ah, then he has arrived?

GWENDOLENE: Yes. And I believe that he is more fond of Lady Beauvedere than people think. I shouldn't wonder if, after all . . .

VENDRAMINI: (*agitated*) I say it is out of the question. He mustn't marry Geraldine . . . it would be – oh, the word – give me the word!

GWENDOLENE: Madness?

VENDRAMINI: No, sentimentality! He may marry for hate, for money, for power, for independence, for despair, but never, never for sentimentality. I must stop this. (*Rises and paces the room*)

GWENDOLENE: How can you?

VENDRAMINI: (*agitated*) We must distract him. Any woman rather than Geraldine – *any* woman!

GWENDOLENE: But why?

VENDRAMINI: (*returning to centre*) Because we have both known him for the same number of years!

GWENDOLENE: (*softly*) Dear Princess!

VENDRAMINI: I am jealous.

GWENDOLENE: I am so sorry!

VENDRAMINI: I could bear *that*, but she has not the kindness, the tact, the *savoir faire* and *savoir vivre* to show the smallest jealousy of *me*! It is insulting!

GWENDOLENE: That's the hardest part!

VENDRAMINI: Naturally. Oh, if I could see her jealous! Is there no one? St Orbyn is capricious, fastidious to a degree – past all calculations.

GWENDOLENE: There is no one new or interesting here – except Juliet.

VENDRAMINI: (*approaching to* GWENDOLENE)
Of course! But of course! *Juliet*. An inspiration! (*Sinks into a reverie*)

GWENDOLENE: (*frightened*) You won't do anything . . . anything?

VENDRAMINI: *Mon ange*, leave all to me. (*Crosses and pauses*) Shed no more tears and go. (GWENDOLENE *hesitates*) Go. (*Stamps her foot*)

[*Exit* GWENDOLENE]
(THE PRINCESS *laughs contemptuously, then stands listening as though for a footstep. She moves forward smiling as the door opens and* ST ORBYN *enters*)

ST ORBYN: (*astonished*) My dear Princess! I know now that prayers are answered!

VENDRAMINI: Why?

ST ORBYN: Are you not in Paris when I am in Paris?

VENDRAMINI: We both come, I fear, on the same mission!

ST ORBYN: Amazing creature! Are you arranging another war?

VENDRAMINI: In a way – yes. I have come to offer my congratulations on a friend's engagement!

ST ORBYN: Oh, that marriage! (*She shakes her head*) What do you think?

VENDRAMINI: *Mon Dieu*! (*Goes up to table and pours out tea*)

ST ORBYN: Ah, I feared you would take that view – but I like a man who makes a fool of himself about a woman. (*Approaches the tea-table*)

VENDRAMINI: How you must hate yourself!

ST ORBYN: Why?

VENDRAMINI: Because you merely let women make fools of themselves about *you*!

ST ORBYN: Ah, no, those days are over, dearest Princess. I had my faults, but now, in these matters, I am a child (*He hands her tea*) – any one could deceive me – even you. Try!

VENDRAMINI: Oh no! I loved you once, but never again! It gave me three wrinkles, and no man on earth is worth even one.

ST ORBYN: (*piqued*) Well, to flirt with spirit, one must be either too young to think or too wise to trust oneself to think.

VENDRAMINI: I halt between the two conditions. I am not yet old, and not yet wholly wise. (*Sits in chair next piano drinking tea*)

ST ORBYN: Amazing creature? Women should never be either old or wise. They were born to make men happy and each other jealous!

VENDRAMINI: (*handing him her cup, which he places on tea-table*) No. They were born to trust – and to be confounded! Will you never regard me seriously?

ST ORBYN: (*putting his own cup on table*) I can't.

VENDRAMINI: Why not?

ST ORBYN: Beause you make me sad, and I'm only serious . . .

VENDRAMINI: (*eagerly*) When?

ST ORBYN: When I'm joking.

VENDRAMINI: (*agitated and rising*) Oh, you only see me in my lighter moods, listening to scandal, talking nonsense, grinning at this one's disappointment, sighing at that one's success, civil to men whom I distrust, distant to others I dare not – like! (*Going up to him*)

ST ORBYN: Who is the fortunate man who has aroused your discretion?

VENDRAMINI: Cruel . . . But we are forgetting our poor friends.

ST ORBYN: An unpremeditated kindness on my part, I assure you!

VENDRAMINI: Do you know, I have a little plan by which we may help them.

ST ORBYN: As unscrupulous as ever.

VENDRAMINI: Listen. This girl – Juliet Gainsborough – is young, impressionable, ambitious. It would not hurt you to distract her attention, and she – no wiser than the rest of her sex – would be dazzled.

ST ORBYN: Act I., she is dazzled – and now Act II.?

VENDRAMINI: Hoping for a better match, she breaks off her engagement with dear Bill.

ST ORBYN: Act III.?

VENDRAMINI: Well, you will be like the wise knight in the poem—

'Adieu for evermore
My Love!
And adieu for evermore!'

ST ORBYN: Oh, I couldn't find the heart to do it!

VENDRAMINI: *Heart* is not required. You have done nothing else all your life!

ST ORBYN (*stopping her*) Do you defy me – do you dare me?

VENDRAMINI: I could never have believed you so backward in a little intrigue.

ST ORBYN: (*seized by the idea*) Gad! I'll do it!

VENDRAMINI: But what?

ST ORBYN: If the girl is *not* worldly, she will come out of the adventure with flying colours. Why, now I think of it, I may even render her a service by proving to you all that she is sincerely, deeply, wholly in love with that prodigious bore – her inestimable Intended!

VENDRAMINI: But, if, on the other hand, she is worldly – as I think her?

ST ORBYN: In that case, we shall both know how to wish each other *Goodbye*. I shall press her hand. I shall say – 'For the last time.' . . . She will look at me. She will be clever enough to smile. I shall be clever enough to sigh. She will control a sob – I shall control a grin! I shall wish her – sincerely – every happiness. She will wish me – sincerely – to the devil! And there, dearest lady, the matter will end.

VENDRAMINI: Oh, the wickedness of men!

ST ORBYN: Oh, the perfidy of women!

VENDRAMINI: Albert.

ST ORBYN: Yes, Rosamund?

VENDRAMINI: Has the wind ruffled my hair? (ST ORBYN *draws near and examines her face and coiffure very carefully but without emotion*) Well?

ST ORBYN: (*seriously*) I think it's all right. (*Turns away from her*)

VENDRAMINI: Have I changed much since I was a girl?

ST ORBYN: Not a bit.

VENDRAMINI: Don't you think I'm a good deal paler?

ST ORBYN: I hate a blowsy complexion.[6] Yours was always delicate.

VENDRAMINI: (*after a pause*) Haven't you noticed that the expression of my mouth has altered? Some people say it has grown severe!

ST ORBYN: Let me see. No. I should never have dreamed of calling it severe. A shade malicious, perhaps . . . (*Looks at it in silence*)

VENDRAMINI: (*petulantly*) Oh, Albert! you are too . . .

(*Crosses the room and meets* JULIET, *who enters with a telegram in her hand, which she is reading evidently with much concern.*

She greets the PRINCESS *mechanically.* ST ORBYN *advances*)

JULIET: (*crossing to the* PRINCESS) How do you do, Princess? Does Lady Beauvedere know that you are here? (*Going up to* ST ORBYN) This must be Lord St Orbyn. I am Juliet Gainsborough. May I give you some tea?

ST ORBYN: (*much struck*) Thank you, I have had my tea.

JULIET: (*looking at telegram*) This is from Bill. (*Crossing to table*) He has got his leave earlier than he expected. He is now on his way from Berlin to Paris. (*Seems petrified with astonishment*)

VENDRAMINI: (*aside to* ST ORBYN) What do you think of her? (*He is too absorbed to reply*)

JULIET: I suppose Bill would not get any letter that was posted yesterday?

VENDRAMINI: Of course not. But when he sees you he will not want letters.

JULIET: But the letter would be forwarded?

VENDRAMINI: Of course.

JULIET: (*repeating*) Oh yes, . . . (*Seats herself*) It will be forwarded. Will you excuse me for a moment? I must send for my sister. (*Writes*)

ST ORBYN: (*looking at* JULIET) So that is Juliet!

VENDRAMINI: Yes . . . are you disappointed?

ST ORBYN: (*firmly but very quietly*) Princess . . .

VENDRAMINI: Well?

ST ORBYN: (*with quiet force*) If I should ever say anything to her . . . if I should ever lead her to suppose that she was more to me than other women . . . (*with a pause*) . . . I say . . . *if* . . .

VENDRAMINI: Yes? . . . Yes?

ST ORBYN: (*with point*) If I said so – remember this: it would be in earnest. It would be for me – all the world to nothing. (*Quickly*) I say . . . (*After a pause*) . . . *if*.

JULIET: (*to herself*) Of course it would be forwarded.

VENDRAMINI: (*to* ST ORBYN) What is the matter? Is this your first love?

ST ORBYN: (*staring*) No – my last!

Act II

The conservatory at LADY BEAUVEDERE'S. *Dim lights. A fountain (with goldfish) playing in the centre. Several couples in the conservatory. As curtain rises, waltz music is heard. Some of the couples go back to the ball-room. Ball-room seen beyond. A small group of chaperons are near the front of the stage.* LADY BEAUVEDERE, *beautifully dressed, very elegant, adorned with few pearls, etc., stands by fountain.* THE DUCHESS OF HAMPSHIRE *in mauve brocade, lace lappets, diamonds, etc.* LADY BASLER, LADY ULLWEATHER, MRS DASNEY, *with an enormous tiara, very gorgeous, are seated on cane sofa and rout seats*

LADY BEAUVEDERE: (*discovered crossing in front of fountain*) I think perhaps, we ought to go back to our posts. (*Looks about her anxiously*)

LADY ULLWEATHER: (*a languid, thin person with a drawl*) You will never spare yourself or others, Geraldine.

LADY BEAUVEDERE: (*vaguely*) Do you know . . . I am afraid . . . I really must . . . if you don't mind. (*She goes out towards ball-room, peering about as if looking for someone*)

LADY BASLER: (*to* LADY ULLWEATHER) Well, what do you think of the bride-elect?

LADY ULLWEATHER: I really forget. One meets so many women nowadays.

DUCHESS: (*seated on a couch*) Oh, how true that is! If they're dull, I call on 'em during Lent; if they're pretty, I keep 'em for my parties at the *end* of the season; if they're rich, I'm civil to 'em all the year round; and if they're clever, I avoid 'em like the plague!

LADY BASLER: How well dear Gwen Marleaze is bearing the disappointment! I admire her *so* much.

LADY ULLWEATHER: So do I. (*Drowsily*) What with her long, long arms – some people *admire* an arm like a pipe-stem – her amazing corpse-like complexion, and her large, mysterious mouth, I think her quite too fascinating!

LADY BASLER: Oh, you wicked creature!

LADY ULLWEATHER: Wicked? I assure you I admire her excessively. It is so difficult to describe a woman fairly. Words are so *bald*. By the by, Edith, I did not see you at the Baron's wedding.

LADY BASLER: I never go where I am not invited, but then *I* am peculiar.

DUCHESS: (*very kindly*) Not when one knows you, dear.

LADY BASLER: (*after a pause*) I cannot think why St Orbyn does not settle down and marry poor old Rosamund Vendramini. Hers is a real affection.

LADY VANRINGHAM: And if they *love* each other, what does it matter to anybody?

DUCHESS: (*to* LADY BASLER) My dear Edith, men of St Orbyn's turn of mind don't want affection, they want amusement.

LADY BASLER: Then why on earth don't he marry *Geraldine*?

MRS DASNEY: Good heavens! Rosamund couldn't stand that! She sooner would send him after Juliet Gainsborough. (*The* DUCHESS *looks at her: all stare at her for speaking – but she goes on undaunted*) I wish he could fancy one of my poor sisters, but he won't (*Sighs*) – he is too poetical.

LADY BASLER: (*addressing* DUCHESS *and ignoring* MRS DASNEY) But he is not a poet in any ordinary sense, dear Duchess. I mean to say, he wouldn't be called *poetical* in his *tastes*. I once spent a day in the country with three poets . . . real poets . . . professionals . . . you know the sort of thing? I have clean forgotten what they *said*, but I know we had lumps of beef and dreadful pickles for supper!

DUCHESS: How unwholesome! (*To* MRS DASNEY, *who has risen*) What's the matter? Are you leaving?

MRS DASNEY: (*crossing room*) I'm rather tired. You see, I dined here!

[*Exit*]

(*Music stops. Looks at* LADY BASLER, *sighs, then rises as though very tired.*)

DUCHESS: I suppose we must go.

(DUCHESS *goes up right of fountain with* LADY VANRINGHAM.
LADY ULLWEATHER *and* LADY BASLER *go up left of fountain.
Then all solemnly walk out abreast. Enter* ST ORBYN *and* JULIET)

ST ORBYN: Stay a little longer. If this is Bill's dance, let him find you.

JULIET: Yes. I wonder . . . (*pauses*) . . . Don't you think that letters which were sent to Berlin on Saturday and missed him ought to be here now?

ST ORBYN: I should think so. Why? (*Jealously*) Are you still worrying about that letter?

JULIET: (*confused*) Oh no, but – I wish he had it.

ST ORBYN: Don't let us think of Bill and his letters now. This is *my* hour.

JULIET: (*as they stroll toward the fountain*) It is certainly most pleasant here and cool . . .

ST ORBYN: (*looking at her*) As an unplucked rose!

JULIET: I have been reading your poems. They are very pretty, but each one of your two hundred and fifty sonnets is dedicated to a different woman.

ST ORBYN: Not at all. It is the same woman, but she has two hundred and fifty different moods!

JULIET: Was she pretty – and did you love her very much?

ST ORBYN: Inexpressibly!

JULIET: How unfortunate!

ST ORBYN: Why?

JULIET: Because, in that case, she could never know . . .

ST ORBYN: Ah, she knows – she must know – she cannot doubt it.

JULIET: How forward of her!

ST ORBYN: Why forward?

JULIET: I think girls find it so hard, as a rule, to believe that they are really loved . . . by the man they . . . might (*meets his glance*) . . . respect.

ST ORBYN: You guess then that she is a *girl*?

JULIET: Oh no; I was merely speaking – as a girl – about girls – in the vaguest way. (*Removing gloves*)

ST ORBYN: Do you like goldfish?

JULIET: Yes, but I often wonder what they were made for!

ST ORBYN: Why, to look pretty and slip through our fingers – as women do.

JULIET: I am afraid you have a hard opinion of women.

ST ORBYN: (*after a pause*) Yesterday, when I was returning from my ride in the Bois, I looked up and said – that is either her face or a lily in the window!

JULIET: I was only standing there scattering cake to the birds.

ST ORBYN: Happy birds to have the unhappy cake dropped by those beautiful hands!

JULIET: Perhaps it was a lily in the window!

ST ORBYN: And that very lily, I swear, is the one thing on earth I ever loved, or could love – that I ever believed in, or could believe in.

JULIET: So much feeling . . . just for a flower?

ST ORBYN: How can I praise more plainly what I love so deeply – so desperately – so wrongly – and so rightly?

JULIET: (*surprised*) Wrongly?

ST ORBYN: Yes . . . because . . . because, having found this star of stars. But why should the star care for the moth?

JULIET: Is she a star now?

ST ORBYN: Yes . . . she is everything! So, having found her, I propose to keep her against all comers – all pretended owners – against the whole world!

JULIET: I don't suppose . . . the flower . . . I mean, the star . . . I mean, the girl . . . would mind . . . (*Moves down left then turns towards* ST ORBYN)

ST ORBYN: (*following her*) Ah, Juliet, I must love you in any case . . . but, may I? (*She turns toward chair*) I wish . . . I dare not say all I wish . . . yet, you will guess. This engagement to Bill is a mistake . . . an error . . . a crime! You don't . . . you cannot love him . . . (*Watches her face*)

JULIET: (*agitated*) I think . . . I don't wish to love any one . . . . Love makes me afraid . . . Oh, I was happier before!

ST ORBYN: Before what?

JULIET: Before . . . when I was only wondering what it meant.

ST ORBYN: Do you know *now*?

JULIET: (*speaking rather to herself than to* ST ORBYN)
I . . . guess . . . and I say – no, no! Let me be as I was. Let me dream – dreams were best.

ST ORBYN: All my life I have been waiting to meet you . . . looking out for you . . . hoping, despairing, and again hoping. At last you come, and not too late. You never shall belong to any one else! (*Taking her hand*) Juliet, would you mind if you didn't?

JULIET: Your love is one of the things I would most wish for . . . but these things never happen! (*Rises*)

ST ORBYN: (*following her*) It has happened. I do love you. I have known you but five days, yet my destiny is in these little hands. (*Kisses them*)

JULIET: Only five days!

ST ORBYN: But the whole world was made in six! I recognised you at first sight. This, I said, is the one . . . (*taking both her hands*) . . . this is my future wife!

JULIET: (*withdrawing both her hands*) Oh, wait – wait – are you in earnest?

ST ORBYN: (*passionately*) Cannot you see that I mean every word?

JULIET: You may mean them – for the minute – but I must remember them – for ever! You see, there's a difference!

ST ORBYN: My dearest Heart! I swear that my whole life depends now upon your answer.

JULIET: (*Taking and pressing his hand to her cheek*) Oh, how happy I could be, if I *might* be! (*Holds his hand*) I shall think of you often – and that means – always!

ST ORBYN: What is this? Not tears? . . . Why tears?

JULIET: *You* mustn't think of *me*. I am poor and unimportant. I have no great relatives. The world would call it a wild marriage. The world would laugh at you and strike me! Oh, I have met the world so often during the last two weeks.

ST ORBYN: Not the world – but his scarecrows!

JULIET: Oh, I should be your stumbling-block!

ST ORBYN: *My stumbling-block*! You mean my crown – the prize of life! These other notions are fancies.

JULIET: They are not fancies. What did people think about my engagement to Sir William? And they would say of you – St Orbyn has married at last, – a little thing without a shilling; she's young and silly; she's a blight on his career!

ST ORBYN: Who cares? Dearest, every man – even the most cynical – has one enthusiasm – he is earnest about some one thing; the all-round trifler does not exist. If there is a skeleton – there is also an *idol* in the cupboard! That idol may be ambition, love, revenge, the turf, the table – but it is there. Now *I* am flippant. . . .

JULIET: Are you?

ST ORBYN: At times. But, on my honour, I have it in me to be scorched, snubbed, and shelved for the sake of the woman I love. (*Rises*) As for the world – the less a man considers it, the better it will treat him. That's my experience. I will please *it* if possible, but my own heart at any rate!

JULIET: Oh, you speak like my dreams!

> Enter SIR WILLIAM *pompous, well-bred, evidently*
> *good-natured, and self-satisfied*

SIR WILLIAM: Oh, there you are! (*He shows no sort of suspicion. To* JULIET.) I think this must be our dance. I am sorry to be so late, but a host, on these occasions, is expected to be here, there, and everywhere. I know you will forgive me.

JULIET: Oh, of course, I . . . I . . . didn't really expect you, but . . . Oh, see . . . (*Holding up her sash*), when I was playing with the goldfish I splashed some water on my sash.

SIR WILLIAM: How careless!

JULIET: (*crosses the room*) I am afraid I must change it before I go back to the ball-room. I shan't be long. Do you mind? (ST ORBYN *hands her her gloves*)

SIR WILLIAM: (*wiping his brow*) There's no hurry. I shall be glad to have a little chat with St Orbyn. (JULIET *goes out*) I have not had a moment with you since I arrived. I always say, if you want to see your friends, meet 'em at some one else's house – not your own! (*Moves over to sofa*) Between ourselves, I am very worried.

ST ORBYN: Why?

SIR WILLIAM: (*seating himself*) I'm in a cursed hard position.

ST ORBYN: How amusin'!

SIR WILLIAM: Oh no; nothing is amusing that can lead to hysterics and fainting fits! You don't know what it is to have two or three women wrangling about one!

ST ORBYN: No! Perhaps not!

SIR WILLIAM: Mama is drinking quinine by the pint, and Gwendolene is shooting out her eyes at me at every turning. What is to be done?

ST ORBYN: That's the very thing, no doubt, that everybody is asking.

SIR WILLIAM: I'm devoted, as you know, to mama. She has sacrificed her whole life to Vivian – and myself. She was left a widow at nineteen.

ST ORBYN: And what a pretty creature she was too!

SIR WILLIAM: She might have married again (*With a long look at* ST ORBYN) . . . but she didn't. Well, on one side I see this noble self-sacrifice, on the other I am driven to ask myself whether this affection for Juliet is a passing and violent fancy. You will own that Juliet has charm?

ST ORBYN: Yes . . . *great* charm!

SIR WILLIAM: But the women – my stepmother's friends, women of high breeding and culture and experience – seem to detect in Juliet a certain note of satire – as though she rather laughed at one – which they say augurs ill for married happiness. Now I cannot disguise from myself . . .

ST ORBYN: No, disguise nothing!

SIR WILLIAM: Juliet has ideas. She says she would die for them.

ST ORBYN: Why not? To *die* for one's great ideas is glorious – and easy. The horror is to *outlive* them. That is our worst capability.

SIR WILLIAM: (*annoyed at the interruption*) Now, I ask you, as a man of the world, do you believe in the general *workableness* of love at first sight?

ST ORBYN: I've known instances of it . . . among my own intimate acquaintance, in fact! One cannot dogmatise on the subject. Sometimes it answers, and sometimes – it doesn't!

SIR WILLIAM: I suppose it is just one of those things which happen.

ST ORBYN: If it turns out badly, no one talks of anything else.

SIR WILLIAM: And if it turns out well . . . ?

ST ORBYN: They won't take the smallest interest in the matter. Those who have made unhappy marriages walk on stilts, while the happy ones are on a level with the crowd. No one sees 'em!

SIR WILLIAM: I cannot think that the anxiety of the last few weeks points to a peaceful issue. I have a little burden on my conscience too!

ST ORBYN: Your conscience! This means, of course, that somebody somewhere is crying!

SIR WILLIAM: How did you guess!

ST ORBYN: I always associate a man's conscience with a woman's tears. They are inseparable.

SIR WILLIAM: I begin to wonder if I have acted well towards Gwendolene.

ST ORBYN: You certainly grew up together with the notion of pleasing your parents by marrying.

SIR WILLIAM: She has behaved in the most touching manner – not a reproach – but, little things tell! She no longer wears a small gift I gave her – a trifle – a *moonstone brooch*.

ST ORBYN: Ah!

SIR WILLIAM: Every time I see her now, I miss it, and it is as though a certain light had gone out of my life.

ST ORBYN: I attach, as you do, *immense* importance to the brooch episode!

SIR WILLIAM: I am glad you agree with me. That simple, unstudied act, I assure you, has cut me to the heart more deeply than any scene, any appeal could ever have done. It is by these means – so artless and so infinitely pathetic – that woman conquer us.

ST ORBYN: True. Oh, how true!

SIR WILLIAM: Turn over my difficulty in your mind. See – on the one side the unswerving love of Gwendolene.

ST ORBYN: (*working on his sympathy*) The friendship of your childhood, the affection of your more mature years.

SIR WILLIAM: She is not pretty . . . she is not accomplished . . .

ST ORBYN: But she is good. She has fine eyes, and then – she's fond of you!

SIR WILLIAM: *Very!*

ST ORBYN: On the other side . . . ?

SIR WILLIAM: There is a fancy, perhaps a purely physical infatuation. I say perhaps. . . .

ST ORBYN: Nothing more likely. Take that for granted.

SIR WILLIAM: (*sighing*) While Juliet herself is, I must say, extremely cold, with all her lively airs.

ST ORBYN: Personally, I should not hesitate for a moment. (*Rises*)

SIR WILLIAM: (*rising*) Then what would you do?

ST ORBYN: Do! I would take the woman I wanted, of course!
'Gather the rose of love whilst yet 'tis time,
Whilst loving thou mightst loved be . . .'[7]
and so on!

SIR WILLIAM: (*sighing*) Yet . . . how delightful she is!

ST ORBYN: Which of 'em?

SIR WILLIAM: Why, Juliet, of course!

ST ORBYN: (*seeing his hesitancy*) Ah, but think of that other poor girl! Think of Gwendolene – her sleepless nights – watching the sun rise and the moon come out. . . .

SIR WILLIAM: Awful!

ST ORBYN: Think of her silent tears! How she has shared in thought and hope every step in your career. Ah, never play with hearts! And then think of her eyes – those mournful eyes full of a great, uncomplaining, ever-devoted love. Upon my word, it would move a Don Juan to fidelity!

SIR WILLIAM: Well, I hope I'm not a Duan Juan! But I grant Gwendolene's claim. And, after all, Juliet told me at the beginning that she did not love me.

ST ORBYN: (*relieved*) Ah, she told you that, did she?

SIR WILLIAM: (*taking* ST ORBYN'S *arm and walking with him*) Yes, with the most amazing candour. I confess I was piqued – deucedly piqued! At the time, I put it down to coquetry, but since my arrival here she has been more distant than ever. We have hardly exchanged a word.

ST ORBYN: (*with veiled sarcasm*) But then, your stepmother has naturally monopolised you to the exclusion of others!

SIR WILLIAM: True. When I saw my stepmother – I had not expected such a change – I felt I ought, in duty, to knock under.

ST ORBYN: My dear Bill, you are right. A broken engagement is a pity, but a wretched marriage is a joke – a hideous, hellish joke! Don't submit the most serious action of your life to the judgment of a parcel of old women, who only think of the presents they have had engraved with your wife's monogram!

SIR WILLIAM: That's all very well, but they rule the set, you know. If they don't happen to like a woman, they can make it very disagreeable for a fellow.

ST ORBYN: I suppose they can – given the fellow!

SIR WILLIAM: All the same, your advice is excellent (*Both walk up stage*), and I am wholly of your opinion, but – how in the world . . .

ST ORBYN: Ah, Princess!

Enter the PRINCESS VENDRAMINI *and* LORD LAVENSTHORPE

SIR WILLIAM: I will leave you.

[*Exit with* LAVENSTHORPE]

VENDRAMINI: (*to* ST ORBYN) Well, have you been happy this evening?

ST ORBYN: Your presence casts a spell over my memory. Now, at last, I am in bliss; I forget all that I was, or have been!

VENDRAMINI: (*seating herself*) Your compliments are a two-edged sword; they hurt both of us!

ST ORBYN: I deserve my wounds. And you, Rosamund . . . ?

VENDRAMINI: I own I am not blameless.

ST ORBYN: It is so hard to know when you speak in mockery and when you speak in earnest.

VENDRAMINI: (*laughing bitterly*) Do you think that any woman can be in earnest when she refers to her own shortcomings? But, speaking of faults, what do you think now of little Gainsborough?

ST ORBYN: She has eyes like woods of autumn, and a voice like the west wind among roses!

VENDRAMINI: Little minx! Why don't you trust me, and speak out? Madame de Savigny and Princess Zoubaroff both say . . .

ST ORBYN: (*sitting right of her*) No names! Mention no names, I entreat you. The one safe theme in diplomatic circles is Ancient History. Talk of Caesar, George IV, Henry VIII., or Queen Anne, and mean . . . whom you please. But don't speak of your friends — friends with whom we dine, have dined, and hope again to dine!

VENDRAMINI: I believe that little thing has bewitched you! Gwen Marleaze told me as much just now.

ST ORBYN: Poor Gwen! She is youngish, prettyish . . .

VENDRAMINI: (*tartly*) And foolish!

ST ORBYN: (*thoughtfully*) It is a great embarrassment, but there seems no lively way of describing the virtues!

VENDRAMINI: (*peevishly*) The virtues aren't women at all.

ST ORBYN: What are they?

VENDRAMINI: Allegories.

ST ORBYN: Your sex, then, consists of the Graces, the Muses, and the Dowdies!

VENDRAMINI: You shan't change the subject! I call Gwen Marleaze a cat! Upon my word, I would sooner Bill married Juliet after all.

ST ORBYN: There I can't agree with you. The more I see of Miss Gainsborough, the more I feel convinced that Sir William is *not* the man to make her happy!

VENDRAMINI: Nonsense!

ST ORBYN: But he could never appreciate her: that shy, delicate humour; that innocent roguery . . . that pearly flesh tint round the chin!

VENDRAMINI: *Mon Dieu!* The flame this time has been extinguished by the moth! She has got the better of you. Who would have believed it! She has fooled you!

ST ORBYN: Not at all. You will not deny that she is just nineteen. *You* will know, because I think she told me you were present at her christening!

VENDRAMINI: (*falling into the trap*) Nineteen! She is *not* nineteen. She is barely seventeen . . . if that . . .

ST ORBYN: Delighted to hear it! Again, you own she is lovely to look at?

VENDRAMINI: I admit she possesses certain attractions of a superficial kind.

ST ORBYN: Exactly. A fine complexion, beautiful hair, and pretty features are unquestionably on the surface. I thank my stars they are! One would not be well advised to take them, like the soul, for granted! (*Rises and moves centre*) But come, can you resist this music?

VENDRAMINI: I could resist the music . . . but you – alas! (*Sighs*)

ST ORBYN: Shall we go?

> (*She accepts his arm, and they return to the ball-room*
> *as* SIR WILLIAM *and* JULIET *enter by arch;* JULIET *is*
> *carrying some letters*)

JULIET: (*to* SIR WILLIAM) As I was passing through the hall, I found these letters. They are from Berlin. I thought they might be important. There is one I sent on Saturday, which missed you. I should like you to read it.

SIR WILLIAM: Why read it when you are here yourself? I can read this at any time – when I am alone.

JULIET: (*in a low voice*) I would rather you read it now, because it is really rather important.

SIR WILLIAM: (*peevishly*) I tell you, I am not in the mood. I am greatly distressed about Mama and one or two other things. I am not myself . . . I . . .

> *Enter* VIVIAN *hurriedly, pale and greatly agitated*

VIVIAN: (*to* SIR WILLIAM)

Bill! I must see you at once. It is a matter of life and death. Please leave us alone, Juliet.

SIR WILLIAM: (*pompously*) This is absurd. What is the matter. I cannot go into it now. I can conceive of nothing so inopportune!

JULIET: Do see him, Bill. I can wait here. I shall like resting. (*Putting her hand on his arm*) Be kind to him, won't you? (*She glides away to the side and sits up left*)

SIR WILLIAM: (*to* VIVIAN) Well, what is it? (*Crosses and sits on couch*)

VIVIAN: (*standing over* SIR WILLIAM) I'm in the most awful fix. You know Hugo Lascelles?

SIR WILLIAM: I have heard of the person.

VIVIAN: He's been very decent to me . . . . He let me play cards with him.

SIR WILLIAM: Indeed!

VIVIAN: Just at first I won a good deal.

SIR WILLIAM: Well?

VIVIAN: Then I began to lose . . . a good deal more than I won.

SIR WILLIAM: Of course! Well . . . ?

VIVIAN: You know Mama has been too ill to read her letters lately. The other day a cheque came from Didcomb for £500. It so happened that I put it in my breast-pocket.

SIR WILLIAM: Well . . . ?

VIVIAN: Last night I lost £500 to Lascelles.

SIR WILLIAM: Lost £500! . . . Good Gad! . . . Good Gad! (*Stands up*) . . . Good Gad!

VIVIAN: What is the use of Good Gad-ing about the place? I thought I should win it back in no time . . . so I played again this afternoon. I lost more. . . .

SIR WILLIAM: Well?

VIVIAN: There were several fellows there. . . . I had promised Lascelles the money. So . . . without meaing it . . . I thought of the cheque.

SIR WILLIAM: Go on!

VIVIAN: Well . . . I endorsed it in Mama's name . . . and gave it him.

SIR WILLIAM: You mean to say you forged Mama's name?

VIVIAN: I tell you I didn't mean to do it. It was one of those sudden impulses. . . . It just came into my head . . . I tell you it seemed the only way out of the scrape. I thought you wouldn't mind paying in the money to Mama's account, so that she wouldn't miss it. I have acknowledged the cheque to Didcomb. He's all right. I can arrange the details later . . . but . . .

SIR WILLIAM: You expected me to be a party to this abominable deception . . . *me*! (*Paces the room*)

VIVIAN: (*following him*) I'll pay it all back again – honour bright – when I come of age. What's a little beastly five hundred pound to you? I don't ask it for my sake either, but for her – to save her – when she is so ill and worried about you. You might be willing to spare her the disappointment about me. She wouldn't mind the

money. It's the way I've got it. She told me to break off with
Lascelles – but she told *you* to break off with *Juliet* . . .

SIR WILLIAM: (*springing to his feet indignantly*) Not another word!

VIVIAN: I say it isn't so easy as it seems to go about breaking off. You
might be decent for this once and pay the money – and jaw, if you
like, afterwards.

SIR WILLIAM: (*after some hesitation*) No. On principle! No!

VIVIAN: I say, you don't mean that? You're an awfully goodhearted
chap, really.

SIR WILLIAM: This flattery is nauseating. I say Mama has indulged you
to the most absurd degree. Let her observe the disastrous effect of a
fond bringing up.

VIVIAN: (*half in tears*) What is the good of going on like this? Lascelles,
I tell you, has got the cheque. He will pay it in tomorrow morning.

SIR WILLIAM: Tell me no more about it. On principle, I wash my hands
of the matter.

VIVIAN: Then I shall blow my brains out – that's all! (*Excited*)

SIR WILLIAM: These vulgar threats, my dear Vivian, are unavailing.

VIVIAN: But I tell you . . .

SIR WILLIAM: Silence, I say. Here is your wretched mother.

Enter LADY BEAUVEDERE

LADY BEAUVEDERE: Bill, Vivian, surely you have partners. You
cannot be spared from the ball-room. Several of the best dancers
have left already. I believe that dreadful Major Lascelles is giving a
party himself this evening, merely to vex me and entice away my
men.

SIR WILLIAM: I find it hard to believe that any of your friends would
prefer Lascelles' society to ours. But (*With a pointed glance at*
VIVIAN), one can be sure of nothing. (*To* LADY BEAUVEDERE) I will
come with you.

LADY BEAUVEDERE: (*taking* SIR WILLIAM'S *arm*) Come, dear Vivie.

VIVIAN: I'm coming . . . in a minute.

(LADY BEAUVEDERE *and* SIR WILLIAM *go back to the ball-room.*
VIVIAN *remains staring after them*)

VIVIAN: All right . . . I say, all right. (*Takes a small pocket-pistol from
his pocket*) I'm not such a fool as I look. I know the quickest way
out of every scrape. (*Handles the pistol*)

JULIET: (*rushing forward from her place of semi-concealment*)
Vivian! What are you doing?

VIVIAN: (*hiding the pistol*) I was . . . just thinking, that's all.

JULIET: (*embarrassed*) Vivie . . . I couldn't help hearing . . . some of the things. . . . Bill talks rather loud, and I was so afraid lest some one else should hear, that I nearly interrupted him.

VIVIAN: (*huskily*) Don't be sorry. Every dog has his day. I've had mine . . . I've had a very good time, take it all round. I ain't complaining.

JULIET: (*moving near to him*) I wish I could help you. I haven't a penny of money myself, but Major Lascelles would be kind, I know, if you asked him.

VIVIAN: Ah, you don't know Lascelles.

JULIET: Oh yes, I do!

VIVIAN: You do!

JULIET: I've known him ever since I can remember.

VIVIAN: (*apparently struck with an idea*) Does he like you?

JULIET: (*simply*) I think so.

VIVIAN: Would you have the pluck to . . . no, you wouldn't . . .

JULIET: (*eagerly*) Yes, I would . . . but what for?

VIVIAN: He will do nothing for men. He is as hard as the devil with men, but they say he will do any mortal thing for a pretty woman.

JULIET: You want me to ask him not to present that cheque?

VIVIAN: That's it. What a clever girl you are, after all!

JULIET: I'll write him a note in the morning.

VIVIAN: A note . . . that won't do . . . you must *see* him.

JULIET: Very well, then I'll go and see him tomorrow.

VIVIAN: But . . . tomorrow will be too late. You must go tonight.

JULIET: Tonight! Why, it's nearly three o'clock already.

VIVIAN: Ah, I knew you wouldn't have the pluck! But, think how easy it will be. He has a party this evening.

JULIET: Yes.

VIVIAN: So . . . I know you will find him at home.

JULIET: Yes.

VIVIAN: You can get out through that gate. (*Points to conservatory door*)

JULIET: Yes.

VIVIAN: Run across the garden to his house.

JULIET: I see.

VIVIAN: Send up your name on a card.

JULIET: Yes.

VIVIAN: Ask to see him . . . and tell the concierge that you have an appointment.

JULIET: Well . . . what else?

VIVIAN: He'll see you, be quite sure of that. *Make* him give you back the cheque into your own hands. Don't come away *without* it.

JULIET: I'll do it.

VIVIAN: You will!

JULIET: I'll do it . . . not for you – but, for your mother.

VIVIAN: Ah, you wouldn't like to see her heart broken, would you?

JULIET: I say I will do it on her account. Have you got the key of the garden gate?

VIVIAN: (*taking it from his pocket*) Yes, I use it . . . rather often.

JULIET: Oh, Vivie!

VIVIAN: My dear girl, a man can't run around holding his mother's hand all day! (*Gives her the key*)

JULIET: Quick! quick! (*He moves to door and opens it*) Will you wait here to let me in when I come back? Oh, Vivie, it is very dangerous . . . if any one were to see me, how could I explain? (*Follows him to door*)

VIVIAN: They won't see you. They've never caught me yet. Make haste.

JULIET: I see the way now . . . straight across the garden through the gate. (*She puts scarf round her head*) Oh, Vivie, why did you do it? Your poor mother!

> (*She darts out, and he closes the door. At this moment the music ceases. The couples pour in. Among them is* GWENDOLENE, *looking very pale, on* SIR WILLIAM'S *arm, followed by* LADY BEAUVEDERE)

GWENDOLENE: I feel a little faint. . . . Could you take me to the door? . . . The air . . .

SIR WILLIAM: (*opening the door*) There . . . are you better, dear Gwendolene?

LADY BEAUVEDERE: Fetch her my salts – quickly.

> [*Exit* SIR WILLIAM]

GWENDOLENE: Thank you . . . so much better . . . (*She lifts her head, looks out into the garden, suddenly seems amazed, rubs her eyes, seizes* LADY BEAUVEDERE'S *arm*) Lady Beauvedere, do you see that white figure? . . . running . . . is . . . look quickly. . . .

LADY BEAUVEDERE: (*peering*) Where, Gwen? . . . It is . . . !

GWENDOLENE: Can it be . . . Juliet? Where is she going?

LADY BEAUVEDERE: Where *is* she going?

GWENDOLENE: There are lights in Major Lascelles' windows. . . .

LADY BEAUVEDERE: What has *she* to do with Major Lascelles?

GWENDOLENE: She met him this morning. . . . I caught her waving to him from the drawing-room.

LADY BEAUVEDERE: (*quickly*) Not a word of this to Bill. . . . Leave it all to me. . . . Not a word. . . . (*She goes out into the garden*)

(SIR WILLIAM returns with the smelling-bottle. GWENDOLENE
closes the door hurriedly)

SIR WILLIAM: (*anxiously to* GWENDOLENE) Are you better?

GWENDOLENE: (smiling) So *much* better!

Act III

At MAJOR LASCELLES' *residence in the Champs Elysées. It is about 3 a.m. Room furnished in the Renaissance style: heavily gilded ceiling, dark wood chairs; prevailing tints, gold and blue and red. As curtain rises great noise of laughing and chattering. Supper table is seen with remains of very elaborate supper. About six guests besides* LASCELLES *himself. Four are women. As curtain rises* MISS KATIE *and* MISS YOLANDE TAYLORSON, *two young girls, with hair down their backs, dressed fantastically in accordion-pleated baby dresses, are standing in front of supper table wrapt in contemplation of a song being sung by* TOTO, *a young man, accompanied by* MISS MAMIE TAYLORSON *the eldest daughter of* MRS TAYLORSON. MRS TAYLORSON, *an elderly lady very weary, in black silk of the utmost respectability, watches her daughters with pride. This group to convey an impression of candid vulgarity as opposed to vicious, or merely fashionable vulgarity. At conclusion of song all clap hands*

LORD REGGIE: (*seated right of table*) And now, Miss Katie, won't you dance?

MRS TAYLORSON: Why, yes, Katie, you can do that little skirt dance for Lord Reggie.

KATIE: Why, yes – if you'll (*to* MAMIE) play. (*Talks to* LORD REGGIE) (MAMIE *begins to play opening bars of the* Sonata Pathétique)

KATIE: Oh, Mamie, not that one! That's the tune the old cow died of!

MAMIE: (*with indignation*) Did you expect me to play anything different? My style is Classic.

KATIE: Oh, well, I know that, but try how I will, I can't dance worth a cent to really good music. Please play something vulgar just for this once!

MAMIE: (*with a deep sigh*) Well, I will. (*Plays*)
          (KATIE *dances most decorously; while she is dancing*
                    enter ST ORBYN)

LASCELLES: O, le bienvenu! How did you escape so soon? (*Leaning on back of piano*) Was the widow's ball a bore?

ST ORBYN: (YOLANDE *goes to him*) I could not love 'ma belle cousine' so much loved I not dullness more! (*Shakes hand with* YOLANDE)

YOLANDE: Pshaw! Mama, Lord St Orbyn always calls me cousin!

MRS TAYLORSON: Why, that's very kind!

KATIE: Mama, let me present Lord St Orbyn. (MRS TAYLORSON *rises*) Lord St Orbyn, this is my mother, Mrs Whitcomb J. Taylorson. (*Crosses and speaks to* YOLANDE)

MRS TAYLORSON: Happy to meet you, Lord St Orbyn.

ST ORBYN: (*to* MRS TAYLORSON) Delighted to meet the charming mother of the Muses.

(YOLANDE *sits on the supper table*)

MRS TAYLORSON: (*very practically*) Oh, now, Lord St Orbyn! You know Mamie? (LORD ST ORBYN *bows to* MAMIE) If you would just put in a word (*confidentially*) for Yolande and Katie at the Grand Opera House, I'd be real grateful to you. You know they're studying their voices here for the stage. Mamie, of course, is at the Conservatoire, studying the piano.

MAMIE: For the Lamoureux Concerts . . . nothing less!

MRS TAYLORSON: Yolande's had elegant offers, but she won't marry. She's an artiste by temperament. Art with her is all in all.

YOLANDE: (*with her mouth full, still sitting on table and taking up a dish of pastry*) I live for Art. Marriage is like a good pie spoilt in the baking. Everything is admirable except the result! It is very heavy . . . very, very heavy! (*Bursts into laughter and throws plate on the floor*)

KATIE: Why, Yolande, how you do act! I sh' think you'd be ashamed!

YOLANDE: Get along! He's not the only pebble on the beach!

ST ORBYN: (*going over to* LASCELLES *at piano*) Just get rid of them for a moment. Send them into the billiard-room. I want a few minutes with you. I must be quiet. (*Crosses up into recess*)

LASCELLES: Here, Reggie, just go into the billiard-room a little while.

[*Exeunt* REGGIE, YOLANDE *and* KATIE]

LASCELLES: Here, Toto, just go with the other children into the next room.

TOTO: (*eating stolidly at head of table*) Oh no; I'm still too hungry!

LASCELLES: I thought of that. There is another supper in there. (*Gives his arm to* MRS TAYLORSON)

MRS TAYLORSON: Why, how lavish!

[*Exeunt* MRS TAYLORSON, TOTO *and* MAMIE]

LASCELLES: Yolande is a great dear! Awful straight goer too! Isn't she amusing?

ST ORBYN: (*coming down with a sigh of relief, and sitting in chair*) Oh, I dare say, when one is in the right vein.

LASCELLES: Why, what is the matter?

ST ORBYN: It's a wise man that knows his own imbecility!

LASCELLES: But this is serious. When Yolande begins to bore a man, I know what to expect. You must be contemplating marriage.

ST ORBYN: (*irritably*) No doubt. If anything on earth would fairly *kick* one into marriage, it would be Yolande! But, I'm not thinking about her at all.

LASCELLES: Of course not. (*Gets chair from table and sits*) Has she blue eyes, this time, or brown? Has she a cruel parent, or a brutal husband? Is she tender, or is she proud?

ST ORBYN: *This* is altogether a new experience! *This* . . . this is the real thing! I have often been taken, often fallen in love, if you like, for all sorts of reasons; but, *this* time I am not conscious of any particular reason one way or the other. It is destiny . . . destiny!

LASCELLES: If you once begin to talk about destiny, you know . . .

ST ORBYN: I am not a romantic boy with a head full of rhymes and a liver full of illusions. . . .

LASCELLES: I'd rather be ruled by a liver than by love!

ST ORBYN: A liver lasts longer! Oh, I know my world – I know women. I know their *faults*. I know their good points too. Women may be whole oceans deeper than we are, but they are also a whole paradise better! She may have got us out of Eden, but as a compensation she makes the earth very pleasant! If I have not married, it is not because I didn't believe in women.

LASCELLES: Why, then?

ST ORBYN: Because I have not believed in *myself*!

LASCELLES: And now?

ST ORBYN: Oh, now I begin to understand my own poetry! That's *something*, you know – hang it! that's a good deal; indeed, that's half the battle!

LASCELLES: You have certainly written a lot of poetry about love.

ST ORBYN: Well, it was all imagination. It was not from my own experience.

LASCELLES: They say the nightingale sings divinely during his courtship, but once mated, he can only croak.

ST ORBYN: That may be my case. At any rate, I have at last met the one woman I can worship . . . do you hear – *worship*? . . . (*Rises*) What do you know about worship? . . . Nothing!

LASCELLES: I am having an object-lesson now. (*Turning chair towards* ST ORBYN)

ST ORBYN: Guess who it is?

LASCELLES: I must decline that indiscretion.

ST ORBYN: (*sitting at supper table, and moving things about nervously*) Think of the ass she is engaged to. Think of the dull, portentous bore with the brain of a . . . a . . . lobster and the heart of a . . . a . . . spring onion! (*Takes a piece of lobster and a spring onion out of the salad bowl*) Think of *him*.

LASCELLES: By Jove! you don't mean . . .

ST ORBYN: Yes, I do. There is but one.

LASCELLES: Good Lord! What is going to happen?

ST ORBYN: (*sitting right of table*) A row, of course.

LASCELLES: But seriously . . . you mean Bill Beauvedere?

ST ORBYN: Not seriously – *superfluously*! That is all – *superfluously*. He must be removed. He can't be permitted: he is an unnecessary person!

LASCELLES: That's all very well, but this is going to be awkward.

ST ORBYN: By no means. A little friendly jobbery, that's all! I know his mother, I know the girl – such a nice, good, plain girl – he ought to marry. It is just a simple case of a *plus* b *plus* x *minus* x – a mere matter of subtraction. These problems are nothing to me.

LASCELLES: I have every confidence in your skill, but these things work out better on paper then they do in the flesh.

ST ORBYN: Bosh! Flesh? Who cares for the flesh? My godmother renounced all that for me at my baptism!

LASCELLES: Ah! there is where you diplomatists come to grief; you are always backing the devil against the world . . . and the rest of it.

ST ORBYN: The devil is a very poor creature. I have no opinion of him . . . I wouldn't put a shilling on him; a low, tenth-rate, rank outsider! Faust called in all hell in order to ruin one simple girl, and she, by her prayers to Heaven, saved his soul! No, love will get the better of the devil every time; love is the supreme power; love, my dear fellow, is . . . simply tremendous; love is the one thing that always wins, and must win; love has wings, do you hear? . . . wings!

LASCELLES: Yes . . . to fly away!

ST ORBYN: No, no. That's so vulgar; everybody says that who has backed a wrong'un! No, love has wings to lift one out of every trouble, every disaster; love . . .

LASCELLES: If this fancy comes to a crisis, I suppose you know what will happen?

ST ORBYN: No.

LASCELLES: Miss Gainsborough is a charming girl, and beautiful – but she's no match! She is all that a woman should be – high-minded, virtuous, exquisite, but – she's no match.

ST ORBYN: (*rising*) No match!

LASCELLES: She has, perhaps, five thousand pound, all told. The Duke of Drumdrosset, her grandfather, is a recluse; few people have even heard of him – at any rate he's not a bit of good! It would be a foolish marriage. It would, indeed. No candid friend of yours could say otherwise.

ST ORBYN: (*satirically, moving towards fireplace*) And yet – she is all that a woman should be, charming, beautiful, high-minded, virtuous, exquisite!

LASCELLES: Well, aren't there other women equally delightful, but who have money into the bargain, and who have influence in the right quarters? What I ask is this – does your private fortune, quite apart from your salary, allow you to play Prince Charming to Cinderella?

ST ORBYN: (*to himself*) No match! Good Lord! No match! (*Laughs*)

LASCELLES: I know the Foreign Office. They will take you away from Rome. You will never get Paris or Petersburg – never! But they will give you something dingy and feverish, God knows where!

ST ORBYN: (*seating himself*) Let 'em! Fine appointments are rare, but a good wife is rarer. The Foreign Office, my dear fellow, is not, and never has been the master of my fate. I do my work honestly, and if they can find a better fellow for *their* business, let 'em send for him by all means. But my marriage is *my* business. Miss Gainsborough is a lady who, if she consents to join her life with mine, will do me the greatest honour that existence can give. Do you understand me now?

LASCELLES: I do! (*Rises, gets cigarette-box from table*)

ST ORBYN: Moreover, say that my private means *are* small, well, when I retire, I can live in what people call a small way. I can do admirably on £2,000 a year – and bills!

LASCELLES: Bills! That is what I am thinking of. With your tastes, your habits (*Handing him cigarette from box on table*), your friends! This is all very well and pretty, but at your age and with your experience. . . .

ST ORBYN: I don't care. It is just because I *am* at my age and have *had* my experience that I am determined to have my own way. With £2,000 a year one can take a little place in the country, and what with one's books and one's garden . . . and a friend or two to stay with one now and again . . .

LASCELLES: Oh, charming – for a short time! But it is very difficult to live on £2,000 a year all the year round! And then your ambition?

ST ORBYN: What of that? In the age of chivalry one's devotion to a sweetheart was as necessary as one's glory in the fight. A man was no man unless he could be determined in love. Well, it's the same today. A man is still a man. And when you see a fellow really making his mark, really feared by his enemies and liked by his friends, you will find . . .

LASCELLES: What?

ST ORBYN: You will find that he has had, among other things, the sense to marry for love.

LASCELLES: But love-matches don't always make for happiness!

ST ORBYN: Never mind that. The great thing is to love – not to be happy. Love is for both worlds. Perfect happiness is for the other only.

LASCELLES: Well, say you are very fond of Miss Gainsborough. . . .

ST ORBYN: I'm *not* 'very fond' of her . . . I *love her! My* part is sure at any rate. The rest is for Providence or Fate.

LASCELLES: My goodness!

ST ORBYN: I take her for better for worse, for richer for poorer. (*Naïvely*) There is nothing about happiness or the Foreign Office in the marriage vows! And, moreover . . . (*perceiving* DUVAL *enter, changes whole tone*) . . . Yes, as you were saying, it is clear as daylight that the Government desires to see the whole question settled. (*Crosses the room*)

(DUVAL *hands* LASCELLES *a card*)

LASCELLES: (*without reading the card; grinning*) Oh, this is Tina – dear little Tina! She's killing! But fancy the puss sending up a card. (*To* DUVAL) Show her up.   [*Exit* DUVAL]

(LASCELLES *takes card to lamp, reading it to himself*)

Good Lord! . . .

ST ORBYN: What is the matter?

LASCELLES: It isn't Tina, after all! It's some one . . . some one . . . else.

ST ORBYN: (*languidly*) Can't you pack her into the billiard-room with the others?

LASCELLES: Well, I needn't see her here. I'll tell you what I'll do – I'll . . . (*walks to door*)

(*Just as he is going to the door,* DUVAL *ushers in* JULIET, *who has a lace scarf over her head. As she enters, she throws back the scarf.* ST ORBYN *springs to his feet on recognising her. Both bow low – then* ST ORBYN *goes in the billiard-room, leaving* LASCELLES *and* JULIET *together*)

JULIET: Major Lascelles, you will be greatly surprised . . .

LASCELLES: No, no. Pray sit down. I am only sorry that . . .

(*Loud peals of laughter from the billiard-room*)

JULIET: (*starting and speaking eagerly*) I came to ask a favour . . . It is something I cannot write, because there is not a moment to be lost – not an instant.

LASCELLES: You have only to ask it.

JULIET: It is about Vivian. He was here this afternoon, *wasn't he?* And you very kindly allowed him to join . . . to join one of your amusing games, *didn't* you? And in the excitement . . . he . . . *inadvertently* gave you something by mistake . . . *didn't* he?

LASCELLES: (*very quietly*) I knew . . . at the time, that it was, as you say, a mistake . . . there is no occasion for anxiety. (*Goes to escritoire and unlocks it, and takes out envelope*) The error . . . is in that.

JULIET: But the debt?

LASCELLES: The debt? That's Vivian's lesson. You know there's a time to be young, there's a time to be foolish.

JULIET: Oh, how can I thank you! I was so anxious, because his mother does not understand . . . games and things, as *you* do.

LASCELLES: She shall never know.

JULIET: It was a mistake, after all, any one might make, *wasn't* it?

LASCELLES: Oh, yes, quite a common occurrence. Never gave it a second thought!

JULIET: How good you are! And . . . now, I have to ask something else. (*With great difficulty*) Don't explain my reason for coming here to Lord St Orbyn.

LASCELLES: (*taking her hand*) Is that your wish, because . . . he might think . . .

JULIET: It *is* my wish. Don't explain on *any* account.

LASCELLES: I promise you.

JULIET: Thank you. (*Shakes hands with him. Laughter heard from the billiard-room*) May I go now? (*Moves to door below sofa.* LADY BEAUVEDERE *knocks at door*)

LASCELLES: Who is that?

LADY BEAUVEDERE: (*entering*) May I come in?

JULIET: (*with a cry of terror*) Ah! . . . Lady Beauvedere!

LADY BEAUVEDERE: (*advancing*) Major Lascelles, I must apologise for this intrusion. It is made, as you may believe, against my will; but I thought Juliet ought not to be here alone. . . . (*She pauses*)

LASCELLES: I hope you don't think . . .

LADY BEAUVEDERE: (*haughtily*) If you ask me what I *think*, I can only say that I know *nothing*, that I understand nothing, and, on the other hand, that I can conceive of nothing that would explain this.

JULIET: (*To* LASCELLES, *seeing him about to speak*)
Please . . . please! Let me see Lady Beauvedere alone for a few minutes.

LASCELLES: But Lady Beauvedere may not be aware that your father is one of my oldest friends.

(*Billiard-room door bursts open and* YOLANDE *runs in, sees visitors*)

YOLANDE: Great Caesar!

(*Bangs door and goes out, giggling loudly*)

LADY BEAUVEDERE: (*controlling her indignation*) No doubt Miss Gainsborough finds a party of *old* friends more amusing than one among new acquaintances!

JULIET: (*to* LASCELLES) Please leave us.

LADY BEAUVEDERE: I am unable to remain here, Major Lascelles. I have stolen away, as it is, from my own house, my own guests, in order to save this reckless girl from the worst consequences of this conduct. I blame you more (*to* LASCELLES), but I blame her sufficiently.

(*Singing from billiard-room;* LASCELLES *goes to door to quiet them, and remains at back of stage, by the writing table*)

JULIET: (*to* LADY BEAUVEDERE)

(*This scene to be taken at a quick pace. The words must come, as it were, like hailstones*)

Wait, wait! I know I must seem foolish, and . . . everything else. I know that, and I can never explain, never. But, you need not be so sorrowful because I am no longer engaged to Bill.

LADY BEAUVEDERE: (*astonished*) No longer engaged to Bill! Has he broken off the engagement?

JULIET: (*smiling sadly*) No, I wrote to him before he came from Berlin. Five days ago. The letter missed him, unfortunately, but he has got the letter this evening. I know that he has it, for I gave it to him myself.

LADY BEAUVEDERE: But what did he say? My poor boy, how did he bear it?

JULIET: (*firmly*) Nothing that he could *say* would alter me, and I am sure he will bear it in the way you would most desire!

LADY BEAUVEDERE: But – why did you do this . . . why?

JULIET: (*with spirit*) Because I saw that you were miserable: because I knew . . . suddenly . . . that I did not love him well enough because I felt, all at once, that we could never, *never* make each other happy – that it was most unfair to him, to you, to all of us, from beginning to end: that is the reason why!

LADY BEAUVEDERE: Had you seen any one else?

JULIET: No, I had not seen any one else *then*, except my sister.

LADY BEAUVEDERE: My poor child! (*After a struggle with herself*)

Still this is madness. What will people think? Will they believe that you broke it off? Such good prospects! It is but fair to give you warning. You are young and romantic. You have no mother to advise you. (*Firmly*) It is but fair to give you warning.

JULIET: Oh, I know that Sir William is rich. I know that he could give me everything that *money* can buy! But *I* am thinking of the things that money *cannot* buy! – my ideals – my dreams.

LADY BEAUVEDERE: Ideals! – dreams! Good Heavens! (*In a tone of self-mockery*)

JULIET: Yes – the ideals that men and women have died for, for which they have been burnt – tortured – martyred. Are they nothing in the world? Shall I give up these treasures?

LADY BEAUVEDERE: Oh, when one is young, one is full of these enthusiasms.

JULIET: Have you none yourself? Don't you ever feel there is something lacking in these big parties? Do you never get tired of these smart friends? – friends who would tear your soul to ribbons if it would make a lunch more lively! Do you always like these brutal jokes – this hateful scramble to go one better and be, at any cost, amused? It's horrid, it is contemptible!

LADY BEAUVEDERE: My dear child, do you find *me* contemptible?

JULIET: No; unhappy!

LADY BEAUVEDERE: (*laughing uneasily*) Me, unhappy! What a notion!

JULIET: You are, you must be. (*Touching her arm*) You are too good, too gentle, to be contented with such a stifling life. You must long for the free, fresh air, to watch the sky, to hear a little of the music of the woods and fields. . . .

LADY BEAUVEDERE: Woods and fields. . . . (*Stares blankly into space*)

JULIET: Don't you want one human heart at least on which you can always depend?

LADY BEAUVEDERE: I have my boy. I ask for no more. I have Vivian. He is my best.

JULIET: (*sorrowfully*) Oh, yes, I know how dearly you love him.

LADY BEAUVEDERE: Dearly is not the word. It is idolatry. Sometimes I fear it is wrong. But he is mine, and when all the worldly maxims are said, when all is done, the love between mother and child is real; children do not care whether one is looking one's best or one's worst; whether one is young, old, pretty, or plain. Vivian is all I have – all!

JULIET: I know . . . I know. . . .

LADY BEAUVEDERE: (*with feeling*) And all I *want*.

JULIET: (*a little surprised*) Yes . . .

LADY BEAUVEDERE: (*looking at her*) Oh, Juliet, what an enigma! what a contradiction! (*Takes her hand in hers*) I was beginning to care for you, I was beginning to understand you. I had no daughter of my own. Oh, Juliet, what an enigma!

JULIET: (*standing*) Oh, no, it is all simple enough, *if* it could be all told. But it *cannot* be told. One may stop wondering about it, and, if possible, forget it . . .

LADY BEAUVEDERE: (*standing*) Juliet, I won't wonder about you. I won't ask you any questions. (*Holds out both her hands*) But, will you come back with me?

JULIET: Oh, why are people always kind to each other – too late?

LADY BEAUVEDERE: Don't say that, dear Juliet. No one, not even Bill, shall ever hear of this . . . escapade: but, come back again with me. Tomorrow we can part, perhaps not to meet again, but let us part friends. Will you come? (*Moves a little towards her*)

JULIET: (*looking at her*) You are very good.

LADY BEAUVEDERE: Don't hesitate, my dear child, come. (*Goes up to her and takes her hand*) I feel, I *know* . . . something tells me that . . . (*Kisses her*) . . . that perhaps we shall never really like each other: we are so different. But, I trust you, I *do* trust. I don't know why, but I do. (*Puts her arm round her*)

JULIET: (*after a moment's pause*) Yes, I will come . . . till tomorrow.
(*They go out in silence, each wondering at the other, without heeding* LASCELLES)

LASCELLES: (*looking after them*) I shall never, no, *never* understand good women. I suppose they will go back to the ball, and smile at each other like angels of light till – they part for ever by the first possible train on the morrow.
(*He goes up to door, opens it, and calls* ST ORBYN, *who enters rather grave, but otherwise inscrutable; says nothing, but picks up newspaper and sits down to it*)

LASCELLES: Here is a fine scandal, and the worst of it is – I hope you won't mind – but Miss Gainsborough has made me promise not to give you the smallest explanation of her visit here.

ST ORBYN: (*springing to his feet, radiant*) Ah, I knew it! Dear, innocent little creature. I knew it, I knew it all along!

LASCELLES: (*astonished*) Knew what?

ST ORBYN: My dear fellow, if she had *not* been innocent, she would have insisted on nothing *but* explanations for the rest of your life and mine! . . . Goodnight! (*Advances to door*)

LASCELLES: What! Are you going?

ST ORBYN: Going! I should think so. I am going after her. (*Goes to door, but comes back again*) Are the lights still burning over the way?

LASCELLES: (*going to window and opening it*) Yes. The ball is in full swing. Can't you hear 'The Jewel of Asia'?

ST ORBYN: Thank Heaven! (*Goes out and comes back*) Lascelles!

LASCELLES: What?

ST ORBYN: Isn't she a dream? (*Disappears*)

LASCELLES: What is happening to the world! One would think you were a boy out of school!

ST ORBYN: (*coming back*) I will tell you all about it tomorrow. (*Going*)

LASCELLES: You will be late if you don't hurry.

ST ORBYN: (*opening door*) Not I! (*Starts back*) Good Heavens! No wonder I could not cross the threshold. (*Stoops and picks up something*)

LASCELLES: What is the matter?

ST ORBYN: A rosette from her shoe! The darling rosette from her precious shoe! (*Kisses it, then to* LASCELLES) You dull, moping dog, jealous. . . .

>   (*Loud laughter from billiard-room, and all the guests rush in, followed by* MRS TAYLORSON)

YOLANDE: Your Excellency must not leave us!

ST ORBYN: (*thrusting hand with rosette into breast, and bowing low*) I go, dear lady, because I dare not stay.

YOLANDE: But the fun . . . the fun is *just* beginning!

ST ORBYN: Dear lady, no doubt! But I seek the nightingale, and not the lark! (*Kisses his hand and goes out, leaving the guests dancing*)

Act IV

The garden outside drawing-room at LADY BEAUVEDERE'S. *It is planted in the Italian style with parterres, gravel walks, statuary, and a few acacia-trees. The dawn is just appearing in the sky, and a few stars are still to be seen. Lights are within the house, and the garden is moderately illuminated. The hour is 4 a.m. As the curtain rises* VIVIAN *is watching at the garden gate in great anxiety. He looks at his watch*

VIVIAN: Will she never come? What has happened? How late it is! She will be missed to a dead certainty . . . She will be missed.

    (*At this moment* GWENDOLENE *and* SIR WILLIAM *appear on the wide step with balcony rail which leads from the conservatory into the garden.* VIVIAN *retires into the house unobserved*)

GWENDOLENE: How sweet it is out here!

SIR WILLIAM: Yes, and I hope not damp.

GWENDOLENE: I hope, as you say, not damp.

SIR WILLIAM: Gwen, why do you no longer wear the brooch I gave you?

GWENDOLENE (*hanging her head*) I thought I needed . . . no further reminder of our . . . of our friendship.

SIR WILLIAM: Don't say that! We must always be friends, Gwen.

GWENDOLENE: In time we may be, but, just now . . . it is too hard.

SIR WILLIAM: You are awfully fond of me, aren't you, Gwen?

GWENDOLENE: Is this right, Bill – Is this kind?

SIR WILLIAM: Would I ask it if I entertained the smallest doubt as to its propriety?

GWENDOLENE: I . . . I suppose not.

  (SIR WILLIAM *leads* GWENDOLENE *to seat and then stands by her*)

SIR WILLIAM: Gwen, Juliet has given me back my freedom. I have been free without knowing it for very nearly five days. I could not in the circumstances ask her to reconsider the matter. She never loved me . . . at least as you do!

GWENDOLENE: Oh, Bill!

SIR WILLIAM: (*seating himself by her*) Gwen, perhaps in two . . . or three . . . possibly *four* years' time we may marry, you and I, and gather a circle of the very nicest people round us, and exercise the best influence upon Society.

GWENDOLENE: What happiness, dearest Bill!

SIR WILLIAM: It ought to be . . . I think it will be.

GWENDOLENE: And shall we go to Italy for our honeymoon?

SIR WILLIAM: Most probably. One soon gets tired of a place that is *merely* climate! One wants something to look at . . . to keep one interested, and all that . . . (*Feeling the arm of the seat*) Is the dew falling? (*rises*)

GWENDOLENE: (*rises*) Won't you kiss me, Bill!

SIR WILLIAM: (*approaching her*) I thought I did. (*Kisses her cheek and walks up centre, leaving her*)

GWENDOLENE: (*after a pause*) Yes, it does seem rather chilly. Shall we go in?

SIR WILLIAM: You know we are such friends, dear Gwen, that you would not expect *raptures*, would you?

GWENDOLENE: No . . . no . . . not exactly raptures!

SIR WILLIAM: It is much more sensible, really, not to want you to catch cold.

GWENDOLENE: (*walks up to him and looks into his face*) It must have been on such a night as this when Romeo climbed the wall of Juliet's garden. Oh, Bill, you do like me a little, don't you? People seem to think we are such icebergs!

SIR WILLIAM: That's because people are fools. (*With sudden and genuine feeling, embracing her*) I am simply awfully fond of you. (*Kisses her*) There, will that satisfy you?

GWENDOLENE: Oh, quite!

SIR WILLIAM: Shall we go in?

    (*They go in.* VIVIAN *comes out again from the shadow*)

VIVIAN: Will she never come? I hope there has been no mistake. Lascelles has just opened his window . . . I believe he is there. What on earth has happened? . . . (*Rattle of key heard in the door*) At last! (*He rushes forward as door is opened and* LADY BEAUVEDERE *enters followed by* JULIET. VIVIAN *falls back in astonishment. To* LADY BEAUVEDERE) You!

LADY BEAUVEDERE: (*smiling with a strong effort*) Did I startle you, darling? Juliet and I have just been out for a little air. It seems so very close this evening. Surely we have not been long?

VIVIAN: (*stammering*) I . . . I . . . don't know . . . I should say . . . no. Why?

LADY BEAUVEDERE: (*handing him her scarf*) Put my scarf over there. I don't need it. (*He takes scarf and places it on seat. While he crosses the stage* LADY BEAUVEDERE *addresses* JULIET) For your own sake, say nothing. I will not betray you. You may trust me. I have given you my word. (JULIET *merely inclines her head*)

Enter SIR CHARLES DE LORME *from house*

SIR CHARLES: Ah, Lady Beauvedere, I have been seeking you. . . .

LADY BEAUVEDERE: How wrong of me! I stole out into the garden. These April nights are so delicious!

SIR CHARLES: Alas! I have not got an April chest! I cannot take these enjoyments. But, they are forming a cotillon: I believe they wait for us.

LADY BEAUVEDERE: Then let us go at once.

[*They go into house*]

VIVIAN: (*comes up to* JULIET *when his mother has gone,* JULIET *is standing motionless, looking on the ground*) Is it all right?

JULIET: (*sitting down mechanically*) Yes . . . all right . . . He gave it me.

VIVIAN: What, the cheque? (JULIET *merely bows her head*) Thank God! Oh, Juliet, I have been mad. I have been half dead with anxiety. Why *were* you so long?

JULIET: Yes . . . it must have seemed . . . a long while.

VIVIAN: Was he disagreeable?

JULIET: Oh no . . . He was very kind.

VIVIAN: How did you meet my mother? What an escape!

JULIET: I didn't escape.

VIVIAN: What do you mean?

JULIET: I didn't escape, Vivian. She must have seen me go or, some one told her. She followed me.

VIVIAN: Where?

JULIET: Into the house . . . Into the very room.

VIVIAN: (*horrified*) Into the very room . . . Then . . . she knows . . .

JULIET: She knows nothing.

VIVIAN: But what excuse did you make?

JULIET: None.

VIVIAN: That must have been devilish awkward!

JULIET: Yes, it was . . . awkward.

VIVIAN: What does she think?

JULIET: (*in tears*) Don't ask me. I have done all that was possible for both of you. Be satisfied.

VIVIAN: Mama is not easily satisfied. She would think, you know, all sorts of things.

JULIET: Oh, leave me . . . leave me alone. I cannot tell you any more. I have tried to love an enemy . . . now let me pay the price, without a regret, do you understand, without a single regret. I want to feel that I should do it all again, willingly, and that isn't easy. Don't ask me any more.

Enter LORD LAVENSTHORPE *a pale, insipid young man*
with a silly smile

LORD LAVENSTHORPE: Really, Miss Gainsborough, I have been looking for you everywhere. You promised to go into supper with me. Have you forgotten?

JULIET: (*rising*) Oh no. I was just hoping you had forgotten (*Perceiving her mistake*) . . . I mean . . .

LAVENSTHORPE: Yes, what *did* you mean?

JULIET: Oh, I was afraid that you would get so hungry – that's all.

[*She goes out on* LAVENSTHORPE'S *arm*]

VIVIAN: (*clenching his hands*) Oh, I can't have this. It's too cowardly. I would sooner make a clean breast of the whole thing – I can't have a girl suffer all this just because I have been such a fool. (*Garden door opens*) Who is that? (*He retires*)

Enter ST ORBYN *with a quick step, humming a lively air*

ST ORBYN: Hullo! Is that Vivian?

VIVIAN: (*coming forward*) Yes, I . . . I . . . Oh, Lord St Orbyn, I am so beastly miserable.

ST ORBYN: Why? What is the matter? Come to the light. (*Studies his face*) This won't do. Are you in love? Are you jealous? or, what is a far more serious thing, is *she* jealous?

VIVIAN: Oh, it's nothing pleasant like that! I have got Juliet into an awful scrape.

ST ORBYN: Juliet! How can this be?

VIVIAN: She is the most splendid brick of a girl I have ever heard of.

ST ORBYN: What has she done?

VIVIAN: She went to Lascelles to get me out of a . . . devil of a hole. And Mama followed her there, and Juliet never explained!

ST ORBYN: Yes, yes, but you can explain! What is it? Make haste! Don't try to talk well – just splutter it out anyhow! When a man has facts he needn't be clever.

VIVIAN: Mama, you know, hates Lascelles, and I have been playing cards with him . . . and . . .

ST ORBYN: (*smoothly*) At first you won, and then you lost, and then you could not pay your losses with perfect convenience at that particular moment! That's simple enough. (*His puts his hat on a chair*) And then?

VIVIAN: I got over-excited.

ST ORBYN: Most natural thing in the world!

VIVIAN: (*eagerly*) Yes, you know how it is. I had always heard what a frightful disgrace it was not to pay debts of honour, and so . . .

ST ORBYN: You adopted certain measures . . .

VIVIAN: Yes . . . but . . .

ST ORBYN: (*kindly*) Somehow you feel that you can never again be so happy as you were before.

VIVIAN: (*half in tears*) It was all that rotten cheque.

ST ORBYN: Cheque belonging to the family, I suppose?

VIVIAN: Ye . . . s . . . by way of being a family cheque.

ST ORBYN: And you put . . . a sort of family name on the back?

VIVIAN: Yes, but I knew it was not the sort of thing that fellows do . . . as a rule.

ST ORBYN: Not as a rule! But it is done. It may be rather distinguished and out of the way. One shouldn't do it again. But, what is the rest?

VIVIAN: Juliet got it for me . . . the cheque, I mean. Lascelles gave it to her. Awfully decent of Lascelles.

ST ORBYN: Where is it now?

VIVIAN: Here is the beastly thing.

ST ORBYN: Give it to me. (VIVIAN *does so.* ST ORBYN *looks at it, tears off the endorsed half, and burns it with a match, sitting on seat*) Well, go on. What else happened?

VIVIAN: Well, of course when Mama came bouncing in Juliet could not explain *why* she was at Lascelles', because she wouldn't give me away! And so . . . and so, poor Juliet is quite misunderstood. Mama is such a stickler for etiquette and chaperons, and all that rot?

ST ORBYN: What do you propose to do?

VIVIAN: Oh, I must see Mama and put it all square. I can't have a girl suffer on my account. That's playing very low down.

ST ORBYN: (*rising and moving towards* VIVIAN) My boy, leave all this to me. Say nothing, and I promise you that no harm will come to any one. Let me see your mother, and I will make the thing look as well . . . as such a thing can look!

VIVIAN: Oh, you are good.

ST ORBYN: One word. Remember the words of the poet: 'Oh, Nemesis, let me never crave anything so wildly that I would desire to seize it from its legitimate possessor.' Recollect this always, and then you will find existence most enjoyable. Whenever we meet, let us remind each other of this. Go back to your dancing . . . and don't be wretched any more. Everybody always forgets . . . everything. I usually do myself. In fact, it is one of my rules. The only one I ever keep. Go back to your dancing. (*Crosses garden*)

VIVIAN: I say, you are, you know, the most awfully understanding person I've ever met!

ST ORBYN: That will do . . . that's all right.

VIVIAN: I know what you think of me, you know.

ST ORBYN: I never think about anybody. I merely look at 'em and make up my mind.

VIVIAN: Well, don't make up your mind about me just yet.

ST ORBYN: Well, we'll put it this way – I haven't *changed* my mind about you.

VIVIAN: Thanks! (*Seizes his hand*) I shall find Juliet, and tell her you know everything – that you are simply the most splendid friend. . . . (*Goes out with a smothered sob, blowing his nose violently*)

ST ORBYN: (*taking the rosette from his pocket and kissing it*) A *plus* b *plus* x *minus* x. What is to be done – what is to be done with that odious minus x?

(LADY BEAUVEDERE *appears on the steps and calls*)

LADY BEAUVEDERE: Is Juliet there? Is Bill there?

ST ORBYN: Ah, my dear Geraldine, do come out. This is enchanting. Byron was quite wrong when he said that the early dawn did not suit women. I have never seen you looking better.

LADY BEAUVEDERE: I am not well. (*She comes down the steps*) I am dreadfully tired.

ST ORBYN: Come, put this round you (*Takes up scarf* VIVIAN *left on seat*), and sit down here with me. (*She sits down*) But, before we begin to talk nicely, and before I forget it, do you see this? (*Holds up half of the cheque*)

LADY BEAUVEDERE: Good gracious! (*Taking cheque*) Where did you find that?

ST ORBYN: In the oddest way. You remember the day I wrote, against my judgment, at your desk?

LADY BEAUVEDERE: Perfectly?

ST ORBYN: Well, among other strange possibilities, that *may* have been caught up among my papers! At any rate, there it is, and I have not the smallest doubt that I have destroyed the other half!

LADY BEAUVEDERE: How amusing! I did miss it, as a matter of fact, and I was a little anxious . . . Such an awkward thing to speak about!

ST ORBYN: And now, what a charming ball this has been!

LADY BEAUVEDERE: I am glad you think so.

ST ORBYN: I have never enjoyed myself so much before. But, wait, I knew there was something else. (*Walks to right of seat*) I have a little message for you from Vivian.

LADY BEAUVEDERE: (*frightened*) Vivian! What can it be?

ST ORBYN: My dear Geraldine, a trifle to us, but to these children a great affair.

LADY BEAUVEDERE: Oh, Bertie, he does not want to *marry* anybody, does he?

ST ORBYN: Gently, gently. You are still a girl in your emotions. You are always in a nervous flutter about some one marrying or not marrying.

LADY BEAUVEDERE: But so many trying things have happened this evening. I am quite unstrung.

ST ORBYN: Well, listen to me and I may account for some of these mysteries. It seems there has been a little misunderstanding between Vivian and Lascelles. You know the sort of heady, absurd . . .

LADY BEAUVEDERE: Yes, yes. Dear Vivian is so impulsive.

ST ORBYN: Precisely. He is too impulsive. Without going into the merits of the case . . . (*Watching her closely*) . . . it might have led, managed badly, to a duel!

LADY BEAUVEDERE: Oh, heavens!

ST ORBYN: The matter came to Miss Gainsborough's ears. Her first thought was, naturally, for you: she offered to intercede, to make peace.

LADY BEAUVEDERE: Noble-hearted girl!

ST ORBYN: She went to Lascelles. She pleaded her cause, effected a reconciliation, was about to return with her good news to Vivian, when . . . perhaps you know the rest . . .

LADY BEAUVEDERE: Oh, how wrong I have been, how unjust! (*Rises*) But I trusted her, I told her so, I did, really. And she did it all to save me! Oh, Bertie, where is she? Let me thank her on my knees. (*Looking vaguely round*)

ST ORBYN: Yes; she is worth it.

LADY BEAUVEDERE: And now, just as I was beginning to appreciate her, and understand her, and love her: it is all too late . . . too late. What a world it is! I am so vexed, so *dreadfully* vexed.

ST ORBYN: Vexed? Why?

LADY BEAUVEDERE: She has broken off her engagement with Bill.

ST ORBYN: (*controlling his astonishment, rises, walks a little, then speaks*) But, you know, I rather expected that!

LADY BEAUVEDERE: She wrote to him, it seems, the very day we were all saying horrid things about her. (*Rises and crosses to him*) Dear Bertie, you are so clever. Let us do our utmost to bring these two together again.

ST ORBYN: Bring them together again!

LADY BEAUVEDERE: Yes, it may be a mere lover's tiff. Make peace between them. You manage these things so wonderfully.

ST ORBYN: Geraldine, I will be frank with you. I cannot dissemble, as you know.

LADY BEAUVEDERE: I do indeed. I always feel I can read you like a book!

ST ORBYN: (*a little sorry for her*) Y . . . e . . . s . . . of course! But, to be honest, I would do anything to further your happiness, yet, in this instance, I must think of my own.

(LADY BEAUVEDERE *reseats herself*)

ST ORBYN: The fact is there is an obstacle . . . an unsurmountable obstacle.

LADY BEAUVEDERE: What is that, pray?

ST ORBYN: There's another man. (*Sits by her side*)

LADY BEAUVEDERE: (*As though a sudden suspicion had struck her*) Oh, surely not.

ST ORBYN: There is. I can deal with any other fellow, but this particular one is the plague of my life. The trouble he has given me from time to time is past belief. (*Sits*) Yet I have a sort of liking for him too! I feel bound to say he would make Juliet the best of husbands!

LADY BEAUVEDERE: (*Still struggling with suspicion*) Who is the person? I don't know him.

ST ORBYN: Yes, you do, Geraldine. I may know him better, perhaps, but you know him well enough.

LADY BEAUVEDERE: You say he is in love with Juliet?

ST ORBYN: He is crazy about her, absolutely crazy. And the man who thinks of a wife, you know, is a very strict observer.

LADY BEAUVEDERE: You cannot mean . . .

(*The birds begin to twitter*)

ST ORBYN: Yes, I do, Geraldine. (*Rises*) I don't sleep, I don't eat, I can't think, my ears ring, my heart dances. I was never so ill, so ridiculous, or so utterly happy in all my life! When I met her . . .

LADY BEAUVEDERE: Do you mean Juliet?

ST ORBYN: Yes. When I first met her here, five days ago, I was just verging on that mood when life seems to have shown one all its prizes – and none of them appear worth while. Do you know that state of mind?

LADY BEAUVEDERE: (*sighing*) Oh yes.

ST ORBYN: Love is the only thing, Geraldine! When I say love, I don't mean all this nonsense about sighing and dying, wild kisses, sobs and throbs! I mean affection, devotion, a deep, unwavering trust, I mean . . .

LADY BEAUVEDERE: (*rising and crossing to him*) You mean in fact what every bachelor means when he grows weary of flirtation, and wants to marry some pretty young woman who knows nothing about him. Men, I believe, to be truly happy must have, at least, one simple heart, which they can always impose upon. This process they call trust and sympathy! Sir, you are all born impostors!

ST ORBYN: It is because you have these views of us that I have never had the smallest wish to deceive you!

LADY BEAUVEDERE: To think that you love Juliet! . . . Oh, how do these things happen?

ST ORBYN: Well, say it's a fine day in spring. You suggest a walk. . . .

LADY BEAUVEDERE: Alone?

ST ORBYN: Of course not. . . . Say she's pretty – say that you find yourself wishing that she would look you straight in the eyes again. . . .

LADY BEAUVEDERE: (*in a low voice*) Say she does. . . .

ST ORBYN: Then you find yourself wishing she hadn't?

LADY BEAUVEDERE: But why?

ST ORBYN: Because it's dangerous.

LADY BEAUVEDERE: I don't understand.

ST ORBYN: I can't explain.

LADY BEAUVEDERE: Was that how you came to love Juliet?

ST ORBYN: No . . . that's how I came to love so many others in the past.

LADY BEAUVEDERE: Then where is the point?

ST ORBYN: The point is – now that I have met Juliet – it shall never happen again . . . in the future.

LADY BEAUVEDERE: Hear the birds. . . . How happy they must be! Winged creatures – nearer the sky than we are! (*Sighs*)

ST ORBYN: Aren't *you* happy, Geraldine!

LADY BEAUVEDERE: Not especially!

ST ORBYN: Yet, you are young, accomplished, beautiful.

LADY BEAUVEDERE: Bah! I'd rather look old and ugly to some purpose than be as I am – in vain!

ST ORBYN: In vain!

LADY BEAUVEDERE: (*passionately*) Yes! In vain! Beauty in some cases is a humiliation – nothing more.

ST ORBYN: *This* from a woman with the world at her feet!

LADY BEAUVEDERE: I prefer a friend for my heart. (*Gives him her hand*)

ST ORBYN: But you have got friends. *I* am one of 'em!

LADY BEAUVEDERE: You! What is it to you whether I'm lovely or hideous?

ST ORBYN: Nothing! I think only of your soul!

LADY BEAUVEDERE: (*releasing his hand and looking indignant*) There! I knew it. (*Changes her tone to laugher*) How droll!

ST ORBYN: Sometimes I believe you wish you hadn't got a soul!

LADY BEAUVEDERE: Oh, I like my soul well enough, but – it never seems to belong to me – to be *me* . . . myself. Now my face is *me*. . . . do you understand?

(PRINCESS VENDRAMINI *appears on step above them*)

VENDRAMINI: Goodbye, dear Lady Beauvedere. I must be going.

LADY BEAUVEDERE: (*dazed*) What! so early?

VENDRAMINI: It is four o'clock now, and in a few hours' time I leave Paris for Constantinople. (*To* ST ORBYN) Shall we say, Au revoir?

ST ORBYN: (*kissing her hand*) Oh, Princess, we always meet too late, and part too soon.

VENDRAMINI: (*in a low voice inaudible to* LADY BEAUVEDERE) Oh, Albert, to think you have preferred that little girl to me . . . to *me*! We two together could have ruled the destinies of Europe!

ST ORBYN: (*kissing her hand again*) Only we didn't want to rule 'em, did we? Europe is becoming such a bore!

(PRINCESS VENDRAMINI *crosses to* LADY BEAUVEDERE.
JULIET'S *laughter is heard within. She appears with* LAVENS-
THORPE.
*They stand to admire the sunrise. Other couples also come
out, and scatter behind the various bushes*)

JULIET: (*to* LAVENSTHORPE) Isn't it pretty where the light strikes the trees? There is just one star left; do you see?

LAVENSTHORPE: No.

JULIET: Then come this way. (*She comes down and crosses stage with*
LAVENSTHORPE)

(ST ORBYN *watches her as if fascinated, and is about to follow*)

LADY BEAUVEDERE: (*calling*) Bertie!

ST ORBYN: Did you call?

LADY BEAUVEDERE: Will you take Rosamund to her carriage?

(ST ORBYN *conceals his chagrin, offers his arm to the*
PRINCESS, *and they go out.* LADY BEAUVEDERE *watches them till
they are out of sight, then she sits down and rests her face on her
hand, seeming lost thought.*)

JULIET: Leave me here with Lady Beauvedere. I am afraid she is very tired.

(LAVENSTHORPE *bows and leaves her*)

JULIET: (*coming down timidly*) Are you tired? (*Kneels at her feet*)

LADY BEAUVEDERE: (*rousing herself*) Is that you, Juliet? I can't say much . . . Lord St Orbyn has told me everything about Vivian . . . and . . . you behaved very nobly. I want you to . . . forgive me. (*Bites her lip*)

JULIET: Oh, please, never think of that again!

LADY BEAUVEDERE: (*Takes her hands, looks into her face*) You *lucky* girl!

JULIET: (*astonished*) Why?

LADY BEAUVEDERE: But – he is very fickle. I must say that – very fickle.

JULIET: (*innocently*) Do you mean Bill?

ST ORBYN enters

LADY BEAUVEDERE: (*perceiving him*) Bertie (*Crosses to him*), I was just warning her that a man we all know is fickle, and she asks – Do I mean Bill? (*She joins their hands*) Will you tell her who I mean? (*She laughs and goes up steps into house. When she is out of their observation, her face alters. She is in misery*)

   (ST ORBYN *and* JULIET *stand hand in hand, awkwardly looking at each other. Sun grows brighter as dialogue proceeds, the birds sing softly*)

JULIET: (*after a pause*) But . . . oughtn't one to be dancing?

ST ORBYN: Not yet . . . Oh, Juliet.

JULIET: Yes.

ST ORBYN: I want to tell you how much – but if I could say how much it would be little – I love you!

JULIET: Why?

ST ORBYN: Because you are pretty . . . and yet that's not the reason.

JULIET: What, then?

ST ORBYN: Because you are honest . . . that's not the reason either.

JULIET: Well, guess again!

ST ORBYN: Because . . . Oh, Juliet, it is because you make me forget the reason why!

JULIET: Then remember the reasons why not. I am poor . . .

ST ORBYN: So are the angels.

JULIET: And then . . .

ST ORBYN: Well, dearest?

JULIET: . . . You make me forget the reasons why not!

ST ORBYN: Juliet! (*He moves to embrace her*)

(*At this moment music is heard within: last waltz beginning. Couples emerge from behind every bush, and out of every corner*)

ST ORBYN: Aren't we alone? (*Looking round*)

JULIET: (*nervously*) Oughtn't one to be dancing?

NOTES

1 **a guinea-pig**: a person receiving a fee (possibly a sinecure) paid in guineas, particularly a company director.

2 *The Upper Ten*: a magazine – gossip sheet – concerned with the lives of the upper classes, the aristocracy, that is the 'upper ten thousand'.

3 **dower-house**: house occupied by a widow, often a smaller house on an estate close to the big house, forming part of the widow's dower.

4 **Moon-rakers**: possibly another name for moon- or ox- eye daisies – *Chrysanthemum leucanthemum*.

5 **Le doux printemps . . . aimerez demain!**:

> Gentle spring drank from the hollow of her hand
> The first tear which dawn dropped in the wood,
> You will love tomorrow, you who did not yet love,
> And you who no longer love, you will love tomorrow!

6 **a blowsy complexion**: red-faced, coarse-looking, even slatternly.

7 **Gather the rose of love . . .**: quotation from Spenser's *The Faerie Queen* (1596) book II, canto 12, stanza 75:

> Gather the rose of love, whilst yet is time,
> Whilst loving thou mayest lovèd be with equal crime.

Joanna Baillie

Despite her importance as the pre-eminent female playwright of her generation, there is a relative scarcity of critical material relating to her career as it connects to the nineteenth-century stage, critics being more interested in Baillie's contribution to and engagement with Romanticism. Nevertheless, readers may find particular interest in the following letter written to Joanna Baillie by Walter Scott describing the scene in the Edinburgh Theatre Royal on the opening night of *The Family Legend*:

My dear Miss Baillie, – You have only to imagine all that you could wish to give success to a play, and your conceptions will still fall short of the complete and decided triumph of *The Family Legend*. The house was crowded to a most extravagant degree; many people had come from your native capital of the West [Glasgow]: everything that pretended to distinction, whether from rank or literature, was in the boxes, and in the pit such an aggregate mass of humanity as I have seldom if ever witnessed in the same space. It was quite obvious from the beginning, that the cause was to be very fairly tried before the public, and that if anything went wrong no effort, even of your numerous and zealous friends, could have had much influence in guiding or restraining the general feeling. Some good-natured persons had been kind enough to propagate reports of a strong opposition, which, though I considered them as totally groundless, did not by any means lessen the extreme anxiety with which I waited the rise of the curtain. But in a short time I saw there was no ground whatever for apprehension, and yet I sat the whole time shaking for fear a scene shifter, or a carpenter, or some of the subaltern actors should make some blunder. The scene on the rock struck the utmost possible effect into the audience, and you heard nothing but sobs on all sides. The banquet scene was equally impressive, and so was the combat. [Henry] Siddons announced the play *for the rest of the week*, which was received not only with a thunder of applause, but with cheering and throwing up of hats and handkerchiefs. Mrs Siddons supported her part incomparably, Siddons himself played Lorne very well indeed, and moved and looked with great spirit. A Mr Terry, who promises to be a fine performer, went through the part of the Old Earl with great taste and effect. [Letter from Walter Scott to Joanna Baillie, 30 January 1810. Reproduced by James C. Dibdin, *The Annals of the Edinburgh Stage* (Edinburgh: Richard Cameron, 1888): 261–2]

Baillie was a popular and influential figure, whose *oeuvre* was respected by many of her contemporaries. For example:

Miss Mitford ascribed to Miss Baillie's tragedies 'a boldness and grasp of mind, a firmness of hand, and resonance of cadence that scarcely seem within the reach of a female writer.' 'Miss Baillie,' wrote Hazlitt, 'has much of the power and dramatic spirit of dramatic writing, and not the less because, as a woman, she has been placed out of the vortex of philosophical and political extravagances.' [W. Davenport Adams, *A Dictionary of the Drama*, volume 1 (London: Chatto and Windus, 1904): 100]

The first substantial account of her work is completed by Margaret S. Carhart in 1923. In her study *The Life and Work of Joanna Baillie*, she mentions the opinions of some of Baillie's notable admirers:

'If I had to present any one to a foreigner as a model of an English Gentlewoman,' said William Wordsworth, 'it would be Joanna Baillie.' And this was the same Joanna Baillie whom Sir Walter Scott called 'the best dramatic writer' Britain had produced since the days of Shakespeare and Massinger. [. . .]

On September 6, 1813 he [Byron] wrote to Miss Milbanke: 'Nothing could do me more honor than the acquaintance of that Lady [Joanna Baillie], who does not possess a more enthusiastic admirer than myself. She is our only dramatist since Otway and Southerne; I don't except Home.' [Margaret S. Carhart, *The Life and Work of Joanna Baillie* (New Haven: Yale University Press and London: Humphrey Milford and OUP, 1923): 1 and 38–9]

Byron's admiration for Baillie continued, for in 1815 he wrote to Moore:

Women (save Joanna Baillie) cannot write tragedy; they have not seen enough nor felt enough of life for it. [Byron quoted by Timothy Webb, 'The Romantic Poet and the Stage: a Short, Sad, History', *The Romantic Theatre: an International Symposium*, edited by Richard Allen Cave (Gerrards Cross: Smythe, 1986): 9–46, 41]

More recent scholarship has had to work hard to claim for her any substantial reputation, but those willing to attempt the struggle are increasingly convincing. Daniel P. Watkins has this to say about her relationship to Romanticism:

> While her major dramatic effort is suggested in the title of her *Series of Plays; in which it is attempted to delineate the stronger passions of the mind*, she does not treat human passion in the abstract. Rather she situated it among social and historical pressures of immense complexity: specific details and material situations disclose the inner workings of social life during the Romantic period. Further, despite her awareness of the limitations of theatre in her day, she chooses drama to reveal, in ways lyric poetry cannot, the ideological conflicts disturbing and shaping the passions that constitute her primary thematic and psychological interest. As a genre in decline, drama in the romantic age is at once weighted with nostalgia and desire for the once-powerful and stable social world that had brought it to prominence, and, at the same time, pressured by the confidence, individualism, and sheer defiance of the social energies struggling to assert (like Keats's Apollo) their new found power and authority. Baillie's imagination intervenes powerfully in this social, historical, *and* formal generic crisis, tracking the complex intersections of psychological, social, and imaginative motion in an intense moment of historical – specifically class and gender – anxiety, when one structure of authority and belief is on the verge of displacement by another. [Daniel P. Watkins, 'Class, Gender and Social Motion in Joanna Baillie's *De Montford*', *The Wordsworth Circle* volume 23 n. 2 (Spring 1992): 109–17, 109]

Marie-Thérèse De Camp

Marie-Thérèse De Camp is even less well-served by critics and commentators than is Joanna Baillie. However, readers will find in descriptions of her persona and acting career an unexpected angle on her career as a writer. In the *Examiner* (8 January 1815) Leigh Hunt makes clear his enthusiasm for her abilities as a performer, although he makes no mention of her skills as a writer:

> Mrs Charles Kemble is a still more useful actress than either of those ladies [Mrs Davison or Mrs Edwin], and, we suspect, a much more intelligent woman. There is no description of character, tragic, comic, or pantomimic, old or young, speaking, singing, or dancing, which she cannot undertake, and for which she would not gain a certain degree of applause; but not withstanding the effect she has had in some characters, and the display she gives to most, we are inclined to attribute her success more to the superior intellect above-mentioned, and a certain general readiness of apprehension, than to any actual

talent for the stage. She seldom performs, we believe, now; and had latterly got into some parts which tended to lead the natural vigour of her temperament into the masculine; but they who remember her not many years back in the parts of romantic heroines and melodramatic nymphs and goddesses, will not easily forget the graceful pomp of her action, her striking features, her beautiful figure, her rich profusion of hair, and her large black eyes looking upon you with a lamping earnestness. [Leigh Hunt, 'Sketches of the Performers: The Comic Actresses', originally published as 'Theatrical Examiner', *Examiner*, 8 January 1815: 25–6. Reproduced in *Leigh Hunt's Dramatic Criticism: 1808–1831*, edited by Lawrence Huston Houtchens and Carolyn Washburn Houtchens (New York: Columbia University Press, 1949): 89–90]

Influential though Hunt's unbiased opinions may have been, readers may find the thoughts of Marie-Thérèse De Camp's daughter, Fanny Kemble, just as interesting. She writes that:

Whatever qualities of mind or character I inherit from my father's family I am persuaded that I am more strongly stamped with those I derived from my mother, a woman, who, possessing no specific gift in such perfection as the dramatic talents of the Kembles, had in a higher degree than any of them the peculiar organisation of genius. To the fine senses of a savage rather than a civilised nature, she joined an acute instinct of criticism in all matters of art, and a general quickness and accuracy of perception, and a brilliant vividness of expression that made her conversation delightful. Had she possessed half the advantages of education which she and my father laboured to bestow on us, she would, I think, have been one of the most remarkable persons of her time. [Frances Anne Kemble, *Records of a Girlhood*, volume 2 (London: Richard Bentley, 1878): 2]

One may further encounter De Camp in the several biographies of her daughter, although few mention her career as a playwright in any greater depth than that managed by J. C. Furnas, who comments, briefly and perhaps rather chauvinistically, that:

Several of Thérèse's adaptations (one, *Smiles and Tears*, was based on Mrs Opie's novel, *Father and Daughter*, with 'la-sir' comedy interpolated to relieve the mawkishness) were published; their sprightly and chewy dialogue shows how well she had got the hang of English. [J. C. Furnas, *Fanny Kemble: Leading Lady of the Nineteenth-Century Stage* (New York: Dial Press, 1982): 38–9]

Fanny Kemble

The critic of the *Times* presents an immediate reaction to the opening night of *Francis the First*:

> The boldness of the attempt in an author so young might very reasonably bespeak for it somewhat more than the ordinary indulgence which is granted to very early efforts; but it is mere justice to say, that it stands in need of no such favour, and that it displays so much spirit and originality, so much of the true qualities which are required in dramatic composition, that it may fairly stand upon its own intrinsic worth, and that the author may fearlessly challenge a comparison with any other modern dramatist. The chief fault which is discovered is that the interest is not sufficiently concentrated, and this is the more sensibly felt, because the historical characters, and the incidents which belong to them, are not sufficiently familiar to an English audience to supply the deficiency. On the other hand, it is extremely well written, the dialogue is well sustained and characteristic, and there occur frequent passages of remarkable beauty, and occasionally great force. The characters are developed with extraordinary skill and discrimination, and in this, more than in any other part of the drama, the author's genius, and her accuracy of observation are most strikingly displayed.

The critic is particularly enthusiastic about the scene between the Queen and Bourbon, roles played by Fanny and Charles Kemble. He writes that the scene:

> [. . .] is very skilfully constructed, and written with a nicety of discrimination which holds out great promise for the author's future efforts. The well-suppressed emotion of Louisa at Bourbon's entrance, [. . .] Bourbon's mistake of her meaning at first, and the outbreak of his fiery spirit when he discovers it, are introduced in natural and powerful succession; and it should be added, that the scene was very admirably acted. [*Times*, 16 March 1832:5]

Fanny Kemble's autobiographical writings throw light on many aspects of her life including an appealingly modest assessment of her first play:

> The success of *Francis I* was one of entirely indulgent forbearance on the part of the public. An historical play, written by a girl of seventeen, and acted by the authoress at one and twenty was not unnaturally, the subject of some curiosity; and, as such, it filled the house for a few nights. Its entire want of real merit, of course, made it impossible that it should do anything more. [Fanny Kemble, *Records of a Girlhood*, volume 3 (London: Richard Bentley, 1878): 194]

Her endearing humility perhaps effaces her determination to write a good and interesting play. Dorothy Marshall describes Kemble's resolution:

> Fanny set to work [on *Francis the First*] with great enthusiasm. She told Harriet [St Leger] that the project was not 'one of the soap bubbles which I am so fond of blowing, admiring and forgetting'. The first three acts were quickly written, the fourth more slowly, but the young authoress had difficulty with the fifth act, which the convention of the day required. Finally, in a mood of grim determination, writing furiously between six in the evening and eleven-thirty at night, Fanny finished her play. Next she had to brace herself for the ordeal of reading it to her parents, who, to her enormous joy, thought well of it . . . Her father suggested the possibility of it being produced at Covent Garden, but Fanny favoured its being published by a bookseller. [Dorothy Marshall, *Fanny Kemble* (London: Weidenfeld and Nicolson, 1977): 27]

J. C. Furnas comments on the play and describes the reaction of her friends:

> Fanny's plan to write a historical novel about Françoise de Foix, a romantic, harried figure from the sixteenth century [. . .] was not thought absurd by her family. When, after drafting, she decided to make it a play about the lady, no Kemble need have been surprised. When she read the end product to them, there was no tactless astonishment, merely pleasure; even Thérèse [her mother, Marie-Thérèse De Camp] allowed its merits. Between that draft and the version eventually published came polishing and rearranging, but even in that first form it was probably a credit to a girl of seventeen. It was also absurd for her at that age to summon from the vasty deep these overweening emotions – raging jealousy, middle-aged concupiscence, revulsionary treason, and carnal lust. James Spedding, one of brother John Mitchell's scholarly cronies at Cambridge, liked the rhetoric and pacing but mistrusted these 'darker passions [. . .] reflected from Shakespeare – I do not believe that she is a whit more familiar with that than you and I, who know them out of the Bard of Avon, Walter Scott, and Don Juan [. . .] as for anything else we are as innocent as lambs unborn.' [J. C. Furnas, *Fanny Kemble: Leading Lady of the Nineteenth-Century Stage* (New York: Dial Press, 1982): 39. Furnas quotes Mrs Charles Brookfield's *The Cambridge 'Apostles'* (New York: Charles Scribner, 1906): 262]

Dorothy Marshall summarises usefully the opinions of several contemporary critics:

When *Francis I* appeared the majority of literary critics were kind. Arthur Hallam pronounced it 'a remarkable production for seventeen. The language is very pure, free, elegant English and strictly dramatic.' With this last opinion Crabbe Robinson was not in agreement. When the play was finally produced at Covent Garden [two years later] in the April of 1832, he wrote in his diary 'A sad disappointment it would have been if I had expected anything from a girl of nineteen who aspired to write a Shakespearean historical play.' As Fanny's own aspirations were literary she professed herself delighted with the reviews, declaring that she thought the one in the *Quarterly Review* was very handsome and that it should satisfy 'my most unreasonable friends. It more than satisfied me, for it made me out a great deal cleverer than I ever thought I was, or ever, I am afraid, shall be.' [Marshall, *op. cit.*: 65–6]

Anna Cora Mowatt

Mowatt's own Preface to the 1850 London edition of *Fashion* provides a useful introduction:

> The comedy of *Fashion* was intended as a good-natured satire upon some of the follies incident to a new country, where foreign dross sometimes passes for gold, while native gold is cast aside as dross; where the vanities rather than the virtues of other lands are too often imitated, and where the stamp of *Fashion* gives currency even to the coinage of vice. [Anna Cora Mowatt, Preface, *Fashion* (London: W. Newbery, 1850]

The most sustained contemporary criticism of Mowatt as both playwright and performer is that of Edgar Allen Poe in his role as drama critic for the *Broadway Journal*. His reviews and essays are collected in *The Complete Works of Edgar Allen Poe*, edited by James A. Harrison. The extracts given below are from the 1902, seventeen-volume, Virginia edition.

Rather surprisingly for modern readers, Poe first reviews the play text of *Fashion* in advance of its premiere. His essay on 'The New Comedy by Mrs Mowatt' appeared in the *Broadway Journal* on 29 March 1845:

> It is a pretty-well arranged selection from the usual *routine* of stage characters, and stage manoeuvres – but there is not one particle of any nature beyond green-room nature about it. No such events ever happened in fact, or ever could happen, as happen in 'Fashion' [. . .]
> It must be understood that we are not condemning Mrs Mowatt's

comedy in particular, but the modern drama in general. Comparatively, there is much of merit in 'Fashion', and in many respects (and
those of a *telling* character) it is superior to any American play. It has,
in especial, the very high merit of simplicity in plot [. . .] The necessity
for verbose explanation on the part of Trueman at the close of
'Fashion' is, however, a serious defect. The *dénouement* should in all
cases be full of *action* and nothing else. Whatever cannot be explained
by such action should be communicated at the opening of the play.

The colloquy in Mrs Mowatt's comedy is spirited, generally terse,
and well seasoned at points with sarcasm of much power. The
management throughout shows the fair authoress to be thoroughly
conversant with our ordinary stage effects, and we might say a good
deal in commendation of some of the 'sentiments' interspersed: – we
are really ashamed, nevertheless, to record our deliberate opinion that
if 'Fashion' succeed at all (and we think upon the whole that it will) it
will owe the greater portion of its success to the very carpets, the very
ottomans, the very chandeliers, and the very conservatories that gained
so decided a popularity for that most inane and utterly despicable of all
modern comedies – the 'London Assurance' of Boucicault.

The above remarks were written before the comedy's representation
at the Park, and were based on the author's MS. [Edgar Allen Poe, *The
Complete Works of Edgar Allen Poe*, volume 12 (New York: Crowell,
1902): 117–20]

Poe returns to the subject of *Fashion* in the subsequent edition of the
Broadway Journal (5 April 1845):

So deeply have we felt interested in the question of 'Fashion's success or
failure, that we have been to see it every night since its first production;
making careful note of its merits and defects as they were more and
more distinctly developed in the gradually perfected representation of
the play [. . .] In one respect, perhaps, we have done Mrs Mowatt
unintentional injustice. We are not quite sure, upon reflection, that her
entire thesis is not an original one. We can call to mind no drama, just
now, in which the design can be properly stated as the satirizing of
fashion *as* fashion. Fashionable follies, indeed, as a class of folly in
general, have been frequently made the subject of dramatic ridicule –
but the distinction is obvious – although certainly too nice a one to be
of any practical avail save to the authoress of the new comedy.
Abstractly we may admit some pretension to originality of plan – but,
in the presentation, this shadow of originality vanishes.

We cannot, if we would, separate the *dramatis personae* from the
moral they illustrate; and the characters overpower the moral. We see
before us only personages with whom we have been familiar time out

of mind: – when we look at Mrs Tiffany, for example, and hear her speak, we think of Mrs Malaprop in spite of ourselves, and in vain endeavour to think of anything else. The whole conduct and language of the comedy, too, have about them the unmistakable flavour of the green-room. We doubt if a single *point* either in the one or the other, is not a household thing with every play-goer. Not a joke is any less old than the hills – but this conventionality is more markedly noticeable in the sentiments, so-called [. . .] We are delighted to find, in the reception of Mrs Mowatt's comedy, the clearest indications of a revival in the American drama – that is to say of an earnest disposition to see it revived. [Poe, *The Complete Works of Edgar Allen Poe*, volume 12: 124–6]

Mowatt's *Fashion* was revived in London in 1929. The production was generally and favourably reviewed. The *New Statesman* considered that:

Although the characters of the play are all stock types [. . .] nevertheless Mrs Mowatt handles her puppets with a certain vivacity and ingenuity, and the play has a certain fidelity which makes it an interesting example of social comedy. [. . .] What an extraordinary period it was, and how much further away it seems than the eighteenth century or even the Elizabethan age! When Gertrude's lover, Colonel Howard, thinks that she has been deceiving him with the bogus count because they are found together in the conservatory, he announces that he will never marry now, and that he is going to Africa to shoot lions. This solemn declaration was, naturally, received by the audience at the Gate Theatre with shrieks and shouts of laughter; but in 1850 it would have been received in a hushed, awed silence, or with fervent cheers. ['A new "Fashion" at the Gate Theatre' by J.B-W, *New Statesman*, 12 January 1929, volume 32: 440–1]

Fashion has also received the attentions of scholars and academic critics. In the 1920s Arthur Hobson Quinn found that:

Fashion deserved its success. It is that rare thing, a social satire based on real knowledge of the life it depicts, but painting it without bitterness, without nastiness, and without affectation. It is true to the manners of the time and place, but it is based on human motives and failings that are universal, and when it is placed on the stage today it is as fresh as when it delighted the audiences of the Park Theatre in 1845. [. . .]

But the great merit of *Fashion* is the way in which it provides scope for capable acting, and if it is a 'shell,' as Poe declared in his unsympathetic and not very discriminating review, certainly when the shell is vivified by clever actors it presents a fine counterfeit of life. [Arthur Hobson Quinn, *A History of the American Drama: From the Beginning to the Civil War* (New York and London: Harper, 1923): 312 and 315]

In his 1973 study of early American comedy, *The Columbian Muse of Comedy*, Daniel F. Havens argues that Mowatt's play presents 'an image of the American-dream-gone-sour' where ambition is a corrupt and 'decadent extreme of the Jacksonian promise.' He continues:

Foreign affectation [. . .] defines Mrs Tiffany's character: her blatant denial of her own middle-class origins [. . .] and those of her husband [. . .] now that she is numbered among New York's 'upper ten thousand' is sufficient proof [. . .]

The satire of these affectations, some obviously imported but many just as clearly indigenous to the new American society, reveal Mrs Mowatt's concern for a social problem rooting deeper than the surface of universal foibles and follies, the traditional target of comic playwrights. Examining the play's positive values, such as sane social conservatism, romantic (or sentimental) love, the dignity of honest labour, the republican principle of individual merit regardless of social class, and above all common sense – all embodied in Trueman and Gertrude – one finds it difficult to agree with Poe's criticism, that the play was merely a facile imitation of *The School for Scandal* and that its success was attributable to its theatricality [. . .] perceptive critic though he often was, Poe was perhaps too close to the problem of the jaded American Dream to see it beneath the bright glitter, which is, after all, part of the show in the tradition of manners comedy.

But *Fashion* is more than manners comedy. The heroine, Gertrude, and the hero, Adam Trueman, function as characters fully aware of the seriousness of the corrupted ethics underlying certain fashions in their society. Both are, in a sense, outsiders and therefore able to bring a more objective judgement to the pursuits of New York society. Both are independent, freed from the necessity of compromise with folly as they see it. To them, the doings of Mrs Tiffany's circle are not an artificial game, the rules of which they seek to learn, but a sign of moral corruption: the enemy. Gay though its comedy is, and preposterously happy though its ending is [. . .] the play takes a serious view of folly and seeks to reform the attitudes responsible for it. Thus, *Fashion* is a social comedy. [Daniel F. Havens, *The Columbian Muse of Comedy: the Development of a Native American Tradition in Early American Comedy. 1787–1845* (Carbondale: Southern Illinois University Press, 1973): 133–4]

Interest in Mowatt's work has not waned. Her career features in

Walter J. Meserve's multi-volume history of American drama, in which he notes that:

> After opening night even indulgent viewers had reservations, for good and specific reasons. Clearly reflecting the popular interest in spectacular melodrama, the *Spirit* noted that Mrs Mowatt 'possesses few qualifications for dramatic writing, as she lacks the essentials – vigor and ingenuity.' 'The dialogue of *Fashion*,' the critic continued, 'is unpolished, spiritless and disjointed; the satire is dealt out in unconnected items, much after the manners of newspaper squibs; the plot is entirely too light for the dialogue, and the action, although not encumbered by an underplot, is cut up by unnecessary deviations.' 'The piece, taken as a comedy, is a dreadful failure.'
>
> [. . .] Like all her peer playwrights, however, Mowatt wrote *Fashion* to succeed on-stage, not in the library. Even by design it would not meet the vague standards chosen by contemporary magazine editors and literary critics. It was, indeed, a fusion of melodrama and farce exhibiting the follies of fashionable life in New York. As a play of 1845, *Fashion* held something for everyone – moral commentary, a nationalistic theme, society caricatures, witty epigrams, a country Yankee, an American hero, a Negro servant, patriotic sentiments, a temperance issue, a French count and a French maid, and satire throughout. For what *Fashion* lacked in spectacle – although there is a ballroom scene – a variety of action, style and characters compensated. [Walter J. Meserve, *Heralds of Promise: the Drama of the American People During the Age of Jackson, 1829–1849* (New York, et al: Greenwood Press, 1986): 129–31]

In 1993 Gary A. Richardson was enthusiastic about *Fashion*:

> The rural character that forms the corner stone of both the frontier and Yankee plays is utilized to more substantial purpose and with greater sophistication in the best comedy of the pre-Civil War period, Anna Cora Mowatt's *Fashion* (1845). The action of the play is rather straightforward, though complicated by the usual intrigues of drawing room comedies [. . .] The central issue in the play is the nature of fashionable American culture in mid-nineteenth-century New York. Like [Royall] Tyler sixty years before, Mowatt comes down firmly on the side of traditional republican pieties, but unlike Tyler, Mowatt extends her vision beyond the particulars of affectation to include a pointed satire on the economic bases which contribute to it. In this way, Mowatt confronts one of the fundamental questions that has consumed American writers ever since – the relationship between culture and economics in a capitalist society. Mowatt's social satire is

wide-ranging and delightful, but it is her enlivening portraits of the various American types that gives the play its power. Her single plot, while providing few scenic counterpoints, gives her play a strict focus and lends persuasiveness to the play's indictment. [. . .] Fashion, Mowatt suggests, is potentially a tool for reshaping society along aristocratic lines, and it is this political element of the satire which receives increasing emphasis in the course of the play. By the play's end the relationship between political freedom and moral probity has been so firmly reiterated that Tiffany's reinstitution of traditional 'American' values carries with it a reassurance of the political future of the nation. [Gary A. Richardson, *American Drama from the Colonial Period through World War I: a Critical History* (New York: Twayne, 1993): 99–100]

Mrs Henry Wood

The phenomenal success of Mrs Henry Wood's novel *East Lynne* was in some measure assured after it was reviewed in the *Times*. There follows extracts from this detailed and influential piece, written, it is generally agreed, by Samuel Lucas:

East Lynne, by a comparatively unknown authoress, is the best novel of the season. [. . .]

[However] Its motive power is often inadequate to its events, which are so fortuitous in their succession and bearings that the story reads like a chapter of accidents, which have the singularity of suiting the author's convenience. It is startling to observe how the characters come together, even from the ends of the earth, at the opportune moment [. . .] If in fiction such liberties are in some degree allowable, there is a tendency to take them too frequently here [. . .] the villain of the piece [. . .] is a very weak and commonplace villain, and in some respects unequal to the part assigned him. Let us premise that he has to do double duty as the perpetrator of an undiscovered murder, and the seducer and heartless deserter of the heroine [. . .] An ordinary dandy, encumbered with debt, he not only commits extraordinary havoc among female hearts and reputations (in fact he numbers *four* victims among the limited circle of characters here depicted), but he concentrates on his head all the wrath of the gods by tearing from her sphere the heroine of the story, a high-born, loved, and devoted wife, whom he carries off in a pet, under the influence of groundless jealousy. He abandons her and her child, equally without motive or remorse, when he could have rehabilitated the one and legitimized the other, and he marries some one else, though the consequence is, that he is hated or despised by nearly all of his acquaintance, not excepting even the woman he espouses [. . .] All this crime and retribution for an ordinary performer who is merely up to the standard of a walking gentleman is excessively onerous [. . .]

On the other hand, his victim and dupe, Lady Isabel Carlyle, a gentle and ingratiating person, is unsatisfactory also, in the readiness with which she yields to a causeless and frivolous jealousy. She is loved by her husband, who has every quality to secure love, and she loves him in return sufficiently to render her solicitous that every thought, every word, every attention should be hers. That under the circumstances she should abandon him and her children, that she should shoot madly from her sphere at the first suggestion of her seducer, is equally a violation of moral probabilities [. . .]

We next come to the leading subject of the book [. . .] and we observe that it involves a prima-facie improbability, that a divorced wife should return to her husband's home, and should superintend in disguise the education of her own children. Let us allow that detection is all but certain, but let us add that the authoress has described a set of circumstances under which the imagination is able to conceive that detection is not absolutely inevitable [. . .]

The reader cannot fail to take an interest in [Lady Isabel's] fate, nor to be satisfied with the demeanour of her husband on her deathbed. The feelings of the latter are just indicated to the point to which analysis may fairly go, and then the authoress retires with a wise and decorous reticence. Balzac would have gone further, and would have handled and squeezed each throbbing heartstring, as his manner was, in making his morbid preparations. But our authoress has better taste and a chaster purpose [. . .] she evinces the tact of a gentlewoman even in the passages where less equable and chastened temperaments have a natural tendency to literary hysterics. The deathbed of Lady Isabel's child is an example of this self-command, where the child is repre-sented as asking a child's questions under circumstances where others would have made him a precocious angel [. . .] With all its artistic defects *East Lynne* is a first-rate story. ['East Lynne', *Times*, 25 January 1862: 6]

Adeline Sergeant, while equally favourable, acknowledges Mrs Wood's tendency toward the sentimental:

The faults of Mrs Henry Wood's style, its occasional prolixity and commonplaceness, the iteration of the moral reflections, as well as the triteness and feebleness sometimes of the dialogue, very nearly disappear from view when we resign ourselves to a consideration of this tragic situation. It cannot be denied that there is just a touch of mawkishness now and then, just a slight ring of false sentiment in the pity accorded to Lady Isabel, who was certainly one of the silliest women that ever existed in the realms of fiction. Nevertheless the spectacle of the mother nursing the dying boy, who does not know her, is one that will always appeal to the heart of the ordinary reader, and will go far to account for the extraordinary popularity of *East Lynne*. ['Mrs Henry Wood' by Adeline Sergeant, in *Women Novelists of Queen Victoria's Reign: a Book of Appreciations* by Mrs Oliphant, Mrs Lynn Linton, Mrs Alexander, Mrs Macquaid, Mrs Parr, Mrs Marshall, Charlotte M. Yonge, Adeline Sergeant and Edna Lyall (London: Hurst and Blackett, 1897): 178–9.]

More recent scholarship has found Mrs Wood's potent narrative worthy of serious study. Lynda Hart offers a complex reading of 'The Victorian Villainess and the Unconscious' which she begins by quoting from *Women who Kill* by Ann Jones:

> Common sense and [Caesar] Lombroso's own experiences told him that there were only [. . .] two kinds of women in the world – bad and good – but he seemed haunted by the fear that an apparently good woman might, at any unexpected moment, turn out to be bad.

If Victorian patriarchs shared this concern with the father of criminal anthropology, the popular fare of the nineteenth-century melodramatic stage frequently allayed this anxiety by reversing the formula. For the most part, at their worst Victorian heroines were fallen but recuperable. In Lombroso's typology of 'female offenders', most Victorian villainesses would have been categorized as 'occasional offenders', women like the immensely popular Lady Isabel of *East Lynne* (1862) whose unrestrained passion meets unparalleled punishment. After the spectacle of Isabel's abjection, the explicit warning – 'Lady-wife-mother! should you ever be tempted to abandon your home, so will you awake!' – is almost subversive in its superfluity. It would appear to serve not only to remind female spectators of the shaky foundation upon which their own claims to respectability had been erected, but also to blur the distinction between 'bad' and 'good' women. The message that any woman might become a Lady Isabel if she lost her footing may have struck terror in the hearts of women, but it also might have provoked more anxiety in the eyes of men. The trajectory of 'normal' femininity and that of 'fallen' womanhood were not two parallel lines incapable of meeting; on the contrary, a slippery slope lay between the two states. This could not have failed to disconcert the keepers of the social order who relied on a stable and circumscribed image of woman. Like Lombroso's troublesome occasional offenders, who were repentant and open to rehabilitation, fallen women differ only in circumstances to normal women. [Lynda Hart, *Fatal Women: Lesbian Sexuality and the Mark of Aggression* (Princeton: Princeton University Press, 1994): 29]

Florence Bell and Elizabeth Robins

J. T. Grein's 'Preface' to the published version of *Alan's Wife* is a useful place to start a study of criticism. Revealing that the secret of the play's authorship has been withheld even from the management of the Independent Theatre Society, he writes that:

> For a long time no play has elicited so much comment, such high praise, and such virulent abuse, as this psychological and physical study of a woman's character [. . .] We do not dive into the question whether those who have condemned the play have done so rightly; but we cannot refrain from stating that it is a great shame that in certain newspapers every play produced at the Independent Theatre is howled down and stigmatised as abominable. It is unworthy that men who rule over large mouthpieces of public opinion should allow such prejudice, such absolute dishonesty, for the simple reason that the Independent Theatre endeavours to cut new paths. [. . .]
>
> What we admire so greatly in *Alan's Wife* is the utter simplicity, the wonderful mixture of light and shade [. . .] If ever tragedy has been written by a modern Englishman [sic], *Alan's Wife* has a right to claim that title. We know but one more powerful, modern play, equally sad and equally simple: Ibsen's *Ghosts* – that is all. [J. T. Grein, Preface, *Alan's Wife* (London: Henry and Co, 1893): vi–vii]

Grein mentions the almost universal condemnation reviewers cast on the play's theme, but even the most damning of reviews felt able to praise Robins's performance in the title role. The *Era* admits the importance of the emergence of the independent sector:

> The *raison d'être* of the Independent Theatre is the exhibition of curiosities. The friendliness of several of our leading managers towards the institution proves that they have realised the truth of our contentions when the Independent Theatre was started, viz. that it could not be a commercial rival to their own speculations, and that it might serve as a useful 'trotting-out' ground for young and ambitious actors and actresses. The production of *Alan's Wife* [. . .] for instance, gave that interesting actress Miss Elizabeth Robins an opportunity for some very powerful acting. The arrangement of the piece is extremely eccentric. The form is amateurish; the process of artistic selection has not been employed in the proportioning of the three acts. Yet there are imagination and power in certain scenes of *Alan's Wife*. [. . .]
>
> The intention of the author, Elin Ameen, upon whose story *Alan's Wife* is founded, would seem to be to show an individual, with what

Schopenhauer calls 'the will to live' strongly developed, converted from optimism to pessimism by a sudden change of fortune. But, in the healthy individual, instinct always dominates reason. Cato and his kind are exceptions even in their sex. A mother who murders her baby because it is likely to grow up deformed is simply a monster, with whom we can feel no sympathy whatever. Mothers have killed their babes because they were living tokens of their shame, or because they (the women) were temporarily insane. But Jean is distinctly *compos mentis*. She reasons logically, so far as her superstition will allow, concerning the child's heavenly future; and it is only by supposing her to be without maternal instinct, and, consequently, as we have said, a monster, that we can account for her action. She is simply an ignorant, cruel, and presumptuous person [. . .] The scene of the murder is nevertheless awesome. Miss Elizabeth Robins rose to a fine height of tragic expression in the child murder scene, and thrilled her audience by the intensity and poignancy of her acting; and, in the last division of the piece, her stony indifference and dumb show were deeply impressive. ['The Independent Theatre: *Alan's Wife*', *Era*, 6 May 1893: 8]

A. B. Walkey in *The Speaker* was less circumspect and declared that he found in the play:

no intellectual or artistic quality at all [. . .] it is not artistic because who says art says pattern, arrangement, selection, the refraction of nature through a temperament [. . .] there is no intellectual quality in this play. It presents no ethical thesis, no *crux*, not even any development of character [. . .] I submit that this play ought never to have been written [. . .] the recollection of the play hangs on me like a nightmare; and if the Independent Theatre proposes to pursue this line of dramatic experiment, I shall have to take refuge in the circus. [*Speaker*, 6 May 1893: 512]

The *Athenaeum* agreed:

It is not the aspects of irregular passion Independent dramatists seek to set before us; it is the squalor and revolt of poverty [. . .] We have been so often depressed and harrowed at the Independent Theatre that, if only as a change, we should like, with more sanguine subscribers, to be a little shocked.
    Alan's Wife [. . .] does not pretend to be a play. It consists of three disconnected scenes, the links between which are easily supplied by the audience [. . .] The anonymous writer gives as its source a story by Elin Ameen. That the treatment is in a sense potent few will be found to deny; the psychology is conceivable, and the determination impressive. In *A Doll's House* we are shown a mother leaving her children because

she finds out that her husband is a weak and contemptible Pharisee; in *Alan's Wife* a mother, who has married her husband for his Viking stature and beauty, and has dreamed that his child [. . .] will resemble him in physical gifts, slays him when she finds him puny and deformed. She does this out of love, and the state of mind in which the deed is committed may be conceived [. . .] The whole is shudderingly nude, and its truth of detail is revolting. We make no strong protest [. . .] We wish, however, that our new dramatists would put a little light into the picture. All action does not pass in a cavern. There is a joy in the life the heroin boasts, and it is her delight in this that apparently brings on her punishment. [*Athenaeum*, 6 May 1893: 581–2]

Recent commentators have been more enthusiastic, claiming for the play a central place in the development of feminist theatre. Linda Fitzsimmons champions the play but is cautious enough to recognise that:

By today's standards, there are problems with the play, such as Jean delighting in Alan's being her 'master', and the suggestion that she kills the child out of some eugenicist notion that he is too imperfect to live. But her decision to smother the baby comes out of love for him and her recognition that she will be unable always to protect and provide for him. The play shows that it is women who are left with the responsibility to provide, and asks what they can do with their guilt when they are unable to. Jean's killing of her child, and silently accepting her death-sentence in punishment, are an indictment of an uncaring society. Jean accepts her responsibility and takes control in the only way she sees possible. [Linda Fitzsimmons, Introduction, *New Women Plays*, edited by Fitzsimmons and Viv Gardner [London: Methuen, 1991): 5]

In her biography of Elizabeth Robins, Angela V. John provides an interesting context for our understanding of the play:

The original Swedish story was called *Befriad* meaning 'Released' or 'Set Free', the title Florence [Bell] would have preferred. The more innocuous-sounding title *Alan's Wife* [. . .] denoted possession [. . .]
    For much of the [final] scene her words are not actually spoken but are written out for the actress to convey the feelings, emotions apparently 'speaking' for themselves, Jean's feelings transcending everyday speech and theatrical conventions. The stage direction 'silent' is given in brackets eleven times yet in most cases written words follow; for example:

Jean: (*silent – stares vacantly into space*) I can tell him nothing.

Here is illustrated Elizabeth's belief in the power of women's silence, and a technique which could well have been prompted by her appreciation of Ibsen's use of the unspoken text between the lines in his plays. The play is bold in its assertion of Jean's choice: against her mother who had wanted her to marry the puny minister, in her acknowledgement of the sexual attraction of Alan and finally in the act of infanticide. Its celebration of the healthy and strong at the expense of the weak and disabled – the fittest may not literally survive but his naturally mutilated offspring is condemned – makes us uneasy today [. . .]

Yet it was with Ibsen's *Ghosts* that contemporaries drew comparisons, another play which to many appeared to defy all decency. *Alan's Wife* both puzzled and disturbed, clearly justifying the decision of the society lady and the eminent actress to remain anonymous. Infanticide was then and still remains a delicate subject, raising fundamental questions about the delineation and labelling of the 'bad mother'. [Angela V. John, *Elizabeth Robins: Staging a Life*, 1862–1952 (London and New York: Routledge, 1995): 87–8]

Pearl Craigie

Craigie's comedy *The Ambassador* was generously reviewed on its premiere but has received little interest from modern commentators. Of contemporary reviews, the *Era* is particularly enthusiastic:

The immense advance which has been made in the last twenty or thirty years in the science of representation on the stage was accentuated most emphatically by Mr George Alexander's production of *The Ambassador* at the St James's last Thursday [2 June 1898]. What a gulf lies between this almost photographic reproduction of society and the crude caricatures of contemporary life given in such a play as *Money*, for instance! At the St James's on Thursday the stage was an idealised and improved reflection of the stalls. The 'fashionables' who crowd to all Mr Alexander's premières saw themselves in the mirror which 'John Oliver Hobbes,' assisted by costumiers and scenic artists, held up. The likeness, however, was a flattering one. Fine ladies in real life are just as fond of scandal and detraction as those in Mrs Craigie's play; only they have not, as a rule, the brilliant wit of the authoress of *Some Emotions and a Moral*. And we may reasonably doubt if, at any smart 'functions,' as many pretty women – or, at least, many women as pretty – could be gathered together to display Worth's wondrous conceptions and their own charms. So the 'great world' may thank 'John Oliver Hobbes' and Mr George Alexander quite heartily. For have they not represented society as much more amusing than it is, and quite as picturesque?

We must not merely apply to *The Ambassador* our usual method of giving a scenario, for the delight given by the play is not created in cleverly-planned intrigue or strong situations. Nor is *The Ambassador* a mere display of verbal 'fireworks.' There is an agreeable abundance of squibs and Catherine-wheels – Mrs Craigie never descends to the plebeian 'cracker' – but the charm of the piece is the purity of its general tone. The dialogue is certainly 'sparkling,' but we would give all the epigrams in *The Ambassador* for the delicate grace of the love-scenes between Lord St Orbyn and Juliet Gainsborough, and the humour of the character of Sir William Beauvedere. Mrs Craigie and Mr Alexander managed on Thursday to bewitch us all. We forgot we were sitting at a play, and spent the evening in delightful company, smiling at witty converse, sympathising with sweet sentiment, and staring at the pretty women in the fashionable 'frocks.' [. . .]

Mrs Craigie, clever in everything, has been specially clever in providing the actor-manager with a character to his latest taste. Lord St Orbyn [. . .] is serene, a little cynical, and at heart honest and affectionate [. . .] We have already alluded to Mr Alexander's being supplied with a part after his own heart; and those who have seen how supremely excellent he is in such characters can imagine the mingled suavity and sarcasm, the alternations of diplomatic reserve and youthful expansiveness, the courteous dignity, and the impassioned energy which he displays as Lord St Orbyn.

[. . .] The artistic taste and refined beauty of the scenery of Messrs Hann and Hall, and the splendour of the dresses must be seen to be appreciated – they 'beggar description.' The authoress was twice led before the curtain by Mr Alexander, who, at first judiciously declining to make a speech, was forced by the enthusiasms of the audience to utter a few words of thanks for the reception of *The Ambassador*. The play is one of the brightest and most agreeable 'entertainments of the stage' which we have seen for some time; and it is certain to have a very long run at the St James's. ['*The Ambassador*', *Era*, 4 June 1898: 13]

In the *Athenaeum* the critic was cautiously positive:

the new drama is as sweet, pleasant, guileless, primitive, artless a piece of work as has ever been placed on the stage. It enchanted a public sated with stronger fare just by reason of its very innocence [. . .] John Oliver Hobbes must not, however, led away by her triumph, jump to the conclusion that she has written a good play. She has written a nice, presentable, sympathetic entertainment, to which, according to the phrase of the day, 'a girl may take her mother,' and has supplied it with dialogue at once epigrammatic, appropriate, and unforced. There is, moreover, a vein of good-humoured cynicism. Add to these things that the management has supplied an excellent interpretation and a lovely *mise en scène*, and the secret of success is apparent. In its expiring years the nineteenth century is aiming, apparently, at rivalling the elegance and distinction of the eighteenth, with perhaps a little less unblushing effrontery and a more scientific use of the fan. From this point of view *The Ambassador* is excellent. It has, however, neither dramatic logic nor sequence [. . .] We do not comprehend the sudden infatuation of the hero for the heroine, do not understand the heroine herself, and can see no reason whatever for her headlong rush into a compromising situation [. . .] We have not, however, the least disposition to censure. Yielding to the influences of the surrounding atmosphere, we enjoyed ourselves, and were in no mood for fault-finding. But it will be a pity if John Oliver Hobbes thinks she has struck upon a lode when she has only discovered a chance nugget. [*Athenaeum*, 4 June 1898: 767–8, 768]

A. B. Walkey, in *The Speaker*, had similar doubts and reached a similar conclusion:

A very dainty and [. . .] a very 'distinguished' thing this comedy by 'John Oliver Hobbes'. It has more grace than strength; its characters have more 'manners' than substance; while it leaves the deeps of passion unexplored, it gently stirs sentiment to a ripple; it skims very pleasantly the surface of moods, *états d'âme*, hopes and disappointments [. . .] it is a sentimental comedy which hovers around the edge of drama, and, just as you thought it was going to topple over the edge, recovers itself with a roguish laugh and a pretty little pout at your alarm.

[. . .] On reflection, I find it somewhat difficult to account for the keen pleasure this play afforded me. Both hero and heroine are somewhat colourless personages [. . .] There is no dramatic relationship between the two men. The dialogue is witty, although the strain for wit is frequently too perceptible. But here and there one has a scene which only a woman could have written – a scene which gives a glimpse into the little tragi-comedies of women's lives. [*Speaker*, 11 June 1898: 729–30]

Margaret Maison's biography of Craigie contains this brief, if revealing, section on *The Ambassador*:

Graceful, elegant, witty and Wilde-ish, [*The Ambassador*] took the West End by storm. It starred George Alexander, the celebrated actor-manager and matinée idol, and the cast included such famous names as Henry Irving, Fred Terry and Violet Vanburgh.

Since her very first taste of theatrical success with *Journeys End in Lovers Meeting*, Pearl's ambition had been to become a famous playwright, and although many of her friends [. . .] considered that it was not her true *métier*, she persevered with her attempts in this direction. She often found the construction too difficult for her, and felt obliged to look for a collaborator. (It was for this purpose that her association with Moore had begun). Once, in desperation, she even appealed to Arthur Pinero for assistance, but he declined, assuring her that 'the stamp of her own individuality' would be of more value than 'mere mechanical excellence'. He was proved right, and in 1898 Pearl's own unaided effort was crowned with success. [Margaret Maison, *John Oliver Hobbes: Her Life and Work* (The Eighteen Nineties Society, London, 1976): 38]

SUGGESTIONS FOR FURTHER READING

The nineteenth century has been well-served by theatre scholars and cultural historians. Interested readers will find much to occupy them.

A general introduction to the period's theatre might be found in two volumes of *The Revels History of Drama in English*, edited by Michael R. Booth, et al. (London: Methuen, 1975–83): volume 6 covers the period 1750–1880 and volume 7, 1880 to the present. Michael R. Booth's *Theatre in the Victorian Age* (Cambridge: Cambridge University Press, 1991) is a comprehensive examination of the major aspects of theatre practice and literature in Britain at this time.

Readers with a particular interest in the American stage during the nineteenth century might choose to begin their investigations with volume 8 of the *Revels* series which focuses on the American stage, before turning to Walter J. Meserve's multi-volume study, and in particular the volumes *An Emerging Entertainment: the Drama of the American People to 1828* (Bloomington and London: Indiana University Press, 1977) and the subsequent *Heralds of Promise: the Drama of the American People During the Age of Jackson, 1829–1849* (New York, et al.: Greenwood Press, 1986). Readers will be surprised and challenged by Bruce McConachie's *Melodramatic Formations: American Theatre and Society, 1820–1870* (Iowa City: University of Iowa Press, 1992) and Jeffrey D. Mason's *Melodrama and the Myth of America* (Bloomington and Indianapolis: Indiana University Press, 1993).

Claire Tomalin has written two highly accessible biographies that those interested in the changing role of women as actresses in nineteenth-century stage will find fascinating. *Mrs Jordan's Profession: the Story of a Great Actress and a Future King* (London: Viking, 1994) tells the incredible story of Dorothy Jordan, a remarkable actress, considered her generation's finest comedienne who was also the mother of some thirteen children – ten by her long-time lover the Duke of Clarence, later William IV. *The Invisible Woman: the Story of Nelly Ternan and Charles Dickens* (London: Penguin, 1991) is a surprising biography of the mid-century actress who became Dickens's lover; the opening section paints a vivid portrait of the nineteenth-century stage, particularly as experienced by actresses.

Tracy C. Davis is one of the most respected theatre historians working on this period. She offers a very different type of analysis of the same industry in her revisionist study of *Actresses as Working Women: their Social Identity in Victorian Culture* (London: Routledge, 1991).

Jackie Bratton is equally erudite on the period, being particularly interested in women in popular entertainment. She is the editor of a fascinating account of the culture of the music hall, *Music Hall: Performance and Style* (Milton Keynes: Open University Press, 1986). Its companion piece *Music Hall: the Business of Pleasure*, edited by Peter Bailey (Milton Keynes: Open University Press, 1986) is equally interesting.

The Profession of the Playwright: British Theatre, 1800–1900 (Cambridge: Cambridge University Press, 1992) by John Russell Stephens is a scholarly study of the emerging cultural and economic power of the playwright: readers will look in vain, however, for reference to women writers. Instead they might turn to the bibliographical guide, *Women and the Drama to 1900: a Bibliography of American and British Writers* (London: Mansell, 1992) edited by Gwenn Davis and Beverly A. Joyce, which lists almost three thousand plays written by women to 1900, and also contains a useful bibliography of secondary material.

The development of the new, radical and political theatre institutions of the late-century are discussed in *Resistible Theatres: Enterprise and Experiment in the Late-Nineteenth Century* by John Stokes (London: Elek, 1972). The new role of women in theatre and society is considered in *The New Woman and Her Sisters: Feminism and Theatre, 1850–1914*, edited by Viv Gardner and Susan Rutherford (London, et al.: Harvester Wheatsheaf, 1992).

Particularly important anthologies of plays include Michael R. Booth's five-volume *English Plays of the Nineteenth Century* (Oxford: Oxford University Press/Clarendon Press, 1969–76) which contains some thirty-three plays of many different genres with interesting introductory and editorial material: readers will find no works by women in this collection. Michael Kigarriff's collection of *The Golden Age of Melodrama: Twelve Nineteenth-Century Melodramas* (London: Wolfe, 1974) contains Oxenford's adaptation of Mrs Henry Wood's *East Lynne*. Readers may easily find the works of contemporary playwrights Planché, Boucicault, Taylor, Robertson, Byron,

Reade, Gilbert, Pinero, Jones, Wilde and Shaw published separately and in anthologies. The increasingly politicised writing by women at the turn of the century is to be found in *New Women Plays*, edited by Linda Fitzsimmons and Viv Gardner (London: Methuen, 1991) and the plays of the subsequent decades in *How the Vote was Won and other Suffragette Plays*, edited by Carole Haymen and Dale Spender (London: Methuen, 1985).

Joanna Baillie's rather retiring lifestyle does not make her the stuff of exciting biography and interested readers may have to be satisfied by the brief 'Life of Joanna Baillie' which introduces the 1853 edition of her *Collected Works* (London: Longman, Brown, Green and Longmans) and Margaret S. Carhart's 1923 account of *The Life and Work of Joanna Baillie* (New Haven: Yale University Press and London: Humphrey Milford and Oxford University Press) or meet her as a secondary character in studies of Scott. Her context within Scottish literature might be deduced from *The History of Scottish Literature: volume 3, the Nineteenth Century*, edited by Douglas Gifford (Aberdeen: Aberdeen University Press, 1988), her place within Romantic drama may be drawn from Terence Hoagwood's 'Prolegomen for a theory of Romantic drama,' *The Wordsworth Circle* v23 n2 (Spring 1992): 49–64. Readers also should investigate Richard Allen Cave's volume *The Romantic Theatre: an International Symposium* (Gerrards Cross: Smythe, 1986); Catherine Burrough's essay on 'English Romantic Women Writers and Theatre Theory: Joanna Baillie's Prefaces', in Joel Haefner and Carol Shiner Wilson's *Revisioning Romanticism: British Women Writers, 1776–1837* (Philadelphia: University of Pennsylvania Press, 1994): 274–96; and Daniel P. Watkin's 'Class, Gender and Social Motion in Joanna Baillie's *De Montford*', *The Wordsworth Circle* v23 n2 (Spring 1992): 109–17.

Marie-Thérèse De Camp has not yet been the subject of a major biographical or critical study but her life – and that of several of her siblings – is described in the comprehensively entitled *A Biographical Dictionary of Actors, Actresses, Musicians, Dancers, Managers and other Stage Personnel in London, 1660–1800*, edited by Philip H. Highfill, jr., Kalman A. Burnim and Edward A. Langhan (Carbondale and Edwardsville: Southern Illinois University Press, 1973–93) and one can find passing reference to her in the several biographical studies of other members of the Kemble dynasty.

Fanny Kemble's own journals and memoirs offer a fascinating insight into her life and the society she encountered during her long career and extensive travels. These have been edited by Eleanor Ransome in *The Terrific Kemble: a Victorian Self-Portrait from the Writings of Fanny Kemble* (London: Hamish Hamilton, 1978). There are a number of biographies but most readers will find two more recent volumes both perfectly adequate: Dorothy Marshall's *Fanny Kemble* (London: Weidenfeld and Nicolson, 1977) is certainly comprehensive and interesting, but is neither annotated nor does it contain a bibliography; J. C. Furnas's *Fanny Kemble: Leading Lady of the Nineteenth-Century Stage* (New York: Dial Press, 1982) is more scholarly, equally accessible and thorough.

Anna Cora Mowatt's own *Autobiography of an Actress; or, Eight Years on the Stage* (Boston: Ticknor and Fields, 1856) is an indispensable introduction to her life and the state of the American stage during the 1840s and 1850s, a milieu that acts as background for her novels *Mimic Life; or, Before and Behind the Curtain* (Boston: Ticknor and Fields, 1856) and *Twin Roses* (Boston: Ticknor and Fields, 1857).

   Criticism has found her a worthy subject and at least passing reference is made to her in almost all the histories of nineteenth-century American theatre. Readers will find *The Modern American Drama: the Female Canon* edited by June Schlueter (Cranbury: Associated University Press, 1990) a rewarding volume, with Mowatt featuring prominently in Doris Abramson's essay on ' "The New Path": Nineteenth-Century American Women Playwrights'. One of the most sustained analyses of *Fashion* is to be found in Daniel F. Haven's *The Columbian Muse of Comedy: the Development of a Native American Tradition in Early American Comedy, 1787–1845* (Carbondale: Southern Illinois University Press, 1973). Other interesting essays included James M. Hutchinsson's 'Poe, Anna Cora Mowatt and T. Tennyson Twinkle' in *Studies in the American Renaissance* (1993): 245–54. This essay makes an intriguing point that Mowatt deliberately parodied Edgar Allen Poe in the character of her 'drawing room appendage'.

East Lynne, a Domestic Drama in a Prologue and Four Acts, is adapted from Mrs Wood's novel by T. A. Palmer. Although concentrating on the novel, an interesting analysis is to be found in Laurie Langbauer's 'Women in White, Men in Feminism', *Yale Journal of Criticism* volume 2 n.2: 219–44. Readers should also investigate Elaine Showalter's *A Literature of their Own: British Women Novelists from Brontë to Lessing* (Princeton: Princeton University Press, 1977) and in particular an essay in that volume, 'Subverting the Feminine Novel: Sensationalism and Feminine Protest', and Lynda Hart's chapter on 'The Victorian Villainess and the Patriarchal Unconscious' in her *Fatal Women: Lesbian Sexuality and the Mark of Aggression* (Princeton: Princeton University Press, 1994) 29–46.

Florence Bell and Elizabeth Robins are to be encountered in various studies of the *fin de siècle* and the early 1900s. Lady Bell's anthology *Landmarks: a Reprint of Some Essays and Other Pieces Published Between the Years 1894 and 1922* is useful for, among other things, an essay on Elizabeth Robins, whose own writings are impressive and constantly engaging: they include *Ibsen and the Actress* (London: Hogarth, 1928), *Theatre and Friendship* (London: Cape, 1932) and *Both Sides of the Curtain* (London: Heinemann, 1940). Of particular interest is Angela V. John's biography of *Elizabeth Robins: Staging a Life* (London and New York: Routledge, 1995), which, of course, contains some comment on the relationship between Robins and Bell. As a leading champion of Ibsen and as William Archer's lover, Robins features prominently in *Prophet of the New Drama: William Archer and the Ibsen Campaign* by Thomas Postlewait (London: Greenwood, 1986) and in *William Archer: a Biography* by Peter Whitebrook (London: Methuen, 1993). An essential assessment on the play is Catherine Wiley's 'Staging Infanticide: the Refusal of Representation in Elizabeth Robins's *Alan's Wife*', *Theatre Journal* volume 42, n.4 (December, 1990): 432–46.

Pearl Craigie's life is clearly, if simply, told in Margaret Maison's, *John Oliver Hobbes: Her Life and Work* (London: The Eighteen-Nineties Society, 1976). Of her own writings her travelogue, *Imperial India: Letters from the East* (London: T. Fisher Unwin, 1903), is both delightful and fascinating.

The Family Legend by Joanna Baillie

Act I, scene i – The Maclean castle, Isle of Mull, Scotland

A peace has been negotiated between the two warring clans of the Macleans and the Campbells. Maclean, the youthful clan chief has wed Helen, daughter of the Campbell Earl of Argyll and a son and heir has been born. Benlora, fiercest and bravest of the Macleans, has been released from two years imprisonment by the Campbells. He finds the peace shameful and the match dishonourable. Eliciting the help of Lochtarish and Glenfadden he sets upon a plan to renew hostilities.

Act I, scene ii – An apartment in the castle

Morton, Maclean's steward and Rosa, Helen's maid, discuss the unpopularity of their lady. They agree that she might be at risk from Maclean's lieutenants. Benlora, Lochtarish and Glenfadden arrive to sue for mercy for Allan of Duras. Maclean refuses clemency but Helen moved to pity intercedes and his banishment is rescinded. Morton tells Helen that he has seen her brother, the Lord of Lorne, and another noble stranger in hiding close by. Helen realises that the second man is Sir Hubert De Grey, 'the man I must not see.'

Act II, scene i – An apartment in the castle. Evening

John of Lorne and Sir Hubert enter, disguised as peasants, for a secret meeting with Helen. Sir Hubert speaks of his love for Helen. It is revealed that she sacrificed her true love for him to make the politically expedient match with Maclean. Lorne tells Helen that he fears for her safety as he has heard of a plot amongst Maclean's nobles. Helen reassures her brother who leaves hurriedly to escape discovery.

Act II, scene ii – A cave

Lochtarish, Benlora and Glenfadden, along with several other nobles are discovered. They agree upon a plot to murder Helen, with the double-intent of ridding the Maclean castle of the influence of Argyll and throwing the two clans into war. Maclean arrives, suspicious of such a clandestine meeting. The conspirators entreat him to abandon Helen. He refuses but they threaten to overthrow his command if he does not consent. Maclean protests but finally consents, begging that they do not harm Helen. The traitors assure him that they 'will not shed her blood.'

Act III, scene i – A small island

Helen is abandoned by the traitors on a rocky islet. She is left to drown.

Act III, scene ii – Another small island

Sir Hubert, awaiting the return of Lorne and onward travel to the mainland, hears some fishermen talk of a mysterious lamentation they have heard from a nearby rocky island. Sir Hubert dispatches them to investigate.

Act III, scene iii – A fisherman's house on the mainland

Lorne is anxious to travel on to Argyll's castle, while Sir Hubert will wait for the arrival of the fishermen. When they arrive it is with the exhausted Helen whom they have rescued from drowning.

Act IV, scene i – A hall in Argyll's castle

Helen, Lorne and Sir Hubert arrive at Argyll's castle where Helen is reunited with her father.

Act IV, scene ii –The garden of the castle

Argyll, Lorne and Sir Hubert consider how vengeance might be won. Lorne is intent upon immediate and bloody revenge but Argyll and Sir Hubert, thinking of the infant child, counsel caution. They agree that news of Helen's safe arrival at the castle be kept a close secret.

Act IV, scene iii – A court within the castle

Rosa, Helen's maid, arrives at the castle. She has escaped confinement at the hands of the Macleans and comes with news that the Macleans are to announce the death of her mistress. However, she is suspicious of foul play. Sir Hubert tells Argyll that he is to travel to Northumberland to visit his ailing father. A messenger indeed arrives from Maclean with news of the death of Helen.

Act IV, scene iv – An apartment in the castle

Sir Hubert and Rosa discuss the imminent arrival of Maclean and his lieutenants. Sir Hubert says that he intends to use this opportunity to travel to Mull to rescue the infant from the house of Lochtarish's mother. Sir Hubert and Helen make a tender farewell.

Act V, scene i – The vestibule of Argyll's castle

Argyll and Lorne meet Maclean and his entourage.

Act V, scene ii – A small room adjoining a gallery

Lochtarish and Glenfadden voice suspicion over their welcome at the castle. They agree that if things go badly they will abandon both Maclean and Benlora and retreat to Mull. Argyll and Lorne subject Maclean to close questioning as to the death of Helen. He assures them that she was carried off by a sudden illness and that she indeed died in his embrace.

Act V, scene iii – The great hall set for a feast

Argyll announces the presence of a new mistress of the castle and a veiled lady enters the room. She throws off her disguise and is revealed as Helen. The company are astonished. Benlora draws his sword and calls the Macleans to arms. Argyll casts them from his company. Helen foresees great bloodshed on her account.

Act V, scene iv – Before the castle gates

Lorne and Maclean do battle. Lorne kills his opponent and imprisons his lieutenants. Benlora attacks his captors, is mortally wounded and dies. Lochtarish says that he and his men must be released for if they fail to return to Mull within the week Helen's son will be murdered. Helen despairs and begs Argyll to release the Macleans. Sir Hubert arrives with the faithful Morton. They have rescued the child who is reunited with his mother. Argyll condemns the treacherous Macleans and looks forward to an era of peace and reconciliation.

Smiles and Tears; or, The Widow's Stratagem by Marie-Thérèse De Camp

Act I, scene i – Delaval's apartments

Delaval, a foolish and, apparently, dissolute young man, has lost a letter from his father Lord Glenthorn which states that his relationship with Cecil Fitzharding will cost his inheritance, and suggests his agreement to marry another. He is greatly in debt and, being recently defeated in a parliamentary election, is being pursued by creditors from that quarter. He is joined by Sir Henry Chomley who confesses his love for an unknown woman he met a masquerade. It is concluded that the woman is Lady Emily Gerald, niece of Stanly, and object of Delaval's hopeful plans to marry into money. Both leave in pursuit of the beautiful and rich lady.

Act I, scene ii – A room in Lady Emily's house

Lady Emily and her uncle, Mr Stanly, discuss her several suitors. Lady Emily dismisses Delaval as a 'cold-hearted libertine', preferring the good, if hot-headed, Colonel O'Donolan. Lady Emily's poor opinion of Delaval is confirmed by her servant Mrs Jefferies, who tells the pair of the tragic tale of the Fitzhardings, previous owners of Stanly's Richmond home. Delaval effected an affair and elopement with Cecil Fitzharding who, along with her illegitimate child, was subsequently abandoned by the young man. This scandal, it is generally agreed, has precipitated her father's decline into madness. It is further revealed that Mrs Belmore, a young widow and house guest of Stanly and Lady Emily, is involved with a long-running, and increasingly costly, lawsuit brought by Sir Henry Chomley's late father. Lady Emily has set upon a plan to bring the two parties together and end the suit. A letter arrives from Sir Henry who has discovered the name and now the address of the masked-woman he has fallen in love with. Lady Emily replies, inviting him to her home, but demanding that he call under the assumed name of 'Grenville'. She tells Mrs Jefferies that, as Sir Henry has never seen her face, she plans 'to pass Mrs Belmore upon him for myself.'

Act II, scene i – A room in a neat cottage

Delaval comes to visit Cecil at her meagre lodgings only to find that she has renounced him and fled his seeming dishonesty. Jeffries brings news of Lord Glenthorn's death and Delaval's consequent ascendancy. He despairs of ever being reunited with Cecil, whom, it is revealed, he truly loves.

Act II, scene ii – Stanly's house at Richmond

Lady Emily and Mrs Belmore discuss the lawsuit that the latter is engaged in with Sir Henry, Mrs Belmore revealing that she and Sir Henry have never met and that the suit was entered into by her husband and Sir Henry's father, both now dead. Colonel O'Donolan enters, telling of his devotion to Lady Emily, but also of his frustration at her determination to be out in society. In particular, he is jealous of her attendance at a masked ball where she met with 'Grenville'. He is appalled to hear that he is to call upon Lady Emily and, in a fit of temper, renounces her and leaves, bidding her 'eternally farewell.' Lady Emily's stratagem continues. She tells Mrs Belmore that she cares nothing for 'Grenville' and hopes to win back O'Donolan's affections by convincing him of the affair as an elaborate charade. She presses Mrs Belmore to meet 'Grenville', but to pretend that she is the masked 'Lady Emily'. Mrs Belmore readily agrees.

Act III, scene i – Stanly's house at Richmond

Sir Henry arrives in the guise of 'Mr Grenville'. He indeed assumes that Mrs Belmore is Lady Emily, whose face, of course, he has never seen.

Declaring his love for the lady, he is interrupted first by the real Lady Emily, who teases him further, and then by Mrs Jefferies who announces that Stanly has been accosted by an escapee from the asylum and is badly shaken. Sir Henry has been successfully duped. As he leaves for an appointment with his lawyers, he declares 'Lady Emily, I adore you! Mrs Belmore, I detest you!'

Act III, scene ii – Richmond Park

Cecil, with her infant son, laments her abandonment by Delaval, and the fate of her father. She is approached by a lunatic. It is her father, escaped from custody and pursued by guards. As Cecil looks on Fitzharding is recaptured and bundled away by his captors. She despairs.

Act IV, scene i – Stanly's house

Cecil visits Stanly to beg for his intervention in the care of Fitzharding, allowing her to tend him in the asylum. Her sincerity touches Stanly deeply, who immediately takes pity on her and admits her to his protection.

Act IV, scene ii – Stanly's house

The two lovers, O'Donolan and Sir Henry, meet at Stanly's. Thinking they are both in love with 'Lady Emily', they quarrel. Although O'Donolan knows his true identity Sir Henry is determined to maintain his charade as 'Grenville'. He leaves to ensure that his servants do not let his true identity be known. Mrs Belmore enters and O'Donolan tells all, thus exposing 'Grenville' as Sir Henry. Mrs Belmore realises the dupe affected by Lady Emily. O'Donolan is delighted and determines reconciliation with Lady Emily, arguing that Mrs Belmore should also marry Sir Henry. Mrs Belmore determines upon another stratagem: O'Donolan is to reveal nothing of what has happened to Lady Emily. He agrees saying that her exposing Lady Emily's deception has made him 'the happiest man in the world'. Lady Emily overhears his pledge and assumes that O'Donolan has asked Mrs Belmore to marry him. O'Donolan is in consternation, for his promise to Mrs Belmore means that he cannot explain his actions.

Act V, scene i – Stanly's house

The distraction of Fitzharding and the contrite devotion of Cecil are discussed by Stanly and Lady Emily. Delaval, now Lord Glenthorn, arrives still trying to find Cecil and declaring his love for her true and his repentance sincere. Stanly agrees to take him to Cecil, if only to test his honesty. After more confusions, the two pairs of lovers, Emily and O'Donolan, and Mrs Belmore and Sir Henry are finally united.

Act V, scene ii – The asylum

Fitzharding tells Cecil (as yet unknown to him) that he has cast off his wayward daughter as punishment for her sins and to him she is dead.

Act V, scene iii – The asylum

Cecil and Delaval meet. Delaval convinces Cecil of his repentance and determination to make amends with her. She says she intends to devote herself only to the care of Fitzharding and she consigns the child to his protection so that he might not be tainted by her sins nor demeaned by her reputation. Delaval realises that he has lost her.

Act V, scene iv – Stanly's house

O'Donolan and Sir Henry discuss what it is to be in love. Emily, O'Donolan and Sir Henry initiate their plan to help Cecil and Fitzharding.

Act V, scene v – Stanly's house

Fitzharding's sanity is recovered and he is reconciled with Cecil.

Francis the First by Fanny Kemble

Act I, scene i – A court of the Louvre

Members of the French court discuss the Queen's new confessor Gonzales, the imminent arrival from Italy of the heroic de Bourbon and the advancement of de Bonnivet to the position of prime minister.

Act I, scene ii – The Queen Mother's apartment

The Queen is distracted anticipating the arrival of de Bourbon. She reveals to Gonzales that she loves de Bourbon, and that it was she who recalled him from Italy. She has suggested to her son, the King, that de Bourbon is overly ambitious and was using his position in Italy to establish a powerbase from which to attack Francis. Alone Gonzales reveals himself as a Spanish spy intent on revenge for an unnamed personal wrong.

Act I, scene iii – The Princess Margaret's chamber

The Queen's daughter, Margaret, speaks of her love for de Bourbon.

Act I, scene iv – The lists

The courtiers Lautrec and Laval discuss the mysterious Gonzales. Laval declares his love for Lautrec's sister, Françoise. Lautrec agrees to Laval pursuing the match. The King arrives and sees Françoise in the crowd and praises her beauty lavishly. He discovers that she is betrothed to Laval.

Act II, scene i – An apartment of the Princess Margaret's

De Bourbon tells Margaret of his love for her and of his anger at being recalled from Italy by the Queen.

Act II, scene ii – An apartment of the Queen Mother's

The Queen tempts de Bourbon with the throne through marriage to her. He refuses and the Queen plots her revenge with Gonzales.

Act II, scene iii – A gallery in the palace

Lautrec tells Françoise he has found for her in Laval a noble bridegroom. She consents, despite her devotion to her brother and her suspicions that Francis holds a passion for her.

Act II, scene iv – An anteroom in the palace

Francis dispatches Clement with a letter for Françoise.

Act II, scene v – Council Chamber

Lautrec is appointed to de Bourbon's former command in the defence of the Italian states. The Queen humiliates de Bourbon by asking for the return of his sword of command that it might be given to Lautrec. In fury de Bourbon breaks the sword and curses the French troops and court. He is arrested as a traitor. Françoise tells Lautrec her fears for his safety in Italy. He reassures her and commends her to the protection of Margaret. Françoise begs to be allowed to return to their family home whilst Lautrec is at war. He consents. Laval declares the depth of his love of Françoise. Alone Françoise reveals that she wishes to flee the court because she fears the passionate attentions of Francis.

Act III, scene i – The Royal Chamber

Clement tells Francis that his letter to Françoise was received badly, that she turned from him with horror at the tone of the note. Francis dismisses Clement's chastisements and determines to 'woo this pretty saint until she yield.'

Act III, scene ii – A small apartment in the Louvre

Gonzales is delighted that de Bourbon has been arrested. The Queen commissions him to bring de Bourbon to her chambers.

Act III, scene iii – A prison

Margaret despairs at de Bourbon's fate. He tells her of her mother's plot. Gonzales enters and turns de Bourbon's anger against France offering him a position in Charles of Spain's army. De Bourbon sees an opportunity for revenge and agrees. Gonzales reveals himself as Garcia, a Spanish knight intent on revenge upon Laval. De Bourbon is freed and sets off for Spain.

Act III, scene iv – The Royal Apartment

Francis receives the news of defeats to his armies in Italy and the desertion of Lautrec, whom he curses as a coward. A messenger arrives telling of the arrest of Lautrec and his desire to speak with Francis. The Queen tells Francis that de Bourbon has escaped and that it is only a matter of time until he joins the Spanish force in Italy. Francis is distracted by his passion to win Françoise.

Act III, scene v – An apartment in the Chateau de-Foix
Françoise receives a letter from Lautrec begging her to intercede with Francis on his behalf. She sets off for Paris.

Act III, scene vi – A room in the palace
Francis receives news of the death of Laval in battle. Françoise arrives to beg for her brother's life. Francis is unmoved by her pleas but suggests that pardon might be won for Lautrec if Françoise were to acquiesce to his desire. The scene is interrupted by the entrance of the Queen. Angrily, Francis turns on her, insisting on his independence, status and prerogative as king. She is furious, seeing her power dissipating. She turns her plots against her son by commissioning Gonzales to murder Françoise. He readily consents as the scheme fits his own plans for revenge upon Laval.

Act III, scene vii – A gallery in the palace
Françoise understands that to save her brother's life she must immediately submit herself to the King's suit. She determines to consent.

Act IV, scene i – An apartment in the Chateau-de-Foix
Françoise's actions have lead to the release of Lautrec but she remains guilt-ridden and distracted. Gonzales is called to tend her seeming madness. He sees in this further opportunity to attack Laval.

Act IV, scene ii – An inner court in the Chateau-de-Foix
Francis speaks of his love for Françoise and his determination to take her as his wife. Gonzales affirms his plans for revenge. Laval returns intent on seeing Françoise.

Act IV, scene iii – An apartment in the Chateau-de-Foix
Francis, determined to tell Françoise of his love, is concealed in her apartment. She is visited by Laval and Gonzales who tells Laval that his bride has betrayed him with the King. Françoise denies this, insists on her love for Laval but kills herself. Francis rushes out – he and Laval draw swords. The Queen and her guards enter and Laval is arrested. Gonzales delights in the success of his politicking and reveals his true identity to the assembly. He has wrought revenge on Laval for the wrongs of his father who destroyed Gonzales' sister. Laval curses the King for wronging the

noble Françoise. The Queen condemns the spy to death – but Gonzales first reveals the treachery of the Queen. Francis places her under close arrest and sets off for the war in Italy.

Act V, scene i – A wide encampment
De Bourbon is in command of the Spanish forces in Italy. Lautrec enters with news of the death of Françoise and that of the heartbroken Laval. De Bourbon and Lautrec are both determined to kill Francis.

Act V, scene ii – The King of France's tent before the walls of Pavia
Francis talks of the forthcoming battle, inspiring his knights. However news arrives that de Bourbon has advanced and that his army is about to fall upon the French.

Act V, scene iii – The battlefield
In a scene of confusion de Bourbon's army continues to advance.

Act V, scene iv – Another part of the battle field
Francis is injured. Lautrec falls upon him but is restrained by de Bourbon's lieutenant. Francis and his allies are taken prisoner.

Act V, scene v – The inside of a church
Francis admits his errors and surrenders to de Bourbon.

Fashion; or, Life in New York by Anna Cora Mowatt

Act I – Mrs Tiffany's drawing room
Mrs Tiffany, a social parvenu who effects a façade of sophistication and old money, is determined to be amongst the New York 'ee-light', despite the impossible financial burden placed upon her husband and the presence of her sister, Prudence, constantly reminding her of her lowly beginnings as a milliner. Millinette, Mrs Tiffany's French maid, introduces the new footman, Zeke, to his duties: Mrs Tiffany finds the name common and dubs him 'Adolph'. Mrs Tiffany entertains a number of her daughter's suitors to tea. Among them is Count Jolimaitre, to whom she is determined to marry Seraphina. Adam Trueman, an old friend of Mr Tiffany and a country farmer, arrives. Mrs Tiffany is embarrassed by his blunt manners and rustic clothes.

Act II, scene i – Mr Tiffany's office
Guilty of minor forgeries, Mr Tiffany is being blackmailed by his clerk, Snobson. His price is the hand of Seraphina. Trueman arrives.

Act II, scene ii – A conservatory at Mrs Tiffany's house

Colonel Howard woos Gertrude, Seraphina's young governess. Jolimaitre, too, pursues Gertrude, proposing that she becomes his mistress while he marries Seraphina for her money. Trueman interrupts the scene. Trueman questions Prudence about Gertrude's character and virtue. Prudence sets her cap at the old man.

Act III, scene i – Mrs Tiffany's parlour

Tiffany begs his wife to be more frugal in her habits. He tells her of his wish that Seraphina marry Snobson. Mrs Tiffany is appalled and becomes ever more determined that her daughter marry Count Jolimaitre. Snobson arrives but his suit is interrrupted by the arrival of Jolimaitre. Millinette seems to recognise Jolimaitre. He proposes to Seraphina who accepts but agrees to keep the engagement secret.

Act III, scene ii – The housekeeper's room at Mrs Tiffany's house

Millinette confronts Jolimaitre: he is neither French nor a count but her former lover, the cook Gustave. She threatens to expose him. Gertrude is suspicious of Jolimaitre's ungentlemanly behaviour. Her doubts are confirmed when she overhears part of the conversation between Jolimaitre and Millinette. She determines to expose the truth behind his pretence. She confronts Jolimaitre with his duplicity but his audacity is too much for her slender evidence.

Act IV, scene i – The ballroom at Mrs Tiffany's house

Gertrude implements her plan to expose Jolimaitre. Adopting a French accent she disguises herself as Millinette and, intending to find out the truth of the count's identity, meets him in secret. Unfortunately, she is followed by the suspicious Prudence, keen to ingratiate herself with Trueman.

Act IV, scene ii – The housekeeper's room at Mrs Tiffany's house

Jolimaitre meets Gertrude, disguised as Millinette. Prudence has alerted Mrs Tiffany, Trueman and Colonel Howard who angrily descend upon the scene. Jolimaitre claims that Gertrude has lured him to the tryst. Gertrude's reputation seems lost and Mrs Tiffany dismisses her.

Act V – Mrs Tiffany's drawing room

Gertrude convinces Trueman of her innocence, and he effects a reconciliation between her and Howard. Prudence reads a note from Seraphina announcing that she has eloped with Jolimaitre. Mrs Tiffany is disappointed that there is to be no grand wedding, but consoles herself with the knowledge that her daughter is a countess. Tiffany is more distressed, imagining that with his daughter's marriage to another, Snobson will immediately expose his forgeries. Trueman is assured of Gertrude and Howard's true and mutual love. He therefore tells Gertrude that she is his granddaughter, and thereby heir to his great fortune. Gertrude tells Mrs Tiffany of Jolimaitre's deception. She refuses to believe the story, until Millinette admits that she, too, knows he is an impostor. Snobson arrives, drunk and furious that Seraphina has married another. He exposes Tiffany's forgery. Seraphina arrives to collect her jewels for Jolimaitre: she is, as yet, unwed. Tiffany begs her to save the family by marrying Snobson. When all seems blackest Trueman intervenes. He scares off Snobson by revealing that he must be an accessory to Tiffany's crime and, as such, equally culpable. Snobson backs down determining to leave, seeking his fortune in California. Trueman announces that he will pay off Tiffany's debts and set him in a new business far from the city of New York. Jolimaitre returns and cheerfully admits his deception. Trueman says that he will set him up in a restaurant if he will call upon society in his true guise as a cook. He roguishly agrees while taking Millinette's hand. Affectations of any description are scorned by Trueman's philosophy of native worth and the vapid and illusory value of fashion.

East Lynne by T. A. Palmer, after Mrs Henry Wood

Prologue, scene i – The library at Castle Marling
Lord Mount Severn has inherited title and debts from his cousin, Isabel Vane's father. Isabel is now in his family's protection but Mount Severn's wife is jealous of her youth and beauty. Isabel seems besotted with the unprincipled Levison. Isabel is visited by the lawyer Archibald Carlyle, who is moved by her dependent position within the Mount Severn family. He proposes marriage. Isabel agrees to consider the offer.

Prologue, scene ii – A room in Hare's house
Barbara Hare tells her father that Carlyle has bought Isabel's family home, East Lynne. Barbara reveals that she is in love with Carlyle.

Prologue, scene iii – In Lynne wood
Richard Hare visits Afy Hallijohn to deliver a gun to her father. She will not let him enter her cottage and he suspects that she is being visited by 'Thorne'. Richard loves Afy but cannot marry because of family disapproval. Afy's father, Hallijohn, enters. There is a struggle during which 'Thorne' shoots and kills Hallijohn. This is witnessed by Otway Bethell. 'Thorne' gives him £50 to buy his silence and Bethell foresees more to come as he has recognised the murderer as Sir Francis Levison.

Richard sees 'Thorne' escaping and goes to confront Afy with her unfaithfulness. He finds the dead Hallijohn and picks up the nearby murder weapon, which is, of course, his own gun. Just then Locksley, a poacher, enters. He and Afy see Richard with the gun bending over the dead Hallijohn and assume that Richard is the murderer. Richard's father, Hare, and a number of villagers enter. Fearing their wrath, Richard flees the scene. Hare promises that he will not protect his son and determines to bring Richard to justice.

Act I, scene i – The garden of Carlyle's estate at East Lynne

Four years have passed and Isabel has married Carlyle. Levison prevails upon Carlyle to intercede with his uncle for more money. Carlyle agrees for Levison is Isabel's cousin. Barbara enters with news that Richard is in hiding close by: in the interim the coroner's inquest has found him guilty of Hallijohn's murder. Levison suggests to Isabel that Carlyle has been unfaithful to her and is secretly enarmoured of Barbara.

Act I, scene ii – An apartment at East Lynne

Isabel overhears a conversation between the servants Wilson and Joyce which seems to confirm the suspicions suggested by Levison. Barbara is still in love with Carlyle and hates Isabel. Isabel grows ever more suspicious. Carlyle enters and protests that he never loved Barbara. Isabel begs him that if anything should happen to her he does not marry Barbara for she believes that she would not love her children. Carlyle decides to send Isabel abroad to recover her spirits. Cornelia, Carlyle's sister, disapproves of this idea as mere coquetry. Levison declares his love for Isabel. A letter arrives from Barbara insisting on Carlyle's help in concealing Richard. He rushes away. Isabel recovers the note from the fire and assumes that Carlyle has gone to Barbara. She despairs of Carlyle's love. Levison sees his opportunity.

Act I, scene iii – A chamber in East Lynne

Richard begs Carlyle to help him as he has seen 'Thorne', the true villain. Cornelia enters. She disbelieves of Richard's story, but because no one has found or even heard of 'Thorne', she agrees to help him.

Act I, scene iv – An apartment at East Lynne

Isabel leaves for a party alone. Levison sees Richard. He foresees his exposure as the real murderer and determines that if he must be exiled he will take Isabel with him. Barbara arrives and Levison sees means of confirming Isabel's suspicions. Barbara and Carlyle appear in close conversation planning how to save Richard. Levison returns with Isabel and presents her with the scene insisting that Carlyle has been unfaithful with Barbara and that the planned trip to Trouville was designed merely to remove Isabel from East Lynne. Isabel despairs and decides to leave Carlyle for the protection of Levison. Carlyle, innocent of his role in Isabel's flight, sees his family disgraced.

Act II, scene i – A chamber at Hare's

Time has passed and Carlyle is divorced from his unfaithful wife. He tells Barbara that he will never remarry for he is bound 'until *death* do us part'. Hare enters. He declares his annoyance with Barbara for not agreeing to marry any of her suitors and reaffirms his promise to bring Richard to justice.

Act II, scene ii – A chamber

Time has passed and Isabel is visited by the untrue Levison. He has abandoned her when he inherited the title and estates of his uncle. Isabel has been left carrying their illegitimate child: although it is not clear, this child is now, or is soon to be, dead. Isabel refuses his offer of an allowance and dismisses him from her company. Isabel is visited by the noble Lord Mount Severn, who offers to support her.

Act III, scene i – An apartment at East Lynne

Mount Severn and Cornelia discuss Carlyle's marriage to Barbara, permitted when news arrived of Isabel's death in a train accident in France. Cornelia disapproves of the match, thinking Barbara scheming. Barbara enters and they discuss the children's new governess, a Madam Vine. Cornelia comments on her likeness to Isabel but this is dismissed. When she enters it is clear to the audience that Vine is indeed Isabel in disguise. Hare arrives to propose Carlyle as a parliamentary candidate. Isabel talks to her ailing son, Willie, of her love for him but despairs at not being able to reveal to him her true identity.

Act III, scene ii – The garden of Carlyle's estate at East Lynne

Hare reveals to Mount Severn, Carlyle and Cornelia that Levison is to stand in opposition to Carlyle at the forthcoming election. Carlyle determines to face and defeat his adversary.

Act III, scene iii – A bed-chamber at East Lynne

Willie is dying. He talks to Isabel (disguised as Vine) of his feelings for his father, his siblings and his lost mother. He dies. In her despair she reveals her true identity to Joyce.

Act IV, scene i – A lane or street in the suburbs of East Lynne

Cornelia learns that Richard is in the town disguised as a sailor and that

Levison is about to be exposed as the mysterious 'Thorne' by Otway
Bethell. Levison is arrested and confronts Bethell with his betrayal. Bethell
admits that he accepted a bribe from Levison but upon hearing that an
innocent man was being sought for the murder returned instantly from
Norway where he had lately been in exile. Richard is reconciled with his
father.

Act IV, scene ii – A bed-chamber at East Lynne
Isabel is dying. Carlyle visits and recognises her as his wife. Isabel begs
that he forgive her before she dies. She explains that she left because she
suspected him of being false but had to return in disguise so as to be near
her children. With Carlyle's forgiveness won, Isabel dies.

Alan's Wife by Florence Bell and Elizabeth Robins

Scene i – A village street
Mrs Holroyd discusses with a neighbour the love-match made between
her daughter Jean and Alan Creyke, a good but poor factory worker,
revealing that she had hopes that Jean would marry Jamie Warren, a
childhood friend and now minister in the parish. Jean and Mrs Holroyd
wait for Alan to come home from the factory for lunch. Jamie, on his way
to the local school, passes the time of day with the women. Jean
anticipates the pleasures of motherhood and envisions Alan as a good
father and an infant as strong and capable as he. A commotion begins.
There has been an accident at the factory. Jamie comes with news of
Alan's death.

Scene ii – A room in Jean's cottage
Time has passed and Jean has given birth to a physically disabled but
seemingly sturdy child. She seems very depressed and takes little to do
with the care of the child, leaving such things to Mrs Holroyd and a
neighbour Mrs Ridley. Alone she declares her love for the child. Jamie
arrives and, finding Jean depressed, assures her of God's love and mercy.
Jean despairs at the life the child will have. Leaving, Jamie promises to
pray for the infant. Jean is evermore distracted and calls on God to punish
her not the child. She foresees an unhappy and frustrated life for the child
and, first baptising him 'Alan', determines to smother him.

Scene iii – A room in the prison
Jean is imprisoned awaiting execution for infanticide. The governor,
Colonel Stuart, is keen to find extenuating circumstances that might give
grounds for a reprieve but Mrs Holroyd declares that Jean was merely

hard-hearted and killed the child because 'it wasn't strong and sturdy' like Alan. Jean refuses to offer any defence, saying that she 'knew well enough' what she did and will not ask for clemency. Jamie arrives with news that the sentence will not be commuted and begs Jean to turn to God to ask for mercy and confess her crime. Jean denies that her action was a crime and anticipates being reunited with Alan and her child in heaven.

The Ambassador by Pearl Craigie

Act I – At Lady Beauvedere's residence in the Champs-Elysées, Paris. Saturday

Juliet Gainsborough is engaged to Sir William Beauvedere. She is fond of Sir William but does not love him, agreeing to the engagement only because she feels obligated to the Beauvedere family. Juliet knows that Sir William is loved by another, one Gwendolene Marleaze. She writes to Sir William in Berlin to call off the relationship. Lady Beauvedere, Sir William's young stepmother, and her own son, Vivian, discuss the invitation list for her forthcoming birthday celebration. Vivian wants to invite Hugo Lascelles, but Lady Beauvedere refuses, insisting that he is a gambler and a ne'er-do-well. Lady Beauvedere is visited by a number of friends who discuss Sir William's engagement. Lord St Orbyn arrives. It is clear that Lady Beauvedere holds something of a flame for this old friend. Juliet and Gwendolene discuss Lascelles, who, it transpires, is a friend of Juliet's family. St Orbyn admits his love for Juliet to his confidante, Princess Vendramini.

Act II – Conservatory at Lady Beauvedere's. Four days later

It is the evening of Lady Beauvedere's ball. St Orbyn and Juliet discuss love and the sexes. Sir William arrives – he has not received Juliet's letter. However, he discusses with St Orbyn his doubts as to his relationship with Juliet, revealing that he knows that Juliet does not love him. Juliet's letter is delivered and she entreats Sir William to read it. Vivian enters in great distraction – he has lost at cards to Lascelles. To settle his debt he has stolen a cheque for £500 intended for his mother. Despite his appeals Sir William refuses to lend him any money to settle this and his further debts. Overhearing the exchange Juliet offers to intervene with Lascelles on Vivian's behalf. Vivian insists that she visit him immediately to prevent Lascelles presenting the cheque and so revealing the debt to Lady Beauvedere. As Juliet slips into Lascelles's garden she is spotted by Lady Beauvedere and Gwendolene.

Act III – At Major Lascelles's residence in the Champs-Elysées. Same morning

St Orbyn has left Lady Beauvedere's party and is now at Lascelles', whom he tells of his love for Juliet. Juliet arrives and Lascelles agrees to forget Vivian's debt. However, just as she is leaving Lady Beauvedere enters. She suggests scandal in Juliet's unchaperoned presence in Lascelles' private apartments. Juliet, however, denies all impropriety and tells Lady Beauvedere that she has called off her engagement to Sir William. Although Juliet refuses to explain her presence at Lascelles' (for fear of incriminating Vivian) the two are partially reconciled and return to the ball, followed by the besotted St Orbyn.

Act IV – Garden at Lady Beauvedere's. Same morning

Sir William and Gwendolene declare their mutual fondness and agree to marry at some point in the future. Juliet tells Vivian that Lascelles has agreed to forego the debt and that Lady Beauvedere suspects impropriety in her visit to his home. Vivian tells St Orbyn of Juliet's intercession and of his concern that his actions have damaged her reputation. St Orbyn explains all to Lady Beauvedere, who realises that she has been unfair to Juliet. She plans to reconcile Juliet with Sir William, but St Orbyn admits his love for Juliet. Concealing her own disappointment, Lady Beauvedere gives her blessing to the union. St Orbyn admits his love to Juliet.

ACKNOWLEDGMENTS

Substantial work for this volume was undertaken during the tenure of a British Academy Postdoctoral Fellowship and was further supported by the award of a Personal Research Grant from the Academy. Research was facilitated by a number of libraries and archives and I wish to acknowledge the expertise and kindess of the staff at the Library of Trinity College, Dublin (principally those in the Department of Early Printed Books), Glasgow University Library, the National Library of Scotland, the British Library (especially staff in the Manuscripts Collection), the Library of Congress, Washington, D.C., and the Huntington Library, San Marino, California. In addition, Mabel Smith of the Backsettown Trustees was more than encouraging in bringing about the reproduction of *Alan's Wife*.

Particular thanks must go to Paddy Lyons, Senior Lecturer in the Department of English Literature at the University of Glasgow, who first suggested the project and has proved an enthusiastic supporter, and to Claude Schumacher, Reader in Theatre Studies at the University of Glasgow, who offered much useful advice as to the role and the skills of the editor. My gratitude to these and the many others who provided information, comment and advice.

A final note of indebtedness must go to Alasdair Cameron, Senior Lecturer in the Department of Theatre, Film and Television Studies, also at the University of Glasgow, who died before this project was completed. He supported and inspired my work for the ten years I knew him and offered valuable advice, as well as sympathetic encouragement, for this volume and the other aspects of my career. He showed by example the responsibilities and the fun of scholarship and I would like to dedicate this volume to him in celebration of his role as a friend and a teacher. His vitality, humour and love is missed by his many friends.

WOMEN'S WRITING
IN EVERYMAN

Poems and Prose
CHRISTINA ROSSETTI
A collection of her writings, poetry and prose, published to mark the centenary of her death
£5.99

Women Philosophers
edited by Mary Warnock
The great subjects of philosophy handled by women spanning four centuries, including Simone de Beauvoir and Iris Murdoch
£6.99

Glenarvon
LADY CAROLINE LAMB
A novel which throws light on the greatest scandal of the early nine- teenth century – the infatuation of Caroline Lamb with Lord Byron
£6.99

Women Romantic Poets
1780–1830: An Anthology
edited by Jennifer Breen
Hidden talent from the Romantic era rediscovered
£5.99

Memoirs of the Life of Colonel Hutchinson
LUCY HUTCHINSON
One of the earliest pieces of women's biographical writing, of great historic and feminist interest
£6.99

The Secret Self 1: Short Stories by Women
edited by Hermione Lee
'A superb collection' The Guardian
£4.99

The Age of Innocence
EDITH WHARTON
A tale of the conflict between love and tradition by one of America's finest women novelists
£4.99

Frankenstein
MARY SHELLEY
A masterpiece of Gothic terror in its original 1818 version
£3.99

The Life of Charlotte Brontë
ELIZABETH GASKELL
A moving and perceptive tribute by one writer to another
£4.99

Victorian Women Poets
1830–1900
edited by Jennifer Breen
A superb anthology of the era's finest female poets
£5.99

Female Playwrights of the Restoration: Five Comedies
edited by Paddy Lyons
Rediscovered literary treasure in a unique selection
£5.99

All books are available from your local bookshop or direct from:
Littlehampton Book Services Cash Sales, 14 Eldon Way, Lineside Estate,
Littlehampton, West Sussex BN17 7HE (*prices are subject to change*)

To order any of the books, please enclose a cheque (in sterling) made payable to
Littlehampton Book Services, or phone your order through with credit card details (Access,
Visa or Mastercard) on 01903 721596 (24 hour answering service) stating card number
and expiry date. (*Please add £1.25 for package and postage to the total of your order.*)

In the USA, for further information and a complete catalogue call 1-800-526-2778

DRAMA
IN EVERYMAN

The Oresteia
AESCHYLUS
*New translation of one of the
greatest Greek dramatic trilogies
which analyses the plays in
performance*
£5.99

**Everyman and Medieval
Miracle Plays**
edited by A. C. Cawley
*A selection of the most popular
medieval plays*
£4.99

Complete Plays and Poems
CHRISTOPHER MARLOWE
*The complete works of this great
Elizabethan in one volume*
£5.99

Restoration Plays
edited by Robert Lawrence
*Five comedies and two tragedies
representing the best of the
Restoration stage*
£7.99

**Female Playwrights of the
Restoration: Five Comedies**
edited by Paddy Lyons
*Rediscovered literary treasures
in a unique selection*
£5.99

**Plays, Prose Writings
and Poems**
OSCAR WILDE
*The full force of Wilde's wit
in one volume*
£4.99

**A Dolls House/The Lady from
the Sea/The Wild Duck**
HENRIK IBSEN
introduced by Fay Weldon
*A popular selection of Ibsen's
major plays*
£4.99

**The Beggar's Opera and
Other Eighteenth-Century Plays**
JOHN GAY et. al.
Including Goldsmith's She Stoops
To Conquer *and Sheridan's* The
School for Scandal, *this is a volume
which reflects the full scope of the
period's theatre*
£6.99

**Female Playwrights of the
Nineteenth Century**
edited by Adrienne Scullion
*The full range of female nineteenth-
century dramatic development*
£6.99

All books are available from your local bookshop or direct from:
Littlehampton Book Services Cash Sales, 14 Eldon Way, Lineside Estate,
Littlehampton, West Sussex BN17 7HE (*prices are subject to change*)

To order any of the books, please enclose a cheque (in sterling) made payable to
Littlehampton Book Services, or phone your order through with credit card details (Access,
Visa or Mastercard) on 01903 721596 (24 hour answering service) stating card number
and expiry date. (*Please add £1.25 for package and postage to the total of your order.*)

In the USA, for further information and a complete catalogue call 1-800-526-2778

SHORT STORY COLLECTIONS
IN EVERYMAN

The Strange Case of Dr Jekyll and Mr Hyde and Other Stories
R. L. STEVENSON
An exciting selection of gripping tales from a master of suspense
£1.99

Nineteenth-Century American Short Stories
edited by Christopher Bigsby
A selection of the works of Henry James, Edith Wharton, Mark Twain and many other great American writers
£6.99

The Best of Saki
edited by MARTIN STEPHEN
Includes Tobermory, Gabriel Ernest, Svedni Vashtar, The Interlopers, Birds on the Western Front
£4.99

Souls Belated and Other Stories
EDITH WHARTON
Brief, neatly crafted tales exploring a range of themes from big taboo subjects to the subtlest little ironies of social life
£6.99

The Night of the Iguana and Other Stories
TENNESSEE WILLIAMS
Twelve remarkable short stories, each a compelling drama in miniature
£4.99

Selected Short Stories and Poems
THOMAS HARDY
Hardy's most memorable stories and poetry in one volume
£4.99

Selected Tales
HENRY JAMES
Stories portraying the tensions between private life and the outside world
£5.99

The Best of Sherlock Homes
ARTHUR CONAN DOYLE
All the favourite adventures in one volume
£4.99

The Secret Self 1: *Short Stories by Women*
edited by Hermione Lee
'A superb collection' The Guardian
£4.99

All books are available from your local bookshop or direct from:
Littlehampton Book Services Cash Sales, 14 Eldon Way, Lineside Estate, Littlehampton, West Sussex BN17 7HE (*prices are subject to change*)

To order any of the books, please enclose a cheque (in sterling) made payable to *Littlehampton Book Services*, or phone your order through with credit card details (Access, Visa or Mastercard) on 01903 721596 (24 hour answering service) stating card number and expiry date. (*Please add £1.25 for package and postage to the total of your order.*)

In the USA, for further information and a complete catalogue call 1-800-526-2778

CLASSIC FICTION
IN EVERYMAN

**The Impressions of
Theophrastus Such**
GEORGE ELIOT
*An amusing collection of character
sketches, and the only paperback
edition available*
£5.99

Frankenstein
MARY SHELLEY
*A masterpiece of Gothic terror in
its original 1818 version*
£3.99

East Lynne
MRS HENRY WOOD
*A classic tale of melodrama,
murder and mystery*
£7.99

**Holiday Romance and
Other Writings for Children**
CHARLES DICKENS
*Dickens's works for children,
including 'The Life of Our Lord'
and 'A Child's History of England',
with original illustrations*
£5.99

The Ebb-Tide
R. L. STEVENSON
*A compelling study of ordinary
people in extreme circumstances*
£4.99

The Three Impostors
ARTHUR MACHEN
*The only edition available
of this cult thriller*
£4.99

Mister Johnson
JOYCE CARY
*The only edition available of this
amusing but disturbing twentieth-
century tale*
£5.99

The Jungle Book
RUDYARD KIPLING
*The classic adventures of Mowgli
and his friends*
£3.99

Glenarvon
LADY CAROLINE LAMB
*The only edition available of the
novel which throws light on the
greatest scandal of the early nineteenth century – the infatuation of
Caroline Lamb with Lord Byron*
£6.99

**Twenty Thousand Leagues
Under the Sea**
JULES VERNE
*Scientific fact combines with
fantasy in this prophetic tale
of underwater adventure*
£4.99

All books are available from your local bookshop or direct from:
Littlehampton Book Services Cash Sales, 14 Eldon Way, Lineside Estate,
Littlehampton, West Sussex BN17 7HE (*prices are subject to change*)

To order any of the books, please enclose a cheque (in sterling) made payable to
Littlehampton Book Services, or phone your order through with credit card details (Access,
Visa or Mastercard) on 01903 721596 (24 hour answering service) stating card number
and expiry date. (*Please add £1.25 for package and postage to the total of your order.*)

In the USA, for further information and a complete catalogue call 1-800-526-2778

CLASSIC NOVELS
IN EVERYMAN

The Time Machine
H. G. WELLS
*One of the books which defined
'science fiction' – a compelling
and tragic story of a brilliant
and driven scientist*
£3.99

Oliver Twist
CHARLES DICKENS
*Arguably the best-loved of
Dickens's novels. With all the
original illustrations*
£4.99

Barchester Towers
ANTHONY TROLLOPE
*The second of Trollope's
Chronicles of Barsetshire,
and one of the funniest of all
Victorian novels*
£4.99

The Heart of Darkness
JOSEPH CONRAD
*Conrad's most intense, subtle,
compressed, profound and
proleptic work*
£3.99

Tess of the d'Urbervilles
THOMAS HARDY
*The powerful, poetic classic
of wronged innocence*
£3.99

Wuthering Heights and Poems
EMILY BRONTË
*A powerful work of genius – one of
the great masterpieces of literature*
£3.99

Pride and Prejudice
JANE AUSTEN
*Proposals, rejections, infidelities,
elopements, happy marriages –
Jane Austen's most popular novel*
£2.99

North and South
ELIZABETH GASKELL
*A novel of hardship, passion
and hard-won wisdom amidst the
conflicts of the industrial revolution*
£4.99

The Newcomes
W. M. THACKERAY
*An exposé of Victorian polite
society by one of the nineteenth-
century's finest novelists*
£6.99

Adam Bede
GEORGE ELIOT
*A passionate rural drama enacted
at the turn of the eighteenth
century*
£5.99

All books are available from your local bookshop or direct from:
Littlehampton Book Services Cash Sales, 14 Eldon Way, Lineside Estate,
Littlehampton, West Sussex BN17 7HE (*prices are subject to change*)

To order any of the books, please enclose a cheque (in sterling) made payable to
Littlehampton Book Services, or phone your order through with credit card details (Access,
Visa or Mastercard) on 01903 721596 (24 hour answering service) stating card number
and expiry date. (*Please add £1.25 for package and postage to the total of your order.*)

In the USA, for further information and a complete catalogue call 1-800-526-2778

POETRY
IN EVERYMAN

Amorous Rites: Elizabethan Erotic Verse
edited by Sandra Clark
Erotic and often comic poems dealing with myths of transformation and erotic interaction between humans and gods
£4.99

Selected Poems
JOHN KEATS
An excellent selection of the poetry of one of the principal figures of the Romantic movement
£6.99

Poems and Prose
CHRISTINA ROSSETTI
A new collection of her writings, poetry and prose, marking the centenary of her death
£5.99

Poems and Prose
P. B. SHELLEY
The essential Shelley in one volume
£5.99

Silver Poets of the Sixteenth Century
edited by Douglas Brooks-Davies
An exciting and comprehensive collection
£6.99

Complete English Poems
JOHN DONNE
The father of metaphysical verse in this highly-acclaimed collection
£6.99

Complete English Poems, Of Education, Areopagitica
JOHN MILTON
An excellent introduction to Milton's poetry and prose
£6.99

Women Romantic Poets 1780–1830: An Anthology
edited by Jennifer Breen
Hidden talent from the Romantic era rediscovered
£5.99

Selected Poems
D. H. LAWRENCE
An authoritative selection spanning the whole of Lawrence's literary career
£4.99

The Poems
W. B. YEATS
Ireland's greatest lyric poet surveyed in this ground-breaking edition
£7.99

All books are available from your local bookshop or direct from:
Littlehampton Book Services Cash Sales, 14 Eldon Way, Lineside Estate,
Littlehampton, West Sussex BN17 7HE (*prices are subject to change*)

To order any of the books, please enclose a cheque (in sterling) made payable to
Littlehampton Book Services, or phone your order through with credit card details (Access,
Visa or Mastercard) on 01903 721596 (24 hour answering service) stating card number
and expiry date. (*Please add £1.25 for package and postage to the total of your order.*)

In the USA, for further information and a complete catalogue call 1-800-526-2778